American Politics

*Classic and
Contemporary
Readings*

American Politics

Classic and Contemporary Readings

Third Edition

Allan J. Cigler
University of Kansas

Burdett A. Loomis
University of Kansas

Houghton Mifflin Company   **Boston**   **Toronto**
Geneva, Illinois   Palo Alto   Princeton, New Jersey

Sponsoring Editor: Jean Woy
Senior Associate Editor: Frances Gay
Associate Project Editor: Nicole Ng
Production/Design Coordinator: Jennifer Waddell
Senior Manufacturing Coordinator: Priscilla Bailey

Cover Credit: Susan Slyman. *Fourth of July on the River*, 1985, acrylic on canvas, courtesy of Jaro Art Galleries, New York, NY.

Cover Design by Catherine Hawkes.

Text credits begin on page A-20.

Library of Congress Catalog Card Number: 94-76495

ISBN
Student text: 0-395-70833-8
Examination text: 0-395-71670-5

56789–B–98 97

Contents

Topic Correlation Chart

Although the chapters of this book of readings have been organized to mesh with the coverage of most American government textbooks, many subjects receive attention in more than one chapter. The following chart permits student and instructors to locate relevant readings for twenty-five subjects, ranging (in alphabetical order) from the bureaucracy to the Washington establishment.

Topic:	Covered in:
Bureaucracy	Chapter 12; 5.3 (The Power of One); 14.1 (Sign It, Then Mind It); 14.4 (The Rhetoric of Reform)
Campaigns and Elections	Chapter 7; 5.1 (Voter Turnout in America: Ten Myths); 6.2 (The Politics of Repudiation); 8.3 (Is There [a] . . . Media Tilt?)
Civil Liberties/ Civil Rights	Chapter 3; 8.2 (The Mass Media: Free and Independent?); 13.3 (The Framers and Original Intent); 14.3 (Wild Pitch: "Three Strikes, You're Out" . . .)
Clinton Presidency	11.3 (On Health, Clinton Finds Heaven . . .); 13.5 (The Political Court); 14.2 (Health Care Reform: Six Questions . . .); 14.3 (Wild Pitch; "Three Strikes, You're Out" . . .)
Congress	Chapter 10; 7.2 (Campaign Finance Reform: Some Lessons from the Data); 7.3, 7.4 (Debate on Term Limits . . .); 9.4 (The "Buying" of Public Policy); 14.3 (Wild Pitch: "Three Strikes, You're Out" . . .)
The Constitution	Chapters 1 and 13; 2.2 (*McCulloch v. Maryland*); 3.3 (*Griswold v. Connecticut*)
Domestic Policy	Chapter 14; 2.4 (Federal Government Mandates: Why the States . . .); 3.6, 3.7 (Debate on Affirmative Action . . .); 9.4 (The "Buying" of Public Policy); 11.3 (On Health, Clinton Finds Heaven . . .); 12.3 (Down on the Farm)
Federalism	Chapter 2; 9.1 (*Federalist* 10)
The Founding	Chapter 1; 9.1 (*Federalist* 10); 13.1 (*Federalist* 78)
Interest Groups	Chapter 9; 5.3 (The Power of One); 12.3 (Down on the Farm)
Leadership	Chapter 11; 1.1 (The Founding Fathers: A Reform Caucus in Action); 1.2 (The Founding Fathers: An Age of

Realism); 5.3 (The Power of One); 8.1 (Lowering the Political Hero to Our Level); 10.4 (Can Congress Govern?)

Mass Media   Chapter 8; 7.1 (Politicking Goes High-Tech); 10.1 (Congress-bashing Through the Ages)

Participation   Chapter 5; Chapter 6; 9.2 (The Changing Nature of Interest Group Politics)

Policymaking Process Chapter 14; 7.2 (Campaign Finance Reform: Some Lessons from the Data); 9.4 (The "Buying" of Public Policy); 10.2 (Housebroken); 10.3 (The Changing Textbook Congress); 10.4 (Can Congress Govern?); 11.1 (The Power to Persuade); 11.3 (On Health, Clinton Finds Heaven . . .); 11.4 (The No-Hands Presidency); 12.2 (From Ouagadougou to Cape Canaveral); 13.4 (What Am I? A Potted Plant?)

Political Culture   1.2 (The Founding Fathers: An Age of Realism); 3.1 (*Near v. Minnesota*); 4.1 (They've Got Your Number); 4.2 (The Shifting Sands of Public Opinion); 5.2 (A Lost Political Generation?)

Political Ideology   1.3 (An Economic Interpretation of the Constitution); 4.2 (The Shifting Sands of Public Opinion); 8.3 (Is There [a] . . . Media Tilt?)

Political Parties   Chapter 6; 8.3 (Is There [a] . . . Media Tilt?); 10.3 (The Changing Textbook Congress); 10.4 (Can Congress Govern?)

Presidency   Chapter 11; 13.5 (The Political Court); 14.2 (Health Care Reform: Six Questions . . .)

Public Opinion   Chapter 4; 6.2 (The Politics of Repudiation); 6.3 (Americans Want and Need a New Political Party); 8.3 (Is There [a] . . . Media Tilt?); 10.1 (Congress-bashing through the Ages)

Reform   1.1 (The Founding Fathers: A Reform Caucus in Action); 6.3 (Americans Want and Need a New Political Party); 7.2 (Campaign Finance Reform); 7.3 (Debate on Term Limits . . .); 12.2 (Constraints on Public Managers); 12.3 (Down on the Farm); 14.1 (Sign It, Then Mind It); 14.2 (Health Care Reform: Six Questions . . .); 14.4 (The Rhetoric of Reform)

Representation   1.1 (The Founding Fathers: A Reform Caucus in Action); 1.2 (The Founding Fathers: An Age of Realism);

PREFACE

As in the first two editions of this book, we have sought to combine classic and contemporary readings that would be accessible to students while still challenging them. Emphasizing readability, content, and usefulness within an introductory course, we have strived to assemble the best possible collection of articles—both established "classics" and important recent pieces—that will flesh out the complexities of American politics. In addition, we have chosen articles that reflect many of the major concerns of the 1990s, such as health care, crime, federal mandates, and, in numerous settings, proposed reforms of the political process.

We employed several overlapping criteria for selecting the final set of 54 articles (27 holdovers, 27 new pieces). First, we included acknowledged classics, by authors such as Richard Neustadt, Charles Beard, and Robert Dahl. Along these lines, we also think we've identified some classics in the making; these include Charles Peters on the bureaucracy and Kenneth Shepsle on the "textbook Congress." Second, we looked for readable and recent treatments of key elements of American politics. Articles in this category include those written by Steven Roberts on technology, Jeff Birnbaum on lobbyists, Martha Derthick on federal mandates, and Larry Sabato on the media. Third, we searched for articles that would foster discussion, and these are often incorporated in pairs like the pieces by Herbert Hill and Shelby Steele on affirmative action and those by Bill Frenzel and Thomas Mann on term limits. Fourth, we consciously sought to include presentations from authors with widely varied backgrounds. Thus, we have a substantial number of journalists (Maureen Dowd, Steven Roberts, Jeffrey Birnbaum), some practitioners (former Rep. Bill Frenzel, Judge Richard Posner), numerous academics, and a fair number of think-tank scholars (Thomas Mann, Ruy Teixeira, Michael Malbin).

Finally, many users have asked that the book be shorter. While maintaining broad coverage, we have sought to be a bit more incisive in this edition, both by editing some of the longer selections and by reducing the number of items in a few chapters. The result is that the book is about 20 percent shorter this time.

The selections in *American Politics: Classic and Contemporary Readings*, Third Edition, are divided into fourteen chapters that correspond to the organization of most American government texts. Each chapter begins with an essay that sets out the themes of that section. Headnotes introduce all selections, which are immediately followed by summary questions. With these devices we hope to provide context for students and direct their attention to the most important issues.

The book also includes two useful additional features. First, each selection is annotated, so that difficult terms and unfamiliar historical references are clarified. Second, we have produced an extensive topic correlation chart (see page xiii) that provides cross-references on twenty-five subjects, such as the Clinton presidency, political reform, and political culture. In addition, we reprint the full texts of the Declaration of Independence and the U.S. Constitution.

Complementing *American Politics* is an *Instructor's Resource Manual with Test Items*, once again prepared by Joel Paddock of Southwest Missouri State University. This manual includes selection summaries, suggestions for classroom use, and sets of multiple-choice and essay questions for all readings.

Houghton Mifflin has consistently obtained excellent reviewers for this project; this year was no exception. They all provided us with thoughtful critiques and sound suggestions for improvement. We are greatly in their debt, and we offer our sincere thanks to them all:

Cary R. Covington, University of Iowa
Tom Denyer, Texas A & M University
John C. Domino, Sam Houston State University
Dale Grimnitz, Normandale Community College
J. Scott Johnson, St. John's University
Grant Reeher, Syracuse University
Peter G. Renstrom, Western Michigan University
Charles Shipan, University of Iowa
Robert J. Spitzer, State University of New York at Cortland
Alan J. Wyner, University of California, Santa Barbara

As always, the Houghton Mifflin editorial staff has immeasurably improved the quality of this book. Our thanks go to Frances Gay, Margaret Seawell, Nicole Ng, and Jean Woy. Our families, as always, have supported our work, and our gratitude goes to Beth and Kirsten Cigler and Michel and Dakota Loomis. Finally, we've survived editing seven books together. Who said this marriage couldn't last?

A.J.C.
B.A.L.

 Part I

CONSTITUTIONAL FOUNDATIONS

 Chapter 1

THE CONSTITUTION AND FOUNDING

The framing of the Constitution serves as one of the anchors of American politics. The Constitution was written, under pressure, by an extraordinary band of political leaders, whose accomplishments at the Philadelphia convention have proven so workable and lasting that it is difficult not to see them as mythical figures. Still, with the possible exception of George Washington, these were people, not demigods. And Washington's elevated status proved useful to the framers: As they devised the presidency and later pushed for ratification, they, along with the great body of citizens, could easily envision Washington as the first incumbent of the office.

It is difficult to exaggerate the scope of the problems the framers faced. They confronted a system of government under the Articles of Confederation that emphasized the sovereignty of the individual states at the expense of a coherent national identity and hindered the development of the nation. An armed insurrection in Massachusetts (Shays's Rebellion) demonstrated the weakness of the states in coming to terms with problems of commerce, currency, and credit. In addition, this uprising brought home the supposed dangers of the masses within a democratic state. The possible "tyranny of the majority" was a real fear. Domestic challenges were no greater than those from abroad. The United States may have won its war of independence, but European powers certainly did not see American sovereignty as immutable. Throughout the country's first few decades, there were numerous plots to compromise American independence (for example, the XYZ Affair and Aaron Burr's plan for a separatist state in the Southwest).

In writing the Constitution and securing its ratification, the framers proved themselves skillful political engineers and propagandists. John P. Roche describes these individuals as comprising a "reform caucus," a label that aptly captures the essentially political nature of their task. Nevertheless, their purposes were more radical than merely carrying out a set of reforms. As Roche notes, "The Constitutionalists went forth to subvert the Confederation," not to enact some modest changes.

Just as the American Revolution has been characterized as conservative, the same can be said of the writing of the Constitution. As historians Charles A. Beard and Richard Hofstadter emphasize, protecting property rights played a central role in the framers' thinking. Given their status as part of the new nation's elite, this is understandable. Still, protecting property rights represented more than a simple appeal to self-interest; for the framers, such safeguards were important guideposts in assessing the reach of governmental power. Property rights could best be protected by creating a central government that was strong enough to ensure orderly commerce but not so strong that it impinged on the rights of the minority. As Hofstadter points out, "Freedom for property would result in liberty for men—perhaps not for all men, but at least for all worthy men."

A governmental structure that could protect property rights without becoming oppressive would not only have to make sense theoretically; it would have to win the approval of the states in the ratification process. To address these necessities, the framers created a series of checks and balances, most notably federalism (see Chapter 2) and the separation of powers. In *The Federalist,* James Madison argues that liberty can be protected only where the executive, legislative, and judicial functions are divided, although the division need not be, and cannot be, complete; there will always be some sharing of powers. Rather, he notes in *The Federalist,* No. 47, "where the *whole* power of one department is exercised by the same hands which possess the *whole* power of another department, the fundamental principles of a free constitution are subverted."

One test of a "fundamental principle" of any constitution is its staying power. The separation of powers has not gone unchallenged over the course of the American republic. The most common conflict has arisen between the executive and the legislature, with critics often arguing that the executive branch needs more power to carry out its electoral mandate and to implement a coherent foreign policy. Since the election of 1968, the separation of powers has undergone another test—that of accommodating a long-term dose of divided government in which Republicans control the presidency and Democrats dominate the Congress. Of course, nothing dictated that one party control both these branches of government, but until 1969 divided control reflected short-lived changes in the partisan balance of power. How well American enterprise functions under an extended division between admittedly weakened parties remains to be seen, even as President Bill Clinton struggles to build majorities for such far-reaching proposals as reform of the health care and welfare systems.

The Founding Fathers: A Reform Caucus in Action

John P. Roche

After two hundred years, the American Constitution remains a vital document, subject to continuing reinterpretation in the courts. At the same time, its status in American mythology has become more firmly enshrined. A balance between tangible and symbolic elements has been central to the success of the Constitution, but we need to put down our rose-colored glasses to view its creation in ways that contribute to both our contemporary and our historic understanding of it.

In this selection, John P. Roche argues that the framers of the Constitution were above all "superb democratic politicians" who constituted an elite—but a democratic elite. Roche objects to viewing the framers solely through the lens of *The Federalist,* the collection of articles in support of ratification that he regards as a brilliant set of post hoc rationalizations. Instead, James Madison should be seen as a clever tactical politician and an "inspired propagandist," whose writing in *The Federalist* only incidentally emerges as brilliant political theory. We might well wonder what our political system would have looked like, absent the framers' political acumen.

The Convention has been described picturesquely as a counter-revolutionary junta and the Constitution as a *coup d'état,* but this has been accomplished by withdrawing the whole history of the movement for constitutional reform from its true context. No doubt the goals of the constitutional elite were "subversive" to the existing political order, but it is overlooked that their subversion could only have succeeded if the people of the United States endorsed it by regularized procedures. Indubitably they were "plotting" to establish a much stronger central government than existed under the Articles, but only in the sense in which one could argue equally well that John F. Kennedy was, from 1956 to 1960, "plotting" to become President. In short, on the fundamental *procedural* level, the Constitutionalists had to work according to the prevailing rules of the game. . . .

John P. Roche is a professor of political science at Tufts University.

I

The history of the United States from 1786 to 1790 was largely one of a masterful employment of political expertise by the Constitutionalists as against bumbling, erratic behavior by the opponents of reform. Effectively, the Constitutionalists had to induce the states, by democratic techniques of coercion, to emasculate themselves. To be specific, if New York had refused to join the new Union, the project was doomed; yet before New York was safely in, the reluctant state legislature had . . . to take the following steps: (1) agree to send delegates to the Philadelphia Convention; (2) provide maintenance for these delegates . . . ; (3) set up the special *ad hoc* convention to decide on ratification; and (4) concede to the decision of the *ad hoc* convention that New York should participate. New York admittedly was a tricky state, with a strong interest in a *status quo* which permitted her to exploit New Jersey and Connecticut, but the same legal hurdles existed in every state. . . . that the *only* weapon in the Constitutionalist arsenal was an effective mobilization of public opinion.

The group which undertook this struggle was an interesting amalgam of a few dedicated nationalists with the self-interested spokesmen of various parochial bailiwicks. The Georgians, for example, wanted a strong central authority to provide military protection for their huge, underpopulated state . . . ; Jerseymen and Connecticuters wanted to escape from economic bondage to New York; the Virginians hoped to establish a system which would give that great state its rightful place in the councils of the republic. . . . There was, of course, a large element of personality in the affair: there is reason to suspect that Patrick Henry's opposition to the Convention and the Constitution was founded on his conviction that Jefferson was behind both, and a close study of local politics elsewhere would surely reveal that others supported the Constitution for the simple (and politically quite sufficient) reason that the "wrong" people were against it.

To say this is not to suggest that the Constitution rested on a foundation of impure or base motives. It is rather to argue that in politics there are no immaculate conceptions, and that in the drive for a stronger general government, motives of all sorts played a part. Few men in the history of mankind have espoused a view of the "common good" or "public interest" that militated against their private status; even Plato with all his reverence for disembodied reason managed to put philosophers on top of the pile. Thus it is not surprising that a number of diversified private interests joined to push the nationalist public interest; what would have been surprising was the absence of such a pragmatic united front. And the fact remains that, however motivated, these men did demonstrate a willingness to compromise their parochial interests in behalf of an ideal which took shape before their eyes and under their ministrations.

As Stanley Elkins and Eric McKitrick have suggested in a perceptive essay, what distinguished the leaders of the Constitutionalist caucus from their enemies was a "Continental" approach to political, economic and military issues. To the extent that they shared an institutional base of operations, it was the Continental

Congress (thirty-nine of the delegates to the Federal Convention had served in Congress), and this was hardly a locale which inspired respect for the state governments. . . . "Continental" ideology developed which seems to have demanded a revision of our domestic institutions primarily on the ground that only by invigorating our general government could we assume our rightful place in the international arena. Indeed, an argument with great force—particularly since Washington was its incarnation—urged that our very survival in the Hobbesian* jungle of world politics depended upon a reordering and strengthening of our national sovereignty. . . .

The great achievement of the Constitutionalists was their ultimate success in convincing the elected representatives of a majority of the white male population that change was imperative. A small group of political leaders with a Continental vision and essentially a consciousness of the United States' *international* impotence, provided the matrix of the movement. To their standard other leaders rallied with their own parallel ambitions. Their great assets were (1) the presence in their caucus of the one authentic American "father figure," George Washington, whose prestige was enormous; (2) the energy and talent of their leadership (in which one must include the towering intellectuals of the time, John Adams and Thomas Jefferson, despite their absence abroad), and their communications "network," which was far superior to anything on the opposition side; (3) preemptive skill which made "their" issue The Issue and kept the locally oriented opposition permanently on the defensive; and (4) the subjective consideration that these men were spokesmen of a new and compelling credo: *American* nationalism, that ill-defined but nonetheless potent sense of collective purpose that emerged from the American Revolution. . . .

The Constitutionalists got the jump on the "opposition" (a collective noun: oppositions would be more correct) at the outset with the demand for a Convention. Their opponents were caught in an old political trap: they were not being asked to approve any specific program of reform, but only to endorse a meeting to discuss and recommend needed reforms. If they took a hard line at the first stage, they were put in the position of glorifying the *status quo* and of denying the need for *any* changes. Moreover, the Constitutionalists could go to the people with a persuasive argument for "fair play"—"How can you condemn reform before you know precisely what is involved?" Since the state legislatures obviously would have the final say on any proposals that might emerge from the Convention, the Constitutionalists were merely reasonable men asking for a chance. Besides, since they did not make any concrete proposals at that stage, they were in a position to capitalize on every sort of generalized discontent with the Confederation.

---

* Thomas Hobbes (1588–1679) was an English philosopher who viewed human nature as brutish and self-seeking to the point of anarchy. The state, with an absolute ruler, thus becomes an agency for maintaining peace and order.

Perhaps because of their poor intelligence system, perhaps because of over-confidence generated by the failure of all previous efforts to alter the Articles, the opposition awoke too late to the dangers that confronted them in 1787. Not only did the Constitutionalists manage to get every state but Rhode Island . . . to appoint delegates to Philadelphia, but when the results were in, it appeared that they dominated the delegations. Given the apathy of the opposition, this was a natural phenomenon: in an ideologically nonpolarized political atmosphere those who get appointed to a special committee are likely to be the men who supported the movement for its creation. Even George Clinton, who seems to have been the first opposition leader to awake to the possibility of trouble, could not prevent the New York legislature from appointing Alexander Hamilton—though he did have the foresight to send two of his henchmen to dominate the delegation. Incidentally, much has been made of the fact that the delegates to Philadelphia were not elected by the people; some have adduced this fact as evidence of the "undemocratic" character of the gathering. But put in the context of the time, this argument is wholly specious: the central government under the Articles was considered a creature of the component states and in all the states but Rhode Island, Connecticut and New Hampshire, members of the national Congress were chosen by the state legislatures. This was not a consequence of elitism or fear of the mob; it was a logical extension of states'-rights doctrine to guarantee that the national institution did not end-run the state legislatures and make direct contact with the people.

II

With delegations safely named, the focus shifted to Philadelphia. While waiting for a quorum to assemble, James Madison got busy and drafted the so-called Randolph or Virginia Plan with the aid of the Virginia delegation. This was a political master-stroke. Its consequence was that once business got underway, the framework of discussion was established on Madison's terms. There was no interminable argument over agenda; instead the delegates took the Virginia Resolutions—"just for purposes of discussion"—as their point of departure. And along with Madison's proposals, many of which were buried in the course of the summer, went his major premise: a new start on a Constitution rather than piecemeal amendment. This was not necessarily revolutionary—a little exegesis could demonstrate that a new Constitution might be formulated as "amendments" to the Articles of Confederation—but Madison's proposal that this "lump sum" amendment go into effect after approval by nine states (the Articles required unanimous state approval for any amendment) was thoroughly subversive. . . .

Basic differences of opinion emerged, of course, but these were not ideological; they were *structural*. If the so-called "states'-rights" group had not accepted the fundamental purposes of the Convention, they could simply have pulled out and by doing so have aborted the whole enterprise. Instead of bolting, they returned day after day to argue and to compromise. An interesting symbol of this basic homogeneity was the initial agreement on secrecy: these professional politicians did not want to become prisoners of publicity; they wanted to retain that freedom of maneuver which is only possible when men are not forced to take public stands in the preliminary stages of negotiation. There was no legal means of binding the tongues of the delegates: at any stage in the game a delegate with basic principled objections to the emerging project could have taken the stump (as Luther Martin did after his exit) and denounced the convention to the skies. Yet Madison did not even inform Thomas Jefferson in Paris of the course of the deliberations and available correspondence indicates that the delegates generally observed the injunction. Secrecy is certainly uncharacteristic of any assembly marked by strong ideological polarization. This was noted at the time: the *New York Daily Advertiser*, August 14, 1787, commented that the ". . . profound secrecy hitherto observed by the Convention [we consider] a happy omen, as it demonstrates that the spirit of party on any great and essential point cannot have arisen to any height."

Commentators on the Constitution who have read *The Federalist* in lieu of reading the actual debates have credited the Fathers with the invention of a sublime concept called "Federalism." Unfortunately *The Federalist* is probative evidence for only one proposition: that Hamilton and Madison were inspired propagandists with a genius for retrospective symmetry. Federalism, as the theory is generally defined, was an improvisation which was later promoted into a political theory. . . .

It is indeed astonishing how those who have glibly designated James Madison the "father" of Federalism have overlooked the solid body of fact which indicates that he shared Hamilton's quest for a unitary central government.* To be specific, they have avoided examining the clear import of the Madison-Virginia Plan, and have disregarded Madison's dogged inch-by-inch retreat from the bastions of centralization. The Virginia Plan envisioned a unitary national government effectively freed from and dominant over the states. The lower house of the national legislature was to be elected directly by the people of the states with membership proportional to population. The upper house was to be selected by the lower, and the two chambers would elect the executive and choose the judges. The national government would be thus cut completely loose from the states.

The structure of the general government was freed from state control in a truly radical fashion, but the scope of the authority of the national sovereign as Madison initially formulated it was breathtaking. . . . The national legislature was to be empowered to disallow the acts of state legislatures, and the central

---

* *Unitary governments* such as that of Great Britain minimize the importance of local or regional units. Most major decisions are made at the national level.

government was vested, in addition to the powers of the nation under the Articles of Confederation, with plenary authority wherever ". . . the separate States are incompetent or in which the harmony of the United States may be interrupted by the exercise of individual legislation." Finally, just to lock the door against state intrusion, the national Congress was to be given the power to use military force on recalcitrant states. This was Madison's "model" of an ideal national government, though it later received little publicity in *The Federalist*.

The interesting thing was the reaction of the Convention to this militant program for a strong autonomous central government. Some delegates were startled, some obviously leery of so comprehensive a project of reform, but nobody set off any fireworks and nobody walked out. Moreover, in the two weeks that followed, the Virginia Plan received substantial endorsement *en principe*; the initial temper of the gathering can be deduced from the approval "without debate or dissent," on May 31, of the Sixth Resolution which granted Congress the authority to disallow state legislation ". . . contravening *in its opinion* the Articles of Union." Indeed, an amendment was included to bar states from contravening national treaties.

The Virginia Plan may therefore be considered, in ideological terms, as the delegates' Utopia, but as the discussions continued and became more specific, many of those present began to have second thoughts. After all, they were not residents of Utopia or guardians in Plato's Republic who could simply impose a philosophical ideal on subordinate strata of the population. They were practical politicians in a democratic society, and no matter what their private dreams might be, they had to take home an acceptable package and defend it—and their own political futures—against predictable attack. On June 14 the breaking point between dream and reality took place. Apparently realizing that under the Virginia Plan, Massachusetts, Virginia and Pennsylvania could virtually dominate the national government—and probably appreciating that to sell this program to "the folks back home" would be impossible—the delegates from the small states dug in their heels and demanded time for a consideration of alternatives. One gets a graphic sense of the inner politics from John Dickinson's reproach to Madison: "You see the consequences of pushing things too far. Some of the members from the small States wish for two branches in the General Legislature, and are friends to a good National Government; but we would sooner submit to a foreign power than . . . be deprived of an equality of suffrage in both branches of the Legislature, and thereby be thrown under the domination of the large States."

. . . Now the process of accommodation was put into action smoothly—and wisely, given the character and strength of the doubters. Madison had the votes, but this was one of those situations where the enforcement of mechanical majoritarianism could easily have destroyed the objectives of the majority: the Constitutionalists were in quest of a qualitative as well as a quantitative consensus. This was hardly from deference to local Quaker custom; it was a political imperative if they were to attain ratification.

III

According to the standard script, at this point the "states'-rights" group intervened in force behind the New Jersey Plan, which has been characteristically portrayed as a reversion to the *status quo* under the Articles of Confederation with but minor modifications. A careful examination of the evidence indicates that only in a marginal sense is this an accurate description. It is true that the New Jersey Plan put the states back into the institutional picture, but one could argue that to do so was a recognition of political reality rather than an affirmation of states'-rights. A serious case can be made that the advocates of the New Jersey Plan, far from being ideological addicts of states'-rights, intended to substitute for the Virginia Plan a system which would both retain strong national power and have a chance of adoption in the states. The leading spokesman for the project asserted quite clearly that his views were based more on counsels of expediency than on principle; said Paterson on June 16: "I came here not to speak my own sentiments, but the sentiments of those who sent me. Our object is not such a Governmt. as may be best in itself, but such a one as our Constituents have authorized us to prepare, and as they will approve." This is Madison's version; in Yates' transcription, there is a crucial sentence following the remarks above: "I believe that a little practical virtue is to be preferred to the finest theoretical principles, which cannot be carried into effect." . . .

This was a defense of political acumen, not of states'-rights. In fact, Paterson's notes of his speech can easily be construed as an argument for attaining the substantive objectives of the Virginia Plan by a sound political route, *i.e.*, pouring the new wine in the old bottles. With a shrewd eye, Paterson queried:

> Will the Operation and Force of the [central] Govt. depend upon the mode of Representn.—No—it will depend upon the Quantum of Power lodged in the leg. ex. and judy. Departments—Give [the existing] Congress the same Powers that you intend to give the two Branches [under the Virginia Plan], and I apprehend they will act with as much Propriety and more Energy . . .

In other words, the advocates of the New Jersey Plan concentrated their fire on what they held to be the *political liabilities* of the Virginia Plan—which were matters of institutional structure—rather than on the proposed scope of national authority. Indeed, the Supremacy Clause of the Constitution first saw the light of day in Paterson's Sixth Resolution; the New Jersey Plan contemplated the use of military force to secure compliance with national law; and finally Paterson made clear his view that under either the Virginia or the New Jersey systems, the general government would ". . . act on individuals and not on states." From the states'-rights viewpoint, this was heresy: the fundament of that doctrine was the proposition that any central government had as its contituents the states, not the people, and could only reach the people through the agency of the state government.

Paterson then reopened the agenda of the Convention, but he did so within a distinctly nationalist framework. Paterson's position was one of favoring a strong central government in principle, but opposing one which in fact *put the big states in the saddle*. (The Virginia Plan, for all its abstract merits, did very well by Virginia.) As evidence for this speculation, there is a curious and intriguing proposal among Paterson's preliminary drafts of the New Jersey Plan:

> Whereas it is necessary in Order to form the People of the U.S. of America in to a Nation, that the States should be consolidated, by which means all the Citizens thereof will become equally intitled to and will equally participate in the same Privileges and Rights . . . it is therefore resolved, that all the Lands contained within the Limits of each state individually, and of the U.S. generally be considered as constituting one Body or Mass, and be divided into thirteen or more integral parts.
>
> Resolved, That such Divisions or integral Parts shall be styled Districts.

This makes it sound as though Paterson was prepared to accept a strong unified central government along the lines of the Virginia Plan if the existing states were eliminated. He may have gotten the idea from his New Jersey colleague Judge David Brearley, who on June 9 had commented that the only remedy to the dilemma over representation was ". . . that a map of the U.S. be spread out, that all the existing boundaries be erased, and that a new partition of the whole be made into 13 equal parts." According to Yates, Brearley added at this point, ". . . then a government on the present [Virginia Plan] system will be just."

This proposition was never pushed—it was patently unrealistic—but one can appreciate its purpose: it would have separated the men from the boys in the large-state delegations. How attached would the Virginians have been to their reform principles if Virginia were to disappear as a component geographical unit (the largest) for representational purposes? Up to this point, the Virginians had been in the happy position of supporting high ideals with that inner confidence born of knowledge that the "public interest" they endorsed would nourish their private interest. Worse, they had shown little willingness to compromise. Now the delegates from the small states announced that they were unprepared to be offered up as sacrificial victims to a "national interest" which reflected Virginia's parochial ambition. Caustic Charles Pinckney was not far off when he remarked sardonically that ". . . the whole [conflict] comes to this"[:] "Give N. Jersey an equal vote, and she will dismiss her scruples, and concur in the Natil. system." What he rather unfairly did not add was that the Jersey delegates were not free agents who could adhere to their private convictions; they had to take back, sponsor and risk their reputations on the reforms approved by the Convention— and in New Jersey, not in Virginia. . . .

IV

On Tuesday morning, June 19, . . . James Madison led off with a long, carefully reasoned speech analyzing the New Jersey Plan which, while intellectually vigorous in its criticisms, was quite conciliatory in mood. "The great difficulty," he observed, "lies in the affair of Representation; and if this could be adjusted, all others would be surmountable." (As events were to demonstrate, this diagnosis was correct.) When he finished, a vote was taken on whether to continue with the Virginia Plan as the nucleus for a new constitution: seven states voted "Yes"; New York, New Jersey, and Delaware voted "No"; and Maryland, whose position often depended on which delegates happened to be on the floor, divided. Paterson, it seems, lost decisively; yet in a fundamental sense he and his allies had achieved their purpose: from that day onward, it could never be forgotten that the state governments loomed ominously in the background and that no verbal incantations could exorcise their power. Moreover, nobody bolted the convention: Paterson and his colleagues took their defeat in stride and set to work to modify the Virginia Plan, particularly with respect to its provisions on representation in the national legislature. Indeed, they won an immediate rhetorical bonus; when Oliver Ellsworth of Connecticut rose to move that the word "national" be expunged from the Third Virginia Resolution ("Resolved that a *national* Government ought to be established consisting of a *supreme* Legislative, Executive and Judiciary"), Randolph agreed and the motion passed unanimously. The process of compromise had begun.

For the next two weeks, the delegates circled around the problem of legislative representation. The Connecticut delegation appears to have evolved a possible compromise quite early in the debates, but the Virginians and particularly Madison (unaware that he would later be acclaimed as the prophet of "federalism") fought obdurately against providing for equal representation of states in the second chamber. There was a good deal of acrimony and at one point Benjamin Franklin—of all people—proposed the institution of a daily prayer; practical politicians in the gathering, however, were meditating more on the merits of a good committee than on the utility of Divine intervention. On July 2, the ice began to break when through a number of fortuitous events—and one that seems deliberate—the majority against equality of representation was converted into a dead tie. The Convention had reached the stage where it was "ripe" for a solution (presumably all the therapeutic speeches had been made), and the South Carolinians proposed a committee. Madison and James Wilson wanted none of it, but with only Pennsylvania dissenting, the body voted to establish a working party on the problem of representation.

The members of this committee, one from each state, were elected by the delegates—and a very interesting committee it was. Despite the fact that the Virginia Plan had held majority support up to that date, neither Madison nor Randolph was selected (Mason was the Virginian) and Baldwin of Georgia, whose shift in position had resulted in the tie, was chosen. From the composition, it was clear that this was not to be a "fighting" committee: the emphasis in membership was on what might be described as "second-level political entrepreneurs." On the basis of the discussions up to that time, only Luther Martin of Maryland could be described as a "bitter-ender." Admittedly, some divination enters into this sort of analysis, but one does get a sense of the mood of the delegates from these choices—including the interesting selection of Benjamin Franklin, despite his age and intellectual wobbliness, over the brilliant and incisive Wilson or the sharp, polemical Gouverneur Morris, to represent Pennsylvania. His passion for conciliation was more valuable at this juncture than Wilson's logical genius, or Morris' acerbic wit.

. . . It should be reiterated that the Madison model had no room either for the states or for the "separation of powers": effectively *all* governmental power was vested in the national legislature. The merits of Montesquieu did not turn up until *The Federalist*; and although a perverse argument could be made that Madison's ideal was truly in the tradition of John Locke's *Second Treatise of Government*, the Locke whom the American rebels treated as an honorary president was a pluralistic defender of vested rights, not of parliamentary supremacy.*

It would be tedious to continue a blow-by-blow analysis of the work of the delegates; the critical fight was over representation of the states and once the Connecticut Compromise† was adopted on July 17, the Convention was over the hump. . . . Moreover, once the compromise had carried (by five states to four, with one state divided), its advocates threw themselves vigorously into the job of strengthening the general government's substantive powers—as might have been predicted, indeed, from Paterson's early statements. It nourishes an increased respect for Madison's devotion to the art of politics, to realize that this dogged fighter could sit down six months later and prepare essays for *The Federalist* in contradiction to his basic convictions about the true course the Convention should have taken. . . .

VI

Drawing on their vast collective political experience, utilizing every weapon in the politician's arsenal, looking constantly over their shoulders at their constituents, the delegates put together a Constitution. It was a makeshift affair; some sticky issues (for example, the qualification of voters) they ducked entirely; others they mastered with that ancient instrument of political sagacity, studied ambiguity (for example, citizenship), and some they just overlooked. In this last category, I suspect, fell the matter of the power of the federal courts to determine the constitutionality of acts of Congress. When the judicial article was formulated (Article III of the Constitution), deliberations were still in the stage where the legislature was endowed with broad power under the Randolph formulation, authority which by its own terms was scarcely amenable to judicial review. In

---

* John Locke (1632–1704) was an English philosopher whose writings served as a basis for government rooted in a social contract between citizens and their rulers. Montesquieu (1689–1755) was a French political philosopher whose work emphasized checks and balances in the exercise of authority.

† The Connecticut Compromise advanced the solution of a two-chamber legislature, with each state receiving two senators and House representation in proportion to its population.

essence, courts could hardly determine when ". . . the separate States are incompetent or . . . the harmony of the United States may be interrupted"; the National Legislature, as critics pointed out, was free to define its own jurisdiction. Later the definition of legislative authority was changed into the form we know, a series of stipulated powers, *but the delegates never seriously reexamined the jurisdiction of the judiciary under this new limited formulation.* All arguments on the intention of the Framers in this matter are thus deductive and *a posteriori,* though some obviously make more sense than others.

The Framers were busy and distinguished men, anxious to get back to their families, their positions, and their constituents, not members of the French Academy devoting a lifetime to a dictionary. They were trying to do an important job, and do it in such a fashion that their handiwork would be acceptable to very diverse constituencies. No one was rhapsodic about the final document, but it was a beginning, a move in the right direction, and one they had reason to believe the people would endorse. In addition, since they had modified the impossible amendment provisions of the Articles (the requirement of unanimity which could always be frustrated by "Rogues [Rhode] Island") to one demanding approval by only three-quarters of the states, they seemed confident that gaps in the fabric which experience would reveal could be rewoven without undue difficulty. . . .

Madison, despite his reservations about the Constitution, was the campaign manager in ratification. His first task was to get the Congress in New York to light its own funeral pyre by approving the "amendments" to the Articles and sending them on to the state legislatures. Above all, momentum had to be maintained. The anti-Constitutionalists, now thoroughly alarmed and no novices in politics, realized that their best tactic was attrition rather than direct opposition. Thus they settled on a position expressing qualified approval but calling for a second Convention to remedy various defects (the one with the most demagogic appeal was the lack of a Bill of Rights). Madison knew that to accede to this demand would be equivalent to losing the battle, nor would he agree to conditional approval (despite wavering even by Hamilton). This was an all-or-nothing proposition: national salvation or national impotence with no intermediate positions possible. Unable to get congressional approval, he settled for second best: a unanimous resolution of Congress transmitting the Constitution to the states for whatever action they saw fit to take. . . .

VII

. . . Victory for the Constitution meant simultaneous victory for the Constitutionalists; the anti-Constitutionalists either capitulated or vanished into limbo— soon Patrick Henry would be offered a seat on the Supreme Court and Luther Martin would be known as the Federalist "bull-dog." And irony of ironies, Alexander Hamilton and James Madison would shortly accumulate a reputation as the formulators of what is often alleged to be our political theory, the concept of "federalism." Also, on the other side of the ledger, the arguments would soon appear over what the Framers "really meant"; while these disputes have assumed the proportions of a big scholarly business in the last century, they began almost before the ink on the Constitution was dry. One of the best early ones featured Hamilton versus Madison on the scope of presidential power, and other Framers characteristically assumed positions in this and other disputes on the basis of their political convictions.

Probably our greatest difficulty is that we know so much more about what the Framers *should have meant* than they themselves did. We are intimately acquainted with the problems that their Constitution should have been designed to master; in short, we have read the mystery story backwards. If we are to get the right "feel" for their time and their circumstances, we must, in Maitland's phrase, ". . . think ourselves back into a twilight." Obviously, no one can pretend completely to escape from the solipsistic web of his own environment, but if the effort is made, it is possible to appreciate the past roughly on its own terms. The first step in this process is to abandon the academic premise that because we can ask a question, there must be an answer.

Thus we can ask what the Framers meant when they gave Congress the power to regulate interstate and foreign commerce, and we emerge, reluctantly perhaps, with the reply that . . . they may not have known what they meant, that there may not have been any semantic consensus. The Convention was not a seminar in analytic philosophy or linguistic analysis. Commerce was *commerce*—and if different interpretations of the word arose, later generations could worry about the problem of definition. The delegates were in a hurry to get a new government established; when definitional arguments arose, they characteristically took refuge in ambiguity. If different men voted for the same proposition for varying reasons, that was politics (and still is); if later generations were unsettled by this lack of precision, that would be their problem. . . .

The Constitution, then, was not an apotheosis of "constitutionalism," a triumph of architectonic genius; it was a patch-work sewn together under the pressure of both time and events by a group of extremely talented democratic politicians. They refused to attempt the establishment of a strong, centralized sovereignty on the principle of legislative supremacy for the excellent reason that the people would not accept it. They risked their political fortunes by opposing the established doctrines of state sovereignty because they were convinced that the existing system was leading to national impotence and probably foreign domination. For two years, they worked to get a convention established. For over three months, in what must have seemed to the faithful participants an endless process of give-and-take, they reasoned, cajoled, threatened, and bargained amongst themselves. The result was a Constitution which the people, in fact, by democratic processes, did accept, and a new and far better national government was established. . . .

To conclude, the Constitution was neither a victory for abstract theory nor a great practical success. Well over half a million men had to die on the battlefields of the Civil War before certain constitutional principles could be defined—a baleful consideration which is somehow overlooked in our customary tributes to the farsighted genius of the Framers and to the supposed American talent for "constitutionalism." The Constitution was, however, a vivid demonstration of effective democratic political action, and of the forging of a national elite which literally persuaded its countrymen to hoist themselves by their own boot straps. American pro-consuls would be wise not to translate the Constitution into Japanese, or Swahili, or treat it as a work of semi-Divine origin; but when students of comparative politics examine the process of nation-building in countries newly freed from colonial rule, they may find the American experience instructive as a classic example of the potentialities of a democratic elite.

Summary Questions

1. How does Roche's approach to the framers affect our contemporary understanding of the Constitution? How might the framers have confronted difficult problems such as abortion and affirmative action?
2. What does Roche mean by a *democratic elite*? Is this phrase a contradiction in terms, or does it have real meaning?

 1.2

The Founding Fathers: An Age of Realism

Richard Hofstadter

If the framers were, in John P. Roche's words, "a reform caucus," they were also realists who had witnessed more than a decade of severe economic, social, and political turbulence. They wanted some greater certainty for themselves and their new nation. At the same time, they remained steadfast in their desire to retain the liberty they had so recently won.

Historian Richard Hofstadter examines the interplay among liberty, stability, and property rights in this brief essay. As the framers saw it, the key to the long-term success of a democratic state (if it was to be possible) was to ensure that

Probably the pre-eminent American historian of his time, Richard Hofstadter (1916–1970) was DeWitt Clinton Professor of American History at Columbia University.

substantial numbers of citizens had a stake in the government and in the state. If that were so, people's "rapacious self-interest" might well be reconciled with freedom. This tenuous balance of self-interest and property rights seems an unlikely brace for a government, but it has proven adequate for more than two hundred years.

It is ironical that the Constitution, which Americans venerate so deeply, is based upon a political theory that at one crucial point stands in direct antithesis to the main stream of American democratic faith. Modern American folklore assumes that democracy and liberty are all but identical, and when democratic writers take the trouble to make the distinction, they usually assume that democracy is necessary to liberty. But the Founding Fathers thought that the liberty with which they were most concerned was menaced by democracy. In their minds liberty was linked not to democracy but to property.

What did the Fathers mean by liberty? What did Jay mean when he spoke of "the charms of liberty"? Or Madison when he declared that to destroy liberty in order to destroy factions would be a remedy worse than the disease? Certainly the men who met at Philadelphia were not interested in extending liberty to those classes in America, the Negro slaves and the indentured servants, who were most in need of it, for slavery was recognized in the organic structure of the Constitution and indentured servitude was no concern of the Convention. Nor was the regard of the delegates for civil liberties any too tender. It was the opponents of the Constitution who were most active in demanding such vital liberties as freedom of religion, freedom of speech and press, jury trial, due process, and protection from "unreasonable searches and seizures." These guarantees had to be incorporated in the first ten amendments because the Convention neglected to put them in the original document. Turning to economic issues, it was not freedom of trade in the modern sense that the Fathers were striving for. Although they did not believe in impeding trade unnecessarily, they felt that failure to regulate it was one of the central weaknesses of the Articles of Confederation, and they stood closer to the mercantilists than to Adam Smith.* Again, liberty to them did not mean free access to the nation's unappropriated wealth. At least fourteen of them were land speculators. They did not believe in the right of the squatter to occupy unused land, but rather in the right of the absentee owner or speculator to pre-empt it.

The liberties that the constitutionalists hoped to gain were chiefly negative. They wanted freedom from fiscal uncertainty and irregularities in the currency,

---

* *Mercantilist theory* emphasized state control of the economic process to accumulate as much of value as possible. Achieving positive trade balances became a principal element of national policy. Scottish economist Adam Smith, in *The Wealth of Nations* and other writings, opposed this theory and developed his own ideas on the division of labor, laissez-faire (free market) economics, and the ultimate increase in value as more labor is expended in the production process.

from trade wars among the states, from economic discrimination by more powerful foreign governments, from attacks on the creditor class or on property, from
popular insurrection. They aimed to create a government that would act as an
honest broker among a variety of propertied interests, giving them all protection
from their common enemies and preventing any one of them from becoming too
powerful. The Convention was a fraternity of types of absentee ownership. All
property should be permitted to have its proportionate voice in government.
Individual property interests might have to be sacrificed at times, but only for the
community of propertied interests. Freedom for property would result in liberty
for men—perhaps not for all men, but at least for all worthy men. Because men
have different faculties and abilities, the Fathers believed, they acquire different
amounts of property. To protect property is only to protect men in the exercise of
their natural faculties. Among the many liberties, therefore, freedom to hold and
dispose property is paramount. Democracy, unchecked rule by the masses, is sure
to bring arbitrary redistribution of property, destroying the very essence of liberty.

The Fathers' conception of democracy, shaped by their practical experience
with the aggressive dirt farmers in the American states and the urban mobs of the
Revolutionary period, was supplemented by their reading in history and political
science. Fear of what Madison called "the superior force of an interested and
overbearing majority" was the dominant emotion aroused by their study of
historical examples. The chief examples of republics were among the city-states
of antiquity, medieval Europe, and early modern times. Now, the history of these
republics—a history, as Hamilton said, "of perpetual vibration between the
extremes of tyranny and anarchy"—was alarming. Further, most of the men who
had overthrown the liberties of republics had "begun their career by paying an
obsequious court to the people; commencing demagogues and ending tyrants."

All the constitutional devices that the Fathers praised in their writings were
attempts to guarantee the future of the United States against the "turbulent"
political cycles of previous republics. By "democracy," they meant a system of
government which directly expressed the will of the majority of the people,
usually through such an assemblage of the people as was possible in the small area
of the city-state.

A cardinal tenet in the faith of the men who made the Constitution was the
belief that democracy can never be more than a transitional stage in government,
that it always evolves into either a tyranny (the rule of the rich demagogue who
has patronized the mob) or an aristocracy (the original leaders of the democratic
elements). "Remember," wrote the dogmatic John Adams in one of his letters to
John Taylor of Carolina, "democracy never lasts long. It soon wastes, exhausts,
and murders itself. There never was a democracy yet that did not commit
suicide." Again:

> If you give more than a share in the sovereignty to the democrats, that is, if you give
> them the command or preponderance in the . . . legislature, they will vote all property
> out of the hands of you aristocrats, and if they let you escape with your lives, it will be
> more humanity, consideration, and generosity than any triumphant democracy ever

displayed since the creation. And what will follow? The aristocracy among the demo-crats will take your place, and treat their fellows as severely and sternly as you have treated them.

Government, thought the Fathers, is based on property. Men who have no property lack the necessary stake in an orderly society to make stable or reliable citizens. Dread of the propertyless masses of the towns was all but universal. George Washington, Gouverneur Morris, John Dickinson, and James Madison spoke of their anxieties about the urban working class that might arise some time in the future—"men without property and principle," as Dickinson described them—and even the democratic Jefferson shared this prejudice. Madison, stating the problem, came close to anticipating the modern threats to conservative republicanism from both communism and fascism:

> In future times, a great majority of the people will not only be without landed but any other sort of property. These will either combine, under the influence of their common situation—in which case the rights of property and the public liberty will not be secure in their hands—or, what is more probable, they will become the tools of opulence and ambition, in which case there will be equal danger on another side.

What encouraged the Fathers about their own era, however, was the broad dispersion of landed property. The small landowning farmers had been trouble-some in recent years, but there was a general conviction that under a properly made Constitution a *modus vivendi* could be worked out with them. The pos-session of moderate plots of property presumably gave them a sufficient stake in society to be safe and responsible citizens under the restraints of balanced government. Influence in government would be proportionate to property; mer-chants and great landholders would be dominant, but small property-owners would have an independent and far from negligible voice. It was "politic as well as just," said Madison, "that the interest and rights of every class should be duly represented and understood in the public councils," and John Adams declared that there could be "no free government without a democratical branch in the constitution."

The farming element already satisfied the property requirements for suffrage in most of the states, and the Fathers generally had no quarrel with their enfran-chisement. But when they spoke of the necessity of founding government upon the consent of "the people," it was only these small property-holders that they had in mind. For example, the famous Virginia Bill of Rights, written by George Mason, explicitly defined those eligible for suffrage as all men "having sufficient evidence of permanent common interest with and attachment to the commu-nity"—which meant, in brief, sufficient property.

However, the original intention of the Fathers to admit the yeoman into an important but sharply limited partnership in affairs of state could not be perfectly realized. At the time the Constitution was made, Southern planters and North-ern merchants were setting their differences aside in order to meet common dangers—from radicals within and more powerful nations without. After the

Constitution was adopted, conflict between the ruling classes broke out anew, especially after powerful planters were offended by the favoritism of Hamilton's policies to Northern commercial interests. The planters turned to the farmers to form an agrarian alliance, and for more than half a century this powerful coalition embraced the bulk of the articulate interests of the country. As time went on, therefore, the mainstream of American political conviction deviated more and more from the antidemocratic position of the Constitution-makers. Yet, curiously, their general satisfaction with the Constitution together with their growing nationalism made Americans deeply reverent of the founding generation, with the result that as it grew stronger, this deviation was increasingly overlooked.

There is common agreement among modern critics that the debates over the Constitution were carried on at an intellectual level that is rare in politics, and that the Constitution itself is one of the world's masterpieces of practical statecraft. On other grounds there has been controversy. At the very beginning contemporary opponents of the Constitution foresaw an apocalyptic destruction of local government and popular institutions, while conservative Europeans of the old regime thought the young American Republic was a dangerous leftist experiment. Modern critical scholarship, which reached a high point in Charles A. Beard's *An Economic Interpretation of the Constitution of the United States,* started a new turn in the debate. The antagonism, long latent, between the philosophy of the Constitution and the philosophy of American democracy again came into the open. Professor Beard's work appeared in 1913 at the peak of the Progressive Era, when the muckraking fever was still high;* some readers tended to conclude from his findings that the Fathers were selfish reactionaries who do not deserve their high place in American esteem. Still more recently, other writers, inverting this logic, have used Beard's facts to praise the Fathers for their opposition to "democracy" and as an argument for returning again to the idea of a "republic."

In fact, the Fathers' image of themselves as moderate republicans standing between political extremes was quite accurate. They were impelled by class motives more than pietistic writers like to admit, but they were also controlled, as Professor Beard himself has . . . emphasized, by a statesmanlike sense of moderation and a scrupulously republican philosophy. Any attempt, however, to tear their ideas out of the eighteenth century context is sure to make them seem starkly reactionary. Consider, for example, the favorite maxim of John Jay: "The people who own the country ought to govern it." To the Fathers this was simply a swift axiomatic statement of the stake-in-society theory of political rights, a moderate conservative position under eighteenth-century conditions of property distribution in America. Under modern property relations this maxim

---

* The Progressive Era, from roughly 1900 to 1920, was marked by reformist movements against governmental corruption and political machines. Crusading journalists (muckrakers) and insurgent mayors and governors attempted to inject professionalism and merit into government.

demands a drastic restriction of the base of political power. A large portion of the modern middle class—and it is the strength of this class upon which balanced government depends—is propertyless; and the urban proletariat, which the Fathers so greatly feared, is almost one half the population. Further, the separation of ownership from control that has come with the corporation deprives Jay's maxim of twentieth century meaning even for many propertied people. The six hundred thousand stockholders of the American Telephone & Telegraph Company not only do not acquire political power by virtue of their stock-ownership, but they do not even acquire economic power; they cannot control their own company.

From a humanistic standpoint there is a serious dilemma in the philosophy of the Fathers, which derives from their conception of man. They thought man was a creature of rapacious self-interest, and yet they wanted him to be free—free, in essence, to contend, to engage in an umpired strife, to use property to get property. They accepted the mercantile image of life as an eternal battleground, and assumed the Hobbesian war of each against all; they did not propose to put an end to this war, but merely to stabilize it and make it less murderous. They had no hope and they offered none for any ultimate organic change in the way men conduct themselves. The result was that while they thought self-interest the most dangerous and unbrookable quality of man, they necessarily underwrote it in trying to control it. They succeeded in both respects: under the competitive capitalism of the nineteenth century America continued to be an arena for various grasping and contending interests, and the federal government continued to provide a stable and acceptable medium within which they could contend; further, it usually showed the wholesome bias on behalf of property which the Fathers expected. But no man who is as well abreast of modern science as the Fathers were of eighteenth century science believes any longer in unchanging human nature. Modern humanistic thinkers who seek for a means by which society may transcend eternal conflict and rigid adherence to property rights as its integrating principles can expect no answer in the philosophy of balanced government as it was set down by the Constitution-makers of 1787.

Summary Questions

1. What is the connection between property and liberty? Does it still hold true today?
2. How would widespread property ownership contribute to the stability of government?

1.3

An Economic Interpretation of the Constitution of the United States

Charles A. Beard

One central problem in establishing a new constitutional order in 1787 was that of limiting the power of the majority within a centralized political system that drew ultimate legitimacy from the approval of its citizens. Indeed, this was a major task that the framers addressed in writing and seeking ratification for the document. Charles A. Beard argues that the framers, "by the force of circumstances, [were] compelled to convince large economic groups that safety and strength [lay] in the adoption of the new system." This was a neat trick given Beard's assessment of the framers as economic elitists who relentlessly pursued their own interests throughout the process.

Among interpreters of the creation of the Constitution, few scholars have had more impact than Charles Beard. Despite shortcomings in Beard's analysis, his approach has been extremely important in opening up the subject to subsequent demythologizing interpretations. In addition, you should bear in mind Hofstadter's assertion that the framers saw prosperity as virtually essential for the protection of liberty.

The Constitution as an Economic Document

It is difficult for the superficial student of the Constitution, who has read only the commentaries of the legists,* to conceive of that instrument as an economic document. It places no property qualifications on voters or officers; it gives no outward recognition of any economic groups in society; it mentions no special privileges to be conferred upon any class. It betrays no feeling, such as vibrates through the French constitution of 1791; its language is cold, formal, and severe.

Charles A. Beard (1874–1948), a professor of history at Columbia University, helped found the New School for Social Research in New York City.

* A *legist* is one learned in law, and particularly ancient and Roman law.

The true inwardness of the Constitution is not revealed by an examination of its provisions as simple propositions of law; but by a long and careful study of the voluminous correspondence of the period, contemporary newspapers and pamphlets, the records of the debates in the Convention at Philadelphia and in the several state conventions, and particularly, *The Federalist,* which was widely circulated during the struggle over ratification. The correspondence shows the exact character of the evils which the Constitution was intended to remedy; the records of the proceedings in the Philadelphia Convention reveal the successive steps in the building of the framework of the government under the pressure of economic interests; the pamphlets and newspapers disclose the ideas of the contestants over the ratification; and *The Federalist* presents the political science of the new system as conceived by three of the profoundest thinkers of the period, Hamilton, Madison, and Jay.

Doubtless, the most illuminating of these sources on the economic character of the Constitution are the records of the debates in the Convention, which have come down to us in fragmentary form; and a thorough treatment of material forces reflected in the several clauses of the instrument of government created by the grave assembly at Philadelphia would require a rewriting of the history of the proceedings in the light of the great interests represented there. But an entire volume would scarcely suffice to present the results of such a survey, and an undertaking of this character is accordingly impossible here.

The Federalist, on the other hand, presents in a relatively brief and systematic form an economic interpretation of the Constitution by the men best fitted, through an intimate knowledge of the ideals of the framers, to expound the political science of the new government. This wonderful piece of argumentation by Hamilton, Madison, and Jay is in fact the finest study in the economic interpretation of politics which exists in any language; and whoever would understand the Constitution as an economic document need hardly go beyond it. It is true that the tone of the writers is somewhat modified on account of the fact that they are appealing to the voters to ratify the Constitution, but at the same time they are, by the force of circumstances, compelled to convince large economic groups that safety and strength lie in the adoption of the new system.

Indeed, every fundamental appeal in it is to some material and substantial interest. Sometimes it is to the people at large in the name of protection against invading armies and European coalitions. Sometimes it is to the commercial classes whose business is represented as prostrate before the follies of the Confederation. Now it is to creditors seeking relief against paper money and the assaults of the agrarians in general; now it is to the holders of federal securities which are depreciating toward the vanishing point. But above all, it is to the owners of personalty* anxious to find a foil against the attacks of levelling democracy, that the authors of *The Federalist* address their most cogent arguments in favor of ratification. It is true there is much discussion of the details of the new frame-

---

* *Personalty* is a legal term for personal property.

work of government, to which even some friends of reform took exceptions; but Madison and Hamilton both knew that these were incidental matters when compared with the sound basis upon which the superstructure rested.

In reading the pages of this remarkable work as a study in political economy, it is important to bear in mind that the system, which the authors are describing, consisted of two fundamental parts—one positive, the other negative:

I. A government endowed with certain positive powers, but so constructed as to break the force of majority rule and prevent invasions of the property rights of minorities.

II. Restrictions on the state legislatures which had been so vigorous in their attacks on capital.

Under some circumstances, action is the immediate interest of the dominant party; and whenever it desires to make an economic gain through governmental functioning, it must have, of course, a system endowed with the requisite powers.

Examples of this are to be found in protective tariffs, in ship subsidies, in railway land grants, in river and harbor improvements, and so on through the catalogue of so-called "paternalistic" legislation. Of course it may be shown that the "general good" is the ostensible object of any particular act; but the general good is a passive force, and unless we know who are the several individuals that benefit in its name, it has no meaning. When it is so analyzed, immediate and remote beneficiaries are discovered; and the former are usually found to have been the dynamic element in securing the legislation. Take, for example, the economic interests of the advocates who appear in tariff hearings at Washington.

On the obverse side, dominant interests quite as often benefit from the prevention of governmental action as from positive assistance. They are able to take care of themselves if let alone within the circle of protection created by the law. Indeed, most owners of property have as much to fear from positive governmental action as from their inability to secure advantageous legislation. Particularly is this true where the field of private property is already extended to cover practically every form of tangible and intangible wealth. This was clearly set forth by Hamilton:

> It may perhaps be said that the power of preventing bad laws includes that of preventing good ones. . . . But this objection will have little weight with those who can properly estimate the mischiefs of that inconstancy and mutability in the laws which form the greatest blemish in the character and genius of our governments. They will consider every institution calculated to restrain the excess of law-making, and to keep things in the same state in which they happen to be at any given period, as more likely to do good than harm. . . . The injury which may possibly be done by defeating a few good laws will be amply compensated by the advantage of preventing a number of bad ones.

The Underlying Political Science of the Constitution

Before taking up the economic implications of the structure of the federal government, it is important to ascertain what, in the opinion of *The Federalist*, is

the basis of all government. The most philosophical examination of the foundations of political science is made by Madison in the tenth number. Here he lays
down, in no uncertain language, the principle that the first and elemental
concern of every government is economic.

1. "The first object of government," he declares, is the protection of "the
diversity in the faculties of men, from which the rights of property originate." The
chief business of government, from which, perforce, its essential nature must be
derived, consists in the control and adjustment of conflicting economic interests.
After enumerating the various forms of propertied interests which spring up
inevitably in modern society, he adds: "The regulation of these various and
interfering interests forms the principal task of modern legislation, and involves
the spirit of party and faction in the ordinary operations of the government."

2. What are the chief causes of these conflicting political forces with which
the government must concern itself? Madison answers. Of course fanciful and
frivolous distinctions have sometimes been the cause of violent conflicts; "but the
most common and durable source of factions has been the various and unequal
distribution of property. Those who hold and those who are without property
have ever formed distinct interests in society. Those who are creditors, and those
who are debtors, fall under a like discrimination. A landed interest, a manufacturing interest, a mercantile interest, a moneyed interest, with many lesser
interests grow up of necessity in civilized nations, and divide them into different
classes actuated by different sentiments and views."

3. The theories of government which men entertain are emotional reactions
to their property interests. "From the protection of different and unequal faculties of acquiring property, the possession of different degrees and kinds of property immediately results; *and from the influence of these on the sentiments and views
of the respective proprietors, ensues a division of society into different interests and
parties.*" Legislatures reflect these interests. "What," he asks, "are the different
classes of legislators but advocates and parties to the causes which they determine." There is no help for it. "The causes of faction cannot be removed," and
"we well know that neither moral nor religious motives can be relied on as an
adequate control."

4. Unequal distribution of property is inevitable, and from it contending
factions will rise in the state. The government will reflect them, for they will have
their separate principles and "sentiments"; but the supreme danger will arise from
the fusion of certain interests into an overbearing majority, which Madison, in
another place, prophesied would be the landless proletariat—an overbearing
majority which will make its "rights" paramount, and sacrifice the "rights" of the
minority. "To secure the public good," he declares, "and private rights against the
danger of such a faction and at the same time preserve the spirit and the form of
popular government is then the great object to which our inquiries are directed."

5. How is this to be done? Since the contending classes cannot be eliminated
and their interests are bound to be reflected in politics, the only way out lies in
making it difficult for enough contending interests to fuse into a majority, and in

balancing one over against another. The machinery for doing this is created by the new Constitution and by the Union. (a) Public views are to be refined and enlarged "by passing them through the medium of a chosen body of citizens." (b) The very size of the Union will enable the inclusion of more interests so that the danger of an overbearing majority is not so great. "The smaller the society, the fewer probably will be the distinct parties and interests composing it; the fewer the distinct parties and interests, the more frequently will a majority be found of the same party. . . . Extend the sphere, and you take in a greater variety of parties and interests; you make it less probable that a majority of the whole will have a common motive to invade the rights of other citizens; or if such a common motive exists, it will be more difficult for all who feel it to discover their strength and to act in unison with each other."

Q.E.D. [which was to be demonstrated], "in the extent and proper structure of the Union, therefore, we behold a republican remedy for the diseases most incident to republican government."

The Economic Conflict over Ratification as Viewed by Contemporaries

. . . No one can pore for weeks over the letters, newspapers, and pamphlets of the years 1787–1789 without coming to the conclusion that there was a deep-seated conflict between a popular party based on paper money and agrarian interests, and a conservative party centered in the towns and resting on financial, mercantile, and personal property interests generally. It is true that much of the fulmination in pamphlets was concerned with controversies over various features of the Constitution; but those writers who went to the bottom of matters, such as the authors of *The Federalist,* and the more serious Anti-Federalists,* gave careful attention to the basic elements in the struggle as well as to the incidental controversial details.

The superficiality of many of the ostensible reasons put forth by the opponents of the Constitution was penetrated by Madison. Writing to Jefferson, in October, 1788, he says: "The little pamphlet herewith inclosed will give you a collective view of the alterations which have been proposed by the State Conventions for the new Constitution. Various and numerous as they appear, they certainly omit many of the true grounds of opposition. The articles relating to Treaties, to paper money, and to contracts, created more enemies than all the errors in the system, positive and negative, put together."

Naturally the more circumspect of the pamphleteers who lent their support to the new system were careful about a too precise alignment of forces, for their

---

* The term *antifederalists* has attached itself to opponents of the Constitution. Ironically, Madison and Hamilton were nationalists who appropriated the federalist title. True federalists, who desired more power for the states, were left with the less attractive antifederalist label.

strength often lay in the conciliation of opponents rather than in exciting a more deep-seated antagonism. But even in such conciliatory publications the material advantages to be expected from the adoption of the Constitution are constantly put forward.

Take, for example, this extract from a mollifying "Address to the Freemen of America" issued while the Convention was in the midst of its deliberations:

> Let the public creditor, who lent his money to his country, and the soldier and citizen who yielded their services, come forward next and contribute their aid to establish an effective federal government. It is from the united power and resources of America only that they can expect permanent and substantial justice. . . . Let the citizens of America who inhabit the western counties of our states fly to a federal power for protection [against the Indians]. . . . Let the farmer who groans beneath the weight of direct taxation seek relief from a government whose extensive jurisdiction will enable it to extract the resources of our country by means of imposts and customs. Let the merchant, who complains of the restrictions and exclusions imposed upon his vessels by foreign nations, unite his influence in establishing a power that shall retaliate those injuries and insure him success in his honest pursuits by a general system of commercial regulations. Let the manufacturer and mechanic, who are everywhere languishing for want of employment, direct their eyes to an assembly of the states. It will be in their power only to encourage such arts and manufactures as are essential to the prosperity of our country. . . .

Conclusions

. . . The movement for the Constitution of the United States was originated and carried through principally by four groups of personalty interests which had been adversely affected under the Articles of Confederation: money, public securities, manufactures, and trade and shipping.

The first firm steps toward the formation of the Constitution were taken by a small and active group of men immediately interested through their personal possessions in the outcome of their labors.

No popular vote was taken directly or indirectly on the proposition to call the Convention which drafted the Constitution.

A large propertyless mass was, under the prevailing suffrage qualifications, excluded at the outset from participation (through representatives) in the work of framing the Constitution.

The members of the Philadelphia Convention which drafted the Constitution were, with a few exceptions, immediately, directly, and personally interested in, and derived economic advantages from, the establishment of the new system.

The Constitution was essentially an economic document based upon the concept that the fundamental private rights of property are anterior to government and morally beyond the reach of popular majorities.

The major portion of the members of the Convention are on record as recognizing the claim of property to a special and defensive position in the Constitution.

In the ratification of the Constitution, about three-fourths of the adult males failed to vote on the question, having abstained from the elections at which delegates to the state conventions were chosen, either on account of their indifference or their disfranchisement by property qualifications.

The Constitution was ratified by a vote of probably not more than one-sixth of the adult males.

It is questionable whether a majority of the voters participating in the elections for the state conventions in New York, Massachusetts, New Hampshire, Virginia, and South Carolina, actually approved the ratification of the Constitution.

The leaders who supported the Constitution in the ratifying conventions represented the same economic groups as the members of the Philadelphia Convention; and in a large number of instances they were also directly and personally interested in the outcome of their efforts.

In the ratification, it became manifest that the line of cleavage for and against the Constitution was between substantial personalty interests on the one hand and the small farming and debtor interests on the other.

The Constitution was not created by "the whole people" as the jurists have said; neither was it created by "the states" as Southern nullifiers long contended; but it was the work of a consolidated group whose interests knew no state boundaries and were truly national in their scope.

Summary Questions

1. Compare Roche's and Beard's characterizations of the framers. Do these scholars reach fundamentally different conclusions, or are they essentially in accord on the nature of the framers' actions and motivations?
2. Why was a strong central government so important for a propertied economic elite? Do you think the framers acted solely on economic grounds?

1.4

The Federalist, No. 51

James Madison

As we have seen, among the formidable tasks the framers faced in writing the Constitution was establishing a strong central government while minimizing the possibility that this authority would be abused. The resulting system of checks and balances relies heavily on the separation of powers and a multiple-level, federal relationship between the states and the national government.

James Madison, Alexander Hamilton, and John Jay led the fight for ratification through a series of newspaper articles, *The Federalist.* In the following selection from these papers, Madison articulates a sophisticated understanding of the actual operation of central authority divided into legislative, executive, and judicial branches. Madison observes that regardless of the formal separations embodied within a constitution, the different branches in fact will share powers. Such a realistic assessment is reflected today in continuing arguments over the legislature's role in foreign policy (for example, passing legislation to implement the North American Free Trade Agreement) and the Supreme Court's willingness to range beyond narrow constitutional interpretations, as in its 1973 *Roe* v. *Wade* abortion decision.

To the People of the State of New York: To what expedient, then, shall we finally resort for maintaining in practice the necessary partition of power among the several departments as laid down in the Constitution? The only answer that can be given is, that as all these exterior provisions are found to be inadequate, the defect must be supplied by so contriving the interior structure of the government as that its several constituent parts may, by their mutual relations, be the means of keeping each other in their proper places. Without presuming to undertake a full development of this important idea, I will hazard a few general observations, which may perhaps place it in a clearer light, and enable us to form a more correct judgment of the principles and structure of the government planned by the convention.

In order to lay a due foundation for that separate and distinct exercise of the difficult powers of government, which to a certain extent is admitted on all hands

---

James Madison, who was the chief drafter of the Constitution, became the fourth president of the United States.

to be essential to the preservation of liberty, it is evident that each department should have a will of its own; and consequently should be so constituted that the members of each should have as little agency as possible in the appointment of the members of the others. Were this principle rigorously adhered to, it would require that all the appointments for the supreme executive, legislative, and judiciary magistracies should be drawn from the same fountain of authority, the people, through channels having no communication whatever with one another. Perhaps such a plan of constructing the several departments would be less difficult in practice than it may in contemplation appear. Some difficulties, however, and some additional expense would attend the execution of it. Some deviations, therefore, from the principle must be admitted. In the constitution of the judiciary department in particular, it might be inexpedient to insist rigorously on the principle: first, because peculiar qualifications being essential in the members, the primary consideration ought to be to select that mode of choice which best secures these qualifications; secondly, because the permanent tenure by which the appointments are held in that department must soon destroy all sense of dependence on the authority conferring them.

It is equally evident, that the members of each department should be as little dependent as possible on those of the others for the emoluments annexed to their offices. Were the executive magistrate or the judges not independent of the legislature in this particular, their independence in every other would be merely nominal.

But the great security against a gradual concentration of the several powers in the same department, consists in giving to those who administer each department the necessary constitutional means and personal motives to resist encroachments of the others. The provision for defence must in this, as in all other cases, be made commensurate to the danger of attack. Ambition must be made to counteract ambition. The interest of the man must be connected with the constitutional rights of the place. It may be a reflection on human nature, that such devices should be necessary to control the abuses of government. But what is government itself, but the greatest of all reflections on human nature? If men were angels, no government would be necessary. If angels were to govern men, neither external nor internal controls on government would be necessary. In framing a government which is to be administered by men over men, the great difficulty lies in this: you must first enable the government to control the governed; and in the next place oblige it to control itself. A dependence on the people is, no doubt, the primary control on the government; but experience has taught mankind the necessity of auxiliary precautions.

The policy of supplying, by opposite and rival interests, the defect of better motives might be traced through the whole system of human affairs, private as well as public. We see it particularly displayed in all the subordinate distributions of power, where the constant aim is to divide and arrange the several offices in such a manner as that each may be a check on the other—that the private interest of every individual may be a sentinel over the public rights. These inventions of prudence cannot be less requisite in the distribution of the supreme powers of the state.

But it is not possible to give to each department an equal power of self-defence. In republican government the legislative authority necessarily predominates. The remedy for this inconveniency is to divide the legislature into different branches; and to render them, by different modes of election and different principles of action, as little connected with each other as the nature of their common functions and their common dependence on the society will admit. It may even be necessary to guard against dangerous encroachments by still further precautions. As the weight of the legislative authority requires that it should be thus divided, the weakness of the executive may require, on the other hand, that it should be fortified. An absolute negative on the legislature [i.e., veto] appears, at first view, to be the natural defence with which the executive magistrate should be armed. But perhaps it would be neither altogether safe nor alone sufficient. On ordinary occasions it might not be exerted with the requisite firmness, and on extraordinary occasions it might be perfidiously abused. May not this defect of an absolute negative be supplied by some qualified connection between this weaker department and the weaker branch of the stronger department, by which the latter may be led to support the constitutional rights of the former, without being too much detached from the rights of its own department?

If the principles on which these observations are founded be just . . . and they be applied as a criterion to the several state constitutions and to the federal Constitution, it will be found that if the latter does not perfectly correspond with them, the former are infinitely less able to bear such a test.

There are, moreover, two considerations particularly applicable to the federal system of America, which place that system in a very interesting point of view.

First. In a single republic, all the power surrendered by the people is submitted to the administration of a single government; and the usurpations are guarded against by a division of the government into distinct and separate departments. In the compound republic of America,* the power surrendered by the people is first divided between two distinct governments, and then the portion allotted to each subdivided among distinct and separate departments. Hence a double security arises to the rights of the people. The different governments will control each other, at the same time that each will be controlled by itself.

Second. It is of great importance in a republic not only to guard the society against the oppression of its rulers, but to guard one part of the society against the injustice of the other part. Different interests necessarily exist in different classes of citizens. If a majority be united by a common interest, the rights of the minority will be insecure. There are but two methods of providing against this evil: the one by creating a will in the community independent of the majority—that is, of the

---

* For the framers, a *republic* was essentially a representative democracy. A *compound republic* placed representative authority at two levels, state and national.

society itself; the other by comprehending in the society so many separate descriptions of citizens as will render an unjust combination of a majority of the whole very improbable, if not impracticable. The first method prevails in all governments possessing an hereditary or self-appointed authority. This, at best, is but a precarious security; because a power independent of the society may as well espouse the unjust views of the major, as the rightful interests of the minor party, and may possibly be turned against both parties. The second method will be exemplified in the federal republic of the United States. Whilst all authority in it will be derived from and dependent on the society, the society itself will be broken into so many parts, interests and classes of citizens, that the rights of individuals or of the minority will be in little danger from interested combinations of the majority. In a free government the security for civil rights must be the same as that for religious rights.* It consists in the one case in the multiplicity of interests and in the other in the multiplicity of sects. The degree of security in both cases will depend on the number of interests and sects; and this may be presumed to depend on the extent of country and number of people comprehended under the same government. This view of the subject must particularly recommend a proper federal system to all the sincere and considerate friends of republican government, since it shows that in exact proportion as the territory of the Union may be formed into more circumscribed confederacies or states, oppressive combinations of a majority will be facilitated; the best security under the republican forms for the rights of every class of citizens will be diminished; and consequently the stability and independence of some member of the government, the only other security, must be proportionally increased. Justice is the end of government. It is the end of civil society. It ever has been and ever will be pursued until it be obtained, or until liberty be lost in the pursuit. In a society under the forms of which the stronger faction can readily unite and oppress the weaker, anarchy may as truly be said to reign as in a state of nature, where the weaker individual is not secured against the violence of the stronger; and, as in the latter state even the stronger individuals are prompted, by the uncertainty of their condition, to submit to government which may protect the weak as well as themselves; so, in the former state will the more powerful factions or parties be gradually induced by a like motive to wish for a government which will protect all parties, the weaker as well as the more powerful. It can be little doubted that if the state of Rhode Island was separated from the Confederacy and left to itself, the insecurity of rights under the popular form of government within such narrow limits would be displayed by such reiterated oppressions of factious majorities that some power altogether independent of the people would soon be called for by the voice of the very factions whose misrule had proved the necessity of it. In the

---

* Madison and his colleagues did not incorporate a separate bill of rights into the Constitution; rather, they relied on the "multiplicity of interests" to protect these rights. In part, a guarantee that a bill of rights would be passed was essential to ratification, especially at New York's convention, where the document won a narrow 30–27 victory.

extended republic of the United States and among the great variety of interests, parties, and sects which it embraces, a coalition of a majority of the whole society could seldom take place on any other principles than those of justice and the general good; and there being thus less danger to a minor from the will of a major party, there must be less pretext, also, to provide for the security of the former, by introducing into the government a will not dependent on the latter, or, in other words, a will independent of the society itself. It is no less certain than it is important, notwithstanding the contrary opinions which have been entertained, that the larger the society, provided it lie within a practical sphere, the more duly capable it will be of self-government. And happily for the *republican cause*, the practicable sphere may be carried to a very great extent by a judicious modification and mixture of the *federal principle*.

Summary Questions

1. Could governmental powers ever be completely separated into three distinct branches?
2. Madison claims that the legislative branch will be the strongest. Why would this be so? Does such a contention hold true today?

Chapter 2

Federalism and Intergovernmental Relations

Federalism is a way of organizing a political system so that authority is shared between a central government and state or regional governments. Individuals living in Pennsylvania, for example, are citizens of both that state and the United States, are under the legal authority of both governments, and have obligations (such as paying taxes) to each government.

A country is federal only if the subnational units exist independently of the national government and can make some binding decisions on their own. Some nations, like Britain and France, have unitary forms of government, in which regional and local units exist only to aid the national administration. Such subnational units can be abolished or altered at any time by the national government. In contrast, the central government in the United States (commonly referred to as the federal government) can never abolish a state. Also, the Constitution protects states by providing for two senators and at least one member of the House of Representatives from each state.

The United States embraced the concept of federalism in the Constitution more than two hundred years ago, amid much debate. The Articles of Confederation had proved inadequate because of the weakness of the central government and the almost total autonomy of the states. The nation's domestic economy was chaotic, as individual states' trade restrictions, tariff barriers, and currency weaknesses led to local depressions and encouraged citizens to move from state to state to escape debt obligations. At the same time, neither the central government nor the states could protect citizens from foreign threats or even from domestic insurrection. At the Constitutional Convention in 1787, the founders agreed that the existing government was inadequate; debate arose over the amount of power the central government should be given and how certain aspects of state autonomy could be ensured.

Federalism resulted from a compromise between those seeking a more powerful and efficient central government and those who feared such a government and valued state independence. The founders hoped the national government would act on matters concerning the common good, such as defense, trade, and financial stability, yet not become so strong that it threatened individual liberty and reduced diversity among the states. Federalism as it was understood then, and as it operated until the twentieth century, essentially meant dual federalism: Governmental functions were divided between the state and the national government, each of which was autonomous in its own sphere. For example, the national government had a monopoly on delivering the mail and conducting foreign relations, whereas state governments were in charge of areas such as education and law enforcement.

The framers tried to be as clear as possible in defining the powers possessed by the national government (Article 1, Section 8 of the Constitution). But with some exceptions, such as state control of the conduct of elections, they said little about state powers or about what should happen when national and state authorities collide.

In general, the trend has been to expand the central government's powers beyond those enumerated in the Constitution and thus to erode state power and independence. Supreme Court decisions have played a crucial role here, opening the door for the federal government's involvement in many traditionally state functions. In the landmark case of *McCulloch* v. *Maryland* (1819), the Court affirmed the supremacy of the national government over the states and introduced the notion of implied powers. The Court ruled that the purpose of the Constitution is not to prevent Congress from carrying out the enumerated powers; Congress has the authority to use all means "necessary and proper" to fulfill its obligations. For example, broad interpretations of the commerce clause not only have given Congress the authority to regulate commerce with foreign nations and among the states but also have provided it with a basis for intervention within state boundaries on matters such as racial relations.

The variety and scale of the federal government's actions have changed over the years. Since the Civil War (which definitively settled the question of national supremacy), the relationships between the states and the federal government have become increasingly characterized by cooperative federalism, in which governmental powers and policies are shared. Cooperative federalism often involves sharing the costs of needed programs or projects, which requires state and local officials to adhere to federal guidelines. Franklin Roosevelt's New Deal, with its expanded national economic and social agenda, had an especially marked impact on intergovernmental relations. Both states and citizens became dependent on Washington for aid, for many states were incapable of dealing with poverty on their own. In addition, the problems of an industrial society that did not stop at state boundaries, such as water and air pollution, necessitated federal government action.

By the 1960s, American citizens seemed unwilling to let states and localities thwart the national will, and the central government was viewed as an entity to be encouraged rather than feared. Perhaps the greatest cost of federalism has been the systematic oppression of blacks by localities and states, first as slaves and then as a separate class. The Great Society programs of the Johnson years attempted to eliminate racism and poverty through national initiatives, and federal aid to the states rose greatly during the 1960s and 1970s. By 1980, Daniel Elazar, a leading scholar of federalism, concluded that

> we have moved to a system in which it is taken as axiomatic that the federal government shall initiate policies and programs, shall determine their character, shall delegate their administration to the states and localities according to terms that it alone determines, and shall provide for whatever intervention on the part of its administrative agencies it deems necessary to secure compliance with those terms.

Still, the boundaries between state and national authority, originally inspired by a fear of a strong central government, have never been fixed, and political conflict between national and state governments has existed since the nation's founding.

There is a great deal of evidence to support the notion that the role of the states was enhanced during the 1980s. But forces such as the mass media and economic interdependence among nations are leading to an increasingly national culture. Further, it is unlikely that the states will have the protection of the courts in defending their rights, as has often been the case in the past. In *Garcia* v. *San Antonio Metropolitan Transit Authority* (1985), the Supreme Court ruled that no constitutional limits contained in the Tenth Amendment or any other section of the Constitution may limit the national government's power over commerce. States' rights, therefore, are to be found only in the structure of the government, such as equal state representation in the Senate. In a sense, states are now considered equivalent to other special interest groups asking for favors and protection from the national government in Washington.

The four readings in this chapter illustrate various aspects of the controversy over the meaning and changing nature of federalism. *The Federalist,* No. 39, reflects James Madison's views on the relations between states and the national government under the new constitution and on the importance of the governmental structure as an American innovation. The landmark case *McCulloch* v. *Maryland* resolved two key issues left open by the Constitution: which level of government is supreme when state and national policies clash and whether the federal government is limited by the Tenth Amendment to those powers explicitly enumerated in the Constitution.

The final two selections look at federalism in practice. H. G. Nicholas explores some of federalism's costs or disadvantages in American government. Martha Derthick views with dismay the tendency of federal authority to erode state power, and suggests efforts should be made to prevent the states from becoming totally subordinate units to the federal government.

2.1

The Federalist, No. 39

James Madison

At the time of the framing of the Constitution, the founders were aware of two basic forms of government: a national government, with total central domination, and a confederation, a loose alliance of states in which the central government has virtually no power. When the Constitution and *The Federalist* were written, a "federal" government and a "confederation" were synonymous. The governmental form that has come to be called *federalism,* in which authority is divided between two independent levels, was the invention of the founders, though the label came later.

Critics of the Constitution believed the document gave so much power to the central government that it was in fact "national" in character. In *The Federalist,* No. 39, James Madison refutes this charge and asserts that the new government is "neither a national nor a federal Constitution, but a composition of both." Being a politician, Madison took great pains to point out that the national government's powers are strictly limited to those enumerated in the Constitution and that the residual sovereignty of the states is greater than that of the national government. The first part of this paper can also be regarded as an elegant statement of what Madison meant by the term *republic.*

*T*o the People of the State of New York: The first question that offers itself is, whether the general form and aspect of the government be strictly republican?* It is evident that no other form would be reconcilable with the genius of the people of America; with the fundamental principles of the revolution; or with that honorable determination, which animates every votary [devotee] of freedom, to rest all our political experiments on the capacity of mankind for self-government. If the plan of the Convention therefore be found to depart from the republican character, its advocates must abandon it as no longer defensible.

---

* A *republican* form of government is one in which power resides in the people but is formally exercised by their elected representatives.

What then are the distinctive characters of the republican form? Were an answer to this question to be sought, not by recurring to principles, but in the application of the term by political writers, to the constitutions of different States, no satisfactory one would ever be found. Holland, in which no particle of the supreme authority is derived from the people, has passed almost universally under the denomination of a republic. The same title has been bestowed on Venice, where absolute power over the great body of the people, is exercised in the most absolute manner, by a small body of hereditary nobles. Poland, which is a mixture of aristocracy and of monarchy in their worst forms, has been dignified with the same appellation. The government of England, which has one republican branch only, combined with a hereditary aristocracy and monarchy, has with equal impropriety been frequently placed on the list of republics. These examples, which are nearly as dissimilar to each other as to a genuine republic, show the extreme inaccuracy with which the term has been used in political disquisitions.

If we resort for a criterion, to the different principles on which different forms of government are established, we may define a republic to be, or at least may bestow that name on, a government which derives all its powers directly or indirectly from the great body of the people; and is administered by persons holding their offices during pleasure, for a limited period, or during good behaviour. It is *essential* to such a government, that it be derived from the great body of the society, not from an inconsiderable proportion, or a favored class of it; otherwise a handful of tyrannical nobles, exercising their oppressions by a delegation of their powers, might aspire to the rank of republicans, and claim for their government the honorable title of republic. It is *sufficient* for such a government, that the persons administering it be appointed, either directly or indirectly, by the people; and that they hold their appointments by either of the tenures just specified; otherwise every government in the United States, as well as every other popular government that has been or can be well organized or well executed, would be degraded from the republican character. According to the Constitution of every State in the Union, some or other of the officers of government are appointed indirectly only by the people. According to most of them the chief magistrate himself is so appointed. And according to one, this mode of appointment is extended to one of the coordinate branches of the legislature. According to all the Constitutions also, the tenure of the highest offices is extended to a definite period, and in many instances, both within the legislative and executive departments, to a period of years. According to the provisions of most of the constitutions, again, as well as according to the most respectable and received opinions on the subject, the members of the judiciary department are to retain their offices by the firm tenure of good behaviour.

On comparing the Constitution planned by the Convention, with the standard here fixed, we perceive at once that it is in the most rigid sense conformable to it. The House of Representatives, like that of one branch at least of all the State

Legislatures, is elected immediately by the great body of the people. The Senate, like the present Congress, and the Senate of Maryland, derives its appointment indirectly from the people.* The President is indirectly derived from the choice of the people, according to the example in most of the States. Even the judges, with all other officers of the Union, will, as in the several States, be the choice, though a remote choice, of the people themselves. The duration of the appointments is equally conformable to the republican standard, and to the model of the State Constitutions. The House of Representatives is periodically elective as in all the States: and for the period of two years as in the State of South-Carolina. The Senate is elective for the period of six years; which is but one year more than the period of the Senate of Maryland; and but two more than that of the Senates of New-York and Virginia. The President is to continue in office for the period of four years; as in New-York and Delaware, the chief magistrate is elected for three years, and in South-Carolina for two years. In the other States the election is annual. In several of the States however, no constitutional provision is made for the impeachment of the Chief Magistrate. And in Delaware and Virginia, he is not impeachable till out of office. The President of the United States is impeachable at any time during his continuance in office. The tenure by which the Judges are to hold their places, is, as it unquestionably ought to be, that of good behaviour. The tenure of the ministerial offices generally will be a subject of legal regulation, conformably to the reason of the case, and the example of the State Constitutions.

Could any further proof be required of the republican complexion of this system, the most decisive one might be found in its absolute prohibition of titles of nobility, both under the Federal and the State Governments; and in its express guarantee of the republican form to each of the latter.

But it was not sufficient, say the adversaries of the proposed Constitution, for the Convention to adhere to the republican form. They ought, with equal care, to have preserved the *federal* form, which regards the union as a *confederacy* of sovereign States; instead of which, they have framed a *national* government, which regards the union as a *consolidation* of the States. And it is asked by what authority this bold and radical innovation was undertaken. The handle which has been made of this objection requires, that it should be examined with some precision.

Without enquiring into the accuracy of the distinction on which the objection is founded, it will be necessary to a just estimate of its force, first to ascertain the real character of the government in question; secondly, to enquire how far the Convention were authorised to propose such a government; and thirdly, how far the duty they owed to their country, could supply any defect of regular authority.

---

* The Seventeenth Amendment, adopted in 1913, changed the election procedure for senators from indirect election by state legislatures to direct election by the people of each state.

First. In order to ascertain the real character of the government it may be considered in relation to the foundation on which it is to be established; to the sources from which its ordinary powers are to be drawn; to the operation of those powers; to the extent of them; and to the authority by which future changes in the government are to be introduced.

On examining the first relation, it appears on one hand that the Constitution is to be founded on the assent and ratification of the people of America, given by deputies elected for the special purpose; but on the other, that this assent and ratification is to be given by the people, not as individuals composing one entire nation; but as composing the distinct and independent States to which they respectively belong. It is to be the assent and ratification of the several States, derived from the supreme authority in each State, the authority of the people themselves. The act therefore establishing the Constitution, will not be a *national* but a *federal* act.

That it will be a federal and not a national act, as these terms are understood by the objectors, the act of the people as forming so many independent States, not as forming one aggregate nation, is obvious from this single consideration that it is to result neither from the decision of a *majority* of the people of the Union, nor from that of a *majority* of the States. It must result from the *unanimous* assent of the several States that are parties to it, differing no other wise from their ordinary assent than in its being expressed, not by the legislative authority, but by that of the people themselves. Were the people regarded in this transaction as forming one nation, the will of the majority of the whole people of the United States would bind the minority; in the same manner as the majority in each State must bind the minority; and the will of the majority must be determined either by a comparison of the individual votes; or by considering the will of a majority of the States, as evidence of the will of a majority of the people of the United States. Neither of these rules has been adopted. Each State in ratifying the Constitution, is considered as a sovereign body independent of all others, and only to be bound by its own voluntary act. In this relation then the new Constitution will, if established, be a *federal* and not a *national* Constitution.

The next relation is to the sources from which the ordinary powers of government are to be derived. The house of representatives will derive its powers from the people of America, and the people will be represented in the same proportion, and on the same principle, as they are in the Legislature of a particular State. So far the Government is *national* not *federal*. The Senate on the other hand will derive its powers from the States, as political and co-equal societies; and these will be represented on the principle of equality in the Senate, as they now are in the existing Congress. So far the government is *federal*, not *national*. The executive power will be derived from a very compound source. The immediate election of the President is to be made by the States in their political characters. The votes allotted to them are in a compound ratio, which considers them partly as distinct and co-equal societies; partly as unequal members of the same society. The eventual election again is to be made by that branch of the Legislature which consists of the national representatives; but in this particular act, they are to be thrown into the form of individual delegations from so many distinct and co-equal bodies politic. From this aspect of the Government, it appears to be of a mixed character presenting at least as many *federal* as *national* features.

The difference between a federal and national Government as it relates to the *operation of the Government* is supposed to consist in this, that in the former, the powers operate on the political bodies composing the confederacy, in their political capacities: In the latter, on the individual citizens, composing the nation, in their individual capacities. On trying the Constitution by this criterion, it falls under the *national*, not the *federal* character; though perhaps not so compleatly, as has been understood. In several cases and particularly in the trial of controversies to which States may be parties, they must be viewed and proceeded against in their collective and political capacities only. So far the national countenance of the Government on this side seems to be disfigured by a few federal features. But this blemish is perhaps unavoidable in any plan; and the operation of the Government on the people in their individual capacities, in its ordinary and most essential proceedings, may on the whole designate it in this relation a *national* Government.

But if the Government be national with regard to the *operation* of its powers, it changes its aspect again when we contemplate it in relation to the *extent* of its powers. The idea of a national Government involves in it, not only an authority over the individual citizens; but an indefinite supremacy over all persons and things, so far as they are objects of lawful Government. Among a people consolidated into one nation, this supremacy is compleatly vested in the national Legislature. Among communities united for particular purposes, it is vested partly in the general, and partly in the municipal Legislatures. In the former case, all local authorities are subordinate to the supreme; and may be controuled, directed or abolished by it at pleasure. In the latter the local or municipal authorities form distinct and independent portions of the supremacy, no more subject within their respective spheres to the general authority, than the general authority is subject to them, within its own sphere. In this relation then the proposed Government cannot be deemed a *national* one; since its jurisdiction extends to certain enumerated objects only, and leaves to the several States a residuary and inviolable sovereignty over all other objects. It is true that in controversies relating to the boundary between the two jurisdictions, the tribunal which is ultimately to decide is to be established under the general Government.* But this does not change the principle of the case. The decision is to be impartially made, accord-

---

* The tribunal to resolve boundary disputes became the Supreme Court (see *McCulloch* v. *Maryland,* which follows this selection).

ing to the rules of the Constitution; and all the usual and most effectual precautions are taken to secure this impartiality. Some such tribunal is clearly essential to prevent an appeal to the sword, and a dissolution of the compact; and that it ought to be established under the general rather than under the local Governments; or to speak more properly, that it could be safely established under the first alone, is a position not likely to be combated.

If we try the Constitution by its last relation, to the authority by which amendments are to be made, we find it neither wholly *national*, nor wholly *federal*. Were it wholly national, the supreme and ultimate authority would reside in the *majority* of the people of the Union; and this authority would be competent at all times, like that of a majority of every national society, to alter or abolish its established Government. Were it wholly federal on the other hand, the concurrence of each State in the Union would be essential to every alteration that would be binding on all. The mode provided by the plan of the Convention is not founded on either of these principles. In requiring more than a majority, and particularly, in computing the proportion by *States*, not by *citizens*, it departs from the *national*, and advances towards the *federal* character: In rendering the concurrence of less than the whole number of States sufficient, it loses again the *federal*, and partakes of the *national* character.

The proposed Constitution therefore is in strictness neither a national nor a federal constitution; but a composition of both. In its foundation, it is federal, not national; in the sources from which the ordinary powers of the Government are drawn, it is partly federal, and partly national; in the operation of these powers, it is national, not federal; in the extent of them again, it is federal, not national. And finally, in the authoritative mode of introducing amendments, it is neither wholly federal, nor wholly national.

Summary Questions

1. According to Madison, why was the new U.S. Constitution neither a "national" nor a "federal" document? Which of its features were designed to curb the national government's domination of the states?
2. Madison believed the Constitution set up a republican rather than a democratic form of government. What features of the document were designed to give the people an indirect rather than a direct influence on public policy?

2.2

McCulloch v. Maryland (1819)

In many areas, the framers of the Constitution were explicit about the powers granted to the national government and to the states. In other areas, however, such as the power to tax, the two were given many of the same responsibilities. The Constitution leaves open the relationship of state and national authority when their policies conflict. In 1819, *McCulloch* v. *Maryland** settled the issue in favor of the national government.

In 1791 Congress created a national bank to print money, make loans, and engage in a variety of banking activities. The bank was deeply resented by a number of state legislatures, which held that Congress did not have the authority to charter a bank, and in 1818 Maryland passed a law that taxed its Baltimore branch $15,000. James McCulloch, a cashier at the bank, refused to pay and was sued in state court. The state's tax was upheld, and the bank appealed to the U.S. Supreme Court.

Chief Justice John Marshall delivered a landmark opinion for the Court with a decision that markedly expanded the powers of the national government over those explicitly stated in the Constitution and affirmed the supremacy of the national government over the states. According to the Court, Congress had the power to charter a national bank because it had been granted the power "to make all laws which shall be necessary and proper for carrying into execution" the expressed powers. In short, Congress has a number of implied powers in addition to its enumerated powers. Further, because the power to tax could be used to destroy an institution that is necessary for the operations of the national government, Maryland's attempt to levy a tax on the national bank was unconstitutional. The Court upheld the supremacy of the national government when policies collide.

M r. Chief Justice Marshall[†] delivered the opinion of the Court.
 In the case now to be determined, the defendant, a sovereign State, denies the obligation of a law enacted by the legislature of the Union, and the plaintiff, on his part, contests the validity of an act which has been passed

---

* 4 Wheaton 316 (1819).

[†] John Marshall became chief justice of the United States in 1801. He is probably most famous for his opinion in *Marbury* v. *Madison* (see Chapter 13), which established the principle of judicial review—the power of the Court to declare laws unconstitutional.

by the legislature of that State. The constitution of our country, in its most interesting and vital parts, is to be considered; the conflicting powers of the government of the Union and of its members, as marked in that constitution, are to be discussed; and an opinion given, which may essentially influence the great operations of the government. . . .

The first question made in the case is, has Congress power to incorporate a bank? . . .

The power now contested was exercised by the first Congress elected under the present constitution. The bill for incorporating the bank of the United States did not steal upon an unsuspecting legislature, and pass unobserved. Its principle was completely understood, and was opposed with equal zeal and ability. After being resisted, first in the fair and open field of debate, and afterwards in the executive cabinet, with as much persevering talent as any measure has ever experienced, and being supported by arguments which convinced minds as pure and as intelligent as this country can boast, it became a law. The original act was permitted to expire; but a short experience of the embarrassments to which the refusal to revive it exposed the government, convinced those who were most prejudiced against the measure of its necessity, and induced the passage of the present law. It would require no ordinary share of intrepidity to assert that a measure adopted under these circumstances was a bold and plain usurpation, to which the constitution gave no countenance. . . .

In discussing this question, the counsel for the State of Maryland have deemed it of some importance, in the construction of the constitution, to consider that instrument not as emanating from the people, but as the act of sovereign and independent States. The powers of the general government, it has been said, are delegated by the States, who alone are truly sovereign; and must be exercised in subordination to the States, who alone possess supreme dominion.

It would be difficult to sustain this proposition. The Convention which framed the constitution was indeed elected by the State legislatures. But the instrument, when it came from their hands, was a mere proposal, without obligation, or pretensions to it. It was reported to the then existing Congress of the United States, with a request that it might "be submitted to a Convention of Delegates, chosen in each State by the people thereof, under the recommendation of its Legislature, for their assent and ratification." This mode of proceeding was adopted; and by the Convention, by Congress, and by the State Legislatures, the instrument was submitted to the people. They acted upon it in the only manner in which they can act safely, effectively, and wisely, on such a subject, by assembling in Convention. It is true, they assembled in their several States—and where else should they have assembled? No political dreamer was ever wild enough to think of breaking down the lines which separate the States, and of compounding the American people into one common mass. Of consequence, when they act, they act in their States. But the measures they adopt do not, on that account, cease to be the measures of the people themselves, or become the measures of the State governments.

From these Conventions the constitution derives its whole authority. The government proceeds directly from the people; is "ordained and established" in the name of the people; and is declared to be ordained, "in order to form a more perfect union, establish justice, ensure domestic tranquillity, and secure the blessings of liberty to themselves and to their posterity." The assent of the States, in their sovereign capacity, is implied in calling a Convention, and thus submitting that instrument to the people. But the people were at perfect liberty to accept or reject it; and their act was final. It required not the affirmance, and could not be negatived, by the State governments. The constitution, when thus adopted, was of complete obligation, and bound the State sovereignties.

It has been said, that the people had already surrendered all their powers to the State sovereignties, and had nothing more to give. But, surely, the question whether they may resume and modify the powers granted to government does not remain to be settled in this country. Much more might the legitimacy of the general government be doubted, had it been created by the States. The powers delegated to the State sovereignties were to be exercised by themselves, not by a distinct and independent sovereignty, created by themselves. To the formation of a league, such as was the confederation, the State sovereignties were certainly competent. But when, "in order to form a more perfect union," it was deemed necessary to change this alliance into an effective government, possessing great and sovereign powers, and acting directly on the people, the necessity of referring it to the people, and of deriving its powers directly from them, was felt and acknowledged by all.

The government of the Union, then (whatever may be the influence of this fact on the case) is, emphatically, and truly, a government of the people. In form and in substance it emanates from them. Its powers are granted by them, and are to be exercised directly on them, and for their benefit.

This government is acknowledged by all to be one of enumerated powers. The principle, that it can exercise only the powers granted to it, would seem too apparent to have required to be enforced by all those arguments which its enlightened friends, while it was depending before the people, found it necessary to urge. That principle is now universally admitted. But the question respecting the extent of the powers actually granted, is perpetually arising, and will probably continue to arise, as long as our system shall exist. . . .

If any one proposition could command the universal assent of mankind, we might expect it would be this—that the government of the Union, though limited in its powers, is supreme within its sphere of action. This would seem to result necessarily from its nature. It is the government of all; its powers are delegated by all; it represents all, and acts for all. Though any one State may be willing to control its operations, no State is willing to allow others to control them. The nation, on those subjects on which it can act, must necessarily bind its component parts. But this question is not left to mere reason: the people have, in express terms, decided it, by saying, "this constitution, and the laws of the United States, which shall be made in pursuance thereof, . . . shall be the supreme law of the land," and by requiring that the members of the State legislatures, and the officers of the executive and judicial departments of the States, shall take the oath of fidelity to it.

The government of the United States, then, though limited in its powers, is supreme; and its laws, when made in pursuance of the constitution, form the supreme law of the land, "any thing in the constitution or laws of any State to the contrary notwithstanding."

Among the enumerated powers, we do not find that of establishing a bank or creating a corporation. But there is no phrase in the instrument which, like the articles of confederation, excludes incidental or implied powers; and which requires that every thing granted shall be expressly and minutely described. Even the 10th amendment, which was framed for the purpose of quieting the excessive jealousies which had been excited, omits the word "expressly," and declares only that the powers "not delegated to the United States, nor prohibited to the States, are reserved to the States or to the people;" thus leaving the question, whether the particular power which may become the subject of contest has been delegated to the one government, or prohibited to the other, to depend on a fair construction of the whole instrument. The men who drew and adopted this amendment had experienced the embarrassments resulting from the insertion of this word in the articles of confederation, and probably omitted it to avoid those embarrassments. A constitution, to contain an accurate detail of all the subdivisions of which its great powers will admit, and of all the means by which they may be carried into execution, would partake of the prolixity of a legal code, and could scarcely be embraced by the human mind. It would probably never be understood by the public. Its nature, therefore, requires, that only its great outlines should be marked, its important objects designated, and the minor ingredients which compose those objects be deduced from the nature of the objects themselves. That this idea was entertained by the framers of the American constitution, is not only to be inferred from the nature of the instrument, but from the language. Why else were some of the limitations, found in the ninth section of the 1st article, introduced?* It is also, in some degree, warranted by their having omitted to use any restrictive term which might prevent its receiving a fair and just interpretation. In consideration of this question, then, we must never forget, that it is *a constitution* we are expounding.

Although, among the enumerated powers of government, we do not find the word "bank" or "incorporation," we find the great powers to lay and collect taxes; to borrow money; to regulate commerce; to declare and conduct a war; and to raise and support armies and navies. The sword and the purse, all the external relations, and no inconsiderable portion of the industry of the

---

* Article 1, Section 9, follows the provision enumerating the national government's powers and is a broad list of specific prohibitions that restrain the national government, including the inability to levy taxes or duties on articles from any state or to give preferential treatment to the ports of one state at the expense of another.

nation, are entrusted to its government. It can never be pretended that these vast powers draw after them others of inferior importance, merely because they are inferior. Such an idea can never be advanced. But it may with great reason be contended, that a government, entrusted with such ample powers, on the due execution of which the happiness and prosperity of the nation so vitally depends, must also be entrusted with ample means for their execution. The power being given, it is the interest of the nation to facilitate its execution. It can never be their interest, and cannot be presumed to have been their intention, to clog and embarrass its execution by withholding the most appropriate means. Throughout this vast republic, from the St. Croix to the Gulf of Mexico, from the Atlantic to the Pacific, revenue is to be collected and expended, armies are to be marched and supported. The exigencies of the nation may require that the treasure raised in the north should be transported to the south, *that* raised in the east conveyed to the west, or that this order should be reversed. Is that construction of the constitution to be preferred which would render these operations difficult, hazardous, and expensive? Can we adopt that construction, (unless the words imperiously require it,) which would impute to the framers of that instrument, when granting these powers for the public good, the intention of impeding their exercise by withholding a choice of means? If, indeed, such be the mandate of the constitution, we have only to obey; but that instrument does not profess to enumerate the means by which the powers it confers may be executed; nor does it prohibit the creation of a corporation, if the existence of such a being be essential to the beneficial exercise of those powers. It is, then, the subject of fair inquiry, how far such means may be employed. . . .

But the constitution of the United States has not left the right of Congress to employ the necessary means, for the execution of the powers conferred on the government, to general reasoning. To its enumeration of powers is added that of making "all laws which shall be necessary and proper, for carrying into execution the foregoing powers, and all other powers vested by this constitution, in the government of the United States, or in any department thereof." . . .

We admit, as all must admit, that the powers of the government are limited, and that its limits are not to be transcended. But we think the sound construction of the constitution must allow to the national legislature that discretion, with respect to the means by which the powers it confers are to be carried into execution, which will enable that body to perform the high duties assigned to it, in the manner most beneficial to the people. Let the end be legitimate, let it be within the scope of the constitution, and all means which are appropriate, which are plainly adapted to that end, which are not prohibited, but consist with the letter and spirit of the constitution, are constitutional. . . .

It being the opinion of the Court, that the act incorporating the bank is constitutional; and that the power of establishing a branch in the State of Maryland might be properly exercised by the bank itself, we proceed to inquire—

Whether the State of Maryland may, without violating the constitution, tax that branch?

That the power of taxation is one of vital importance; that it is retained by the States; that it is not abridged by the grant of a similar power to the government of the Union; that it is to be concurrently exercised by the two governments: are truths which have never been denied. But, such is the paramount character of the constitution, that its capacity to withdraw any subject from the action of even this power, is admitted. The States are expressly forbidden to lay any duties on imports or exports, except what may be absolutely necessary for executing their inspection laws. If the obligation of this prohibition must be conceded—if it may restrain a State from the exercise of its taxing power on imports and exports; the same paramount character would seem to restrain, as it certainly may restrain, a State from such other exercise of this power, as is in its nature incompatible with, and repugnant to, the constitutional laws of the Union. A law, absolutely repugnant to another, as entirely repeals that other as if express terms of repeal were used.

On this ground the counsel for the bank place its claim to be exempted from the power of a State to tax its operations. There is no express provision for the case, but the claim has been sustained on a principle which so entirely pervades the constitution, is so intermixed with the materials which compose it, so interwoven with its web, so blended with its texture, as to be incapable of being separated from it, without rending it into shreds.

This great principle is, that the constitution and the laws made in pursuance thereof are supreme; that they control the constitution and laws of the respective States, and cannot be controlled by them. From this, which may be almost termed an axiom, other propositions are deduced as corollaries, on the truth or error of which, and on their application to this case, the cause has been supposed to depend. These are, 1st. that a power to create implies a power to preserve. 2nd. That a power to destroy, if wielded by a different hand, is hostile to, and incompatible with these powers to create and to preserve. 3d. That where this repugnancy exists, that authority which is supreme must control, not yield to that over which it is supreme.

These propositions, as abstract truths, would, perhaps, never be controverted. Their application to this case, however, has been denied; and, both in maintaining the affirmative and the negative, a splendor of eloquence, and strength of argument, seldom, if ever, surpassed, have been displayed.

The power of Congress to create, and of course to continue, the bank, was the subject of the preceding part of this opinion; and is no longer to be considered as questionable.

That the power of taxing it by the States may be exercised so as to destroy it, is too obvious to be denied. . . .

The Court has bestowed on this subject its most deliberate consideration. The result is a conviction that the States have no power, by taxation or otherwise, to retard, impede, burden, or in any manner control, the operations of the constitutional laws enacted by Congress to carry into execution the powers vested in the general government. This is, we think, the unavoidable consequence of that supremacy which the constitution has declared.

We are unanimously of opinion, that the law passed by the legislature of
Maryland, imposing a tax on the Bank of the United States, is unconstitutional
and void. . . .

Summary Questions

1. Why did the Court believe that the national government possessed powers
   beyond those enumerated in the Constitution?
2. Does Marshall's view in this case seem consistent with the view of national-
   state relations expressed by James Madison in *The Federalist*, No. 39?

 2.3

The Price of Federalism

H. G. Nicholas

Federalism can encourage great diversity. States have preceded the national
government in passing legislation to extend civil rights, develop welfare programs,
improve social conditions, and protect the environment. But federalism carries
costs as well. In this article H. G. Nicholas, a British observer of American politics,
discusses some of the disadvantages of a federal structure that encourages
"extreme complexity." The division of power among national, state, and local
authorities makes government liable to contradictions and confusions. According
to Nicholas, a U.S. citizen is faced with "an awful lot of government," and the
frequency of elections, the number of offices to be filled, and the range of issues
submitted for consideration are so great that many citizens are overwhelmed.

Nicholas further argues that a dual system of courts and the proliferation of laws
creates an excess of legalism while contributing to confusion, and ultimately to
lawlessness. Other costs of excessive legalism include time, expense, and an
elevated status for lawyers in society.

H. G. Nicholas is a former Rhodes Professor of American History and Institutions at Oxford
University.

"The Federal system," says Tocqueville, "was created with the intention of combining the different advantages which result from the greater and lesser extent of nations; and a single glance over the United States of America suffices to discover advantages which they have derived from its adoption." "A single glance"—even now the observer needs hardly more. The unique advantage of federalism is that it makes the United States possible. This great invention of the Founding Fathers squarely confronts the two greatest difficulties we have been examining—size and diversity—and, to a degree totally without precedent in history, provides a mechanism by which they can be accommodated within the framework of a single democratic government. The success of the device lay not only in the sensible and elastic division of powers between central and provincial governments, but even more in the provision that both the central and the provincial governments, each within its delimited sphere, should operate directly on the individual citizen. This feature, so novel at the time, is now so familiar as to require no exposition here. Yet without it there would have been no United States; instead, there would have been the balkanization of a continent.

Yet in politics, as in the rest of life, nothing is free, and even the greatest of advances exacts its price. Taking the indispensability of federalism for granted, our object here is to ask what price the United States has had to pay for it. Our enquiry will reveal that many of what at first sight appear to be wanton defects in American government are no more than the inescapable consequences of the federal system. . . .

The most obvious characteristic of a system embracing . . . diversities is its extreme *complexity*. There have to be harmonized at the very least two sovereignties—that of any individual state and that of the federal government—and at the worst fifty-one—all of the states' and the federal government's. The mere idea of harmonized sovereignties is a difficult one to grasp, even when it is not totally repugnant. The facile absolutism of Virginia's John Randolph of Roanoke has immediate appeal: "Asking one of the states to surrender part of her sovereignty is like asking a lady to surrender part of her chastity."* Yet the American system of government asks its citizens not only to accept this central paradox but also to work it. The Constitution which prescribes the system is indeed a model of lucidity and compactness, yet, as Tocqueville remarked, "in examining it . . . one is startled at the variety of information and the amount of discernment that it presupposes in the people whom it is meant to govern." Historically there has been one great and tragic occasion on which the citizens failed to muster the qualities of heart and mind necessary to enable it to function. Yet the example is as notable for its uniqueness as for its enormity and in the main one can certainly

---

* John Randolph, an ardent states'-rights advocate, was a famous orator with a reputation for sarcasm. He was elected to the House of Representatives in 1799, and later to the U.S. Senate. He once fought a duel, in which no one was hurt, with Henry Clay because of his insulting language in the Senate over Clay's appointment as secretary of state.

concur with Tocqueville's tribute: "I have never been more struck by the good sense and the practical judgement of the Americans than in the manner in which they elude the numberless difficulties resulting from their federal constitution."

For the ordinary citizen the most obvious consequence of this complexity is that he is faced by an awful lot of government. For everyone there are three tiers of rule—local, state, and federal. This means three lots of representatives (to say nothing of executives) to elect, three judicial and police jurisdictions to respect, three levels of taxes to pay, three sets of laws or ordinances to observe, three rings of the political circus to watch. (Indeed for most citizens there is a fourth layer of government as well, where a county inserts itself between a municipal and a state government—to say nothing of the various semi-autonomous administrative bodies, such as school boards, which are a feature of American local government.) For a great many people this is simply too much to do. The frequency of elections, the number of offices to be filled, the range of issues submitted for consideration, produce one simple consequence—relatively few people vote. (If it were not for the merciful, extra-constitutional device of the two-party system even fewer would do so.) The three tiers of government compete erratically for the harassed newspaper reader's time—and even more erratically for the television viewer's attention—with now one, now another ring of the political circus stealing the spotlight from the rest. The diversities of the tax system raise tax-dodging—and tax-chasing—to the level of a competitive sport. The police systems, though sometimes co-operating, are often engaged in professional rivalry against a criminal underworld which knows nothing of state lines but a great deal about how to play off competing jurisdictions one against the other.

As far as courts and judges are concerned a similar tripartism prevails. States could, of course, use their powers to co-ordinate the work and jurisdictions of local and state-wide courts, and there are many that do. But unity in judicial organization remains the exception rather than the rule and jurisdiction is often so fragmented that a litigant may have to go to more than one court to get a decision on a single case. As between the state and federal levels the principles of federalism dictate a necessary separation—separate courts, separate appointing or electing agents, separate jurisdictions. The United States, as a truly federal government, can and does accommodate a considerable diversity of state laws, even the civil law of Louisiana with its heavy dependence upon the Code Napoléon.* It has been said with justice that "American law," as such, does not exist. Where differences result in conflict and a decision is required the federal courts, of course, exist to provide it. And of course the Constitution debars the states altogether from legislating in certain areas. But it gives the federal government very little power to oblige the states to take positive action when they have

---

* Louisiana is the only state in which the legal system is based on civil law (laws passed by the state legislature) rather than on common law (laws based on court decisions). In France all the civil laws are combined into a single code, and the French influence in the settlement of Louisiana is reflected in that state's legal procedures.

a mind not to. The overwhelming mass of American law is state-originated and state-enforced without interference by the agencies of federal government. . . .

Behind the fact of federal diversities, but linked with it, lies a paradox at the heart of the American attitude to law itself. It is remarkably and profoundly revered. Of all the marble temples in Washington wherein the spirit of the Republic dwells there is none more splendid, more dazzling, more marbled than that which houses the Supreme Court of the United States. ("We ought to ride in on elephants," Mr. Justice Stone is reported to have said.) Of all the documents enshrined in the National Archives none is so much—or so often—revered by the out-of-town pilgrim as the Constitution of the United States. Nor is it revered as a piece of paper alone; veneration has grown with every year for the Constitution as the central dogma and in the creed of Americanism. And this veneration has the most practical and direct results; it is what enables the people to accept, with a readiness which no other democracy can parallel, the right, even the obligation, of a Supreme Court to nullify the acts of the people's representatives on the grounds that they are unconstitutional. A sentiment which operates to such an end cannot be dismissed as formal or superficial.

Yet along with this sincere regard for constitutionalism goes a serious, recurrent, and surprisingly pervasive lawlessness. The pages of American history bear eloquent testimony to this phenomenon. The institutionalized violence of slavery persisted longer in America than anywhere else in the western world and required the institutionalized violence of civil war to bring it to an end, while the Ku Klux Klan preserved many of its repressive features down to a later day. The history of westward expansion is studded with violence in its most colourful and popularized and frequently successful forms. The legends of the Vigilantes of "the law west of the Pecos," of Jesse James, Billy the Kid, "Wild Bill" Hickok, et al., testify to the blend of odium and admiration which such inextricably mingled symbols of law and lawlessness continue to evoke. . . . The incidence of assassination as the ultimate political weapon has been and continues to be heavy in American public life.

For much of this there are perfectly good reasons which have nothing to do with federalism (and not always even, or exclusively, with the United States). But behind it lies an attitude to law which, if not exclusively American, is recognizably so and is in part at any rate the by-product of the character and complexity of American law itself. Aristotle thought that respect for the law as such was so valuable that even if you might improve a law by changing it it was probable that the harm of the change would outweigh the benefits of the revision. Nothing could be less American. The American polity was formed in an age of almost universal belief in Natural Law,* as a moral code of universal validity. To this the Constitution was deemed to conform and from this it derived much of its binding

---

* In Natural Law, rights are God-given or inherent in the individual; therefore, no government can legitimately take the rights away.

force. But if such moral timbers could be used to underpin fundamental law, they could equally provide a battering ram against ordinary legislative enactments which were deemed less than ideal. Each citizen felt free to judge for himself, on moral grounds, the applicability of any piece of legislation, to determine whether it was "just" or "unjust" and, if "unjust," to disobey it.

Brought up on the spectacle of the mutability and diversity of the laws, the man in the street develops a natural disposition to regard law-abidingness as, at best, a highly conditional virtue. This is a country in which, under the Constitution, all laws are *not* equal. The citizen knows that if he cannot divorce his wife satisfactorily in New York he can in Reno, that if he incorporates his business in New Jersey he will escape many of the onerous requirements that would obtain in New York. When a mere motor drive will bring him under a different legal dispensation is it surprising that he acquires a somewhat relativist attitude to law? He may not go as far as Huey Long with his claim that Louisiana had "the best laws money can buy," but he may rely on doing the next best thing, hiring the best lawyers money can buy. For this is a setting in which the lawyer who can steer through the complexities and make play with the diversities comes into his own. Thus, by a paradox, out of lawlessness emerges the next item on the price list of federalism, *legalism*.

"Federalism is legalism" . . . or, more crudely, "a government of lawyers, not of men." The citizen of a federation contemplating a proposed piece of legislation always has to ask himself two questions:

(a) Is it desirable?

(b) Is it constitutional?

The first point he can answer for himself; for the second he needs a lawyer. Similarly the opponents of a proposal which cannot be defeated merely on political grounds, whose popularity cannot be denied, will always be tempted to fall back on constitutional objections, whether valid or not. Thus the history of American politics is also, at almost every point, a constitutional history and, as often as not, the constitutional conflicts are not the real ones, but the smokescreen behind which the real political differences are being thrashed out.

This often introduces an element of unreality, not to say casuistry and playacting, into the arguments of American politics. The great slavery debate was seldom joined about the merits of slavery as such, much less about the relations of black and white, but rather about whether or not Congress had the right to legislate slavery into or out of the territories. The great and continuing struggle between *laissez-faire* and public control was—and is still—fought in the largely outworn language of states' rights and what the Founding Fathers meant by terms like "general welfare." Historicism enters in—the appeal to history as an arbiter for present-day conflicts. Since it is a document of 1789 that is appealed to there is perpetual harking back to what its authors meant and thought. During the bitter controversies about the constitutionality of the New Deal this was a constant refrain. While the bench explored the constitutional debates of 1787, the magazines were carrying articles and titles like "Madison in America Now" ("He would be alarmed for the future of the Republic"), while partisan groups crusaded under historically evocative labels such as "Jeffersonian Democrats."

This is not altogether a bad thing. It helps to unify by emphasizing the elements of continuity and tradition in the national heritage. It can be to politics what the classics are to education, especially since the Founding Fathers were unusually sagacious, representative, and expressive men. . . .

Another consequence of legalism is expense and delay. Federalism's complexity and the frequent conflicts of laws cost a lot of money to resolve. Delay may be thought good or bad according as one's interest lies in hastening or retarding change. But the uncertainty that accompanies delay is seldom in the public interest, while the cost of litigation hits everyone except the lawyers. They thrive. The United States, with four times the population of the U.K. has ten times as many lawyers. . . .

Twenty-eight of the thirty-nine Presidents have been lawyers by training or practice. ("The profession I chose was politics," wrote Woodrow Wilson. "The profession I entered was the law. I entered the one because I thought it would lead to the other.") Over half of the state governors since the Civil War have been lawyers. Congress pretty consistently runs to over 50 per cent lawyers and these constitute, as Bryce put it, "the better-educated half of the professional politicians." What holds true at the elected level is even more true at the appointed one, where a degree from a law school is the preferred qualification for any serious post in the federal service.

The peculiar cast which this gives to American government is more easily sensed than defined. It matches perfectly another characteristic of American public life, the disposition to move in and out of government employment as circumstances or politics dictate. The lawyer with his permanent licence to practise law for himself, is especially equipped to operate in this way. Abraham Lincoln indeed maintained his law partnership while he was President. No one could do that today, but the lawyer in government, though not a servant of two masters, is, in a useful sense, a master of two servants; and if one, the public service, does not please him he can switch back to the other, his private practice. In this way the law materially assists at that infusion of new blood which is such a marked characteristic of each new Washington administration.

But if the law brings new men and new ideas into government it also brings its own way of doing the work of governing. To the lawyer it is natural to see administration not as a continuous operation to be maintained or conducted throughout successive changes of party, but as a series of problems to be solved, or malpractices to be corrected—in fact as something very like a succession of legal cases to be fought and won (or at least settled in the judge's chambers). This inevitably involves concentration of effort on what he considers to be crucial areas; it put a premium on the immediately realizable; it sets little store by continuity; it breaks up the unity of administration, the seamless web of government, into manageable, discontinuous, not infrequently conflicting segments.

This approach to administration, when combined with the peculiar problems created by the framework of a written federal constitution and judicial review, encourages the lawyer in his professional addiction to ingenious solutions and especially to those which proceed by indirection. *Indirection* is indeed another, almost inescapable, characteristic of federal government. The adjustments in a fixed constitution necessary to keep it abreast of changing requirements can only occasionally be made by formal revision. For most day-to-day purposes they must be made by exploiting the possibilities for evading and circumventing the rigidities of the master plan.

Consider a classic example. Migratory birds are notoriously indifferent to territorial jurisdictions. Thus state legislation for their protection can never be adequate. Consequently in 1913 the U.S. Congress made it a federal offence to slaughter them. The Supreme Court of the period, however, could find no authority in the Constitution such as would permit Congress to legislate in such an area. Conservation-minded lawyers were not to be frustrated. On their advice the President negotiated and the Senate approved a treaty with the United Kingdom (acting at that time, under the British North America Act) by which the USA and Canada agreed to provide the necessary legal protection. Congress then was obligated to pass appropriate legislation to put this into effect and such legislation was judged indubitably constitutional because (Article VI) "All treaties made . . . under the authority of the United States are the supreme law of the land." So an essentially domestic problem was provided with a solution through powers conferred for the regulation of foreign relations.

For different reasons criminals may evade the short arm of justice at the level at which most U.S. criminal law enforcement occurs, the state. Thus Al Capone was able to pursue his career of murder and larceny unchecked in the Chicago of the Prohibition era because murder and extortion are not *per se* federal offences. Fortunately for justice, however, Capone was careless with his federal tax returns; as a result the federal government was able to do what Chicago and Illinois could not, and put him behind bars, if not for his major crimes, at any rate for his income-tax evasion. . . .

There are limits to what indirection can achieve. No one who is a genuine believer in federal government—and most Americans are—will resort to extreme devices of indirection save where no alternative seems available. The normal working of federal government will not depend on them. But, without term, that government will have to reconcile itself to a certain slowness, a deliberation in its movements which reflects the complexity and frequent contradictoriness of its parts. In many spheres, if not all, the pace of a federal government is the speed of its slowest component. It is not merely that the government of a federation is confined to certain fields. It is that even within those fields its action is deliberately retarded and circumscribed. This is most obvious, of course, in foreign relations. Not only does the President's treaty-making require the consent of two-thirds of the Senate. The Senate itself is tilted towards over-representation of the minority. Alaska's half-million residents have the same number of senators

as California's 23 million. Again, the system of presidential selection and election, pivoting as it may on the capture of a few key states, can give a minority
in such states a disproportionate influence on a candidate's chances of victory
or defeat.

These considerations carry through even to the internal organization of the
federal legislature. The committee system breaks down the straight-forward
operation of the majority principle in both chambers, and within each committee
a disproportionate power has flowed into the hands of each chairman; to pursue
this in the context of foreign policy one has only to recall the potency of the
Idaho senator, Borah, who for so many years dominated the Foreign Relations
Committee of the Senate. A less predictable but comparably potent weapon is
the filibuster, similarly if more eccentrically designed to heighten the veto power
of a minority.* Finally, when all other hurdles have been cleared, a popular
measure can still fail as a result of a disagreement between the two houses or
between both houses and the President—clashes which the Constitution has,
ultimately, no powers to resolve.

The Constitution stops short of carrying this principle of minority veto into
the internal organization of the executive branch itself. The President is not told
how his administration should embody the federal idea. But no President can
reach the White House without realizing that his administration must reflect the
elements that elected him and that in a vast and federal country most of these
elements will have a territorial base. Consequently, though he is not obliged, like
the Senate or the House, to find room for representatives of every state, he will
be bound to pay attention, in forming his administration, to the claims of each
region. His Cabinet must reflect what the United Nations has learnt to call
"equitable geographical representation." In filling vacancies in the federal courts
he must note which part of the country feels under-represented. In the major
administrative and diplomatic appointments he must take care that all the plums
do not go to any one section. This, after all, whatever unifying factors are at work,
remains a continental government which must reflect the real individualities of
its regions across an area larger than Europe.

Summary Questions

1. According to Nicholas, what is the price of federalism? How would a defender
   of federalism refute Nicholas's arguments?
2. Why are attorneys so influential in American society? What is the relationship between legalism and lawlessness, according to Nicholas? Do you agree?

---

* The Senate has an unlimited debate rule, and only in extraordinary circumstances are senators
prevented from speaking as long as they wish. Through a filibuster, senators delay action on a
piece of legislation by extended speaking, often on topics unrelated to the business at hand.

2.4

Federal Government Mandates: Why the States Are Complaining

Martha Derthick

The 1980s in some ways witnessed a resurgence of the states as active members in the federal system. A number of factors, ranging from the modernization and professionalization of state government to the decentralizing policies of the Reagan administration, as well as increasing state revenues, combined to create a context conducive to vigorous, progressive state government. Compared to the federal government, which often appeared hopelessly gridlocked and constrained by huge deficits, states appeared innovative and financially sound.

States are still junior partners in the federal arrangement, however, and, according to Martha Derthick, the history of U.S. federalism, "is one of centralization, steady and seemingly irreversible." In her view, as we emerge from recession in the early 1990s, the ever-increasing coercive power of the federal government is again threatening the states' capacities to review and weigh competing claims on state budgets. Particularly troublesome is the tendency of Congress to pass laws ordering states to undertake new programs, yet not providing the money to do so. Such mandates strike at the heart of republican government, since congressional mandates come from a body "not responsible to state electorates."

Derthick believes that "the task of governing so vast a country is too formidable for one government alone, and the case for lodging a large measure of domestic responsibility and discretion with the states and their local subdivisions remains strong."

Hard pressed by recession, state governments have been complaining that Congress keeps passing laws ordering them to undertake expensive new programs—but without providing the money to do so. Complaints about federal mandates are not new. In 1980 New York City Mayor Edward I. Koch wrote bitterly of the "mandate millstone" in an article in *The Public Interest,* giving currency to the term.

The main concern of state officials is political: who will pay the costs of government? But their complaints raise constitutional issues as well. In various

---

Martha Derthick is the Julia Allen Cooper Professor of Government at the University of Virginia.

ways the Constitution protects the states' existence as governments, having their own elected officials and the power to raise taxes and to enact, enforce, and interpret laws. How far can federal mandates be pushed without infringing on the states' governmental character?

The federal government influences state governments in four main ways—through court decrees, legislative regulations, preemptions, and conditional grants-in-aid. As a quick review will show, all four have grown significantly more coercive in the past half century.

Judicial Decrees

Until the mid-1950s federal courts interpreting the Constitution had habitually told the states what they might *not* do. They had struck down literally hundreds of state laws. But they had refrained from telling states what they *must* do. This changed with school desegregation. In 1955, with *Brown v. Board of Education II*, the Supreme Court gave federal district courts responsibility for entering the orders and decrees to desegregate public schools. The Court's ruling initiated a judicial effort to achieve racial integration with affirmative commands, telling school districts how to construct their attendance zones, where to build schools, where to bus their pupils, and how to assign their teachers.

Once courts and litigants discovered what could be done (or attempted) in the schools, other state institutions, especially prisons and institutions for the mentally ill and retarded, became targets. Nearly all state prison systems now operate under judicial decrees that address overcrowding and other conditions of prison life, and federal judges routinely mandate construction programs and modes of prison administration.

Needless to say, federal judicial mandates come without money, because courts have no way of raising money.

Legislative Regulations

Congress is also a source of affirmative commands to the states. When it imposes taxes and regulations—such as social security payroll taxes, wages-and-hours regulation, and emissions limits—on private parties, it must decide whether to cover state governments as well, for they and their local subdivisions are employers and, in some respects, producers.

For much of the nation's history, Congress did not tax and regulate state governments because it conceived of them as separate, sovereign, and equal. In a leading statement of this constitutional doctrine, the Supreme Court ruled in 1871 (*Collector v. Day*) that a federal income tax could not be levied against a county judge in Massachusetts. An earlier decision of the Court (*Dobbins v. The Commissioners of Erie*, 1842) had settled that the states could not tax the salary of an officer of the United States. Under 19th-century conceptions of federalism, it followed that the federal government could not tax the salaries of officers of the states.

When the Social Security Act of 1935 was passed, states as employers were routinely exempted from paying the payroll tax. Similarly, when the Fair Labor Standards Act of 1938 set maximum hours and minimum wages for industrial employers, no one would have imagined extending such regulation to state and local governments. . . .

The Supreme Court overruled *Collector v. Day* in 1939. Eventually, under the nationalizing impact of the New Deal, Congress began regulating state governments just as if they were private parties. For example, Congress extended wages-and-hours regulation to some state and local employees in 1966, to the rest in 1974. The Supreme Court at first upheld the move, but then, in response to the law of 1974, changed its mind. In 1976 the Court forbade Congress from exercising its commerce power so as to "force directly upon the States its choices as to how essential decisions regarding the conduct of integral governmental functions are to be made" (*National League of Cities v. Usery*). But the standard proved impractical and was abandoned in 1985 (*Garcia v. San Antonio Metropolitan Transit Authority*). Speaking for the Court, Justice Blackmun wrote that the "political process ensures that laws that unduly burden the States will not be promulgated." The Court seemed to wash its hands of the subject, leaving the states to the mercy of what Justice O'Connor in dissent called Congress's "underdeveloped capacity for self-restraint."

Preemptions

Preemptions are commands to the states to *stop* doing something and let the federal government do it. They are sanctioned by the supremacy clause of the Constitution, which requires that state laws yield to federal ones in case of conflict. Historically, preemptions have been not so much a calculated technique of intergovernmental relations as something that "just happened" as a byproduct of congressional action. It was left to the courts to rule, in response to litigation, whether preemption had taken place.

Recently preemptions have become both more frequent and more explicit. Congress passed more than 90 new preemptive laws in the 1970s and again in the 1980s, more than double the number for any previous decade. Partly because of pressure from the courts to be explicit, Congress now often does declare an intention to preempt. And the states naturally experience such declarations as coercion, even if they are being prevented from doing things rather than commanded to do them.

There is also a modern variant on the use of preemption, called by students of federalism "partial preemption." In the 1970s, as it enacted a new wave of regulation, Congress hit on a way of making use of the states for administration. It would preempt a field—say, occupational health and safety or surface mining or air pollution control—but permit the states to continue to function providing that they adopted standards at least as exacting as those it stipulated. The Supreme Court upheld this technique (*Hodel v. Virginia Surface Mining and Reclamation Association*, 1981).

Technically, the states can refuse the federal government's invitation to serve as administrators of its regulations. But in practice they have responded. "Each State shall . . . adopt . . . a plan which provides for implementation, maintenance, and enforcement" of federal air quality standards, the Clean Air Act says—and each state does. Better to be subordinate governments than empty ones.

Grant-in-Aid Conditions

Federal grant-in-aid conditions addressed to the states have been around at least since the Morrill Act of 1862, which gave the states land—30,000 acres for each member of Congress—to endow colleges in the agricultural and mechanic arts.

In theory, states have always been able to refuse federal grants. In practice, they have generally found them irresistible. And as time passed, states' dependence increased: aid was habit-forming. In 1965 federal highway grants passed $4 billion a year. In 1970 grants for public assistance, including Medicaid,* passed $7 billion a year. Altogether federal grants in 1970 amounted to nearly 30 percent of states' own-source revenues. It is absurd to hold, as constitutional doctrine formally does, that such grants can be rejected, and the burden of the accompanying conditions thereby avoided.

Over time, the conditions of grant programs expanded in scope and detail. Successful political movements left their mark on grant programs through conditions that apply to all or most grant programs. The rights revolution of the 1960s and 1970s, for example, left a legacy of anti-discrimination requirements; and the environmental movement, a requirement that environmental impact statements be prepared for federally aided projects.

Similarly, conditions have multiplied program by program. Section 402 of Title IV of the Social Security Act of 1935 took 2 brief paragraphs to describe what should be contained in state plans for aid to dependent children. By 1976 section 402 had grown to 9 pages; by 1988, to 27.

Also, Congress in the 1970s began threatening to withhold grants, particularly those for Medicaid and highways, to achieve objectives connected only loosely or not at all to the underlying purpose of the grant. When Congress set a national speed limit of 55 miles per hour in 1974 and a minimum drinking age of 21 in

---

* Medicaid is a federally aided but state-operated and administered health and medical care program directed at certain low-income populations. States are responsible for determining eligibility and coverage for Medicaid and administering the program, subject to federal guidelines.

1984, it did so by threatening to withhold highway grants from states that failed to comply.

Finally, the language of grant-in-aid statutes has become more coercive. Federal law makes some Medicaid services "mandatory" and Congress keeps adding to the list.

From time to time presidents, especially Republicans, have tried to reduce and simplify grant conditions. The revisions that Nixon, Ford, and Reagan achieved, in the form of revenue sharing and block grants, have been modest and, in the case of general revenue sharing, short-lived. Conditioned grants for specific purposes have persisted and always predominated.

Historically, grant-in-aid conditions could be enforced only by administrative action, primarily the threat to withhold the grant. Because withholding was self-defeating, it was not often used. Federal administrators got what compliance they could through negotiation. However, with the rights revolution and the rise of judicial activism, many grant-in-aid conditions became judicially enforceable, particularly in programs of AFDC* and education of handicapped children. A whole new set of commands emanated from an awe-inspiring source, the courts.

As grant conditions became more coercive, grants did not keep pace. Grants as a share of states' own-source revenues reached a peak at 32 percent in 1976 and then began to fall.

Do Mandates Matter?

The rise of the affirmative command, occurring subtly and on several different fronts, constitutes a sea-change in federal-state relations. The states have been converted from separate governments into subordinate ones, arguably mere "agents" in some programs. In constitutional significance, the change is comparable to the transformation by which the federal government ceased over the course of many years to be a government of limited, specified powers and became free to engage in any domestic activity not prohibited by the Bill of Rights.

That mandates developed only in the past 40 years does not necessarily mean that they are contrary to the Framers' intentions. That depends on which Framers one consults. Today's federalism is what the losing side of 1787 feared, but arguably what the winning side hoped for. Madison, after all, went into the Constitutional Convention saying that the states should be retained because they would be "subordinately useful." That is precisely what they have become. And there is at least a hint in *The Federalist* that affirmative commands would be acceptable. Number 27, written by the ardently nationalistic Hamilton, antici-

---

* Aid to Families with Dependent Children (AFDC) is a welfare program that provides federal funds for children living with a parent or relative deemed needy by state standards. Like Medicaid, states operate the program subject to broad federal guidelines.

pated that the federal government would employ the states to administer its laws. It is hard to see how that could have happened in the absence of mandates.

Yet most fundamentally, *The Federalist* saw federalism as a way to safeguard the public against abuses of governmental power and to sustain republicanism, the great central principle of the American regime. As Hamilton argued in number 28, "Power being almost always the rival of power, the general government will at all times stand ready to check the usurpations of the state governments, and these will have the same disposition towards the general government. The people, by throwing themselves into either scale, will infallibly make it preponderate. If their rights are invaded by either, they can make use of the other as the instrument of redress."

Indeed, the institutions of federalism can be used by the people to play different levels of government—and through them different policy choices—off against each other. One sees this happening most vividly in the prolonged contest over abortion policy, in which the federal courts "corrected" the restrictive excesses of state laws in the early 1970s and state legislatures responded by "correcting" the libertarian excesses of *Roe* v. *Wade*, and so on—in a heated intergovernmental exchange that threatens to be endless because the rival political movements are incapable of compromise.

Today mandates come in so many different forms and with so many different purposes that it is difficult to speak of them as a class. Limited, for the sake of discussion, to those that compel expenditure, they clearly raise important questions about republicanism. Judicial mandates come from a body that is not elected at all; congressional mandates, from a body that is not responsible to the various state electorates. When the federal judiciary commands the states to spend more on prisons and Congress commands them to spend more on Medicaid, they are making decisions that state electorates have no way to review. State officials lose their ability to weigh competing claims on state budgets. Of course, no such weighing is done at the federal level, where mandates are produced in isolation from one another. Neither the courts nor Congress, framing commands to the states, asks the question, "how much, compared to what?" that is crucial to rational, responsible policymaking. At some point, federal commands to the states may come to implicate the guarantee clause of the Constitution: "The United States shall guarantee to every state in this Union a Republican Form of Government."

Can Mandates Be Curbed?

How strongly state officials oppose mandates may be questioned. Accepting subordination as a fact of life, they have produced scattered complaints but not concerted or doctrinaire opposition. Although the loss of budgetary discretion is a serious problem for governors, it is hard for all 50 of them to get together on anything, much less take a public stand *for* overcrowded prisons or *against* medical care for pregnant women.

Largely devoid of interest in constitutional issues except for its own battles with the president, today's Congress is not much inclined to contemplate the deeper issues of federalism and to ask, self-critically, whether or where it should exercise restraint in its use of mandates. If it can expand the benefits of government while imposing much of the cost on other governments in the system, why not do it?

By contrast, the Supreme Court, habituated to thinking in constitutional terms, and made conservative by a series of Republican appointments, is engaged in a wide-ranging retreat from the use of mandates. In school desegregation, prison administration, and enforcement of grant-in-aid conditions, not to mention voting rights, [and] abortion, . . . the Court has signaled that it will show more deference to the states. But it is one thing for the Court to practice self-restraint and quite another for it to attempt to restrain Congress. The Court does not lightly challenge a coequal branch of government, nor has it had much success in the past in devising practical and enduring standards to protect the state governments.

There remains, nonetheless, a strong case for federalism, as Alice Rivlin, for one, has urged in the 1991 Webb Lecture before the National Academy of Public Administration and in *Reviving the American Dream*. As Madison foresaw, the task of governing so vast a country is too formidable for one government alone. It is significant that someone as thoughtful and experienced as Rivlin, whose whole career has been based in Washington and devoted to shaping national policy, should conclude that national uniformity is a liability in some areas of government. She names education and skills training, child care, housing, infrastructure, and economic development as activities that are "likely to succeed only if they are well adapted to local conditions, have strong local support and community participation and are managed by accountable officials who can be voted out if things go badly."

Rivlin's vision of revitalized state government calls, appropriately, for interstate equalization of revenues, to be achieved—and here her proposal becomes radical—by the states' adopting "one or more common taxes (same base, same rate) and sharing the proceeds." She suggests a single state corporate income tax or a uniform value-added tax, shared on a per capita basis and substituted for state retail sales taxes. To achieve this, the states would need the "blessing and perhaps the assistance of the federal government."

Indeed. There is no plausible mechanism, formal or informal, by which the 50 states could voluntarily agree on a common tax. It would have to be imposed by Congress in a fresh stroke of centralization—a mandate, if you will—entailing preemption of a particular tax source and dedication of the proceeds to the states, with no conditions attached. The absence of conditions proved not to be politically durable when general revenue sharing was tried in the 1970s. State political leaders might be forgiven if they doubt whether Congress would be willing to take the heat for imposing a new tax while turning the proceeds over to them.

Perhaps no other of our governing institutions has been subject to so much change and yet so resistant to planned, deliberate reform as federalism. Its history is one of centralization, steady and seemingly irreversible. Yet the case for lodging a large measure of domestic responsibility and discretion with the states and their local subdivisions remains strong. So is the case for the states having governments—republican governments chosen by state electorates and accountable to them, and capable of raising their own revenues and deciding how those revenues should be spent. It is one of the ironies of federalism that deliberate acts of decentralization, such as Rivlin proposes, depend on centralization as a precondition.

Summary Questions

1. What devices have been used by the federal government to coerce the states to follow the will of the national authority? Why does Derthick view the increasing use of such devices in such negative terms? What reasons might be put forth to support the position that lodging a significant measure of domestic responsibility and discretion with the states is a good idea?
2. Why is it so difficult to reform American federalism? Why have state officials been so willing to accept subordination to federal authority? What are the prospects for significant reform in the future?

 Chapter 3

CIVIL LIBERTIES AND CIVIL RIGHTS

Abortion. Prayer in public schools. Libel and slander. Busing. Affirmative action and racial quotas. The right to legal counsel. These often-emotional issues strike at the core of the relationship between the citizen and the state. The framers understood the central position of individual rights, seeing them as inalienable— that is, as God-given, neither handed down nor taken away by rulers or the government as a whole. Still, the government serves as the chief agency for protecting individual rights, even though it can effectively deny them as well (for example, through the long history of legal segregation). The framers and subsequent generations of policymakers have thus performed a pair of balancing acts with civil liberties and civil rights issues.

First, they have strived to balance the rights of individuals with the needs of the community at large. On many occasions, the individual and the community are best served by the same policy. For example, the court decision in *Gideon* v. *Wainwright* that guarantees indigents the right to counsel was a victory both for individual poor people and for society as a whole. Frequently, however, the interests of the community and the individual are, or appear to be, at odds. Does the right to freedom of speech and assembly extend to Nazis who wish to march through a predominantly Jewish community like Skokie, Illinois? The list of troubling and important questions in this area is endless and has produced a river of cases for the Supreme Court to wade through.

The second balance policymakers must maintain lies in the relative amounts of power accorded the government and its citizens. The government stands as the ultimate protector of individual liberties, such as the Constitution's enumerated rights of speech, religion, petition, and so forth. At the same time, the government can adopt policies and procedures that deny rights. The actions of an overzealous FBI or CIA have infringed on privacy rights, and many legislative initiatives have overstepped the bounds of propriety in seeking to regulate political organizations and speech. The Supreme Court's willingness to curb the government's assertion of power has varied. The Supreme Court of the 1990s is probably more likely to decide in favor of the government—whether national, state, or local—than it has been at any time since Earl Warren became Chief Justice in 1953.

What makes the study of civil rights and civil liberties so fascinating is the simultaneous timelessness and immediacy of the issues. For example, the notion of freedom of speech is as important today as it was in the eighteenth century, and contemporary controversies place basic issues, such as the potential defamation of a public figure, in new contexts. Likewise, civil rights and civil liberties issues hold our interest because their implications are extensive. Millions of individuals are directly affected by the Supreme Court's ruling in abortion or desegregation cases.

Although the legislative and executive branches play important roles in making and implementing rights policies, it is the judiciary that stands at center stage in this arena. At first such a responsibility may seem incongruous, since the courts are insulated from the influence of most citizens. In the end, however, this very independence from the popular will and the daily intrigues of politics is what renders the judicial branch, especially in its upper reaches, well suited to consider questions of rights. Protecting rights is frequently an unpopular business. In the 1940s and 1950s, for instance, Congress shied away from legislation that challenged racial separation, and the Supreme Court ruled on a series of desegregation cases, culminating in *Brown* v. *Board of Education.*

The direction of the Court is influenced by precedent and societal context as well as by individual appointments. Although the membership of the Court during the last twenty years has become more conservative, its decisions have not dramatically turned away from the expansive civil liberties positions under Chief Justice Earl Warren (1953–1969). For example, on the one hand the Burger (1969–1986) and Rehnquist (from 1986) Courts have gradually expanded the flexibility of the police in carrying out searches and seizures. At the same time, their decisions have not overturned any of the key Warren Court precedents, such as *Mapp* v. *Ohio* (1961), which limited the use of evidence from an illegal search, or *Miranda* v. *Arizona* (1966), which guaranteed that the accused be made aware of their right to counsel and protection from self-incrimination. Still, the increasing willingness of the Rehnquist Court of the 1990s to limit or overturn previous decisions may indicate that some fundamental changes (e.g., overturning *Roe* v. *Wade*) remain possible.

The following selections show the variety of civil rights and civil liberties issues. The first two indicate the conflict over the possibility of limiting free speech. In *Near* v. *Minnesota* (1931), the Supreme Court refused to bar the publication of an irresponsible newspaper that had mounted vicious anti-Semitic attacks on Minneapolis public officials. This decision reflects the Court's great reluctance to order the prior restraint of any publication, even the most despicable. The *Near* decision was notable not for its immediate impact, which was next to nothing, but for the precedent it set. In *Brandenburg* v. *Ohio* (1969) the Court ruled unconstitutional a statute that punished "mere advocacy" of violence in accomplishing a political goal.

Another area of civil liberties is the so-called right to privacy. Unlike enumerated rights, which protect speech, religion, assembly, and so on, the right to privacy is not acknowledged in the Constitution. Such a right has evolved, however, becoming explicit in *Griswold* v. *Connecticut* (1965). The *Griswold* ruling was a focal point in the 1987 confirmation hearings of Robert Bork, President Reagan's unsuccessful nominee for a Supreme Court seat.

Two other cases in the chapter show the changes in the Court's positions on civil rights over the past thirty years. In *Gideon* v. *Wainwright* (1963), the Court altered its previous interpretation of the Sixth Amendment by proclaiming the unconditional right to counsel. *Brown* v. *Board of Education* (1954; 1955) struck down laws that required segregated school systems, denying states the right to act as the agent of discrimination.

The final two selections reflect very different views of the thorny issue of affirmative action. Herbert Hill defends the idea of righting historical wrongs through plans that would advance the interests of certain classes of individuals (minorities) at the expense of those (generally, white males) who historically have been advantaged by a system that condoned discriminatory practices. Shelby Steele, a black academic, argues that affirmative action policies create a stigma of reverse discrimination that is demoralizing both for those who receive the preferences and for the society that condones the practice.

Near v. Minnesota (1931)

Among the rights guaranteed in the Constitution, perhaps the most fundamental is the freedom of expression. Without unfettered speech and a free press, the idea of democracy loses its meaning. Freedom of expression issues emerge in many forms, including controversies over libel, obscenity, and political speech. Even the most exhaustive collection of articles could not capture the range of questions that courts regularly face in deciding freedom of expression cases.

In *Near* v. *Minnesota,* the central question revolves around prior restraint of the press. In 1931, the Supreme Court ruled five to four that Minnesota could not muzzle the publisher of a newspaper that was attacking various Minneapolis public officials. Although any public official who is the subject of a "malicious, scandalous, and defamatory" article can sue for libel, the state could not halt publication of a newspaper merely because it expected that paper to defame public officials.

Mr. Chief Justice Hughes delivered the opinion of the Court. . . . Under this statute, [section one, clause (b)], the County Attorney of Hennepin County brought this action to enjoin the publication of what was described as a "malicious, scandalous and defamatory newspaper, magazine and periodical," known as "*The Saturday Press*," published by the defendants in the city of Minneapolis. The complaint alleged that the defendants, on September 24, 1927, and on eight subsequent dates in October and November, 1927, published and circulated editions of that periodical which were "largely devoted to malicious, scandalous and defamatory articles" concerning Charles G. Davis, Frank W. Brunskill, the *Minneapolis Tribune*, the *Minneapolis Journal*, Melvin C. Passolt, George E. Leach, the Jewish Race, the members of the Grand Jury of Hennepin County impaneled in November 1927, and then holding office, and other persons, as more fully appeared in exhibits annexed to the complaint, consisting of copies of the articles described and constituting 327 pages of the record. While the complaint did not so allege, it appears from the briefs of both parties that Charles G. Davis was a special law enforcement officer employed by a civic organization, that George E. Leach was Mayor of Minneapolis, that Frank W. Brunskill was its Chief of Police, and that Floyd B. Olson (the relator in this action) was County Attorney.

Without attempting to summarize the contents of the voluminous exhibits attached to the complaint, we deem it sufficient to say that the articles charged in substance that a Jewish gangster was in control of gambling, bootlegging and racketeering in Minneapolis, and that law enforcing officers and agencies were not energetically performing their duties. Most of the charges were directed against the Chief of Police; he was charged with gross neglect of duty, illicit relations with gangsters, and with participation in graft. The County Attorney was charged with knowing the existing conditions and with failure to take adequate measures to remedy them. The Mayor was accused of inefficiency and dereliction. One member of the grand jury was stated to be in sympathy with the gangsters. A special grand jury and a special prosecutor were demanded to deal with the situation in general, and, in particular, to investigate an attempt to assassinate one Guilford, one of the original defendants, who, it appears from the articles, was shot by gangsters after the first issue of the periodical had been published. There is no question but that the articles made serious accusations against the public officers named and others in connection with the prevalence of crimes and the failure to expose and punish them. . . .

If we cut through mere details of procedure, the operation and effect of the statute in substance is that public authorities may bring the owner or publisher of a newspaper or periodical before a judge upon a charge of conducting a business of publishing scandalous and defamatory matter—in particular that the matter consists of charges against public officers of official dereliction—and unless the owner or publisher is able and disposed to bring competent evidence to satisfy the judge that the charges are true and are published with good motives and for justifiable ends, his newspaper or periodical is suppressed and further publication is made punishable as a contempt. This is of the essence of censorship.

The question is whether a statute authorizing such proceedings in restraint of publication is consistent with the conception of the liberty of the press as historically conceived and guaranteed. In determining the extent of the constitutional protection, it has been generally, if not universally, considered that it is the chief purpose of the guaranty to prevent previous restraints upon publication. The struggle in England, directed against the legislative power of the licenser, resulted in renunciation of the censorship of the press. The liberty deemed to be established was thus described by Blackstone:* "The liberty of the press is indeed essential to the nature of a free state; but this consists in laying no *previous* restraints upon publications, and not in freedom from censure for criminal matter when published. Every freeman has an undoubted right to lay what sentiments he pleases before the public; to forbid this, is to destroy the freedom of the press; but if he publishes what is improper, mischievous or illegal, he must take the consequence of his own temerity." . . . The distinction was early pointed out

---

* Sir William Blackstone (1723–1780) was an English jurist and legal scholar whose writings served as the core of legal education in the United States during the nineteenth century.

between the extent of the freedom with respect to censorship under our constitutional system and that enjoyed in England. Here, as Madison said, "the great and essential rights of the people are secured against legislative as well as against executive ambition. They are secured, not by laws paramount to prerogative, but by constitutions paramount to laws. This security of the freedom of the press requires that it should be exempt not only from previous restraint by the Executive, as in Great Britain, but from legislative restraint also." . . .

The objection has . . . been made that the principle as to immunity from previous restraint is stated too broadly, if every such restraint is deemed to be prohibited. That is undoubtedly true; the protection even as to previous restraint is not absolutely unlimited. But the limitation has been recognized only in exceptional cases: "When a nation is at war many things that might be said in time of peace are such a hindrance to its effort that their utterance will not be endured so long as men fight and that no Court could regard them as protected by any constitutional right." . . . No one would question but that a government might prevent actual obstruction to its recruiting service or the publication of the sailing dates of transports or the number and location of troops. On similar grounds, the primary requirements of decency may be enforced against obscene publications. The security of the community life may be protected against incitements to acts of violence and the overthrow by force of orderly government. The constitutional guaranty of free speech does not "protect a man from an injunction against uttering words that may have all the effect of force. . . ." These limitations are not applicable here. Nor are we now concerned with questions as to the extent of authority to prevent publications in order to protect private rights according to the principles governing the exercise of the jurisdiction of courts of equity.

The exceptional nature of its limitations places in a strong light the general conception that liberty of the press, historically considered and taken up by the Federal Constitution, has meant, principally although not exclusively, immunity from previous restraints or censorship. The conception of the liberty of the press in this country had broadened with the exigencies of the colonial period and with the efforts to secure freedom from oppressive administration. That liberty was especially cherished for the immunity it afforded from previous restraint of the publication of censure of public officers and charges of official misconduct. . . . Madison, who was the leading spirit in the preparation of the First Amendment of the Federal Constitution, thus described the practice and sentiment which led to the guaranties of liberty of the press in state constitutions:[1]

"In every State, probably, in the Union, the press has exerted a freedom in canvassing the merits and measures of public men of every description which has not been confined to the strict limits of the common law. On this footing the freedom of the press has stood; on this footing it yet stands. . . . Some degree of abuse is inseparable from the proper use of everything, and in no instance is this more true than in that of the press. It has accordingly been decided by the practice of the States, that it is better to leave a few of its noxious branches to their luxuriant growth, than, by pruning them away, to injure the vigour of those yielding the proper fruits. And can the wisdom of this policy be doubted by any who reflect that to the press alone, chequered as it is with abuses, the world is indebted for all the triumphs which have been gained by reason and humanity over error and oppression; who reflect that to the same beneficent source the United States owe much of the lights which conducted them to the ranks of a free and independent nation, and which have improved their political system into a shape so auspicious to their happiness? Had 'Sedition Acts,' forbidding every publication that might bring the constituted agents into contempt or disrepute, or that might excite the hatred of the people against the authors of unjust or pernicious measures, been uniformly enforced against the press, might not the United States have been languishing at this day under the infirmities of a sickly Confederation?* Might they not, possibly, be miserable colonies, groaning under a foreign yoke?"

The fact that for approximately one hundred and fifty years there has been almost an entire absence of attempts to impose previous restraints upon publications relating to the malfeasance of public officers is significant of the deep-seated conviction that such restraints would violate constitutional right. Public officers, whose character and conduct remain open to debate and free discussion in the press, find their remedies for false accusations in actions under libel laws providing for redress and punishment, and not in proceedings to restrain the publication of newspapers and periodicals. The general principle that the constitutional guaranty of the liberty of the press gives immunity from previous restraints has been approved in many decisions under the provisions of state constitutions.

The importance of this immunity has not lessened. While reckless assaults upon public men . . . exert a baleful influence and deserve the severest condemnation in public opinion, it cannot be said that this abuse is greater, and it is believed to be less, than that which characterized the period in which our institutions took shape. Meanwhile, the administration of government has become more complex, the opportunities for malfeasance and corruption have multiplied, crime has grown to most serious proportions, and the danger of its protection by unfaithful officials and of the impairment of the fundamental security of life and property by criminal alliances and official neglect, emphasizes the primary need of a vigilant and courageous press, especially in great cities. The fact that the liberty of the press may be abused by miscreant purveyors of scandal does not make any the less necessary the immunity of the press from previous restraint in dealing with official misconduct. Subsequent punishment

---

* The fear of such legislation was scarcely idle. In 1798 Congress passed the Alien and Sedition Acts, which provided for indicting those who conspired against the administration or who spoke or wrote "with intent to defame" the government. The Sedition Act was enforced against a few individuals before being repealed during the Jefferson administration.

for such abuses as may exist is the appropriate remedy, consistent with constitutional privilege.

In attempted justification of the statute, it is said that it deals not with publication *per se*, but with the "business" of publishing defamation. If, however, the publisher has a constitutional right to publish, without previous restraint, an edition of his newspaper charging official derelictions, it cannot be denied that he may publish subsequent editions for the same purpose. He does not lose his right by exercising it. If his right exists, it may be exercised in publishing nine editions, as in this case, as well as in one edition. If previous restraint is permissible, it may be imposed at once; indeed, the wrong may be as serious in one publication as in several. Characterizing the publication as a business, and the business as a nuisance, does not permit an invasion of the constitutional immunity against restraint. Similarly, it does not matter that the newspaper or periodical is found to be "largely" or "chiefly" devoted to the publication of such derelictions. If the publisher has a right, without previous restraint, to publish them, his right cannot be deemed to be dependent upon his publishing something else, more or less, with the matter to which objection is made.

Nor can it be said that the constitutional freedom from previous restraint is lost because charges are made of derelictions which constitute crimes. With the multiplying provisions of penal codes, and of municipal charters and ordinances carrying penal sanctions, the conduct of public officers is very largely within the purview of criminal statutes. The freedom of the press from previous restraint has never been regarded as limited to such animadversions as lay outside the range of penal enactments. Historically, there is no such limitation; it is inconsistent with the reason which underlies the privilege, as the privilege so limited would be of slight value for the purposes for which it came to be established.

The statute in question cannot be justified by reason of the fact that the publisher is permitted to show, before injunction issues, that the matter published is true and is published with good motives and for justifiable ends. If such a statute, authorizing suppression and injunction on such a basis, is constitutionally valid, it would be equally permissible for the legislature to provide that at any time the publisher of any newspaper could be brought before a court, or even an administrative officer (as the constitutional protection may not be regarded as resting on mere procedural details) and required to produce proof of the truth of his publication, or of what he intended to publish, and of his motives, or stand enjoined. If this can be done, the legislature may provide machinery for determining in the complete exercise of its discretion what are justifiable ends and restrain publication accordingly. And it would be but a step to a complete system of censorship. The recognition of authority to impose previous restraint upon publication in order to protect the community against the circulation of charges of misconduct, and especially of official misconduct, necessarily would carry with it the admission of the authority of the censor against which the constitutional barrier was erected. The preliminary freedom, by virtue of the very reason for its existence, does not depend, as this Court has said, on proof of truth. . . .

Equally unavailing is the insistence that the statute is designed to prevent the circulation of scandal which tends to disturb the public peace and to provoke assaults and the commission of crime. Charges of reprehensible conduct, and in particular of official malfeasance, unquestionably create a public scandal, but the theory of the constitutional guaranty is that even a more serious public evil would be caused by authority to prevent publication. "To prohibit the intent to excite those unfavorable sentiments against those who administer the Government, is equivalent to a prohibition of the actual excitement of them; and to prohibit the actual excitement of them is equivalent to a prohibition of discussions having that tendency and effect; which, again, is equivalent to a protection of those who administer the Government, if they should at any time deserve the contempt or hatred of the people, against being exposed to it by free animadversions on their characters and conduct."[2] There is nothing new in the fact that charges of reprehensible conduct may create resentment and the disposition to resort to violent means of redress, but this well-understood tendency did not alter the determination to protect the press against censorship and restraint upon publication. As was said in *New Yorker Staats-Zeitung v. Nolan* . . . : "If the township may prevent the circulation of a newspaper for no reason other than that some of its inhabitants may violently disagree with it, and resent its circulation by resorting to physical violence, there is no limit to what may be prohibited." The danger of violent reactions becomes greater with effective organization of defiant groups resenting exposure, and if this consideration warranted legislative interference with the initial freedom of publication, the constitutional protection would be reduced to a mere form of words.

For these reasons we hold the statute, so far as it authorized the proceedings in this action under clause (b) of section one, to be an infringement of the liberty of the press guaranteed by the Fourteenth Amendment. We should add that this decision rests upon the operation and effect of the statute, without regard to the question of the truth of the charges contained in the particular periodical.* The fact that the public officers named in this case, and those associated with the charges of official dereliction, may be deemed to be impeccable, cannot affect the conclusion that the statute imposes an unconstitutional restraint upon publication.

Notes

1. Report on the Virginia Resolutions, Madison's Works, vol. iv, p. 544.
2. Madison, *op. cit.*, p. 549.

---

* Note the strength of this declaration. The falsity of a statement does not constitute adequate grounds for imposing prior restraint.

Summary Questions

1. Why should public figures be treated differently when libel or slander is alleged? Is it possible to libel someone as public as the president?
2. In what instances might prior restraint of a publication be appropriate? In wartime? In the case of a consistently obscene magazine?

 3.2

Brandenburg v. Ohio (1969)

Under an Ohio statute that defined as criminal the advocacy of crime or violence in accomplishing industrial or political reform, Charles Brandenburg was convicted of advocating lawless action. He appealed to the Ohio appellate court and lost. The U.S. Supreme Court was faced with distinguishing between advocacy of violent actions and imminent incitement to act. Brandenburg, a Ku Klux Klan leader, contended that his right to free expression had been abridged.

P ER CURIAM.*
The appellant, a leader of a Ku Klux Klan group, was convicted under the Ohio Criminal Syndicalism statute for "advocat[ing] . . . the duty, necessity, or propriety of crime, sabotage, violence, or unlawful methods of terrorism as a means of accomplishing industrial or political reform" and for "voluntarily assembl[ing] with any society, group, or assemblage of persons formed to teach or advocate the doctrines of criminal syndicalism." Ohio Rev. Code Ann. §2923.13. He was fined $1,000 and sentenced to one to 10 years' imprisonment. The appellant challenged the constitutionality of the criminal syndicalism statute under the First and Fourteenth Amendments to the United States Constitution, but the intermediate appellate court of Ohio affirmed his conviction without opinion. The Supreme Court of Ohio dismissed his appeal, *sua sponte,* "for the reason that no substantial constitutional question exists herein." It did not file

---

* A *Per Curiam* decision is an unsigned, usually brief decision handed down by the court as a whole.

an opinion or explain its conclusions. Appeal was taken to this Court, and we noted probable jurisdiction. 393 U.S. 948 (1968). We reverse.

The record shows that a man, identified at trial as the appellant, telephoned an announcer-reporter on the staff of a Cincinnati television station and invited him to come to a Ku Klux Klan "rally" to be held at a farm in Hamilton County. With the cooperation of the organizers, the reporter and a cameraman attended the meeting and filmed the events. Portions of the films were later broadcast on the local station and on a national network.

The prosecution's case rested on the films and on testimony identifying the appellant as the person who communicated with the reporter and who spoke at the rally. The State also introduced into evidence several articles appearing in the film, including a pistol, a rifle, a shotgun, ammunition, a Bible, and a red hood worn by the speaker in the films.

One film showed 12 hooded figures, some of whom carried firearms. They were gathered around a large wooden cross, which they burned. No one was present other than the participants and the newsmen who made the film. Most of the words uttered during the scene were incomprehensible when the film was projected, but scattered phrases could be understood that were derogatory of Negroes and, in one instance, of Jews. Another scene on the same film showed the appellant, in the Klan regalia, making a speech. The speech, in full, was as follows:

> This is an organizers' meeting. We have had quite a few members here today which are—we have hundreds, hundreds of members throughout the State of Ohio. I can quote from a newspaper clipping from the Columbus, Ohio Dispatch, five weeks ago Sunday morning. The Klan has more members in the State of Ohio than does any other organization. We're not a revengent organization, but if our President, our Congress, our Supreme Court, continues to suppress the white, Caucasian race, it's possible that there might have to be some revengeance taken.
>
> We are marching on Congress July the Fourth, four hundred thousand strong. From there we are dividing into two groups, one group to march on St Augustine, Florida, the other group to march into Mississippi. Thank you.

The second film showed six hooded figures one of whom, later identified as the appellant, repeated a speech very similar to that recorded on the first film. The reference to the possibility of "revengeance" was omitted, was one sentence was added: "Personally, I believe the nigger should be returned to Africa, the Jew returned to Israel." Though some of the figures in the films carried weapons, the speaker did not.

The Ohio Criminal Syndicalism Statute was enacted in 1919. From 1917 to 1920, identical or quite similar laws were adopted by 20 States and two territories. E. Dowell, A History of Criminal Syndicalism Legislation in the United States 21 (1939). In 1927, this Court sustained the constitutionality of California's Criminal Syndicalism Act, Cal. Penal Code §§11400–11402, the text of which is quite similar to that of the laws of Ohio. *Whitney v. California*, 274 U.S. 357

(1927). The Court upheld the statute on the ground that, without more, "advocating" violent means to effect political and economic change involves such danger to the security of the State that the State may outlaw it. Cf. *Fiske* v. *Kansas*, 274 U.S. 380 (1927). But *Whitney* has been thoroughly discredited by later decisions. See *Dennis* v. *United States*, 341 U.S. 494, at 507 (1951). These later decisions have fashioned the principle that the constitutional guarantees of free speech and free press do not permit a State to forbid or proscribe advocacy of the use of force or of law violation except where such advocacy is directed to inciting or producing imminent lawless action and is likely to incite or produce such action. As we said in *Noto* v. *United States*, 367 U.S. 290, 297–298 (1961), "the mere abstract teaching . . . of the moral propriety or even moral necessity for a resort to force and violence, is not the same as preparing a group for violent action and steeling it to such action." . . . A statute which fails to draw this distinction impermissibly intrudes upon the freedoms guaranteed by the First and Fourteenth Amendments. It sweeps within its condemnation speech which our Constitution has immunized from governmental control. . . .

Measured by this test, Ohio's Criminal Syndicalism Act cannot be sustained. The Act punishes persons who "advocate or teach the duty, necessity, or propriety" of violence "as a means of accomplishing industrial or political reform"; or who publish or circulate or display any book or paper containing such advocacy; or who "justify" the commission of violent acts "with intent to exemplify, spread or advocate the propriety of the doctrines of criminal syndicalism"; or who "voluntarily assemble" with a group formed "to teach or advocate the doctrines of criminal syndicalism." Neither the indictment nor the trial judge's instructions to the jury in any way refined the statute's bald definition of the crime in terms of mere advocacy not distinguished from incitement to imminent lawless action.

Accordingly, we are here confronted with a statute which, by its own words and as applied, purports to punish mere advocacy and to forbid, on pain of criminal punishment, assembly with others merely to advocate the described type of action. Such a statute falls within the condemnation of the First and Fourteenth Amendments. The contrary teaching of *Whitney* v. *California*, *supra*, cannot be supported, and that decision is therefore overruled.

Reversed.

Summary Questions

1. At what point does advocacy become incitement? Are those who advocate violence ultimately responsible for actions of their followers that might occur at a later date?
2. Those who test the limits of speech often espouse unpopular opinions. Is there a price to pay for a society allowing such speech? How does society benefit from such tolerance?

3.3

Griswold v. Connecticut (1965)

Since the 1960s, one of the most interesting and controversial fields of constitutional law has involved the alleged right of privacy. The Constitution nowhere explicitly spells out any such right, yet preserving privacy is of paramount concern in an increasingly intrusive society.

One key case (not presented here) is *Roe* v. *Wade* (1973), which declared abortion laws in almost all states unconstitutional. Justice Harry A. Blackmun held that the constitutional right to privacy allowed women to determine whether to go ahead with an abortion, although the rights of the mother were to be balanced against the potential right to life of the fetus (which was not a person in a constitutional sense). *Roe* v. *Wade* set off almost ceaseless attempts by pro-life activists to ban abortions. It also became a turning point in the Senate's defeat of Ronald Reagan's Supreme Court nominee, Appeals Court Judge Robert Bork, in 1987.

Griswold v. *Connecticut* (1965) laid the groundwork for *Roe* by giving the right of privacy formal constitutional protection. The decision grew from a challenge to Connecticut's restrictive but rarely enforced birth control laws. Estelle Griswold, executive director of the Planned Parenthood League of Connecticut, was convicted of dispensing birth control information to married people. The Supreme Court overturned the lower court's decision.

Mr. Justice Douglas delivered the opinion of the Court. . . . Coming to the merits, we are met with a wide range of questions that implicate the Due Process Clause of the Fourteenth Amendment. Overtones of some arguments suggest that *Lockner* v. *State of New York* . . . should be our guide. But we decline that invitation. . . . We do not sit as super-legislature to determine the wisdom, need, and propriety of laws that touch economic problems, business affairs, or social conditions. This law, however, operates directly on an intimate relation of husband and wife and their physician's role in one aspect of that relation.

The association of people is not mentioned in the Constitution nor in the Bill of Rights. The right to educate a child in a school of the parents' choice—whether public or private or parochial—is also not mentioned. Nor is the right to study any particular subject or any foreign language. Yet the First Amendment has been construed to include certain of those rights.

By *Pierce* v. *Society of Sisters* . . . , the right to educate one's children as one chooses is made applicable to the States by the force of the First and Fourteenth Amendments. By *Meyer* v. *State of Nebraska* . . . , the same dignity is given the right to study the German language in a private school. In other words, the State may not, consistently with the spirit of the First Amendment, contract the spectrum of available knowledge. The right of freedom of speech and press includes not only the right to utter or to print, but the right to distribute, the right to receive, the right to read (*Martin* v. *City of Struthers* . . .) and freedom of inquiry, freedom of thought, and freedom to teach (see *Wieman* v. *Updegraff* . . .)—indeed the freedom of the entire university community. . . . Without those peripheral rights the specific rights would be less secure. And so we reaffirm the principle of the *Pierce* and the *Meyer* cases.

In *NAACP* v. *State of Alabama* . . . we protected the "freedom to associate and privacy in one's associations," noting that freedom of association was a peripheral First Amendment right. Disclosure of membership lists of a constitutionally valid association, we held, was invalid "as entailing the likelihood of a substantial restraint upon the exercise by petitioner's members of their right to freedom of association." In other words, the First Amendment has a penumbra where privacy is protected from governmental intrusion.* In like context, we have protected forms of "association" that are not political in the customary sense but pertain to the social, legal, and economic benefit of the members. In *Schware* v. *Board of Bar Examiners*, . . . we held it not permissible to bar a lawyer from practice, because he had once been a member of the Communist Party. The man's "association with that Party" was not shown to be "anything more than a political faith in a political party" and was not action of a kind proving bad moral character.

Those cases involved more than the "right of assembly"—a right that extends to all irrespective of their race or ideology. The right of "association," like the right of belief is more than the right to attend a meeting; it includes the right to express one's attitudes or philosophies by membership in a group or by affiliation with it or by other lawful means. Association in that context is a form of expression of opinion; and while it is not expressly included in the First Amendment its existence is necessary in making the express guarantees fully meaningful.

The foregoing cases suggest that specific guarantees in the Bill of Rights have penumbras, formed by emanations from those guarantees that help give them life and substance. Various guarantees create zones of privacy. The right of association contained in the penumbra of the First Amendment is one, as we have seen. The Third Amendment in its prohibition against the quartering of soldiers "in any

---

* Justice William O. Douglas developed the analogy to a penumbra, "the partial shadow surrounding a complete shadow (as in an eclipse)." Douglas found a right to privacy in the "penumbras" of the First, Third, Fourth, Fifth, and Ninth Amendments. Most scholars of the Constitution agree that some right to privacy does exist, but the extension of that right is open to debate.

house" in time of peace without the consent of the owner is another facet of that privacy. The Fourth Amendment explicitly affirms the "right of the people to be secure in their persons, houses, papers, and effects, against unreasonable searches and seizures." The Fifth Amendment in its Self-Incrimination Clause enables the citizen to create a zone of privacy which government may not force him to surrender to his detriment. The Ninth Amendment provides: "The enumeration in the Constitution, of certain rights, shall not be construed to deny or disparage others retained by the people."

The Fourth and Fifth Amendments were described in *Boyd* v. *United States* . . . as protection against all governmental invasions "of the sanctity of a man's home and the privacies of life." We recently referred in *Mapp* v. *Ohio* . . . to the Fourth Amendment as creating a "right to privacy, no less important than any other right carefully and particularly reserved to the people." . . .

The present case, then, concerns a relationship lying within the zone of privacy created by several fundamental constitutional guarantees. And it concerns a law which, in forbidding the use of contraceptives rather than regulating their manufacture or sale, seeks to achieve its goals by means having a maximum destructive impact upon that relationship. Such a law cannot stand in light of the familiar principle, so often applied by this Court, that a "governmental purpose to control or prevent activities constitutionally subject to state regulation may not be achieved by means which sweep unnecessarily broadly and thereby invade the area of protected freedoms." *NAACP* v. *Alabama.* . . . Would we allow the police to search the sacred precincts of marital bedrooms for telltale signs of the use of contraceptives? The very idea is repulsive to the notions of privacy surrounding the marriage relationship.

We deal with a right to privacy older than the Bill of Rights—older than our political parties, older than our school system. Marriage is a coming together for better or for worse, hopefully enduring, and intimate to the degree of being sacred. It is an association that promotes a way of life, not causes; a harmony in living, not political faiths; a bilateral loyalty, not commercial or social projects. Yet it is an association for as noble a purpose as any involved in our prior decisions.

Mr. Justice Goldberg, whom the Chief Justice and Mr. Justice Brennan join, concurring:

I agree with the Court that Connecticut's birth-control law unconstitutionally intrudes upon the right of marital privacy, and I join in its opinion and judgment. Although I have not accepted the view that "due process" as used in the Fourteenth Amendment includes all of the first eight Amendments . . . I do agree that the concept of liberty protects those personal rights that are fundamental, and is not confined to the specific terms of the Bill of Rights. My conclusion that the concept of liberty is not so restricted and that it embraces the right of marital privacy though that right is not mentioned explicitly in the Constitution is supported both by numerous decisions of this Court, referred to in the Court's opinion, and by the language and history of the Ninth Amendment. In reaching the conclusion that the right of marital privacy is protected, as being within the protected penumbra of specific guarantees of the Bill of Rights, the Court refers to the Ninth Amendment. I add these words to emphasize the relevance of that Amendment to the Court's holding. . . . The Framers did not intend that the first eight amendments be construed to exhaust the basic and fundamental rights which the Constitution guaranteed to the people.

While this Court has had little occasion to interpret the Ninth Amendment "[i]t cannot be presumed that any clause in the constitution is intended to be without effect." *Marbury v. Madison.* . . . In interpreting the Constitution, "real effect should be given to all the words it uses." *Myers v. United States.* . . . The Ninth Amendment to the Constitution may be regarded by some as a recent discovery but since 1791 it has been a basic part of the Constitution which we are sworn to uphold. To hold that a right so basic and fundamental and so deep-rooted in our society as the right of privacy in marriage may be infringed because that right is not guaranteed in so many words by the first eight amendments to the Constitution is to ignore the Ninth Amendment and to give it no effect whatsoever. Moreover, a judicial construction that this fundamental right is not protected by the Constitution because it is not mentioned in explicit terms by one of the first eight amendments or elsewhere in the Constitution would violate the Ninth Amendment, which specifically states that "[t]he enumeration in the Constitution, of certain rights shall not be *construed* to deny or disparage others retained by the people." (Emphasis added.) . . . [T]he Ninth Amendment simply lends strong support to the view that the "liberty" protected by the Fifth and Fourteenth Amendments from infringement by the Federal Government or the States is not restricted to rights specifically mentioned in the first eight amendments. . . .

In sum, I believe that the right of privacy in the marital relation is fundamental and basic—a personal right "retained by the people" within the meaning of the Ninth Amendment. Connecticut cannot constitutionally abridge this fundamental right, which is protected by the Fourteenth Amendment from infringement by the States. I agree with the Court that petitioners' convictions must therefore be reversed.

Mr. Justice Black, with whom Mr. Justice Stewart joins, dissenting: . . .

The Court talks about a constitutional "right of privacy" as though there is some constitutional provision or provisions forbidding any law ever to be passed which might abridge the "privacy" of individuals. But there is not. . . .

One of the most effective ways of diluting or expanding a constitutionally guaranteed right is to substitute for the crucial word or words of a constitutional guarantee another word or words, more or less flexible and more or less restricted in meaning. This fact is well illustrated by the use of the term "right of privacy" as a comprehensive substitute for the Fourth Amendment's guarantee against "unreasonable searches and seizures." "Privacy" is a broad, abstract and ambiguous concept which can easily be shrunken in meaning but which can also, on the other hand, easily be interpreted as a constitutional ban against many things other than searches and seizures. I have expressed the view many times that First Amendment freedoms, for example, have suffered from a failure of the courts to stick to the simple language of the First Amendment in construing it, instead of invoking multitudes of words substituted for those the Framers used. For these reasons I get nowhere in this case by talk about a constitutional "right of privacy" as an emanation from one or more constitutional provisions. I like my privacy as well as the next one, but I am nevertheless compelled to admit that government has a right to invade it unless prohibited by some specific constitutional provision. For these reasons I cannot agree with the Court's judgment and the reasons it gives for holding this Connecticut law unconstitutional. . . .

My Brother Goldberg has adopted the recent discovery that the Ninth Amendment as well as the Due Process Clause can be used by this Court as authority to strike down all state legislation which this Court thinks violates "fundamental principles of liberty and justice," or is contrary to the "traditions and [collective] conscience of our people." He also states, without proof satisfactory to me, that in making decisions on this basis judges will not consider "their personal and private notions." One may ask how they can avoid considering them. Our Court certainly has no machinery with which to take a Gallup Poll. And the scientific miracles of this age have not yet produced a gadget which the Court can use to determine what traditions are rooted in the "[collective] conscience of our people." Moreover, one would certainly have to look far beyond the language of the Ninth Amendment to find that the Framers vested in this Court any such awesome veto powers over lawmaking, either by the States or by the Congress. Nor does anything in the history of the Amendment offer any support for such a shocking doctrine. The whole history of the adoption of the Constitution and Bill of Rights points the other way, and the very material quoted by my Brother Goldberg shows that the Ninth Amendment was intended to protect against the idea that "by enumerating particular exceptions to the grant of power" to the Federal Government, "those rights which were not singled out, were intended to be assigned into the hands of the General Government [the United States], and were consequently insecure." That Amendment was passed, not to broaden the powers of this Court or any other department of "the General Government," but, as every student of history knows, to assure the people that the Constitution in all its provisions was intended to limit the Federal Government to the powers granted expressly or by necessary implication. If any broad, unlimited power to hold laws unconstitutional because they offend what this Court conceives to be the "[collective] conscience of our people" is vested in this Court by the Ninth Amendment, the Fourteenth Amendment, or any other provision of the Constitution, it was not given by the Framers, but rather has been bestowed on the Court by the Court. This fact is perhaps responsible for the peculiar phenomenon that for a period of a century and a half no serious suggestion was ever made that the Ninth Amendment, enacted to protect state powers against federal invasion, could be used as a weapon of federal power to prevent state legislatures from passing laws they consider appropriate to govern local affairs. Use of any such broad, unbounded judicial authority would make of this Court's members a day-to-day constitutional convention. . . .

Summary Questions

1. Can a right be fundamental yet not enumerated in the Constitution?
2. Should the state ever have an interest in the relationships and actions between consenting adults? In what instances?

 3.4

Gideon v. Wainwright (1963)

Clarence Gideon, an indigent, was accused of breaking and entering a poolroom, a felony under Florida law. He proclaimed his innocence and requested that he be provided with a lawyer. The trial judge refused this request, Gideon was found guilty, and he was sentenced to a five-year term in the state penitentiary. In a hand-written statement Gideon appealed his case to the Supreme Court, which took the case and appointed Abe Fortas, a prominent Washington attorney and later Supreme Court justice, to represent him.

The Supreme Court had frequently ruled in specific circumstances that the Sixth Amendment guaranteed a right to counsel and that this right was incorporated by the Fourteenth Amendment and was thus applicable to the states. Still, before *Gideon* v. *Wainwright* (1963), the Court had not ruled that there was any general right to counsel. Indeed, the governing rule was that of *Betts* v. *Brady,* a 1942 decision that the right to counsel was not a "fundamental" right. The Court's reconsideration of the Betts rule after only twenty-one years was unusual.

After the decision in this case, Gideon was retried in Florida, with counsel, and found innocent. Subsequently, thousands of prisoners in Florida and elsewhere won their release on the grounds that they had not been represented by counsel at their trials.

M r. Justice Black delivered the opinion of the Court. . . .
. . . Since 1942, when *Betts* v. *Brady* . . . was decided by a divided Court,
the problem of a defendant's federal constitutional right to counsel in a
state court has been a continuing source of controversy and litigation in
both state and federal courts. To give this problem another review here, we
granted certiorari. Since Gideon was proceeding *in forma pauperis*, we appointed
counsel to represent him and requested both sides to discuss in their briefs
and oral arguments the following: "Should this Court's holding in *Betts* v. *Brady*
be reconsidered?" . . .

We think the Court in *Betts* had ample precedent for acknowledging that those
guarantees of the Bill of Rights which are fundamental safeguards of liberty
immune from federal abridgment are equally protected against state invasion by
the Due Process Clause of the Fourteenth Amendment. This same principle was
recognized, explained, and applied in *Powell* v. *Alabama* . . . , a case upholding the
right of counsel, where the Court held that despite sweeping language to the
contrary in *Hurtado* v. *California* . . . , the Fourteenth Amendment "embraced"
those " 'fundamental principles of liberty and justice which lie at the base of all
our civil and political institutions,' " even though they had been "specifically
dealt with in another part of the federal Constitution." . . . In many cases other
than *Powell* and *Betts*, this Court has looked to the fundamental nature of original
Bill of Rights guarantees to decide whether the Fourteenth Amendment makes
them obligatory on the States. . . .

We accept *Betts* v. *Brady*'s assumption, based as it was on our prior cases, that a
provision of the Bill of Rights which is "fundamental and essential to a fair trial"
is made obligatory upon the States by the Fourteenth Amendment. We think the
Court in *Betts* was wrong, however, in concluding that the Sixth Amendment's
guarantee of counsel is not one of these fundamental rights. Ten years before *Betts*
v. *Brady*, this Court, after full consideration of all the historical data examined in
Betts, had unequivocally declared that "the right to the aid of counsel is of this
fundamental character." *Powell* v. *Alabama*. . . . While the Court at the close of
its *Powell* opinion did by its language, as this Court frequently does, limit its
holding to the particular facts and circumstances of that case, its conclusions
about the fundamental nature of the right to counsel are unmistakable. . . .

In light of . . . many other prior decisions of this Court, it is not surprising that
the *Betts* Court, when faced with the contention that "one charged with crime,
who is unable to obtain counsel, must be furnished counsel by the State,"
conceded that "[e]xpressions in the opinions of this court lend color to the
argument. . . ." The fact is that in deciding as it did—that "appointment of
counsel is not a fundamental right, essential to a fair trial"—the Court in *Betts* v.
Brady made an abrupt break with its own well-considered precedents. In returning to these old precedents, sounder we believe than the new, we but restore
constitutional principles established to achieve a fair system of justice. Not only
these precedents but also reason and reflection require us to recognize that in our

adversary system of criminal justice, any person haled into court, who is too poor to hire a lawyer, cannot be assured a fair trial unless counsel is provided for him. This seems to us to be an obvious truth. Governments, both state and federal, quite properly spend vast sums of money to establish machinery to try defendants accused of crime. Lawyers to prosecute are everywhere deemed essential to protect the public's interest in an orderly society. Similarly, there are few defendants charged with crime, few indeed, who fail to hire the best lawyers they can get to prepare and present their defenses. That government hires lawyers to prosecute and defendants who have the money hire lawyers to defend are the strongest indications of the widespread belief that lawyers in criminal courts are necessities, not luxuries. The right of one charged with crime to counsel may not be deemed fundamental and essential to fair trials in some countries, but it is in ours. From the very beginning, our state and national constitutions and laws have laid great emphasis on procedural and substantive safeguards designed to assure fair trials before impartial tribunals in which every defendant stands equal before the law. This noble ideal cannot be realized if the poor man charged with crime has to face his accusers without a lawyer to assist him. . . .The Court in *Betts* v. *Brady* departed from the sound wisdom upon which the Court's holding in *Powell* v. *Alabama* rested. Florida, supported by two other states, has asked that *Betts* v. *Brady* be left intact. Twenty-two States, as friends of the Court,* argue that *Betts* was "an anachronism when handed down" and that it should now be overruled. We agree.

The judgment is reversed and the cause is remanded to the Supreme Court of Florida for further action not inconsistent with this opinion.

Mr. Justice Harlan, concurring:

I agree that *Betts* v. *Brady* should be overruled, but consider it entitled to a more respectful burial than has been accorded, at least on the part of those of us who were not on the Court when that case was decided.

I cannot subscribe to the view that *Betts* v. *Brady* represented "an abrupt break with its own well-considered precedents." In 1932, in *Powell* v. *Alabama* . . . , a capital case, this Court declared that under the particular facts there presented— "the ignorance and illiteracy of the defendants, their youth, the circumstances of public hostility . . . and above all that they stood in deadly peril of their lives"—the state court had a duty to assign counsel for the trial as a necessary requisite of due process of law. It is evident that these limiting facts were not

---

* Various organizations and individuals, such as interest groups or state attorneys general, offer *amicus curiae* (friend of the court) briefs on major cases. Since the 1950s, *amicus* briefs as practiced by groups such as the National Association for the Advancement of Colored People (NAACP) and the American Civil Liberties Union (ACLU) have become a major tool for promoting social change.

added to the opinion as an afterthought; they were repeatedly emphasized, and were clearly regarded as important to the result.

Thus when this Court, a decade later, decided *Betts* v. *Brady*, it did no more than to admit of the possible existence of special circumstances in noncapital as well as capital trials, while at the same time insisting that such circumstances be shown in order to establish a denial of due process. The right to appointed counsel had been recognized as being considerably broader in federal prosecutions, see *Johnson* v. *Zerbst* . . . , but to have imposed these requirements on the States would indeed have been "an abrupt break" with the almost immediate past. The declaration that the right to appointed counsel in state prosecutions, as established in *Powell* v. *Alabama,* was not limited to capital cases was in truth not a departure from, but an extension of, existing precedent.

The principles declared in *Powell* and in *Betts,* however, have had a troubled journey throughout the years that have followed first the one case and then the other. Even by the time of the *Betts* decision, dictum in at least one of the Court's opinions had indicated that there was an absolute right to the services of counsel in the trial of state capital cases. Such dicta continued to appear in subsequent decisions and any lingering doubts were finally eliminated by the holding of *Hamilton* v. *Alabama*. . . .

In noncapital cases, the "special circumstances" rule has continued to exist in form while its substance has been substantially and steadily eroded. In the first decade after *Betts,* there were cases in which the Court found special circumstances to be lacking, but usually by a sharply divided vote. However, no such decision has been cited to us, and I have found none, after *Quicksall* v. *Michigan* . . . , decided in 1950. At the same time, there have been not a few cases in which special circumstances were found in little or nothing more than the "complexity" of the legal questions presented, although those questions were often of only routine difficulty. The Court has come to recognize, in other words, that the mere existence of serious criminal charge constituted in itself special circumstances requiring the services of counsel at trial. In truth the *Betts* v. *Brady* rule is no longer a reality.

This evolution, however, appears not to have been fully recognized by many state courts, in this instance charged with the front-line responsibility for the enforcement of constitutional rights. To continue a rule which is honored by this Court only with lip service is not a healthy thing and in the long run will do disservice to the federal system.

The special circumstances rule has been formally abandoned in capital cases, and the time has now come when it should be similarly abandoned in noncapital cases, at least as to offenses which, as the one involved here, carry the possibility of a substantial prison sentence. (Whether the rule should extend to *all* criminal cases need not now be decided.) This indeed does no more than to make explicit something that has long since been foreshadowed in our decisions. . . .

Summary Questions

1. At what point does having access to counsel become a constitutional right? Is it a right for any felony? What about for a serious misdemeanor?
2. *Gideon* paved the way for the *Miranda* case, which required the police to inform a suspect of his or her constitutional rights, including the right to counsel. Should the police be able to question a suspect without counsel present?
3. Has *Gideon* completely closed the gap between the wealthy and the poor when it comes to obtaining adequate counsel?

 3.5

Brown v. Board of Education (1954; 1955)

No single contemporary court case has had more widespread impact than *Brown v. Board of Education* (1954; 1955). The 1954 case consolidated four suits, from Kansas, South Carolina, Virginia, and Delaware; each state mandated the separate schooling of children by race. The lead case was brought by Oliver Brown, whose daughter Linda attended an all-black school twenty-one blocks from her Topeka home, each day passing by an all-white school five blocks away. In *Brown,* the Court unanimously ruled that such legalized practices were unconstitutional.

The 1954 decision promised so much social change that the justices reheard the case a year later to consider how it should be implemented. In the process, Chief Justice Earl Warren coined the ambiguous phrase "with all deliberate speed" to describe how desegregation should be ended. Warren was sensitive to the fact that the Court cannot easily enforce its decisions, especially when they are controversial and require substantial changes in both laws and patterns of behavior.

1954

M r. Chief Justice Warren delivered the opinion of the Court.
These cases come to us from the States of Kansas, South Carolina, Virginia, and Delaware. They are premised on different facts and

different local conditions, but a common legal question justifies their consideration together in this consolidated opinion.

In each of the cases, minors of the Negro race, through their legal representatives, seek the aid of the courts in obtaining admission to the public schools
of their community on a nonsegregated basis. In each instance, they had been
denied admission to schools attended by white children under laws requiring or
permitting segregation according to race. This segregation was alleged to deprive
the plaintiffs of the equal protection of the laws under the Fourteenth Amendment. In each of the cases other than the Delaware case, a three-judge federal
district court denied relief to the plaintiffs on the so-called "separate but equal"
doctrine announced by this Court in *Plessy v. Ferguson*. . . . Under that doctrine, equality of treatment is accorded when the races are provided substantially
equal facilities even though these facilities be separate. In the Delaware case,
the Supreme Court of Delaware adhered to that doctrine, but ordered that the
plaintiffs be admitted to the white schools because of their superiority to the
Negro schools.

The plaintiffs contend that segregated public schools are not "equal" and
cannot be made "equal," and that hence they are deprived of the equal protection
of the laws. Because of the obvious importance of the question presented, the
Court took jurisdiction. Argument was heard in the 1952 Term, and reargument
was heard this Term on certain questions propounded by the Court.

Reargument was largely devoted to the circumstances surrounding the adoption of the Fourteenth Amendment in 1868. It covered exhaustively consideration of the Amendment in Congress, ratification by the states, then existing
practices in racial segregation, and the views of proponents and opponents of the
Amendment. This discussion and our own investigation convince us that, although these sources cast some light, it is not enough to resolve the problem with
which we are faced. At best, they are inconclusive. The most avid proponents of
the post-War Amendments undoubtedly intended them to remove all legal
distinctions among "all persons born or naturalized in the United States." Their
opponents, just as certainly were antagonistic to both the letter and the spirit of
the Amendments and wished them to have the most limited effect. What others
in Congress and the state legislatures had in mind cannot be determined with any
degree of certainty.

An additional reason for the inconclusive nature of the Amendment's history,
with respect to segregated schools, is the status of public education at that time.
In the South, the movement toward free common schools, supported by general
taxation, had not yet taken hold. Education of white children was largely in the
hands of private groups. Education of Negroes was almost nonexistent, and
practically all of the race were illiterate. In fact, any education of Negroes was
forbidden by law in some states. Today, in contrast, many Negroes have achieved
outstanding success in the arts and sciences as well as in the business and
professional world. It is true that public education had already advanced further
in the North, but the effect of the Amendment on Northern States was generally

ignored in the congressional debates. Even in the North, the conditions of public education did not approximate those existing today. The curriculum was usually rudimentary; ungraded schools were common in rural areas; the school term was but three months a year in many states; and compulsory school attendance was virtually unknown. As a consequence, it is not surprising that there should be so little in the history of the Fourteenth Amendment relating to its intended effect on public education.

In the first cases in this Court construing the Fourteenth Amendment, decided shortly after its adoption, the Court interpreted it as proscribing all state-imposed discriminations against the Negro race. The doctrine of "separate but equal" did not make its appearance in this court until 1896 in the case of *Plessy v. Ferguson, supra,* involving not education but transportation. American courts have since labored with the doctrine for over half a century. In this Court, there have been six cases involving the "separate but equal" doctrine in the field of public education. In *Cumming v. County Board of Education . . .* and *Gong Lum v. Rice . . . ,* the validity of the doctrine itself was not challenged. In more recent cases, all on the graduate school level, inequality was found in that specific benefits enjoyed by white students were denied to Negro students of the same educational qualifications. *Missouri ex rel. Gaines v. Canada; Sipuel v. Oklahoma; Sweatt v. Painter; McLaurin v. Oklahoma State Regents.* In none of these cases was it necessary to reexamine the doctrine to grant relief to the Negro plaintiff. And in *Sweatt v. Painter, supra,* the Court expressly reserved decision on the question whether *Plessy v. Ferguson* should be held inapplicable to public education.

In the instant cases, that question is directly presented. Here, unlike *Sweatt v. Painter,* there are findings below that the Negro and white schools involved have been equalized, or are being equalized, with respect to buildings, curricula, qualifications and salaries of teachers, and other "tangible" factors. Our decision, therefore, cannot turn on merely a comparison of these tangible factors in the Negro and white schools involved in each of the cases. We must look instead to the effect of segregation itself on public education.

In approaching this problem, we cannot turn the clock back to 1868 when the Amendment was adopted, or even to 1896 when *Plessy v. Ferguson* was written. We must consider public education in the light of its full development and its present place in American life throughout the Nation. Only in this way can it be determined if segregation in public schools deprives these plaintiffs of the equal protection of the laws.

Today, education is perhaps the most important function of state and local governments. Compulsory school attendance laws and the great expenditures for education both demonstrate our recognition of the importance of education to our democratic society. It is required in the performance of our most basic public responsibilities, even service in the armed forces. It is the very foundation of good citizenship. Today it is a principal instrument in awakening the child to cultural values, in preparing him for later professional training, and in helping him to adjust normally to his environment. In these days, it is doubtful that any child may reasonably be expected to succeed in life if he is denied the opportunity of an education. Such an opportunity, where the state has undertaken to provide it, is a right which must be made available to all on equal terms.

We come then to the question presented: Does segregation of children in public schools solely on the basis of race, even though the physical facilities and other "tangible" factors may be equal, deprive the children of the minority group of equal educational opportunities? We believe that it does.

In *Sweatt* v. *Painter, supra,* in finding that a segregated law school for Negroes could not provide them equal educational opportunities, this Court relied in large part on "those qualities which are incapable of objective measurement but which make for greatness in a law school." In *McLaurin* v. *Oklahoma State Regents, supra,* the Court, in requiring that a Negro admitted to a white graduate school be treated like all other students, again resorted to intangible considerations: ". . . his ability to study, to engage in discussions and exchange views with other students, and, in general, to learn his profession." Such considerations apply with added force to children in grade and high schools. To separate them from others of similar age and qualifications solely because of their race generates a feeling of inferiority as to their status in the community that may affect their hearts and minds in a way unlikely ever to be undone. The effect of this separation on their educational opportunities was well stated by a finding in the Kansas case by a court which nevertheless felt compelled to rule against the Negro plaintiffs:

> Segregation of white and colored children in public schools has a detrimental effect upon the colored children. The impact is greater when it has the sanction of the law; for the policy of separating the races is usually interpreted as denoting the inferiority of the Negro group. A sense of inferiority affects the motivation of a child to learn. Segregation with the sanction of law, therefore, has a tendency to retard the educational and mental development of Negro children and to deprive them of some of the benefits they would receive in a racially integrated school system.

Whatever may have been the extent of psychological knowledge* at the time of *Plessy* v. *Ferguson,* this finding is amply supported by modern authority. Any language in *Plessy* v. *Ferguson* contrary to this finding is rejected.

We conclude that in the field of public education the doctrine of "separate but equal" has no place. Separate educational facilities are inherently unequal. Therefore, we hold that the plaintiffs and others similarly situated for whom the actions have been brought are, by reason of the segregation complained of, deprived of the equal protection of the laws guaranteed by the Fourteenth Amendment. This disposition makes unnecessary any discussion whether such segregation also violates the Due Process Clause of the Fourteenth Amendment.

---

* The decision in *Brown* v. *Board of Education* was justified in part on psychological and sociological grounds. This line of argument helped Chief Justice Warren obtain a unanimous decision, but it did not provide the strongest legal foundation for attacking desegregation.

Because these are class actions, because of the wide applicability of this decision, and because of the great variety of local conditions, the formulation of decrees in these cases presents problems of considerable complexity. On reargument, the consideration of appropriate relief was necessarily subordinated to the primary question—the constitutionality of segregation in public education. We have now announced that such segregation is a denial of the equal protection of the laws. In order that we may have the full assistance of the parties in formulating decrees, the cases will be restored to the docket, and the parties are requested to present further argument. . . .

1955

Mr. Chief Justice Warren delivered the opinion of the Court.

These cases were decided on May 17, 1954. The opinions of that date, declaring the fundamental principle that racial discrimination in public education is unconstitutional, are incorporated herein by reference. All provisions of federal, state, or local law requiring or permitting such discrimination must yield to this principle. There remains for consideration the manner in which relief is to be accorded.

Because these cases arose under different local conditions and their disposition will involve a variety of local problems, we requested further argument on the question of relief. In view of the nationwide importance of the decision, we invited the Attorney General of the United States and the Attorneys General of all states requiring or permitting racial discrimination in public education to present their views on that question. The parties, the United States, and the States of Florida, North Carolina, Arkansas, Oklahoma, Maryland, and Texas filed briefs and participated in the oral argument.

These presentations were informative and helpful to the Court in its consideration of the complexities arising from the transition to a system of public education freed of racial discrimination. The presentations also demonstrated that substantial steps to eliminate racial discrimination in public schools have already been taken, not only in some of the communities in which these cases arose but in some of the states appearing as *amici curiae*, and in other states as well. Substantial progress has been made in the District of Columbia and in the communities in Kansas and Delaware involved in this litigation. The defendants in the cases coming to us from South Carolina and Virginia are awaiting the decision of this Court concerning relief.

Full implementation of these constitutional principles may require solution of varied local school problems. School authorities have the primary responsibility for elucidating, assessing, and solving these problems; courts will have to consider whether the action of school authorities constitutes good faith implementation of the governing constitutional principles. Because of their proximity to local conditions and the possible need for further hearings, the courts which originally heard these cases can best perform this judicial appraisal.* Accordingly, we believe it appropriate to remand the cases to those courts.

In fashioning and effectuating the decrees, the courts will be guided by equitable principles. Traditionally, equity has been characterized by a practical flexibility in shaping its remedies and by a facility for adjusting and reconciling public and private needs. These cases call for the exercise of these traditional attributes of equity power. At stake is the personal interest of the plaintiffs in admission to public schools as soon as practicable on a non-discriminatory basis. To effectuate this interest may call for elimination of a variety of obstacles in making the transition to school systems operated in accordance with the constitutional principles set forth in our May 17, 1954, decision. Courts of equity may properly take into account the public interest in the elimination of such obstacles in a systematic and effective manner. But it should go without saying that the vitality of these constitutional principles cannot be allowed to yield simply because of disagreement with them.

While giving weight to these public and private considerations, the courts will require that the defendants make a prompt and reasonable start toward full compliance with our May 17, 1954, ruling. Once such a start has been made, the courts may find that additional time is necessary to carry out the ruling in an effective manner. The burden rests upon the defendants to establish that such time is necessary in the public interest and is consistent with good faith compliance at the earliest practicable date. To that end, the courts may consider problems related to administration, arising from the physical condition of the school plant, the school transportation system, personnel, revision of school districts and attendance areas into compact units to achieve a system of determining admission to the public schools on a nonracial basis, and revision of local laws and regulations which may be necessary in solving the foregoing problems. They will also consider the adequacy of any plans the defendants may propose to meet these problems and to effectuate a transition to a racially nondiscriminatory school system. During this period of transition, the courts will retain jurisdiction of these cases.

The judgments below, except that in the Delaware case, are accordingly reversed and the cases are remanded to the District Courts to take such proceedings and enter such orders and decrees consistent with this opinion as are necessary and proper to admit to public schools on a racially nondiscriminatory basis with all deliberate speed the parties to these cases. The judgment in the Delaware case—ordering the immediate admission of the plaintiffs to schools previously attended only by white children—is affirmed on the basis of the principles stated in our May 17, 1954, opinion, but the case is remanded to the Supreme Court of Delaware for such further proceedings as that Court may deem necessary in light of this opinion.

---

* The emphasis on local interpretation of the Court's decision makes sense, but it allowed for great variation in implementation well into the 1970s.

Summary Questions

1. What is wrong with the idea of "separate but equal" facilities? Could this notion ever have some merit?
2. Could the Court have speeded the process of desegregation by handing down a more detailed ruling on how the *Brown* decision was to be implemented? What kinds of problems would such a ruling have faced?
3. *Brown v. Board of Education* concerned legal (de jure) desegregation. Have the courts been as capable of dealing with de facto segregation, such as that produced by housing patterns? Why or why not?

 Debate on Affirmative Action

 3.6

Race, Affirmative Action and the Constitution

Herbert Hill

Other than abortion, it is unlikely that any contemporary civil rights/liberties dispute has engendered as much anger and indignation as that over affirmative action. The very idea of seeking to assist entire categories of the historically disadvantaged seems to work against the American ideal of equal treatment for all. At the same time, no one can seriously contend that generations of American minorities—and especially African-Americans—have been subject to broad discrimination. How, then, are we to reconcile our ideal of a "color-blind" society with the harsh realities of slavery, segregation, and discrimination?

For Herbert Hill the answer is straightforward: We should adopt strong affirmative action policies that mandate quotas and/or timetables. "There must be," he writes, "some benchmark, some tangible measure of change." Not only does this position far exceed what Republican presidents Reagan and Bush have seen as an acceptable notion of affirmative action; it surpasses the standards of many liberal Democrats within the Congress, which in 1991 passed a bill that would formally outlaw quotas.

Herbert Hill is a professor of Afro-American studies and industrial relations at the University of Wisconsin–Madison.

U nder the original Constitution, a system of slavery based on race
◆ ◆ ◆   existed for many generations, a system that legally defined black
            people as property and declared them to be less than human.
Under its authority an extensive web of racist statutes and judicial decisions
emerged over a long period. The Naturalization Law of 1790 explicitly limited
citizenship to "white persons," the Fugitive Slave Acts of 1793 and 1850 made
a travesty of law and dehumanized the nation, and the Dred Scott Decision
of 1857, where Chief Justice Taney declared that blacks were not people but
"articles of merchandise," are but a few of the legal monuments grounded on the
assumption that this was meant to be a white man's country and that all others
had no rights in the law.

With the ratification of the 13th, 14th, and 15th Amendments in 1865, 1868
and 1870 respectively and the adoption of the Civil Rights Acts of 1866, 1870
and 1875, a profoundly different set of values was asserted. This new body of law
affirmed that justice and equal treatment were not for white persons exclusively,
and that black people, now citizens of the nation, also were entitled to "the equal
protection of the laws."

The Civil Rights Amendments and the three related Acts proclaim a very
different concept of the social order than that implicit in the "three-fifths"
clause contained in Section 2 of Article 1 of the Constitution. A concept that
required the reconstruction of American society so that it could be free of slavery,
free of a racism that was to have such terrible long-term consequences for the
entire society.

The struggle to realize the great potential of the Reconstruction amendments
to the Constitution, the struggle to create a just, decent and compassionate
society free of racist oppression, is a continuing struggle that has taken many
different forms in each era since the Reconstruction Period and one that continues today. In our own time the old conflict between those interests intent on
perpetuating racist patterns rooted in the past and the forces that struggle for a
society free of racism and its legacy continues in the raging battle for and against
affirmative action.

During the late 1950's and early 1960's, as a result of direct confrontation with
the system of state imposed segregation, together with the emergence of a new
body of constitutional law on race, a hope was born that the legacy of centuries
of slavery and racism would finally come to an end. But that hope was not yet to
be realized. The high moral indignation of the 1960's was evidently but a passing
spasm which was quickly forgotten.

A major manifestation of the sharp turning away from the goals of justice and
equality is to be found in the shrill and paranoid attacks against affirmative
action. The effort to eliminate the present effects of past discrimination, to
correct the wrongs of many generations was barely underway when it came under
powerful attack. And now, even the very modest gains made by racial minorities
through affirmative action are being erased, as powerful institutions try to turn

the clock of history back to the dark and dismal days of a separate and unequal status for black Americans.

Judging by the vast outcry, it might be assumed that the remedy of affirmative action to eliminate racist and sexist patterns has become as widespread and destructive as discrimination itself. And once again, the defenders of the racial *status quo* have succeeded in confusing the remedy with the original evil. The term "reverse discrimination," for example, has become another code word for resisting the elimination of prevailing patterns of discrimination.

The historic dissent of Justice John Marshall Harlan in the 1883 decision of the Supreme Court in the Civil Rights Cases defines the constitutional principle requiring the obligation of the government to remove all the "badges and incidents" of slavery. Although initially rejected, the rationale of Harlan's position was of course vindicated in later Supreme Court decisions, as in *Brown* v. *Board of Education* in 1954 and *Jones* v. *Mayer* in 1968, among others.

The adoption by Congress of the Civil Rights Act of 1964 further confirmed this constitutional perception of the equal protection clause of the 14th Amendment and reinforced the legal principle that for every right there is a remedy. I believe that what Justice Harlan called the "badges and incidents" of slavery include every manifestation of racial discrimination, not against black people alone, but also against other people of color who were engulfed by the heritage of racism that developed out of slavery.

In this respect, I believe that an interpretation of the law consistent with the meaning of the 13th and 14th Amendments to the Constitution holds that affirmative action programs carry forth the contemporary legal obligation to eradicate the consequences of slavery and racism. In order to do that, it is necessary to confront the present effects of past discrimination and the most effective remedy to achieve that goal is affirmative action. Mr. Justice Blackmun in his opinion in *Bakke** wrote, ". . . in order to get beyond racism, we must first take account of race. There is no other way."

By now it should be very clear, that the opposition to affirmative action is based on narrow group self-interest rather than on abstract philosophical differences about "quotas," "reverse discrimination," "preferential treatment" and the other catch-phrases commonly raised in public debate. After all the pious rhetoric equating affirmative action with "reverse discrimination" is stripped away, it is evident that the opposition to affirmative action is in fact the effort to perpetuate the privileged position of white males in American society.

------

* Allan Bakke was an applicant to the medical school of the University of California–Davis in 1972 and 1973. Although well qualified, he was denied admission on the basis of a quota system that reserved 16 of 100 places in each class for disadvantaged applicants. He sued the university for admission, and the case eventually went to the Supreme Court. In a 5–4 ruling, the Court upheld Bakke's position. At the same time, the Court noted that the admissions process could take race into account, but not with strict quotas. Bakke graduated from the Davis medical school in 1982.

In his dissent in *Bakke*, Justice Thurgood Marshall wrote, "The experience of Negroes in America has been different in kind, not just in degree, from that of other ethnic groups. It is not merely the history of slavery alone but also that a whole people were marked as inferior by the law. And that mark has endured. The dream of America as the great melting pot has not been realized for the Negro; because of his skin color he never even made it into the pot."

I propose to examine some important aspects of the historical process so aptly described by Mr. Justice Marshall. A major recomposition of the labor force occurred in the decades after the Civil War. By the end of the 19th century the American working class was an immigrant working class and European immigrants held power and exercised great influence within organized labor. For example, in 1900, Irish immigrants or their descendants held the presidencies of over fifty of the 110 national unions in the American Federation of Labor. Many of the other unions were also led by immigrants or their sons, with Germans following the Irish in number and prominence, while the president of the AFL was a Jewish immigrant. Records of labor organizations confirm the dominant role of immigrants and their descendants in many individual unions and city and state labor bodies throughout the country at the turn of the century and for decades later.

For the immigrant worker loyalty was to the ethnic collective, and it was understood that advancement of the individual was dependent upon communal advancement. Participation in organized labor was a significant part of that process, and many of the dramatic labor conflicts of the 19th and 20th centuries were in fact ethnic group struggles. For blacks, both before and after emancipation, the historical experience was completely different. For them, systematic racial oppression was the basic and inescapable characteristic of the society, north and south, and it was the decisive fact of their lives. The problems of the white immigrant did not compare with the oppression of racism, an oppression that was of a different magnitude, of a different order.

Initially isolated from the social and economic mainstream, white immigrants rapidly came to understand that race and ethnic identity was decisive in providing access to employment and in the eventual establishment of stable communities. For white immigrant workers assimilation was achieved through group mobility and collective ethnic advancement that was directly linked to the work place. The occupational frame of reference was decisive.

Wages, and the status derived from steady work, could only be obtained by entering the permanent labor force, and labor unions were most important in providing access to the job market for many groups of immigrant workers. In contrast to the white ethnics, generations of black workers were systematically barred from employment in the primary sectors of the labor market, thereby denied the economic base that made possible the celebrated achievements and social mobility of white immigrant communities.

An examination of briefs *amicus curiae* filed in the Supreme Court cases involving affirmative action reveals the active role these two historically interrelated groups, white ethnics and labor unions, have played in the repeated attacks against affirmative action. With some few exceptions, this has been the pattern from *De Funis* in 1974 and *Bakke* in 1978 to the most recent cases. Given the context in which this issue evolved, the historical sources of the opposition to affirmative action are not surprising.

The nineteenth-century European migrations to the United States took place during the long age of blatant white supremacy, legal and extralegal, formal and informal, and as the patterns of segregation and discrimination emerged north and south, the doors of opportunity were opened to white immigrants but closed to blacks and other non-whites. European immigrants and their descendants explain their success as the result of their devotion to the work ethic, and ignore a variety of other factors such as the systematic exclusion of non-Caucasians from competition for employment. As white immigrants moved up in the social order, black workers and those of other non-white races could fill only the least desirable places in a marginal secondary labor market, the only places open to them.

The elimination of traditional patterns of discrimination required by the Civil Rights Act of 1964 adversely affected the expectations of whites, since it compelled competition with black workers and other minority group members where none previously existed. White worker expectations had become the norm and any alteration of the norm was considered "reverse discrimination." When racial practices that have historically placed blacks at a disadvantage are removed to eliminate the present effects of past discrimination, whites believe that preferential treatment is given to blacks. But it is *the removal of the preferential treatment traditionally enjoyed by white workers at the expense of blacks as a class* that is at issue in the affirmative action controversy.

In many different occupations, including a variety of jobs in the public sector such as in police and fire departments, white workers were able to begin their climb on the seniority ladder precisely because non-whites were systematically excluded from the competition for jobs. Various union seniority systems were established at a time when racial minorities were banned from employment and union membership. Obviously blacks as a group, not just as individuals, constituted a class of victims who could not develop seniority status. A seniority system launched under these conditions inevitably becomes the institutionalized mechanism whereby whites as a group are granted racial privileges.

After long delay and much conflict, a new comprehensive body of law is emerging that has a significant potential and gives hope to women and racial minorities in the labor force.

♦ On March 25, 1987, in *Johnson* v. *Transportation Agency*, the Supreme Court issued its fifth affirmative action ruling within an eleven month period. In *Johnson*, the Court upheld a voluntary affirmative action plan for hiring and promoting women and minorities adopted by the Transportation Agency of Santa Clara County, California. *Johnson* firmly supports the conclusion that affirmative action is a valid remedy to eliminate discrimination in public sector employment.

♦ In *United States* v. *Paradise*, the Court upheld a lower court's decision requiring the Alabama Department of Public Safety to promote one black state trooper for each white promoted until either 25 percent of the job category was black or until an acceptable alternative promotion plan was put into place.

♦ *Wygant* v. *Jackson Board of Education*, in which the Court struck down a provision in a collective bargaining agreement which provided that, in the event of teacher layoffs, the percentage of minority personnel laid off would be no greater than the percentage of minority personnel employed by the Jackson, Michigan, school system at the time of the layoffs. However, a majority of the Court agreed that voluntary affirmative action plans by public employers are constitutional in some instances.

♦ *Local 28 of the Sheet Metal Workers International Association* v. *EEOC*, in which the Court upheld a lower court's order requiring a New York construction union to adopt an affirmative action plan, including a special fund to recruit and train minority workers and a 29 percent minority membership goal. This decision was the culmination of almost forty years of struggle in state and federal courts to end the racist practices of this AFL-CIO affiliate. Other cases involving unions in the building trades have a similar history and after years of litigation are still pending in Federal courts. (See for example, *Commonwealth of Pennsylvania and Williams* v. *Operating Engineers, Local 542*, 347 F. Supp. 268, E. D. PA. 1979.)

♦ *Local No. 93, International Association of Firefighters* v. *City of Cleveland*, in which the Court upheld a consent decree which contained promotion goals for minorities and other affirmative action provisions in settlement of a job discrimination suit by minority firefighters.

The adverse decision in *Wygant* notwithstanding, these decisions of the Supreme Court in conjunction with the Court's 1979 decision in *Steelworkers* v. *Weber* make it very clear that the principle of affirmative action applied in several different contexts is well established in the law and recognized as an effective and valid remedy to eliminate traditional discriminatory employment practices. But the opponents of affirmative action continue their attacks. Powerful forces, through a well-orchestrated propaganda campaign, based upon misrepresentation and the manipulation of racial fears among whites continue their efforts to perpetuate discriminatory practices. In this, they have been aided and abetted again and again by the Reagan Administration, the most reactionary administration on civil rights in the 20th century.

In reviewing the attacks upon affirmative action, it is necessary to note the disingenuous argument of those who state that they are not against affirmative action, but only against "quotas." Affirmative action without numbers, whether in the form of quotas, goals, or timetables, is meaningless; there must be some benchmark, some tangible measure of change. Statistical evidence to measure performance is essential. Not to use numbers is to revert to the era of symbolic gesture or, at best, "tokenism."

White ethnic groups and many labor unions frequently argue that affirmative action programs will penalize innocent whites who are not responsible for past discriminatory practices. This argument turns on the notion of individual rights and sounds very moral and highminded. But it ignores social reality. It ignores the fact that white workers benefited from the systematic exclusion of blacks in many trades and industries. As has been repeatedly demonstrated in lawsuits, non-whites and women have been denied jobs, training and advancement not as individuals but as a class, no matter what their personal merit and qualification. Wherever discriminatory employment patterns exist, hiring and promotion without affirmative action perpetuate the old injustice.

Before the emergence of affirmative action remedies, the legal prohibitions against job discrimination were for the most part declarations of abstract morality that rarely resulted in any change. Pronouncements of public policy such as state and municipal fair employment practice laws were mainly symbolic, and the patterns of job discrimination remained intact. Because affirmative action programs go beyond individual relief to attack long-established patterns of discrimination and, if vigorously enforced by government agencies over a sustained period can become a major instrument for social change, they have come under powerful and repeated attack.

As long as Title VII litigation was concerned largely with procedural and conceptual issues, only limited attention was given to the consequences of remedies. However, once affirmative action was widely applied and the focus of litigation shifted to the adoption of affirmative action plans, entrenched interests were threatened. And as the gains of the 1960's are eroded, the nation becomes even more mean-spirited and self-deceiving.

Racism in the history of the United States has not been an aberration. It has been systematized and structured into the functioning of the society's most important institutions. In the present as in the past, it is widely accepted as a basis for promoting the interests of whites. For many generations the assumptions of white supremacy were codified in the law, imposed by custom and often enforced by violence. While the forms have changed, the legacy of white supremacy is expressed in the continuing patterns of racial discrimination, and for the vast majority of black and other non-white people, race and racism remain the decisive factors in their lives.

The current conflict over affirmative action is not simply an argument about abstract rights or ethnic bigotry. In the final analysis it is an argument between those who insist upon the substance of a long-postponed break with the traditions of American racism, and those groups that insist upon maintaining the valuable privileges and benefits they now enjoy as a consequence of that dismal history.

Summary Questions

1. How does Hill's argument on affirmative action relate to Levy's contentions (see Chapter 13) that it is impossible and inadvisable to seek out the framers' "original intent"?
2. In seeking jobs after college, should minority graduates be given preference over nonminorities, even those who have never practiced discrimination? How does Hill justify granting such a preference?

 3.7

Affirmative Action: The Price of Preference

Shelby Steele

Affirmative action policies may well place nonminorities at a disadvantage, but many analysts believe these rules hurt the very individuals they are intended to help. In obtaining a job or admission to a prestigious university, a minority individual may never know whether skin color (or sex or ethnic origin) or merit was the key factor in the employment or admission decision. Thus, such minority achievements are tainted with the implication that standards were lowered to achieve racial (or gender or ethnic) parity. Although many black conservatives voiced such sentiments during the 1980s, this perspective received the most attention with George Bush's appointment of Clarence Thomas to the Supreme Court in 1991.

Shelby Steele, an English professor at San Jose State University, has become a prominent spokesperson for a critical approach to affirmative action. Steele acknowledges past and even present discriminatory practices in American society, but he sees the solution offered by affirmative action as worse than the problem it seeks to address. The difficulty lies in the "implied inferiority" embedded in the preferences granted by affirmative action. Even if blacks believe this implication of inferiority is unjustified, they understand that many whites will

Shelby Steele is an English professor at San Jose State University in California. This excerpt is adapted from *The Content of Our Character: A New Vision of Race in America* (St. Martin's Press, 1990).

interpret affirmative action similarly. Steele offers no easy answers here. He argues for better education, more job training, safer neighborhoods, and increased financial assistance for college for the disadvantaged, but does not explain how this will occur—to say nothing of how it will ultimately achieve the goals pursued by affirmative action. Steele's analysis differs sharply from that of Herbert Hill. Is there any meaningful middle ground in this controversy?

In a few short years, when my two children will be applying to college, the affirmative-action policies by which most universities offer black students some form of preferential treatment will present me with a dilemma. I am a middle-class black, a college professor, far from wealthy, but also well removed from the kind of deprivation that would qualify my children for the label "disadvantaged." Both of them have endured racial insensitivity from whites. They have been called names, have suffered slights and have experienced first hand the peculiar malevolence that racism brings out of people. Yet they have never experienced racial discrimination, have never been stopped by their race on any path they have chosen to follow. Still, their society now tells them that if they will only designate themselves as black on their college applications, they will probably do better in the college lottery than if they conceal this fact. I think there is something of a Faustian bargain in this.

Of course many blacks and a considerable number of whites would say that I was sanctimoniously making affirmative action into a test of character. They would say that this small preference is the meagerest recompense for centuries of unrelieved oppression. And to these arguments other very obvious facts must be added. In America, many marginally competent or flatly incompetent whites are hired every day—some because their white skin suits the conscious or unconscious racial preference of their employers. The white children of alumni are often grandfathered into elite universities in what can only be seen as a residual benefit of historic white privilege. Worse, white incompetence is always an individual matter, but for blacks it is often confirmation of ugly stereotypes. Given that unfairness cuts both ways, doesn't it only balance the scales of history, doesn't this repay, in a small way, the systematic denial under which my children's grandfather lived out his days?

In theory, affirmative action certainly has all the moral symmetry that fairness requires. It is reformist and corrective, even repentant and redemptive. And I would never sneer at these good intentions. Born in the late 1940's in Chicago, I started my education (a charitable term, in this case) in a segregated school, and suffered all the indignities that come to blacks in a segregated society. My father, born in the South, made it only to the third grade before the white man's fields took permanent priority over his formal education. And though he educated himself into an advanced reader with an almost professorial authority, he could only drive a truck for a living, and never earned more than $90 a week in his entire life. So yes, it is crucial to my sense of citizenship, to my ability to identify with the spirit and the interests of America, to know that this country, however imperfectly, recognizes its past sins and wishes to correct them.

Yet good intentions can blind us to the effects they generate when implemented. In our society affirmative action is, among other things, a testament to white good will and to black power, and in the midst of these heavy investments its effects can be hard to see. But after 20 years of implementation I think that affirmative action has shown itself to be more bad than good and that blacks—whom I will focus on in this essay—now stand to lose more from it than they gain.

In talking with affirmative-action administrators and with blacks and whites in general, I found that supporters of affirmative action focus on its good intentions and detractors emphasize its negative effects. It was virtually impossible to find people outside either camp. The closest I came was a white male manager at a large computer company who said, "I think it amounts to reverse discrimination, but I'll put up with a little of that for a little more diversity." But this only makes him a half-hearted supporter of affirmative action. I think many people who don't really like affirmative action support it to one degree or another anyway.

I believe they do this because of what happened to white and black Americans in the crucible of the 1960's, when whites were confronted with their racial guilt and blacks tasted their first real power. In that stormy time white absolution and black power coalesced into virtual mandates for society. Affirmative action became a meeting ground for those mandates in the law. At first, this meant insuring equal opportunity. The 1964 civil-rights bill was passed on the understanding that equal opportunity would not mean racial preference. But in the late 60's and early 70's, affirmative action underwent a remarkable escalation of its mission from simple anti-discrimination enforcement to social engineering by means of quotas, goals, timetables, set-asides and other forms of preferential treatment.

Legally, this was achieved through a series of executive orders and Equal Employment Opportunity Commission guidelines that allowed racial imbalances in the workplace to stand as proof of racial discrimination. Once it could be assumed that discrimination explained racial imbalances, it became easy to justify group remedies to presumed discrimination rather than the normal case-by-case redress.

Even though blacks had made great advances during the 60's without quotas, the white mandate to achieve a new racial innocence and the black mandate to gain power, which came to a head in the very late 60's, could no longer be satisfied by anything less than racial preferences. I don't think these mandates, in themselves, were wrong, because whites clearly needed to do better by blacks and blacks needed more real power in society. But as they came together in affirmative action, their effect was to distort our understanding of racial discrimination. By making black the color of preference, these mandates have reburdened society with the very marriage of color and preference (in reverse) that we set out to eradicate.

When affirmative action grew into social engineering, diversity became a golden word. Diversity is a term that applies democratic principles to races and cultures rather than to citizens, despite the fact that there is nothing to indicate that real diversity is the same thing as proportionate representation. Too often the result of this, on campuses for example, has been a democracy of colors rather than of people, an artificial diversity that gives the appearance of an educational parity between black and white students that has not yet been achieved in reality. Here again, racial preferences allow society to leapfrog over the difficult problem of developing blacks to parity with whites and into a cosmetic diversity that covers the blemish of disparity—a full six years after admission, only 26 to 28 percent of blacks graduate from college.

Racial representation is not the same thing as racial development. Representation can be manufactured; development is always hard earned. But it is the music of innocence and power than we hear in affirmative action that causes us to cling to it and to its distracting emphasis on representation. The fact is that after 20 years of racial preferences the gap between median incomes of black and white families is greater than it was in the 1970's. None of this is to say that blacks don't need policies that insure our right to equal opportunity, but what we need more of is the development that will let us take advantage of society's efforts to include us.

I think one of the most troubling effects of racial preferences for blacks is a kind of demoralization. Under affirmative action, the quality that earns us preferential treatment is an implied inferiority. However this inferiority is explained—and it is easily enough explained by the myriad deprivations that grew out of our oppression—it is still inferiority. There are explanations and then there is the fact. And the fact must be borne by the individual as a condition apart from the explanation, apart even from the fact that others like himself also bear this condition. In integrated situations in which blacks must compete with whites who may be better prepared, these explanations may quickly wear thin and expose the individual to racial as well as personal self-doubt. (Of course whites also feel doubt, but only personally, not racially.)

What this means in practical terms is that when blacks deliver themselves into integrated situations they encounter a nasty little reflex in whites, a mindless, atavistic reflex that responds to the color black with negative stereotypes, such as intellectual ineptness. I think this reflex embarrasses most whites today and thus it is usually quickly repressed. On an equally atavistic level, the black will be aware of the reflex his color triggers and will feel a stab of horror at seeing himself reflected in this way. He, too, will do a quick repression, but a lifetime of such stabbings is what constitutes his inner realm of racial doubt. Even when the black sees no implication of inferiority in racial preferences, he knows that whites do, so that—consciously or unconsciously—the result is virtually the same. The effect of preferential treatment—the lowering of normal standards to increase black representation—puts blacks at war with an expanded realm of debilitating doubt, so that the doubt itself becomes an unrecognized preoccupation that undermines their ability to perform, especially in integrated situations.

I believe another liability of affirmative action comes from the fact that it indirectly encourages blacks to exploit their own past victimization. Like implied inferiority, victimization is what justifies preference, so that to receive the benefits of preferential treatment one must, to some extent, become invested in the view of one's self as a victim. In this way, affirmative action nurtures a victim-focused identity in blacks and sends us the message that there is more power in our past suffering than in our present achievements.

When power itself grows out of suffering, blacks are encouraged to expand the boundaries of what qualifies as racial oppression, a situation that can lead us to paint our victimization in vivid colors even as we receive the benefits of prefer-ence. The same corporations and institutions that give us preference are also seen as our oppressors. At Stanford University, minority-group students—who receive at least the same financial aid as whites with the same need—recently took over the president's office demanding, among other things, more financial aid.

But I think one of the worst prices that blacks pay for preference has to do with an illusion. I saw this illusion at work recently in the mother of a middle-class black student who was going off to his first semester of college: "They owe us this, so don't think for a minute that you don't belong there." This is the logic by which many blacks, and some whites, justify affirmative action—it is something "owed," a form of reparation. But this logic overlooks a much harder and less digestible reality, that it is impossible to repay blacks living today for the historic suffering of the race. If all blacks were given a million dollars tomorrow it would not amount to a dime on the dollar for three centuries of oppression, nor would it dissolve the residues of that oppression that we still carry today. The concept of historic reparation grows out of man's need to impose on the world a degree of justice that simply does not exist. Suffering can be endured and overcome, it cannot be repaid. To think otherwise is to prolong the suffering.

Several blacks I spoke with said they were still in favor of affirmative action because of the "subtle" discrimination blacks were subject to once they were on the job. One photojournalist said, "They have ways of ignoring you." A black female television producer said: "You can't file a lawsuit when your boss doesn't invite you to the insider meetings without ruining your career. So we still need affirmative action." Others mentioned the infamous "glass ceiling" through which blacks can see the top positions of authority but never reach them. But I don't think racial preferences are a protection against this subtle discrimination; I think they contribute to it.

In any workplace, racial preferences will always create two-tiered populations composed of [the] preferred and unpreferred. In the case of blacks and whites, for instance, racial preferences imply that whites are superior just as they imply that blacks are inferior. They not only reinforce America's oldest racial myth but, for blacks, they have the effect of stigmatizing the already stigmatized.

I think that much of the "subtle" discrimination that blacks talk about is often (not always) discrimination against the stigma of questionable competence that affirmative action marks blacks with. In this sense, preferences make scapegoats of the very people they seek to help. And it may be that at a certain level employers impose a glass ceiling, but this may not be against the race so much as against the race's reputation for having advanced by color as much as by competence. This ceiling is the point at which corporations shift the emphasis from color to competency and stop playing the affirmative-action game. Here preference backfires for blacks and becomes a taint that holds them back. Of course one could argue that this taint, which is after all in the minds of whites, becomes nothing more than an excuse to discriminate against blacks. And certainly the result is the same in either case—blacks don't get past the glass ceiling. But this argument does not get around the fact that racial preferences now taint this color with a new theme of suspicion that makes blacks even more vulnerable to discrimination. In this crucial yet gray area of perceived competence, preferences make whites look better than they are and blacks worse, while doing nothing whatever to stop the very real discrimination that blacks may encounter. I don't wish to justify the glass ceiling here, but only suggest the very subtle ways that affirmative action revives rather than extinguishes the old rationalizations for racial discrimination.

I believe affirmative action is problematic in our society because we have demanded that it create parity between the races rather than insure equal opportunity. Preferential treatment does not teach skills, or educate, or instill motivation. It only passes out entitlement by color, a situation that in my profession has created an unrealistically high demand for black professors. The social engineer's assumption is that this high demand will inspire more blacks to earn Ph.D's and join the profession. In fact, the number of blacks earning Ph.D's has declined in recent years. Ph.D's must be developed from preschool on. They require family and community support. They must acquire an entire system of values that enables them to work hard while delaying gratification.

It now seems clear that the Supreme Court, in a series of recent decisions, is moving away from racial preferences. It has disallowed preferences except in instances of "identified discrimination," eroded the precedent that statistical racial imbalances are prima facie evidence of discrimination, and, in effect, granted white males the right to challenge consent degrees that use preference to achieve racial balances in the workplace. Referring to this and other Supreme Court decisions, one civil-rights leader said, "Night has fallen . . . as far as civil rights are concerned." But I am not so sure. The effect of these decisions is to protect the constitutional rights of everyone, rather than to take rights away from blacks. Night has fallen on racial preferences, not on the fundamental rights of black Americans. The reason for this shift, I believe, is that the white mandate for absolution from past racial sins has weakened considerably in the 1980's. Whites are now less willing to endure unfairness to themselves in order to grant special entitlements to blacks, even when those entitlements are justified in the name of past suffering. Yet the black mandate for more power in society has remained unchanged. And I think part of the anxiety many blacks feel over these decisions has to do with the loss of black power that they may signal.

But the power we've lost by these decisions is really only the power that grows out of our victimization. This is not a very substantial or reliable power, and it is important that we know this so we can focus more exclusively on the kind of development that will bring enduring power. There is talk now that Congress may pass new legislation to compensate for these new limits on affirmative action. If this happens, I hope the focus will be on development and anti-discrimination, rather than entitlement, on achieving racial parity rather than jerry-building racial diversity.

But if not preferences, what? The impulse to discriminate is subtle and cannot be ferreted out unless its many guises are made clear to people. I think we need social policies that are committed to two goals: the educational and economic development of disadvantaged people regardless of race and the eradication from our society—through close monitoring and severe sanctions—of racial, ethnic or gender discrimination. Preferences will not get us to either of these goals, because they tend to benefit those who are not disadvantaged—middle-class white women and middle-class blacks—and attack one form of discrimination with another. Preferences are inexpensive and carry the glamour of good intentions—change the numbers and the good deed is done. To be against them is to be unkind. But I think the unkindest cut is to bestow on children like my own an undeserved advantage while neglecting the development of those disadvantaged children in the poorer sections of my city who will most likely never be in a position to benefit from a preference. Give my children fairness; give disadvantaged children a better shot at development—better elementary and secondary schools, job training, safer neighborhoods, better financial assistance for college and so on. A smaller percentage of black high school graduates go to college today than 15 years ago; more black males are in prison, jail or in some other way under the control of the criminal-justice system than in college. This, despite racial preferences.

The mandates of black power and white absolution out of which preferences emerged were not wrong in themselves. What was wrong was that both races focused more on the goals of those mandates than on the means to the goals. Blacks can have no real power without taking responsibility for their own educational and economic development. Whites can have no racial innocence without earning it by eradicating discrimination and helping the disadvantaged to develop. Because we ignored the means, the goals have not been reached and the real work remains to be done.

Summary Questions

1. Can past discrimination against minorities be addressed by present policies that give preferences to these groups? Should such policies be adopted?
2. How do affirmative action policies affect the ways minorities view themselves? Do these alleged psychological injuries justify abandoning the entire notion of affirmative action?

 Part II

PEOPLE AND POLITICS

 Chapter 4

PUBLIC OPINION

At base, politics is the relationship between those who govern and those who are governed. Public opinion plays a crucial role in this relationship. Governments—even totalitarian states—must take into account the attitudes and perspectives of the public, because without the people's support no government can endure.

In modern democracies, the idea that governments should consider the wishes of the governed can be traced to the late seventeenth and eighteenth centuries, particularly to the egalitarian and majoritarian ideas of John Locke and Thomas Jefferson. Governing authority had previously been based on an aristocratic ideology that defended social and legal inequality as a proper and permanent fact of life. The various classes had fixed places in society, and the ruling class devised elaborate justifications for the exclusion of others from politics. But the dissemination of radically different social ideas, plus changes in economic circumstances, broadened the base of political participation. What the growing middle class thought became important, and in the early 1800s the term *public opinion* became commonplace.

In countries that boast democratic forms of government, like the United States, it appears virtually mandatory that the "will of the people" prevail. The difficulty is in determining what the will of the people is—or indeed, whether it exists. "To speak with precision of public opinion," wrote political scientist V. O. Key, "is a task not unlike coming to grips with the Holy Ghost," partly because the distinction between "public" and "private" opinion is not easy to make and is constantly changing. For example, thirty years ago cigarette smoking was a private matter, unregulated by government and absent from the agenda of political debate. By the 1970s, however, when smoking had been identified as a major public health hazard, advertising by tobacco companies was severely curtailed and movements to ban smoking in all public places were afoot. Today smoking is a public matter, and interest groups on both sides of the issue are involved in legislative deliberations. Questions about smoking now are a routine component of national public opinion polls.

The meaning of *opinion* is similarly vague. Opinions, beliefs, and attitudes are often treated as if they were the same, but scholars increasingly make distinctions among these terms. One social scientist, Bernard Hennessy, defines opinions as "immediate orientations toward contemporary controversial political objects," whereas attitudes are "more diffused and enduring orientations toward political objects not necessarily controversial at the moment."

For most purposes, however, it is preferable to think of public opinion in the broadest sense—in Key's definition, as "those opinions held by private persons which governments find it prudent to heed." Public opinion may be expressed in a letter (or many letters) to an elected official or to the editor of a newspaper, turnout at a protest march, the statements of a special interest group, the results of an election, or the findings of survey research. Often public opinion is gathered by impressions—legislators' sense of their districts, what their political intimates tell them, or the number of interest group representatives they see or hear. More and more often, however, public opinion is being derived scientifically from efforts to poll citizens.

Survey research is now a major element of political life, and citizens are constantly bombarded with poll results. Besides independent polling concerns such as the Gallup Organization, which periodically release information concerning public attitudes, the three major television networks have joined with major newspapers to create polling groups. Other efforts abound, and it seems fair to say that polling has become a major way of interpreting public opinion at the state and local as well as national level. Virtually all issues on the public agenda have generated public opinion data.

As opinion-gathering devices, polls are powerful vehicles for those who believe in majoritarian democracy. Unlike other methods of discovering public opinion, polls can represent the entire public, not just those elements with political resources or well-organized interest groups. Polls can be superior even to elections, because they report what everyone thinks rather than only what those who bother to vote think. Since poll results can make politicians aware of citizens' wishes, polls have the capacity to make government more responsible.

But not everyone believes poll-measured public opinion serves democratic ideals well. Often polls solicit opinions (and get them) on subjects on which little or no real opinion exists, such as on foreign policy. Not all polls are accurate, but their scientific aura lends them some credibility. Because all opinions count equally, polls tend to underrepresent intense opinion and give extra influence to the apathetic. Critics tend to believe that polls actually inhibit responsible government by forcing politicians to respond to public wishes that may be ill informed. Political leaders, in their quest for office, may follow poll results even when the long-term interests of the public are not well served.

Overall, both defenders and critics of opinion polls can point to convincing evidence for their views. Politicians probably are somewhat constrained by poll data and are restrained from taking action of which the public would disapprove. Programs such as Social Security, for example, are retained in their current form largely because the public strongly supports them. But it is also true that consistent, overwhelming majorities in the polls do not necessarily dictate public policy. This can be seen in the case of gun control; as early as 1938 the national polls showed that over 80 percent of the public favored hand-gun registration, but the organized efforts of the National Rifle Association have thwarted the passage of such a law.

The reading selections in this chapter were chosen to explain public opinion through the instrument of survey research. Charles Kenney's article "They've Got Your Number" presents some of the basics of polling and includes a set of criteria for evaluating poll results. In the second selection, William Mayer surveys trends in public opinion since the 1960s. He suggests that mass public opinion has shifted markedly a number of times during that period, providing both an opportunity and a danger to politicians who attempt to respond to it.

They've Got Your Number

Charles Kenney

Scientific polling to assess public opinion has been a significant force in American society for over half a century. Although roughly 98 percent of all polling is done for nonpolitical purposes, citizens increasingly come into contact with political polls sponsored by candidates for office, the news media, or special interest groups and organizations. But some polls are highly inaccurate. Consequently, it is important to understand how survey research works in order to be able to assess its level of accuracy.

In this selection, Charles Kenney traces the development of polls in American politics and the growth of the polling industry. Because of our society's growing appetite for predictions, pollsters have become important figures in their own right. Kenney goes on to explore some of the criticisms of political polling and concludes with an outline of how polls are conducted and some suggested guidelines for judging their worth.

America's first great polling fiasco came not during the 1948 presidential campaign, when so many pollsters predicted that Thomas E. Dewey would beat Harry S Truman, but during Franklin Delano Roosevelt's 1936 campaign for reelection. In those days, a New York magazine called *Literary Digest* ran the oldest and most highly publicized survey on presidential campaigns. It had picked the winner of presidential races from 1920 through 1932. In 1936, the *Digest* wanted to conduct the broadest possible survey, so its editors, in a rather spectacular blunder, settled upon two lists: a compilation of names from telephone directories and a list of people who had registered automobiles.

Months before the election, the *Digest* mailed out 10 million mock ballots to people whose names appeared on the two lists. By late October the *Digest* received 2,376,523 completed ballots. On the basis of that information, the *Digest* predicted that Alfred M. Landon would defeat Roosevelt in a landslide, that the president would receive a mere 41 percent of the vote.* (Naturally, Democrats

---

Charles Kenney is a staff writer for the *Boston Globe Magazine*.

* "Alf" Landon was the Republican governor of Kansas at the time of the 1936 race. His daughter, Nancy Landon Kassebaum, is currently a U.S. senator from Kansas.

challenged the *Digest's* findings, none more vigorously than a group of Massachusetts Roosevelt supporters who offered to bet the *Digest's* editors $100,000 that FDR would win. The editors declined the wager.)

As it turned out, of course, Roosevelt won in a landslide, taking 63 percent of the popular vote and winning every state except Maine and Vermont. So spectacularly wrong was the *Literary Digest* poll that it brought down upon itself the swift and fierce wrath of polling skeptics (and partisan Democrats). Only days after the election, Sen. Kenneth D. McKellar, a Tennessee Democrat, proposed a congressional investigation into the *Digest* poll and suggested that the federal government strictly regulate all straw polls. Nonbelievers in the infant quasi-science of polling wondered, along with believers: How could the *Digest* poll have been so wrong?

Henry E. Brady, an associate professor of political science at the University of Chicago and an expert on polling, says the *Digest's* flaw was as obvious as it was fatal. "In the midst of the Depression," says Brady, "only the rich had telephones and automobiles." As a result, he says, the *Digest* wound up with a sample in which there were too many wealthy people and Republicans and not enough poor people and Democrats.

Thus did *Literary Digest* commit polling's mortal sin: It did not base its survey on a random sample of the electorate. Random sampling is the *only* way to conduct an accurate poll because only a purely random sample guarantees that every voter in the population has an equal chance of being questioned.

Since the *Digest* catastrophe delighted polling skeptics 51 years ago, the survey-research business has changed radically. What was then a fledgling business has grown into a massive industry. Where once only a few national pollsters struggled to find buyers for their numbers, today hundreds of polling companies provide tens of thousands of surveys to a seemingly insatiable clientele that includes national, regional, and even local newspapers, and radio and television stations as well as politicians running for every imaginable office. For numbers and analyses that are sometimes insightful, sometimes meaningless, the purchasers of polls pay anywhere from $5,000 to more than $50,000. An average telephone survey—a good one—costs about $20,000.

By far, the greatest number of surveys conducted in the United States these days are not political but market research—on every conceivable type of product from liquid laundry detergents to teen-age movie idols. Our focus here, however, is on political-survey research, where, as the business has grown—particularly during the past 10 to 15 years—the quality of polls has improved. Pre-1970s methods could be maddeningly slow, clumsy, and imprecise. Results published weeks or more after a survey was conducted were as stale as last month's news. Today, largely through the use of computers and telephones, polls are strikingly fast and often as fresh as today's bread. And because today's survey methods are more sophisticated, polls are more reliable than ever before.

Polling is not a science, but it is constructed on a foundation of sound, widely accepted scientific principles. Some of the best pollsters, well grounded in mathematics and probability theory, are also artful analyzers of raw data (the worst pollsters are ignorant of methods *and* politics). The work of the best people can be precisely executed methods that lead to brilliantly inspired insight. Other pollsters, entrepreneurs who have gotten in on the boom times to make a buck, produce polls that are quick and dirty, overnight wonders by schlock operators with shaky methodology.

Polls from the fascinating to the ridiculous, the perplexing to the unfathomable, will be on display during the next 14 months, leading up to the 1988 presidential election, a campaign during which Americans will be inundated with polls as never before. But as you face all those numbers, graphs, and charts, there's no need to throw up your hands and give in to the avalanche. Understanding polls is easier when you know where they come from; why they work (or don't work); how they are conducted; who uses them (and for what); who conducts them; and what distinguishes a good poll from a bad one.

And if you think it odd that this relatively young industry has so captured the American imagination, consider that our hunger for information about ourselves—and even more so for glimpses of what lies ahead—is as old as civilization.

"There is a constant need in society for prediction, forecasting; for what academics call the 'reduction of uncertainty.' People want to know what's going to be around the corner in life,' says Gary Orren, an associate professor at Harvard's John F. Kennedy School of Government.

"Almost every society has an important place for oracles, soothsayers, prophets. You'd be hard-pressed to find any group that doesn't have someone who serves that role of prediction and forecasting. Pollsters are the 20th century's version of soothsayers."

Polls and Possums

Early pollsters were a favorite target for tart-tongued commentators who saw the new business as a fraud. In 1939, a Louisiana newspaper called *The American Progress* reported on a trip by some of George Gallup's interviewers to New Orleans: "Three months ago a half-dozen post-graduate 'Social Science Workers' from Princeton University, augmented by seven or eight East Side New Yorkers who had never in their lives seen a possum, tasted a sweet potato, or chewed a plug of tobacco, arrived in New Orleans to conduct a so-called survey of public opinion.

"After taking a few sightseeing trips, getting some fancy grub at the famous restaurants in New Orleans, looking at some swamps, and sending picture postcards back home, they then wrote some mystic figures in their little black books and hurried back to their boss, a low-ceiling guy with bifocal glasses who sits enthroned way up there in Princeton, New Jersey, like the Wizard of Oz and peers owlishly at figures all day long until he looks like a left-handed figure 4.

"And out of this hocus-pocus of numbers and dope sheets and form charts, lo and behold, if up didn't jump The Gallup Poll!"

A popular target for mockery, Dr. George Gallup Sr. was also probably the most important figure in polling history. The University of Chicago's Brady says Gallup did no less than "institutionalize political polling."

Gallup, who grew up in Iowa, began his survey work during the 1920s, while he was teaching journalism at the University of Iowa. For years he experimented with dozens of different methodologies, finally settling upon a random probability method of interviewing voters—an approach that was the subject of his PhD dissertation in 1928. Using his then-revolutionary methods, Gallup received some national exposure in 1934 when he polled, rather accurately, as it turned out, some of that year's congressional races. The following year Gallup founded his company and began by selling the results of his surveys—in the form of a column that he wrote—to 35 newspapers.

Respect for Gallup soon increased, when, as the *Digest* poll was found to be worthless, Gallup and two other fledgling polling companies—Crossley and Roper—all predicted a landslide for Roosevelt. That inspired some confidence in the new business, but it wasn't long before pollsters suffered a hugely discouraging setback. In the 1948 presidential election, the major survey-research organizations—with Gallup very much in the lead—stopped polling several weeks before the election, in the belief that few voters change their minds late in a campaign. Gallup and the others predicted that Dewey would win. But as Truman triumphantly showed the next morning, in the famous photo with the now-notorious headline announcing a Dewey victory, the pollsters stopped too soon to detect a massive late shift in support for Truman. Dark days followed: Gallup was widely ridiculed, and his client list shrank. A book was mailed to his company entitled *What Dr. Gallup Knows about Polls*. Its pages were blank.

Since that embarrassment of 1948, two devices have improved the speed and quality of polls: computers and telephones. Until the late 1960s, most surveys were conducted by hired interviewers, men and women who visited voters in their homes, clipboards in hand, a process that usually took at least an hour per interview. While long interviews provided pollsters with more information than they could get on the phone, in-person interviewers couldn't be supervised as closely as phone callers, and the possibility of bias—as slight as a knowing glance or rolled eyes during an interview—was always there. The answers from those interviews—mounds of paper—were hand-tabulated, which could take days or even weeks. Today, interviews can be conducted in minutes over the phone, and results can be produced by computer within hours.

"The telephone is a leap forward for public opinion polls," says Geoffrey D. Garin, president of Garin-Hart Strategic Research in Washington. "Because such a large percentage of the American population lives in households equipped with phones—it's up in the 90s—you can contact people very quickly and much less expensively and with relatively little bias. Now we can do things virtually overnight. Between having telephones and computers there are campaigns where we will do the interviewing from 6 in the evening until 9:30 and complete 400 interviews. It will be key punched and processed at my office and by 12 o'clock that night, sitting in front of the results on my computer at home, I can be on the phone with the campaign manager, talking about the results and the implications for the campaign."

How Polls Work: A Layman's Guide

On the face of it, the notion that by talking with 1,500 Americans one can accurately reflect the views of 120 million voters seems preposterous. The idea, however, is rooted in time-honored principles of probability theory. The notion is simply this: If a random sampling of a universe is taken, that sampling will accurately represent the entire universe.

Edward H. Lazarus, a partner in the Washington polling firm of Information Associates, taught political science and survey methodology at Yale before going into the polling business full time. Lazarus says that "a randomly selected sample would be in every way representative of the population at large because every individual in the universe has an equal probability of being picked. If that holds true, your attitudes, demographics, geography will be represented proportionally in the sample."

Garin, of Garin-Hart Strategic Research, explains that the "reliability of a sample is almost never perfect. You can't interview a sample and be absolutely sure the results are identical to what you'd get if you interviewed everybody in the universe. There is a margin of error. If you do everything perfectly right, there is still a margin of error, and the most important part of determining the margin of error is the sample size."

A mathematical formula based on probability and statistical theories places the margin of error for a sample size of 400 at plus or minus 5 percent. Garin says that means that "in 95 out of 100 cases, the difference between the results of the survey and the results of interviewing everybody in the universe would not differ by more than 5 percent in either direction."

Perhaps the most mind-boggling aspect of polling is that the size of the universe being polled is irrelevant to the accuracy of the survey.* Neil Beck, a political science professor at the University of California at San Diego, takes this point a little further, into what might seem like the ionosphere of mathematics. A

---

* This statement is true, but it should also be noted that it may be difficult to gather and list all the members in a large universe. Since the key principle in random sampling is that each member of the universe must have an equal probability of being chosen, having an accurate and inclusive universe is crucial. This is a major reason that most national pollsters sample a universe of phone numbers rather than of individuals; it would be virtually impossible to draw up an inclusive list of the universe of individuals in the United States.

random sampling of 1,000 voters, says Beck, would just as accurately reflect the views of 10,000 voters as it would 20 trillion voters. In fact, he says, the theory of probability assumes the population being studied is an infinite number. Laymen don't understand it, Garin says, "but it's the truth."

Most pollsters, says Garin, don't interview fewer than 400 people because the margin of error rises exponentially as the sample size goes down. When a sample drops to 200, for example, the margin of error rises to 7 percent, a sample of 800 yields a margin of error of about 3.5 percent, while a sample of 1,500—the standard size used in polls of the United States—has a margin of error of about 2.5 percent.

Most pollsters select their sample of people to be interviewed from lists of voters or randomly selected phone numbers (random-digit dialing).* The advantage to using voter lists is that the pollster is sure the people surveyed are eligible to vote, while the advantage of random dialing is that even voters with unlisted numbers may be reached. Both methods are considered reliable.

Modern polling is far from trouble-free, however. Orren says there are three kinds of errors pollsters make. The first, which is the least frequently made, according to Orren, is a sampling error. These aren't as egregious as the *Literary Digest* mistake in '36, but the absence of randomness still renders a survey worthless.

The second type is known as a "measurement error," which usually involves poorly worded questions. For example, some pollsters ask voters whether they rate a politician's performance as excellent, good, fair, or poor. What does a voter who says "fair" mean? asks Orren. " 'Fair' for some people means pretty good." For others it means not so good. Because of the ambiguity, "fair" shouldn't be offered as a category, says Orren.

The third type of mistake, says Orren, is a "specification error," meaning "you've got a bad theory looming behind your questions. It means you might get the right answers to the wrong questions." For example, he says, he once did a survey on busing in a Boston suburb and found that most residents favored busing as a means to achieve school integration. However, he found that many of the people polled didn't much care about the issue. Among those who did care about it—enough to vote for or against a politician based on his position on busing— opposition to busing was overwhelming. Pollsters often make the mistake, says Orren, of conducting polls based on the belief that "everyone cares about everything and that it has the same political consequences for everyone."

---

* Random-digit dialing makes it possible to construct a virtually complete list of all the phone numbers in the United States. Since a phone number has a three-digit area code, a three-digit central office code, and a four-digit local number, pollsters can put together a bank of all the possible numbers in use, including unlisted numbers, that compose the universe. They then randomly select a specified number of the numbers from this bank.

The Making of a Poll

Most of the best and most reputable pollsters follow similar methods in conducting their surveys for clients who are running for public office, using five essential steps:

1. *Draft a questionnaire*. All pollsters ask voters interviewed for standard demographic data such as age, income, race, party identification, and so on. And most also ask about a politician's performance and whether voters like the politician. Once the questionnaire is drafted, the pollster submits it to the politician for approval. Each question adds time on the phone during the interview process—and so to the cost—so Washington pollster Ed Lazarus says that in formulating a question, he asks himself: "What would we or could we do differently if we knew the answer to this question?" If the answer is that very little or nothing would be done differently, he doesn't ask the question.

2. *Generate a sample*. Samples can be drawn in dozens, if not hundreds or thousands, of ways. Some pollsters select their samples from voting lists, others use telephone books. Like many pollsters, Lazarus buys his samples. He pays for a computer-generated list of randomly selected phone numbers—minus most business phones—in the state he's polling. This method is more likely than some others to produce a random sample because it reaches people with unlisted phone numbers. In a statewide race, particularly in a large state, most pollsters do at least 800 interviews. This size sample—which is not dramatically more accurate than one with 400 interviews—permits a pollster to break out subgroups—women, blacks, or residents of a particular media market, for example. If the sample is much smaller than 800, it will probably include too few members of subgroups for a reliable analysis. If Lazarus wants 800 completed interviews, he begins with a list of about 5,000 numbers. Many numbers aren't attached to working phones, some business numbers slip through, some people refuse to talk, others (in the case of random dialing) aren't registered to vote, and still others aren't at home to answer the phone. That makes call-backs crucial. One of the most important features of any good survey is that interviewers always try to call back a voter who is not home on the first try. Says Harrison Hickman, "We want to make sure every person has an equal opportunity to be selected, and you're not doing that if you're only calling each person one time."

3. *Conduct the interviews*. Rare is the pollster these days who has interviews conducted in person. Hiring someone to visit a voter costs about twice as much as a phone interview. Some survey companies have phone banks in their offices and hire and train a cadre of callers. Others, like Lazarus, contract their calls out to a telephone-interviewing service. Lazarus uses a company in suburban Philadelphia to which he ships the phone numbers and the questionnaires. Does it make a difference who makes the calls? A big difference, says Lazarus. "It's important that it be someone who is not going to irritate or annoy you by their voice or diction or language, someone who can establish a rapport quickly so the respondent has an investment in this process." Lazarus says it is important that

the callers not know about or care about the candidates. Callers in Philadelphia aren't concerned with the outcome of a U.S. Senate race in Nevada or California and therefore won't be biased in their interviewing. The longest phone interviews pollsters will conduct run 35 or 40 minutes, and some, like Lazarus, are uncomfortable trying to keep voters on the phone for more than 25 minutes. Surveys conducted early in a campaign take three, four, or even five nights to complete. Near the end of a heated campaign, most pollsters complete a new survey every night, between the hours of 6 and 9:30.

4. *Process the results.* After the interviews are completed, the questionnaires are key punched so the data can be processed by a computer. The computer provides hundreds, sometimes thousands, of pages of data, mostly in the form of cross-tabulations such as the popularity of a candidate among women, the major issue among Hispanics, or the character trait most appealing to undecided voters.

5. *Analyze the results.* The pollster studies the data, searching for particularly salient information. The pollster will then provide the client with answers to major questions, such as job rating and the horse race. Over the course of a few days, or sometimes weeks—particularly if it is *very* early in the campaign—the pollster then prepares a detailed, written report. The report is generally delivered when the pollster makes an oral presentation to the client, which usually lasts for several hours and consists mainly of advice—based on the survey findings—about what direction the campaign should take.

The *real* last step, of course, is getting paid. A statewide telephone survey of 800 interviews with a lengthy questionnaire runs between $20,000 and $30,000. In general, phone surveys cost in the neighborhood of $30 to $35 per interview— about $12,000 to $15,000 for a 400-sample survey; about $45,000 to $55,000 for a 1,500-sample survey.

How Polls Are Used

Newspapers, magazines, and television and radio stations use polls as news items. Candidates use them to formulate strategy. The oft-repeated cynic's cliché about polls holds that candidates read them so they can pander to the populace. But candidates who shift directions with every political zephyr don't often go far in politics—Americans generally see to it that their elected leaders have a bit more heft than that. Do unscrupulous candidates use polls for manipulative purposes? Of course, but probably far less often than doubters suggest.

The cynical notion that politicians use surveys to tailor their positions to the majority of voters has grown rather tired through the years. A politician shifting views on major topics purely to remain in tune with the polls would quickly become transparent. That is not to say that politicians don't use polls to help them get elected—that's precisely what they do. How can a poll help? Let's say, for example, that a candidate for president finds that because of his position on oil-import quotas he has no chance at all of winning Louisiana. But he has a remote shot at taking New Jersey. That small bit of information is valuable because it tells a campaign that it should not waste its major resources—advertising dollars and the candidate's time—in Louisiana but might profitably concentrate on New Jersey.

Or let's say that a state representative is running for mayor of Boston and finds through a poll that he is quite popular throughout the city with one exception—elderly voters don't much like him. Let's say this candidate, as a state rep, had a strong record of supporting causes popular among senior citizens, but, for some reason, the poll reveals that many seniors don't see this candidate as a friend (perception and reality are often at odds in politics). That poll data is of immense value because the problem that has been detected through the survey can be corrected. The candidate can step up activity among the elderly, visiting more senior centers. And the campaign can target direct-mail and radio advertising to the elderly, focusing on the candidate's record on senior-citizens' issues.

Predictably, pollsters get rather grumpy when asked about the use of polls for what some see as manipulation. Harrison Hickman, of Hickman-Maslin Research in Washington, D.C., says polls provide information that allows his clients to be shown in the best possible light. A trace of indignation creeps into Hickman's voice when he poses what he clearly considers an absurd question: "We should be obligated to tell the *worst* side of our client's story?"

Polls are a way for candidates to listen to the voters, says Hickman. And once a candidate has begun executing the strategy—that is, attempting to communicate a specific message about himself or his views through news stories and advertising—a poll is a way to measure whether the message is getting through to voters.

Oddly enough, even though polling had been around for at least 30 years, the first candidate to have a pollster working within his campaign was John F. Kennedy in 1960. His pollster was Louis Harris, leader of one of the oldest and most established polling companies in the nation.

The Big-Name Pollsters

While polling companies have sprouted up around the country to fill the demand of local and regional media outlets and to service candidates for lesser offices, the pollsters who handle the major campaigns could easily fit in a small jet. Most pollsters—Democrat and Republican alike—seem to agree that the best in the business are two well-established, very successful Republicans: Richard Wirthlin of Decision Making Information in Washington, whose best-known client currently occupies the White House [Ronald Reagan], and Robert Teeter, president of Market Opinion Research in Detroit. Both men are considered very smart and thoughtful, and both understand not only the science of polling but political strategy.

Among the Democrats, the well-respected pollsters include Peter Hart of Garin-Hart, William Hamilton, Edward Lazarus, Harrison Hickman, and Edward

Maslin, all based in Washington. Perhaps the most controversial of all American pollsters is Patrick Caddell, who gained fame as a wunderkind barely out of his teens in the 1972 McGovern presidential campaign. Some colleagues consider Caddell a brilliant strategist; others regard him as a has-been.

A number of the major pollsters come from academia, where they studied and taught political science, statistics, and survey methodology. But many other pollsters operating throughout the country have little if any formal training. Polling is an unregulated business. There is no licensing authority or professional association. Anyone with a basic knowledge of polling and a personal computer can open up shop.

Reading Polls Intelligently

At times during the next year or so it may seem that you hear or read about two or three different polls a day. The key to becoming a smart consumer of polling information is to look for a few indications that often reveal the differences between polls you can trust and polls you can't.

Perhaps the most important aspect of any poll is its author. As a general rule, you can feel safe in trusting polls conducted by the likes of Wirthlin, Teeter, or the major national newspapers or television networks.

Next, make sure the precise question asked is printed in full. Read the question carefully. Does it strike you as fair? Or does it seem, through loaded wording, to have an inherent bias that tilts the respondent toward a particular response?

Not all polls provide information about methodology, but look for how the sample was selected. If the people interviewed were selected either from voter lists or through random-digit dialing, you can feel comfortable about it.

Next, look for a sample of at least 600 interviews. If fewer than 400 people were polled, you can skip the survey. If it consists of at least 400 randomly selected people, the overall results may be fine. But if the sample is only 400, or even 600, don't trust results from subgroups. A poll with a sample of 400 would have a subsample of, say, undecided voters, that was simply too small to analyze intelligently.

Also look for a sample where voters are screened so that the results reflect the attitudes of voters who are likely to vote, particularly in primaries. Some pollsters force respondents to pass tough screens. They ask not only whether the voter plans to vote but whether he or she voted in the past few elections, if the voter can name the candidates running for certain offices, and if the voter knows the date of the election.

Finally, see when the poll was conducted. If all the interviews were done over the Labor Day weekend, when people with the opportunity are likely to be away on vacation, chances are very good that the survey overrepresents poor and working people and underrepresents the wealthy. If the interviews were done only during the day, the survey probably oversampled women and older people.

Ours is a healthy if not voracious appetite for polling information, yet there seems little doubt that our collective hunger will be sated by the heaps of polling offered for our consumption during the coming election season. Many of us will even become statistics as we are interviewed by pollsters for whom we, as randomly selected individuals, represent the attitudes, hopes, and frustrations of, say, 80,000 other Americans. That is a heavy responsibility, indeed, and if the soothsayers and oracles of our times are to operate with any intelligence, we ought to cooperate and provide honest responses to their queries.

So even if you are approached by " 'Social Science Workers' from Princeton University, augmented by seven or eight East Side New Yorkers who had never in their lives seen a possum . . . ," you might set skepticism aside momentarily, if not in honor of probability theory, then at least for civility's sake.

Summary Questions

1. What are the major sources of error in public opinion polls? How can such errors be eliminated?
2. How are poll results used in the United States? Are such uses consistent with democratic ideals?
3. What steps are involved in designing and conducting a poll?

 4.2

The Shifting Sands of Public Opinion: Is Liberalism Back?

William G. Mayer

There is a great deal of historical evidence to suggest that the nation's politics has a cyclical quality to it. Eras characterized by relative government inaction are often followed by periods highlighted by major new government initiatives, as authorities respond with vigor to deal with unaddressed problems. Likewise, periods of

---

William G. Mayer is assistant professor of political science at Northeastern University.

activist government may move things too far and too quickly, creating a longing among the citizenry for less disruptive and intense times.

In this article, William G. Mayer provides evidence that mass public opinion over the past three decades possesses such a cyclical feature. He finds that public opinion has shifted three times since the mid-1960s. The period 1966–1973 was characterized by increasing liberalism in public attitudes, especially on such issues as military intervention, regulation of business, and cultural mores. The nation turned to the right during the next period (1974–1980), setting the stage for a military buildup during the early Reagan years and a reaction against cultural liberalism and the excessive growth of the regulatory and welfare state.

Mayer believes that a "liberal resurgence" in the attitudes of the public has taken place since 1981. By the late 1980s, the move to the left in mass public opinion was creating major difficulties for President George Bush, as well as a window of opportunity for Democratic Party candidates advocating new initiatives in areas like education, day care, and health care.

The final polls won't start to close on the night of November 3, 1992 until 7:00 p.m. Eastern Standard Time, but a few hours later, with most of the actual votes still uncounted, politicians and pundits will already be arguing about how to interpret them. Such debates have become a recurrent feature of American elections. Most presidential contests, and even many mid-term elections, are closely scrutinized by our national sages and prognosticators to see what they reveal about the elusive and fickle "mood" of the American public. The general tenor of such analysis is probably familiar to most political observers. In 1960, it was said, the American people were restless, ready for something new. In 1964, they lurched sharply to the left. In 1968, depending on whom one talked to, they had either become liberal because of Vietnam or conservative because of crime. Over the next three elections, they moved right, center, and then right again, a little bit like a drunken sailor.

For most of our nation's history, such speculation was unavoidable. Elections and mass protest movements were our only real clue as to what ordinary citizens (as distinct from political elites) were thinking about the issues of the day. Since the 1930s, however, it has been possible to measure the public pulse with considerably more precision, through the use of mass sample surveys. Even with all of their well-rehearsed limitations (the problems of question wording and question order, the often-disregarded complexities involved in putting together a true probability sample), public opinion polls, properly conducted and interpreted, provide us with a considerably more accurate means of assessing the changes and trends in public opinion than any other alternative.

Surprisingly, however, not until rather recently have pollsters and scholars started to take full advantage of this resource. After the 1980 election, as we will see, there occurred a sharp debate about whether Ronald Reagan's victory signaled a decisive shift to the right in American public opinion. And while significant voices could be heard on both sides of this issue, very few of the disputants ever bothered to examine more than a tiny part of the available evidence. But for those with a serious interest in pursuing such questions, the picture has now become considerably brighter. A number of major survey archives—chief among them, the Roper Center at the University of Connecticut—have collected and catalogued the past results of commercial and academic pollsters. And many survey organizations—in particular, the National Opinion Research Center (NORC) at the University of Chicago—have shown increased appreciation for the value of taking regular, repeated soundings of mass attitudes on a wide range of significant issues. When these data are brought together and analyzed, they provide a fascinating perspective on recent American political history—and on the context of the 1992 elections.

Public Opinion Trends

While many of the most interesting issues in voting analysis are now shrouded in a dense fog of methodological controversy, there is little dispute as to the best procedure for tracking changes in public opinion. One simply looks for cases where a survey question has been asked, with the same wording, on several different occasions over an extended period of time. In 1956, for example, the Gallup Poll asked a national sample of American adults: "Do you favor the death penalty for persons convicted of murder?" Gallup then asked this same question once more in the 1950s, five times in the 1960s, on five occasions in the 1970s, and then six times between 1980 and 1988. Obviously, the results will fluctuate a bit due to sampling error. But if the percentage who say that they favor the death penalty shows a large and sustained increase, we can interpret this as showing that American public opinion became more conservative on this particular issue. Alternatively, if opposition to the death penalty increases, we have evidence that public opinion has moved to the left. In this particular case, public opinion drifted slowly to the left from 1956 to 1966, then broke in a sharply conservative direction. Between 1966 and 1988, support for the death penalty increased by about 35 percentage points.

Drawing on polls from a dozen different survey organizations, I have assembled similar time-series data on almost every major controversy in recent American politics: busing, school prayer, marijuana, abortion, and the ERA; defense spending, arms control, foreign aid, and military intervention; taxes, domestic spending, welfare, regulation, and the environment.*

---

* For the data on which these conclusions are based and a more detailed analysis of specific issues, see William G. Mayer, *The Changing American Mind: How and Why American Public Opinion Changed Between 1960 and 1988* (Ann Arbor: University of Michigan Press, 1992).

The results, summarized in Tables 4.1 to 4.4, show the balance of ideological changes that occurred during four different periods that are generally thought to define the most significant "eras" in recent American politics: 1960–1965, 1966–1973, 1974–1980, and 1981–1988.

1960–1965: Stability

Usable survey data for these years are rather thin (the Gallup Poll was almost the only survey organization doing regular polling during this period), and my interest in them, in any event, was partly as a way of establishing a baseline for the changes in the other three periods. What evidence is available, however, strongly suggests that this was a time of fairly stable attitudes. Liberal trends appear in a small number of issues, including racial equality and capital punishment. With the exception of race, however, the changes were rather small; and they were counter-balanced by an almost equal number of conservative changes.

Particularly striking, in view of the policy changes that occurred during these years, is the total absence of evidence to indicate that public opinion was

Table 4.1
Changes in American Public Opinion Between 1960 and 1965

Issues on which public opinion became more liberal	Issues on which public opinion exhibited little or no change	Issues on which public opinion became more conservative
Capital punishment	Gun registration	Gun ownership
Racial equality	Labor unions	Business
Legal regulation of birth control	Religious beliefs and practices	General opinions of Communist China
	Role and status of women	Regulation
	Balance of military strength	
	Relations with the Soviet Union	
	Admitting Communist China to the UN	
	Taxes	
	Abortion	

becoming more liberal on economic issues. Over the last decade, a small army of left-leaning political scientists has written books and articles vehemently denying that public opinion took a right turn during the 1970s, and complaining bitterly that the "Reagan revolution" was built upon a foundation of misunderstanding, distortion, and manipulation. While I will dispute this verdict below, it is interesting to note that the Great Society* may have been based on just such a misperception. Though many claim that John F. Kennedy inspired the nation to a new commitment to public service, or that Lyndon Johnson's landslide victory over Barry Goldwater showed a growing public determination to expand federal welfare and regulatory programs, such assertions find little support in the available survey data. I can find no indication that the public's thinking about domestic economic issues during the heyday of the New Frontier† and the Great Society changed very much from its position in the 1950s.

1966–1973: Liberal Shift

The late 1960s and early 1970s, by contrast, definitely stand out as a time of increasing liberalism in public attitudes. The popular image of these years as a time of rapid and wrenching social change clearly does have a strong basis in fact. Particularly large changes occurred in a number of cultural issues, such as premarital sex, abortion, racial equality, and the role and status of women; in foreign policy, where popular discontent with the Vietnam War led to noticeably more liberal stances on military intervention, the defense budget, and relations with the Soviet Union; and in growing cynicism about the performance of business.

In 1965, for example, only 15 percent of an NORC sample said that a pregnant woman who did not want any more children should be able to obtain a legal abortion. By 1973, 46 percent supported abortions in this circumstance. Between 1969 and 1973, the number of Americans who felt that "sex relations before marriage" were not wrong jumped from 21 percent to 43 percent. Where only 19 percent of a Gallup sample said that this country was spending too much on national defense in 1960, 46 percent took this position in 1973. The number who agreed that "there's too much power concentrated in the hands of a few large companies" increased from 52 percent in 1965 to 75 percent in 1973.

---

* The Great Society is the label for the domestic programs of the Lyndon Johnson administration during the 1960s. The Johnson program reflected a philosophy that society's economic and social problems could be solved by federal government spending action in a variety of areas, and included major policy initiatives in such areas as civil rights, health care for the elderly and the poor, and education.

† The New Frontier is the term President Kennedy (1961–1963) used to describe his administration's policies. In Kennedy's view, the New Frontier was less a set of specific programs and more a set of challenges to the public to create a stronger and more dynamic nation.

Table 4.2
Changes in American Public Opinion Between 1966 and 1973

Issues on which public opinion became more liberal	Issues on which public opinion exhibited little or no change	Issues on which public opinion became more conservative
Wiretapping	Gun registration	United Nations
Racial equality	Religious beliefs	Gun ownership
Centrality of religious beliefs	Size and power of government	Crime and punishment
Sexual mores		Taxes
Divorce		Federalism
Abortion		Labor unions
Religious practices		Foreign aid
Business		
Military spending		
Legalizing marijuana		
Military intervention		
Government assistance for the poor		
Environmental protection		
Role and status of women		
Conceptions of the family		
Legal regulation of birth control		
School prayer		
Relations with the Soviet Union		
Relations with Communist China		

1974–1980: Right Turn

There are two different "conventional wisdoms" about the changes in public opinion that preceded the 1980 elections. Among practicing politicians and journalistic commentators, Reagan's landslide victory, coupled with the large

Table 4.3
Changes in American Public Opinion Between 1974 and 1980

Issues on which public opinion became more liberal	Issues on which public opinion exhibited little or no change	Issues on which public opinion became more conservative
Racial equality	Gun registration	Crime and punishment
Nuclear energy	Homosexuality	Gun ownership
Premarital sex	Divorce	Military spending
Role and status of women	Abortion	Military intervention
Conceptions of the family	Foreign aid	Taxes
Legalizing marijuana	United Nations	Federalism
	Religious beliefs and practices	Equal Rights Amendment
	Laws regulating sexual behavior	Relations with the Soviet Union
	Wage-price controls	Central Intelligence Agency
	National health insurance	Size and power of government
	Balanced budget amendment	Government assistance for the poor
	Business	Job creation
		Labor unions
		Regulation
		Environmental protection
		Domestic spending
		Causes and cures for inflation

Republican gains in the Senate and the House of Representatives, was widely interpreted as showing a substantial shift to the right in American public opinion. And that perception, in turn, played a major role in Reagan's legislative successes throughout 1981 in cutting social spending, increasing defense spending, and reducing taxes.

But academic studies of the 1980 election took a decisively different view of the matter. The first major academic analyses of the 1980 vote begun to appear in early 1981, and almost without exception, they rejected the contention that American public opinion had become more conservative. To the best of my knowledge, of the numerous books and articles that appeared soon after Reagan's victory, exactly one (published in the *British Journal of Political Science*) showed any sympathy at all with the "right turn" hypothesis. Indeed, there is now a rather substantial secondary literature on the 1980 election that, starting from the assumption that no change in public opinion actually occurred, views the widespread clamor about a new conservative mood as evidence of a right-wing bias in the news media.*

Yet, as I have noted earlier, while many academics denied that a conservative shift had taken place, relatively few bothered to collect or analyze the kinds of data discussed above. Most such studies produced evidence only on the quite different question of whether a partisan realignment had taken place, and thus looked at such matters as party identification, aggregate voting patterns, and economic performance indicators.†

The data I have assembled, however, leave little doubt that the conservative shift was real, substantial, and broad-based. American attitudes really did become more conservative—often substantially more so—about a wide range of issues: crime, the ERA, relations with the Soviet Union, military spending and intervention, taxes, the role of government, domestic spending, regulation, job

---

* See, for example, Michael Parenti, *Inventing Reality: The Politics of the Mass Media* (New York: St. Martin's Press, 1986); and David Paletz and Robert Entman, *Media Power Politics* (New York: Free Press, 1981).

† One book that did try to examine some of these data is Thomas Ferguson and Joel Roger's *Right Turn* (New York: Hill and Wang, 1986). But a number of significant problems limit the usefulness of this work. First, since the authors' concern is primarily to show that policy changes and public opinion moved in divergent directions during the Reagan presidency, most of the data they cite come from the years *after* 1980. Given their own interests, this is a perfectly appropriate procedure. Moreover, I concur with their verdict on these years. But their work is of substantially less utility in establishing the changes *prior* to 1980—though this is the purpose for which it is often cited.

Second, Ferguson and Rogers do find conservative shifts in a number of areas including crime, taxes, and defense spending. In several of these cases, they attempt to argue that these exceptions somehow should not be counted against their thesis, but I find none of their arguments especially plausible. Third, in a number of instances, I think they have selectively chosen data to reinforce their own argument, while ignoring data that would prove the opposite. On the issue of regulation, for example, they include questions showing declining confidence in business, but not the many questions that show increasing dissatisfaction with governmental regulation. They fail to examine the huge changes in public opinion about communism, the Soviet Union, and military intervention that occurred in the late 1970s. They also demonstrate a consistent, and highly questionable, preference for data from the Harris Poll, whose surveys are often tilted in a liberal direction. Finally, much of the data they cite only shows that public opinion is not conservative in an absolute sense, which is a very different question from whether and how such attitudes have *changed*.

creation, the causes of inflation, and environmental protection. In a 1974 Gallup Poll, only 12 percent of the public felt that the United States was spending too little on national defense. By 1980, 49 percent endorsed greater defense spending. In 1970, only 15 percent of Americans said that they were "worse off as a result of government control and regulation" of large corporations—but 40 percent said they were worse off in 1981. Support for American military intervention if the Soviet Union attacked our "major European allies" jumped from 48 percent in 1974 to 74 percent in 1980. In a series of Roper surveys, the number who blamed inflation on "too much government spending on domestic programs" rose from 26 percent in 1973 to 43 percent in 1981.

1981–1988: Liberal Resurgence

To examine the survey record of the late 1970s is to gain a renewed sense of appreciation for the political "antennae" of elected officials. Whatever the source of their judgments—election results, press reports, or conversations with voters—politicians appear to have developed a very accurate portrait of the popular mood (much more accurate than most academic observers), and of the way it changed between the early 1970s and the end of the decade. And it is for precisely this reason that the trends in public opinion between 1981 and 1988 come as such a surprise. For little in the political rhetoric or journalistic commentary of recent years reflects the extent to which this has been a time of generally liberal changes in mass attitudes.

Across a vast range of issues—including military spending and relations with the (now former) Soviet Union, taxes, domestic spending, and environmental protection—liberals have made up much of the ground they lost in the late 1970s. Where a majority of Americans wanted to increase defense spending in 1980, by late 1982 only about 15 percent expressed such a preference. In 1980, 49 percent of the public said that "the government in Washington is getting too powerful for the good of the country and the individual person." In 1988, only 33 percent felt this way. The belief that federal income taxes were too high declined from 68 percent in 1980 to 55 percent in 1988; while support for spending on the environment, health care, education, and even welfare all increased. In late 1980, Americans supported "strip-mining for coal, even if it means damaging the environment," by a 44 percent to 41 percent margin. By 1986, only 20 percent supported strip-mining while 68 percent opposed it.

How can we account for such changes—and for the widespread failure of politicians and journalists to take greater notice of them? In some cases, one can only say that much of the political mythology of the last decade has been exaggerated or mistaken. Take the case of civil rights. Although civil-rights leaders have often claimed that one effect of the Reagan presidency was to relegitimize once-discredited forms of racial prejudice and discrimination, the

Table 4.4

Changes in American Public Opinion Between 1981 and 1988

Issues on which public opinion became more liberal	Issues on which public opinion exhibited little or no change	Issues on which public opinion became more conservative
Racial equality	Gun control	Crime and punishment
Busing	Sexual mores	Legalizing marijuana
Military spending	School prayer	Divorce
Taxes	Business	Abortion
Size and power of government	Central Intelligence Agency	Economic rights and privileges
Nuclear energy	Federalism	Business profits
Domestic spending	Foreign aid	
Discrimination against gays	Religious beliefs and practices	
Relations with the Soviet Union	Government assistance for the poor	
Relations with Communist China	Balanced budget amendment	
Role and status of women	Laws governing social behavior	
Conceptions of the family	United Nations	
Environmental protection	Military intervention	

survey record provides no evidence that this actually occurred. In a few cases, in fact, the Reagan years witnessed advances for the civil-rights cause. For example, almost every year since 1972, NORC has been asking its samples whether they favored or opposed "the busing of black and white school children from one district to another." Between 1972 and 1982, support for busing did not change— but it rose by 13 percentage points between 1982 and 1988.

Determinate Questions v. Comparative Questions

In many cases, however, these changes are probably best interpreted as a kind of backhanded measure of Ronald Reagan's success. In order to understand this point, it is worth drawing a distinction between two different types of survey questions, and how each of them measures ideological change.

Consider, on the one hand, these three survey questions:

1. Are you in favor of the death penalty for persons convicted of murder?
2. Should it be possible for a pregnant woman to obtain a legal abortion if she became pregnant as a result of rape?
3. Do you favor or oppose the Equal Rights Amendment?

Now compare them to these three questions:

1. Do you think we are spending too little, too much, or about the right amount for national defense and military purposes?
2. Do you think there is a need for more government regulation of business, is the present amount of government regulation about right, or do you think there should be less government regulation of business?
3. Do you consider the amount of federal income tax which you have to pay as too high, about right, or too low?

The first set of items are examples of what I have called *determinate* policy questions. They ask respondents for their opinions about specific policy options whose meaning and content remain essentially constant over time. "The death penalty" means the same thing today that it did in the 1930s or the 1950s. The wording of the ERA was the same in 1975 as it was in 1982. The second set of questions, by contrast, are what might be called *comparative* policy questions. Respondents are asked how they would like to change a particular policy as compared to the status quo. Hence, the state of current policy becomes, implicitly or explicitly, an important—and constantly changing—factor in how the public interprets such questions.

Both types of questions do measure real changes in public opinion, but the changes in comparative questions have a more ambiguous meaning, as the defense-spending question quoted above illustrates. Although the Gallup Poll has used this same question wording for the last two decades, in a sense the meaning of those words is constantly changing—because the size of the defense budget is constantly changing. Thus, when the percentage who favor increased defense spending declines, as it did in the 1980s, two interpretations are possible:

1. Americans have decided that the defense build-up that they so urgently wanted in 1980 was a bad idea, after all. Having seen the results of that build-up—its apparent lack of effect in many situations, the horror stories about $700 screwdrivers—Americans have become decisively less militaristic.

2. Public opinion about the ideal level of defense spending has really stayed pretty constant over the last decade. Most Americans have always wanted a level of defense spending that was greater than this country had in 1978—but not as high as many conservatives were proposing in 1984 or 1988. What changed, in other words, was not public attitudes, but the reality that the public was being

asked to evaluate. Most Americans approved of the first several Reagan budgets and the large defense-spending increases they contained. But by about 1982, they had parted company with Reagan. He wanted further increases, whereas they felt that the current defense budget was fine, or even too large.

Reagan's Limited Mandate*

It is this second interpretation, I think, that most accurately describes many of the issues listed in the liberal column of Table 4.4. Ronald Reagan, I have argued, did receive something of a mandate in the 1980 election—but it was a fairly limited mandate. Particularly in the area of economic policy, the public was not asking for a wholesale dismantling of federal welfare and regulatory programs, but for a series of rather modest adjustments: a little less domestic spending (or perhaps a slower rate of growth); a slight relaxation of environmental regulations in order to produce more energy; a little more reliance on individual initiative in dealing with the problems of poverty. And by about 1982 or 1983, substantial parts of the American public seem to have concluded that they had already received most of what they wanted. And who can blame them for drawing this conclusion? The Reagan legislative program of 1981 had, indeed, increased defense spending, reduced the income tax, and imposed at least some cuts in many social programs.

At this point, the public might have reacted with unrestrained joy and gratitude towards Reagan—and in a sense voters did, by overwhelmingly re-electing him. But most survey questions on policy issues are not concerned with "What have you done for me lately?" but with "What should you do for me tomorrow?" And on this score, the survey evidence suggests that voters increasingly came to the conclusion that Ronald Reagan was headed in the wrong direction, particularly in the areas of defense and domestic spending. For whatever their other limitations, comparative survey questions capture one element of the American political system quite accurately. The advocates of zero-based budgeting[†] notwithstanding, the entire federal budget is not debated and constructed anew each year. The starting point is the current budget, and the options discussed are incremental changes: a little more here, a little less there. As elected officials sat down to consider what those marginal changes might look like, they faced a markedly conservative climate of opinion in 1980, but a considerably more liberal one by 1988.

---

* *Mandate* is the perceived popular support for a political program. A mandate is often "assumed" by presidents who are elected by a large electoral margin after running in a campaign where they believe they made their policy preferences clear.

† *Zero-based budgeting* is a budgeting procedure requiring government agencies to justify all spending items each year, in contrast to traditional budgeting procedures (incremental budgeting) which require justification only of changes from the previous year.

Starting in about 1982, then, and building throughout the rest of the 1980s, one begins to see the emergence of a new public mood that might best be summarized as follows: We like Ronald Reagan personally and we approve of most of the policy initiatives he has taken in the past. But we're not sure that we want to *continue* heading in the same direction. We think too much money has been devoted to defense and we're increasingly worried about a growing accumulation of unmet domestic needs in such areas as education, health care, and the environment. We don't like taxes or big government but we're not as concerned or threatened about such matters as we were when Reagan took office.

Some of the best appeals to this mood can be found, ironically, in the 1988 campaign speeches of George Bush. On social and cultural issues, like crime and the Pledge of Allegiance, the Bush strategy plainly rested on an attempt to defend conservative orthodoxy, while painting his opponent as an unrepentant liberal. But on economic issues, the Bush campaign clearly seems to have understood that its candidate could not win simply by promising four more years of Reaganite policies. With the major exception of his pledge not to raise taxes, Bush's speeches were an artful attempt to retain his conservative base while nonetheless distancing himself from substantial parts of the Reagan legacy. He would seek a kinder, gentler nation; make education a top priority; and resurrect the fallen banner of environmentalism. Above all, the Bush presidency would be more than just a holding pattern. As Bush often declared in his campaign speeches, "We are the change."

Prospects for Liberalism

These most recent changes in public opinion, and the new mood they embody, obviously have important implications for the 1992 election. At a minimum, they indicate that new Democratic initiatives in such areas as education, day care, and health care will receive a considerably more sympathetic reception than they would have twelve years earlier. On almost every major policy issue that is relevant to such proposals, recent trends have clearly been in a liberal direction. Not only is public opinion today more supportive of domestic spending, it is also less responsive to such traditional conservative themes as taxes and big government. Of course, the popular "mandate" for such programs is probably just as limited as Reagan's mandate in 1980. Nothing in that the survey data suggests that the public is looking for a massive new expansion of federal domestic programs to rival that of the New Deal or the Great Society. If a Democratic president does get elected in 1992, it is probable that within a few years the public will conclude that he, too, has exceeded his instructions, and public opinion might then start to shift back in the opposite direction. But that problem (if it ever should come to pass) is years in the future. For the present, public attitudes on an important range of economic policy issues have moved a long way from their position in the late 1970s.

The changes summarized in Table 4.4 are not, of course, George Bush's doing. They occurred prior to his own ascension to the presidency. Conceding that, there seems little doubt that Bush has greatly complicated the conservative predicament and considerably magnified the Democratic advantage. True, a president's capacity to mold and shape public opinion is distinctly limited. The dominant trend of public opinion changes during the Nixon, Carter, and Reagan administrations were all in the *opposite* direction to what each president would presumably have preferred. But given any particular constellation of public attitudes, presidents have substantially greater freedom in deciding how to respond to and channel such demands. It was Ronald Reagan's intuitive understanding of this point that helps explain why liberalism was so timid and dormant up through the end of his administration. If Reagan was unable to effect a fundamental restructuring of American economic thinking, he did show the importance of a president's ability to dominate the public debate: to elevate some issues and proposals (and not others) to the center of the national agenda, and to help determine the context in which issues are framed and understood.

It is precisely this power that George Bush has largely abdicated, particularly in the realm of economic policy, over the last three years. By endorsing a tax increase after repeated promises to the contrary, for example, Bush has substantially neutralized the Republicans' strongest counter-argument to new Democratic initiatives. Consider, too, the issue of education. Between 1978 and 1988, the number of Americans who wanted to spend more money for "improving the nation's education system" rose from 48 percent to 64 percent. If Bush has decided, for fiscal reasons, not to comply with this request, he might at least have responded with a significant educational program of his own and then pushed hard for its adoption. Such a course of action might have redirected the debate away from how much should be spent to what the money should be spent on. To those most concerned about the issue, it would have sent the message that the president understood the urgency of problem, and differed only as to the best means for solving it.

In fact, however, Bush's approach to the education issue has oscillated between timidity and boredom. After delaying for several years, he finally delegated the task of policy formation to his secretary of education—and then showed no inclination to push very hard for the package that emerged. Politics, like nature, abhors a vacuum; Bush's lack of leadership on education has helped give the impression (undeserved in my opinion) that conservatives have very little to say about the issue.

In the end, the combination of incumbency, lower interest rates, Bush's record in foreign policy, and public conservatism on social issues may still give the President a substantial re-election victory. In the meantime, however, it is hard to ignore the signs that the long-dormant forces of American liberalism are finally beginning to stir from their slumbers—or to avoid the conclusion that George Bush has played an important role in this reawakening.

Summary Questions

1. Why does the author believe that President Reagan had a "limited mandate" as he began his presidency in 1981? What factors led to a turn to the left in public opinion relatively early during Reagan's presidency?
2. Mayer predicts that if a liberal Democratic president is elected in 1992, it is probable that after a period of time public opinion will turn against the new administration. As you view the performance of the Clinton administration to date, are there any indications that it may eventually have difficulty getting support for its policy initiatives because of changes in public opinion?

 Chapter 5

PARTICIPATION

In a democracy, political participation may take many forms, ranging from efforts by citizens merely to inform themselves about politics to running for and holding public office. Some citizens may even attempt to bypass more conventional modes of participation altogether by engaging in political protest marches or acts of civil disobedience—the nonviolent violation of laws that they believe to be unjust. For most citizens, however, political participation centers around the act of voting in an election.

Participation in free elections provides citizens with many benefits. When people believe they can communicate their needs and wants to those who govern, government becomes both stable and legitimate. Elections teach civic virtues and give citizens a sense of responsibility and personal satisfaction.

The key role of elections, however, is to provide a check on power. As James Madison wrote in *The Federalist,* No. 51, "If Angels were to govern men, neither external nor internal controls on the government would be necessary," but in the absence of heavenly guidance government must be restrained, and "a dependence on the people is, no doubt, the primary control." The ballot box offers the public a way to control those who govern, since people seeking election must further citizens' interests to achieve public office. The public does not rule, but it influences those who do.

Although most Americans probably would be hard-pressed to give a sophisticated answer to the question "Why vote?", most firmly believe that democracy is "rule by the people" and that the cornerstone of popular democracy is free elections. Students are taught that everyone "ought to vote," and voting for the first time is a political rite of passage that serves as a powerful symbol of adulthood and allegiance to the American system. Many Americans hold the view that anyone who doesn't vote has forfeited the right to criticize the government.

In spite of these beliefs and feelings, however, many citizens do not participate in contemporary elections, a fact that could challenge the validity of popular democracy. The United States ranks near the bottom of western democracies in voter turnout. Furthermore, current turnout rates do not compare favorably with those of past elections. For example, in presidential elections in the last half of the 1800s, about 75 percent of eligible voters turned out (nearly 82 percent in the election of 1876), whereas in recent elections only slightly more than 50 percent voted. Turnout rates in off-year state and local elections are often less than 30 percent. President Reagan, who beat President Carter by an overwhelming margin in 1980, was elected by just a little more than 27 percent of the eligible voters in that year.

Comparisons of our own past with that of other nations are fraught with difficulties. A century ago, the electorate included neither women nor blacks. Ballots were not secret, and there were few registration barriers to restrict participation by white males. This created a strong incentive for political parties to mobilize voters, sometimes by herding citizens to the polls and giving them ballots containing only one party's candidates. The eastern cities in particular were dominated by political machines. Consequently, some of the high turnout figures undoubtedly resulted from political corruption.

Similarly, many countries impose a fine for not voting—a policy that would raise turnout rates in the United States but would be interpreted as undemocratic by most Americans. Many western democracies calculate turnout as the percentage of those on the electoral rolls who actually participate in an election, whereas in the United States turnout is calculated by dividing the number who vote by the total potential electorate—all persons of voting age, as determined by the U.S. Bureau of the Census. If this method were applied by other countries, U.S. voting rates would differ little from those of Canada, Great Britain, and Japan.

Surprisingly, voter turnout in the United States has constantly declined since the 1960 presidential election. This period has been marked by rising educational levels, increasingly prominent issues, and the removal of many voting barriers, such as poll taxes and registration and residency requirements. In addition, tremendous amounts of political information have been provided by the mass media, and campaigns have grown enormously in terms of cost and candidate exposure. Newspapers often chastise citizens for being lazy and uninterested in exercising their right to vote, but explanations for the turnout decline are much more complex.

One widely held belief is that, beginning in the mid-1960s, citizens developed mistrust of government officials and a diminished sense that their participation would make a difference. In 1966, about a quarter of the public believed the "people running the country don't care what happens to people like me." By 1977, 60 percent felt this way. By 1978, only 30 percent of Americans believed they could trust the government in Washington "to do what's right." In 1958, a similar poll revealed that 55 percent trusted the government.

Such disillusionment grew from the social disruptions of the 1960s, the assassinations of John F. Kennedy, Robert Kennedy, and Martin Luther King, Jr., the unpopular Vietnam War, the Watergate scandal, and the subsequent resignation of President Nixon. Huge increases in consumer prices in the 1970s and the perceived ineffectiveness of the Carter administration in dealing with the energy crisis and with the Iranian hostage situation also contributed to citizens' perception that leaders were neither trustworthy nor competent. Some scholars suggest that television played a role, too. According to the theory of "video malaise," TV tends to overwhelm viewers with the complexities of political controversies, which convinces the public that individuals are politically ineffective and that problems may be too difficult to solve. Further, the tone of the TV medium has been generally critical of authorities, highlighting the human weaknesses and mistakes of political leaders. Many voters thus question the worthwhileness of political participation.

A second widely accepted explanation for decreasing turnout relies on demographic factors. The arrival of the "baby boomers" at voting age during the mid-1960s, and constitutional changes that enfranchised eighteen- to twenty-year-olds, dramatically expanded the potential electorate between 1960 and 1972. Young voters made up an increasingly high proportion of the total electorate in the 1960s, 1970s, and early 1980s, yet this group participated less than older Americans did. Few saw politics as relevant to their lives. First-time eligible voters have had the lowest participation rates of any age group, perhaps because politics has to compete with schooling, social events, and courtship.

Two of the three readings that follow focus upon citizen involvement in the electoral process. In the first selection, Ruy Teixeira attempts to separate myth from reality in our understanding of turnout decline. He believes many of the standard explanations for decreasing voter participation and its impact are either misleading or incorrect and offers an alternative explanation based upon a generalized detachment that citizens have from politics. In the second selection, Jonathan Cohn explores the factors underlying the participatory patterns of the generation that came of political age in the 1970s and 1980s, a generation often criticized for its lack of political involvement. Finally, Patricia Theiler discusses a different form of individual citizen participation, focusing on the role of "single-issue crusaders" in the policy-making process. She finds that in some cases dedicated individuals can substantially influence policy even in the face of well-funded and organized opposition.

5.1

Voter Turnout in America: Ten Myths

Ruy Teixeira

Few subjects engender more heated discussions during election time than the level of voter turnout and its decline in recent decades. In this selection, Ruy Teixeira challenges some of the "myths" that have evolved concerning why citizens have voted less frequently since 1960. He finds that turnout decline is found in all economic categories and that explanations for low turnout such as the increasing cynicism and levels of citizen satisfaction with government are unconvincing. Nor has turnout decline had major partisan implications. Even major improvements in the turnout levels of strong Democratic support groups, such as blacks, would not have altered the outcome of recent presidential elections won by Republicans.

Teixeira believes that the key to improving turnout is "breaking the extraordinary *detachment* that many citizens have developed from the political process, so that they are connected, in even a minimal way, to the world of politics." He suggests that the campaign process must be made "easier to get involved in, more informative, and less susceptible to political manipulation."

A fter a small improvement in 1984, voter turnout in American presidential elections has resumed its steady decline. With the 3 percentage point reduction in the 1988 election, voter turnout has now dropped almost 13 points since 1960. That puts voter turnout at barely half (50.2 percent) of the voting-age population, below the 51.1 percent mark set by the 1948 Dewey–Truman election and the lowest level since 43.9 percent of age-eligible voters turned out in 1924. The sheer magnitude of nonvoting in contemporary America is staggering: more than 91 million Americans did not bother to participate in 1988.* . . .

Ruy Teixeira is a visiting fellow in the Brookings Governmental Studies Program. This article was written in 1992.

* Turnout improved over 5 percent from 1988 levels in the 1992 presidential election. Research has concluded that nearly half of the increase was due to the presence of Ross Perot on the ballot. Apparently the Perot candidacy provided a "protest" alternative for a number of voters who preferred not to cast a ballot for either Republican George Bush or Democrat Bill Clinton and might not have gone to the polls otherwise.

This dismal situation has occasioned much comment and concern across the political spectrum. The concern is welcome, but it has also been accompanied by a great deal of misunderstanding about the causes and consequences of low voter turnout. Much of the misunderstanding resides in a series of myths about voter turnout that lack any real empirical foundation. Dispelling these myths is, I believe, essential to improving citizen participation levels.

Myth #1: Turnout is going down because the poor are dropping out of politics. According to this myth, declining turnout is primarily due to massive increases in nonvoting among the poor. As a result, the affluent, who continue to vote, dominate the political process while the poor are ignored.

Reality #1: Turnout is going down because all groups—the poor, the middle class and the rich—have become less likely to vote. Although it is true that turnout decline has been sharper among the poorer groups in society, turnout has been falling steadily among all income groups, including the most affluent. For example, if we divide the U.S. electorate into six equal-sized income groups ("sextiles"), we find that, although turnout declined 8 percentage points among the lowest sextile between 1972 and 1988, it also fell 5 points among the highest income group. Results are similar if we look at groups defined by education or occupation: declining turnout has, as it were, been a "team" effort, with all strata of society making a contribution.

Myth #2: Turnout is going down because people see no differences between the Democrats and Republicans. This myth locates the source of turnout decline in the supposedly self-evident fact that no one sees any real differences between the political parties anymore. And, naturally, since citizens now see no differences between the parties, they choose not to vote.

Reality #2: More people see important differences between the Democrats and Republicans than they did three decades ago. Survey data show that the proportion of the electorate that sees important differences between the Republicans and Democrats actually *increased* by 9 percentage points (from 50.3 percent to 59.6 percent) between 1960 and 1988. Now, it is certainly possible that people find it increasingly difficult to know what these differences *mean*, but the fact remains that they are more likely, not less likely, to see differences. It follows that the popular perception of whether the Republicans and Democrats differ has nothing to do with falling turnout levels (indeed, if anything, turnout should have gone up because of this factor).

Myth #3: Turnout is going down because people have become so cynical about politics. Nobody trusts the government anymore. Everybody believes it is controlled by special interests and wastes tax money. Guided by these sentiments, citizens do the appropriate thing: they refuse to vote ("it only encourages them").

Reality #3: Increasing cynicism about politics has little, or nothing, to do with declining turnout. This is not because cynicism about politics hasn't increased. It has, reflected in the ever-larger numbers of Americans who *don't* trust their government and *do* believe the government is controlled by special interests and wastes their tax money. The reason, rather, is that cynicism about politics characterizes all citizens and does little to distinguish voters from nonvoters. For example, statistical analyses show that, all else equal, someone who doesn't trust the government is no less likely to vote than someone who does trust the government. It therefore follows that trust in government can go down drastically (as it has) and still not depress turnout levels.

The attitudes that do lie behind declining turnout appear to have more to do with a general sense that the government is not responsive to ordinary citizens and a feeling that politics is not worth paying attention to, in even the most minimal fashion. It is thus *indifference* to politics that is keeping citizens away from the polling booths, rather than active hostility or lack of trust. The latter is simply the common currency of American public opinion; the former is the particular coin of the electoral dropout.

Myth #4: Nonvoters don't vote because they are satisfied with the way things are. Low turnout is nothing to worry about, since lack of participation simply reflects how happy people are. Why vote, when there's nothing to get upset about?

Reality #4: Levels of satisfaction have nothing to do with turnout. There is simply no evidence that how satisfied people are—with the system, with their personal finances, with their life in general—has anything to do with how likely they are to vote. Therefore, a plethora of happy people cannot explain why U.S. voter turnout is so low.

Conversely, there is no reason to believe that those who do currently vote are the "contented" ones, as John Kenneth Galbraith asserts without a shred of evidence in his recent book, *The Culture of Contentment*. The reasons why people vote are many and complex, but how happy they are does not appear to be one of them.

Myth #5: Nonvoters don't vote because the policies they prefer aren't represented in contemporary politics. People are staying away from the polls because the two major parties aren't providing them with the policy choices they are interested in. Why vote, when the policies you believe in are not advocated by either the Democrats or the Republicans?

Reality #5: Voters and nonvoters differ very little in terms of their policy preferences. Looking across a wide range of issues—the economic role of government, defense, the environment, social issues like abortion—nonvoters' and voters' positions vary only modestly from one another. Specifically, nonvoters are slightly more liberal than voters on the economic role of government and slightly *less* liberal on defense, the environment and social issues. But the differences are nowhere very large and, in some cases, barely there at all.

It therefore follows that nonvoting cannot be attributed to nonvoters' thirst for alternative policy positions, since their views appear quite mainstream. It also follows that current levels of nonvoting have little immediate effect on the policies formulated by government, since the policy preferences of an augmented electorate, including all current nonvoters, would differ little from those of the current electorate. Thus, whatever the pernicious effects of low voter participation, biased public policies, at least in the short run, should not be numbered among them.

Myth #6. Republicans keep getting elected because of low turnout. Because nonvoters are drawn disproportionately from groups—the poor, those with low education, blue collar workers, minorities—that are traditional Democratic constituencies, Republican candidates must be benefiting considerably as increased nonvoting removes more and more reliable Democratic voters from the electorate.

Reality #6: The Republicans would have won anyway. Although low turnout has probably been of marginal assistance to some Republican candidates, there is little evidence that this assistance has made the difference between victory and defeat. The key for the Republicans, instead, has been the relatively high levels of support they have generated among the middle class, broadly defined. With such strong support among the bulk of the electorate, the Republicans would have won these elections anyway, regardless of how high or low the level of turnout.

The presidential elections, won, respectively, by Ronald Reagan and George Bush, provide a good example. If all the nonvoters had voted, would a Democrat be sitting in the White House today? Not according to data from the University of Michigan's National Election Studies. In both cases, the Republican candidate would still have won—except by a larger margin! Not only is it incorrect to assume that widespread nonvoting is putting Republicans in office, it is also incorrect to assume that the Republicans necessarily gain from low turnout (in certain elections, they might actually do *better* if more people showed up on election day).

Myth #7: Low black turnout has really been hurting the Democrats. Everyone knows that blacks heavily support the Democratic party. And everyone knows that blacks vote a lot less than whites. It therefore follows that low black turnout must be a critical factor in the Democrats' current problems.

Reality #7: The Democrats would have lost anyway. While levels of black *support* (generally 85 percent and over) have been important to Democratic candidates, levels of black *turnout* have not been much of a factor, positive or negative, in Democratic fortunes. Democratic losses, in particular, have almost always been attributable to weak support levels among the white middle class, rather than low black turnout.

Consider for example, the 1988 defeat of Michael Dukakis by George Bush. If black turnout and white (non-Hispanic) turnout had been the same (black turnout was about 10 percentage points lower), Dukakis would have gained about

1,442,000 votes. And if black turnout had somehow been 10 points higher than turnout among whites (that is, 20 points higher than it was in reality), the Democratic gain would have amounted to about 2,884,000 votes. But Dukakis lost the election by more than 7 *million votes*.

Nor do these results change if one focuses on state-by-state results in the Electoral College. If black turnout had been 20 points higher in every state that Bush won, only Maryland, Illinois, and Pennsylvania would have been added to the Democratic column. Thus, even under these circumstances—which represent unrealistically high levels of black mobilization—Dukakis still would have suffered a lopsided (367–171) loss in the Electoral College. Low black turnout has not been the Democrats' problem: lack of support among the rest of the electorate has been their Achilles' heel.

Myth #8: A lot of elections are decided by levels of voter turnout. One of the most common nuggets of political wisdom is the assertion, after a given election, that "so-and-so lost the election because of low levels of turnout [of group X]" or "so-and-so won the election because of high levels of turnout [of group Y]." These insights are believed to follow from observations (usually true) that the losing candidate was strongly supported by some group whose turnout was low or that the winning candidate was strongly supported by some group whose turnout was high.

Reality #8: Levels of turnout do not, as a rule, make much of a difference to election outcomes. The statement that "turnout was the key," is one of the most common observations of political pundits—and also one of the least likely to be true. The fact is that the *intensity* of support for different candidates among different groups in the electorate, especially large groups, is far more important than turnout in deciding election outcomes. Indeed, given the Republican and Democratic support levels of different groups (that is, what percentage of white middle class voters supported the Republicans? what percentage of black voters supported the Democrats?), even large increases or decreases in the turnout levels of these groups would be quite unlikely to change the outcome of a typical election.

The contest last year between David Duke and Edwin Edwards for Louisiana governor provides a vivid illustration of this principle. According to many, if not most, reports about the election, Edwards' victory could be attributed to a record high turnout among the black population (and it is true that black turnout was exceptionally high in this election). However, careful analysis of the election results reveals that, given Edwards' support levels among whites (45 percent) and blacks (96 percent), black turnout could have been as low as 16 percent and Edwards *still* would have won. In other words, he could have won the election with a record *low* black turnout, instead of a record high black turnout. This illustrates just how hard it is to change the outcome of an election by raising or lowering the level of turnout.

Myth #9: Registration reform would really help the Democrats. Registration reform would bring millions of Democratic-leaning nonvoters into the political process, proving a tremendous boon for the Democrats and a disaster for the Republicans. (The force of this myth is illustrated by the continuing partisan divisions on this issue in Congress and President Bush's veto of the most recent registration reform bill.)

Reality #9: Registration reform would have virtually no effect on the partisan leanings of the electorate. The political leanings of nonvoters and voters simply do not differ enough for the addition of even millions of nonvoters to make much of a partisan impact. In fact, analysis of survey data reveals that an electorate expanded through registration reform would probably contain only 0.2 percent more voters with Democratic sympathies—hardly enough to justify popping champagne corks down at Democratic headquarters or flying the flag at half-mast at Republican headquarters.

Myth #10: There is nothing we can do to increase voter turnout, given the current sorry state of American politics. Massive nonvoting is a natural response to contemporary American politics, a response we would be foolhardy to try to alter. If people don't want to vote, they won't vote and that's all there is to it.

Reality #10: There are quite a few things we could do to increase voter turnout, some of which are virtually certain to work. The fact of the matter is that most citizens' decisions not to vote are very lightly held and relatively easy to change. For example, simply making it *easier* to vote, by reforming the personal registration system, would probably result in increased levels of voter turnout.* Exactly how much of an increase is not certain, but the weight of the evidence is so strong that we can be virtually certain that the increase would be substantial. My estimate is an increase of about 8 percentage points, which translates into adding about 15 million voters to the electorate—a substantial expansion of citizen participation by any reasonable standard.

It may also be possible to increase turnout by improving voter motivation. It is true that many citizens currently lack even the most elementary political motivation. But we are not talking about turning America's nonvoters into "political junkies" who follow every twist and turn of the campaign. Even a very low level of campaign involvement—perhaps just reading an article or two in the newspaper—or of knowledge about the candidates and issues or of faith the government is paying attention may be enough to turn a nonvoter into a voter. The key is breaking through the extraordinary *detachment* that many citizens have developed from the political process, so that they are connected, in even a minimal way, to the world of politics.

---

* In 1993 the so-called "motor voter law" was passed by Congress mandating states to devise procedures allowing individuals to register at the time they apply for a driver's license or for public assistance or visit a military recruitment office.

There are no sure remedies here, but a lot of plausible ones. They range from campaign finance reform to regulating television campaign commercials to issues-based media coverage of campaigns. The idea is to make the campaign process easier to get involved in, more informative, and less susceptible to political manipulation. We have good reasons to believe that if this goal can be accomplished, more citizens would step forward to participate. It does not take, after all, a great deal of motivation to vote, so even small gains in levels of voter involvement and understanding could pay large dividends on election day.

One might well ask: if myth number 10 is wrong and it's so easy to get more people to vote, why is so little being done to increase voter turnout? Part of the answer lies with the nine other myths. They cast such an aura of confusion around the issue and generate so much partisan haggling that increasing citizen participation has been quite difficult. I believe it's time to jettison these myths and bring tens of millions of Americans into the political process. We have little to lose and much to gain from such a move.

Summary Questions

1. According to Teixeira, why are explanations for declining turnout based on demographic factors and the increasing cynicism of voters inadequate? What factors would he point to as better explanations for why so many voters do not take the time to vote?
2. What kinds of things could be done to improve voter turnout? If turnout were to increase, would Republicans or Democrats be advantaged by the change?

 5.2

A Lost Political Generation?

Jonathan S. Cohn

Citizens who come of political age during particular periods of history often exhibit distinct patterns of political behavior. The New Deal generation, composed of people whose first involvement in politics took place during the first two terms of

Jonathan Cohn is an assistant editor of *The American Prospect*.

the Roosevelt presidency in the 1930s, was overwhelmingly Democratic in its party preference and remained an active, core element of that party's coalition which dominated American politics for nearly half a century. The generation of young citizens who first became active in the 1960s was noteworthy for its initial idealism and commitment to democratic participation and reform found among many of its members.

The political generation composed of citizens who reached political maturity during the 1970s and 1980s appears to be distinct as well. It is politically disengaged, with lower voting turnout rates and a political cynicism that is quite high compared to previous young generations.

In this selection Jonathan Cohn examines the values and political orientations of this most recent generation, a generation of which he is a part, and attempts to pinpoint their causes. He finds, ironically, that the 1970s and 1980s generation is no less idealistic or committed to egalitarian goals than the previous generation. The generation is quite active outside the political realm and is enthusiastic about bringing about social change.

Cohn believes that the political cynicism and disengagement from electoral politics of the recent generation is due largely to its coming of political age during a period in which government was viewed as a problem, not as an avenue for solving social and economic problems and achieving progress. In Cohn's view, to engage his generation politically government "must address some broader goals that embrace our generation's relatively high ideals, and restore to this nation a sense of long term direction."

The Doofus Generation. That's what *The Washington Post* calls those of us in our twenties, who came of political age during the 1970s and 1980s. In the eyes of many observers, we are indifferent and ignorant—unworthy successors to the baby-boom generation that in the 1960s set the modern standard for political activism by the young.

To an extent, they are right. My generation has become acquainted with political realism, and cynicism, early in life. But it is a mistake to equate such cynicism with a lack of moral compassion or concern about public issues. As much as previous generations, we have ideals—strong ones, in fact. Most of us just do not expect to achieve these ideals through electoral politics, and that expectation frames our distinctive generational crisis: Although we want desperately to act according to our ideals, we lack the experiences to turn our idealism into an activist politics.

This perspective on politics transcends traditional ideological labels and is the product, largely, of our historical circumstances. Although we read about Franklin Roosevelt and John Kennedy, the New Deal and the Great Society, we came of age at a time when government neither undertook bold new initiatives nor gave definition to the nation's long-term purpose. Now, reared in an environment

devoid of effective government activism, we have come to see politics as irrelevant to achieving the ideals that matter to us. We remain generally sympathetic
to egalitarian values, but have no patience for government as an instrument
of reform.

If political life in the 1970s and 1980s elicited similar responses from other
generations, its impact on my generation was unique in one crucial respect.
Accounts of the baby boomers tell a story of disaffection, of idealistic expectations gone awry, but we never developed their illusions in the first place.* Unlike
the boomers, we never thought that government could be a positive force in
our lives.

To be sure, my own outlook reflects an upper-middle-class bias. But polling data
and conversations with dozens of young people over the last few months—from
the New Hampshire campaign trail to the New Jersey industrial belt—show these
sentiments are not limited to one end of the socio-economic spectrum. For all of
our differences, we still articulate one strikingly coherent theme: that government is increasingly remote, and that politics is no longer an avenue for achieving
progress.

The mixture of moral idealism and political cynicism that many of us feel is
inherently unstable; how long we can sustain it is difficult to tell. One thing is
certain, however: With few exceptions, we have disengaged from politics, and
that is something that should worry all Americans. Our disaffection should serve
as an imperative for more inspiring national leadership—if not for the sake of
progressive reform, then for the sake of democracy, whose very legitimacy depends on an electorate far more involved with politics than we are

Visions of Camelot

This notorious distaste for politics was not readily apparent in New Hampshire
this winter. Twenty-four years after the invasion of "Clean for Gene" McCarthy
kids, a new army of student volunteers arrived to make their own mark on the
New England landscape.† Drawing sustenance from a steady diet of corn chips,
pizza, and politics, these stubbornly energetic young people—dubbed the "foot
soldiers of democracy" by one local newspaper—dedicated themselves to the
perhaps naive notion that they could change the nation's future. And after one
chilly morning of canvassing through Manchester, a few of these activists took
great offense when confronted by the conventional assessment of our generation's
political commitment.

---

* *Baby boomers* is the term used to represent the generation of Americans born during the two
decades following World War II.

† Senator Eugene McCarthy of Minnesota was a contender for the Democratic presidential
nomination in 1968. His views on political reform and the Vietnam War were particularly popular
on college campuses, and student volunteers formed the core of his campaign organization.

"What, have you been talking to baby-boomers or something?" bristled Stephanie Miner, a twenty-one-year-old volunteer for Bob Kerrey.* Shivering over a cup of coffee—her first nourishment in nearly a day—Miner wrote off the dismissals as more hypocrisy from the hippie-turned-yuppie children of the 1960s. "Here they always talk about how they marched and protested, and now they're the same ones who are stepping over homeless people to buy Rolexes. We're better than that."

"Don't tell me my generation isn't doing anything," agreed Alison Fong. A week after arriving in Manchester, Fong, twenty-three, already showed the symptoms of campaign exhaustion—bleary eyes, a hoarse voice, and a red nose—and offered up her bedraggled condition as proof that the stereotypes are wrong. "We don't wave around huge words and slogans that, in and of themselves, don't get anything done. But we're much more realistic about what we can do. And we do it."

By their own admission, Miner and Fong are atypical. Their enthusiasm for politics (and mine, I suspect) is very much the product of the unusual affluence and education that are standard among New Hampshire volunteers. But the undercurrent of realism in their outlooks reflects the pervasive cynicism that infects most people our age. That cynicism is the basis of our unique generational perspective, and it is what links activists like Miner and Fong to Carolyn Berrios, a shopping mall employee from a working class community near Trenton, New Jersey.

Berrios, eighteen, professes an ignorance of national affairs. When prodded, however, she offers some strongly held opinions on such issues as abortion, the environment, and even the economy. So why not pay attention to the candidates and the parties? "It just doesn't seem to matter," she says. "Maybe if someone like Kennedy were around. From what my parents have told me about him, he really touched people. That would make a difference."

Kennedy, Kennedy, Kennedy. Even before Oliver Stone made his controversial film, and punctuated it with a dedication to the nation's young, the legacy of JFK loomed larger than life over our childhood and adolescence. On college campuses, posters of his likeness adorn dormitory walls (they are among the best-selling items at Harvard's student store, the Coop). On the radio, hit songs resurrect his name (the lyrics from a recent Guns'n'Roses track: "In my first memories they shoot Kennedy . . .").

Whether JFK the man was anything like JFK the myth is the topic of frequent debate. Detractors note his inability to complete a legislative program, his inconsistent foreign policy, and his extramarital affairs. Yet those shortcomings make the obsession with Kennedy all the more telling. Those of us who look to Kennedy as a hero do so because we lack any similarly inspiring figures of our own. If Kennedy has assumed a legendary status disproportionate with his achieve-

---

* Senator Bob Kerrey of Nebraska was one of the early entrants in the 1992 Democratic nomination contest. He dropped out of the race shortly after the New Hampshire primary contest.

ments, it is precisely because his successors in the White House (not coinciden-
tally, I think, his predominantly Republican successors) have so consistently
failed to arouse our passions. "Political leaders are not only failing to impart
citizenship values," observe the authors of "Democracy's Next Generation," a
1989 survey of youth opinion issued by People for the American Way, "they are
actually alienating young people from public life."

My generation woke up to politics amid the worst scandal in American history.
"Mommy, who's that?" I remember asking as I watched the gaunt figure on
television. "That's Tricky Dick," she replied.* "He's bad." And so went a simple
but pointed lesson, taught in millions of households: The President of the United
States was not a man to be respected. Our parents perhaps meant only to indict
one individual, but for a grade-school population still learning the basics of
American government, an indictment of the President was an indictment of the
entire system.

Richard Nixon's successors restored trust in the government. But they did little
else to raise our still malleable expectations about what politics could actually
accomplish. We remember Gerald Ford, if at all, as a bumbling "Saturday Night
Live" caricature. We remember Jimmy Carter as a weak leader, who wore cardigan
sweaters around the White House and let a fanatic Islamic leader hold us hostage
for more than a year. By 1980 our parents lamented how bad things had gotten,
but for us it was just more of the same.

And then there was Ronald Reagan, who told us it was morning in America.
As much as older Americans, we were fans of the Gipper. Unfortunately, the
most basic tenet of Reaganism was a distrust of government, and under Reagan we either came to disrespect government because it did not touch our lives
or respect it for the very same reason. Either way, the effect was the same, as
former Democratic presidential candidate Gary Hart told me recently: "My
generation got into public life the degree to which it did because of John
Kennedy and the inspiration about citizen obligation. The next generation was
turned off to public service . . . [Reagan] in effect told people not to become
involved in government."

Hart is right. Twenty years ago, an inspired baby boom generation came to
politics amid great expectations of their electoral potential. Patrick Caddell,
George McGovern's pollster and later Hart's top adviser, eventually suggested
generational politics as the centerpiece of Democratic strategy in the 1980s. A
platform that appealed to boomers' generational identity and longing for "new
ideas," Caddell said, could put the right candidate over the top.

Of course, those hopes were never fulfilled, as the baby boomers became
increasingly disinterested in politics. Now, lacking a catalyst (a role Hart once
was poised to fill) and with the 1960s fading into historical memory, the chances

---

* *Tricky Dick* was the nickname bestowed on Richard Nixon early in his political career by his
detractors.

Figure 5.1

Change in Presidential Voting Participation Rates by Age, 1972–1988

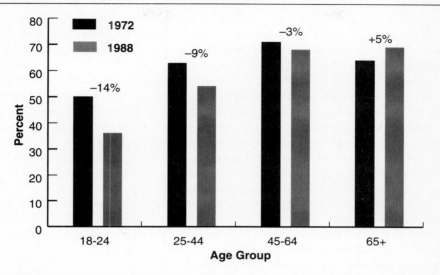

Source: U.S. Bureau of the Census.

that political leaders will ever fully capitalize on the baby boomers' distinctive yearnings seem increasingly remote.

Still, even the boomers never disengaged as dramatically as we have. According to "The Age of Indifference," a 1990 survey conducted by the Times-Mirror Center for the Press and Politics, "Today's young Americans, aged 18 to 30, know less and care less about news and public affairs than any other generation of Americans in the past 50 years." Similarly, Linda and Stephen Bennett, authors of a recent book, *Living with Leviathan*, write that "among the youngest, best-educated segments of our society, the concept of democratic citizenship is in serious decline."

Analyses like these suggest our generation's cynicism about politics is fundamentally different from the cynicism that characterizes the baby boomers, who still have what Caddell once described as a "dormant idealism"—a sense that political leadership, in the right hands, can make a difference. Politicians can appeal to the boomers' sense of civic obligation knowing that somewhere, buried beneath the thinning hair of middle age, the activist flame flickers. That seed of idealism is a crucial ingredient in political enthusiasm, and it is almost completely absent in my generation's consciousness.

When our elders grew up, government was a consistent part of their lives, launching bold initiatives or calling upon citizens for broad sacrifice. The New Deal. The mobilization for World War II. The GI Bill. The Great Society. These government initiatives reinforced the connection between citizen and state and infused young people with a sense that government could advance their lives. We never had such experiences. While the programs of the New Deal and Great Society continued to affect us—arguably, government was more active during our childhoods than ever before—we took those programs for granted, and, absent any new initiatives to grab our attention, we came to believe politics was tangential to our lives.

Other factors have contributed to our sense of distance. Kennedy successfully connected with youth in part because he, too, was young. Since his day, however, the White House has aged along with the country. Every president since Eisenhower was born in the same sixteen-year period from 1908 to 1924, and that has widened the perceived gap between the presidency and the young electorate. "Fresh ideas can come from tired old politicians," says Peter Cleary, a young staffer at the Environmental Defense Fund. "But they don't have the same fresh appeal that will make a difference with young people."

Identifying with government has been even more difficult for women and members of minority groups. Reared in a climate of increasing multiculturalism (particularly on college campuses), they are now heirs to a political establishment inconsistent—particularly at its highest level, the presidency—with their expectations of diversity. As a result, activists like Rusty Terry—a black volunteer for the Tom Harkin* campaign—are very much the exception in places like New Hampshire. "Within the Black Students Union, they don't get involved with politics," says Terry of his classmates at the University of Rochester. "They say it's not for them, so why should they even get involved in the first place?"

In the end, though, this is all part of the same phenomenon: Government for my generation has become a distant, insignificant entity. We are thankful if it is merely free of corruption and expect it to produce little progress that will affect us. That sentiment may belie the extent to which government does improve our lives, but it is the only logical conclusion most of us can draw from our experience.

Liberal Ambivalence

Paul Tsongas is an unlikely generational hero.† Relatively uncharismatic, he relies on a puritanical, "take your medicine" tone to woo voters—hardly a formula for capturing the imaginations of young people. But Tsongas has enjoyed widespread support among youth throughout the campaign. His "Economic Call to Arms" struck a chord with intellectually minded college students early on, and since

---

* Senator Tom Harkin of Iowa was also an early entrant in the 1992 Democratic nomination contest. Like Kerrey, he dropped out early in the race.

† Ex-Senator Paul Tsongas of Massachusetts was probably Bill Clinton's major challenger for the Democratic nomination in 1992. He also dropped out of the race before the nominating convention began.

then his no-frills campaign style has played perfectly to my generation's deep-seated cynicism about slick politicians.

At a New York fund raiser in February, that support was evident. New Hampshire's momentum had brought Tsongas to Astoria, Queens, which boasts one of the largest Greek populations outside Athens. But conspicuous among the boisterous ethnic crowd was a regiment of Tsongas student volunteers—mostly white, pre-professional types from Columbia or New York University. Bitter weather and rush-hour congestion had made the half-hour commute from Manhattan all the more difficult, but the Tsongas message and peculiar brand of charm had the students far too mesmerized to complain.

"I chose this party because it was my parents' party, but I have yet to see a candidate who was forward thinking and was honest about what needed to get done," bubbled Joanie Patterson, a twenty-three-year-old student at Columbia. "Tsongas isn't afraid to tell the truth, and, for the first time, I can vote and enthusiastically support a candidate who has something to say and something to do that will actually make a difference in the country."

Patterson's qualified liberalism is typical of our generation. Although we led the nation in our support for Reagan, we harbor no great love for the Republican Party. In fact, we overwhelmingly reject the social agenda of Republicanism and are comfortable voting for Democrats (indeed, for anyone) who offer us hope of improvement or mere competence. But our disengagement from politics—our refusal to see politics as the path for achieving our ideals—makes us hesitant to embrace platforms of wide-ranging progressive reform. Thus, like Patterson, most of us find more appeal in a Paul Tsongas—as opposed to a Mario Cuomo, a Jerry Brown, or even a Bill Clinton—because his agenda embraces our social attitudes but stops short of affirming government as a positive force.

Most everybody concedes that young America's love affair with Ronald Reagan during the 1980s had more to do with the man and his leadership style than with his conservative social agenda. "I fell in love with Ronald Reagan in the fifth grade," confesses Steve Satran, executive director of College Republicans of America. "He made quite an impression. I just liked the things he said about America and the future." And so did the rest of us. Says CNN's Guy Molyneux, formerly a leading activist with Democratic Socialists of America, "Those party attachments [of the 1980s] were more performance-based than ideology-based. That makes it a lot more fragile."

Well, not totally fragile. Conservatives note correctly that young voters have bought into one prominent area of Republican social ideology: law-and-order issues. We have much less patience for the rights of criminals than our elders did, and give unprecedented support to the death penalty. Also, we oppose legalization of marijuana and profess more concern about drug abuse than did people our age a decade ago.

But the conservative views of law and order are the exception. Strip away our fear of crime and what remains is a generation as liberal as any before it, if not more so, at least on issues not specifically linked to money. According to the

Figure 5.2
Changing Attitudes Among College Freshmen

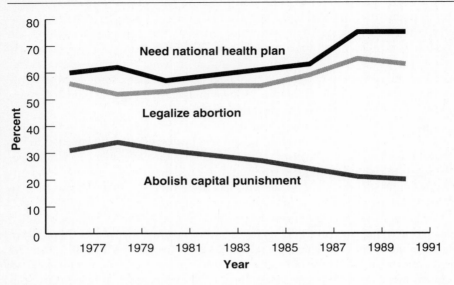

Source: UCLA/American Council on Education National Survey

UCLA/American Council on Education national survey of college freshmen, first conducted in 1966, student support for abortion rights hit 64 percent four years ago and has remained stable ever since. Today, 76 percent of freshmen think health care should be a right—the highest ever—while only 42 percent think government should pass laws banning gay relationships—the lowest ever (although an alarmingly high figure, nonetheless).

Such liberal social attitudes should come as no surprise. Folk wisdom has long held that young adults, still in the throes of post-adolescent rebellion, are the most predisposed toward challenging the status quo. And while this purported receptivity to change is occasionally disputed, there is another, even more plausible explanation for our progressive ideals: We are the product of the most explicitly open-minded culture in American history.

Many of us attended integrated schools, and thus knew only an environment officially, if not actually, intolerant of blatant discrimination. During our lifetimes, Heathcliff Huxtable of "The Crosby Show" replaced Howard Cunningham of "Happy Days" as our national surrogate father, while Magic Johnson and Michael Jordan succeeded Joe Namath and Pete Rose as our national sports heroes. Most of us received from our parents and culture a clear message about social values—a commitment to egalitarianism and tolerance unprecedented in the nation's history. That message may not have meshed with reality, and may have reached some of us more powerfully than others, but it left nearly all of us with something to which we could pin a strong liberal social identity.

But Americans vote with their pocketbooks, too, and it is on the fiscal front my generation's striking conservatism emerges. Although we endorse the philosophy behind the social safety net, we remain skeptical about welfare programs and other specific initiatives. We profess egalitarian attitudes but are unwilling to spend taxpayer money to realize such goals.

One possible explanation for our fiscal attitudes is the difficult economic circumstances that confront us. As young people entering the work force, buying our first cars and maybe even homes, we are particularly vulnerable to the middle-class squeeze. With wages shrinking and job opportunities lacking (thanks to the dwindling industrial sector and the boomers occupying all the good mid-level positions), we have always looked to the financial horizon nervously. Now the recession has realized our worst fears and, so it would seem, made us all the more stingy. According to the ACE/UCLA survey, young people increasingly cite financial well-being as a goal in life (from 44 percent in 1966 to 78 percent in 1992), and show less support for welfare state programs. As Lorraine Voles, press secretary for the Harkin campaign, says, "You'd be surprised at just how conservative young people can be."

But how so? Our fiscal conservatism clearly does not represent a rejection of social or even economic egalitarianism. According to the Bennetts, "measures tapping egalitarian opinions show the young to be more in favor of expanding equality than older cohorts." Citing national election surveys by the University of Michigan's Center for Political Studies, they found that my generation expressed "the most egalitarian opinions" of any. While such a discrepancy between philosophical and actual support for social welfare programs is not unusual, it is telling. It suggests that our low opinion of government—not some crude economic selfishness or a lack of class consciousness—is the major reason we are so skeptical of the social safety net and other government spending programs.

This, of course, is still Republican political territory, and that points to the real problem my generation poses for liberals. Even though our sympathies lie with the liberal causes traditionally championed by the Democratic Party, our refusal to believe in government is positively Reaganesque. Political liberalism requires not only a desire but a willingness to act. By straddling the ideological divide over fiscal and social attitudes, we demonstrate no such willingness. The fact that our attitude reflects a skepticism about government efficacy and not a true sympathy for the status quo is of little relevance once we get to the voting booth.

We are not alone in this disposition. As recent elections have shown, the "centrist" message of social liberalism and fiscal conservatism has broad appeal, particularly among disillusioned baby-boomers. But that, alas, is to be expected. Generations are supposed to get more fiscally conservative as they grow older. My generation has no such excuse. Our acceptance of that outlook while still so young does not bode well for the progressive causes.

The prospects for liberal reform in America, then, rest on one hope: that our egalitarian sensibilities run deeper than our cynicism about politics, and that our sense of social justice makes us uncomfortable bridging this ideological divide. If that is the case, our current disposition may be more unstable than anybody realizes.

Music Video Politics

Two Sundays before the New Hampshire primary, television's talk-show circuit was abuzz with the usual campaign gossip. On ABC, the venerable David Brinkley pressed Bob Kerrey on whether he could win an election on national health care alone. Over at the McLaughlin Group, the feisty Fred Barnes clung to his prediction that Mario Cuomo would enter the race. And on MTV, the trendy Tabitha Soren reported that a well-crafted appeal on education and the environment could swing New Hampshire's youth vote.

Welcome to politics, music video style. Over the last year, MTV—much maligned as the bane of contemporary youth existence—has attempted to resurrect the marriage of pop culture and politics consummated in the 1960s. Sporting, brightly colored attire (Soren seems partial to loud green and orange), the MTV News crews are a conspicuous if irregular presence on the campaign trail, and have managed to produce a considerable body of coverage.

Granted, Soren is no Walter Cronkite. Discussion of economic stimuli and trade policy juxtapose uncomfortably with dizzying cutaways and thumping rhythm tracks. The broadcasts don't exactly challenge the intellect, and person-on-the-street quotes like "I think Dan Quayle is hot" serve primarily to reinforce the most negative stereotypes of our generation.

Yet MTV's broadcasts are refreshingly upstart. Overcommercialized cable networks may be no substitute for underground newspapers, but MTV does reach a lot of us. The mere fact that this profit-minded enterprise would even contemplate a political agenda at all suggests that an audience exists. It suggests that we, too, are uncomfortable with our professed indifference to politics, and that we cannot forever stay disengaged from politics when we want so badly to make a difference.

Our continued activism outside of electoral politics substantiates this prognosis. According to the national survey of freshmen, the probability that we participated in national, state, or local political campaigns during the last year has fallen by nearly half over the last two decades—from 16.5 percent in 1969 to 8.7 percent in 1988. Yet, while this may surprise baby-boomer activists, we are more than twice as likely as they were to have participated in organized demonstrations. In 1966 only 15.5 percent of the survey's respondents reported having participated in a protest during the previous year; by 1990, that proportion had jumped to 39.4 percent. (Oddly, the organized demonstration question was not asked during the late 1960s, when the anti-war movement was at its peak.)

Perhaps the most telling statistic of all is the observation that "students are becoming increasingly interested in bringing about social change." Although interest in electoral politics continues to fall, the percentage who say they want to influence social values has increased from about 35 percent in 1968 to roughly 43 percent in 1991.

In Washington, grass-roots activists tell a similarly confounding story. Ask us to campaign for an elected official or a new bill in Congress, and we respond with what Molyneux terms "a kind of militant apathy." But ask us to work on something in our home or community, and our attitudes change dramatically. Says Cleary of his experience at the Environmental Defense Fund: "Young people, especially, have latched onto the environment as an issue because it's something they feel capable of affecting themselves, in their day-to-day lives."

The same goes for campaigns that channel deep-seated feelings about so-called moral issues into small communities where young people know their voices will be heard. Contemporary college campuses may not witness the Vietnam-inspired revolts that marked the 1960s, but they still see vocal activism on everything ranging from acquaintance rape to faculty diversity. Last fall, Ms. Magazine chronicled the rise of "New Campus Radicals," feminist students committed to changing the social environments at their schools. The article sensed "change is in the air"—a prediction since realized in the politics on acquaintance rape adopted on many campuses.

We profess indifference but hear the call of our socially idealistic upbringing. Activism still captures our imagination. "The problem," says Mary Beth Maxwell, organizing director for the United States Student Association, "is people are not seeing a connection between the ballot box and the issues they care about." Given the extent to which my generation remains interested in issues, this is likely a temporary situation. And if leaders can somehow reestablish the connection between issues and voting, we might well embrace—indeed, insist upon—an activist government committed to our own progressive agenda.

The New Generational Politics

. . . The recession has, for the moment, staved off our civic decline. Like all Americans, we have looked to the government for economic recovery. As a result, people who might not otherwise have given politics a chance—people like Jim Finn, a twenty-five-year-old volunteer with the Kerrey campaign—have waded into the political waters. "I saw that politics in general needed to make a difference. That's why we're all here." "The people here are true believers," adds Bill Crowley, a twenty-three-year-old staffer for Tsongas. "They know they're making a difference. They'd kill or die for the cause."

But crisis-driven civic virtue is not enough, for when the crisis evaporates—as it will eventually—so will the enthusiasm. To save the political spirit of young America, government must do more than cure the current recession. Even as it

acknowledges our low expectations of government activism—an acknowl-
edgment upon which my cynical generation will insist—it must address some
broader goals that embrace our generation's relatively high ideals, and restore to
this nation a sense of long-term direction. Only by doing that can government
capture our attention and enthusiasm.

And only from the left can such initiative come. For all of our conservative
attitudes toward the role of government in society, we have a profoundly different
notion than conservatives do about what our society should look like. Even as we
say we are content to solve public problems without engaging in politics, we long
for the very public solutions—equal economic opportunity, a clean environment—that only politics can achieve.

We want desperately to act, to make a difference in the world during our
lifetimes. A liberal political agenda not only relevant to our daily lives but also
committed to our high ideals would capitalize on this instinct. When government
seems to us both capable of and willing to embrace those goals, we will reengage
with the political world.

Summary Questions

1. What explanations may be offered to explain the paradox of the most recent
   generation's social idealism and egalitarianism on one hand, and its disengagement from politics on the other? What, in the author's view, would it take for
   the paradox to be resolved?
2. The author of this selection believes that only from the political left
   can "government capture our attention and enthusiasm." Do you agree?
   What arguments might political conservatives make to challenge the
   author's assertion?

▦ 5.3

The Power of One

Patricia Theiler

Although electoral participation has undergone serious decline since the early 1960s, citizen involvement in other forms of political influence appears to have increased. The expansion of the group universe (see selection 9.2), especially in the late 1960s and 1970s, has provided numerous opportunities for citizens to influence politics at all governmental levels. Many participants in the expanded group activity have been first-time activists, some involved in protest or movement activity, ranging from farmers who rode their tractors to Washington to protest low commodity prices to pro-choice and pro-life advocates concerned about the nation's abortion policy.

Not all attempts to influence government decision makers take place through the group process, however. In this selection, Patricia Theiler describes the activities of a number of highly-motivated, persistent individuals—"single-issue crusaders"—who have attempted to affect public policy deliberations in Washington. She finds that such involvement is often sparked by a common catalyst—a "personal brush with a senseless death or a blatant injustice" that gives these citizen advocates "a kind of credibility" that can help them compete with sophisticated, well-funded professional lobbyists.

The papers are spread all over the kitchen table—transcripts of congressional hearings, countless letters and piles of accident reports marked with paper clips. The documents include a complaint about the Federal Railroad Administration lodged on the congressional General Accounting Office (GAO) hotline: "I indict the FRA for abuse of the public trust for their refusal to take action when presented with proof of improper accident reporting."

Wayne Bates, soft-spoken author of the complaint and outspoken critic of the FRA, thumbs through the documents. "I'm doing this for my country, for locomotive engineers and for my brother—not necessarily in that order," he says. A former electronic communications specialist for the U.S. Army, Bates, 68, has spent the last 12 years crusading for increased regulation of the railroads, citing

---

Patricia Theiler is a Washington writer and former managing editor of *Common Cause Magazine*. This article was written in 1990.

evidence gleaned from his review of 500 accident reports from across the country. He has been called the "Ralph Nader of the Railways."

Bates's obsession with railroad safety began as concern over the FRA's handling of a 1978 accident involving his brother, J. R. Bates, who worked for the Southern Pacific. Bates was the engineer of a train that was heading from San Antonio, Texas, to Houston and collided with the caboose of another train on a side track. Bates's train derailed, causing injuries to his head, elbow and knee and more than $162,000 in damage.

As Wayne Bates tells it, the accident probably occurred because of a faulty green light—possibly caused by a sudden storm knocking out a signal. But the railroad blamed J. R. for the accident and fired him. The FRA backed up the railroad's finding.

After J. R. filed a grievance, a mediation board called on the railroad to reinstate him. In a separate trial, a jury awarded him $74,800 for his injuries. But, following heart bypass surgery in 1979, he was demoted, over his own and his doctor's objections, for "health reasons."

Wayne Bates says the FRA has never fully exonerated his brother and he wants his "good name cleared—clean as a whistle."

In Bates's quest to clear his brother's name, he says he has found a pattern of flawed investigations by the FRA and unsafe practices by railroad companies that endanger railroad workers and the public.

Bates's opponents are more likely to characterize him as a Don Quixote tilting at windmills than a David packing a slingshot. But single-issue crusaders like Bates shouldn't be dismissed as dreamers. At a time when almost all conceivable interest groups—from the makers of chocolate to the consumers of packaged food—deploy sophisticated platoons of lobbyists, these lone warriors still play a vital role in the political process.

A personal brush with a senseless death or blatant injustice gives these citizen advocates a kind of credibility that can help them best an army of hired guns. And unlike many in the billable-hours world of professional lobbying, these self-styled citizen activists have plenty of time.

Motivated by belief in the justness of their cause, they may be willing to devote years, even decades, to exert pressure for change. They may sacrifice privacy, leisure time and family life to achieve results not for themselves but for the nameless others they believe at risk. Opponents may criticize their tactics and zeal, but it's hard not to admire their particular brand of persistence and courage.

Please Hold

Wayne Bates's interest in railroad safety grew exponentially as he looked into his brother's 1978 accident, then at accidents in San Antonio, Texas, and finally nationwide. "As I study the situation, I get more enthused," Bates explains.

A high-school-educated, self-described "country boy," Bates has mastered the art of filing Freedom of Information Act requests and reading between the lines of accident reports. He uses his findings to pound the FRA not only on his brother's behalf but on larger safety issues, such as railcars that are overloaded or improperly carrying hazardous materials.

During the last Congress, Bates's documentation helped advance legislation to tighten weight distribution standards on railcars. The bill ultimately died but is expected to resurface.

Bates's activities have made him a familiar figure at the FRA. With a note of weariness, Mark Lindsey, chief counsel for the FRA, says Bates is "well known throughout the agency for making his views known," but hasn't brought "any major matters or great discoveries" to the FRA's attention that he is aware of. Lindsey defends the agency, which is small and has limited resources, as "responsible over the years."

Refuting this view of Bates is Lawrence Mann, a lawyer with the Railway Labor Executives Association, an umbrella organization for railroad unions and a Bates ally. Mann dubs Bates the "guru" of railroad safety and says he "has been a great assistance in uncovering [safety] issues." Mann says Bates is a "a real thorn in the FRA because he's been so tenacious in holding them to the fire. He's been very effective—that's why they don't like him."

To say he's a thorn may be an understatement. The FRA's Lindsey says Bates's persistent barrage of letters and calls borders on harassment. "One day he tied up the telephone in the administrator's suite all day," Lindsey complains, adding that the FRA has "taken all the action we intend to take [on the J. R. Bates case]" and the matter should be dropped.

Bates claims he's merely doing what he has to do to get a response from slow-moving bureaucrats. If after 60 days he hasn't received an answer, from, say, J.W. Walsh, FRA associate administrator for safety, he starts calling his office. He may call three times a day until he speaks directly to Walsh. "If I don't get him, I call back," Bates says.

Bates's notoriety extends to the inspector general's office at the Department of Transportation, with which he has also frequently corresponded. This past May, Bates supplemented his usual phone calls and letters with a surprise visit. While waiting in the Transportation Department lobby, Bates noticed a number of people curiously poking their heads out of nearby doorways; staffers were trying to get a firsthand look at the man whose voice on the phone had become so familiar over the years. Finally, one official, perhaps emboldened by some vague sense of kinship, approached. "Are you Mr. Bates?" he asked. "I remember you from the 1981 Vulnerability-of-Assessment-by-the-FRA study."

When Bates isn't on the heels of the FRA, he pursues two other hobbies that reflect his obsession with detail and sleuthing—genealogy (he's editor of a newsletter devoted to descendants of John Bates, who settled in York County, Va., in 1624) and ship reunions, an interest that developed after he and a fellow crew member spent three years tracking down all 400 shipmates of the destroyer they served on during World War II. "I got obsessed with the thing," Bates says characteristically.

It doesn't take long to get a sense of Bates's doggedness. During a single three-week period, he sent this reporter copies of more than a dozen letters from himself or the government, including ones he wrote on July 2, 9, 13, 23, 24 and 26.

"I'm interested in truth," he explains. "I'm interested in facts and figures, and I take pride in proving my facts."

Learning the Ropes

The underfunded political weakling known as the Consumer Product Safety Commission (CPSC) is often the target of concerned parents, irate consumers, and health and safety professionals pushing for crackdowns on everything from hazardous stepladders to defective lawn mowers. A burn unit nurse recently drew attention to the dangers of children playing with cigarette lighters; a medical examiner identified an appalling pattern of infants accidentally drowning in five-gallon buckets; and an accident victim's father won a campaign to ban an outdoor game called lawn darts.

Then there's Bonnie Sumner, of Milwaukee, Wis., whose cause is the all-terrain vehicle (ATV).

Sumner became a critic of ATVs—three- or four-wheel recreational vehicles equipped with oversized tires—after her 14-year-old son Noah suffered severe head, spleen, rib and facial injuries in a 1984 accident. "I literally didn't know what the thing was," says Sumner, whose son was hurt driving a friend's three-wheel ATV. Noah recovered, but following the accident, Sumner started tracking state and federal laws governing ATV sales and use. In the process, she discovered that her son's wasn't a freak accident but part of a pattern of serious injuries, particularly among children.

Sumner criticizes the continued lack of state and federal regulation of ATVs, which have been responsible for more than 1,400 deaths and thousands of accidents since 1982. According to ATV critics, the machines are especially dangerous because their high center of gravity makes it easy for operators to lose control or roll over.

Sumner plunged into lobbying at the national level when she was asked to testify at a 1985 congressional hearing. Back then, she had some trepidation, wondering, "Where do you sit? Who tells you what to do?" Now, after three appearances before congressional subcommittees, she's no longer nervous or unknown because, Sumner says, "I'm a pest." The label doesn't seem to bother her. It means "they're listening," she says.

In 1988, partly in response to pressure from consumer groups, health practitioners and others, ATV makers signed a complex agreement with the CPSC. The industry agreed to stop selling three-wheel ATVs and to prevent dealers from selling adult-sized four-wheel ATVs to children. But consumer groups challenged the agreement as weak and ineffective, claiming the industry was already phasing out three-wheelers. They also were critical because ATV dealers weren't legally bound by the agreement.

Subsequent studies have found that dealers are still encouraging adults to buy the larger models for their children. A 1989 survey conducted by the U.S. Public Interest Research Group (PIRG) found less than half of ATV dealers told potential customers the four-wheel vehicles were inappropriate for children.

Sumner supports not only a ban of three-wheelers but a government recall of ones previously sold. She also urges licensing and training requirements for users. Sen. Joseph Lieberman (D-Conn.), a member of the Senate Governmental Affairs Committee, expressed support for the ban, recall and other measures during hearings in late July.

Sumner says her family has a long history of political involvement and activism on behalf of other people. "That's the way I was brought up," she says. She has "carried on a one-person crusade" in the last two Wisconsin state legislative sessions to win support for a bill that would ban ATV use for children, prohibit passengers, and require helmets for operators.

It's clear that she brings a lot of energy to any task before her. Phone calls with this work-at-home mother-of-four are constantly interrupted by asides to her children, knocks at the door and clicks of her call-waiting signal ("that may be the CPSC"). While Sumner doesn't seem prone to excessive self-study, she says she's thought long and hard about her reaction to her son's accident and discovered that she "likes to be in control," especially when it comes to her children. Her crusade has allowed her to channel her anger toward a constructive goal.

James Baxter, executive director of the Wisconsin All Terrain Vehicle Association, says Sumner is "representative of parents of children who have been hurt and have a tremendous guilt complex because of it."

Wisconsin state Sen. Charles Chvala, sponsor of the ATV safety bill, says that Sumner's personal experience actually adds force to her arguments. He views her as "more rational than many people on the other side of the issue," who typically argue for personal freedom over the lives of children.

The emotional strain on Sumner, nevertheless, is high—whether it comes from painfully "having to retell and relive" her son's trauma or from having the memory rekindled when she hears of another accident. Because her advocacy work sometimes involves travel—she attended the PTA national convention in Indianapolis in July to successfully push for a resolution on ATVs—Sumner and her family pay a financial price as well.

Despite the costs, Sumner says, "I can't *not* do this. This isn't a job I'm going to quit." She now views her work as a calling, saying her commitment and personal experience uniquely qualify her to champion the cause. "No one else is doing this. If I don't do this, it won't get done," she says.

Lucinda Sikes, staff attorney with U.S. PIRG, says Sumner is an effective and articulate advocate and has more credibility than the average lobbyist. U.S. PIRG and the Consumer Federation of America have filed a petition asking the CPSC to ban ATVs for children and establish a mandatory safety standard for ATV stability.

Sumner is meanwhile buoyed by the small successes along the way. When one of her son's classmates volunteered that he and his parents decided not to buy an ATV after they heard her on local television, "that made my day," Sumner says. "I always think, if someone sees me and makes the decision not to buy [an ATV], I'm making headway."

Mac Attack

Most citizen advocates operate in relative obscurity. Not Phil Sokolof, the multimillionaire founder and CEO of Phillips Manufacturing Corp., which produces metal fittings. In 1985 Sokolof, who had suffered a near-fatal heart attack 20 years earlier at age 43, founded the National Heart Savers Association (NHSA) with $1 million of his own money. Since then, cholesterol and the foods that cause it to clog the arteries of Americans have been Sokolof's obsessions. ("I've been a workaholic all my life," Sokolof offers by way of explanation.)

In late 1988 his one-man association began a nationwide "Poisoning of America" campaign, targeting by name food companies that made their products with tropical oils, an ingredient high in saturated fat. The ads carried pictures of the offending products, including Pepperidge Farm Goldfish and Keebler's club crackers. Following the ads, a number of companies announced they would no longer use tropical oils.

Most of his targets say they were already converting their oils when the ads hit. Pepperidge Farm was reformulating its products eight to 10 months before the campaign, says spokesperson Tim Ouellette, and switched "in response to consumer demand," not pressure from negative advertising. But some industry experts give Sokolof credit for raising consciousness. "He has had a tremendous impact on the industry," Joe Simrany, vice president of marketing at Sunshine Biscuits (makers of Hydrox cookies), told *Food Business* last year. "He's really stuck by his convictions. If he's to be criticized at all, it's for some of his tactics."

The silver-haired, pinstripe-suited Sokolof, who got his own cholesterol down to a healthy 150 compared to his pre-heart attack 300 level, obviously relishes the role of "America's No. 1 cholesterol fighter," an epithet used liberally in his press releases.

Because Sokolof has hitched his wagon to one of the trendiest issues of our time, he's generated more coverage of affairs of the heart than Donald Trump. Every phone call is another opportunity for him to gather converts. "Concentrate on pointing out the potential risk of cholesterol," he advised *Common Cause Magazine* at the end of a long conversation.

In April, Sokolof launched the "Poisoning of America, Part III" with plans for $500,000 worth of full-page ads in the *New York Times, USA Today* and other major newspapers. But the campaign hit a roadblock in the form of an American icon—the golden arches. Five major newspapers, including the *Los Angeles Times* and the *Chicago Sun-Times,* refused to run the ads, which charged that Big Macs had "too much fat" and criticized McDonald's for not cooking its French fries in vegetable oil. *Los Angeles Times* spokesperson Terri Niccum says the decision not to run the $30,000 ad was based on "legal" considerations (including the ad's use of the trademark golden arches) and "reasons of good taste." Niccum adds, "There were statements we believed were not true."

McDonald's spokesperson Melissa Oakley says there were a number of inaccuracies, including an incorrect calculation of the saturated fat in a burger and fries. A press release from McDonald's called the ad "reckless, misleading and intended to scare rather than inform. . . ."

"Was McDonald's mad about the ad?" the release asked. "Mad as hell."

Despite the Mac attack, on July 4 Sokolof struck again. In full-page ads in several national newspapers, NHSA charged: "McDonald's, your hamburgers still have too much fat and your French fries still are cooked with beef tallow." The ads also criticized Wendy's and Burger King.

Three weeks later the three chains announced that their French fries would be fried in "cholesterol-free" vegetable oil. Any connection to Sokolof's media blitz? "The timing was coincidental," says a Burger King spokesperson. The switch was "in response to our customers' changing taste and lifestyle," adds McDonald's. "Our customers told us to," echoes Wendy's. Only Hardee's, which the July ad called "the industry leader" for already introducing a leaner hamburger and reformulating its fries, begs to differ. "Obviously he had some influence," observes a Hardee's spokesperson, who hastens to point out Hardee's switched two years ago, long "before Sokolof became the guru of saturated fat."

Sokolof isn't saying his ads were the sole motivation—he is quick to credit the fat-fighting efforts of the well-respected Center for Science in the Public Interest and others. But the ads "triggered the response of the public" in pushing for healthier fast foods, he says.

In contrast to the handwritten yellow "stickem" notes from Bonnie Sumner, Sokolof has a professional media kit, complete with a glossy black and white photo of himself, a "Poisoning of America" poster, several color reprints of articles in major newspapers and slick brochures on cholesterol.

Still, Sokolof claims he's "a little guy" when compared to the corporate giants he's battling. Referring to international press attention, he says, "Here I am in my office in Omaha, Neb., talking, literally, to the world. It shows one person can make a difference."

Despite Sokolof's maverick style, he's an old-fashioned philanthropist at heart. "I've been on two journeys," he told *Advertising Age* magazine. "On the first journey, I made a lot of money. On the second one, I realized that using that money on a good cause is better than making it."

The Never-ending Story

Most advocates operate out of spare bedrooms and basement studies on streets with names like Rocky Run and Lake Drive. News clippings and letters are stuffed in cardboard boxes or piled on desks in family rooms. Mitch Kurman of

Westport, Conn., says you'd need a "U-Haul truck" to move all the information he has collected.

For the past 25 years, Kurman, a retired wholesale furniture salesman, has battled the summer camp industry. In 1965 Kurman's 15-year-old son David died in a boating accident at a YMCA camp in New York. Kurman sued the YMCA and settled for $30,000. But Kurman's campaign didn't stop in court. When he discovered what he considered an appalling lack of state or federal standards for summer camps—among them no life preserver requirements for boats and no training requirements for camp counselors—he made camp safety his lifelong quest.

An estimated four to six million children attend summer camp. Regulation of the industry is largely left to the states, and only about 17 have licensing requirements, health and safety inspections or other standards.

"While there are excellent, wonderful camps," Kurman says, "there is also a very, very substantial number of downright dangerous camps," which don't protect kids against injuries from boating, riflery or other sports.

Kurman has been a crusader for so long that conversations with him are dotted with references to politicians of the past as well as names, middle initials and spellings of dozens of officials and parents he's encountered. He was initially able to build up his archives because of his work as a traveling salesman. Clients would pass on stories of accidents, and Kurman would make a detour to investigate.

In his stream of consciousness style, Kurman catalogs the dates, locations and details of tragic summer camp accidents—from drownings to sexual abuse—that he believes build the case for increased federal involvement in the industry. "This could happen to anybody," he says of his tragedy.

In 1971 Kurman helped win passage of a federal boat safety law, requiring manufacturers to post passenger capacity and safety features on boats. He also helped win passage of state laws in New York, New Hampshire and Connecticut requiring life preservers in camp boats. But Kurman and his wife Betty, whom he has enlisted as an aide-de-camp, have failed to catch the brass ring—establishment and enforcement of federal health and safety standards.

Kurman estimates he's spent $75,000 gathering information and visiting lawmakers. One letter from him included the practical request that the numerous articles, congressional statements and xeroxed letters be returned. In the same seven-page, handwritten missive Kurman admitted to being tired after having worked all night compiling a similar clipping file for a reporter doing a story for a small-town weekly. Despite the limited circulation, Kurman noted, his efforts "invariably have a snowball effect to bring me still more materials to prove the pattern of neglect that must be corrected."

"It's like a bone in your throat," says Betty Kurman. "He can't stop, and I can't either, until we accomplish what we want." While Mrs. Kurman concedes they have made sacrifices, their commitment also has built character. "I was amazed at the qualities that developed [in my husband]," she says.

Kurman had his 15 minutes of fame in the mid-1970s. He was profiled in the *New York Times*, put on page one of the *Wall Street Journal* and appeared on "Good Morning, America." Today he sets his sights closer to home, specifically the *Fairfield County Advocate* near Westport, Conn. Editor Jim Motavalli remembers reading about Kurman when he was growing up in the area. Now, says Motavalli, who recently wrote an article on Kurman, he "practically *lives* here." Despite Kurman's penchant for cornering busy editors, Motavalli firmly believes Kurman's "cause is just."

Justified or not, it's an uphill battle.

As a 1989 GAO report notes, "Little information is available on accidents, illnesses and fatalities that occur in youth camps." Because the government doesn't require summer camps to file federal accident reports, Kurman says he's filling an important need by keeping files on "hundreds of cases."

Rep. Joseph Gaydos (D-Pa.), chairman of the House subcommittee with jurisdiction over the camping industry, says Kurman has done "yeoman's work on the issue" and "contributed valuable information." Nevertheless, Gaydos says the subcommittee concluded recently that the issue is "more of a state problem than a national" one and has no immediate plans to take action.

Kurman isn't likely to let one more politician deter him from the cause he's been fighting since he first persuaded former Sen. Abe Ribicoff (D-Conn.) to take it up in the '60s. "I would love to get this over with," Kurman says wistfully of his crusade, "I'd love to go back to my gardening, to my family. . . ." But Betty Kurman confirms it's unlikely the couple will let up any time soon.

A telling example of the grudging respect such dedication can stir even from adversaries comes from John Miller, executive vice president of the American Camping Association. Miller says that though Mitch Kurman is "misguided," he "has a very legitimate, heart-felt involvement in this issue."

"It's been Mr. Kurman, honestly, that keeps bringing this up at the federal level," inspiring repeated congressional hearings, GAO reports and newspaper editorials, says Miller.

Come now, Mr. Miller, can one person exert that much influence?

"When you're as single-focused and as committed as Mr. Kurman is . . . ," says Mr. Miller, "yes."

Summary Questions

1. What common experiences and resources characterize the "single-issue crusaders" whom the author describes? What motivations do the activists appear to share?

2. Why does the author believe the political activists she describes have an impact on the policymaking process far greater than their numbers? What negative consequences of their activism can you think of?

# Chapter 6

POLITICAL PARTIES

The word *party* is not mentioned in the United States Constitution. The nation's founders, suspicious of special interests, viewed parties as devices to organize factions—"to put in the place of the delegated will of the nation the will of party," as George Washington put it. Yet within a generation of the nation's founding, parties had emerged as instruments for structuring political conflict and encouraging mass participation.

In retrospect, the development of political parties seems almost inevitable. The United States has always harbored a diverse political culture, and the practical necessity of governing demands that majorities be forged among contending interests. Political parties evolved as the only solution to the problem of reconciling individual diversity with majority rule.

The American political party functions as an intermediary between the public and the government. A party can combine citizens' demands into a manageable number of issues, thus enabling the system to focus on society's most crucial problems. The party performs its mediating function primarily through coalition building—in the words of journalist David Broder, "the process of constructing majorities from the broad sentiments and interests that can be found to bridge the narrower needs and hopes of separate individuals and communities."

For example, Franklin Roosevelt's New Deal, forged in the 1930s in the face of deep economic depression, brought about a Democratic coalition that essentially dominated national policymaking for thirty years. Generally speaking, socioeconomic divisions shaped politics in the 1930s. Less affluent citizens tended to support the Roosevelt administration's provisions for social and economic security and government regulation of private enterprise. Those who were better off usually took the opposite position. By and large, the New Deal coalition came to represent northern urban workers, immigrants and ethnic minorities, blacks, Catholics, Jews, and many southerners.

Such coalition building has contributed greatly to the stability of American political life, but the parties also serve as the major vehicle for political change. Political coalitions are never permanent. Old issues are dealt with or decrease in importance, while new issues move onto the agenda. New voters enter the electorate, older ones die, and the economic and social circumstances of groups and regions change.

Confronted with a new political environment, parties may realign—rearrange the bases of their coalitions to reflect new issues and public concerns. Critical realignments usually occur in the midst of an economic crisis such as a depression. Such an event causes sharp and durable changes in voter perceptions and identities because of the parties' differing positions on how to handle the situation. Scholars have concluded that party realignment has taken place a number of times since the early 1800s as the party system has adjusted to the changing issues in politics.

There is a general consensus among political observers that the American party system today is again in the midst of change, but there is little consensus as to its direction. Throughout the system's first 150 years, political realignment took place roughly every thirty-two to thirty-six years, but after the transforming election of 1932, the "expected" rearrangement did not occur by the early 1970s. New Deal political issues had faded in importance by the late 1960s, yet neither party appeared able or willing to build stable coalitions around the new issues.

Civil rights and the Vietnam War deeply divided the dominant Democrats in the 1960s, and divisions among constituent elements intensified in the 1970s as the governing system addressed such questions as women's rights, affirmative action, and consumer and environmental protection. As the party's agenda moved from guaranteeing equality of opportunity to pushing for equality of circumstance, the old coalition became impossible to sustain. Similarly, the Republican party, though experiencing a variety of successes (especially at the presidential level), has not developed a stable electoral and governing coalition. During the Nixon years, the Watergate scandal stopped what many viewed as a long-term shift in the balance of power toward the Republican party. Ronald Reagan's popularity caused some voters to shift party allegiance and may have enticed increasing numbers of young voters to identify with the Republican party, but economic, cultural, and social divisions among Republicans remain a barrier to coalition unity.

The lack of a critical realignment by the party system has caused some political analysts to claim that the system is undergoing "dealignment"—the movement of voters away from both parties. This viewpoint holds that "candidate politics" are more prevalent than "party politics." Some observers even suggest that party politics is not possible in the age of high technology, mass media dominance, and a highly educated electorate that engages in split-ticket voting. Those who believe in dealignment point to the decline of the importance of party identification in voting, to the growth of independence among older voters, and to the nonalignment of young voters entering the electorate. They also note the great stress on the American political system during the past quarter-century. The civil rights movement, the Vietnam War, the energy crisis, the hyperinflation of the late 1970s, and scandals in the highest places in government have both heightened citizen awareness of political affairs and increased mistrust of public officials and political institutions, including parties.

Much of the decline in the importance of parties is blamed on their inability to perform their traditional functions in the electoral process. For example, post-1968 reforms in both parties (but particularly in the Democratic party) mean that delegates to presidential nomination conventions are selected largely in primaries rather than in caucuses and state conventions, thus increasing the number of narrow-issue activists and decreasing the number of elected officials and party professionals. One consequence is that presidential contenders are less likely to be concerned with building broad coalitions than with mobilizing activists concerned with specific issues. Some believe the parties have lost their ability to set the political agenda in the nomination process as well. Candidates no longer have to spend years working within the party hierarchy to become contenders; today fresh faces quickly emerge, thanks to the role played by the media, particularly television, in determining who is or is not a "serious" candidate.

Changes in campaigning and finances have also reduced the parties' traditional role in campaign organization. Campaigns are now largely run by candidate organizations rather than by the parties. The ever-increasing importance of money and the growth of political action committees (PACs) since the Campaign Reform Acts of 1971 and 1974 (which mandated financial reporting by candidate committees) have enabled individuals to rely less on traditional party sources of funds and more on funds made available by special interests. Not surprisingly, those interests play a major role in recruiting candidates, setting issue agendas, and, in some cases, actually mobilizing voters.

Campaigns have also become more oriented toward the media than toward people in recent decades, and independent political consultants are now more likely than party professionals to run campaigns. Candidates for most national or statewide offices routinely place their campaigns in the hands of a comprehensive political consulting firm, which is charged with raising funds, polling, advertising, and designing campaign strategy. One consequence is that office-holders now owe little allegiance to either party organizations or party leaders; they are elected by their own efforts and are accountable to no one but themselves.

In spite of these trends, some political scientists assert that the two major parties are adjusting to the challenge of PAC politics, high technology, and mass media and are staging a resurgence, especially at the national level. Both have taken advantage of the PAC phenomenon by forming loose alliances with some prominent groups. In their emerging role as brokers, the national parties assist PACs in directing contributions to particular campaigns. Likewise, they aid candidates by soliciting contributions from PACs. In addition, the national parties provide professional assistance to candidates in the form of direct mail and polling services.

The readings that follow address various aspects of the changing party system. All three reflect the uncertainty many observers feel in assessing the contributions of contemporary political parties. In the first selection, Kay Lawson, a proponent of what she calls "real" political parties, argues that contemporary parties have been captured by elites and no longer operate as vehicles of influence for the masses. In her view, citizens need once again to take control of political parties. In the second selection, Walter Dean Burnham examines the 1992 election with an eye toward understanding party and electoral change. While his analysis of voting patterns yields much in the way of continuity, Burnham believes the party system is poised for a major reconstruction in the near future. The final selection, by pollsters Gordon and Benjamin Black, is more speculative. They believe that the time is ripe for the rise of a new major party to challenge Republicans and Democrats, parties they see as unable to address the political reforms desired by many voters.

Why We Still Need Real Political Parties

Kay Lawson

While all elected federal officials and almost all state officials continue to run for office under party labels, the role of parties in the process is much diminished compared to earlier in the nation's history. Most political scientists believe that we have moved from an era of "party politics" to an era of "candidate politics," characterized by a heightened role for the media, interest groups, and profes- sional campaign operatives and consultants. Parties have not disappeared, but they are only one interest involved in contemporary electoral politics and probably not the most important one at that.

In this selection, Kay Lawson argues that it was the development of political parties that "made democracy possible" in the United States, and the functions they performed for citizens at an earlier time are just as relevant today. In her view, today's parties have become captured by elites and other insiders, and the citi- zenry no longer views them as valuable institutions to solve social and eco- nomic problems. "Real" political parties are needed, parties controlled by a broad base of citizens, concerned with aggregating interests and addressing policy issues, and able to hold public officials accountable to the party faithful. Professor Lawson, a strong advocate of party renewal, believes that only through citizen activity within parties can they be restored to "democratic usefulness."

What is a "Real Political Party"?

Scholars have as many definitions of party as there are parties. Some have gone so far as to declare that any organization that calls itself a party is a party.[1] Others argue that no clear definition is possible, that mere interest groups can slip in and out of partyhood with such ease and frequency that there is no good way to tell them apart. . . . For still others, myself among them, the line is very clear: A party is an organization that nominates candidates to stand for election to public office. Any group that does this becomes, unambiguously, a party. When it stops nominating candidates, it stops being a party.

Kay Lawson is professor of political science at San Francisco State University. This article was written in 1993.

However, this simple and, I think, useful definition is not what I mean here by the term "real political party." Here, I use the word "real" in the good, strong, popular sense of "the very epitome of what the thing ought to be." The term implies not only an ideal but also a set of qualities upon which there is reasonably wide agreement.

Reasonably wide agreement, not unanimity. For some, I acknowledge, the very notion of an "ideal" political party is an oxymoron. We have become so accustomed to disliking our parties that we can no longer imagine what one we might admire would resemble.[2] Nevertheless, the idea of a "real" political party sets our tribal memories astir. Wasn't there a time . . . didn't Van Buren say . . . what was it that Lincoln suggested . . . I seem to recall that during the Great Depression Roosevelt. . . .[3]

Existentialists all, we define the good by the act that is pleasing to ourselves. A party is judged by the acts it performs. Realists all, we recognize that no organization acts unselfishly. Parties are organizations for acquiring control over powerful offices of government, and they act accordingly. Even when they have no hope of placing their own members in such control, they seek to influence the behavior of those who win elections. However, citizens all, we nevertheless look for parties whose selfish acts at the same time serve our own larger social purposes. Parties that work only for themselves may be real enough in their own evaluations, and in those of scholars intent on studying them regardless of their social usefulness—but they are not sufficiently real to the citizens who need them to do more.

It is no wonder, then, that parties in the United States today have little or no reality for most American citizens. Elite organizations that work only for themselves and fellow elites, they appear to most voters to serve no larger societal functions, or else to serve them so poorly that they no longer merit support. If forced by an inquiring pollster to think about them, we rank political parties at the bottom of any list of public institutions; and normally we don't pay them any attention at all. For that matter, we choose our candidates on the basis of incumbency, media personality, or issue stance rather than on what party labels they wear.[4]

What could political parties do in order to become real again? (The cynic interrupts, and offers to answer for the citizen trapped in a seemingly endless recession: "'Get me a job.'") And, indeed, the idea of Tammany as a "real political party" has its appeal.* William Riordon, in his widely read and humorous interviews of New York District Leader George Washington Plunkitt, taught many of us to think of the machine boss, even when motivated by the basest greed

---

* *Tammany* was a political society, formed after the American Revolution, that dominated New York City politics until well into the twentieth century. Although originally interested in political reform and helping the mass of citizens, by the mid-to-late nineteenth century the organization had been corrupted by its leadership and today is pointed to as a symbol of all that is associated with political machines and boss politics.

and engaged in the rawest expropriation of public moneys, as somehow a rather appealing figure, the "realistic" agent of a personalized democracy.[5] The voter gets a low-paying job, the boss gets the vote and with it access to all that power can buy. Textbook after textbook has accepted the idea that the machine, actually an instrument of oppressive criminality, was a useful if makeshift means of assimilating new citizens into "democracy" and that our most reasonable response to it might well be one of nostalgia for the good old days when that's how politics was done. (The careful scholarship of David Mayhew, who notes that very few cities ever actually had machines of any kind, has largely been ignored.)[6] Nevertheless, the facts are that the United States never had extensive machine politics, and that what it did have, none of us should reasonably want back. Parties that buy our votes with one-on-one material payoffs are not viable alternatives today, and cannot be the real political parties we seek.

The functions of real political parties go back longer in time than to turn-of-the-century machinations. They go back to the very origins of parties themselves. The modern political party came into being as a way to solve the problems raised for candidates by an expanding suffrage. As soon as it became impossible for the candidates to secure election—or reelection—by personally persuading the few persons of one's own elevated class who had the vote, some kind of vote-gathering organization became necessary. Furthermore, that organization had to find grounds on which to appeal to a larger and more economically heterogeneous electorate (racial and sexual heterogeneity came later, much later). In other words, it needed candidates *and* issues that would have a wider appeal. The originators of party naively believed that voters would follow their lead only for good reason. They lacked the mass communication technology and skills for persuading voters that bad reasons—or no reasons at all—could make a fair substitute. Although their own motive, the conquest of power, was the same as any party politician's today, they had a different view of what would motivate the voter: They believed they had to either buy the vote (a practice that began long before Tammany but became less and less feasible the more suffrage expanded) or offer to use that power on behalf of the voters' own interests. Parties became the agencies that made democracy possible because they believed their own fortunes depended on playing the democratic game with some minimal level of rectitude.

In the beginning, then (and it was a beginning that lasted well into the twentieth century), parties were organizations that did not seek to motivate voters solely through materialistic horsetrading; nor did they have the capacity to do so, lacking today's sloganistic media blitz. Instead, parties promised to perform specific functions—and voters who took the job seriously evaluated them on the basis of the quality of that performance. These functions, all of which made pragmatic good sense to vote-seeking organizations with limited funds and skills but all of which were also of great use to budding democracies, were the following:

First, parties *aggregated interests, formulated issues, and proposed programs*. They discovered the concerns of a significant body of voters, worked out necessary compromises, and wrote platforms incorporating this work.

Second, parties *recruited and trained candidates* who would support their programs. Training actually came first; working for and in the party was the best way to learn the delicate arts of competitive politics as well as to demonstrate one's aptitude for public office.

Third, parties *structured the vote*. It was they who gave life and meaning to elections. They did so by making their own nominations and allowing those selected to wear the label of the party—a label that had a consistent meaning, or at least one that changed only gradually over time. They did so by conducting campaigns for their candidates, raising the necessary funds, training volunteers, and canvassing door to door. They helped with registration and they got out the vote. In fact, their constant preparations gave substance to the coming election—specifically, by helping citizens decide to vote, and how.

Fourth, parties *provided a means of holding elected officials accountable*. If elected officials did not carry out the party's program, or the party's program once carried out did not produce the desired results, voters had the option of looking elsewhere—and activists had the option of choosing other candidates. For the voters who were not active party members, this function was performed by the parties together, not one by one: It was in their diversity, in the choice that they collectively made possible, that the noninvolved voters' hope of holding elected officials accountable lay. Those with the time and interest could, however, join and become active in a particular party, and there combine with like-minded others to utilize the organization as an instrument of accountability.

The Perversion of Parties

Do not American parties perform the same four functions today? Is it not, indeed, upon them that we depend for the performance of these tasks? The answers are: no and no, with one minor exception.

Although it makes sense when speaking of "real political parties" to begin with interest aggregation, because that is where the political process ideally begins and rebegins, in order to understand what has happened to our parties today we need to consider first how candidates are recruited—because that is where the political process begins today.

American parties today do not look for candidates to support their programs. Instead, they accept as their candidates whoever has been able to rally the strength to extract the nominations. A party's nomination is no longer its own to bestow. Primary elections ensure that the candidate who can gather the most funds and/or the candidate who is an incumbent running for reelection (and normally the two attributes are found in combination) will normally win the party's nomination without any help from the party whatsoever—and, indeed sometimes against the wishes of the party's active membership and leaders. Furthermore, in the vast majority of American elections, political parties are prevented from presenting candidates at all: More than 85 percent of municipal elections are, by law, nonpartisan. (There are, of course, vastly more city elections than state and national elections—some 19,000 per year in California, for example.) In these elections, the parties may not even make nominations; and in some states, they do not even have the right to endorse or repudiate any of the self-nominated candidates for city office.[7]

It is also less and less likely today that the candidates will have learned the art of politics by taking an active part in party life. Party activism is now rewarded, if at all, more by the opportunities it provides to have firsthand contact with candidates than by any chance to become one. Would-be candidates spend their time more effectively working with wealthy and powerful nonparty persons or groups than by bothering with intraparty activism. It is true that the candidate, having gained the nomination, may well benefit from training in a party-sponsored school for candidates; but that, of course, is a clear case of putting the cart before the horse (in this case, a horse that is already off and running). Today's parties do not perform the second function on our list.

And because they do not perform the second, they do not perform the first. Parties do not aggregate interests, formulate issues, and then propose programs that take stands on those issues that will appeal to a significant body of voters. The situation may look like that, at least in elections at the level of state and nation, but that is not what is going on. At the level of the states, where platforms are often written separately from the conventions, an effort may or may not be made to find out and aggregate the points of view of party members or the public; but even if made, that effort will almost always be limited to issues that have already been determined to be "important"—because either powerful interests or the media (normally both, the second in this case responding to the former) have declared them so and, furthermore, have determined the terms of the debate to be held on them. Ideas that might be excellent and clearly consistent with the party's broad philosophy of government (if one may still be discerned), but that seem likely to lower the income of a bloc of major contributors if ever implemented, are unlikely to gain a fair hearing. The same may be said for those ideas that might require extensive voter education. Proposals explaining a political agenda in detail, even when every detail is easy to understand, are similarly excluded. As the purpose is always to take as many of the votes of the massive number of nonpartisans as well as of the other party's putative supporters as possible, in addition to those of one's own supporters, the rush to the center would break the back—or least the patience—of any animal more sensitive to strain than the American electorate. The final result would be an excellent document, entirely lacking in controversy, almost impossible to implement, and eminently unread.

At any rate, it doesn't matter. The program that *will* eventually matter, at least a little bit, will not be the party's program; it will be the program of the candidate, which may or may not agree with that of the party. As we have already seen, getting the nomination does not depend on concurrence with the party program (an absence of linkage that is true at the national level as well), although the attention given the national party's platform is considerably greater and is part of the work of the nominating convention. "Do you agree with the platform?" a reporter asked President Jimmy Carter after the 1980 Democratic convention. "I agree with most of it," the party's nominee affably replied. How nice someone thought to ask.

With the third function, we come to our minor exceptions. Today's political parties do perform some part of the job of structuring the vote. They do not do so, however, via the meaningfulness of the party label. Inasmuch as they no longer control their own nominations, their labels are now associated only with the transient programs of those who have become their candidates, programs as deliberately substanceless as their own. However, both our major parties have become particularly adept at fund-raising (each in its own way), and even if they have lost control over the choice of candidates for whom the money is being raised, they can sometimes play favorites to useful effect. They help with the task of canvassing, if not door to door, at least sometimes phone to phone. They work very hard indeed on voter registration and getting out the vote. They do all this guided not by their own programs or their own convictions but by the wishes of the candidates and by the candidates' and their own power- ful professional advisers, political consultants whose concern for electoral victory far outweighs any passing dreams of principled formulation of issues with distinc- tive substantive content—and very often has little to do with issues at all. But our parties do help structure the vote. Even though today they share that role more than ever with the media, with the candidates' personal organizations, and with independently spending Political Action Committees (which now spend over $20 million per presidential election year independent of contributions to candidates or parties), it must be granted that they are reasonably efficient electoral machines.[8]

As for the fourth function, surely little need be said. The only force that holds U.S. elected officials accountable is the force that is needed to open a wallet. Parties' wallets are now worth opening, but parties themselves have nothing substantive to which to hold the successful bearers of their name accountable. Candidates are chosen and elected whose loyalty to—or even familiarity with— the party platform is minimal at best. The ability of presidents to distance themselves from their own parties is obvious, but we sometimes imagine we see a measure of party discipline in Congress. To persuade ourselves of this, however, we must consent to a very diluted idea of what constitutes a party. Once inside Congress, those miscellaneous victors who succeeded in wresting the label away from one party or the other and using it to win public office may dutifully call themselves "Democrats" or "Republicans" and may even sometimes cobble to- gether a program of sorts; but that program need have little in common with the program of the party organization that exists outside Congress. Furthermore, the other determinants of congressional votes—constituency pressure, personal friendships, personal convictions, and, above all, campaign donor pressure—are at least as likely to prevail should differences arise.

The Ever-Swifter Descent of the Parties—and Their Complicity Therewith

Because our parties no longer perform most of the functions a democratic society requires from its parties, their place in the affections of the American people drops lower and lower. This is apparent when any question about them is put to the people directly. Their dissatisfaction with the parties is not compensated for ·by a conviction that other institutions are working well: as is apparent not only in opinion polls regarding those institutions, but also in the increased demand for alternative democratic reforms in the political process, and in the decreasing interest of the public at large in any form of political activity whatsoever. Yet the parties themselves appear unconcerned about this decline, even to the point of deliberately fostering it—a phenomenon that is not so surprising as it may seem at first. Let us look at each of these factors in turn.

The first significant study of the declining popularity of the parties was made by Jack Dennis in 1975.[9] Bringing together his own work with that of others, Dennis pointed out such discoveries as the following:

◆ More than 66 percent of Americans thought that party labels should not be on the ballot.
◆ Eighty-five percent said that parties create conflict.
◆ Seventy-eight percent believed that parties confused rather than clarified the issues of the day.
◆ Only 26 percent believed that parties knew how to make the government responsible to citizens.
◆ Only 32 percent believed that parties did what they promised.
◆ Only 35 percent believed that parties wanted to know what citizens thought.
◆ Only 40 percent thought it mattered whether one party or another won an election.

In the seventeen years since Dennis published his study, the situation has not improved. Howard Reiter combined his own calculations with those of other authors to show that between 1974 and 1980 the number of those who believed that "parties help government pay attention to what people think" had fallen by four percentage points, to 18 percent, whereas the number who believed that "parties are only interested in people's votes, but not in their opinions," had risen during the same period by one point to 59 percent.[10] More recent figures confirm the pattern: Asked to give a letter grade to the performance of the two parties in the 1988 presidential campaign, a national sample gave both parties an average grade of C.[11] Other studies suggest that any improvement made by the parties in distinguishing themselves from each other in the voters' minds (a form of improvement that some studies suggested did take place to some extent during the Reagan years) had largely disappeared by 1990 and 1991, when a full 25 percent saw no difference between the parties in "keeping the country prosperous," 30 percent saw none in their ability to keep the nation out of war, and, most significant of all, 41 percent saw none in their ability to handle "the nation's most important problem" (whatever that might have been in their own minds).[12]

Dissatisfaction with the parties cannot be dismissed on the grounds that Americans are satisfied in general with their political system, even if they think the parties are largely worthless. The continuing decline in voter turnout is one index, and it is worthwhile to note not only that voting in presidential elections has dropped to the 50 percent level but also that a mere 33 percent of the voting-age population voted in the midterm elections of 1990 (only Maine, Minnesota, Montana, and Alaska were able to turn out more than 50 percent of those eligible to vote).[13] However, as nonvoting itself is sometimes ascribed to contentment, it is important to go beyond that possibly ambiguous signal. It is not difficult to do so. In October 1990, 66 percent of Americans said they were "dissatisfied with the way things are going in the United States at this time," 68 percent disapproved "of the way Congress is handling its job," and 54 percent were dissatisfied with the performance of the president.[14]

Yet another index of dissatisfaction is the growing interest in alternative means of democratizing our political system. There is now remarkably strong support for the devices of direct democracy, despite growing awareness of their deficiencies as a means of basing public policy on public will.[15] Asked "Should we trust our elected officials to make public decisions on all issues, or should the voters have a direct say on some issues?" a national sample favored giving voters a direct say by 76 percent (only 18 percent were opposed; 6 percent did not know). More specifically, a strong majority (57 percent) supported the idea of a national initiative—that is, a constitutional amendment permitting citizens to gather signatures for a proposed law to be placed on the ballot at the succeeding general election and to become law if a majority approved. Only one-fourth were opposed (18 percent were not sure). Fully two-thirds said they believed the Constitution should be changed to permit the recall of members of Congress, whereas 55 percent specified that it should allow recall of the president.[16]

Support for other reforms is also indicative of popular distress with the performance of our weak-partied political system. Term limits have been adopted in California to ensure that state legislators will not serve more than two consecutive terms in office, and the idea has recently been proposed for members of Congress as well. And the proposals for reforming campaign finance appear as endless as the resistance of the legislators whose votes would be needed for their success—but whose pockets always need more relining than the reforms would be likely to permit.

Yet there is little if any evidence that the parties are interested in making changes that would put themselves back in the ring as leading agencies in the democratic process. Another illustration from California is particularly apt. Parties are as weak in California as they are anywhere in the nation, and weaker than in most states.[17] Voting rates have been dropping, and ardent efforts by both parties to increase registration have had little payoff in terms of turnout. Recently, a body of antiparty law was successfully challenged as unconstitutional by a multipartisan reform group, the Committee for Party Renewal. The 1988 ruling of the U.S. Supreme Court in the case, *Eu v. San Francisco County Democrats*, gave the parties of California the right both to issue endorsements in primary elections and to set their own rules and regulations on important matters hitherto closely controlled by law. California's parties now have unambiguous opportunities to strengthen their ability to carry out several of the key functions identified earlier, becoming more responsive to their membership in the endorsement of candidates, in the writing of the state party platform, in the selection of delegates to the party's national convention, and in all party activities.

However, both major state parties have been extremely reluctant to take advantage of these opportunities. The Republicans have made no changes whatsoever, and the Democrats have instituted a method of endorsing primary contestants that greatly advantages incumbents and keeps final control at the highest echelons of the party. Neither party has made any other changes in internal rules that could be termed party-strengthening. The Democratic party rejected by a 2 to 1 vote a proposal to change to a mixed-delegate-selection system that would have had the undeniably party-building effect of giving California Democrats a strong say in the party's selection of its presidential candidate. (Half of California's delegates would have been picked in March caucuses—rather than all, as at present, at a June primary that takes place well after the national nominee has been clearly identified in other, earlier primaries.) The national Democratic party actively campaigned, along with the present state party leadership, for the rejection of this plan, even while acknowledging that the proposal did not contradict national party rules and that the state party did have the right to make the change if it wished. The opponents of the plan argued that it would be too expensive and time consuming, although evidence presented from other states suggested that the cost would have been minimal and that the party-building effects would have justified the time required. But what the plan *would* have done is give local party activists a much stronger say in candidate selection.[18]

A further example from California of a party insisting on maintaining its own weakness is the refusal (at present writing) of the state Democratic party to support a second lawsuit that, if successful, will give California's parties the right to issue endorsements in local elections. This despite the fact that nothing contributes more to the weakness of parties—or is more patently unconstitutional—than refusing them their First Amendment right of free speech in local elections, as is presently the law in California.[19]

Why should the parties in the nation's most populous state—or in any state—be so eager to maintain themselves as agencies incapable of performing the functions of responsive intermediary between people and the state? The answer is not hard to find. Our current parties are not impersonal organizations; they are elite organizations operating on behalf of themselves and fellow elites. As such, they seek power; and our electoral system gives that power not to those who win the support of a majority of the electorate but to those who win a plurality of the vote. So long as victory is won, by however small a percentage of the potential electorate, the fewer who take part in politics the better for the parties. With the advent of mass communication, the parties do not need mass participation to win and do not want it. It is helpful to have a stable and docile work force that can be convoked when needed to carry out, for no pay, the tedious jobs of registration and getting out the vote. But beyond that it is very difficult to know what to do with activists, especially those who are concerned about social problems. It is hard to keep them from expecting to play a role in issue formulation and candidate recruitment, and hard to keep them from figuring out ways to hold representatives accountable to a broader public than that represented by the most powerful PACs. The tears our parties' leaders occasionally weep, over declining public support and loss of membership, should suggest to us that donkey and elephant might both well be replaced by crocodile.

Why We Still Need Real Parties

If the political parties of the United States have degenerated into mere fund-raising electoral machines working on behalf of candidates who represent ever more narrow interests, with no need for or interest in serving as responsive intermediaries between people and the state, and if the general public is at the same time contemptuous and disinterested, is there any point in trying to change the situation, and if so, how?

The first question is easier to answer than the second. The point in trying to do something to change the parties is that the status quo provides us with a set of conditions that should be intolerable to any citizenry committed to its own democratic governance. The parties have become the tool—and merely one among many that are stronger—of persons much more interested in taking power for personal advantage than in resolving the problems from which we as a nation suffer. A report that documented our deficiencies in child care, education, race relations, health care, treating the AIDS epidemic, caring for the aged poor, and addressing the problem of abuse of women and children would contain enough human suffering to break the heart of any sensitive reader, yet would leave out as much as it included. As of 1990, by conservative official estimate nearly 7 million job-seekers were unable to find employment.[20] Nearly 1.5 million violent crimes are committed per year, in addition to nearly 11 million crimes against property.[21] Every year 1.25 million persons are admitted to alcohol treatment centers.[22]

There are nearly 400,000 cocaine addicts in New York City alone.[23] Demands for shelter by homeless families are increasing at the rate of approximately 20 percent per year.[24] And the list goes on. We are a nation in desperate crisis, as most of our potential electorate is well aware, all too often from firsthand experience. Non-voting cannot be construed as a sign of contentment in today's America; it is much more likely a silent scream of despair.

Furthermore, the continuing inability of our political system to treat these problems effectively is rife with the danger that democracy itself will be cast casually aside by those who do continue to vote, and who are clearly becoming ever more prepared to accept any form of leadership that seems to promise succor. We have already gone a very long way in that direction by so drastically overextending the powers of the presidency in recent years. Lacking the methods and arenas that real parties might provide us for articulating our problems, for exploring practicable political solutions, and for placing men and women in office who are dedicated to enacting those solutions, we now sign over all power to those we do not know and who do not know us; we call them "leaders" and keep them in office so faithfully that it is no wonder they lose all interest in knowing what precisely we would have them do.

Sometimes, of course, we become so overwhelmed by the immensity of a particular problem that we feel we must "do something." But normally we can think of nothing better to do than write a check on behalf of the appropriate single interest group that, even if it works hard on the problem in question (an assumption that is not always well founded), is very likely to do so by refusing the degree of compromise with other interests that is essential to produce a national agenda composed of interconnected and harmonized policies moving steadily in a consistent direction. Yes, we still need real political parties. Is there any way, however, to get them? Certainly there is little point in asking them to please reform themselves. Citizens must use the weapons they have at their command, to serve their own purposes. And what weapons are those? We have, above all, the possibility of using our intelligences to recognize not only the seriousness of the situation but also our own responsibility for effecting change. We have the vote, and we might learn to use it—and to withhold it—more wisely, refusing to support any party that does not offer to take at least a few steps in the direction of responsible performance of the functions that parties have always been expected to perform in democracies. Voting for a minor party that has no chance of victory can send a stronger message for change to the major parties than accepting, year after year, the dreary burden of deciding which of two barely distinguishable evils is the lesser.

However, these are weak arms against the arsenals accumulated by the major parties over the years in the battle for power. The real weapons are inside the major parties. All we really have to do is go in and take them. Thus far the major parties have contented themselves with merely discouraging our participation; they have not closed their gates altogether. They are open to us, and if we dared to enter them as citizens bent on restoring them to democratic usefulness, we could no doubt succeed in turning them back into agents of our will. Such an effort is within the realm of the possible, and given our current predicament, may be the only way to recreate our democracy. . . .

Notes

1. Thomas Hodgkin, *African Political Parties* (London: Penguin, 1961), p. 16.
2. The American habit of disliking parties began even before the institution had been well established. "There is nothing," said our first vice-president, John Adams, "I dread so much as the division of the Republic into two great parties, each under its leader. . . . This . . . is to be feared as the greatest political evil under the Constitution.
3. For what Van Buren said, see Richard Hofstadter, *The Idea of a Party System* (Berkeley: University of California Press, 1969), pp. 223–231.
4. As of the midterm elections of 1990, incumbency reelection rates had reached 96.9 percent in the Senate and 96.0 percent in the House. Only fifteen House incumbents and one incumbent Senator were defeated for reelection. See *Congressional Quarterly Almanac*, 1990, pp. 903–906.
5. William T. Riordon, *Plunkitt of Tammany Hall* (New York: E. P. Dutton, 1963).
6. David Mayhew, *Placing Parties in American Politics: Organization, Electoral Settings, and Government Activity in the Twentieth Century* (Princeton, N.J.: Princeton University Press, 1986).
7. In one of the more recent examples, a Superior Court judge in San Francisco issued a restraining order on November 27, 1991, against the Democratic Party of San Francisco, barring it from endorsing Mayor Art Agnos for reelection. See Richard Winger, "Democratic Party Muzzled," *Ballot Access News* (newsletter privately published in San Francisco), December 9, 1991, p. 3.
8. For figures on PAC independent expenditures, see *Statistical Abstract of the United States 1990* (U.S. Department of Commerce: Bureau of the Census, 1990), p. 267.
9. Jack Dennis, "Trends in Public Support for the American Party System, *British Journal of Political Science* 5 (April 1975): 187–230.
10. Howard Reiter, Parties and Elections in Corporate America (New York: St. Martin's, 1987); Warren E. Miller, Arthur H. Miller, and Edward J. Schneider, *American National Election Studies Data Sourcebook, 1952–1978* (Cambridge: Harvard University Press, 1980). It should be noted that, with regard to believing that the parties care about people's opinions, the 1980 figure was actually an improvement over that of 1978—62 percent.
11. *The People, The Press and Politics 1990* (Los Angeles: Times-Mirror Center for the People and the Press), November 16, 1990.
12. *Gallup Poll Monthly*, September 1990, no. 300, p. 32, and May 1991, no. 308, p. 36.
13. *Congressional Quarterly Almanac*, vol. 46, 1990.
14. *Gallup Poll Monthly*, October 1990, no. 302, pp. 34–40.
15. Thomas E. Cronin, *Direct Democracy: The Politics of Initiative, Referendum, and Recall* (Cambridge, Mass.: Harvard University Press, 1989).
16. Ibid., pp. 80, 174, and 132.
17. Kay Lawson, "How State Laws Undermine Parties," in A. James Reichley, ed., *Elections American Style* (Washington, D.C.: Brookings Institution, 1987).
18. Kay Lawson, "Questions Raised by Recent Attempts at Local Party Reform," paper presented at the Workshop on Political Organizations and Parties, Annual Meeting of the American Political Science Association, Washington, D.C., August 28, 1991.
19. Winger, "Democratic Party Muzzled," p. 3.
20. *Statistical Abstract of the United States 1990*, p. 381.
21. Ibid., p. 170.
22. *State Resources Annual* (Washington, D.C.: National Association of State Alcohol and Drug Abuse Directors, August 1990), p. 25.

23. Katherine McFate, "Failing to Meet the Demand for Drug Treatment," *Focus* (Joint Center for Political and Economic Studies), November/December 1990, p. 4.
24. *Status Report on Hunger and Homelessness in America's Cities, 1990* (Washington, D.C.: U.S. Conference of Mayors, December 1990), p. 23.

Summary Questions

1. Why does the author believe that contemporary American parties have ceased to be "real" political parties? What functions should parties perform in a political system?
2. Why does Lawson believe that there is "little if any evidence that parties are interested in making changes that would put themselves back in the ring as leading agencies in the democratic process?" What does she believe must be done for parties to again become important political institutions?

 6.2

The Politics of Repudiation

Walter Dean Burnham

The future direction of the party system is far from clear. The 1992 presidential election yielded mixed signals. Although Arkansas Governor Bill Clinton's victory represented a break in the pattern of electing a Republican to the nation's highest office while also selecting a Democratic Congress, Clinton received less than 43 percent of the popular vote, hardly an indication that voters were enthusiastically endorsing a Democrat in the White House. Even more surprising was the strong showing of independent candidate Ross Perot, who garnered nearly 19 percent of the total vote.

In this selection, Walter Dean Burnham examines the results of the 1992 presidential election from the historical perspective of the changing party system. In a narrow sense, the election represented continuity, as both Bush and Clinton ran strongest among the demographic groups that typically support their party's candidates. There was little evidence of voter realignment.

Walter Dean Burnham is a professor of political science at the University of Texas at Austin.

In a broader sense, the public mood in 1992 was one demanding "change," but the direction of such change was confused and unfocused. The public appeared dissatisfied with the policy implications of both the interest-group liberalism that has characterized the Democratic Party in recent decades as well as with the unfettered capitalism represented by recent Republican presidents. In Burnham's view, the Perot candidacy, which eroded the support of both the Republican and Democratic presidential contenders, was indicative of a high level of voter aliena-tion directed toward political parties and political elites, a "pervasive public sense that Washington insiders and powerful interest groups had stolen the political system from the people."

For a generation the United States has experienced a complex and deepening crisis of its political and economic order. Three pivotal and highly abnormal elections have punctuated this crisis. In 1968, undermined by the Vietnam War and the civil rights revolution, the New Deal order collapsed. A new electoral regime emerged from the ruins, marked by three main features: normal Republican control of the presidency; divided government as the (unprece-dented) norm; and a candidate-dominated "permanent campaign," in which a capital-intensive personalism crowded out labor-intensive political parties.

In the 1970's, severe economic crisis replaced Vietnam as a driving issue. Its effects (stagnation and price-inflation coupled with low real interest rates) were reinforced by signs of foreign policy weakness and the emergence of the socio-religious right. The stage was set for Ronald Reagan and right-wing "conviction politics" designed to stop the rot on all fronts. A massive policy realignment ensued as Reagan and his allies launched their brand of political, economic, and social revitalization, confident that their new regime was both viable and durable.

But the 1992 election repudiated that attempted synthesis and its rhetorical, coalitional, and public-policy regime. Its policy consequences will long outlive the political order—particularly public debt exceeding 50 percent of the 1992 gross domestic product. Even Republicans agree that the Reagan-Bush era in American political history is over, mainly because it failed economically. The promises and dreams of the 1980s were liquidated not only by persistent recession but by its association with a massive, structural downsizing of American capital-ism. More than any of its postwar predecessors, this recession has raised acute anxiety within the broad American middle class—anxiety not just for their own future but for their children's. Average real family income eroded under George Bush and growth was lower across this presidential term than in any during the past sixty years.

Considering that two entire political worldviews and regime orders associated with them had achieved bankruptcy within the space of a dozen years, we should hardly wonder that public demands for "change" were as loud as they were un-clear or confused. Nor is it surprising that the general political atmosphere

among the electorate in 1992 was so disturbed and filled with rage against politicians or that for a few weeks in early summer Ross Perot led *both* major-party
candidates in the polls.

To a quite unusual extent, 1992 presents a broad panorama of analytic issues
associated with American presidential elections. An incumbent president running for reelection was defeated, but this was no ordinary defeat. Both his conduct
in office and his defeat at the polls identify for us just what kind of incumbent
George Bush was. Ross Perot, capitalizing on an immense breadth of public
discontent with the existing order and its leadership, won the third largest share
of the total vote ever secured by a nonmajor-party candidate in American history.
Our task here is to attempt to provide a reasonably integrated account of what
happened and why in the pivotal election of 1992.

The Permanent Campaign and the Interregnum State

Out of the crisis of the 1960s, a genuine critical realignment crystallized, unlike
any in previous history. Its main characteristic was not a shift in voting preferences but the partial dissolution of the traditional linkages between elite and
public, mediated by the traditional party system. At the presidential level, the
McGovern-Fraser commission reforms led to direct primaries at the center of the
nominating process.* This formed a major break with the past and seemingly
energized grass-roots voting participation. But at almost the same moment, a
series of other "reforms" stimulated political action committees and other forms
of political entrepreneurship. These combined with the rapid growth of campaign technology—polling, focus groups, targeting, paid ads, and personalist
campaigns—to shift the entire system away from voting participation and toward
financial participation. In what Sidney Blumenthal was the first to call the
"permanent campaign," congressional incumbents made sure that no reform
was undertaken that could give their challengers an even break, and the money
rolled in.

The decline of party in turn led to a decline in the competitiveness of congressional seats (one sees glimmerings as early as the 1966 congressional elections). Apart from temporary upticks in 1974 and 1982, this trend continued
from the late 1960s through 1988, a year when incumbents in House races
seeking reelection numbered more than 400 of the 435 members of the House,
and their reelection rate hit 98.5 percent. More generally, as a comparison of
presidential and senatorial election outcomes also clearly demonstrates, for the

---

* The McGovern-Fraser Commission, a Democratic Party task force formed after the contentious
1968 Democratic presidential nominating convention, was the first in a series of reform vehicles
that developed rules making the party internally more open and democratic. Besides expanding
the role of primary elections in the nominating process, the McGovern-Fraser Commission is also
credited with increasing the role played by women, blacks, and youth in the party.

first time in American history discrete electoral coalitions—different ones for different offices—emerged. Thus in 1984 Ronald Reagan was the winner in 375 congressional districts, only 182 of which also elected Republican representatives. How did incumbents on the Democratic side do so well? It was easy: All they had to do was run *on average* 19 percentage points ahead of Walter Mondale in their districts.

This intersected with the chief, *governing* feature of this sixth electoral era,* which I call the "interregnum state": the *divided government* that has lately intrigued political scientists. (See Richard Valelly, "Divided They Govern," *TAP,* Fall 1992). The critical realignment of the late 1960s led to a normal Republican majority in presidential elections—five out of six elections, twenty of twenty-four years since 1968–1969. For six years during this period, a quarter of the time, Republicans also enjoyed a majority in the U.S. Senate, but never in the House. The Madisonian separation of powers and its policy-fragmenting implications were thus reinforced by changed behavior in the electorate; the opposite of what the traditional party system (at its best) was designed to produce. Instead, by 1989 George Bush entered office with fewer partisan supporters in Congress than any of his predecessors across two centuries of American politics.

The Republican House minority in 1981 was large enough, in conjunction with Republican control of the Senate, to enact the major features of Ronald Reagan's tax-and-budget "revolution." But these forces were not strong enough to permit a complete clinical experiment in squaring the policy circle: cutting taxes, raising defense spending, and cutting enough outlay elsewhere to keep the budget deficit from exploding. This was to have long-term political consequences, not least of which was the Perot candidacy of 1992. On an increasingly exaggerated scale, divided government produced a bizarre mix of collusion, collision, and buck-passing in public policy—the very negation of accountability.

It is no wonder that the first omnibus budget resolution presented to the House in October 1990, after months of tortuous negotiations among top congressional and executive leaders, was voted down in a wave of resentment among ordinary members of Congress who had been cut out of the whole process. It is no wonder that a key factor in the collapse of public support for George Bush in 1992 was his repudiation of his 1988 pledge, "Read my lips: No new taxes." It is no wonder that by 1991, the Kettering Foundation should find extraordinary levels not of apathy but of anger, rage even, against politics and politicians, captured so well

---

* Readers interested in the previous five eras should consult the author's *Critical Elections and the Mainsprings of American Politics* (New York: W. W. Norton, 1970), which suggests that the political history of the United States can be divided roughly into chronological eras, "systems," or regime orders, each separated from the other by a "critical realignment" of voting preferences, sociopolitical cleavages, and issue coalitions. These eras are: (1) the early Federal period (circa 1780–1824); (2) the democratizing or Jacksonian era (1828–1860); (3) the Civil War era or "system" (1854/60–1892); (4) the industrial-capitalist era or "System of 1896" (1894/6–1932); (5) the New Deal era (1932–1968).

in E. J. Dionne's *Why Americans Hate Politics*. Ordinary Americans, like ordinary members of Congress, strongly resent being dealt out of a political system that affects their lives while being expected to pick up the tab or provide the votes. Nor, given all this, is it any wonder that the voters of all fourteen states that had term-limits proposals on their ballots in November 1992 approved them. This may be (as I believe) a bad idea whose time is rapidly coming. But it represents an enduring truth of American politics—that for every action that closes off the elite world within the Beltway from the voters outside, there is likely sooner or later to be an equal and opposite reaction arising from said voters.

Significantly, while surveys throughout the 1980s indicated popular support for divided government, polls in 1992 showed a swing in attitude: most Americans now preferred that candidates of the same party win the presidency and control Congress too. In the foreseeable structure of electoral politics, this party can only be the Democratic Party. It remains to be seen whether its new team can govern effectively, but for the moment the electorate is giving it the chance. Thus there is an implicit "race" underway between the willingness of the voters to entrust government to the Democrats and the current passion for term limits. The latter is the latest upsurge of a basic idea-set going back to the Progressive era at the turn of the century: that mechanically imposed, immaculately conceived structural solutions can work to cure the ills of American democracy. The former places real contestation at the heart of politics through parties that are vital and coherent enough to address the problems of the country. We shall see, across Bill Clinton's term and later, how this race will be decided in our own time.

From 1961 through 1981, the country endured five aborted presidencies in a row, four of which were repudiations (Johnson, Nixon, Ford, Carter): a sequence also without historical precedent. Now it has repudiated yet another. There do appear to be rare occasions in American political history when a consensus develops that we simply cannot go on like this any longer, that the impasse in our collective affairs has become insupportable. Some such consensus crystallized between the extraordinarily revealing Pennsylvania Senate election of November 1991 and the spring of 1992, and it was to be fatal to George Bush's bid for reelection.* Nor was this a narrow loss: measured in sheer quantitative terms, George Bush's loss of 15.9 percentage of the total vote between his first election and his second was exceeded only three times in *all* of American history: In 1932, when Herbert Hoover's share of the total vote declined 18.6 percent from 1928;

---

* In the fall of 1992 Bryn Mawr College president Harris Wofford, a Democrat, defeated Bush's attorney general, Richard Thornburgh, who had entered the race as the overwhelming favorite. Wofford won with 55 percent of the vote, the first Democrat to win election to the U.S. Senate in Pennsylvania since Joseph Clark in 1962. In the campaign, Wofford stressed economic issues, including the need for a national health-care program, and did extremely well among middle-class, suburban, and normally Republican voters. Many political analysts viewed the election as a warning that if Bush did not pay attention to the economically stressed middle class he would have difficulty in his reelection efforts.

in 1800, when John Adams experienced a decline of 20.4 percent from 1796; and in 1912, when (with Theodore Roosevelt stealing more than half of the Republican electorate) William Howard Taft suffered an erosion of 28.4 percent of the total vote from his 1908 level. Whatever else 1992 may have been, it was a classic case of a landslide vote of no confidence in an incumbent president and the regime he led. Of twenty-nine incumbents seeking reelection or election to a full term across two centuries of American history, in terms of this measure of interelection swing, George Bush in 1992 ranked twenty-sixth, no mean feat that.

Thus in less than a generation, two whole ways of doing our political business, interest-group liberalism and now Reaganite capitalism redux, have been swept into the discard. . . .

Bush: A Third-Term Understudy

If Jimmy Carter had many of the attributes of a historical accident (as I think he did), George Bush seems almost a historical inevitability. He is a near-classic exemplar of a category of presidents extending across political history—the failed understudy.

In twenty-four of the fifty-two presidential elections held since 1789, incumbents originally elected to a full term have run to succeed themselves. Of these, fifteen won, while nine lost their bids for another term. Five of these losers, along with a narrow winner (Madison in 1812), form a distinct subset. Each was chosen to carry on the policies of a recently successful and policy-innovative regime, under conditions where the previous leaders of this regime are unavailable for an additional term themselves. George Bush is the first of them in sixty years. These six "understudy" or "conservator" candidates are: John Adams (Federalist, 1797–1901), succeeding George Washington; James Madison (Democratic-Republican, 1809–1817), succeeding Thomas Jefferson; Martin Van Buren (Democrat, 1937–1841), succeeding Andrew Jackson; William Howard Taft (Republican, 1909–1913), succeeding Theodore Roosevelt; Herbert Hoover (Republican, 1929–1933), succeeding Calvin Coolidge; and George Bush succeeding Ronald Reagan.

What else do these men have in common? For one thing, all faced crises that grew directly out of the policies of their predecessors and their regimes, which buffeted the understudies' term of office. Second, each of them (with perhaps the admitted exception of Hoover) succeeded presidents who were regarded as heroic, charismatic or successful in their own time: acts that were indeed hard to follow, sorcerers whose apprentice successors would have had to be truly remarkable to fill the voids left behind. But, third, each of them was selected precisely to give "four more years" of the same, not to engage in even timely innovations on any large scale. George Bush, for example, was selected (and elected) precisely because he was expected to preserve the Reagan legacy in as nearly pure and undefiled a form as possible. People chosen as understudies, one may assume, are chosen precisely because they are *not* innovators, and the "vision thing" seems much less of a problem when the point of the exercise is conservation of the political gains and commitments secured during the immediate past.

Fourth, each of them came to office replete with exceptional *résumés*. Adams, Washington's vice president, had been a key intellectual and actor before the establishment of the constitutional order in 1787. Madison had been Jefferson's secretary of state, as had Van Buren (in addition to the latter's additional services as vice president). A superb insider politician who was a true innovator in building party organization to channel the new mass electorate, Van Buren had extensive partisan experience as well. Taft had been selected initially to be governor-general of the newly acquired Philippines, a job he loved, and subsequently became Theodore Roosevelt's secretary of war. His is the classic case of being hand-picked by his predecessor to succeed him. Hoover, with impressive credentials in organizing relief efforts in Belgium and Russia, served Harding and Coolidge faithfully as secretary of commerce—an important job in the age of corporatism. George Bush had perhaps the most glittering *résumé* of all: not only Ronald Reagan's vice president for eight years, but before that Republican national chairman and (under Gerald Ford) director of the CIA.

The *résumés* underscore the integral and basic relationship between the understudy and the regime he comes to represent. These men were anything but political outsiders. But they also tended to share a fifth characteristic: As insiders they not only lacked the common touch but were often perceived at the time— sometimes even by themselves (Madison and Taft, for example)—as lacking elemental qualities needed for effective presidential leadership. Each in his own way was conspicuously vulnerable to attack as elitist, out of touch with the public, and indifferent to the plight of ordinary Americans—a charge that was reinforced in most cases by their rigidity and inadaptability.

The sixth and final attribute of these understudies follows: All but Madison lost their bids for reelection. (He was saved by the unique structural characteristics of the so-called "first party system" and the hegemonic position of the Jeffersonian Republican Party in it.) But, Van Buren apart, these were no ordinary losses. Their share of the total vote from their first to their second races collapsed by a mean of 16.9 percent. This contrasts with a decline of 6.8 percent for the five other incumbents losing their seats, and an increase averaging just under 4 percent for the eighteen incumbents (excluding Madison) who were re-elected. All five of the bottom-swing presidents (those with the largest losses from their first to their second election) were third-term understudies. The only other presidents who came close were Gerald Ford in 1976 (–12.7 percent from Nixon's total in 1972), who had never been elected nationwide even as vice president, and Jimmy Carter in 1980 (–9.1 percent, as compared with Bush's –15.9 percent in 1992.)

The 1992 Republican campaign was true to context. Exceptionally clear warning had been given to Bush and his campaign staff by Harris Wofford's trouncing of Richard Thornburgh in the Pennsylvania Senate race one year earlier. . . . Nothing worthwhile was done in response, thought many Republicans who were keenly aware of what was going on. The party convention at Houston, with its dramatic and off-putting stress on family values and the agenda of the socio-religious right, puts its worst foot forward just as did the 1964 Goldwater convention and the 1972 Democratic convention that nominated George McGovern. But these had been *out-party* assemblies; here, in 1992, an *in-party* was providing a symbolically similar, off-putting show, something the Republicans had previously avoided even in the pits of 1932.

Thereafter, anything-but-the-economy—chiefly stressing doubts about Bill Clinton's character and trustworthiness—became the overriding theme of George Bush's message to the voters. After all, something similar had worked in 1988, hadn't it? But in 1992, voters weren't buying, and remarkably, in the second presidential debate a small number of them in the room forced the thematics back onto substantive economic issues. It was in this debate, when Bush kept looking at his watch and stumbled when asked how he personally had been affected by the recession, that his defects as a candidate were brought home—literally—to tens of millions of viewers; he was "out of touch" and he "just didn't get it." In the end, he broke another kind of historic record. Receiving just 37.5 percent of the total 1992 vote, he ranked twenty-eighth of the twenty-nine incumbents running for a full term across two centuries. Only Taft in 1912, with less than half of his party still behind him, and a former President as the third party candidate, did worse (23.2 percent). Even Hoover in 1932 managed to hold on to 39.6 percent of those voting in that election.

Bill Clinton and the "New Democrats"

After the dazzling success of Operation Desert Storm, which pushed Bush's approval rating to 90 percent,* the presumed heavy hitters on the Democratic side found one reason or another not to present themselves for consideration, and by very early 1992 a group of secondary candidates had emerged. One of these was the "obscure" governor of a small and backward state, Bill Clinton of Arkansas. Now is hardly the time for any kind of extensive review of the entire campaign, which in any case has already been covered remarkably well by the print media in the public domain. Through thick and thin, good times and bad, Bill Clinton—like the Energizer bunny in the TV ads—just kept on going and going and going. Demolishing his opponents within the party, his successful tactical choice for the general-election campaign was to take the high road and focus on what his campaign manager, James Carville, had tacked up in the

---

* Operation Desert Storm was the designation of the U.S. military operation in the 1991 Persian Gulf War.

campaign office: "The economy, stupid." He had given abundant evidence that he was very smart, capable of absorbing vast amounts of information and making some sense of it, gifted (perhaps at times too gifted) with words, and perhaps one of the really great natural hands-on politicians of our day. All this was not enough to still persistent public doubts about him (hence one reason for the size of Ross Perot's vote), or to give the public a clear sense of who the "real" Bill Clinton was. But it was more than enough to win, especially in the context we have been describing.

Bill Clinton's rise does represent a real break with the Democratic Party's past, but the nuances of that break have yet to be defined. When Ross Perot bowed out of the race on July 16, citing as a reason a "revitalized Democratic party," he was pointing to a situation in which a candidate less liberal than the party as a whole (and, except perhaps for Jimmy Carter, than its previous nominees) had been selected as its standard-bearer. It was no coincidence that Clinton had been a leading figure in the Democratic Leadership Council (DLC), an intraparty group whose aim was to move the party and its choice of nominee toward the center of the American political spectrum. With old-style interest-group liberalism dead beyond retrieval as a dominant part of any winning presidential coalition, and with its coffin double-sealed by debt, deficit, and basic economic-reproduction problems left behind as a prime legacy of the Reagan-Bush era, the specific 1992 conjuncture was especially favorable for producing a nominee who could win a presidential election, even though a Democrat. As usual in such cases, the man and the moment met: Clinton carried the suburbs, won pluralities in all family-income groups under $75,000 per year, won the support of far more than half of the Democrats who had voted for Ronald Reagan in 1984 (69 percent to 31 percent for Bush on a two-party basis), held Bush to a tie among white voters as a whole, and otherwise enjoyed an exceptionally broad plurality sweep over the incumbent everywhere except the South and isolated pockets elsewhere.

Yet the apparent rightward shift is more complex than that advertised by the DLC. For Clinton believes in activist government, is married to a feminist, and began his tenure as president-elect by reaffirming his support for gays serving in the military. Although he made the necessary inroads into the middle class, he did it without writing off blacks, gays, feminists, greens, or trade unionists—the dreaded "liberal fundamentalists" in the dismissive phrase of DLC demonologists William Galston and Elaine Ciulla Kamarck. Indeed, his support among traditional liberals was about normal, or even better.

The most enduring reality of modern American electoral politics—at least where economic issues are concerned—is that the Democrats have been the pro-state party and the Republicans the anti-state party. Clinton and his coalition of supporters will have as a prime objective the reclamation of his heritage, while overcoming their image as the party of bureaucracy. Despite the Democratic Leadership Council's embrace of Clinton and its own resolute centrism, government once again is to be seen as capable of making positive, indeed essential, contributions to a twenty-first century American economy in a thoroughly competitive and interdependent world.

What such a vision has going for it, in truth, is not the clarity of its program (yet) but simply the force of circumstances, *la forza del destino*. To remain competitive in the longer run with our economic rivals and to revitalize the domestic economy and thereby the well-being of the country's inhabitants and their progeny, some such development of a new role for the state will be a major part of the price. It could just happen that, with success along these lines, the older Republican state-as-(necessary?)-evil ideology will become as *passé* as the once-sacred doctrines of isolation became in the 1940s and 1950s. But to succeed, Clinton will have to take on sacred programmatic cows, which could make him enemies in Congress. If he doesn't redefine a convincing, affirmative role for government, he will not be doing his job of building the harmonistic political economy that is central to this new effort to find a way out of crisis and decline.

Clinton of course takes office as a minority president, elected by just 42.9 percent of those who went to the polls. Leaving aside the special case of John Quincy Adams in the free-for-all of 1824, fifteen of our fifty-two presidential elections have produced minority winners. Clinton's support ranks third from the bottom in this category: only Woodrow Wilson in 1912 (41.8 percent) and Abraham Lincoln in 1860 (39.8 percent) were elected with a narrower base of support.

On the positive side, it is noteworthy that in terms of an elected minority president's percentage lead over the runner-up, Clinton finishes a robust fourth out of these fifteen cases (5.5 percent); and if percentages of the electoral vote are used as a criterion, Clinton (at 68.8 percent) comes in a strong second only to Wilson in 1912 (81.9 percent). Moreover, Wilson (at least in his first term) and Lincoln, below him in the share of the vote, had personal qualities and political contexts favorable to active and highly successful presidencies. Even Nixon, just above him at 43.4 percent, was both a reasonably strong and reasonably successful president until ruination set with the disclosure of the Watergate affair early in his second term.

However, Clinton, with a considerably smaller working majority in Congress than they enjoyed, would seem to have far less room for maneuver than Wilson or Lincoln. The budget deficit will also hem in his programmatic running room, as will his tightrope act between the old and new Democrats. Clinton has a clear constitutional mandate. Any more extensive mandate will have to be fought for and won.

Alienation, Television, and Perot

Whenever major third entrants appear in presidential elections, they reflect a breakdown of the system's legitimacy: the greater the share secured by such candidates, the greater the breakdown. This has happened ten times in American political history, with twelve cases of significant insurgency (1860 and 1912 produced two significant-insurgency candidacies). With 18.9 percent of the total vote, Ross Perot finished a strong third among these twelve. Moreover, the other two cases involved major fragments of organized major parties—Millard Fillmore and the Whig-Americans of 1856 (21.5 percent) and Theodore Roosevelt and his Progressive wing of the Republican Party in 1912 (27.4 percent). Perot's showing is by far the most impressive ever achieved by that other category of third movements, the pure-outsider or "protest" surge.

The data in the *New York Times'* early postelection survey makes it clear that, with few exceptions, Perot's support cut remarkably evenly across the whole spectrum. Perot was strongest among partisan independents, young men, liberal Republicans (a chemical trace in a sample these days!), and a few other categories, and weakest among blacks, Jews, the elderly, and a number of white Democratic voting groups. Regionally there were important differentials. Perot was strongest in New England—his best state was Maine, where fully 30.1 percent voted for him and he edged out Bush for second place—and in the Plains states and Mountain West. He was weakest in the greater South, except for the burgeoning states of Texas and Florida. Yet the general impression is that his appeal cut broadly across most voter categories without (unlike George Wallace in 1968) being concentrated very heavily in any. At the very end, the *USA Today*/CNN Gallup poll reported that when Perot voters were asked how they would have voted if Perot were not in the race, the response was 38 percent for Clinton, 36 percent for Bush, and 6 percent for "others"; 15 percent would not have come to the polls and another 5 percent gave no response. So Perot did not change the outcome. Had he not run, the only notable effect would have been to reduce the turnout from about 56 percent to 54 percent. As there is a distinct historic pro-Republican cast to those groups and areas most penetrated by Perot, this may be one more bit of evidence for our general case that Bush suffered a vote of no confidence in 1992—though in this hypothetical exercise no landslide would have been involved.

Perot represents something quite new in American politics: the *enragé* billionaire Lone Ranger who demonstrated a near-perfect appreciation and use of television to build his following and sell his message. This message concentrated concretely on that part of the poisonous legacy of the past dozen years that produced the deficit and a hugely swollen national debt. But in more general terms, his claim was that the political system as such was broken. In a real sense, he virtually acted out the script that E. J. Dionne and others had been writing for some time: it was necessary to transcend the politics of deadlock and finger-pointing, it was necessary to find some immaculate way of producing correct policy without traditional politics getting in the way.

The extraordinary breadth of his support across the land reflects at least two facts of contemporary political life in the U.S. The first of these is the power of "infomercials" and last-minute TV blitzkrieg backed by unlimited reserves of money to reach and appeal to "common sense." The second is the uncanny fit between Perot's general political symbolism and the pervasive public sense that

Washington insiders and powerful interest groups had stolen the political system from the people.

This candidacy is a warning. It reflects some sort of dialectical acceleration in the decay of traditional parties and channels of authentic mass political action, a decay that I and others have discussed with growing alarm for the past twenty years. Vast numbers of Americans are now poised on the brink of taking a great leap into the unknown as they seek a savior from endless crises and an equally endless squeeze on their living standards. More than nineteen million did so in 1992. . . .

Demographics and the Vote

The 1992 election was a repudiation, but not a radical realignment. Elections are won as a rule by shifts at the margins. Bill Clinton's 53.4 percent of the two-party vote is impressive under the circumstances, but it was no popular-vote landslide. And there have been considerably larger two-party swings in our recent past than the 7 percent pro-Democratic swing that occurred nationally from 1988 to 1992. The basic long-term demographic patterns within which this election was decided go back a generation; the overhang from the past is impressively power- ful. Notwithstanding the collapse of both Carter and Bush, more than three- quarters of the variance in the 1992 distribution of votes can be explained by the aggregate voter-group preferences in 1976; in terms of basic voting align- ments, not much has changed in sixteen years. When we ask which groups line up which way, the short answer is that given by Captain Louis Renault in *Casablanca*: Round up the usual suspects. Groups (very often overlapping, of course) that gave Clinton more than 60 percent of the two-party vote include, in order, blacks (88 percent); Jews (87 percent); voters in the lowest family- income bracket, less than $15,000 per year (72 percent); Hispanics (71 percent); members of union households (70 percent); the unemployed (70 percent); voters in the lowest education level, less than completed high school (66 percent); first-time voters (62 percent); and unmarried voters (60 percent). At the other end of the distribution are those groups in which Bush prevailed over Clinton. These include, in order, white voters (49 percent Democratic); those with a completed college education (49 percent); voters in the medium-high family- income bracket, $50,000–$74,999 (49 percent); voters in the South (49 per- cent); white men (47 percent); voters in the top income bracket, $75,000 and over (43 percent); white Protestants (42 percent); and white born-again Chris- tians (27 percent). There are very few surprises in either list. The survey also makes clear that partisanship coupled with ideology forms a far more powerful long-term continuity factor than demographics.

Even without regard for the moment to the Perot presence in the race, the differentials in the 1988–1992 swing across voter groups make it clear that Bill Clinton's strategy of focusing on the economy and targeting his main appeal to the white middle class was brilliantly successful. This election was above all a revolt of the moderates, a point which the relative strengths and weaknesses of Perot's candidacy in the electorate simply underscores. Demographic and political groups with a two-party Democratic swing of 10 percent or more include Jews (+22); first-term voters (+14); moderate partisan independents (+12); members of union households (+12); voters with complete college educations (+12); voters aged 18–29 (+11); voters with some college education (+11); white men (+11); partisan independents, as a whole (+10); and moderates, as a whole (+10). Groups showing the least Democratic swing include liberal Republicans (–2); blacks (0); Hispanics (+1); liberals (+1); liberal Democrats (+2); conservative Republicans (+2); conservatives as a whole (+3); Republicans as a whole (+3); voters with complete high-school educations (+5); and voters with second lowest family incomes, $15,000–$29,999 (+5). And, according to a *USA Today* survey, Clinton carried suburban voters over Bush. Among Democrats voting for Reagan in 1984, their 1992 choice was Clinton, 55 percent; Bush, 25 percent; and Perot, 20 percent—a two-party Democratic lead of 38 points. Careful readers examining the Democratic percentages in the most-Republican groups discussed earlier will probably be less impressed by the expected (their relative ranking) than by the fact that Bush's lead over Clinton was generally very thin indeed.

With Perot in the race, net voter support for both major-party candidates declined from the two-party 1988 contest, but Bush's decline was more than five times as large as was that on the Democratic side (–16 percent versus –3 percent). George Bush lost 29 percent of his 1988 voting base, one of the largest single-election declines of its sort ever seen. This relative collapse covers a very wide and remarkably heterogenous list of voter groups, being notably limited only among blacks (–8 percent) and Hispanics (–17 percent). And as Perot represented one considerable part of the public's overall judgment that George Bush had been weighed in the balance and found wanting, so his last-minute mini-surge reflected another basic reality of 1992: Bill Clinton had not completely closed his sale of himself as the agent of change from the rejected *status quo* of 1992.

Nonetheless, the highest strategic marks should be given to Governor Clinton, his master tactician James Carville, and other key actors in his campaign. To win, Clinton had to develop an appeal to "middle America" that recent Democratic nominees have lacked. He was successful in this, and in distancing himself from tight relationships with core interest-group liberal constituencies, yet without disavowing them—a debt balancing act. Ross Perot helped by drawing from segments of the electorate that might otherwise have drifted back to George Bush. The strategy was deplored by some urban liberals, but it may have been the only way through the maze to success in 1992. Despite his huge 1988–1992 losses, George Bush might very well have won this election confronted by a less dynamic opponent pursuing a more traditional Democratic campaign strategy. The key to success lay in capitalizing effectively on the revolt of the moderates, the preponderant majority of whom had voted for Reagan and Bush over the past three elections. Even in 1992, this could not have been done by just any Democratic nominee.

The Robust Republicans

Before the actual returns came in, the question hovered in the air as to whether this election was another 1932. It wasn't, because the old partisan voting linkages just aren't there any more and new ones have not been cemented. Republicans gained nine seats in the House contests and broke even in the Senate races. By contrast, the Republicans lost eighty-two incumbent congressmen in 1932. In 1860–61, Lincoln's position as a national minority president was much improved when more than seventy Southern representatives and twenty-one senators left the union with their states. With FDR, Wilson, and Lincoln, overwhelming legislative majorities accompanied the new administration into office. This is not the case this year. If 1992 was a landslide rejection of an incumbent Republican president, his party was scarcely affected.

This can be read in a variety of ways, of course. Republicans were chagrined that a "golden," post-reapportionment, post-scandal opportunity had been lost to make far greater gains that this. There were more open seats in the House (91) than at any time since the First World War. Considering the levels of public rage against incumbents the polls had monitored all year, a real slaughter of sitting Democrats seemed perfectly possible. Turnovers of as many as 150 House seats were contemplated. The payoff on election day, however, was surprisingly modest. Thirteen Democratic incumbents were ousted, as were six Republicans, while another three Democrats and a Republican lost to their opponents where apportionment forced them to run against each other. As for the open seats, Democrats won them by a 57–34 margin and partisan switches in this category canceled each other out. The Republicans' great expectations were once again dashed; but they were hardly irrational.

Following the civil rights act of 1982, Republicans pursued a very often successful "aggregation" strategy of drawing districts designed to elect blacks or Latinos and thus draw off votes on which many white Democrats had relied for their election. Many of the competitive seats narrowly won by Democrats in 1992 probably represent "land mines" for the future. Thus the 176 Republicans in the next Congress represent a situation that, from Clinton's point of view, could have been worse, and may very well become so across the 1990s.

The congressional election was notable on a number of dimensions. The number of House seats where there was no major-party opposition plummeted to 29, the lowest number (and proportion) since 1990. The number and proportion of competitive contests rose to the highest level in incumbent-held seats in nearly thirty years. Perhaps most notable of all was the strong pro-Republican vote shift in the South. This produced a situation where, for the first time in American history, the Democratic share of the congressional two-party vote was lower in the South (51.9 percent) than it was outside it (52.9 percent). This region's secular realignment toward the Republicans, speeded up in 1984 and 1988, is still under way; it has now fully rejoined the Union, and then some.

Still, despite seeming change, the overall impression is one of remarkable continuity. This is the more remarkable when one considers the "everything-up-

for-grabs" atmosphere that was reported in the polls and reflected in a good deal
of pre-election analysis. And if I have not spent any great time discussing the
Senate contests, it is because the continuity level is greater still. In the end, only
four incumbents lost their seats (Fowler, D-Ga.; Kasten, R-Wis.; Sanford, D-
N.C.; and Seymour, R-Calif., the latter an appointee). The candidate domination
that is a central theme of the sixth electoral era's "permanent campaign" remains
alive and in fine health in 1992. This is one very strong reason for believing that
while this election ended the Reagan-Bush era, it made no more than an
occasional dent on the relationship between candidates and voters that so mark
this particular era in American history. To the extent that this is so, the electoral
regime set up in and after the critical realignment of the late 1960s has not yet
run its course or been replaced by something basically different.

Interest group liberalism, in the sense first used by the political scientist
Theodore Lowi in 1969 as an alliance between constituent groups and a benevolent state, has faltered because the state no longer effectively serves the demands
of the groups and the groups no longer provide consistently reliable electoral
support for the (Democratic) governing coalition. Yet at the same time, as the
electoral continuities demonstrate, most of the groups are still there (only
organized labor is notably weaker); indeed, the old interest groups have been
joined by several new fervently active groups—feminists, gays, Hispanics, greens,
disabled people, among others. And most still look, however, skeptically, to
the Democrats.

However, the state today is far less able than before the year 1968 either to
provide tangible benefits or to broker satisfactory compromises—hence the
frustration and the interregnum. Interest group liberalism as a viable regime order
may be dead, but as the 1990 election data show, the Democratic Party still
depends heavily on a coalition of liberal interest groups, traditional and new.
Indeed, leaving aside the white South, the Clinton coalition of 1992 looks
remarkably like the Roosevelt coalition of 1940. What remains to be seen is
whether Clinton can cement their allegiance, while simultaneously defining a
transcendent national interest, to create a seventh durable electoral era and
governing consensus. . . .

Summary Questions

1. Why does the author believe that President Bush's defeat in the 1992 election
   was "almost a historical inevitability?" What were some of the factors that
   contributed to Bush's defeat?
2. Burnham argues that the 1992 election represented a "revolt of moderates,"
   with candidate Bill Clinton doing particularly well among the middle class.
   What kinds of difficulties will President Clinton face in trying to retain the
   support of this group, while simultaneously responding to the core liberal

elements of the Democratic party? Have any of these difficulties revealed themselves during his first term as president?

 6.3

Americans Want and Need a New Political Party

Gordon S. Black and Benjamin D. Black

New political parties have not had much success in American presidential elections. Since the 1850s Democrats and Republicans have dominated electoral politics, and while third parties have frequently appeared on the ballot since that time, none has ever replaced or seriously challenged the political hegemony of the two major parties.

Gordon and Benjamin Black believe that there now exists a "market" for the appearance of a new political party. Using data from a nationwide political survey administered in the 1992 election year, they find that a high proportion of the electorate support meaningful reform of the political system, ranging from enacting term limitations to public funding of elections under certain conditions. At the same time a substantial portion of the public believes that the current parties and their incumbents are unlikely to ever support the much-needed reforms. Their poll results indicate voter sentiment for supporting a new political party if the party's positions matched their own.

The authors contend that the existing two-party system can be successfully challenged despite strong historical evidence to the contrary. In their view, while both major parties have "conspired to artificially maintain the status quo," leadership, organization, and ballot obstacles can be overcome.

With the lone exception of the Republicans, new political parties in the United States have achieved limited success. Anyone who approaches this topic must acknowledge that the historical evidence suggests that

Gordon S. Black is chairman and CEO, Gordon S. Black Corporation; Benjamin D. Black is manager of survey services, Voter Research and Surveys. This article was written in 1992.

those who today believe a new major party is needed are likely to be disappointed in their quest. We should not forget, however, that history is best used to explain the past. It's rarely effective in predicting the future.

A successful new political party will almost certainly arise someday in American politics, just as the Republicans did in the 1850s. When that happens, the historical evidence will "seem" just as convincing as it does now, but the party will arise despite it. The conventional wisdom will prove decidedly wrong at that point, because someone or some group will have figured out why the ancient precedents don't apply. Yet another element needs to be considered. Many political parties have in fact been successful in electing people to local and state offices—although not for a century and a third has a new party won the presidency or gained control of Congress.

At issue, then, is not whether a new party can have some success—many have—but the *extent* to which it can succeed. The latter is determined by whether or not certain basic conditions are present in the country.

Condition 1: The presence of a "market."   The first condition for the emergence of a political party is that there must be a market for it. The size of this market is determined by the answers to a few key questions:

What percentage of the population is dissatisfied with the policies of the existing political parties?

Given substantial dissatisfaction with existing parties, what percentage of the population would be attracted by a new party with certain issue attributes?

How strongly are they attracted by this potential party? Conversely, how actively are they repelled by attributes of the existing parties?

The answers to these questions are empirical. If 90% of the population in a democracy dislikes an existing party, that party can't long persist as a major force. All over eastern Europe, for example, communist parties collapsed abruptly when the people were finally given a voice in their political affairs.

The first question was easy to answer. We conducted a feasibility study of 1,600 registered and likely voters in late May 1992 and found that over half of all voters were angry with both major parties. Nearly half the voters concluded that neither party was likely to provide them with the type of public policies they wanted. We asked four separate questions concerning the desire to have a new party. Thirty percent of the electorate answered all four questions in the affirmative. (The question wordings and the responses are shown in Table 6.1, items 1–4.) Other surveys have come up with similar findings. For example, a CBS News poll in June 1992 found 31% of the public agreeing that the "two political parties have become obsolete," while 58% agreed that "the country needs a new political party to compete with the Democratic and Republican parties."

If one computes the impact of our potential new party on the two old parties, it appears that they might be left with about equal shares of the electorate—25% or so each. The new party, by contrast, might attract 30% of voters.

Table 6.1

Broad Backing for a New Political Party

	All Respondents	Those Inclined to Back Perot at Time of Survey	New Party Voters*
1. Agree, if Democrats and Republicans continue to run things, we'll never get reform.	46%	64%	76%
2. Agree, need a new political party to reform American politics.	47%	67%	100%
3. Yes, would like to see new national party run candidates.	57%	75%	100%
4. Agree, neither party can get things going; need new party.	50%	72%	100%
5. Agree, current incumbents will never reform political process.	69%	83%	87%
6. Yes, angry at both political parties and their candidates.	56%	79%	84%
7. Would switch and vote new party if positions match their own.	65%	81%	100%

*New party voters are those answering "yes" to items 2, 3, 4, and 7.

Questions:

1. The following are some negative things people are saying about state and national politics these days. For each one, please tell me whether you agree or disagree with the statement. . . . If the Democrats and Republicans continue to run things, we'll never get real reform.

2. (Same preface as 1) . . . We need a new political party to reform American politics.

3. Would you like to see a new national political party form, and run candidates for office?

4. Some people are saying that neither the Democrats nor the Republicans are capable any longer of getting this country going in the right direction, and that we need a new national political party. Do you strongly agree, moderately agree, moderately disagree, or strongly disagree?

5. (Same preface as 1) . . . The current incumbents in office will never reform the political process.

6. Some people are angry at both political parties and their candidates. Would you say that describes how you feel right now?

7. Suppose that a new reform-oriented political party is created to run candidates for Congress, the Senate, and even your state legislature. Assuming for a moment that this new party was supporting YOUR positions on many of the issues you care about, would you be MOST likely to vote for the candidates of the new reform party or would you be MOST likely to continue to vote either for the Republican or the Democratic candidates?

Source: Survey by Gordon S. Black Corporation, May 1992.

The second question has to do with the issue attributes of the new party. Voters will not join a new party just for the sake of joining. We examined a whole range of issues where we had reason to believe that the voters, particularly those disaffected, would be prepared to support positions in overwhelming numbers. We found the base for a political party involved a commitment to fundamental electoral, governmental, and policy reform. (See Tables 6.2 and 6.3.)

The final question is whether voters will actually defect to the candidates of a new political party. Those whom we surveyed indicated by a margin of 65% to 22% that they would jump ship to a new, "reform-oriented" party—assuming the new party supports most of their positions on the major issues (Table 6.1, item 7).

Table 6.2
Support for Reform of the Electoral Process

	All Respondents	Those Inclined to Back Perot at Time of Survey	New Party Voters
1. Limit terms of members of Congress, senators, governors, state legislators to 12 years.	77%	82%	86%
2. House elections run every four years instead of every two years.	58%	62%	58%
3. Prohibit campaign contributions from PACS.	66%	72%	77%
4. Prohibit campaign contributions from foreign governments, corporations, or individuals.	78%	80%	82%
5. Favor public funding—if it would encourage better candidates against incumbents.	79%	81%	84%
6. Favor public funding—if tied to elimination of PAC contributions.	76%	79%	80%

Note: Percentages shown are those approving of the proposal.

Questions:
1. The following are proposed changes in election laws. For each one, please tell me whether you approve or disapprove of the proposal. . . . Limit the terms of office of members of Congress, senators, governors, and state legislators to 12 years.
2. (Same preface as 1) . . . Have members of the House of Representatives run every four years, instead of every two years as the constitution currently requires.
3. (Same preface as 1) . . . Prohibit campaign contributions from the Political Action Committees.
4. (Same preface as 1) . . . Prohibit campaign contributions from foreign governments, foreign corporations, or foreign individuals.
5. If public funding of campaigns would encourage more good people to run against incumbents, would you favor or oppose public funding of congressional and senatorial candidates?
6. If public funding were tied to the elimination of all special interest campaign contributions, would you favor or oppose public funding?

Source: Survey by Gordon S. Black Corporation, May 1992.

Table 6.3
Support for Direct Democracy

	All Respondents	Those Inclined to Back Perot at Time of Survey	New Party Voters
1. Give citizens in your state the right of "initiative."	92%	96%	96%
2. Establish the right of initiative for federal legislation.	85%	90%	90%
3. Provide for a referendum on annual state budget.	80%	82%	85%
4. Provide for constitutional amendment requiring national referendum on federal tax increases.	72%	77%	80%
5. Provide for recall elections of public officials.	84%	89%	91%
6. Provide for constitutional amendment requiring balanced budget every year.	84%	89%	91%

Note: Percentages shown are those approving of the proposal.

Questions:
1. There are several other rights that some states give their citizens to provide them with a way of influencing their government. The right of citizens to sign a petition to have a law placed on the ballot for a vote by everyone is called the "initiative." In general, do you favor or oppose giving citizens the initiative in your state?
2. Would you favor or oppose giving citizens the right to petition the federal government to have a law placed on the ballot for national elections?
3. In some states certain proposals must be on the ballot so that everyone has an opportunity to vote on them. This is called a "referendum." In general, do you favor or oppose requiring a referendum on the annual budget of your state?
4. Would you favor or oppose a constitutional amendment to require that any federal tax increase be voted on in a national referendum by the general public?
5. Some states permit citizens to sign petitions asking for a recall election for an elected public official. When enough signatures are obtained, a special election is held where the voters can vote a public official out of office. Would you favor or oppose giving citizens the rights to have a recall election where they can vote an elected state or local official out of office?
6. Would you favor or oppose a constitutional amendment that would require Congress and the President to provide a balanced budget every year?

Source: Survey by Gordon S. Black Corporation, May 1992.

The reasons for so high a willingness to switch are simple. Party loyalty continues to erode, due in part to shortcomings of both the Republicans and Democrats. They have engaged in a whole range of behavior that has turned off many voters.

Voters, as political consumers, are little different from the car-buying public, which defected by the millions to the Japanese when the American car manufacturers failed to give them the quality product they wanted. The support for Perot at his peak proves that people are more than willing to look outside the old two-party system.

As a test of the validity of the spring 1992 survey, many of the same questions were asked in a smaller sample of 600 in August. The only statistical significant difference was that the percentage of people angry with the Democratic party had dropped from 59% to 50%.

Is there a "potential market" for a new, reform-oriented, centrist political party? The research produced an affirmative answer about as unequivocally as any study could possibly produce. A majority of the public is fed up with two established political parties, with Congress, the president, and state office holders. They see the parties having collaborated to produce many of the problems of the past two decades. The Democrats and Republicans, of course, blame each other with great vehemence, and the public thinks it's about the only thing they can get right.

In 1990, 72% of the seats in the House of Representatives were considered locked up by one or the other of the major parties. As a result, there was no significant challenge to the party in power in those districts. However, in the remaining districts (28%) where there was a significant challenge to the incumbent in power, the 1990 exit polls shows that 63% of voters went against the incumbent. If voters are given a real choice, rather than a sacrificial lamb, they are more than willing to reject their congressman. A third party mounting such challenges is likely to have broad success.

Condition 2: Creating the new party organizationally. The existence of a "market" is a necessary but not a sufficient condition for the creation of a new party. Organizationally, a political party is "people with resources and motivation." Without the right kind of active participants it's impossible to create a successful party. But what kinds of people? The organizing leadership must be people with:

* High and sustainable motivation.
* Access to resources, including money; access to others; organizational skills; substantive knowledge with regard to public policy.
* Income that can sustain their independent activities; or a willingness to forgo income for a time.
* Broad agreement on political interests and values.

A political party that can tap such leadership can succeed for the long haul. One doesn't need many people with these skills and resources to make things happen in most metropolitan areas. Collect 10 to 15 of them in a metropolitan area of one million people, coupled with a market like the one described above, and a political party can be created rapidly. The question of whether a new party can attract 2,500 to 3,000 such persons nationally is again an empirical question, and one for which we do not yet have a complete answer. The organizers of the Independence Party have a well-developed list of more than 20,000 such activists. They performed a randomized market test from this list with a sample of 400. Their "success rate" in terms of preliminary recruitment exceeded 15%, which clearly would produce more than enough leaders from a list of 20,000. The final answer will only come, of course, when they approach the full list.

Condition 3: Getting on the ballot. Getting on the ballot is nothing more than a matter of resources. With money, a party can get on the ballot everywhere. Ross Perot has shown that he could gain access to the ballot, albeit at a cost of 18 million dollars. But even minor party efforts have proved successful. The courts have been lowering the barriers to ballot access, and the legal suits are one of the best ways to show publicly how the established parties have rigged the system.

Condition 4: Avoiding a situation where the new party's positions are preempted. Our political parties have had years to deal with many of the problems that outrage the electorate, but they haven't done much at all about them. Some of the main problems with both parties stem from the constituencies that control them. The Gordon S. Black Corporation has performed surveys of national convention delegates for NBC News and USA Today, and we were ourselves surprised at how skewed these activists' views are toward certain special interests. Two statistics capture this unrepresentativeness: Of the Republican delegates in Houston, 46% said they were "born again" Christians; over two-thirds of the delegates were conservative to very conservative. Of the Democratic delegates in New York City this year, 45% said they were employed by government in some form or capacity.

In other words, we have one political party—the Republicans—dominated by a moral minority who would impose their views of morality on the rest of us. We have a second party—the Democrats—dominated by those who are in the direct employ of most of the programs the public would reform. The Democratic wolves are running the government chicken factories. The only way to convince voters that the system can be changed is to challenge it from outside.

Will the major parties reform themselves? Is that a gamble the public is willing to take with its time, money, and energy? We know that two out of every three voters believe that the current incumbents are never going to reform the system, and nearly half believe that the political parties are incapable of reforming anything.

Apologists for the Two Party System

As Theodore Lowi of Cornell University has pointed out (*New York Times Magazine*, August 23, 1992), many observers who argue against the potential for a new national party are in fact advocates of the virtues of two-party democracy. They naturally would want any new party effort to fail.

Our two-party system, as we have practiced it since 1965, is about as big a failure as any system can be. In the process of failing, the parties have managed to antagonize and alienate two out of every three voters. The party system has become one gigantic payoff system, with candidates accepting large electoral bribes in exchange for delivering the public policy sought by the PACs and other interest groups. The much ballyhooed turnover this year in Congress is substantially (over half) a product of Congress's "bribing" members to retire by allowing them to retain huge campaign war chests for their personal use.

The analogy between former Soviet communism and the American two-party system, though absurd on the surface, is frighteningly pertinent. Both systems have conspired to artificially maintain the status quo. Communism survived by threat of force; the two-party system, by eliminating voter choice through gerrymandering, by attracting huge amounts of PAC money, and through incumbent perks. In addition, both systems have existed through eliminating (or in the US, greatly curbing) the ability of challengers to gain access to the ballot. A New York voter, for example, does not have a choice when 147 of the 190 incumbents for the state senate are unopposed. But now there is reason to take heart: Ten years ago the collapse of communism seemed far more unlikely than the creation of a third political party in the United States does today.

Summary Questions

1. What leads the authors to believe that a "market" now exists for the formation of a new political party? Why do they believe that a new political party can be successful? What arguments can be raised to refute their position?
2. What kinds of political reform does the American public desire? According to the authors, why do the existing political parties appear incapable or unwilling to respond to such concerns?

Chapter 7

Campaigns and Elections

Few aspects of American politics have changed as much in recent decades as the ways in which candidates campaign for national office. A generation ago, electioneering was dominated by political parties, which were the main means of communication between candidates and voters. Party parades, mailings, rallies, and door-to-door canvassing were the essential ingredients of campaigns. Party affiliation, based on strong bonds of ethnic, class, regional, or religious identity, was the key factor in determining how voters cast their ballots. Ticket splitters who voted for a president from one party and senators or House members from another were a small minority.

Today's campaigns are candidate centered. An individual politician's campaign organization raises funds, mobilizes activists, advertises on television, conducts sophisticated direct mailing operations, and polls voters, all largely independent of party organization. Political consultants, pollsters, and outside strategists have replaced the party bosses as central figures in campaigns. Candidates' issue positions and personal attractiveness have challenged party loyalties as key factors in voters' decisions. Split-ticket voting is now quite common.

The new style of campaigning is especially apparent in presidential elections. A generation ago, candidates were nominated by party professionals who were usually chosen through state conventions or caucuses tightly controlled by the party organization. The eventual nominee typically had worked his way up the party hierarchy over a long period, had served in a number of elected positions in government, and was able to put together a coalition of state party delegations to win the nomination. Once such a person was nominated, the presidential campaign was usually run by the national party organization. Between 1952 and 1968, for example, at least one of the party campaigns was run by the national committee staff in each election; in 1956 and 1964, both campaigns were run by the national party organizations.

The contemporary route to the presidency is quite different. Nominations are often won or lost on the basis of the personal appeal of candidates on television and their ability to put together effective campaign organizations. Traditional party factors are far less influential, as candidates with commanding media presence can gain recognition and stature almost overnight. Having held elected political office is now no longer a prerequisite to becoming a serious candidate, as demonstrated by the campaigns of television evangelist Pat Robertson and preacher/activist Jesse Jackson in 1988. Moreover, the nominating delegates are often amateurs in politics, motivated more by issues than by party loyalty. After the nomination, the presidential campaign is run by the candidate's organization rather than by the national party. (Since 1972, no general election campaign has been run by either the Republican or the Democratic national committee staffs.)

A number of factors have contributed to the new style of campaign politics. Some reflect social changes, such as rising levels of education, which have created an electorate far more independent and unwilling to follow party labels blindly. Others have resulted from reforms in the political parties, especially the Democratic party, which are now far more open and democratic. New people have the opportunity to enter politics despite little partisan background. Perhaps most important has been the emergence of television as the primary political communications medium and of technological improvements in direct mail techniques, polling, and other practices.

In general, there has been a shift in the nature of key campaign resources. The skill and labor of party functionaries, who are often volunteers, are less important; financial resources, so necessary in purchasing the services and skills of the new campaign operatives, consultants, pollsters, and media specialists, have become crucial. Expensive campaign travel by jet is now the norm, and the cost of network television advertising is exorbitant.

Not surprisingly, there has been a tremendous escalation in the costs of national campaigns. The exception is a decline in general election expenditures for the presidential race since 1972, when Richard Nixon probably spent over $60 million on his successful race. The financial abuses of the Nixon re-election effort played a major role in the adoption of public funding for presidential elections. In 1992, $55.2 million was allocated to each of the major party candidates. Increases in campaign spending for the presidency are now most evident in the nomination process, in which Ronald Reagan, who was uncontested for the 1984 nomination, spent $35 million "securing" the nomination. The long, drawn-out nomination process, characterized by a large number of primaries, necessitates extensive television advertising. Well over half of all expenditures in both the nomination and general election processes are for television advertising, and the percentage increases during each election cycle.

Senate and House races have been affected by the new style of campaigning as well. Senate contests are often highly competitive, typically attracting wealthy, prominent challengers and inspiring huge expenditures of funds, particularly for television advertising. Five-million-dollar Senate races are common. In 1984, incumbent Senator Jesse Helms, a Republican from North Carolina, spent a record $16.5 million in defeating challenger James Hunt, who spent $9.5 million. Much of Helms's spending went to pay for 150 different television ads (broadcast thousands of times) in the year and a half preceding the election.

House races are far less competitive than their Senate counterparts. Challengers are often relatively unknown, and they find it difficult to get funding and free media attention. Incumbents, in contrast, stay in the public eye through their work in Congress and their actions to help constituents. Also, their large victory margins in elections attract contributions for future campaigns. Despite the fact that incumbent safety in the House appears to be greater than at any time in history, House elections have not escaped huge campaign expenditures. According to Federal Election Commission figures, in 1974 the average House incumbent spent about $56,000 and the average challenger, $40,000. By 1992 incumbents were outspending challengers on the average of three and a half to one, with the average incumbent spending over $560,000.

The readings that follow focus on the new style of political campaigning and suggested reforms. The selection by Steven V. Roberts first examines a hotly contested 1986 U.S. Senate race, which illustrates the new style of campaigning and the crucial role played by TV in elections. Michael Malbin then examines the impact of money in congressional elections, especially the financial disadvantages faced by challengers. He concludes that an overhaul of the campaign finance laws is needed, including the possibility of some sort of public funding in congressional races. Finally, the possibility of an even more drastic political reform, limiting congressional term limits by law or constitutional amendment, is considered. Former congressman Bill Franzel and political scientist Thomas Mann explore this issue in a debate format.

7.1

Politicking Goes High-Tech

Steven V. Roberts

The past few decades have witnessed a major change in the manner in which candidates run for public office. Campaigns are now candidate centered rather than party centered. They require great expenditures of money and rely on campaign professionals more than on volunteers. Political consultants and campaign management firms, many from New York City and Washington, now dominate most statewide races and employ sophisticated targeted direct mail strategies, continuous polling, and mass media productions.

Races for the U.S. Senate have perhaps been most affected by the new high-technology politics. Both Senate incumbents and challengers are typically well funded, and because statewide constituencies are often diverse, sophisticated strategies to reach different groups of voters are necessary.

In this article, Steven V. Roberts describes a 1986 Missouri Senate race that exemplifies the use of modern campaign strategy and technology. Outside consultants altered campaign strategies on virtually an hour-by-hour basis to respond to subtle changes in the electorate's attitudes and orientations. Particularly important as an electioneering tool was the political spot (a thirty- or sixty-second commercial) designed to appeal to the emotions of voters.

W hen the Senate race in Missouri entered the homestretch early last month campaign strategists for Republican Christopher S. (Kit) Bond began to take nightly readings of the voters' mood. As soon as they learned that the Reagan-Gorbachev meeting in Iceland had collapsed on Sunday, October 12, they inserted three new questions into their polls.* On Monday night, the President spoke to the nation about the meeting; by

Steven V. Roberts is currently a reporter for *U.S. News and World Report*. This article appeared in print two days before the November 1986 election.

* At the Iceland summit, President Reagan insisted that the Strategic Defense Initiative (the "Star Wars" defense system) not be one of the items on the bargaining table, much to the chagrin of Soviet leader Mikhail Gorbachev. In the eyes of some, Reagan's position was a barrier to a nuclear arms treaty. Others, however, viewed it positively, as "standing up to the Russians."

Tuesday night, Don Sipple, Mr. Bond's media adviser, sensed he was onto something big.

What he read in the polls astounded him: Missouri voters were backing the President by margins of 6 and 7 to 1. Mr. Bond was already running a television commercial that stressed his support for the Strategic Defense Initiative (the President's space-based missile shield) and attacked the arms-control policy of his Democratic opponent, Harriett Woods. Mr. Sipple decided to recast the spot to take advantage of the talks. By Wednesday morning, the consultant had sent Mr. Bond a new introduction, emphasizing that the President had been able to negotiate in Iceland from a "position of strength." By Friday, the revised commercial was on the air.

With the use of increasingly sophisticated polling methods, videotape machines and satellite technology, political consultants like Don Sipple can now monitor the public mood on an hour-by-hour, day-to-day basis, searching for a cresting emotion that might sway a bloc of marginal voters. Today's media whiz then tries to capture, and manipulate, that emotion in a new television commercial that can be put on the air overnight. "It used to take two or three weeks for information to reach the voters," says the pollster Harrison Hickman, "but now it's film at 11. Clearly, we've pushed the edge of the envelope on this stuff."

During the current battle for control of the Senate this high-tech, high-stakes struggle by consultants and pollsters for the hearts and minds of the voting public has reached a new level of importance and visibility. When voters cast their ballots in Missouri and other states on Tuesday, they will be making choices based largely on impressions created by these media consultants. Marshall McLuhan was right: the medium is the message. In American politics today, the medium is television, and that medium is dominated by an elite of highly paid but unelected consultants. The democratic ideal, of a candidate talking directly to the voters and appealing for support, has been profoundly distorted.

These electronic contests sometimes resemble a new form of television game show—one could call them "Spot Wars"—and the cost is staggering. Kit Bond and Harriett Woods will each spend about $4 million on their campaigns, with 60 percent going toward buying television time.

The Missouri Senate race has attracted national interest for a number of reasons. Both of the contestants are tough, seasoned campaigners. Kit Bond, a 47-year-old lawyer, is a moderate conservative who won his first statewide race for auditor at age 31 and has served two terms as Governor. Harriett Woods, who is 59 and a journalist by profession, peppers her liberal stance with populist swipes at the big banks and corporations that have contributed heavily to her rival. She lost a close Senate race in 1982 to John C. Danforth, but was elected Lieutenant Governor in 1984.

Moreover, both parties feel that the larger battle for control of the Senate next year hinges on a handful of key races. And Missouri, where the retirement of

Democrat Thomas F. Eagleton gives the Republicans a chance to pick up a vacant seat, is one of them.*

Not surprisingly, the race attracted the top guns in the consulting business and promised to be the Super Bowl of media advisers. Mr. Bond's man, Don Sipple, is a partner in the Washington firm of Bailey, Deardourff, Sipple, which has a superb track record in selling Republicans. The Woods team at the outset was led by the hottest name on the Democratic side, Robert Squier, who is also based in Washington. Top guns do not come cheap. Mr. Squier, for example, charges a $60,000 fee plus 15 percent of the "media buy," or another $350,000, in a state like Missouri.

Consultants, of course, also work in gubernatorial and House campaigns, but those races do not usually involve the sort of media warfare that dominates the major Senate contests; there is much less money available for the candidates since many national contributors are more interested in senatorial campaigns. The cost of television advertising, however, has grown so rapidly that today, Senate campaigns design most of their tactics for one of three purposes, and sometimes all three: generating free television and radio coverage, raising money to finance paid commercials, and energizing supporters to go out and raise more money.

In Missouri, one 30-second spot on the popular evening game show "Wheel of Fortune" costs about $3,000, and as the race moved into the final hectic month, both candidates were spending about $250,000 a week apiece on television alone. The financial pressures have grown so great that candidates can spend up to half their time appealing for funds, often on the phone with individual donors. "The price of running for the Senate today," says Harriett Woods, "is spending more time than you'd like to spend asking people for more money than they'd like to give."

The Woods campaign actually started organizing its fund-raising effort in March 1985. "Without money," explained Jody Newman, the campaign manager, "we couldn't be on TV, and without TV, we couldn't win."

Fund raising in any senatorial campaign takes place on both the local and national levels. Within the home state, the techniques have remained standard: breakfasts and lunches, pool parties and cocktail parties that charge anywhere from $10 to $500 a head. The pitch is generally about local issues, because the contributors are more interested in what the candidates will do for the state than in the way they will affect policy in Washington.

No Senate candidate, however, can raise enough at home these days to finance a campaign. So, while the elections are generally decided by local issues, the money used to publicize those issues must be raised in Los Angeles and Detroit, Chicago and Houston and, above all, in New York and Washington.

---

* Although nearly two-thirds of Missouri's voters are registered Democrats, most are conservative, particularly outside the St. Louis and Kansas City areas. President Reagan ran extremely well in the state in both 1980 and 1984.

During their campaigns, both Kit Bond and Harriett Woods have made regular trips to New York City in search of money. While the Republican mainly worked the Wall Street crowd, the Democrat concentrated on the city's large liberal community, and Harriett Woods was continually running into other candidates in Manhattan. "We follow one another through the same art galleries and restaurants and living rooms," she said.

But no city is more important in the fund-raising game than Washington, and few Senate campaigns this year are without a new breed of Washington consultant, who does nothing but pry money out of the political action committees, or PACs. There are now more than 4,000 PACs, providing almost one-quarter of all contributions to Senate campaigns.

When Mrs. Woods scheduled a party for PAC representatives in September, her Washington fund-raiser, Sara G. Garland, was up at 5 a.m. for several days, addressing the invitations by hand. Ms. Garland also asked the Democratic Senators who signed the invitation to call special friends in the PACs and urge them to buy tickets. As one veteran fund-raiser put it, "In Washington, nothing happens until the fifth phone call."

The evening garnered $130,000, enough for perhaps four days of commercials, and Mrs. Woods was back again in October for a final dip into the Washington money pool. Ms. Garland also organized a series of smaller meetings between Mrs. Woods and groups of PACs devoted to specific subjects. For example, at one breakfast meeting last July, the guest list included PACs related to health, a major Woods concern. The hosts for the event were Representative Henry A. Waxman of California and Senator Max Baucus of Montana, senior Democrats on the committees handling health issues.

One PAC official resisted all appeals until Ms. Garland said, "This is an opportunity for you. I promise you a seat next to the Senator." The response was immediate: "I'm coming."

These days, Republicans enjoy an obvious fund-raising advantage. Ronald Reagan's farm and trade policies might not be popular in Missouri, but the President raised $450,000 for Mr. Bond at one luncheon in St. Louis. Some PACs hedge their bets and back both candidates, but most choose sides, and the competition is fierce. For example, Mr. Bond received help from John Danforth, who, as chairman of the influential Senate Commerce Committee, has "closed a few doors for us," according to Ms. Garland. "A lot of PACs are going to support Bond because Danforth talked to the C.E.O. or made a call to the vice president for government relations," she said.

Once their fund-raising efforts were in gear, both camps started exploring campaign themes. In the fall of 1985, Don Sipple organized "focus groups" around the state—small gatherings of about a dozen voters. "Focus groups give you a feel you can't get from any polling," said Mr. Sipple, who once served on Mr. Bond's staff in the Missouri Statehouse.

What Mr. Sipple discovered was that voters saw Mr. Bond as a "good guy, a good Governor," but not as an inspiring leader. Accordingly, Mr. Sipple reasoned, the Bond campaign should play to the candidate's strength by emphasizing the "comfort level" he had achieved with many voters.

The focus groups told Mr. Sipple that there were some "very clear differences" between the two candidates on a range of issues, particularly budget and fiscal matters, and the strategist thought he could label Mrs. Woods a "tax and spend" Democrat. The groups also indicated that Mrs. Woods was coming across as "too harsh" and "too liberal," but that information had to be handled delicately. "It was infinitely easier for us to work on the liberal thing than on the harsh thing," Mr. Sipple explained. "When you engage in attacks on personal qualities, that can be very dangerous."

Meanwhile, Mrs. Woods had hired Harrison Hickman and Paul Maslin, two poll-takers based in Washington, who took a survey for her in February. Mrs. Woods was the preference of 47 percent of those polled, as opposed to 44 percent for Mr. Bond. But that early in a campaign, political experts are more interested in what they call "internals," answers to specific questions that reveal a candidate's particular strengths and weaknesses. One of the key findings was that Mrs. Woods rated high on questions of personal character.

The poll revealed a major Bond weakness: his image as a wealthy "country-club Republican." But Messrs. Hickman and Maslin also uncovered evidence of Mr. Bond's strength. On the question of who has the "experience and qualifications a Senator needs," Mr. Bond led 2 to 1.

Bob Squier is a Washington celebrity, widely quoted in the press and seen at the best parties, a charming self-promoter with a good record in close races. In 1984, he worked for Paul Simon of Illinois, one of only two Democrats to oust an incumbent Republican Senator. Mr. Squier actively sought the Missouri assignment, because it promised to be one of the top races of the year, and Mrs. Woods and her staff were flattered by his attention. He would give them instant credibility in Washington and leverage with the PACs. He had a seasoned organization that offered a full range of services, from debate preparation and research to a music composer and editing facility.

By contrast, Joe Slade White, who had worked for Mrs. Woods in her previous campaigns, was practically a one-man operation, with little experience in major Senate races. In explaining the choice of Bob Squier over Joe White, Jody Newman, Mrs. Woods's campaign manager, said: "What often happens in races like this is that you have a fight over the airwaves. One candidate puts on a message, and the other has to decide how to respond. At times you have to rely on experience and instinct, and you have to have the capability of getting on the air instantly."

Nonetheless, while they wanted Mr. Squier's contacts and his organization, Mrs. Woods and her close-knit core of advisers were not prepared to take his advice. Ms. Newman has devoted much of her professional life to promoting Mrs.

Woods, and she approached the campaign with a simple, heartfelt premise: "If people really knew Harriett, they would vote for her." But Mr. Squier and the poll-takers had looked at the numbers. They knew their client's weaknesses as well as her strengths, and they were not ready to canonize her. During one planning meeting with the Woods staff, Bob Squier turned to Harrison Hickman and muttered, "All they have to do is pin wings on her and she'll fly to the Senate."

One key question in any Senate campaign is: Which side goes on the air first with paid commercials? The Woods team agreed to let Mr. Bond take the lead. He had more money, so the shorter the campaign, the better for Mrs. Woods. A longer campaign was also likely to tarnish Mrs. Woods's "halo effect," as Mr. Hickman put it. "She would look more and more like a politician."

Don Sipple was reading the situation in the same way, and decided to begin Mr. Bond's media campaign in May. "We wanted to draw her out," he said. "We wanted to make her spend more money than she wanted to before the primary in August."

The initial Bond spots were low-key. In one, he wandered through a field, talking to a farmer about agricultural issues, and casually mentioned that ladybugs help control aphids in a field of alfalfa. "That comment just said so much," said Mr. Sipple. "In a highly charged political environment, when the farm issue will be a political football, let's find out who knows about agriculture."

A second aim of the ads, added Mr. Sipple, was to "tighten up" his candidate's elitist image. Mr. Bond attended prep school at Deerfield, Mass., college at Princeton and law school at the University of Virginia—not exactly a man of the people. So the television spots invariably showed him in a checked sports shirt, speaking directly to ordinary voters, who nodded sympathetically. During a trip to a state fair, where Mr. Bond was going to film some commercials, the candidate doffed his lawyer's shirt and tie in the car and put on one of his made-for-television plaids—with the price tag still on it.

Don Sipple also prepared a second package of spots that focused on Missouri's troubled economy, taking care to separate Kit Bond from the Administration on such issues as trade policy.* The White House offered to provide the Bond campaign with a videotape of President Reagan meeting with the Republican, but "we passed," said the consultant, "much to the consternation of the White House."

The Bond media campaign was functioning smoothly, so well in fact that a Woods poll in early June showed that the Democrat had lost 11 points and was

---

* Trade policy is an especially sensitive issue in Missouri because of a large auto industry and the large number of farmers who have not done well financially in recent years. These two elements have supported policies to curb imports of automobiles and agricultural goods, in opposition to the free trade position of the Reagan Administration. Missouri farmers were divided in the Senate election: The conservative Missouri Farm Bureau endorsed Bond, while smaller, more radical groups such as the American Agriculture Movement strongly supported Woods.

behind, 48 to 40. More importantly, there was a marked decline in her advantage on character questions, the strongest element of her appeal. The original strategy had been to run a series of positive spots after Mr. Bond's initial wave, but the poll results forced a re-evaluation. It was time for something dramatic.

The Woods camp had received a juicy piece of information: Kit Bond sat on the board of an insurance company, Mutual Benefit Life, that held farm loans in Missouri and had foreclosed on local farmers. After a Kansas City paper ran a story on one of the families, David and Marilyn Peterson of Maysville, Mr. Squier took a film crew to their house for an interview.

During the filming, David Peterson broke into sobs while talking about his lost dairy herd. The Woods campaign, in Harrison Hickman's words, thought they had found a "silver bullet." Mr. Squier edited the material into a three-part series that ended with an attack on Kit Bond for opposing a moratorium on farm foreclosures. The consultants recommended skipping the original positive spots and coming straight out with the negative "crying farmer" spots. Mrs. Woods and her staff agreed.

The first two in the series began running in mid-June. The third spot, with Mr. Peterson's outburst and the attack on Mr. Bond, followed. That night, a group of Bond staff members gathered in Kansas City to watch the commercial. Katie Boyle, Mr. Bond's press secretary, felt as if someone had punched her.

Warren Erdman, Mr. Bond's campaign manager, immediately called Don Sipple. The two men decided to hold their fire and try to determine how the ad was affecting voters. Mr. Erdman traveled to his hometown of Higginsville and showed the commercials to a focus group. "As they watched the third spot, I watched their eyes. I wanted to see their expressions," said Mr. Erdman. When the citizens of Higginsville expressed distaste for the attack on Kit Bond, Mr. Erdman breathed easily for the first time in days.

A strategy was then formulated. Katie Boyle would express sympathy for the Petersons, but would denounce the Woods campaign for "gutter" politics. The Bond camp also encouraged critical stories in the news media about the Woods spot. With a tip from Katie Boyle, Mike Reilly, a reporter for the *Columbia Daily Tribune*, tracked down the Petersons and, after a lengthy interview with Marilyn Peterson, wrote a story quoting her as saying, "I kinda felt like we had been used" by the Woods campaign.

Miss Boyle rushed copies of the article to the Kansas City television stations and two of them used it on the air that night. Within days, the outcry against the spot had reached a crescendo around the state. It was, Bob Squier later conceded, a masterful job of using the news media.

The Woods camp was reeling. Jody Newman was on the phone with Bob Squier, saying that supporters were upset about the negative tone of the ad. The candidate herself was complaining about how she looked. Messrs. Hickman and Maslin took a quick poll and found decidedly mixed results. In the St. Louis area, Mr. Bond had actually increased his overall lead to 10 points. But many voters who said their income was dependent on agriculture like the spots and shifted in favor of Mrs. Woods.

In a private memo accompanying the poll, Messrs. Hickman and Maslin said it would be a "tragic error" for the Woods campaign to back away from the attack. Bob Squier told Mrs. Woods and her other advisers that negative ads always cause a critical reaction at first, but are effective in the long run. "The voting public is like an organism," said Mr. Squier. "It tries to reject information that is unpleasant." In fact, the consultant had assumed that Mr. Bond would attack the commercials as dirty politics, and he had a follow-up spot ready to go, pointing out that Mr. Bond had received $26,000 for serving on the insurance company board and had failed to report the income on his Senate ethics report. (Mr. Bond later said the omission was valid because the fee went directly to his law firm.)

But Jody Newman, in a fury, told the consultants, "We've spent eight years building up Harriett Woods's image, and you've ruined it in a month." When Mr. Squier insisted that the campaign stick to the game plan, he was dismissed. (It is a sign of the times that the dumping of Bob Squier made front-page news, and Mrs. Woods complained that reporters were more interested in his status than in her speeches.)

Messrs. Hickman and Maslin, who agreed with Bob Squier, resigned a few days later. Ms. Newman hurriedly contacted the man who had worked on Mrs. Woods's earlier campaigns, Joe White, at his vacation house on Long Island and asked him to replace Mr. Squier. Mr. White was in St. Louis the next day, and within a few days a new series of Woods spots were on the air.

This time, the candidate took center stage. Against a soundtrack vaguely evocative of "Chariots of Fire," a voice praised her "character and courage." Mrs. Woods was delighted with the spots. "Joe White has always made me look good," she said.

The Washington hotshots were gone and the campaign staff in St. Louis was in charge again. "In our judgment," said Ms. Newman, "Joe White would do things the way we wanted to do them."

But the "spot wars" were just heating up. After Joe White's first ads went on the air, Don Sipple saw an opening for a counterattack. He flew into St. Louis late one evening, and by the next morning he had produced a new spot, featuring the negative news clippings about the Woods commercial—clippings the Bond campaign had helped generate. That night it was on the air. By using the newspaper clips to make the point, and not Mr. Bond himself, Mr. Sipple got others to do the campaign's dirty work.

One of the articles quoted in Mr. Sipple's spot had called Mrs. Woods's tactics "sleazy and shallow," and Mr. White, in turn, thought he saw a target of opportunity. He put together another commercial, saying that Mr. Bond "couldn't take the truth" about his ties to the insurance company.

At that point, in mid-August, both camps lapsed into an exhausted silence. But as Labor Day approached, Joe White knew he had a big problem. Mrs. Woods was trailing Mr. Bond by 8 points in most polls. There was only one thing to do: Go negative.

Mr. White decided to attack Mr. Bond's strongest point, his reputation for sound fiscal management. Mr. Bond's own commercials boasted that, as

Governor, he had taken a budget deficit and turned it into a surplus. In his commercial for Mrs. Woods, Mr. White used the first 10 seconds of the Bond spot, with its claim of financial wizardry, and froze the frame. A somber voice came on saying, "That's what Kit Bond says. What he doesn't say is the truth." The truth, the commercial concluded, was that Mr. Bond actually inherited a surplus as Governor and had to raise taxes to keep the state afloat. (The facts lie somewhere in between, and depend on the accounting method used.)

"All candidates overreact to negatives," noted Mr. White. "They tend to believe the voters will turn against them. So a negative ad throws an opponent off guard. It also gives them the problem of how to respond, and that occupies their time and resources."

The morning in early September that the spot was first televised, Kit Bond was being interviewed at a Kansas City television station, and a reporter asked for his reaction. Mr. Bond made a quick comment and privately told Katie Boyle he wanted to talk to Don Sipple. But Mr. Sipple had already called Mr. Bond at the station, leaving a number in Illinois where he was working on another campaign.

Mr. Bond was late for an appearance in St. Joseph, but once on the highway, his van pulled over at a convenience store, where two adjoining phone booths were unoccupied. On one phone, Mr. Bond called headquarters and talked to his campaign manager, Warren Erdman, who was negotiating with the Woods forces over future debates. On the other phone, his press secretary, Katie Boyle, reached Mr. Sipple in Illinois and discussed the Woods ad. At one point, as some local farmers looked on in amazement, Mr. Bond had a phone in each ear, talking to both advisers at once.

While Mr. White succeeded in initially rattling his opponents, the Bond team, after sniffing the bait, decided not to take it. Demanding that Woods withdraw her commercial would sound like a "lawyer's trick," said Mr. Sipple, and would admit that the ad had "drawn blood." Instead, Miss Boyle made a statement rebutting the charges in the commercial.

Mr. White also made seven other spots, detailing Mrs. Woods's views on such issues as drugs in the schools. Mr. White argued that since the baby-boom generation was now having kids, issues relating to children would play well. Some of the spots were only 10 seconds long, with Mrs. Woods talking directly into the camera. Because short spots are half the cost of 30-second ads, the campaign flooded the airwaves with them, hoping to show that Harriett Woods was knowledgeable on many subjects.

The Bond camp had been caught napping. Mrs. Woods was outspending them 2 and 3 to 1 on television time, and the attack on the Republican's fiscal record "softened up" his support with marginal voters, said Mr. Sipple. "She just kind of drowned us out." By purchasing so much air time in early September, the Woods camp hoped to influence the next round of polls. The strategy worked. The *St. Louis Globe-Democrat* showed Mrs. Woods pulling even with Mr. Bond at 40 percent apiece, with 20 percent undecided. Even before the poll was published,

Ms. Garland was on the phone in Washington, using the results to encourage PACs to contribute to Mrs. Woods. She raised $15,000 in one day.

Within days, Kit Bond was fighting back. One commercial showed ordinary voters—most of them women—attacking Mrs. Woods's "sneaky, rotten campaign tactics." Another ad said Mrs. Woods was rewriting the history of Mr. Bond's Governorship. Both commercials ran on a heavy schedule for eight days and, by the end, said Mr. Sipple, "we had pretty much stopped her move." New polls at the end of September showed Mr. Bond back in front by 7 points.

Mr. White acknowledged that Bob Squier had been right last spring in saying that Mrs. Woods could win only by undermining Mr. Bond's solid image of reliability. So for the final weeks of the campaign he produced a series of negative ads, capped by a renewed attack on the Republican's connection to the insurance industry. The point was simple: to identify Mr. Bond with "big money, out-of-state bad guys." Joe White also took a gamble, producing a spot in which Mrs. Woods talked frankly about her support for a woman's right to have an abortion. The point was to stress the character issue, her concern for average people.

Don Sipple entered the final weeks with a similar strategy. Stress Mr. Bond's strength with spots that highlight his deep roots in Missouri and attack Mrs. Woods's weak points by having him identify with President Reagan's tough stance in Iceland. But that ad—by saying that Mrs. Woods favored a test ban without verification—also triggered a controversy. The Democrat fired back with her own spot, accusing Mr. Bond of telling "an outright lie."

In the last 10 days of the campaign, Mr. Bond tried to capitalize on the President's post-summit popularity by appearing in a rally with him in Springfield, and running a new spot with a Presidential endorsement. At that point, Kit Bond held a 9-point lead in two polls, but the Woods camp argued that the gap was closing. In "Spot Wars," the television audience at home gets to pick the winner. . . .*

Summary Questions

1. According to the article, why are modern campaigns so expensive? Where and how do candidates raise the large amounts they need to conduct such campaigns?
2. What is the major purpose of spot announcements? Why have candidates become so reliant on them?

------

* Kit Bond defeated Harriett Woods 53 to 47 percent. Many post-election observers, such as then retiring Senator Eagleton, believed the independence of Woods's staff and the decision to fire Squier were the biggest mistakes of the campaign. Of Squier's seven other candidates in 1986, six were winners. A Republican won the Senate race in Missouri, but across the country the Democrats gained enough seats to take back the Senate control they had lost in 1980.

7.2

Campaign Finance Reform: Some Lessons from the Data

Michael J. Malbin

Politicians and political observers alike believe that money is the "mother's milk of politics." Candidates well understand that those with ready access to campaign funds have a great advantage electorally. Predictably, during every election year campaign finance reform is a major issue, and the public, the media, and the candidates seem to agree that something must be done. Yet meaningful reform has remained elusive.

In this 1993 article Michael Malbin contends that the fundamental goal of any campaign reform should be to increase electoral competition. In his view, the best way to accomplish this is not to limit the amount spent by incumbents, since spending limits can be easily circumvented, but to ensure that challengers can raise an adequate amount of money to run a serious campaign. Malbin finds that it would cost at least $200,000 for a candidate for Congress to "cross the threshold of visibility and credibility" in order to become potentially competitive.

To Malbin, "the source of the money matters little. What matters is the money." The money could come from a public cash subsidy, letting the parties give more to challengers, or any other device (such as free air time for all general election candidates) that would put money in the hands of the challenger.

I t is amazing how little the debate over campaign finance has changed over the past 20 years. Two decades ago, the public's attention was riveted by the Senate Watergate hearings. After those hearings, Congress adopted a package for congressional and presidential elections that included imperfect but reasonably effective disclosure, an independent Federal Election Commission, and limits on campaign contributions. For presidential elections, the federal law provided public financing for qualified candidates who agreed to limit their campaign spending.

The original 1974 law also required congressional candidates to limit their spending, without giving those candidates any public funding in return. But the

Michael Malbin is professor of political science at the State University of New York at Albany.

Supreme Court ruled in *Buckley* v. *Valeo*[1] that mandatory spending limits violated a candidate's right of free speech. At the same time, however, the *Buckley* case upheld spending limits for presidential elections because those candidates did not have to adhere to a spending limit under the law unless they voluntarily chose to do so in order to get public campaign funds.

Since the *Buckley* case, almost all attempts at changing the federal law have involved efforts to extend a presidential-style public funding system, combined with spending limits, to Congress. State and local reform efforts have also tended to focus on similar kinds of packages. This includes, but is not limited to, New York. For example, the New York State Assembly in 1993 passed a bill at the request of the Governor (Assembly Bill No. 1) that included a public matching grant system, and spending limits, that in many respects looks like the package that already exists for presidential primaries. Similar bills were filed in at least 13 different states in the early 1990s. This is in addition to the nine states that already have a version of partial public financing for some candidates—most of which, like the federal program, are experiencing financial difficulty.

The fact that similar provisions are being offered in different jurisdictions is not be itself a problem. What is a problem is how little change there has been in the arguments and evidence offered by so many of the participants who appear on all sides of this ongoing debate. That is a pity. The federal law has been working for five presidential and nine congressional election cycles. Over the course of these 18 years, the Federal Election Commission (FEC)* has become a highly professional, dependable, and sophisticated source of computer-generated information on federal campaign finance. Because of the wealth of FEC material available on paper, on computer tape, and directly from the FEC's computer over a modem, we now have solid empirical evidence that bears upon some of the key assumptions made on both sides of the debate. Instead of repeating the old "common sense" arguments, therefore, it would be better if all participants—whether at the national, state, or local level—began sorting out their assumptions on the basis of what we now know.

I shall not pretend that the empirical evidence will settle all issues. On the contrary: the remainder of this article is likely to stimulate controversy about the impact of money on the level of competition between congressional incumbents and challengers. Supporters and opponents of the standard reform bills will find me disagreeing with at least some of the premises on which their positions usually rely. My only request is that the conclusions not be rejected out of hand, without a hard look at the data.

---

* The Federal Election Commission (FEC) was established by the Federal Election Campaign Act of 1971 to enforce federal campaign laws. The six-member commission monitors campaign fundraising and spending in federal elections, and facilitates the public disclosure of campaign financial records.

Underfinanced Challengers

Spending for congressional election campaigns was almost 50 percent higher in 1992 than in 1990. Moreover:

1. Much of the spending increase for House elections was made up of increased spending by incumbents, signaling a continued deterioration in the relative financial strength of challengers compared to incumbents (see Figure 7.1).
2. In addition, the relative weakness of the challengers seems to have been reflected in the results. Only 19 House incumbents lost to challengers in the general election, despite the uncertainties caused by redistricting, and despite the general anti-incumbency mood shown by the success of 14 out of 14 term limit initiatives on statewide ballots.

Taken in isolation, these figures seem to support the proposition that the reason so few incumbents lose is that they are getting too rich and blowing the competition away. I would argue, however, that the real problem is not that incumbents have too much money, but that challengers have too little. A few numbers from the 1992 congressional elections will show just how far away most challengers are

Figure 7.1
Challenger-Incumbent Spending Ratios, 1976–1992 (in percentages)

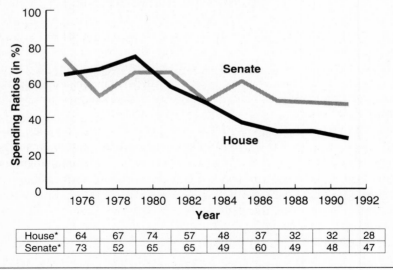

	1976	1978	1980	1982	1984	1986	1988	1990	1992
House*	64	67	74	57	48	37	32	32	28
Senate*	73	52	65	65	49	60	49	48	47

*Mean challenger spending as percentage of the mean spending by incumbents.
Source: N. Ornstein, T. Mann, and M. Malbin, *Vital Statistics on Congress, 1993–94*, p. 81. Copyright © 1993. Used by permission.

from having to worry about how much their opponents spend. The 288 major party, general election challengers in 1992 raised an average of $167,891. That was barely the same nominal amount that the average challenger was able to raise eight years before—without even correcting for inflation. The problem becomes even more stark if we look at realistic threshold figures for mounting a campaign.

During the past several election cycles, the average successful congressional challenger has had to spend at least $450,000–$500,000 to defeat a sitting incumbent. In 1992, 252 congressional candidates were able to spend $500,000. Of these, 184 were incumbents, 53 were open-seat candidates, and only 15 were challengers.

Or consider a lower hurdle. In most congressional districts, it would cost a candidate at least $200,000 to cross the threshold of visibility and credibility. There were 548 candidates who spent $200,000 or more in 1992: 324 incumbents, 135 open-seat candidates, and 89 challengers. In other words, even in an allegedly anti-incumbent year, almost three-quarters (250 of 349) of the incumbents in the 1992 general election did not have to face a challenger who could afford to spend $200,000.

These numbers alert us to a basic fact: if you want to predict how competitive an election is likely to be, the single most important campaign finance number to know is the amount of money the challenger has raised.[2] Nothing about the incumbent is as important or as revealing as the condition of the challenger. In every election since public disclosure, there has been a clear correlation between challenger fund raising and challenger success. To put the point simply, challengers who do well tend to spend *much* more money than ones who do poorly—an average of $281,261 for losing challengers who received 40–49 percent of the 1992 vote, versus $87,931 for those who received less than 40 percent (see Figure 7.2). In addition, challengers who win tend to spend more—$451,201 in 1992—than those who lose.

Winning challengers have to be good fund raisers, but they do *not* have to spend as much as their incumbent opponents to win. Defeated incumbents spent an average of $965,537 in 1992, more than twice as much as the challengers who beat them. Even more surprisingly, how much money the incumbents spend does not tell you how well they will do. In 1992, the average defeated incumbent spent $965,537; incumbents with 50–59 percent of the vote spent $784,303; incumbents with 60 percent or more spent $486,681. In other words, what really seems to matter is the amount of money challengers can raise and not the amount spent by incumbents.

Paradox Explained

It almost looks, political scientist Gary C. Jacobson once wrote, as if the more an incumbent spends, the worse the incumbent will do.[3] Of course, that is an overstatement: very few candidates actually hurt themselves by spending more

Figure 7.2
Incumbent and Challenger Spending in 1992 House Races, by Margin of Victory

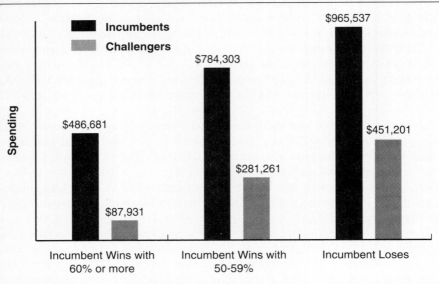

Source: Derived from Federal Election Commission data.

money. Nevertheless, a little knowledge about congressional elections can go a long way toward explaining why money means more to the challenger than it does to the incumbent.

The average House member spends about $500,000 per year ($1,000,000 per two-year election cycle) for the salaries of the members of his or her personal staff. Since a full one-third of personal House staffs are based in congressional district offices, and since a fair amount of the time of Washington-based press secretaries, legislative correspondents, and the like, is also spent on district business, it seems conservative to estimate that the average member devotes at least half of his or her office staff allotment to constituency communication. That comes to about $500,000 per election cycle per member. Add another $175,000 or so per election cycle for the average member's franked postage costs, then throw in subsidized television studios, computerized mail systems, and highly favorable local press coverage, and you begin to understand something of the advantage that incumbents have before the campaign even begins.

This advantage is reflected in surveys of congressional voters. According to the American National Election Studies, more than 90 percent of the voters typically can recognize the name of their incumbent Member of Congress, compared to barely 50 percent who can recognize the name of the challenger. Campaign funds may not be useless for an incumbent, but there is little that spending can do to boost an incumbent's name recognition. As Figure 7.3 shows, raising an incumbent's expenditures from $1,000 to $500,000 will only shift the recognition rate from 88 to 92 percent. By contrast, the challenger would shift from 22 percent to 75 percent rate of recognition with a comparable shift in expenditure levels.

Only after a challenger's name becomes known can he or she begin drawing contrasts with the incumbent and shift the campaign to more substantive issues. Once the campaign centers on such issues, the situation is more fluid than when it merely pits the incumbent's well-known, comfortable personality against a little-known challenger. An incumbent with effective opposition naturally will spend more money than an incumbent whose opposition is unknown. That explains why higher spending incumbents do worse than incumbents who spend less. They do worse because the challengers have managed to shift the debate to more meaningful grounds.

It follows, therefore, that if the aim is to make elections more competitive, more challengers will need to have enough money to mount serious campaigns. The money could come from a public cash subsidy (the Democratic approach), letting the parties give more to challengers (the Republican approach) or any

Figure 7.3
Probability that a Voter Will Recognize a Candidate's Name (1984)

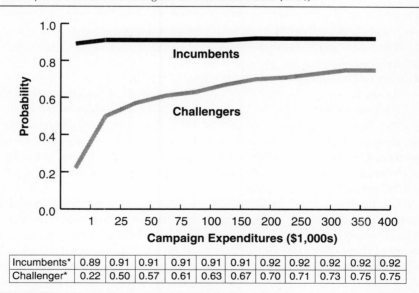

	1	25	50	75	100	150	200	250	300	350	400
Incumbents*	0.89	0.91	0.91	0.91	0.91	0.91	0.92	0.92	0.92	0.92	0.92
Challenger*	0.22	0.50	0.57	0.61	0.63	0.67	0.70	0.71	0.73	0.75	0.75

*The probability that a voter will recognize an incumbent or a challenger at each spending level.
Source: Data taken from Gary C. Jacobson, *Congressional Elections*, 2nd ed. Boston: Little, Brown, 1987, p. 125.

other device (such as free postage or air time for all general election candidates) that would get more money to challengers. The source of the money matters little. What matters is the money.

Spending Limits

Spending limits are another matter entirely. At their best, they are largely irrelevant. With members of Congress spending at least three-quarters of a million dollars in office funds to enhance their own reputations, equal campaign spending would not do anything to improve a challenger's chances for victory. Of course, that does not settle whether spending limits should be enacted. The proponents of limits put forward additional reasons for supporting the concept, such as the claim that the limits will reduce the time office holders devote to raising money.

Some of these additional reasons undoubtedly have merit, but they also need to be weighed against the problems uncovered by 18 years worth of federal experience. The record shows that if the limits are set low enough to cramp spending significantly, highly motivated politicians will find ways to get around them.

Over the course of five elections, the presidential candidates, national political parties, and their supporters have all but perfected the art of legally evading the limits. As a result, the level of spending has increased in every presidential election since public funding began, with more and more of the money going off the books and into the legal underground. The official, publicly funded candidates' campaigns now make up less than half of what is spent to support a major party, general election campaign for the presidency.[4]

If politically active, potential contributors care enough about an election, they will find ways to get involved. If they are wealthy, well organized, and cannot contribute directly, then they will look at independent expenditures, or delegate committees, or registration and get-out-the-vote drives, or communicating with members, or buying issue ads that publicize the position of an incumbent without directly advocating election or defeat, or any of a dozen other devices, some of which have not yet been invented.

Off-the-book activities like these have become a more significant part of every election since 1976. Some of them can be regulated, but there is no way they all can be eliminated without running roughshod over the First Amendment. Moreover, all of these devices favor the well-organized and the powerful over smaller participants. What the limits seem to be doing in presidential elections, therefore, is to encourage the powerful to engage in subterfuge and legal gamesmanship, leading to activities that end up being poorly disclosed. As a cure for cynicism or corruption, this is truly bizarre. It undermines the one item, disclosure, without which everything else in the law becomes meaningless.

Analysis and the Policy Process

The proposals that flow from the above analysis seem almost to write themselves:

* Give all general election candidates some public funding, free postage (to be paid for by reducing the postage available to officeholders), or free airtime (to be required of broadcasters as a condition for gaining monopoly use of a frequency).
* If public money is not acceptable, use differential contribution limits to permit nonincumbents to accept larger seed-money contributions early in the campaign.
* Do not impose spending limits.
* Retain and strengthen existing disclosure rules and contribution limits.

But politics, like the rest of life, is never as straightforward as academic policy analysis. The problem is that most Democrats in Congress have decided that "real reform" has to include spending limits whether or not there is money for challengers, and most Republicans—joined by some southern Democrats—are deeply opposed to public financing. Why so many Democrats have made spending limits the *sine qua non* of reform is beyond this author's conjecture, but the substantive difficulty of their position has already been explored.

The position of the Republicans in Congress is equally hard to understand. To some extent, it is an extension of an instinctive GOP skepticism toward new spending programs. But, as our earlier discussion of office expenses should have made clear, it is naive to think public funds are not being used now to help election campaigns. The problem is that the public only pays for the incumbents! In fact, if publicly funded staff were not so effective at building up the power of incumbency, challengers would not be in the desperate position most are now in.

But whatever my own position may be, it is a lot easier politically to put together a coalition of Democrats and Republicans who support spending limits than it is to find one that wants more money for challengers. That is exactly what happened in the U.S. Senate in June, and is likely to happen again when a bill reaches the House floor. Senate Democrats gave up on the public money that would help challengers, while the Republicans who joined them to break a filibuster were able to preserve their anti-public financing purity. What came out was a bill that had limits, but no money—the exact opposite of what I think would be most beneficial for the democratic process.

All this is a long way of pointing out that the heat of a legislative battle is not the best time to ask people to take a fresh look at the evidence and rethink their premises. If serious rethinking is going to occur, the work should start now. That would be particularly useful in state legislatures where the issue is not on the immediate agenda—where there still is some time for rethinking before the final coalition building is at hand.

Notes

1. *Buckley* v. *Valeo* 424 U.S. 1 (1976).
2. This point was first made by Gary C. Jacobson, *Money in Congressional Elections*. New Haven, CT: Yale University Press, 1980.
3. Ibid.
4. Herbert E. Alexander and Monica Bauer, *Financing the 1988 Election*. Boulder, CO: Westview, 1991.

Summary Questions

1. Why does Malbin believe that limiting campaign spending would not be an effective political reform?
2. According to Malbin, what changes in campaign finance laws would help make congressional elections more competitive? Why have such reforms not been seriously considered in the past? What is the likelihood that such changes will become law in the future?
3. Is public funding of congressional elections a good idea?

▦ Debate on Term Limits

The idea of limiting the number of congressional terms by law or by constitutional amendment has been around since the nation's founding. In the late 1980s and early 1990s the idea again gained momentum as citizens in a number of states, frustrated with the domination of the electoral system by career politicians and believing effective political reform would not be forthcoming from legislative incumbents, organized to limit terms of either state legislators and/or members of Congress. If term-limits advocates had their way, legislators in Washington would typically be limited to serving no more than twelve years.

The possibility of limiting congressional terms has sparked a vigorous debate. In this selection, composed of two 1992 articles presented in a debate format, Bill Frenzel, a former congressman, and Thomas Mann, a congressional scholar, present some of the more compelling reasons to support or oppose the enactment of term limits. In Frenzel's view, accountability is at the heart of the American political system, enforced through the device of competitive elections which, he believes, are infrequent today because of the many advantages of incumbency. From his perspective, the fundamental reason to enact term limitations is "to unrig a rigged system, end automatic reelection, and make Congress mortal again." Mann strongly disagrees. He believes that "term limits are the wrong medicine for what ails the congressional election system," and questions whether term limits would increase political accountability. He is particularly concerned about the side effects of term limitations, including the elimination of many able legislators, the possible power shift to unelected officials and private interests, and a strengthened executive branch at the expense of Congress.

 7.3

Term Limits and the Immortal Congress: How to Make Congressional Elections Competitive Again

Bill Frenzel

The idea of limiting the number of terms a member of Congress may serve has been rattling around since the Constitution was a gleam in the eye of the framers. But until 1990 it was just another idea whose time had not come.

In 1990 California, Colorado, and Oklahoma all passed referendums providing severe term limits on their state legislatures. One of them, Colorado, also set limits on the terms of its representatives in the U.S. Congress. Only in California, where ballot initiative contests have become a major contact sport, was there any real resistance. There a well-organized $5 million opposition campaign kept the vote close. In the two other states, term limits was a runaway winner.

The referendums were a stentorian wake-up call for state and federal legislators who had slumbered through earlier warnings and who had somehow failed to notice that their collective popular approval rating had sunk to levels usually reserved for used car salesmen. For some time, polls had been showing strong popular support for term limits. Nearly a year before the 1990 election one poll had shown 70 percent support running uniformly through regions, parties, sexes, and ages.

Bill Frenzel, a guest scholar at the Brookings Governmental Studies Program, retired from the U.S. House of Representatives voluntarily in January 1991.

With latent enthusiasm for term limits ignited across the country, fledgling state term limits movements arose. They quickly became active everywhere, hyperactive in states that provide for ballot access for initiatives. Term limit bills were introduced in most states, and campaigns got under way in most of the initiative states.

Then last November a funny thing happened. Term limits suffered an unexpected, serious setback. The voters of Washington state defeated a ballot initiative with retrospective effect that would have limited congressional service almost immediately. Opposition forces, thought to be disheartened by unpleasant publicity about the lax personal banking habits of U.S. House members, rallied under the leadership of House Speaker Tom Foley, himself a Washingtonian, to defeat the initiative.

The Washington initiative proved that the term limits juggernaut was not irresistible. It gave the counterforces strong momentum going into the 1992 elections, which are expected to produce about a dozen initiatives. But the term limits forces are still powerful. With both sides gearing up, 1992 is certain to be a lively election year.*

Incumbent Reelection Success

The appeal of term limits, most often proposed as a limit of 12 years, springs from the extraordinarily high, and rising, reelection rates of congressional incumbents. Historically, U.S. House incumbents have never had much trouble getting reelected, but from the middle of the nineteenth century, the reelection rate has crept up steadily to its current average of better than 94 percent in the past ten elections and better than 97 percent in the past three elections.

Until 1914 senators were spared the indignity of elections. Since then they have generally done less well than House members. Even so, their increasing success has produced a reelection rate of better than 88 percent in the past five elections and an astounding 97 percent in the last election. Congress has become almost immortal.

Winning margins are increasing too. Nowadays most members of Congress face only token opposition, if any. In 1990 only one in twenty races for U.S. House seats could be described as competitive—that is, with a winning margin of less than 4 percent. That year four out of five House incumbents got more than 60

---

* In the 1992 elections fourteen states adopted some form of term limitations, but the question of whether term limits could be imposed by state electorates on federal elections remained unclear. After the election a federal district court in the state of Washington ruled that only an amendment to the U.S. Constitution could add conditions to the qualifications for federal office (current constitutional conditions include age, citizenship, and residency requirements). Most political observers believe that the issue will ultimately be resolved by the Supreme Court, most likely in the direction of requiring an amendment to the Constitution before any term limits may be imposed on members of the House or the Senate.

percent of the votes in their districts. Sixty-nine incumbents, or 16 percent, had either no major party opposition or no opposition at all. Four senators (12 percent) were so blessed.

The growing victory margins mean that reelection rates have not peaked yet. It is impossible to break the House record of 1792, when 100 percent of House incumbents who sought reelection were successful (thankfully, 37 percent did not run), but we are headed in that direction. Meanwhile, challengers are not stupid. As long as they know 97 percent of them will lose, their campaigns will be token. Good challengers simply will not file. They know the odds are better at Las Vegas.

Accountability is the heart of our system. Yet the 97 percent success rate has decimated congressional accountability. In days of yore, when members of Congress went home to face the voters, some of them would face the music. The music has stopped. The principal check and balance on the House was its election contests. Today there are no contests.

Congressional Turnover

Election defeats have always represented the smallest fraction of congressional turnover. In the first 100 years of our republic, House reelection rates were in the 70–90 percent range, but a quarter to a half of all incumbents did not seek reelection. That high rate of voluntary retirement kept total turnover in the 40–50 percent range. Each new House was about half rookie and half veteran. By the turn of the century retirement turnover had already declined to about 15 percent, and it continued to decline thereafter. In the past four elections, retirement turnover averaged about 31 members, about 7 percent. Total House turnover, including election defeats, was about 10 percent, an historic low.

In the Senate, retirement turnover is even lower. Senators must love their jobs. On average, over the past five elections, about four senators retired. Last year one retired. Total turnover for the Senate, including election defeats, over the past five elections was about 8 percent. For 1990 it was 2 percent.

The turnover that supplied vitality and inhibited rigidity in the early days of the House is gone, a victim of the incentives of the seniority system, and, more recently, of sure-fire reelection.

Declining Voter Participation

In 1990 the United States held an election party, but only one-third of the voting age population showed up. One-half showed up for the presidential election of 1988. Both those figures are the lowest in 60 years, and voting participation has been headed down for the past 30 years. The drop has come at a time when the United States and the individual states have made substantial efforts to lower barriers to voting (the Voting Rights Act, improved registration systems, better access to voting sites, absentee ballots, lowering the voting age to 18).

Even Americans who can tolerate 97 percent reelection rates with high voter turnout blanch when they understand that Congress is being immortalized by one-third of the eligible voters. As long as reelection certainty is being sustained by a small and declining fraction of the voters, protests are inevitable.

The Term Limits Protagonists

In the states, proponents of term limits belong to all parties and to none. They are liberal and conservative, often close to the ends of the spectrum. They are bound together by the common feeling that they are outsiders, estranged from a system that is rigged against them.

The opponents of term limits are easier to identify. They are the ins and their friends—incumbents, staff, lobbyists, and close observers. They have a stake in the present system or know it and are comfortable with it. They do not believe "their" system is broken, and they see dangers in fixing it.

Congressmen and ex-congressmen, by huge margins, oppose term limits regardless of party affiliation. (A few former members of Congress dot the letterheads of national term limits groups, but they are overwhelmed by the long, prestigious lists of opponents.) A powerful opposition force, the group was an idle resource until awakened by the Foley campaign in Washington state.

If one believes party platforms, Republicans are for term limits. A canvass of GOP members of Congress, past and present, however, would reveal little fidelity to that platform. In the states, some Republicans think that term limits might make their party a majority in the legislatures. Even so, party activity has not been encouraged by Republican members of Congress.

Although polls generally show equal ratios of Democrats and Republicans opposing and supporting term limits, the Democratic party actively and officially opposed initiatives in California and Washington. It may not believe that control of the legislatures will change, but, as the majority party, it sees no reason to take either the trouble or the risk to find out.

Arguments Pro and Con

Enthusiasm often overwhelms reason on both sides of the term limits debate. Much of the campaign rhetoric is speculative. Some of it is specious. Those who favor term limits claim miraculous powers for it. Those who oppose it see in it the demise of the republic.

Reasonable people are probably not going to be persuaded that term limits is the magic bullet that will produce smarter congressmen, better ideas, improved oversight, a balanced budget, or affordable health care, or that it will put "our" side (either liberal or conservative) in control of Congress. Neither are they likely to be convinced by counterarguments that the present system provides ample challenger opportunity, that there is insufficient talent in the United States to service higher turnover, that incumbents are the only ones who can do the job, or that legislative rookies will be pushovers for staff, lobbyists, and bureaucrats.

The simple, essential reason for congressional term limits is to unrig a rigged system, end automatic reelection, and make Congress mortal again.

Many Americans cling to the now lost idea of the citizen-legislator. Term limits can't completely recreate this extinct creature. But it will take us a couple of paces backward and away from the professional congressman-for-life. It will also allow more citizens to serve in Congress, and it could reduce some of the advantages of incumbency, even during the 12-year term.

Predicting the inner workings of Congress is highly speculative, but, at the least, the seniority system will be truncated and weakened by term limits. At best, it may yield to another system that could provide more equal opportunities for leadership for all members and less entrenched regionalism.

Known retirement dates would allow challengers to get their affairs in order and plan their campaigns in advance. That would mean better campaigns, better candidates, and more competition. Incumbents could continue to give themselves more reelection insurance in the form of greater perks and new campaign laws, but competition cannot get worse. If it improves, accountability will also improve.

Voter participation is a complicated subject, but more competition ought to improve it too. Congressional term limits would also restore balance to our system by extending to the legislative branch the noble precedent of term limits applied by the 22nd Amendment to the executive branch only. Both branches need limits.

With less career time to be consumed with the petty details of legislative work and less time to ponder the defense of turf, Congress may begin to look at the forest again, rather than each leaf. The now-compelling urge to micro-manage and extend one's own power and programs far past their usefulness to the republic will be reduced.

Perhaps the essential objection to term limits is that it restricts voter choice. For the purist, that will be a problem, but, alas, there are few purists in politics. A 12-year limit is surely a tiny restriction. The Constitution already contains three other small restrictions on voting for Congress, as well as the presidential term limit. Congressional term limits would be a mere scratch on the body politic compared with the running sore of current congressional immortality.

Opponents worry that Congress will lose good members. It will. But it will also gain good members. All the titans of Congress were pea-green freshmen once. They were good when they got there. Experience (seniority) did not make them smarter. It just gave them more staff and made them harder to say no to. There is plenty of talent that can't get to Congress under the present rules. Today

Congress survives the infrequent retirement of its titans. It can survive an accelerated process too.

There are complaints that the legislative branch will lose power to the executive. That is possible, but not necessarily probable and certainly not inevitable. There is no rule forcing one branch to grow long whiskers before it can stand up to another.

Lame ducks, it is said, are not accountable. Yet studies of lame ducks show no substantial changes in voting patterns. There is no evidence to show unbeatable ducks are more accountable than lame ones.

Finally, opponents suggest that "other changes" will cure the system. That is probably true, but no such changes are in eminent danger of enactment. Usually the "other changes" are reforms in campaign law. That won't help because no legislature has ever passed a campaign law that made it harder for incumbents to get reelected.

The Future

Term limits enjoy wide popular support. But that does not mean that they will see the light of day. The Balanced Budget Amendment* and the Line Item Veto,† both of which enjoyed majority public support and yet were not adopted, are testament to Congress's ability to defend itself. Congress merely toyed with them until the intensity of their supporters petered out. Possessed of nearly infinite staying power and an irresistible urge for self-preservation, Congress is prepared to dally term limits to death too.

Following the Washington state defeat, proponents will have to prove that they can regain their lost momentum. Even if they can succeed in their initiative strategy, most constitutional scholars suggest that states cannot limit the terms of their congressmen, and that a constitutional amendment is required. If so, a term limits strategy must be a very long-term proposition.

---

* In the face of budgetary deficit problems, Congress in recent years has considered a number of proposals to amend the Constitution to require that federal budgetary receipts be equal to or greater than outlays. Such proposals are much debated and receive much media attention, but none has passed. Although supporters of the balanced budget amendment believe its enactment would force the government not to deficit spend, critics contend that such an amendment would not achieve its desired goals even if passed, since Congress could circumvent the spirit of the law by various kinds of "off-budget" spending.

† Many state governors have the power to veto separate items in a legislative bill, but the president does not. Supporters of the presidential line-item veto believe the power would help eliminate wasteful legislative spending by targeting special interest or pork barrel provisions of bills. Opponents are concerned that the executive line-item veto would limit their discretion and make passage of certain pieces of legislation necessitating bargaining and compromise within the legislature more difficult to achieve.

If the term limits movement can recapture its successes in the states, it can elect some pro-term limits congressmen, just as it has begun to seat some friendly state legislators. Making a majority in Congress is a long process, but other factors will help. State limits will give state legislators more incentive to run for Congress, and more incentive to create districts in which their success is more likely. This process will create a new class of more credible challengers in primaries as well as general elections. . . .

Wagering the rent money on term limits for Congress is surely not in order now. The movement is for real, and it is making an impact. However, it must match its high intensity with unprecedented staying power before it can achieve the muscle to force Congress to begin stripping away elements of its own immortality.

In some sort of national debate, Americans must decide what kind of representation they want. The framers wisely made system changes difficult to achieve. It's not enough for Americans to want term limits badly. To get them, they have to want them over the long haul.

 7.4

The Wrong Medicine: Term Limits Won't Cure What Ails Congressional Elections

Thomas E. Mann

B ill Frenzel's case for congressional term limits is disarmingly attractive. No fire and brimstone about the corruption of Congress. No grandiose claim that limits will produce higher quality members or more effective national policymaking. No expedient assertion that states can limit congressional terms without a constitutional amendment. Instead, Frenzel embraces term limits as the only available means of achieving an important but limited objective— namely, restoring competition, turnover, and accountability to an electoral system that has essentially lost all three.

But Frenzel's judicious approach to term limits should not obscure the radical character of his proposed reform. The burden of proof—diagnosing the problem

Thomas E. Mann is director of governmental studies at Brookings and holds the W. Averell Harriman Chair in American Governance.

and demonstrating that the cure is likely to work without debilitating side effects—properly falls on those who would alter the constitutional order. My view is that a persuasive case for term limits has not been made.

Legislatures under Siege

Congress and state legislatures are suffering from extraordinarily (if not unprecedentedly) low levels of popular support. With only a fourth of the electorate approving of the job these representative bodies are doing, the soil is fertile for the burgeoning term limit movement. But it would be a mistake to infer that declining competition and turnover in legislatures are responsible for the drop in public esteem, that the public's embrace of term limits is in any way novel, or that the term limit movement reflects a spontaneous uprising by the public to restore accountability in legislative elections.

Public confidence in legislatures is low because the news coming out of Washington and state capitals has been bad. Recent stories on state legislatures by Alan Ehrenhalt in *Governing* and on Congress by Richard Cohen in the *National Journal* are remarkably parallel in this respect. A stagnant economy, declining real wages and limits on upward mobility for many working-class Americans, suffocating budget deficits, and chronic crime and poverty in our cities have constrained effective policymaking and frustrated citizens. At the same time several developments in the political system have further damaged the reputation of legislatures. Divided government, now the norm in two-thirds of the states as well as in Washington, invites public squabbling between the branches, which diminishes the stature of both. The increasing focus on scandal, fueled by ethics and public disclosure statutes, tough law enforcement against public officials, and a press inclined toward feeding frenzies, leads the public to believe (incorrectly) that legislatures and politicians are more and more corrupt. And the situation is made even worse by negative campaigning—the growing tendency of politicians to cast their electoral and legislative opponents in the worst possible light.

Uncompetitive elections and low turnover are at most sidebars to the big story of the public loss of confidence in Congress and state legislatures. Using term limits to increase competition and turnover is unlikely to alter the public image of these institutions.

Indeed, the public's support for term limits predates the contemporary disrepute of Congress and state legislatures. Polls taken 40 years ago found roughly the same level of support as exists today. No surprise here. Term limits are irresistible to poll respondents: they provide a simple, no-cost means of registering skepticism and unhappiness with politics and politicians in general.

What's different today is that activists have mobilized to bring term limit initiatives before the electorate. Frenzel portrays these activists as Democrats and

Republicans, liberals and conservatives, united only in their status as outsiders, "estranged from a system that is rigged against them." My own view of the term limit movement is slightly less benign. The energy and resources of the movement come overwhelmingly from conservative, libertarian business and ideological interests who share a strong distaste for government and a wish to control or weaken legislatures now dominated by Democrats.

Politics does make strange bedfellows, and there are a handful of Democrats and liberals who are working on behalf of term limits. But I believe any fair accounting would reveal that the struggle for term limits is more about political power than good government. We are in the midst of a national campaign to limit legislative terms not because the public is in open revolt against a rigged electoral system but because the intense ideological and partisan battles of our time have been moved to a new venue.

What's Wrong with Congressional Elections?

Frenzel correctly notes the incredibly high reelection rates of congressional incumbents and their substantial margins of victory. The study of the "vanishing marginals" and the advantages of incumbency has been a cottage industry in political science, and Frenzel is not alone in his concern that the threat of defeat is no longer real for congressional incumbents.

The problem is greater in the House than in the Senate. Although there has been a long-term decline in competitiveness in Senate elections and only one incumbent was defeated in 1990, a third to a half of senators running for reelection routinely attract strong, well-funded challengers. Large-scale defeat of Senate incumbents led to a change in party control of the chamber twice in the 1980s, something that had not been seen since the 1950s.

House elections lack credible challengers. More and more House elections go uncontested; most of the others feature relatively unknown and woefully underfinanced challengers. Fundraising by House challengers has declined precipitously since 1984 while the cost of campaigning and incumbent spending has sharply increased. As the minority party in the House, the Republicans have suffered disproportionately, but Democratic opposition to Republican incumbents is also increasingly anemic.

The absence of credible challengers in the 1990 elections kept House incumbent losses to 15, in spite of an unprecedented drop in the vote margins of both parties' incumbents. A slightly stronger field of opponents could easily have converted the expressed public discontent with Congress into double or triple the number of incumbent defeats.

The 1990 experience highlights an important lesson about congressional elections. Robust competition requires both strong, well-financed challengers and public antipathy to the status quo. The quiescent House elections after 1982 reflected in large part the relatively benign national political environment. From "It's morning again in America" in 1984 to "Keep the recovery going" in 1988, there was no clarion call to throw the rascals out. Absent a scandal or serious political misstep, voters had little incentive to reject their representative. At the same time, potential challengers had no reason to believe that conditions were ripe for a political upset. Their reluctance to run reinforced the public passivity and ensured good times for congressional incumbents.

But it would be a mistake to conclude that these conditions are permanent, that the recent pattern of competition and turnover in congressional elections will continue. No simple linear trend line fits the history of congressional elections. Between 1974 and 1982 the membership of the House and Senate was almost entirely replaced as a result of retirements and incumbent defeats. By the early 1980s three-fourths of senators and representatives had served fewer than 12 years. That tumultuous decade in congressional elections was followed by the placid years after 1982, which saw a drop in voluntary retirements and election defeats and therefore a much more stable membership.

We are about to enter another period of rapid membership turnover. Redistricting, a surge in retirements, more successful candidate recruitment, and a high level of public angst may well produce 80 to 100 new members of the House in 1992, with 30 to 40 reaching office by defeating an incumbent. The volatile Senate class of 1992 could see a dozen of its members replaced in the November elections.* And it is easy to imagine conditions under which rapid turnover continues in the 1994 midterm elections. A massive increase in competitiveness is not prerequisite to a healthy flow of new blood into the legislature.

But what of the charge that the incredibly high success rate of incumbents has destroyed the system of accountability essential to a democracy? There are ample grounds for concern here. Uncontested elections and halfhearted challengers are unlikely to have a bracing effect on incumbents and over time may breed an unhealthy feeling of invulnerability and arrogance. Yet most members of Congress remain unbelievably insecure about their political futures and highly responsive to the interests of their constituencies. One big reason incumbents are so successful is that electoral accountability is alive and well: representatives conform to the wishes of their constituents and are in turn rewarded with reelection.

The problem is not individual accountability. Voters show no signs of suffering from inattentive or unresponsive representatives. If anything, members of Congress are too solicitous of their constituencies and insufficiently attentive to broader national interests, too consumed with their personal standing in their district or state and too little dependent on their political party.

---

* In the 1992 elections incumbents again fared very well. Only 24 incumbents in the House and 4 in the Senate were beaten in the general election. Additionally, 19 House incumbents had lost in the primaries. Overall, however, turnover was exceptionally high in 1992, as 110 new members of the House were elected, most of whom campaigned in open seats to replace voluntary retirees.

What's needed is a change in the electoral system that once again allows the outcome of hundreds of congressional elections to cumulate to a meaningful national decision. We should aspire to elections that are more party-based, less candidate-centered—and capable, on occasion, of changing the majority party in the House and of putting a single party in control of the government in Washington.

Term Limits in Congressional Elections

If my analysis is correct, term limits are the wrong medicine for what ails the congressional election system. There is no compelling reason to insist on 100 percent turnover in Congress every 12 years when 50 to 75 percent of the members of the House and Senate are routinely replaced every decade. Natural turnover (from voluntary retirement, progressive ambition, and election defeat) is preferable to an arbitrary scheme that unnecessarily restricts a democratic electoral process.

Would term limits increase the competitiveness of congressional elections? If more competitiveness means lower reelection rates for incumbents, the answer is clearly no. A term limit would very likely turn into a floor, with would-be candidates deferring their challenge and awaiting the involuntary retirement of the incumbent. If a norm of deference to the term-limited incumbent took root, elections would be contested only in open seats, and then only those not safe for one political party or the other.

Indeed, there is little reason to think that congressional term limits would produce anything approaching a surge in high-quality, well-financed challengers, which is essential for increased competitiveness. More targeted interventions are required to produce that result. (On the other hand, term limits for state legislators, however harmful their effects on state government, would increase the supply of experienced politicians seeking election to Congress.)

Finally, would congressional term limits increase accountability? Would the personal standing of representatives and senators become less important and their political party more so? Would Republicans have a better shot at taking control of Congress when they won the presidency? Having more open seats might marginally increase the ties between presidential and congressional voting. And Republicans would have a better chance of climbing out of their near permanent minority status in the House if the cohort of veteran Democratic legislators were forced to give up their seats without a fight.

Yet reformers would be disappointed by the likely consequences of term limits. The candidate-centered character of our elections would not disappear in a world of shortened congressional careers. The personal vote for incumbents materializes in their first reelection campaign. And while Republicans fare better in open seats than in those contested by an incumbent, even here their performance falls short of the Democrats'.

Term limits just won't get the job done. What's needed are a Republican party determined to build from the bottom up rather than the top down, with a public philosophy that encourages men and women to seek legislative office under the Republican banner; a reformed campaign finance system that puts more resources (money, cheaper mail, less expensive access to television) into the hands of the challengers; additional restrictions on franked mail and other advantages of incumbency; and creative strategies to shift the focus of officeholders and voters from position-taking on parochial matters to collective efforts that grapple with serious national problems. Frenzel is skeptical that any such changes will ever be achieved. I believe we have no choice but to cajole, shame, and threaten politicians into doing the right thing.

Side Effects

These other measures should be pursued not only because they have a better chance of making congressional elections more competitive, but also because they lack term limits' potentially debilitating side effects.

Frenzel is surely correct to note the inflated rhetoric of proponents and opponents of term limits. The republic has survived the limit on presidential terms imposed by the 22nd Amendment and is unlikely to perish if congressional term limits are added to the Constitution.

Nonetheless, it is not unreasonable to be concerned that term limits might eliminate many of the members most inclined to legislate in the national interest; shift power from elected politicians to unelected officials and private interests; and strengthen the executive branch at the expense of Congress. These questions are not easily answered, but they should not be summarily dismissed.

The road to constitutional change, Frenzel approvingly observes, is long and difficult. Let's hope the journey enlightens the public and channels its energy into more productive forms of political participation.

Summary Questions

1. In your view, do the potential benefits of limitations on congressional terms outweigh the costs?
2. Which political interests support limiting congressional terms? Which oppose term limits? Which political party would benefit most from the enactment of term limits on national legislators?

Chapter 8

THE MASS MEDIA

Information is the lifeblood of a democratic system, and the communication of information is essential to democratic politics. Citizens need trustworthy, diverse, and objective information to perform their electoral role adequately. Decision makers need reliable information about the values, preferences, and opinions of citizens to respond intelligently to them. The mass media play a crucial role in the relationship between citizens and their government. Yet their potential impact on political life leaves many people feeling ambivalent.

On the one hand, the mass media have the potential to help the nation realize its democratic possibilities. They can expand the range of public debate and broaden the attentive audience, which creates an informed public. If they perform as a watchdog over elected officials, political accountability can be greatly improved.

On the other hand, the mass media's potential to propagandize and to manipulate the public could undermine the democratic process. In Politics in the Media Age, Ronald Berkman and Laura W. Kitch point out that even in the nineteenth century some people were worried that "by seeking the sensational and simplifying political matters," the mass media could "divert the attention of the masses, arouse irrational passions, and lower the level of political debate." In this century, government management of the news during both world wars exposed the danger that entire populations could be swayed. Government regulation of radio and television in our own period, as well as control over many of the sources of the news, raises concerns that the mass media are at best dependent on, and at worst captives of, the very institutions they scrutinize. The increasing concentration of media ownership, particularly in the past decade, suggests that diverse political information is hard to come by.

It is not surprising that media critics are found at both ends of the political spectrum. Social conservatives claim that violence and sexually suggestive material on television have undermined the American family and contributed to a decline in morals. Social liberals assert that television's depiction of women and minorities perpetuates unflattering stereotypes and limits social progress. Economic conservatives worry that the media's focus on business abuses and tight-fisted bankers will undermine the capitalist system. Economic liberals

243

bemoan the fact that the media can never be a force for economic justice and equality because they draw their revenue from commercial sources.

Of course, when our nation was founded there was no such thing as the mass media. The newspapers that existed were partisan forums, directed toward narrow groups of elite supporters. It was not until the Jacksonian era of the late 1820s and 1830s that American politics developed its mass character and the first mass circulation newspapers came into being.

Today, of course, the mass media are a fact of life. What we know about politics and government comes largely from the media. A. C. Nielsen reports that 98 percent of American families own at least one television set and that the nation has more radios than people. Few of us acquire political information from other people; instead, strangers decide what information most of us receive.

Television is particularly pervasive. By the time the average American reaches eighteen years of age, he or she has probably spent more time in front of a TV set than in a classroom (roughly 15,000 hours). Television is highly credible because it utilizes both sight and sound. Although television is primarily an entertainment medium, many programs have either explicit or implicit political content. News programs and documentaries are obviously political, and entertainment shows that deal with, say, the police or education have some underlying orientation toward the institution in question. Even a show such as "Sesame Street" reveals strong values about politically relevant subjects such as race relations. Advertisements too are full of politically relevant content, particularly in terms of the stereotypes they convey.

Because there are so many potential influences on political behavior and values, it is difficult to assess what effect such factors have. The mass media's impact is often inferred from their content, but the relationship is difficult to pin down. The one apparent truism is that the media exert the least influence when they attempt to affect people's views and preferences directly, especially through such devices as political endorsements. In 1936, for example, Republican Alf Landon was endorsed by over 80 percent of the daily newspapers in the country, but Democrat Franklin Roosevelt achieved one of the biggest electoral landslides in U.S. history.

Media impact appears to be strongest in ambiguous, unstructured situations in which individuals have little prior information. Because most people know little about most political subjects, the media can set agendas, not so much by telling the public what to think as by telling it whom and what to think about. A good example is the presidential nomination process. By focusing citizens' attention on the actions of certain individuals and particular issues, the media can confer status (one candidate is "the strong frontrunner") and create disadvantage (another candidate "has little experience"). Audiences learn not only what the campaign issues are but how much importance to attach to them.

Research on the subject has yielded mixed results, suggesting the media are neither as benign as their supporters have argued nor as damaging as many critics have claimed. We need to distinguish among the various types of media and to specify the conditions under which they do influence political orientations and behavior. Their effect will remain a controversial subject, as the selections in this chapter exemplify.

In the first selection, Joshua Meyrowitz makes a strong case that the electronic media have greatly affected our perceptions of political leadership, making it difficult for Americans to find leaders they respect and trust. The second and third essays, from extremely different perspectives, deal with bias in the news. Michael Parenti regards the American news media as businesses that are strongly biased in favor of conservative capitalism and thus not free to perform their watchdog role in an objective manner. Larry Sabato examines news bias in the 1992 presidential race, focusing on the charge made by Bush and Perot supporters throughout the campaign that the media had favored Bill Clinton in its reporting.

8.1

Lowering the Political Hero to Our Level

Joshua Meyrowitz

Image has always been important in politics. Whether an individual is viewed as honest or untrustworthy, hard-working or lazy, tough or mean, has much to do with that person's political success. Moreover, the use of the electronic media, particularly television, has dramatically altered how the public views political figures, and has especially affected the image of elected leadership.

According to Joshua Meyrowitz, before the invention of the electronic media, the public held political leaders in awe. Politicians' images were based on mystification and careful management of public impressions. Political figures operated at a great distance from the public, who had limited access to them.

Radio and television, however, "reveal too much and too often." Television in particular appears to make politicians available for public inspection. This clouds the distinction between politicians' "onstage" and "backstage" behavior. Their human frailties are highlighted, as TV cameras show them sweating or reacting with anger or tears. National politicians no longer have the opportunity to test their presentations, they appear to the whole nation at the same time, and so they are more likely to make mistakes. Ill-chosen words or the inevitable inconsistencies that arise during a campaign are exaggerated, which calls into question a politician's honesty and competence.

In the end, "the familiarity fostered by electronic media all too easily breeds contempt." According to Meyrowitz, mystification is necessary for an image of strong leadership, yet disclosure eliminates mystery. As a result, few contemporary political leaders are universally revered in their own lifetime.

A ll our recent Presidents have been plagued with problems of "credibility." Lyndon Johnson abdicated his office; Richard Nixon left the presidency in disgrace; Gerald Ford's "appointment" to the presidency was later rejected by the electorate; Jimmy Carter suffered a landslide defeat after being strongly challenged within his own party; and even the comparatively popular

Joshua Meyrowitz is a professor of communication at the University of New Hampshire.

Ronald Reagan has followed his predecessors in the now familiar roller coaster ride in the polls.*

We seem to be having difficulty finding leaders who have charisma and style and who are also competent and trustworthy. In the wish to keep at least one recent leader in high esteem, many people have chosen to forget that in his thousand days in office, John Kennedy faced many crises of credibility and accusations of "news management."

During the 1990 campaign, *Newsweek* analyzed recent political polls and concluded that "perhaps the most telling political finding of all is the high degree of disenchantment voters feel about most of the major candidates."[1] Of course, every horse race has its winner, and no matter how uninspiring the field of candidates, people will always have their favorites. The obsession with poll percentage points and the concern over who wins and who loses, however, tend to obscure the more fundamental issue of the decline in the image of leaders in general.

There are at least two ways to study the image and rhetoric of the presidency. One is to examine the content and form of speeches and actions; in other words, to look at specific strategies, choices, and decisions. Another method is to examine the situations within which Presidents perform their roles. This second method requires a shift in focus away from the specific rhetorical strategies of individual politicians and toward the general environment that surrounds the presidency and is therefore shared by all who seek that office.

This [article] employs the latter method to reinterpret the causes of the political woes of some of our recent national politicians and to shed some light on our leadership problem in general. I suggest that the decline in presidential image may have surprisingly little to do with a simple lack of potentially great leaders, and much to do with a specific communication environment—a communication environment that undermines the politician's ability to behave like, and therefore be perceived as, the traditional "great leader."

The Merging of Political Arenas and Styles

Before the widespread use of electronic media, the towns and cities of the country served as backstage areas of rehearsal for national political figures. By the time William Jennings Bryan delivered his powerful "cross of gold" speech to win the nomination for President at the 1896 Democratic convention, for example, he had already practiced the speech many times in different parts of the country.

The legendary oratory of Bryan and the treasured images of many of our other political heroes were made possible by their ability to practice and modify their

---

* Ronald Reagan, especially after 1982 and before 1987, enjoyed levels of public regard that were exceptional among recent presidents and presidential contenders.

public performances. Early mistakes could be limited to small forums, minor changes could be tested, and speeches and presentations could be honed to perfection. Politicians could thrill many different crowds on different days with a single well-turned phrase. Bryan, for example, was very fond of his closing line in the 1896 speech ("You shall not press down upon the brow of labor this crown of thorns, you shall not crucify mankind upon a cross of gold")—so fond, in fact, that he had used it many times in other speeches and debates. In his memoirs, Bryan noted his early realization of the line's "fitness for the conclusion of a climax," and after using it in smaller public arenas, he "laid it away for a proper occasion."[2]

Today, through radio and television, the national politician often faces a single audience. Wherever the politician speaks, he or she addresses people all over the country. Major speeches, therefore, cannot be tested in advance. Because they can be presented only once, they tend to be relatively coarse and undramatic. Inspiring lines either are consumed quickly or they become impotent clichés.

Nineteenth century America provided multiple political arenas in which politicians could perfect the form and the substance of their main ideas. They could also buttress their central platforms with slightly different promises to different audiences. Today, because politicians address so many different types of people simultaneously, they have great difficulty speaking in specifics. And any slip of the tongue is amplified in significance because of the millions of people who have witnessed it. Those who analyze changing rhetorical styles without taking such situational changes into account overlook a major political variable.

Many Americans are still hoping for the emergence of an old-style, dynamic "great leader." Yet electronic media of communication are making it almost impossible to find one. There is no lack of potential leaders, but rather an overabundance of information about them. The great leader image depends on mystification and careful management of public impressions. Through television, we see too much of our politicians, and they are losing control over their images and performances. As a result, our political leaders are being stripped of their aura and are being brought closer to the level of the average person.

The impact of electronic media on the staging of politics can best be understood by analyzing it in relation to the staging requirements of any social role. . . . Regardless of competence, regardless of desire, there is a limit to how long any person can play out an idealized conception of a social role. All people must eat, sleep, and go to the bathroom. All people need time to think about their social behavior, prepare for social encounters, and rest from them. Further, we all play different roles in different situations. One man, for example, may be a father, a son, a husband, an old college roommate, and a boss. He may also be President of the United States. He needs to emphasize different aspects of his personality in order to function in each of these roles. The performance of social roles, therefore, is in many ways like a multistage drama. The strength and clarity of a particular onstage, or "front region," performance depend on isolating the audience from the backstage, or "back region." Rehearsals, relaxations, and behaviors from other onstage roles must be kept out of the limelight. The need to shield backstage behaviors is especially acute in the performance of roles that rely heavily on mystification and on an aura of greatness—roles such as those performed by national political leaders.

Yet electronic media of communication have been eroding barriers between the politician's traditional back and front regions. The camera eye and the microphone ear have been probing many aspects of the national politician's behavior and transmitting this information to 225 million Americans. By revealing to its audience both traditionally onstage and traditionally backstage activities, television could be said to provide a "sidestage," or "middle region," view of public figures. We watch politicians move from backstage to onstage to backstage. We see politicians address crowds of well-wishers, then greet their families "in private." We join candidates as they speak with their advisors, and we sit behind them as they watch conventions on television. We see candidates address many different types of audiences in many different settings.

By definition, the "private" behaviors now exposed are no longer true back region activities precisely because they are exposed to the public. But neither are they merely traditional front region performances. The traditional balance between rehearsal and performance has been upset. Through electronic coverage, politicians' freedom to isolate themselves from their audiences is being limited. In the process, politicians are not only losing aspects of their privacy—a complaint we often hear—but, more important, they are simultaneously losing their ability to play many facets of the high and mighty roles of traditional leaders. For when actors lose parts of their rehearsal time, their performances naturally move toward the extemporaneous.

The sidestage perspective offered by television makes normal differences in behavior appear to be evidence of inconsistency or dishonesty. We all behave differently in different situations, depending on who is there and who is not. Yet when television news programs edit together videotape sequences that show a politician saying and doing different things in different places and before different audiences, the politician may appear, at best, indecisive and, at worst, dishonest.

The reconfiguration of the stage of politics demands a drive toward consistency in all exposed spheres. To be carried off smoothly, the new political performance requires a new "middle region" role: behavior that lacks the extreme formality of former front region behavior and also lacks the extreme informality of traditional back region behavior. Wise politicians make the most of the new situation. They try to expose selected, positive aspects of their back regions in order to ingratiate themselves with the public. Yet there is a difference between *coping* with the new situation and truly *controlling* it. Regardless of how well individual politicians adjust to the new exposure, the overall image of leaders changes in the process. The new political performance remains a performance, but its style is markedly changed.

Mystification and awe are supported by distance and limited access. Our new media reveal too much and too often for traditional notions of political leadership to prevail. The television camera invades politicians' personal spheres like a spy in back regions. It watches them sweat, sees them grimace at their own ill-phrased remarks. It coolly records them as they succumb to emotions. The camera minimizes the distance between audience and performer. The speaker's platform once raised a politician up and away from the people—both literally and symbolically. The camera now brings the politician close for the people's inspection. And in this sense, it lowers politicians to the level of their audience. The camera brings a rich range of expressive information to the audience; it highlights politicians' mortality and mutes abstract and conceptual rhetoric. While verbal rhetoric can transcend humanity and reach for the divine, intimate expressive information often exposes human frailty. No wonder old style politicians, who continue to assume the grand postures of another era, now seem like clowns or crooks. The personal close-up view forces many politicians to pretend to be less than they would like to be (and, thereby, in a social sense, they actually become less).

Some people were privy to a sort of "middle region" for politicians before television. Through consistent physical proximity, for example, many reporters would see politicians in a multiplicity of front region roles and a smattering of back region activities. Yet, the relationship between politicians and some journalists was itself a personal back region interaction that was distinguished from press accounts to the public. Before television, most of the news stories released were not records of this personal back region relationship or even of a "middle region." The politician could always distinguish for the press what was "on" the record, what was "off" the record, what should be paraphrased, and what must be attributed to "a high government official." Thus, even when the journalists and the politicians were intimates, the news releases were usually impersonal social communications. Print media can "report on" what happens in one place and bring the report to another place. But the report is by no means a "presentation" of the actual place-bound experience. The print reporters who interviewed Theodore Roosevelt while he was being shaved, for example, did not have an experience "equivalent" to the resulting news reports. Because private interactions with reporters were once distinct from the public communications released in newspapers, much of a politician's "personality" was well hidden from the average citizen.

Private press-politician interactions continue to take place, but electronic media have created new political situations that change the overall "distance" between politician and voter. With electronic coverage, politicians lose a great deal of control over their messages and performances. When they ask that the television camera or tape recorder be turned off, the politicians appear to have something to hide. When the camera or microphone is on, politicians can no longer separate their interaction with the press from their interaction with the public. The camera unthinkingly records the flash of anger and the shiver in the cold; it determinedly shadows our leaders as they trip over words or down stairs.

And, unlike the testimony of journalists or of other witnesses, words and actions recorded on electronic tape are impossible to deny. Thus, while politicians try hard to structure the *content* of the media coverage, the *form* of the coverage itself is changing the nature of political image. The revealing nature of television's presentational information cannot be fully counteracted by manipulation, practice, and high-paid consultants. Even a staged media event is often more personally revealing than a transcript of an informal speech or interview. When in 1977, President Carter allowed NBC cameras into the White House for a day, the result may not have been what he intended. As *The New York Times* reported:

> Mr. Carter is a master of controlled images, and he is obviously primed for the occasion. When he isn't flashing his warm smile, he is being soothingly cool under pressure. But the camera ferrets out that telltale tick, that comforting indication of ordinary humanity. It finds his fingers nervously caressing a paperclip or playing with a pen. It captures the almost imperceptible tightening of facial muscles when the President is given an unflattering newspaper story about one of his sons.[3]

Some politicians, of course, have better "media images" than others, but few can manipulate their images as easily as politicians could in a print era. The nature and the extent of this loss of control become even clearer when back and front regions are not viewed as mutually exclusive categories. Most actions encompass both types of behavior. In many situations, for example, an individual can play a front region role while simultaneously giving off covert back region cues to "teammates" (facial expressions, "code" remarks, fingers crossed behind the back, etc.). . . . Because expressions are constant and personal, an individual's exuding of expressions is a type of on-going back region activity that was once accessible only to those in close physical proximity. Thus, the degree of control over access to back regions is not simply binary—access/no access—but infinitely variable. Any medium of communication can be analyzed in relation to those personal characteristics it transmits and those it restricts.

Print, for example, conveys words but no intonations or facial gestures; radio sends intonations along with the words but provides no visual information; television transmits the full audio/visual spectrum of verbal, vocal, and gestural. In this sense, the trend from print to radio to television represents a shrinking shield for back region activities and an increase in the energy required to manage impressions. Further, Albert Mehrabian's formula for relative message impact—7% verbal, 38% vocal, and 55% facial and postural—suggests that the trend in media development not only leads to revealing more, but to revealing more of more. From the portrait to the photograph to the movie to the video close-up, media have been providing a closer, more replicative, more immediate, and, therefore, less idealized image of the leader. "Greatness" is an abstraction, and it fades as the image of distant leaders comes to resemble an encounter with an intimate acquaintance.

As cameras continue to get lighter and smaller, and as microphones and lenses become more sensitive, the distinctions between public and private contexts continue to erode. It is no longer necessary for politicians to stop what they are doing in order to pose for a picture or to step up to a microphone. As a result, it is increasingly difficult for politicians to distinguish between the ways in which they behave in "real situations" and the ways in which they present themselves for the media. The new public image of politicians, therefore, has many of the characteristics of the former backstage of political life, and many once informal interactions among politicians and their families, staff, reporters, and constituents have become more stiff and formal as they are exposed to national audiences. . . .

Most politicians, even Presidents, continue to maintain a truly private backstage area, but that area is being pushed further and further into the background, and it continues to shrink both spatially and temporally.

Writing and print not only hide general back region actions and behaviors, they also conceal the act of producing "images" and messages. Presidents once had the time to prepare speeches carefully. Even seemingly "spontaneous" messages were prepared in advance, often with the help of advisors, counselors, and family members. Delays, indecision, and the pondering of alternative solutions in response to problems were hidden in the invisible backstage area created by the inherent slowness of older media. Before the invention of the telegraph, for example, a President never needed to be awakened in the middle of the night to respond to a crisis. A few hours' delay meant little.

Electronic media, however, leave little secret time for preparations and response. Because messages *can* be sent instantly across the nation and the world, any delay in hearing from a President is apparent. And in televised press conferences, even a few seconds of thought by a politician may be seen as a sign of indecisiveness, weakness, or senility. More and more, therefore, the public messages conveyed by officials are, in fact, spontaneous.

Politicians find it more difficult to hide their need for time and for advice in the preparation of public statements. They must either reveal the decision process (by turning to advisors or by saying that they need more time to study the issue) or they must present very informal, off-the-cuff comments that naturally lack the craftsmanship of prepared texts. The new media demand that the politician walk and talk steadily and unthinkingly along a performance tightrope. On either side is danger: A few seconds of silence or a slip of the tongue can lead to a fall in the polls.

The changing arenas of politics affect not only the perceptions of audiences but also the response of politicians to their own performances. In face-to-face behavior, we must get a sense of ourselves from the ongoing response of others. We can never see ourselves quite the way others see us. On videotape, however, politicians are able to see exactly the same image of themselves as is seen by the public. In live interactions, a speaker's nervousness and mistakes are usually politely ignored by audiences and therefore often soon forgotten by the speaker too. With television, politicians acquire permanent records of themselves sweating, stammering, or anxiously licking their lips. Television, therefore, has the power to increase a politician's self-doubt and lower self-esteem.

Highly replicative media are demystifying leaders not only for their own time, but for history as well. Few leaders are universally revered in their own lifetime. But less replicative media allowed, at least, for greater idealization of leaders after they died. Idiosyncrasies and physical flaws were interred with a President's bones, their good deeds and their accomplishments lived after them. Once a President died, all that remained were flattering painted portraits and the written texts of speeches. An unusual speaking style or an unattractive facial expression was soon forgotten.

If Lincoln had been passed down to us only through painted portraits, perhaps his homeliness would have faded further with time. The rest of the Lincoln legend, however, including Lincoln's image as a dynamic speaker, continues to be preserved by the *lack* of recordings of his unusually high, thin voice, which rose even higher when he was nervous. Similarly, Thomas Jefferson's slight speech impediment is rarely mentioned. Through new media, however, the idiosyncrasies of Presidents are preserved and passed down to the next generation. Instead of inheriting only summaries and recollections, future generations will judge the styles of former Presidents for themselves. They will see Gerald Ford lose his balance, Carter sweating under pressure, and Reagan dozing during an audience with the Pope. Presidential mispronunciations, hesitations, perspiration, and physical and verbal clumsiness are now being preserved for all time.

Expressions are part of the shared repertoire of all people. When under control and exposed briefly, expressive messages show the "humanity" of the "great leader." But when they are flowing freely and constantly, expressive messages suggest that those we look up to may, after all, be no different from ourselves. The more intense our search for evidence of greatness, the more it eludes us.

There is a demand today for two things: fully open, accessible administrations and strong, powerful leaders. Rarely do we consider that these two demands may, unfortunately, be incompatible. We want to spy on our leaders, yet we want them to inspire us. We cannot have both disclosure *and* the mystification necessary for an image of greatness. The post-Watergate fascination with uncovering cover-ups has not been accompanied by a sophisticated notion of what will inevitably be found in the closets of all leaders. The familiarity fostered by electronic media all too easily breeds contempt.

Notes

1. David M. Alpern, "A Newsweek Poll on the Issues," *Newsweek*, 3 March 1980, 29.
2. William Jennings Bryan and Mary Baird Bryan, *The Memoirs of William Jennings Bryan, Vol. I*, Reprint of 1925 edition (Port Washington, New York: Kennikat, 1971), 103.
3. John J. O'Connor, "TV: A Full Day at the White House," *The New York Times*, 14 April 1977.

Summary Questions

1. Why does the author believe that "old style" political heroes are no longer possible?
2. It has been said that American voters prefer a "candidate of the people, but not like the people." What does this mean? Would Meyrowitz agree with this assertion?

 8.2

The Mass Media: Free and Independent?

Michael Parenti

It is usually conceded that the mass media set the agenda for public debate, but there is a great deal of disagreement over the extent of the agenda. Are important issues left out? Are certain ideas systematically excluded from public considera- tion? How free are the media to act as a watchdog by addressing items that are potentially embarrassing to government and important economic interests?

Michael Parenti believes that the American media simply cannot either seriously scrutinize government and economic elites or facilitate genuinely open political debate. He sees mass communications essentially as a business, run by busi- nesspeople for profit and increasingly concentrated in the hands of a few corpo- rations. One result is that the media favor business and capitalism and discredit opposing views or fail to give them a fair hearing. This orientation extends to coverage of foreign affairs. In Parenti's view, government manipulation of the press is common, and government agencies have a long history of suppressing information they do not want the public to have.

For all the talk about a free press, it comes as a shock to some people to discover that the major media are an increasingly concentrated component of corporate America, being themselves giant companies or subsidiaries of conglomerates controlled by a small number of top banks and corporations, and

Michael Parenti received his Ph.D. from Yale University and has taught political science at a number of colleges and universities.

a handful of rich conservative tycoons like Rupert Murdoch and Walter Annenberg. Murdoch, for instance, owns major newspapers in England, Australia, New York, and Chicago, a European cable network, and is co-owner of 20th Century Fox and a chain of television stations in the United States. Another example: the Tribune Company owns, besides the *Chicago Tribune* and the Chicago Cubs, television stations in Los Angeles, Atlanta, New Orleans, and Denver, five radio stations, fifteen cable television systems, and the *New York Daily News*. As Charles Perlik, president of the Newspaper Guild, observed: "The news industry has always been a business, run by businessmen—and an occasional businesswoman. Today it is in danger of being run—and overrun—by financiers."[1]

Of the "independent" television stations, 80 percent are affiliates of one of the three major networks, NBC, CBS, and ABC. Except for the local news, practically all the shows they run are network programs. Most of the remaining "independents" are affiliated with NET, the "educational" network, which receives most of its money from the Ford Foundation (controlled largely by the Morgan and Rockefeller banks) and a few allied foundations. The Ford Foundation picks NET's board of directors and reserves the right to inspect every program produced with Ford money.

Newspapers show a similar pattern of ownership. Two-thirds of the 1700-odd dailies, controlling 80 percent of circulation, are owned by chains like Gannett and Knight-Ridder. The trend in ownership concentration continues unabated, as the large chains buy not only independent papers but other chains. The "free and independent American press" is largely a monopoly press. Less than 4 percent of American cities have competing newspapers under separate ownership; and in cities where there is a "choice," the newspapers offer little variety in ideological perspective and editorial policy. In general, newspapers vary mostly from moderately conservative to ultraconservative, with a smaller number that are centrist or tepidly liberal.

Most of the "independent" dailies rely on the wire services and big-circulation papers for stories, syndicated columnists, and special features. Like television stations, they are independent more in name than content. Coverage of national and local affairs is usually scant, superficial—consisting of a few brief "headline" stories and a number of conservative or simply banal commentaries and editorials.

Along with the accelerated concentration of ownership is the growing trend toward cross-media conglomerates, as corporations and banks engage in mammoth multibillion-dollar takeovers of newspapers, television and radio stations, magazines, publishing houses, and movie studios. What fuels these record-breaking mergers? As one conservative publication explains: "The profits are almost unbelievable."[2] Like other businesses, the media corporations are diversified and multinational, controlling print, broadcast, and film outlets throughout Latin America, Asia, and the Middle East—as well as in Europe and North America.

Government coercion and official censorship are not the only threats to freedom of the press. As a report by one group of scholars noted, protection against the state is not enough: "The owners and managers of the press determine which person, which facts, which version of the facts, and which ideas shall reach the public."[3] The pro-business, conservative, and centrist biases of the mainstream media are readily evident. Given the media's pattern of ownership and dependency on big-business advertising, labor unions have few opportunities to present programs on the needs and struggles of working people. Peace activists seldom get a chance to challenge the military-industrial complex. Information favorable to existing socialist countries is systematically suppressed. . . .

Of the many interesting documentaries made by independent film producers, dealing critically with racism, women's oppression, labor oppression, corporate environmental abuse, the FBI, and U.S. imperialism in Central America and elsewhere, few if any have ever gained access to commercial movie houses or major television networks. In 1986, for instance, the documentary *Faces of War*, revealing the destructive U.S.-supported counterinsurgency waged against the people of El Salvador, was denied broadcast rights in twenty-two major television markets.

Journalists express concern about having their stories killed, about getting reassigned, passed over for promotion, and fired. *New York Times* columnist Tom Wicker testifies:

> When I was *Times* bureau chief in Washington, I was a member of the League of Gentlemen [i.e., the established elite]; otherwise I never would have been bureau chief. Time after time, good reporters . . . complained about not being able to get stories in the paper. And time after time I said to them, "You're just not going to get *that* in the *New York Times* . . . it's too reliant on your judgment rather than on official judgment, it's too complex, it contradicts the official record more flagrantly than the conventions of daily journalism allow."[4]

News reports on business rely mostly on business sources and allow little space for the views of antibusiness critics, or the communities and individuals afflicted by business. Reports about State Department or Pentagon policies rely heavily on State Department and Pentagon releases. Media coverage of the space program uncritically accepts the government's claims about the program's desirability and seldom gives exposure to the arguments made against it.

An Official Press

Far from being vigilant critics, most news organizations share the counterrevolutionary, anticommunist assumptions and vocabulary of the media magnates who own them. For years the press has supported cold-war policies, indulging in an unremitting Soviet-bashing and a hatred and fear of existing socialist societies that is so formidable in its ideological monopoly as to permeate even much of the American left. The Vietnam War was portrayed in the media as a noble but ill-conceived venture, with little attention given to the underlying class interests and to the horrendous devastation wreaked by U.S. forces upon the Vietnamese people and their society and environment. . . .

For twenty-five years, the Shah of Iran, a friend of the U.S. oil companies and a product of the CIA, maimed and murdered tens of thousands of dissident workers, students, peasants and intellectuals. For the most part, the American press ignored these terrible happenings and portrayed Iran as a citadel of stability and the Shah as an enlightened modernizer. However, when the Polish government cracked down on the Solidarity union in Poland in December 1981, resulting in the death of several miners and the incarceration of several thousand other people, every network, newspaper, and newsmagazine gave these events top-story play for weeks on end. . . .

The business-owned media treats the atrocities of U.S.-sponsored rightist regimes with benign neglect while casting a stern, self-righteous eye on popular revolutions, as in Nicaragua. Generally the press defames leftist movements and governments and supports those right-wing pro-capitalist dictatorships that are clients of the multinational corporations.

When seven political parties participated in elections in Nicaragua in 1984, with each accorded funds and free television time by the government during a campaign judged to be fair and open by teams of observers from neutral countries, the U.S. media—following the White House line—treated the election as a rigged affair conducted under "unfair conditions." The news media never provided evidence to support that conclusion, but simply repeated the charges in successive news stories and editorials. That same year, however, the U.S.-sponsored election held in El Salvador between two right-wing candidates, under highly coercive and restricted conditions—including the lack of secret ballots—was hailed in the U.S. press as a great blossoming of democracy (in a country where most of the labor-union leadership had been assassinated along with thousands of other opponents of the regime). . . .

The workings of the capitalist political economy remain another area uncharted by the news media. The need to invest surplus capital; the tendency toward a falling rate of profit; the drive toward profit maximization; the instability, recession, inflation, and underemployment—these and other such problems are treated superficially, if at all, by newspersons and commentators who have neither the knowledge nor the permission to make critical analyses of multinational corporatism. Instead, economic adversity is ascribed to innocent and unavoidable causes, such as "hard times." One television commentator put it this way: "Inflation is the culprit and in inflation everyone is guilty." When economic news is reported, it is almost always from management's viewpoint.

Each evening the network news programs faithfully report the Dow Jones stock-exchange averages, but stories deemed important to organized labor are scarcely ever touched upon, according to a study made by union members. Reporters fail to enlist labor's views on national questions. Unions are usually noticed only when they go on strike, but the issues behind the strike, such as job security, occupational and public safety, and resistance to loss of benefits are seldom acknowledged. The misleading impression is that labor simply turns down "good contracts" because it wants too much for itself.

There are few militantly progressive and no avowedly socialist commentators and editorialists in the mass media. Of the liberal columnists and commentators, most take care to present themselves as judiciously moderate—that is, they avoid class issues and direct confrontations with class power, knowing full well who their employers are and under what limits they are working. Some liberal commentators have been refused radio spots even on the relatively infrequent occasions they have had sponsors who would pay. When independent liberal groups manage to muster enough money to buy broadcasting time or newspaper space, they still may be denied access to the media—as has happened to those wanting to run ads against the Vietnam War, the nuclear arms buildup, and U.S. intervention in Central America.

Denied access to the major media, the political left has attempted to get its message across through little magazines and radical newspapers, publications that suffer chronic financial difficulties and sometimes harassment from police, FBI, rightist vigilantes, the IRS, and the U.S. Postal Service. Dissenters also attempt to make themselves heard by mobilizing great numbers of people in public protest. But popular demonstrations against official policies are often trivialized, undercounted, and accorded minimal coverage by the business-owned media. The September 1981 march on Washington, in which a half million working people protested Reagan's policies, was the largest ever to take place in that city. In June 1982, upwards of a million people marched in New York to protest nuclear armaments in the largest demonstration in U.S. history. However, neither historic event received direct coverage (unlike the marriage of England's Prince Charles or the funeral of Monaco's Princess Grace). The networks preferred to concentrate on sporting events on those days, giving but a few minutes of evening news to these massive expressions of popular sentiment.

This is not to say that the press is entirely immune to mass pressures. If, despite the media's misrepresentation and neglect, a well-organized and persistent public opinion builds around an issue or set of issues, the press eventually feels compelled to acknowledge its existence. If the popular opinion is strong and widespread and *if it does not attack the capitalist system as a system*, it can occasionally break through the media-controlled sound barrier, albeit with selected images. On occasion, acts of skulduggery and cover-up are committed in high places involving no class-wide interest as such but leaving prominent personages—presidential cabinet members or even the president—vulnerable before the law. When elite power is thus weakened for a time and held accountable to law in a democratic way, then it is hard to keep the press from digging into the story, especially an important one like the Watergate scandal or the Iran-contra connection. In such instances, conservatives are convinced the press is a liberal conspiracy dedicated to wrecking the system. . . .

To combat what they see as the ideological "softness" of the centrist media, hardcore ultraconservatives have launched repeated attacks on specific newspersons and have induced corporations to withdraw their advertising support from certain programs. They have organized corporate proxy fights against those news organizations deemed not sufficiently sympathetic to the right's message, and have poured millions of dollars into building new media outlets to compete with the centrist media; these include the religious right's radio network, consisting of 1,300 local stations, and two national networks, PTL and CBN; each has almost as many affiliates as ABC. Spreading the gospel is only one concern of the Christian rightists; most of the programming is economically conservative, militaristic, phobically anticommunist, antiunion, and hostile toward the needs of minorities.

It is said that a free and independent press is a necessary condition for democracy, and it is frequently assumed that the United States is endowed with such a press. While the news in "totalitarian" nations is controlled, we Americans supposedly have access to a wide range of competing sources. In reality, the controls exerted in the United States, while more subtle than in some other countries, leave us with a press that is far from "free" by any definition of the word. When it comes to getting the other side of the story, Americans are a rather deprived people. U.S. programs can be heard throughout Eastern Europe via Voice of America. American films are regularly shown in socialist countries. Twenty percent of the television shows in Poland come from the United States. American novels and other books are translated and widely read in the Soviet Union and Eastern European countries. Cubans can watch Miami television and listen to a half dozen U.S. radio stations and to Spanish-language Voice of America programs. But how many Americans are exposed to the media and literature of socialist countries? More importantly, how many Americans get information about their *own* country, from *within* their own country, that is contrary to the capitalist orthodoxy? . . .

The Politics of Entertainment

While the entertainment sector of the media, as opposed to the news sector, supposedly has nothing to do with politics, entertainment programs in fact undergo a rigorous political censorship. Shows that treat controversial, antiestablishment subjects often have trouble getting sponsors and network time. The censorship code used by Procter & Gamble, the largest television advertiser in the United States, for programs it sponsors states in part: "Members of the armed forces must not be cast as villains. If there is any attack on American custom, it must be rebutted completely on the same show."[5] Truly radical themes are eschewed by both the networks and Hollywood. On the rare occasions a leftist film is produced, such as *1900*, or *Reds*, or *Burn*, it is likely to be accorded a limited distribution.

But entertainment shows contain plenty of politics of their own. Be it adventure film, prime-time drama, or soap opera, adversities are caused by ill-willed individuals rather than by the economic and social system in which they live, and problems are solved by individual effort within the system rather than collective effort against it. Evening soap operas like "Dallas" and "Dynasty" depict a corporate world of ruthless tycoons engaged in an amoral pursuit of wealth, power, and sex—but the audience is invited to identify with, rather than reject, it all.

Revolutionaries and foreign agents are seen as menacing our land, and the military and police as protecting it. Movies like *Rambo* glorify the killing of Communists and depict Russians as subhumans who delight in torture and atrocity. Other films like *Red Dawn* and *Invasion USA*, and television specials like ABC's "Amerika," offer fantasy depictions of the conquest of the United States by Soviet troops—assisted by Cubans and Nicaraguans. The message is clear: the Soviets are our inexorable enemy and we had better not expect to live in peace and friendship with them. . . .

In the media, women appear less often than men and primarily in subsidiary roles as housewives, secretaries, and girlfriends, who are usually incapable of initiating responsible actions of their own. In media advertisements it is even worse: women seem predominantly concerned with being cheery, mindless handmaidens who shampoo a fluffy glow into their hair, wax floors shiny bright, make yummy coffee for hubby, and get Junior's grimy clothes sparkling clean. One-fifth of all television time is taken up with commercials that often characterize people as loudmouthed imbeciles whose problems are solved when they encounter the right medication, cosmetic, or cleanser. In this way, industry confines the social imagination and cultural experience of millions, teaching people to define their needs and life-styles (and those of hubby, wifey, and baby) according to the dictates of the commodity market.

For years, characters who were Afro-American, Latino, or some other ethnic minority were given little exposure except in unflattering stereotyped roles. When minorities have made appearances in cop shows, it has been most often as crooks, pimps, informers, or persons in need of assistance from White professionals. Working people in general, be they White, Black, Latino, or whatever, have little representation in the entertainment media except as uncouth, simple persons, hoodlums, sidekicks, and other stock characters. The tribulations of working-class people in this society—their struggle to make ends meet; the specter of unemployment; the lack of decent recreational facilities; the victimization by unscrupulous landlords and realty developers; the loss of pensions and seniority; the bitter strikes and the historical and ever-present battle for unionization, better wages, and work conditions; the dirty, noisy, mindless, dangerous quality of industrial work; the lives wrecked by work-connected injury and disease—these and other realities are given little if any dramatic treatment in the business-owned media.

In recent years, however, partly in response to the public pressure of a more politically advanced audience, there have been changes for the better. Various television series like "Hill Street Blues," "St. Elsewhere," "Cagney and Lacey,"

"Who's the Boss," and "Hail to the Chief" have offered plots with some social content and have projected women and minorities as intelligent and capable persons, sometimes as doctors, lawyers, district attorneys, police lieutenants, or as occupying other positions of authority and empowerment. Situation comedies continue to be loaded with a contrived and frenetically aggressive or downright silly humor. But in some of the better ones, like "The Cosby Show," minorities are portrayed as intelligent, likable, and decent people. And in a few rare films, such as *Norma Rae*, the struggles of working people have been given respectful attention.

Not all air time is given to commercial gain. The Federal Communications Commission requires that broadcasters devote some time to public-service announcements. Like the free space donated by newspapers and magazines, this time is monopolized by the Advertising Council, a group composed of representatives from the networks and big business. No public-interest groups are represented. While supposedly "nonpolitical," the Council's "public service" commercials laud the blessings of free enterprise and falsely claim that business is "doing its job" in hiring veterans, minorities, and the poor. Workers are exhorted to take pride in their work and produce more for their employers—but nothing is said about employers paying more to their workers. The ads blame pollution on everyone (but not on industry) and treat littering as the major environmental problem. In general, social and political problems are reduced to individual failings or evaded altogether. Air time that could be used by conservationists and labor, consumer, and other public-interest groups has been preempted by an Advertising Council that passes off its one-sided ads as noncontroversial and nonpartisan.

Repressing the Press

On those rare occasions when the news media expose the murky side of official doings, they are likely to encounter serious discouragements from public authorities. Government officeholders treat news that places them in an unfavorable light as "slanted" and criticize reporters for not presenting the "accurate" and "objective" (that is, uncritical and supportive) viewpoint. These kinds of attacks allow the media to appear as defenders of free speech against government pressure, instead of supporters of the established order as they more commonly have been.

The federal government has used the FBI to harass and arrest newspersons who persist in writing troublesome news reports. The Justice Department won a Supreme Court decision requiring reporters to disclose their information sources to grand-jury investigators, in effect reducing the press to an investigative arm of the courts and the prosecution—the very officialdom over whom it is supposed to act as a watchdog. Dozens of reporters have since been jailed or threatened with prison terms on the basis of that decision. On repeated occasions the government has subpoenaed documents, tapes, and other materials used by news media. Such interference imposes a "chilling effect" on the press, a propensity—already evident in news reports—to slide over the more troublesome aspects of a story and censor oneself in order to avoid censorship by those in power.

To offer one of numerous recent examples: in May 1986, William Casey, then CIA director, threatened to prosecute NBC, the *Washington Post,* and other media, for printing stories that supposedly violated "national security." One of these stories concerned an American who was charged with selling the Soviets information about how U.S. submarines were spying in Soviet harbors. But if the Soviets already knew about this, then suppressing the story would only keep it from the American people. While the U.S. government attempts to prevent unauthorized leaks to the press, it itself continually leaks information when it serves official purposes. As *New York Times* columnist James Reston noted, the administration "leaks the baloney it thinks people will swallow, and threatens to sue anybody who publishes information it wants to suppress."[6]

In 1986 the Reagan administration admitted that it had generated misinformation against Libyan leader Colonel Qaddafi as part of a campaign to overthrow him. This revelation evoked shocked comments from newspaper editors and executive producers of news shows—as if it were the first time the government had ever tried to manipulate the press. In fact, most American presidents and other top officials have attempted to manipulate the news flow. . . .

In 1983, the White House refused to let reporters cover the U.S. invasion of Grenada, thus making certain that the public would get only the official version. This was the first time in U.S. history the press had been banned from covering a war. "The exclusion of reporters during the first days of the Grenada invasion gave new meaning to the concept that no country can limit the freedom of others without also limiting it for itself."[7] While these curbs were supposed to be temporary, the government came up with a set of guidelines in October 1984 that were to be imposed on all future surprise military operations; these included limiting the number of reporters to a select pool, imposing press blackouts, and restricting coverage. . . .

Government manipulation of the press is a constant enterprise. Every day the White House, the Pentagon, and other agencies release thousands of self-serving statements and reports to the media, many of which are then uncritically transmitted to the public as information from independent news sources. White House staffers meet regularly with network bosses and publishers to discuss and complain about specific stories and reporters. They withhold information or feed misleading data to troublesome journalists. And in the 1980s the administration increased its control over what becomes news by severely reducing reporters' expectations about having full access. As the *New York Times*'s Washington editor, Bill Kovach, stated: "[The administration's] whole attitude is that government information belongs to the government." Helen Thomas of UPI, dean of the White House press corps, complained: "They [the administration] pick the story every day. They pick the one that will almost invariably wind up on the nightly news, and that's the one they answer questions on or give access to information about. [On] a lot of events, we're absolutely blacked out, and if you don't like it, too bad. The whole attitude is: We will tell you what we think you should know."[8]

From what has been said so far it should be clear that one cannot talk about a "free press" apart from the economic and political realities that determine who owns and controls the media. As [Herbert] Schiller asks: "How may at least a part of the nation's information and cultural apparatus be rescued from near-total corporate control and made accountable and accessible to the viewing, listening and reading public?"[9]

There is no such thing as unbiased news. All reports and analyses are selective and inferential to some inescapable degree—all the more reason to provide a wider ideological spectrum of opinions and not let one bias predominate. If in fact we do consider censorship to be a loathsome danger to our freedom, then we should not overlook the fact that the media are already heavily censored by those who own and control them. The very process of selection allows the cultural and political biases and class interests of the selector to operate as a censor. Some measure of ideological heterodoxy could be achieved if public law required all newspapers and broadcasting stations to allot substantial portions of space and time to a diverse array of political opinion, including the most progressive and revolutionary. But given the interests the law serves, this is not a likely development.

An existing statute, known as the Fairness Doctrine, requires that unpaid time be given to an opposing viewpoint—only if a particular editorial opinion is voiced, which discourages some stations from engaging in discussions of political questions. The law makes no requirement as to the diversity of the opposing viewpoints, so usually the range is between two slightly different establishment stances. In the 1980s, the Reagan administration all but ceased enforcing the Fairness Doctrine, with the consequence that advocacy advertising by corporations and well-financed conservative private organizations rose dramatically.* In 1985, these interests spent an estimated $1.8 billion to communicate their views on a variety of public issues. Advocacy ads tend to be emotionally charged appeals paid by corporate sponsors who often hide behind public-service sounding names. . . .

---

* In 1985 the Federal Communications Commission, reflecting the Reagan administration's deregulation policy, declared that the Fairness Doctrine unduly restricted the broadcast media in comparison with the print media. The FCC further argued that the plurality of media in American society makes the Fairness Doctrine unnecessary. The doctrine was not immediately scrapped, however, because the Commission was not sure whether Congress had mandated the requirement. A 1986 federal appeals court ruled that Congress had never fully embraced the rule, and the FCC no longer applies it. Attempts within Congress to reinstate the requirements have been unsuccessful.

With few exceptions, those who own the newspapers and networks will not relinquish their hold over private investments and public information. Ordinary citizens will have no real access to the media until they come to exercise control over the material resources that could give them such access, an achievement that would take a different kind of economic and social system than the one we have. In the meantime, Americans should have no illusions about the "free press" they are said to enjoy.

Notes

1. Charles Perlik, address before the Newspaper Guild, reprinted in the *Daily World*, November 7, 1985. As of the 1980s, the majority of all American newspapers, magazines, radio and television stations, publishing houses, and movie studios were controlled by fifty giant corporations, which themselves interlocked financially with massive industries and major banks: Ben Bagdikian, *The Media Monopoly* (Boston: Beacon Press, 1983).
2. *U.S. News and World Report*, May 13, 1985.
3. Report by the Commission on Freedom of the Press, quoted in Robert Cirino, *Don't Blame the People* (New York: Vintage, 1972), 47.
4. Quoted in Kevin Kelly, " 'League of Gentlemen' Rates Media," *Guardian*, February 13, 1985.
5. Eric Barnouw, *The Television Writer* (New York: Hill and Wang, 1962), 27.
6. *New York Times*, May 21, 1986.
7. Mike Zagarell, "News Reporting—the Military Vies for Command," *World Magazine*, November 1, 1984, p. 8.
8. Both Kovach and Thomas are quoted in *Washington Post*, June 10, 1985.
9. Herbert Schiller, "Beyond the Media Merge Movement," *Nation*, June 8, 1985, pp. 696–98.

Summary Questions

1. According to Parenti, what items should be on the nation's political agenda that are not? Why does he believe political dialogue through the nation's mass media is one-sided?
2. In Parenti's view, how is censorship practiced in the United States? Why is it difficult for the media to resist censorship attempts by business and government?

8.3

Is There an Anti-Republican, Anti-Conservative Media Tilt?

Larry Sabato

Given the importance of mass communications in modern campaigns, it is not surprising that charges of media bias are frequently leveled by candidates and their supporters who feel that opponents are being aided by the content and tone of the news. In 1992 supporters of incumbent President George Bush and independent candidate Ross Perot felt particularly aggrieved, believing that the national news media were wittingly hostile to their respective choices while presenting news coverage that portrayed Democrat Bill Clinton in a favorable light.

In this article, Larry Sabato surveys the empirical evidence from the press coverage in the last presidential election and finds that, on the whole, "the press was certainly a Clinton ally in 1992." Besides a much higher proportion of negative to positive references to Bush or Perot compared to Clinton in press and network news stories, the media tilt was enhanced by late-night comics and some prime-time entertainment shows, such as "Murphy Brown," which bashed Republicans and promoted Democrats. Particularly costly to the Bush campaign was the media's coverage of the economy: instead of focusing upon economic data that pointed to a recovery from the recession, coverage emphasized the negative—especially unemployment rates.

Sabato believes that although the ideology and partisan identity of reporters played a role in the liberal, pro-Democrat slant of the media, in addition, George Bush was not well liked personally by reporters. Still another problem for Bush was the fact that "the press is traditionally tougher on an incumbent administration, whatever its party affiliation, especially so in hard times." Sabato concludes that the election results, however, did not hinge on media coverage since "press tilt has a marginal-to-moderate effect, no more and no less."

A surprising number of prominent journalists and commentators, not all from the conservative wing of their profession, insist that in the 1992 general election the press leaned heavily in Bill Clinton's direction. Republicans are overwhelmingly of this opinion, having long ago consigned

Larry Sabato is professor of political science at the University of Virginia.

journalists to the rung of hell reserved for Democrats. The Perotists would concur: George Bush and Ross Perot may not agree on much, but dislike for those Bush called the "nutty talking heads" and Perot termed "jerks" and "teenage boys" is one unifying element. (The first half of Bush's favorite slogan. "Annoy the Media—Reelect Bush" could easily have been adopted by Perot.)

Naturally enough, much of the media establishment disagrees with Bush, Perot, and the bold journalists whose critiques are cited above. NBC's political director, Bill Wheatley, declared, "I don't believe there was an active bias at work," while his network colleague, anchor Tom Brokaw, offered his own sound bite to dampen the controversy: "Bias, like beauty, is most often in the eye of the beholder." Thus, fairness prevailed, say most of the news business's high priests, and the press did not defeat Bush; Bush beat Bush.

The more one studies the remarkable case of 1992, the greater the likelihood of judging both sides of this debate partly correct. For 1992, the conclusions about the press tilt are essentially the same as they were in earlier years: "of course" the news media are biased, but "press tilt has a marginal-to-moderate effect, no more and no less. . ."

Broadcasters for Clinton

Television viewers could be forgiven for sometimes believing the acronyms ABC, NBC, and CBS stood for the American Broadcasters for Clinton, the National Broadcasters for Clinton, and the Clinton Broadcasting System. From Labor Day to Election Day the Center for Media and Public Affairs found that 71 percent of the substantive comments made about George Bush on ABC, NBC, and CBS by reporters and other "nonpartisan" sources were negative. Bill Clinton's evaluations among the same group were 52 percent positive. These totals excluded "horse race" remarks about who was likely to win the election—portrayals that favored Clinton by an even greater margin.

Another study, by PR Data Systems and Mead Data Center, suggests that print news organizations exhibited a similar bias. A painstaking content analysis of AP, UPI, and eleven major U.S. daily newspapers over the general election period showed that nearly three-quarters (72 percent) of all negative characterizations made in presidential debate stories and accompanying headlines were about Bush. Clinton garnered just 15 percent of these unfavorable mentions, and Perot only 13 percent. By contrast, Clinton was the beneficiary of almost half (48 percent) of the glowing characterizations and headlines, while Perot garnered 30 percent of the positive mentions and Bush a paltry 22 percent. Most observers rated Perot the best performer in the first debate, Clinton in the second, and Bush in the third, so even a healthy frontrunner's bonus could scarcely entitle Clinton to such a lion's share of kudos if fairness prevailed. The tilt to Clinton in the news pages was matched on the editorial pages, too, as Clinton became the first

Democrat since Lyndon Johnson in 1964 to win more newspaper editorial endorsements than the Republican nominee.

Seemingly, everywhere one looked in the summer and autumn of 1992, Bush
and Quayle were being bashed and Clinton and Gore were being hailed in the
media. The *Washington Post* certainly fit the pattern, and when its ombudsman,
Joann Byrd, scrutinized the newspaper's contents (including headlines and photographs) covering the campaign's last two and a half months, she reached the
conclusion that her paper had a "very lopsided" tilt in Clinton's direction. For
instance the *Post*'s Style section featured a glowing account of a Clinton-Gore
bus trip headlined, "New Heartthrobs of the Heartland." And in one of the most
embarrassing juxtapositions of the campaign, the *Post* hyped its mid-September
public opinion poll showing a 21 percentage point lead for Clinton with a front
page, top-left headline, "Clinton's Lead Appears Solid, May Be Growing." Just a
week later, when its next poll revealed a much narrower 9-point lead for Clinton,
the *Post* buried the story inside page A6 with the amusingly protective headline, "Clinton Slide in Survey Shows Perils of Polling." The news media tilt was
supplemented by late-night comics and even some prime-time entertainment
shows, such as "Murphy Brown," which piled on the Republicans and promoted
the Democrats.

There were notable exceptions, of course. Broadcast personality Rush Lim-
baugh, with a weekly radio audience of over 12 million, aimed daily broadsides
at the Clinton bandwagon. The *Washington Times* was slanted against Clinton
from its masthead to its classified ads, with headlines and news stories so enthusiastically pro-Bush that at times it appeared to be a throwback to the nineteenth
century's cheerleading party press. And many of the news approaches to Hillary
Rodham Clinton suffered from a subtle—and sometimes blatant—sexism. But
added together, these anti-Clinton transgressions are still no match for the collective pro-Clinton fare of the leading networks and newspapers.

Covering the Economy

Everyone agrees that the economy torpedoed Bush and elected Clinton. But was
it the economy itself or the media depictions of it that turned voters against Bush?
No one can say with any certainty, but the networks' descriptions of economic
conditions sounded more like the Great Depression than the moderate recession
and prolonged period of sluggish growth that characterized 1990–1992. Fully 96
percent of the economic evaluations on the evening newscasts during much of
the general election were negative, as were 83 percent of the predictions about
the economy's future performance. The latter undoubtedly helped to drive down
consumer confidence still further, and make Bush's predictions of recovery seem
fanciful and "out of touch" to voters.

These media characterizations of the economy were no minor matter. The state
of the economy was unquestionably the central issue of the campaign and the

Late-night Political Humor in the 1992 Campaign

Candidate	Total No. of Letterman, Leno, and Arsenio Hall Jokes	Examples
George Bush	608	On Bush's alleged affair: "Wouldn't it be ironic if Barbara got a chance to throw him out of the White House before we got a chance to?" (Jay Leno, June 25, 1992).
		"Bush is now being accused of manufacturing the current crisis with Iraq. If it's true, it'll be the first manufacturing job he's brought to the U.S. in years." (Jay Leno, September 2, 1992).
		On Bush meeting with the postmaster general: "It wasn't an emergency or anything. Bush just needed one of those change-of-address kits." (Jay Leno, October 27, 1992).
Bill Clinton	423	"Top Ten Surprises in the United Nations' Sex Study: No. 10—Of the 100 million acts of love daily, most occur in Bill Clinton's campaign van." (David Letterman, June 25, 1992).
		"Bill Clinton said yesterday, 'It's not appropriate to go after someone's wife in the media.' He said, 'Going after someone's wife is better done discreetly, like at a cocktail party.' " (Jay Leno, August 25, 1992).
		On Clinton saying he's capable of commanding the U.S. military because he's headed the Arkansas National Guard: "Isn't that like saying you can fly the Space Shuttle because you've seen every episode of Star Trek?" (Jay Leno, August 31, 1992).
Dan Quayle	357	On Quayle being like Hamburger Helper: "You know he's in the Cabinet. You just hope you never have to use him." (Jay Leno, June 19, 1992).
		On Quayle's trip to Los Angeles: "Just what L.A. needs— another dumb blond." (Arsenio Hall, June 24, 1992).
		On Quayle meeting with Ronald Reagan: "That must have been interesting—someone who doesn't know what he's doing meeting with someone who can't remember what he did." (Jay Leno, September 9, 1992).
		"Top Ten ways Quayle prepared for the vice presidential debate: No. 7—Read book of inspirational stories about dumb guys who went up against smart guys—and won. No. 2— Reread his 'how a bill becomes a law' comic book." (David Letterman, October 13, 1992).

Late-night Political Humor in the 1992 Campaign (*continued*)

Candidate	Total No. of Letterman, Leno, and Arsenio Hall Jokes	Examples
Ross Perot	334	"I haven't seen a guy so mixed up about being in a race since Michael Jackson." (Arsenio Hall, September 25, 1992).
		"If he is not elected president he should go out to the airport. He'd make a great Hare Krishna." (Jay Leno, October 8, 1992).
		"Top Ten reasons Clinton is losing his lead: No. 2—More and more people like the idea of a tiny, insane millionaire running things." (David Letterman, October 29, 1992).
Jerry Brown	106	On Brown's showing in the New York primary: "He finished fifth, behind Clinton, Tsongas, uncommitted, and the older, fatter Elvis." (Johnny Carson, April 8, 1992).
		On Brown's 800 Number: "They put you on hold and play a recording of his concession speech." (David Letterman, April 26, 1992).
		On a break-in at Brown's campaign headquarters: "Not too serious, I understand. The thieves got away with three mood rings, two lava lamps, some magic crystals, [and] a couple of beaded curtains." (Jay Leno, June 22, 1992).
Al Gore	49	On Al Gore, Sr.'s comment that his son was raised for the job of vice president: "How do you raise someone [for that]? Do you put them in their room with nothing to do? Take them to a funeral and let them hang around? (Jay Leno, July 10, 1992).
		On Gore's speaking style: "I never thought I'd miss the charisma of Paul Tsongas." (Jay Leno, October 13, 1992).

Note: Other politicians (and total number of 1992 late-night jokes) who were frequent targets include: Edward Kennedy (59), Patrick Buchanan (56), Ronald Reagan (53), and Paul Tsongas (51).
Sources: Numbers of jokes on the "Tonight Show with Jay Leno," "Late Night with David Letterman," and the "Arsenio Hall Show" were compiled by the Center for Media and Public Affairs. All of calendar year 1992 was surveyed. The joke examples were selected from campaign issues of *Hotline* from January 1, 1992 to November 3, 1992.

chief source of President Bush's woes. A positive press spin suggesting economic recovery could have helped Bush regenerate lost momentum and would have undercut Clinton's major campaign thrust. But not only did Bush not receive an assist, the news media repeatedly ignored or downplayed nearly every encourag-

---

Media Comments on the 1992 Campaign

"Indeed, coverage of the campaign vindicated exactly what conservatives have been saying for years about liberal bias in the media."

Jacob Weisberg, *The New Republic*

"I sensed and observed a bias toward Clinton and more liberal policies and positions."

Richard Benedetto, *USA Today*

"There seems little doubt—at least in this corner—that press coverage was tilted against Bush during much of the campaign."

David Gergen, *U.S. News & World Report*

"[The pro-Clinton] bias of reporters, editors, the whole crew . . . brought about a tilt that was more pervasive and obvious than I've ever seen."

Hugh Sidney, *Time*

"The coverage has not been equal, not been fair."

Reid Collins, CNN

---

ing sign of an ongoing recovery that was slowly picking up steam. Near the end of the campaign, when the U.S. gross domestic product was announced to have grown by a strong 2.7 percent in the third quarter, most major media outlets pooh-poohed the news, some even implying the government's books had been cooked to make Bush look good at a critical moment. After the election, when the government released the final revised GDP growth rate for the third quarter, the statistic turned out to be 3.4 percent—an even better showing than Bush had been able to trumpet.

Was this just an isolated incident, one where skeptical reportorial juices were flowing freely as election day approached? Not according to a number of experienced financial reporters who attended the Commerce and Labor Departments' briefings throughout the campaign. Some colleagues, they noted, openly cheered bad economic statistics and booed good ones, hoping for the best spin from Clinton's perspective. These personal reactions would be revealing but harmless enough, as long as the resulting stories were not affected by the bias. Yet many news reports of economic statistics seemed to share the same slant. When the civilian unemployment rate rose, the headlines logically reflected that bad news. But when it fell in the summer and autumn, that fact was sometimes de-emphasized or even buried in print stories, with more obscure, unfavorable jobless statistics—such as private, nonfarm payroll employment—highlighted in the headlines. For example, in early September when overall unemployment edged down a tenth of a point, to 7.6 percent, the front pages of both the *Washington Post* and the *New York Times* headlined instead the loss of 167,000 private nonfarm jobs. Said one financial reporter for a major news service, "Financial markets paid attention to the [private nonfarm] number, but even professional economists weren't uniformly focused on that drop. and I have never [before] seen a paper lead with it in a general news report."

The Big Tilt

The media's Democratic tilt is not new to many voters. A post-election survey by the Times-Mirror Center for the People and the Press found that 35 percent of the voters believed the press had been unfair to George Bush, while just 19 percent termed the press unfair to Bill Clinton. Even many reporters acknowledged as much. An October 1992 study by the *Times-Mirror* center revealed that 55 percent of the journalists surveyed believed Bush's candidacy was damaged by press coverage, while only 11 percent thought Clinton was similarly harmed.

True, the press targeted Clinton early on, thanks to Gennifer Flowers, the draft charges, and marijuana non-inhaling—but this was the time when key reporters had tagged Clinton "easy meat" for the Republicans in the fall and many news persons were privately hoping a "stronger" Democrat would enter the fray. Once Clinton was the nominee and alternative to four more years of Bush, the tone of his coverage changed markedly. Adding to Clinton's advantage was the shame and regret many reporters felt about their handling of the Flowers affair, not to mention embarrassment about their mispredictions of Clinton's "inevitable" demise.

What motivated the tilt? The obvious but incomplete candor is party preference and ideology. A Freedom Forum survey of journalists revealed that journalists are predominantly and increasingly Democratic: 44 percent of reporters in 1992 called themselves Democrats, up from 38 percent in 1982, while only 16 percent identified with the Republican party, down from 19 percent ten years earlier. Whether Democratic, Republican, or independent, most reporters are ideologically liberal, especially on social issues. Thus, the Democratic National Convention platform was almost universally labeled "moderate" despite containing an absolutist pro-choice position on abortion and, for the first time ever, controversial pledges to end the ban on gays in the military and seek civil rights legislation for homosexuals. (President Clinton and the news media were to discover just how explosive the proposal on gays in the military was shortly after the new president's inauguration.) By contrast, the Republican National Convention platform was repeatedly characterized as right-wing and extreme even though it was little changed from the ones with which Ronald Reagan and George Bush won landslide Electoral College victories in 1980, 1984, and 1988.

The abortion issue in particular generated an extra shove in the Democratic direction in 1992, since another GOP presidential victory could have eventually provided the fifth Supreme Court vote to overturn *Roe* v. *Wade*, the decision guaranteeing abortion rights. Many reporters claim their personal views on abortion and other issues do not influence coverage, but this assertion rings more true for some than others. Journalists are not automatons, and at the very least their personal preferences influence the kinds of subjects they choose to cover and the approach they take to that coverage. A few newspersons are quite blunt about the influence their views have on coverage. Margaret Carlson, *Time's* deputy bureau chief in Washington who once worked in the Carter administration, explained: "You couldn't have fought the battles you have fought to get to where you are and not find what the Republicans say about women offensive—it's not possible, you cannot be that objective." Of course, most Republicans find Carlson's statement not only offensive but proof positive of press bias. Another example often cited by the GOP is the statement by ABC New's Carole Simpson that she "believed Anita Hill" in her 1991 charges of sexual harassment against Supreme Court Justice-to-be Clarence Thomas. This declaration came less than a week before Simpson was to moderate the second presidential debate in Richmond, Va. on October 16.

The Scent of a Loser

Other factors besides ideology were also at work in 1992. The press is traditionally tougher on an incumbent administration, whatever its party affiliation, especially so in hard times. The White House occupant's flaws are always well known, and the press's battles with him have usually left tender bruises that are easily inflamed or require the revenge of the pen. By contrast, the challenger is relatively unsullied, his transgressions less known or threatening. George Bush was an irresistibly inviting target because he had blown a massive lead and become unpopular with most viewers and readers—a development that actually predated the nasty turn in his press coverage. Bush took on the unmistakable look of a potential loser, and the possible fall of a once-invincible leader became a compelling story that shaped the context in which all other reporting was done. The scent of losing also emboldened enemies from the president's own party and ideology to carp and lash out, without fear of retribution, which made it all the more difficult for Bush to communicate a persuasive message. After all, the news media often only echo and amplify the biting criticism they readily find in the pundit class or on the campaign trail, and the source can as easily be on the right (Bush critics Patrick Buchanan, William Safire, and George Will, for instance) as on the left. In fact, the most dismissive, vicious remarks about Bush came from conservative, not liberal, commentators; the president's right flank was breathtakingly exposed, and relatively few ardent defenders of the Bush faith could be found to counteract the torrent of abuse heaped upon him.

Surprisingly, given Bush's apparent congeniality, many senior reporters also dislike him personally—and this group extends well beyond Dan Rather. Various explanations were offered privately, including Bush's inaccessibility, perceived favoritism, and even reverse class snobbery (the old "preppie factor" that long dogged the upper-crust Bush). Some journalists also harbored resentment about the way in which Bush won the presidency in 1988, especially his team's shrewd manipulation of the media and the use of Willie Horton,* the pledge-of-allegiance issue, and the like; 1992 became the payback, the just dessert for 1988. But whatever the cause, the press usually gives more favorable treatment to politicians they personally like (Bill Clinton, Ronald Reagan) than ones they do not like (Gary Hart, George Bush), regardless of ideology.

In addition, the newsrooms across America are now dominated by the baby boomers, and in the main they identify with the Democrats' young and hip boomer ticket. The forty-six-year-old Clinton's Fleetwood Mac, saxophone, and experiences in the '60s counterculture era had more resonance and relevance to youthful journalists than the sixty-eight-year-old Bush's country music, horse-shoes, and World War II.

Perhaps most fundamentally, journalists' careers and personal satisfaction depend in good part on the importance of the news they cover. The defeat of an incumbent president, the end of the Reagan-Bush era, and the election of a Kennedyesque successor with the accompanying massive changes in policy and personnel was simply better news, with the promise of years of drama and upheaval to come. More than a few newspersons who did the reporting on candidate Clinton knew they would likely win the assignment to cover President Clinton, sharing the White House limelight and—with visions of Ben Bradlee advising JFK dancing in their dreams—maybe even the Oval Office. Most of us just hope for change that will benefit our professions or businesses; journalists are in a position to assist their kind of change to fruition.

Newsroom Diversity

So on the whole, the press was certainly a Clinton ally in 1992. But George Bush probably could still have won the election had he held fast to his "no new taxes" pledge, capitalized early on his Persian Gulf victory, focussed purposefully on domestic ills, and spent the campaign convincing Americans of the worth of his recovery plan instead of mainly attacking Clinton's character and record. Bush and his managers ignored a fundamental lesson of American presidential elections: voters cast ballots retrospectively, and any contest for the White House inevitably becomes a referendum on the performance of the incumbent administration, not the challenger. So the fault, dear George, lay less in your press

---

* When Bush's Democratic opponent in 1988, Michael Dukakis, was governor of Massachusetts, he supported a program that allowed weekend furloughs for prison inmates. One inmate who took advantage of the program was Willie Horton, a black man who had been convicted of first-degree murder. While on a weekend furlough, Horton escaped to Maryland, where he was captured after beating a white man and raping his fiancée. The Bush campaign used the image of Willie Horton in a very effective campaign advertisement to portray Dukakis as soft on crime. A number of prominent members in the national press believed that the ads were inappropriate because of underlying racist overtones.

clippings than in yourself and your truly awful campaign—one of the most inept in modern history.

This is not to exonerate the press. Consumers have a right to expect more balance and fairness than they get in campaign coverage. Once again, vigorous ombudsmen who relentlessly challenge their news organizations can play a vital role, and the need for video ombudsmen is especially apparent in this area. The television networks need internal critics even more than most newspapers, where a variety of opinions is regularly available. It would also help if more conservative-minded young people could be attracted to news reporting; if news accounts and agendas are inevitably biased, perhaps readers and viewers would benefit from an ideological mix. "Diversity," after all, is the holy buzzword of the '90s. Why not the newsroom, too?

Summary Questions

1. What factors does the author believe were responsible for the negative media coverage of Bush in 1992? Did media coverage have a major effect on the eventual outcome of the election?
2. Why do news organizations tend to exhibit a liberal bias? What, according to the author, can be done to encourage a more balanced presentation of the news?

 Chapter 9

INTEREST GROUPS

The United States has always been a nation of joiners, and more interest groups are active in our governmental affairs than in any other nation. Still, Americans have never been comfortable with special interest politics. Ever since James Madison first warned of the "mischiefs of faction" in *The Federalist,* No. 10 (the first selection in this chapter), citizens, politicians, and scholars have debated the role of special interests in policymaking.

The conflict between special interests and the public interest has been especially evident when the government has seemed to be functioning ineffectively. During the Progressive Era, for example, the influence of railroads, oil companies, and insurance firms drew the attention of scholars and the popular press; consequently, regulation of lobbyists became a major aim of the reformers. During the New Deal, in contrast, relatively little attention was paid to special interests. The dominant view of scholars during and after that period was pluralism—the belief that competition among groups is healthy for democracy.

By the 1960s, however, it had become obvious that such competition was highly distorted; some special interests almost always lost in the political process, and others—especially those with money, access, or inside information—usually won. The interest group universe had a blatant representational bias, as well; some interests, such as business, were well represented in the process, whereas others (minorities, the poor, and consumers) were seriously underrepresented.

Renewed attention to the role of interest groups grew stronger in the 1970s and 1980s. The tremendous expansion in the number of interest groups, the decline of political parties, and the heightened visibility of interest groups in the electoral and policymaking processes appeared to parallel government's inability to deal with economic and social problems. From the inability of Congress and the president to work together during the Carter years to the $200 billion deficits and influence-peddling scandals of the Reagan presidency, interest groups have been accused of being at the heart of the problem of contemporary government.

Depending on one's perspective, the United States is either blessed or cursed with many special interests. The constitutional guarantees of free speech, free association, and petition are basic to group formation. Because political organizations often parallel government structure, federalism and the separation of powers have encouraged a multiplicity of groups as interests organize around various local, state, and national access points. Societal cleavages also help foster interest group development. Differences in economics, climate, culture, tradition, and in racial, ethnic, and religious backgrounds create ready-made interests within American life. Finally, our cultural values may well play a role. As Alexis de Tocqueville observed 150 years ago, values such as individuality and personal achievement underlie the propensity of citizens to join groups.

There is a difference, however, between the existence of special interests and the emergence of special interest groups—associations of individuals who share attitudes or goals and attempt to influence public policy. In a simple society there is little need for interest groups, because people have no political or economic reason to organize when they work only for their families. It was not until the mid-to-late nineteenth century that interest groups started to appear regularly on the American political scene. As the nation became economically and socially complex, new interests were created and old ones redefined. Farming, for example, became specialized, commercialized, and dependent on other economic sectors. U.S. trade policies appeared to affect southern cotton farmers and midwestern grain producers, and it soon made sense for such people to organize.

Many political scientists argue that new interest groups are a natural consequence of a growing society. Groups develop both to improve individuals' positions or to protect existing advantages. For example, mobilization of business interests in the 1960s and 1970s often resulted from threats posed by consumer groups and environmentalists. The post–World War II era, especially since 1960, has witnessed a dramatic increase in the number of special interests that have organized for political purposes. New groups have crowded into areas such as business and agriculture, which already were well organized, but the most rapid expansion has taken place in areas that were poorly organized or not organized at all. Women, blacks, environmentalists, consumers, and other nonoccupational interests are now actively represented by groups.

Such changes have been so extensive that even the term *interest group* no longer seems appropriate. Much of the business lobbying in Washington, for example, is now done by representatives of individual companies as well as by "peak" associations, such as the National Association of Manufacturers, which represent groups of companies. Many institutions, even colleges and universities, have their own lobbyists. Some of the so-called groups operating in Washington are not mass membership organizations governed by a board of elected directors; one study of public interest groups discovered that 40 percent of the groups had fewer than one thousand members and 30 percent had no members at all. A large number of active groups are staff organizations, composed of a handful of individuals who are funded by foundation resources. Some are totally private concerns, like Ralph Nader's organization Public Citizen, which claims to lobby for all consumers.

Lobbying has become a growth industry. From 1975 to 1985, the number of registered lobbyists in Washington doubled; the number of attorneys more than tripled between 1973 and 1983, rising to more than 37,000. Washington now abounds with lobbying firms, which contract with companies and groups to represent their interests. Some have more than fifty clients, ranging from individual companies to entire nations. Some plan and manage political campaigns, as well as advise specialized interests.

New techniques of influence have also appeared as lobbyists have embraced technology. Orchestrated mass mailings to legislators or the president can be put in motion within minutes by some of the more sophisticated lobbies. The Campaign Finance Acts of 1971 and 1974 have made it possible for almost all groups to create political action committees (PACs) to coordinate financial contributions to candidates for public office. In 1990, nearly 4,200 PACs were registered.

To provide a sense of the controversy over interest groups and a flavor of today's environment, this chapter includes a diverse range of selections. *The Federalist,* No. 10, is a classic statement of the dilemma special interests posed to the framers, who sought to control the detrimental effects of factions, especially "majority factions." As the authors point out in "The Changing Nature of Interest Group Politics," the Madisonian solution may have contributed to today's problem: how to find the public interest when so many minority factions exist.

Then the two selections which follow deal with the role of special interest money in American politics, albeit from very different perspectives. Jeffrey Birnbaum surveys the history of lobbying in America, focusing upon some of the scandals that have given lobbyists an unsavory reputation. Finally, the controversy over PAC contributions is examined by Frank Sorauf, who suggests that their impact on legislators' voting behavior is hard to demonstrate and may be exaggerated.

9.1

The Federalist, No. 10

James Madison

There is an inherent tension in any democratic society. Liberty demands that citizens be allowed to pursue their special interests, even if those interests are offensive and selfish; yet the pursuit of special interests may conflict with the public interest. The nation's founders were well aware of this dilemma and directed many of their efforts toward constructing a government that respected personal freedom but was capable of acting for the collective good.

This paper is perhaps the best statement of what the founders thought about special interests or factions. At base they feared all special interests, especially "majority factions," which had the potential to tyrannize the system. Madison realized, however, that special interests "are sown in the nature of man," and any attempt to eliminate them would involve the destruction of liberty, a remedy "worse than the disease." Madison's solution was to limit the effects of factions by promoting competition among them and designing a government with an elaborate system of checks and balances to reduce the power of any single, strong group, whether made up of a majority or a minority of citizens.

Among the numerous advantages promised by a well constructed Union, none deserves to be more accurately developed than its tendency to break and control the violence of faction.* The friend of popular governments, never finds himself so much alarmed for their character and fate, as when he contemplates their propensity to this dangerous vice. He will not fail therefore to set a due value on any plan which, without violating the principles to which he is attached, provides a proper cure for it. The instability, injustice and confusion introduced into the public councils, have in truth been the mortal diseases under which popular governments have every where perished; as they continue to be the favorite and fruitful topics from which the adversaries to liberty derive their most specious declamations. The valuable improvements

---

* Madison used the term *faction* to denote any special interest, including parties. Although interest groups did exist, they were not organized in the sense in which we think of them today. Interest "groups" representing special interests were not common until after the Civil War.

made by the American Constitutions on the popular models, both ancient and modern, cannot certainly be too much admired; but it would be an unwarrantable partiality, to contend that they have as effectually obviated the danger on this side as was wished and expected. Complaints are every where heard from our most considerate and virtuous citizens, equally the friends of public and private faith, and of public and personal liberty; that our governments are too unstable; that the public good is disregarded in the conflicts of rival parties; and that measures are too often decided, not according to the rules of justice, and the rights of the minor party; but by the superior force of an interested and over-bearing majority. However anxiously we may wish that these complaints had no foundation, the evidence of known facts will not permit us to deny that they are in some degree true. It will be found indeed, on a candid review of our situation, that some of the distresses under which we labor, have been erroneously charged on the operation of our governments; but it will be found, at the same time, that other causes will not alone account for many of our heaviest misfortunes; and particularly, for that prevailing and increasing distrust of public engagements, and alarm for private rights, which are echoed from one end of the continent to the other. These must be chiefly, if not wholly, effects of the unsteadiness and injustice, with which a factious spirit has tainted our public administrations.

By a faction I understand a number of citizens, whether amounting to a majority or minority of the whole, who are united and actuated by some common impulse of passion, or of interest, adverse to the rights of other citizens, or to the permanent and aggregate interests of the community.

There are two methods of curing the mischiefs of faction: the one, by removing its causes; the other, by controlling its effects.

There are again two methods of removing the causes of faction: the one by destroying the liberty which is essential to its existence; the other, by giving to every citizen the same opinions, the same passions, and the same interests.

It could never be more truly said than of the first remedy, that it is worse than the disease. Liberty is to faction, what air is to fire, an aliment without which it instantly expires. But it could not be a less folly to abolish liberty, which is essential to political life, because it nourishes faction, than it would be to wish the annihilation of air, which is essential to animal life, because it imparts to fire its destructive agency.

The second expedient is as impracticable, as the first would be unwise. As long as the reason of man continues fallible, and he is at liberty to exercise it, different opinions will be formed. As long as the connection subsists between his reason and his self-love, his opinions and his passions will have a reciprocal influence on each other; and the former will be objects to which the latter will attach themselves. The diversity in the faculties of men from which the rights of property originate, is not less an insuperable obstacle to a uniformity of interests. The protection of these faculties is the first object of Government. From the protection of different and unequal faculties of acquiring property, the possession of different degrees and kinds of property immediately results: and from the influence of these on the sentiments and views of the respective proprietors, ensues a division of the society into different interests and parties.

The latent causes of faction are thus sown in the nature of man; and we see them every where brought into different degrees of activity, according to the different circumstances of civil society. A zeal for different opinions concerning religion, concerning Government and many other points, as well of speculation as of practice; an attachment to different leaders ambitiously contending for pre-eminence and power; or to persons of other descriptions whose fortunes have been interesting to the human passions, have in turn divided mankind into parties, inflamed them with mutual animosity, and rendered them much more disposed to vex and oppress each other, than to co-operate for their common good. So strong is this propensity of mankind to fall into mutual animosities, that where no substantial occasion presents itself, the most frivolous and fanciful distinctions have been sufficient to kindle their unfriendly passions, and excite their most violent conflicts. But the most common and durable source of factions, have been the various and unequal distribution of property. Those who hold, and those who are without property, have ever formed distinct interests in society. Those who are creditors, and those who are debtors, fall under a like discrimination. A landed interest, a manufacturing interest, a mercantile interest, a monied interest, with many lesser interests, grow up of necessity in civilized nations, and divide them into different classes, actuated by different sentiments and views. The regulation of these various and interfering interests forms the principal task of modern Legislation, and involves the spirit of party and faction in the necessary and ordinary operations of Government.

No man is allowed to be a judge in his own cause; because his interest would certainly bias his judgment, and, not improbably, corrupt his integrity. With equal, nay with greater reason, a body of men, are unfit to be both judges and parties, at the same time; yet, what are many of the most important acts of legislation, but so many judicial determinations, not indeed concerning the rights of single persons, but concerning the rights of large bodies of citizens; and what are the different classes of legislators, but advocates and parties to the causes which they determine? Is a law proposed concerning private debts? It is a question to which the creditors are parties on one side, and the debtors on the other. Justice ought to hold the balance between them. Yet the parties are and must be themselves the judges; and the most numerous party, or, in other words, the most powerful faction must be expected to prevail. Shall domestic manufactures be encouraged, and in what degree, by restrictions on foreign manufactures? are questions which would be differently decided by the landed and the manufacturing classes; and probably by neither, with a sole regard to justice and the public good. . . .

It is in vain to say, that enlightened statesmen will be able to adjust these clashing interests, and render them all subservient to the public good. Enlightened statesmen will not always be at the helm: Nor, in many cases, can such an adjustment be made at all, without taking into view indirect and remote considerations, which will rarely prevail over the immediate interest which one party may find in disregarding the rights of another, or the good of the whole.

The inference to which we are brought, is, that the causes of faction cannot be removed; and that relief is only to be sought in the means of controlling its *effects*.

If a faction consists of less than a majority, relief is supplied by the republican principle, which enables the majority to defeat its sinister views by regular vote: It may clog the administration, it may convulse the society; but it will be unable to execute and mask its violence under the forms of the Constitution. When a majority is included in a faction, the form of popular government on the other hand enables it to sacrifice to its ruling passion or interest, both the public good and the rights of other citizens. To secure the public good, and private rights, against the danger of such a faction, and at the same time to preserve the spirit and the form of popular government, is then the great object to which our enquiries are directed: Let me add that it is the great desideratum, by which alone this form of government can be rescued from the opprobrium under which it has so long labored, and be recommended to the esteem and adoption of mankind.

By what means is this object attainable? Evidently by one of two only. Either the existence of the same passion or interest in a majority at the same time, must be prevented; or the majority, having such co-existent passion or interest, must be rendered, by their number and local situation, unable to concert and carry into effect schemes of oppression. If the impulse and the opportunity be suffered to coincide, we well know that neither moral nor religious motives can be relied on as an adequate control. They are not found to be such on the injustice and violence of individuals, and lose their efficacy in proportion to the number combined together; that is, in proportion as their efficacy becomes needful.

From this view of the subject, it may be concluded, that a pure Democracy, by which I mean, a Society, consisting of a small number of citizens, who assemble and administer the Government in person, can admit of no cure for the mischiefs of faction. A common passion or interest will, in almost every case, be felt by a majority of the whole; a communication and concert results from the form of Government itself; and there is nothing to check the inducements to sacrifice the weaker party, or an obnoxious individual. Hence it is, that such Democracies have ever been spectacles of turbulence and contention; have ever been found incompatible with personal security, or the rights of property; and have in general been as short in their lives, as they have been violent in their deaths. Theoretic politicians, who have patronized this species of Government, have erroneously supposed, that by reducing mankind to a perfect equality in their political rights, they would, at the same time, be perfectly equalized and assimilated in their possessions, their opinions, and their passions.

A Republic, by which I mean a Government in which the scheme of representation takes place, opens a different prospect, and promises the cure for which we are seeking. Let us examine the points in which it varies from pure Democracy, and we shall comprehend both the nature of the cure, and the efficacy which it must derive from the Union.

The two great points of difference between a Democracy and a Republic are, first, the delegation of the Government, in the latter, to a small number of citizens elected by the rest: secondly, the greater number of citizens, and greater sphere of country, over which the latter may be extended.

The effect of the first difference is, on the one hand to refine and enlarge the public views, by passing them through the medium of a chosen body of citizens, whose wisdom may best discern the true interest of their country, and whose patriotism and love of justice, will be least likely to sacrifice it to temporary or partial considerations. Under such a regulation, it may well happen that the public voice pronounced by the representatives of the people, will be more consonant to the public good, than if pronounced by the people themselves convened for the purpose. On the other hand, the effect may be inverted. Men of factious tempers, of local prejudices, or of sinister designs, may by intrigue, by corruption or by other means, first obtain the suffrages, and then betray the interests of the people. The question resulting is, whether small or extensive Republics are most favorable to the election of proper guardians of the public weal: and it is clearly decided in favor of the latter by two obvious considerations.

In the first place it is to be remarked that however small the Republic may be, the Representatives must be raised to a certain number, in order to guard against the cabals of a few; and that however large it may be, they must be limited to a certain number, in order to guard against the confusion of a multitude. Hence the number of Representatives in the two cases, not being in proportion to that of the Constituents, and being proportionally greatest in the small Republic, it follows, that if the proportion of fit characters, be not less, in the large than in the small Republic, the former will present a greater option, and consequently a greater probability of a fit choice.

In the next place, as each Representative will be chosen by a greater number of citizens in the large than in the small Republic, it will be more difficult for unworthy candidates to practise with success the vicious arts, by which elections are too often carried; and the suffrages of the people being more free, will be more likely to centre on men who possess the most attractive merit, and the most diffusive and established characters.

It must be confessed, that in this, as in most other cases, there is a mean, on both sides of which inconveniencies will be found to lie. By enlarging too much the number of electors, you render the representative too little acquainted with all their local circumstances and lesser interests; and by reducing it too much, you render him unduly attached to these, and too little fit to comprehend and pursue great and national objects. The Federal Constitution forms a happy combination in this respect; the great and aggregate interests being referred to the national, the local and particular, to the state legislatures.

The other point of difference is, the greater number of citizens and extent of territory which may be brought within the compass of Republican, than of Democratic Government; and it is this circumstance principally which renders factious combinations less to be dreaded in the former, than in the latter. The smaller the society, the fewer probably will be the distinct parties and interests composing it; the fewer the distinct parties and interests, the more frequently will a majority be found of the same party; and the smaller the number of individuals composing a majority, and the smaller the compass within which they are placed, the more easily will they concert and execute their plans of oppression. Extend the sphere, and you take in a greater variety of parties and interests; you make it less probable that a majority of the whole will have a common motive to invade the rights of other citizens; or if such a common motive exists, it will be more difficult for all who feel it to discover their own strength, and to act in unison with each other. . . .

Hence it clearly appears, that the same advantage, which a Republic has over a Democracy, in controling the effects of faction, is enjoyed by a large over a small Republic—is enjoyed by the Union over the States composing it. Does this advantage consist in the substitution of Representatives, whose enlightened views and virtuous sentiments render them superior to local prejudices, and to schemes of injustice? It will not be denied, that the Representation of the Union will be most likely to possess these requisite endowments, Does it consist in the greater security afforded by a greater variety of parties, against the event of any one party being able to outnumber and oppress the rest? In an equal degree does the encreased variety of parties, comprised within the Union, encrease this security? Does it, in fine, consist in the greater obstacles opposed to the concern and accomplishment of the secret wishes of an unjust and interested majority? Here, again, the extent of the Union gives it the most palpable advantage.

The influence of factious leaders may kindle a flame within their particular States, but will be unable to spread a general conflagration through the other States: a religious sect, may degenerate into a political faction in a part of the Confederacy; but the variety of sects dispersed over the entire face of it, must secure the national Councils against any danger from that source: a rage for paper money, for an abolition of debts, for an equal division of property, or for any other improper or wicked project, will be less apt to pervade the whole body of the Union, than a particular member of it; in the same proportion as such a malady is more likely to taint a particular county or district, than an entire State.

In the extent and proper structure of the Union, therefore, we behold a Republican remedy for the diseases most incident to Republican Government. And according to the degree of pleasure and pride, we feel in being Republicans, ought to be our zeal in cherishing the spirit, and supporting the character of Federalists.

Summary Questions

1. What is Madison's view of human nature? What factors led him to this conclusion?

2. According to Madison, why is a republic preferable to a democracy as a form
    of government?
3. What is the Madisonian solution to the problem of dealing with the excesses
    of faction? What are some of the costs of this solution?

 9.2

The Changing Nature of Interest
Group Politics

Burdett A. Loomis and Allan J. Cigler

Special interests have always played a central role in American politics, but recent
decades have witnessed a tremendous growth, both in number of groups and in
scope. Few areas in society have gone untouched, and it is difficult to identify any
interest that does not have some form of representation in Washington.

In this essay, the authors examine the forces that have led to this rapid growth.
The expanding role of the national government has been particularly influential. As the nation's policy agenda has broadened, increasingly specialized
interests have descended on Washington to defend and further enhance their
benefits. Recent technological changes, especially computer-based direct mailing techniques, have also played an important part in new-group formation.

The authors believe that recent changes in interest group politics have had both
positive and negative consequences. Politics has become much more representative, but government has become more complex, and it is increasingly difficult for officials to respond to the public interest.

From James Madison to Madison Avenue, political interests have played a
central role in American politics. But this great continuity in our political experience has been matched by the ambivalence with which citizens,
politicians, and scholars have approached interest groups. James Madison's warnings on the dangers of faction echo in the rhetoric of reformers ranging from

Burdett A. Loomis and Allan J. Cigler are both professors of political science at the University
of Kansas.

Populists and Progressives near the turn of the century to contemporary so-called public interest advocates.

   If organized special interests are nothing new in American politics, can to-day's group politics be seen as having undergone some fundamental changes? Acknowledging that many important, continuing trends do exist, we seek to place in perspective a broad series of changes in the modern nature of interest group politics. Among the most substantial of these developments are:

1. a great proliferation of interest groups since the early 1960s;
2. a centralization of group headquarters in Washington, D.C., rather than in New York City or elsewhere;
3. major technological developments in information processing that promote more sophisticated, timelier, and more specialized grassroots lobbying;
4. the rise of single-issue groups;
5. changes in campaign finance laws (1971, 1974) and the ensuing growth of political action committees (PACs);
6. the increased formal penetration of political and economic interests into the bureaucracy (advisory committees), the presidency (White House group representatives), and the Congress (caucuses of members);
7. the continuing decline of political parties' abilities to perform key electoral and policy-related activities;
8. the increased number, activity, and visibility of public interest groups, such as Common Cause, and the Ralph Nader-inspired public interest research organizations;
9. the growth of activity and impact by institutions, including corporations, universities, state and local governments, and foreign interests; and
10. a continuing rise in the amount and sophistication of group activity in state capitals.

   All these developments have their antecedents in previous eras of American political life; there is little genuinely new under the interest group sun. Political action committees have replaced (or complemented) other forms of special interest campaign financing. Group-generated mail directed at Congress has existed as a tactic since at least the early 1900s. And many organizations have long been centered in Washington, members of Congress traditionally have represented local interests, and so on.

Contemporary Interest Group Politics

Several notable developments mark the modern age of interest group politics. Of primary importance is the large and growing number of active groups and other interests. The data here are sketchy, but one major study found that most current groups came into existence after World War II and that group formation has accelerated substantially since the early 1960s. Also since the 1960s groups have increasingly directed their attention toward the center of power in Washington, D.C., as the scope of federal policymaking has grown, and groups seeking influence have determined to "hunt where the ducks are." As a result, the 1960s and 1970s marked a veritable explosion in the number of groups lobbying in Washington.

A second key change is evident in the composition of the interest group universe. Beginning in the late 1950s political participation patterns underwent some significant transformations. Conventional activities such as voting declined, and political parties, the traditional aggregators and articulators of mass interests, became weaker. Yet at all levels of government, evidence of citizen involvement has been apparent, often in the form of new or revived groups. Particularly impressive has been the growth of citizens' groups—those organized around an idea or cause (at times a single issue) with no occupational basis for membership. Fully 30 percent of such groups have formed since 1975, and in 1980 they made up more than one-fifth of all groups represented in Washington.

In fact, a participation revolution has occurred in the country as large numbers of citizens have become active in an ever-increasing number of protest groups, citizens' organizations, and special interest groups. These groups often comprise issue-oriented activists or individuals who seek collective material benefits. The "free-rider" problem has proved not to be an insurmountable barrier to group formation, and many new interest groups do not use selective material benefits to gain support.*

Third, government itself has had a profound effect on the growth and activity of interest groups. Early in this century, workers found organizing difficult because business and industry used government-backed injunctions to prevent strikes. By the 1930s, however, with the prohibition of injunctions in private labor disputes and the rights of collective bargaining established, most governmental actions directly promoted labor union growth. In recent years changes in the campaign finance laws have led to an explosion in the number of political action committees, especially among business, industry, and issue-oriented groups. Laws facilitating group formation certainly have contributed to group proliferation, but government policy in a broader sense has been equally responsible.

Fourth, not only has the number of membership groups grown in recent decades, but a similar expansion has occurred in the political activity of many

---

* Individuals who have a common interest are sometimes reluctant to join an organization that addresses their concern. This leads to the "free rider" problem: Citizens choose not to bear the participation costs (time, membership dues) because they can enjoy the benefits (such as favorable legislation) whether or not they join. If farm subsidies increase because of the efforts of farm interest groups, for example, all farmers benefit, not just those who belong to the groups. As a result, groups that pursue collective benefits have great difficulty surviving. To remain viable, many groups depend on the development of selective benefits, such as travel discounts and low-cost insurance, that are available only to group members.

other interests such as individual corporations, universities, churches, governmental units, foundations, and think tanks. Historically, most of these interests have been satisfied with representation by trade or professional associations. Since the mid-1960s, however, many of these institutions have chosen to employ their own Washington representatives. Between 1961 and 1982, for example, the number of corporations with Washington offices increased tenfold. The chief beneficiaries of this trend are Washington-based lawyers, lobbyists, and public relations firms. The number of attorneys in the nation's capital, taken as a rough indicator of lobbyist strength, tripled between 1973 and 1983, and the growth of public relations firms was dramatic. The lobbying community of the 1990s is large, increasingly diverse, and part of the expansion of policy domain participation, whether in agriculture, the environment, or industrial development.

Governmental Growth   Since the 1930s the federal government has become an increasingly active and important spur to group formation. A major aim of the New Deal was to use government as an agent in balancing the relationship between contending forces in society, particularly industry and labor. One goal was to create greater equality of opportunity, including the "guarantee of identical liberties to all individuals, especially with regard to their pursuit of economic success." For example, the Wagner Act, which established collective bargaining rights, attempted to equalize workers' rights with those of their employers. Some New Deal programs did have real redistributive qualities, but most, even Social Security, sought only to ensure minimum standards of citizen welfare. Workers were clearly better off, but "the kind of redistribution that took priority in the public philosophy of the New Deal was not of wealth, but a redistribution of power."[1]

The expansion of federal programs has accelerated since 1960. In what political scientist Hugh Heclo termed an "Age of Improvement," the federal budget has grown rapidly (from nearly $100 billion in 1961 to well over a trillion dollars in 1991) and has widened the sweep of federal regulations. Lyndon Johnson's Great Society—a multitude of federal initiatives in education, welfare, health care, civil rights, housing, and urban affairs—created a new array of federal responsibilities and program beneficiaries. The growth of many of these programs has continued, although it was slowed markedly by the Reagan administration. In the 1970s the federal government further expanded its activities in the areas of consumer affairs, environmental protection, and energy regulation, as well as redefined some policies, such as affirmative action, to seek greater equality of results.

Many of the government policies adopted early in the Age of Improvement did not result from interest group activity by potential beneficiaries. Several targeted groups, such as the poor, were not effectively organized in the period of policy development. Initiatives typically came from elected officials responding to a variety of private and public sources, such as task forces composed of academics and policy professionals.

The proliferation of government activities led to a mushrooming of groups around the affected policy areas. Newly enacted programs provided benefit packages that served to encourage interest group formation. Consider group activity in the field of policy toward the aging. The radical Townsend Movement, based on age grievances, received much attention during the 1930s, but organized political activity focused on age-based concerns had virtually no influence in national politics. Social Security legislation won approval without the involvement of age-based interest groups. Four decades later, by 1978, roughly $112 billion (approximately 24 percent of total federal expenditures) went to the elderly, and it is projected that in fifty years the outlay will be 40 percent of the total budget. The development of such massive benefits has spawned a variety of special interest groups and has encouraged others (often those formed for nonpolitical reasons) to redirect their attention to the politics of the aging.

Across policy areas two types of groups develop in response to governmental policy initiatives: *recipients* and *service deliverers*. In the elderly policy sector, recipient groups are mass-based organizations concerned with protecting—and if possible expanding—old-age benefits. The largest of these groups—indeed, the largest voluntary association represented in Washington—is the American Association of Retired Persons (AARP).

Federal program growth also has generated substantial growth among service delivery groups. In the health care sector, for example, these range from professional associations of doctors and nurses to hospital groups to the insurance industry to suppliers of drugs and medical equipment. Not only is there enhanced group activity, but many individual corporations (Johnson and Johnson, Prudential, Humana, among many others) have strengthened their lobbying capacities by opening Washington offices or hiring professional representatives from the capital's unending number of lobbying firms.

Federal government policy toward the aging is probably typical of the tendency to "greatly increase the incentives for groups to form around the differential effects of these policies, each refusing to allow any other group to speak in its name."[2] The complexity of government decision making increases under such conditions, and priorities are hard to set. Particularly troublesome for decision makers concerned with national policy is the role played by service delivery groups. In the area of the aging, some groups are largely organizational middlemen concerned with their status as vendors for the elderly. The trade associations, for example, are most interested in the conditions surrounding the payment of funds to the elderly. For example, the major concern of the Gerontological Society, an organization of professionals, is to obtain funds for research on problems of the aged. Middleman organizations do not usually evaluate government programs according to the criteria used by recipient groups; rather, what is important to them is the relationship between the program and the well-being of their organizations. Because many service delivery groups offer their members vitally important selective material incentives (financial advantages and job opportunities), they are usually far better organized than most recipient groups (the elderly in this case, the AARP notwithstanding). As a result, they sometimes speak for the recipients. This is particularly true when recipient groups represent disadvantaged people, such as the poor or the mentally ill.

Middleman groups have accounted for a large share of total group growth since 1960, and many of them are state and local government organizations. Since the late 1950s the federal government has grown in expenditures and regulations, not in personnel and bureaucracy. Employment in the federal government has risen only 20 percent since 1955, while that of states and localities has climbed more than 250 percent. Contemporary federal activism largely involves overseeing and regulating state and local governmental units, which seek funding for a wide range of purposes. The intergovernmental lobby, composed of such groups as the National League of Cities, the International City Manager Association, the National Association of Counties, the National Governors' Association, and the U.S. Conference of Mayors, has grown to become one of the most important in Washington. In addition, many local officials such as transportation or public works directors are represented by groups, and even single cities and state boards of regents have established Washington offices.

Not only do public policies contribute to group proliferation, but government often directly intervenes in group creation. This is not an entirely new activity. In the early twentieth century, relevant governmental officials in the Agriculture and Commerce Departments encouraged the formation of the American Farm Bureau Federation and the U.S. Chamber of Commerce, respectively. Since the 1960s the federal government has been especially active in providing start-up funds and sponsoring groups.

Government sponsorship also helps explain the recent rise of citizens' groups. Most federal domestic legislation has included provisions requiring some citizen participation, which have spurred the development of various citizen action groups, including grass-roots neighborhood associations, environmental action councils, legal defense coalitions, health care organizations, and senior citizens' groups.

Government funding of citizens' groups takes numerous forms. Several federal agencies—including the Federal Trade Commission (FTC), Food and Drug Administration (FDA), and Environmental Protection Agency (EPA)—have reimbursed groups for participation in agency proceedings. At other times the government makes available seed money or outright grants. Interest group scholar Jack Walker found that nine citizens' groups in ten (89 percent) received outside funding in their initial stages of development. Not all the money was from federal sources, but much did come from government grants or contracts.

Citizens' groups, numbering in the thousands, continually confront the free-rider problem since they are largely concerned with collective goods and rarely can offer the selective material incentives so important for expanding and maintaining membership. With government funding, however, the development of a stable group membership is not crucial. Increasingly, groups have appeared that are essentially staff organizations with little or no membership base.

Government policies contribute to group formation in many *unintended* ways as well. Policy failures can impel groups to form, as happened with the rise of the American Agriculture Movement in the wake of the Nixon administration's grain export policies.* An important factor in the establishment of the Moral Majority was the perceived harassment of church-run schools by government officials. And, as for abortion, the 1973 Supreme Court *Roe* v. *Wade* decision played a major role in right-to-life group mobilization, as did the 1989 *Webster* decision in the creation of pro-choice groups.†

Finally, the expansion of government activity itself often *inadvertently* contributes to group development and the resulting complexity of politics. Here a rather obscure example may prove most instructive: the development of the Bass Anglers Sportsman Society (yes, the acronym is BASS).

It all began with the Army Corps of Engineers, which dammed enough southern and midwestern streams to create a host of lakes, thereby providing an inviting habitat for largemouth bass. Anglers arrived in droves to catch their limits, and the fishing industry responded by creating expensive boats filled with specialized and esoteric equipment. The number and affluence of bass aficionados did not escape the attention of Ray Scott, an enterprising soul who began BASS in 1967. In 1990, with its membership approaching 1 million (up from 400,000 in 1982), BASS remained privately organized, offering its members selective benefits such as a slick magazine filled with tips on how to catch their favorite fish, packages of lures and line in return for joining or renewing their memberships, instant information about fishing hot spots, and boat owners' insurance. BASS also provided a number of solidary benefits, such as the camaraderie of fishing with fellow members in specially sanctioned fishing tournaments and the vicarious excitement of fishing with "BASS pros," whose financial livelihood revolved around competitive tournament fishing. The organization is an excellent example of Robert Salisbury's exchange theory approach to interest groups, as it provides benefits to both members and organizers in a "mutually satisfactory exchange."

---

* The early Nixon administration had an aggressive export policy that encouraged maximum grain production and led to high prices in the face of strong worldwide demand. When demand dropped in the mid-1970s, however, American farmers were confronted with overproduction and a subsequent collapse in grain prices. Many farmers were forced into bankruptcy. The American Agriculture Movement was organized in 1977 to challenge government policy. It received wide publicity for its "tractorcades" in Washington in 1978 and 1979, when large numbers of farmers drove their tractors to the Capitol to talk with government officials. The AAM is now evolving from an ad hoc protest group into a more traditional interest group; it retains a Washington office, has a PAC, and is active in lobbying on agricultural issues.

† The Court decision in *Roe* v. *Wade* declared that a state ban on all abortions was an infringement of a woman's constitutional right to personal privacy. In *Webster* v. *Reproductive Health Services,* the Court majority opined that states could limit the circumstances under which abortions would be permitted.

Like most groups, BASS did not originate as a political organization, and, for the most part, it remains a sportsman's group. Yet, BASS has entered politics. *BassMaster* has published political commentary and in both 1980 and 1988 endorsed George Bush for president. It also has called for easing travel restrictions to Cuba, where world-record catches may lurk.

Most groups claim that access is their major goal within the lobbying process, and here BASS has succeeded beyond its wildest dreams. President George Bush has been a life member of BASS since 1978 and has labeled *BassMaster* his favorite magazine. Scott has used his relationship with Bush to lobby for a number of concerns to the fishing community in general and BASS in particular. In March 1989 Scott visited the White House and, during a horseshoe match, indicated his concern about rumors that the Office of Management and Budget (OMB) planned to limit the disbursement of $100 million in trust funds for various fisheries management projects. The next morning Bush informed Scott that "all of *our* monies are secure from OMB or anyone else."

Scott and BASS have increased their political activities in other ways as well. The group now sponsors VOTE (Voice of the Environment), which lobbies on water quality issues, and the group has filed class-action lawsuits on behalf of fishermen against environmental polluters.

Regardless of the entrepreneurial skills of Ray Scott, however, there would probably be no BASS if it were not for the federal government and the Army Corps of Engineers. (Indeed, there would be far fewer largemouth bass.) Fifty years of dam building by the Corps has altered the nature of fish populations. Damming of rivers and streams has reduced the quality of fishing for coldwater species such as trout and pike and has enhanced the habitat for largemouth bass, a game fish that can tolerate the warmer waters and mud bottoms of man-made lakes. Finally, because many of these lakes are located close to cities, the government has made bass fishing accessible to a large number of anglers.

From angling to air traffic control, the federal government has affected, and sometimes dominated, group formation. Governmental activity does not, however, exist in a vacuum, and many other forces have contributed to group proliferation, often in concert with increased public sector involvement.

Growth of Interest Groups   Although it may be premature to formulate a theory that accounts for spurts of growth, we can identify several factors fundamental to group proliferation in contemporary politics. Rapid social and economic changes, powerful catalysts for group formation, have produced both the development of new interests (for example, the recreation industry) and the redefinition of traditional interests (for example, higher education). The spread of affluence and education, coupled with advanced communication technologies, further contribute to the translation of interests into formal group organizations. Postindustrial changes have generated a large number of new interests, particularly among occupational and professional groups in the scientific and technological arenas.

For instance, genetic engineering associations have sprung up in the wake of recent DNA discoveries.

Perhaps more important, postindustrial changes have altered the pattern of conflict in society and created an intensely emotional setting composed of several groups ascending or descending in status. Ascending groups, such as members of the new professional-managerial-technical elite, have both benefited from and supported government activism; they represent the new cultural liberalism, politically cosmopolitan and socially permissive. At the same time, rising expectations and feelings of entitlement have increased pressures on government by aspiring groups and the disadvantaged. The 1960s and early 1970s witnessed wave after wave of group mobilization based on causes ranging from civil rights to women's issues to the environment to consumer protection.

Abrupt changes and alterations in status, however, threaten many citizens. Middle America, perceiving itself as downwardly mobile, has grown alienated from the social, economic, and cultural dominance of the postindustrial elites, on one hand, and resentful toward government attempts to aid minorities and other aspiring groups, on the other. The conditions of a modern, technologically based culture also are disturbing to more traditional elements in society. Industrialization and urbanization can uproot people, cutting them loose from familiar life patterns and values and depriving them of meaningful personal associations. Fundamentalist elements feel threatened by various technological advances (such as test-tube babies) as well as by the more general secular liberalism and moral permissiveness of contemporary life. And the growth of bureaucracy, both in and out of government, antagonizes everyone at one time or another.

Postindustrial threats are felt by elites as well. The nuclear arms race and its potential for mass destruction fostered the revived peace movement of the 1980s and its goal of a freeze on nuclear weapons. In addition, the excesses and errors of technology, such as oil spills and toxic waste disposal, have led to group formation among some of the most advantaged and ascending elements of society.

Illustrating the possibilities here is the growth in the mid-1980s of the animal rights movement. Although traditional animal protection organizations such as the Humane Society have existed for decades, the last fifteen years have "spawned a colorful menagerie of pro-animal offspring" such as People for Ethical Treatment of Animals (PETA), Progressive Animal Welfare Society (PAWS), Committee to Abolish Sport Hunting (CASH), and the Animal Rights Network (ARN). Reminiscent of the 1960s, there is even the Animal Liberation Front, an extremist group. Membership in the animal rights movement has increased rapidly and approached 2 million by 1990. PETA, founded in 1980, grew from 20,000 in 1984 to 250,000 in 1988.

One major goal of these groups is to stop, or greatly retard, scientific experimentation on animals. Using a mix of protest, lobbying, and litigation, the movement has contributed to the closing of several animal labs, including the Defense Department's Wound Laboratory and a University of Pennsylvania facility involved in research on head injuries. In 1988 Trans-Species, a recent addition to the animal rights movement, forced the Cornell University Medical College to give up a $600,000 grant, which left unfinished a fourteen-year research project in which cats had to ingest barbiturates.

While postindustrial conflicts generate the issues for group development, the massive spread of affluence also systematically contributes to group formation and maintenance. In fact, affluence creates a large potential for "checkbook" membership. Issue-based groups have done especially well. Membership in such groups as PETA and Common Cause might once have been considered a luxury, but the growth in discretionary income has placed the cost of modest dues within the reach of most citizens. For a $15–$25 membership fee, people can make an "expressive" statement without incurring other organizational obligations. Increasing education also has been a factor in that "organizations become more numerous as ideas become more important."

Reform groups and citizens' groups depend heavily upon the educated, white middle class for their membership and financial base. A 1982 Common Cause poll, for example, found that members' mean family income was $17,000 above the national average and that 43 percent of members had an advanced degree. Other expressive groups, including those on the political Right, have been aided as well by the increased wealth of constituents and the community activism that result from education and occupational advancement.

Groups can overcome the free-rider problem by finding a sponsor who will support the organization and reduce its reliance upon membership contributions. During the 1960s and 1970s private sources (often foundations) backed various groups. Jeffrey Berry's 1977 study of eighty-three public interest organizations found that at least one-third received more than half of their funds from private foundations, while one in ten received more than 90 percent of its operating expenses from such sources. Jack Walker's 1981 study of Washington-based interest groups confirmed many of Berry's earlier findings, indicating that foundation support and individual grants provide 30 percent of all citizens' group funding. Such patterns produce many staff organizations with no members, raising major questions about the representativeness of the new interest group universe. Finally, groups themselves can sponsor other groups. The National Council of Senior Citizens (NCSC), for example, was founded by the AFL-CIO, which helped recruit members from the ranks of organized labor and still pays part of NCSC's expenses.

Postindustrial affluence and the spread of education also have contributed to group formation and maintenance through the development of a large pool of potential group organizers. This group tends to be young, well educated, and from the middle class, caught up in a movement for change and inspired by ideas or doctrine. The 1960s was a period of opportunity for entrepreneurs, as college enrollments skyrocketed and powerful forces such as civil rights and the antiwar movement contributed to an idea-orientation in both education and politics. Communications-based professions—from religion to law to university teaching—attracted social activists, many of whom became involved in the formation of groups. The government itself became a major source of what James Q. Wilson called "organizing cadres." Government employees of the local Community Action Agencies of the War on Poverty and numerous VISTA volunteers were active in the formation of voluntary associations, some created to oppose government actions.*

Compounding the effects of the growing number of increasingly active groups are changes in what organizations can do, largely as a result of contemporary technology. On a grand scale, technological change produces new interests, such as cable television and the silicon chip industry, which organize to protect themselves as interests historically have done. Beyond this, communications breakthroughs make group politics much more visible than in the past. Civil rights activists in the South understood this, as did many protesters against the Vietnam War. Of equal importance, however, is the fact that much of what contemporary interest groups do derives directly from developments in information-related technology. Many group activities, whether fund-raising or grass-roots lobbying or sampling members' opinions, rely heavily on computer-based operations that can target and send messages and process the responses.

Although satellite television links and survey research are important tools, the technology of direct mail has had by far the greatest impact on interest group politics. With a minimum initial investment and a reasonably good list of potential contributors, any individual can become a group entrepreneur. These activists literally create organizations, often based on emotion-laden appeals about specific issues, from Sarah Brady's Handgun Control to Randall Terry's Operation Rescue. To the extent that an entrepreneur can attract members and continue to pay the costs of direct mail, he or she can claim—with substantial legitimacy—to articulate the organization's positions on the issues, positions probably defined initially by the entrepreneur.

In addition to helping entrepreneurs develop organizations that require few (if any) active members, information technology also allows many organizations to exert considerable pressure on elected officials. The Washington-based interests increasingly are turning to grass-roots techniques to influence legislators. Indeed, by the mid-1980s, these tactics had become the norm in many lobbying efforts.

Information-processing technology is widely available but expensive. Although the Chamber of Commerce can afford its costly investment in extensive television facilities, many groups simply cannot pay the cost of much technology, at least beyond their continuing efforts to stay afloat with direct mail solicitations. Money remains the mother's milk of politics. Indeed, one of the major impacts of technology may be to inflate the costs of political action, especially given group support for candidates engaged in increasingly expensive election campaigns.

---

* Volunteers in Service to America (VISTA) was created as the domestic equivalent of the Peace Corps. Volunteers were particularly active in inner-city and rural poverty areas.

Group Impact on Policy and Process

Assessing the policy impact of interest group actions has never been an easy task. We may, however, gain some insights by looking at two different levels of analysis: a broad, societal overview and a middle-range search for relatively specific patterns of influence (for example, the role of direct mail or PAC funding). Considering impact at the level of individual lobbying efforts is also possible, but even the best work relies heavily on nuance and individualistic explanations.

Although the public at large often views lobbying and special interest campaigning with distrust, political scientists have not produced much evidence to support this perspective. Academic studies of interest groups have demonstrated few conclusive links between campaign or lobbying efforts and actual patterns of influence. This does not mean, we emphasize, that such patterns or individual instances do not exist. Rather, the question of determining impact is exceedingly difficult to answer. The difficulty is, in fact, compounded by groups' claims of impact and decision makers' equally vociferous claims of freedom from any outside influence.

The major studies of lobbying in the 1960s generated a most benign view of this activity. Lester Milbrath, in his portrait of Washington lobbyists, painted a Boy Scout-like picture, depicting them as patient contributors to the policy-making process. Rarely stepping over the limits of propriety, lobbyists had only a marginal impact at best. Similarly, Raymond Bauer, Ithiel de Sola Pool, and Lewis Dexter's lengthy analysis of foreign trade policy, published in 1963, found the business community to be largely incapable of influencing Congress in its lobbying attempts. Given the many internal divisions within the private sector over trade matters, this was not an ideal issue to illustrate business cooperation, but the research stood as the central work on lobbying for more than a decade—ironically, in the very period when groups proliferated and became more sophisticated in their tactics.

The picture of benevolent lobbyists who seek to engender trust and convey information, although accurate in a limited way, does not provide a complete account of the options open to any interest group that seeks to exert influence. Lyndon Johnson's long-term relationship with the Texas-based construction firm of Brown & Root illustrates the depth of some ties between private interests and public officeholders. The Washington representative for Brown & Root claimed that he never went to Capitol Hill for any legislative help because "people would resent political influence." But Johnson, first as a representative and later as a senator, systematically dealt directly with the top management (the Brown family) and aided the firm by passing along crucial information and watching over key government-sponsored construction projects.

> [The Johnson–Brown & Root link] was, indeed, a partnership, the campaign contributions, the congressional look-out, the contracts, the appropriations, the telegrams, the investment advice, the gifts and the hunts and the free airplane rides—it was an alliance

of mutual reinforcement between a politician and a corporation. If Lyndon was Brown & Root's kept politician, Brown & Root was Lyndon's kept corporation. Whether he concluded that they were public-spirited partners or corrupt ones, "political allies" or cooperating predators, in its dimensions and its implications for the structure of society, their arrangement was a new phenomenon on its way to becoming the new pattern for American society.[3]

Subsequent events, such as the savings and loan scandal demonstrate that legislators can be easily approached with unethical and illegal propositions; such access is one price of an open system. More broadly, the growth of interest representation in the late 1980s and early 1990s has raised long-term questions about the ethics of ex-government officials acting as lobbyists.

Contemporary Practices

Modern lobbying emphasizes information, often on complex and difficult subjects. Determining actual influence is, as one lobbyist noted, "like finding a black cat in the coal bin at midnight," but we can make some assessments about the overall impact of group proliferation and increased activity.

First, more groups are engaged in more forms of lobbying than ever before —both classic forms, such as offering legislative testimony, and newer forms, such as mounting computer-based direct mail campaigns to stir up grass-roots support. As the number of new groups rises and existing groups become more active, the pressure on decision makers—especially legislators—mounts at a corresponding rate. Thus, a second general point can be made: congressional reforms that opened up the legislative process during the 1970s have provided a much larger number of access points for today's lobbyists. Most committee (and subcommittee) sessions . . . remain open to the public, as do many conference committee meetings. More roll-call votes are taken, and congressional floor action is televised. Thus, interests can monitor the performance of individual members of Congress as never before.

Conclusion

The ultimate consequences of the growing number of groups, their expanding activities both in Washington and in state capitals, and the growth of citizens' groups remain unclear. From one perspective, such changes have made politics more representative than ever before. While most occupation-based groups traditionally have been well organized in American politics, many other interests have not. Population groupings such as blacks, Hispanics, and women have mobilized since the 1950s and 1960s; even animals and the unborn are well represented in the interest group arena, as is the broader "public interest," however defined.

Broadening the base of interest group participation may have truly opened up the political process, thus curbing the influence of special interests. For example, agricultural policy making in the postwar era was almost exclusively the prerogative of a tight "iron triangle" composed of congressional committee and subcommittee members from farm states, government officials representing the agriculture bureaucracy, and major agriculture groups such as the American Farm Bureau. Activity in the 1970s by consumer and environmental interest groups changed agricultural politics, making it more visible and lengthening the agenda to consider such questions as how farm subsidies affect consumer purchasing power and how various fertilizers, herbicides, and pesticides affect public health.

From another perspective, more interest groups and more openness do not necessarily mean better policies or ones that genuinely represent the national interest. "Sunshine" and more participants may generate greater complexity and too many demands for decision makers to process effectively. Moreover, the content of demands may be ambiguous and priorities difficult to set. Finally, elected leaders may find it practically impossible to build the kinds of political coalitions necessary to govern effectively, especially in an era of divided government.

This second perspective suggests that the American constitutional system is extraordinarily susceptible to the excesses of minority faction—in an ironic way a potential victim of the Madisonian solution of dealing with the tyranny of the majority. Decentralized government, especially one that wields considerable power, provides no adequate controls over the excessive demands of special interest politics. Decision makers feel obliged to respond to many of these demands, and "the cumulative effect of this pressure has been the relentless and extraordinary rise of government spending and inflationary deficits, as well as the frustration of efforts to enact effective national policies on most major issues."[4]

In sum, the problem of contemporary interest group politics is one of representation. For particular interests, especially those that are well defined and adequately funded, the government is responsive to the issues of their greatest concern. But representation is not just a matter of responding to specific interests or citizens; the government also must respond to the collective needs of a society, and here the success of individual interests reduces the possibility of overall responsiveness. The very vibrancy and success of contemporary groups help contribute to a society that finds it increasingly difficult to formulate solutions to complex policy questions.

Notes

1. Samuel H. Beer, "In Search of a New Public Philosophy," in *The New American Political System*, ed. Anthony King (Washington, D.C.: American Enterprise Institute, 1978), 10.
2. Hugh Heclo, "Issue Networks and the Executive Establishment," in *The New American Political System*, 96.

3. Ronnie Dugger, *The Politician* (New York: W. W. Norton, 1982), 286.
4. Everett Carll Ladd, "How to Tame the Special Interest Groups," *Fortune*, October 1980, p. 6.

Summary Questions

1. What forces have led to the tremendous proliferation of interest groups in Washington in the past three decades?
2. According to the authors, how has the Madisonian solution contributed to the difficulty of policymaking in the public interest? Do you agree with their position?

 9.3

Lobbyists—Why the Bad Rap?

Jeffrey H. Birnbaum

Lobbying activity has a long history in the United States, protected by constitutional provisions that give citizens "the right to petition the government for a redress of grievances." At the dawn of the republic this right was often expressed literally, as citizens signed and formally presented to elected representatives written petitions describing their problems. The petitioning process was all but forgotten shortly thereafter: individuals quickly learned that traveling to Washington and dealing directly with public officials was a much more effective way to influence the new government on a range of concerns, from procuring jobs to policy. Today, it is estimated that roughly 80,000 lobbyists operate in Washington.

In this selection, Jeffrey Birnbaum surveys the colorful history of lobbying in the nation's capital. He finds that many incidents of unethical, if not illegal, behavior by special interest representatives in D.C. have contributed to the unsavory stereotype of the Washington lobbyist. According to Birnbaum, well-financed

Jeffrey H. Birnbaum is a reporter in *The Wall Street Journal's* Washington bureau. This essay is adapted from his recent book, *The Lobbyists* (Time Books, 1992).

American business and manufacturing interests have long used their resources to dictate public policy, their activities largely unregulated and undisclosed.

Birnbaum believes that the relationship between lobbyists and public officials has changed in recent decades, "representing a complex symbiosis of lobbyists and politicians." Lobbyists still seek influence, and money is still important, but blatant bribery by those seeking favors is now uncommon: more common are attempts to influence legislators through devices such as campaign contributions. And often it is the legislators rather than the lobbyists who initiate contact in attempts to raise money for their reelection campaigns. Lobbying techniques have changed as well. Grass-roots lobbying, which involves mobilizing a legislator's home constituents, has emerged as one of the most effective ways for special interests to influence public policy.

I n the past 10 years, the number of lobbyists in Washington has, by some estimates, more than doubled. This modern army of 80,000 uses techniques that are as old as the republic, but its forces wield influence with a precision and sophistication that is purely high tech. Right behind the commanders are divisions of specialists: economists, lawyers, direct-mail producers and telephone salespeople, public relations experts, pollsters, and even accountants, all marching to the time-honored First Amendment–guaranteed beat of petitioning the government for redress of grievances. What follows is a look at the history of lobbying, which lobbyists themselves concede has not always been commendable. It explains in short why lobbying has a bad rap.

Booze, Broads, and Bribes

Lobbying in the early days of the republic was not performed with a great deal of finesse. The first attempt at mass pressure on the U.S. government—during a meeting of the First Continental Congress in Philadelphia in 1783—featured fixed bayonets. Several hundred soldiers from the local garrison felt they were due extra compensation and threatened the assembled legislators with their rifles. The Congress disagreed with them but boldly adjourned to meet again to consider the aggrieved soldiers' requests—at a safe distance, in Princeton, New Jersey. Business interests of the time used more subtle lobbying tactics. After the Continental Congress concluded its meetings each day, hogsheads of wine and port flowed without restraint at sumptuous meals. Wealthy merchants picked up the check.

Blatant bribery was swiftly added to the lobbyists' repertoire. One of the new Congress's major debates was whether to fund the national debt and to assume the debts of the states. Some historians believe that Rep. John Vining of

Delaware sold his deciding vote to the money changers who stood to profit most from the action. Rumor had it that the bribe was 1,000 English guineas, but Sen. William Maclay of Pennsylvania wrote in his journal that Vining's vote was probably purchased for a "tenth part of the sum."

The word "lobbyist" comes from Britain, where the journalists who stood in lobbies of the House of Commons waiting to interview newsmakers were so dubbed. It was first used in America in 1829 during Andrew Jackson's presidency when privilege seekers in New York's capital, Albany, were referred to as lobby-agents. Three years later, the term was abbreviated to "lobbyist" and has been heard frequently ever since, mostly as an expression of reproach.

President Jackson was the first of many American presidents to rail against lobbyists and their business patrons. He sought to deflate financier Nicholas Biddle's power by withdrawing federal deposits from his Second Bank of the United States. But Biddle was not without supporters, notably the illustrious Daniel Webster, who would go on to become secretary of state. The ardency of Webster's convictions on the issue was bolstered not so much by principle as by cash. On December 21, 1833, Webster, then senator from Massachusetts, wrote to Biddle: "If it is wished that my relation to the bank should be continued, it may be well to send me the usual retainers." After an especially eloquent speech by Webster, Biddle paid him $10,000, Webster received in total $32,000 in what would be seen as bribes today but was then considered business as usual.

Lobbying flourished as America grew. Washington was swarming with so many big-business lobbyists by 1852 that future president James Buchanan wrote to his friend, future president Franklin Pierce, that "the host of contractors, speculators, stockjobbers, and lobby members which haunt the halls of Congress . . . are sufficient to alarm every friend of this country. Their progress must be arrested." The influence of business was so strong that at the close of one congressional session, Sen. J. S. Morrill sarcastically moved to appoint a committee to inquire if the president of the Pennsylvania Railroad, skulking in the outer lobby, wanted Congress to consider any further legislation before adjournment.

One of the most heavy-handed corporate lobbyists at the time was Samuel Colt, the famous gun manufacturer. Colt paid a "contingent fee" of $10,000 to one congressman and probably many others to refrain from attacking a patent-extension bill that would have helped his company's sales. To supplement the effort, Colt's high-living lobbyist, Alexander Hay, distributed beautifully decorated revolvers to lawmakers. Other more attractive gratuities were also dispensed: to wit, three young women known as Spiritualists, who, according to one account, were very active in "moving with the members" of Congress on Colt's behalf. Other women of less spiritual natures called "chicks" were also available upon request.

Washington was flooded with even more lobbyists in the wake of the financial panic of 1857. "Everywhere," wrote historian Roy Franklin Nichols, "there was importunity." The most underhanded lobbying battle raged between railroad and steamship companies as lobbyists for each side fought bitterly to reduce government subsidies to the other. Commodore Cornelius Vanderbilt himself led the steamship companies' campaign, often from the gaming tables of a night spot called Pendleton's Gambling House. Hapless lawmakers would fall into debt there and be forced to surrender their votes under threat of exposure or demand for payment. Other times, lawmakers would be allowed to win—as long as they agreed to vote the right way.

The 1850s' most powerful lobbyist was an imposing man named Thurlow Weed. His diverse background included working as a printer and newspaper editor, crusading against the perfidy of corporate power. But for the price of $5,000, Weed switched allegiances and began to lobby for lower duties on wool for the Bay State Mills of Lawrence, Massachusetts. His predecessor had come to Washington armed with facts and figures and was laughed out of town: Weed came armed with cold cash and stayed for years. Weed also has the distinction of being the first lobbyist to hire a journalist in a lobbying campaign, David M. Stone of New York's *Journal of Commerce*.

The Court Steps In

Washington got a new "King of the Lobby," Samuel Ward, after the Civil War. He reigned for 15 years as the undisputed master of dinner-table deceit. "The way to a man's 'Aye' is through his stomach," he said. Ward's pedigree was impeccable: he was the great-great-grandson of Richard Ward, a colonial governor; the great-grandson of Samuel Ward, one of the framers of the Constitution, and the great nephew of General Francis Marion, the famous "Swamp Fox" of the Revolutionary War. His father headed the New York banking firm of Prime, Ward and King, and his sister, Julia Ward Howe, wrote "The Battle Hymn of the Republic."

Washington suited Ward's penchant for living well, and he quickly proved he could charm the natives for profit. With his balding pate, sweeping mustache, and diamond-studded shirts, he was a striking figure, hosting dinners and breakfasts of ham boiled in champagne and seasoned with wisps of newly mown hay.

Ward's clients ran the gamut. He was hired for $12,000 plus dinner expenses by Hugh McCulloch, an Indiana banker who later became President Lincoln's treasury secretary, to "court, woo, and charm congressmen, especially Democrats prone to oppose the war." He was also associated with Joe Morrissey, the lottery boss. It seemed incongruous, but Morrissey retained Ward to promote a bill that would impose a tax on lotteries. Morrissey believed that he could afford the levy but that it would drive his less prosperous rivals out of business.

Ward could be quite conniving, despite his elegant manners. He once wrote to his friend, Henry Wadsworth Longfellow: "When I see you again I will tell you how a client, eager to prevent the arrival at a committee of a certain member before it should adjourn, offered me $5,000 to accomplish this purpose, which I did, by having [the congressman's] boots mislaid while I smoked a cigar and condoled with him until they could he found at 11:45. I had the satisfaction of a good laugh [and] a good fee in my pocket."

When a congressional committee questioned Ward about his activities, he deflected their inquiries with erudition and humor. "Talleyrand says that diplomacy is assisted by good dinners," he responded. "At good dinners people do not talk shop, but they give people a right, perhaps, to ask a gentleman a civil question and get a civil answer." Ward insisted that he refused to take on issues that were meritless, but he also conceded that "the profession of lobbying is not commendable," a characterization still echoing today.

Under the weak presidencies that followed the Civil War, lobbying reached new heights—and depths. Two of the most jarring events were the Crédit Mobilier scandal in 1872, in which millions of federal dollars earmarked for a transcontinental railroad were diverted into the pockets of representatives, senators, and even a future president, James Garfield; and Jay Gould and Jim Fisk's attempt to corner the gold market in 1869. This latter effort, which ultimately failed, implicated the president himself.

The Supreme Court heard a rare case in 1875 involving a lobbyist, *Trist* v. *Child,* during Ulysses Grant's troubled presidency. The High Court refused to uphold the lobbyist's claim for payment after he had fulfilled his part of a contract to influence legislation. The ruling denied the payment on the ground that such an undertaking was contrary to "sound policy and good morals." The opinion continued: "If any of the great corporations of the country were to hire adventurers who make market of themselves in this way, to propose passage of a general law with a view to promotion of their private interests, the moral sense of every right-minded man would instinctively denounce the employers and employed as steeped in corruption and employment as infamous. If the instances were numerous, open, and tolerated they would be regarded as a measure of decay of public morals and degeneracy of the time. No prophetic spirit would be needed to foretell the consequences near at hand." Notably absent from the learned decision was the simple, telling observation that lobbyists and lobbying had become so enmeshed in the fabric of the government that an aggrieved lobbyist did not hesitate to go to the highest court in the land for redress.

That same year, lobbying moved further into the modern age with the first recorded instance of grass-roots lobbying. Instead of simply relying on individual adventurers in Washington, business interests began to reach back to the states and districts of congressmen for constituents to support their causes. The bellowing of home-state voices became so loud that Rep. George Frisbie Hoar forced a resolution through his Judiciary Committee requiring for the first time public disclosure by lobbyists about their activities. Hoar said he offered the resolution because four people from different parts of the country representing an important corporation had accosted and tried to sway four of his committee members. The resolution went nowhere, but grass-roots lobbying became a standard tool of the lobbyists' trade.

The first president to seriously challenge the business lobby was Woodrow Wilson, who had prominently featured its villainy in his 1912 campaign. Wilson had studied lobbyists' impact in Washington as a Princeton professor and concluded that it was dangerous. In a scholarly paper, he noted that special interests could not buy an entire legislature but could purchase individual committees, which was where the real power resided anyway. Such observations became grist for his presidential campaign speeches: "The masters of the government of the United States are the combined capitalists and manufacturers. It is written over every intimate page of the records of Congress; it is written all through the history of conferences at the White House. . . . The government of the United States is a foster child of the special interests. It is not allowed to have a will of its own."

Wilson told the lobbyists to get out of town when he took office in 1913, and for the most part, they did. A few diehards stayed, but according to Cordell Hull, they "became less pestiferous when they discovered just what our policy was and saw they could not influence us."

A story printed in the *New York World* by Martin M. Mulhall, the top lobbyist for the National Association of Manufacturers, soon demonstrated exactly why Wilson was so eager to banish lobbyists. Mulhall held no public title, but, as a powerful lobbyist, he had his own private office in the Capitol. He wrote that he paid the chief page of the House $50 a month and maintained a close association with Rep. John Dwight, the House minority leader, and with Rep. James T. McDermott, a Democrat from Chicago, whom he paid $1,500 to $2,000. These well-placed lawmakers gave him advance information about legislation and helped him dictate appointments to key committees.

Finis J. Garrett, a Tennessee Democrat and the House's minority leader, chaired a four-month inquiry into Mulhall's revelations that eventually censured McDermott. Garrett later proposed legislation that would require lobbyists to register with the clerk of the House and to disclose their employers. The bill passed the House but died in the Senate, not to become law, despite many intervening scandals, for another 33 years.

Lobbyists, scandals, and the harried congressional committees investigating them had all roared back by the 1920s. The Caraway Committee, launched in 1927 by Sen. Thaddeus Caraway (D-Ark.), rocked the city with the contention that most lobbying was simply fraud. Fully 90 percent of the nearly 400 lobbying groups listed in the Washington telephone directory were "fakes" whose primary aim was not to affect legislation but to bilk clients, said the committee.

At the end of the investigation, Caraway recommended yet another bill to register lobbyists. He wanted lobbying defined as "any effort in influencing Congress upon any matter coming before it, whether it be by distributing literature, appearing before committees of Congress, or seeking to interview members of either the House or Senate" and a lobbyist as "one who shall engage, for pay, to attempt to influence legislation or to prevent legislation by the national Congress." The Senate passed the stringent measure without dissent, but it died in the House because of lobbyists' pressure.

Former government and party officials began running on the cash-paved track of lobbying in the late 1920s and 1930s, setting a precedent that continues today. Women started to become full-fledged lobbyists during this time period, too. Mabel Walker Williebrandt, once assistant attorney general in charge of enforcing Prohibition laws, traded in her experience for bananas, oranges, apples, and cherries as counsel to Fruit Industries, Ltd. Quite simply, lobbying power resided with people who had personal connections to government.

According to journalist and lobbying historian Kenneth Crawford: "In the Hoover days, one who wanted to put on the fix saw James Francis Burke, secretary of the Republican National Committee; C. Bascom Slemp, who had been secretary to President Coolidge; or Edward Everett Gann, husband of the redoubtable social warrior, Dolly Gann, sister of Vice President Charles Curtis. Early in the Roosevelt administration, the men to get things done were Bruce Kremer, a friend of the attorney general; Robert Jackson of New Hampshire, long-time treasurer of the Democratic National Committee; Arthur Mullen, National Committeeman from Nebraska; and Joe Davies, later ambassador to Russia and Belgium."

Senator Hugo L. Black (D-Ala.) who was later a Supreme Court justice, introduced a bill to register and regulate lobbyists after a particularly egregious display of lobbying power in a debate over regulation of public utilities. This time, it passed both chambers of Congress—but it died in a House-Senate conference committee, thanks to the efforts of hundreds of lobbyists. Lobbyists didn't escape unscathed, however, and for the first time, utility lobbyists were required to make limited disclosure of their activities under terms of the final Public Utilities Holding Company Act.

Congress finally got around to regulating the business of lobbying as a whole in the 1930s and 1940s, starting with the vast and influential shipping industry. The Merchant Marine Act of 1936 required shipping agents to file disclosures with the Commerce Department before working to influence marine legislation or administrative decisions. Two years later, amid reports of Fascist and Nazi propaganda circulating in the United States, the Foreign Agents Registration Act was passed, requiring anyone who represented a foreign government or individual to register with the Justice Department.

In 1946, Congress passed the Federal Regulation of Lobbying Act as part of the Congressional Reorganization Act, requiring all lobbyists to register in Congress and report the amount and sources of their income from lobbying. There was no attempt to limit lobbying; that would violate the First Amendment's right to petition the government. It defined a lobbyist as a person or organization whose job is to influence the passage or defeat of legislation and who receives money for that purpose.

Like all previous lobbying strictures, the law was ignored at first. In 1950, spurred by complaints from President Harry Truman, a committee headed by Rep. Frank M. Buchanan, Democrat from Pennsylvania, investigated a wide range of lobbying abuses. The Congress of the time, the president complained, was "the most thoroughly surrounded . . . with lobbies in the whole history of this great country of ours. . . . There were more lobbyists in Washington, there was more money spent by lobbyists in Washington, than ever before." The committee requested detailed information about lobbying from 200 corporations, labor unions, and farm groups. The 152 organizations that replied said they had spent $32 million on lobbying from January 1, 1948, through May 31, 1950, and fewer than 50 of them had disclosed a single dime of it as required by the new lobbying law.

The Buchanan report also noted that lobbying had changed over the years. In effect, it said, lobbying had become less blatant and, in this view, more insidious. In 1948, there were 1,016 registered lobbyists. Two years later, the number had more than doubled to 2,047. Buchanan said the figures "reflect a significant picture of tremendous amounts of time and money being expended by pressure groups and pressure interests through the country in seeking to influence actions by Congress."

In the 1870s and 1880s, he continued, "lobbying meant direct, individual solicitation of legislators, with a strong presumption of corruption attached . . . [but] modern pressure on legislative bodies is rarely corrupt. . . . It is increasingly indirect, and [it is] largely the product of group rather than individual effort. . . . The printed word is much more extensively used by organizations as a means of pursuing legislative aims than personal contact with legislators by individual lobbyists."

The Buchanan Committee recommended strengthening the lobbying law, but no action was taken. Instead, in 1954, the Supreme Court weakened the already porous lobbying statute by exempting many types of lobbyists from the law's disclosure requirements. The Court decided that only those who solicited and collected money specifically with lobbying in mind need comply and that organizations need register only if they had lobbying as their "principal purpose" when they collected the funds. What's more, only direct contacts with legislators were considered lobbying; indirect pressure, such as the growing practice of grass-roots lobbying, was excluded.

A Complex Relationship

In the late 1940s and 1950s, it was "often hard to tell where the legislator [left] off and the lobbyist begins," according to lobbying expert James Deakin. Entire pieces of legislation were drafted by lobbyists. According to Rep. Arthur Klein, a Democratic member of the House Labor Committee, the primary author of the Taft-Hartley Act of 1947,* which restricted labor union activities, was neither Taft nor Hartley but William G. Ingles, a $24,000-a-year lawyer and highly labor-dependent lobbyist for Allis-Chalmers, Fruehauf Trailer, J. I. Case, and Inland Steel.

The unprecedented expansion of government after the war was accompanied by a rapid growth in the number of lobbyists. Sensing their advantage, lawmakers began to play one off against the other. "Everything in Washington is a two-way street," Deakin wrote: "The legislators use the lobbyists as much as the lobbyists use them. A cocktail party—like an office conversation—may give the congressman information he needs. Or it may give him something he needs even more: cash. The Washington party has become an increasingly utilitarian institution. Invited to a reception, the lobbyist may find that he is giving more than he gets. The pressure boy is pressured. As he leaves, pleasantly oiled, his attention is directed to a hat in which he is expected to drop $50 or $100 for the congressman's campaign. . . . Washington is a very practical town, and money and votes mean more than liquor. In the final analysis, this is why bribes, blondes, and booze don't rank as high as they once did in the lobbyist's scheme of things. They just aren't as important to the congressman (to his political survival, which is his first law) as votes and money with which to get votes. The legislator may accept the lobbyist's entertainment, and gladly, but he is far more likely to do what the lobbyist wants if votes are involved."

The 1940s and 1950s were also the heyday of the brilliant, brash Thomas "the Cork" Corcoran, former law clerk to Oliver Wendell Holmes and President Franklin Roosevelt's chief legislative operative. Corcoran helped write much of the New Deal legislation, including the Securities and Exchange Act. He also supplied Roosevelt with the phrase, "This generation has a rendezvous with destiny." He made enemies when he tried to help Roosevelt pack the Supreme Court,† and he was blocked from the job he most coveted, becoming the U.S. solicitor general. He became instead a high-priced lobbyist for corporate interests,

---

* The Taft-Hartley Act of 1947 was technically a series of amendments to the National Labor Relations (Wagner) Act of 1935, which many members of the business community felt was too pro-union. A major provision of the Taft-Hartley Act included allowed states to pass right-to-work laws, which in effect banned "closed shop" requirements (making it mandatory that employers hire only members of unions). Taft-Hartley also delineated various unfair labor practices by unions (the 1935 Act only listed unfair labor practices by employers).

† President Franklin Roosevelt, frustrated with the Supreme Court's reluctance to uphold major pieces of New Deal legislation, proposed a plan in 1937 to expand the size of the Court by appointing a new member for each sitting justice who had reached seventy years of age. If the plan had been approved, Roosevelt could have immediately appointed six justices, making the Court a fifteen-member body. The Congress and the nation's press were strongly against the measure, viewing it as a thinly-veiled attempt to "pack" the court to create a liberal majority.

cementing what has since become a well-established route from White House adviser to Washington lobbyist.

Top executives of corporations were increasingly enlisted as lobbyists during the 1960s, but always under the strict guidance of their Washington consultants. Lobbying had come far since the early days of the republic, representing a complex symbiosis of lobbyists and politicians—but traditional, big-money lobbyists still wooed, and occasionally brought crashing down, lawmakers. The most famous victim of lawmakers' penchant for fancy living was Robert G. (Bobby) Baker, whose route from Pickens, South Carolina, to riches on the banks of the Potomac River was eased by lobbyists. Baker was secretary to the Democratic majority in the Senate. With a salary of $19,600 a year, he managed to accumulate assets of $2,166,886 in less than nine years.

Improper contacts with lobbyists also helped bring down Richard M. Nixon's presidency. Investigations revealed that a number of corporations violated the federal law that prohibits them from contributing to the campaigns of federal office seekers. Some of those funds found their way into the hands of the Republican operatives who broke into Democratic Party headquarters in Washington's Watergate complex on June 17, 1972.

Foreign interests have increasingly hired Washington lobbyists in recent years. This foreign money led to the 1976 Koreagate scandal. The *Washington Post* reported that South Korean agents gave between $500,000 and $1 million a year in cash and gifts to members of Congress to help maintain a "favorable legislative climate" for South Korea. The Koreans, led by businessman and socialite Tongsun Park, sought to bribe U.S. officials and buy influence among journalists, funneling illegal gifts to as many as 115 lawmakers. In 1978, the House voted to reprimand three California Democrats for their part in the scandal, and Richard T. Hanna, a former California congressman, was sentenced to prison.

Subtlety Wields Influence

During the 1980s, lobbying was rarely so heavyhanded, yet it became astonishingly effective. Communications techniques reached new heights of sophistication and complexity, and with them lobbyists were able to mobilize thousands of ordinary citizens for the first time. When Congress was considering increasing milk price supports in 1980, for example, lawmakers heard not just from lobbyists for the dairy farmers who wanted the subsidy hiked but also from thousands of worried managers of fast-food restaurants spurred on by an "action alert" newsletter distributed by the fast-food industry's trade association.

The break-up of American Telephone & Telegraph spurred one of the decade's biggest grass-roots lobbying efforts. Legislators heard from thousands of telephone company managers and employees; not only had AT&T put out an action alert but so had the Communications Workers of America, 90 percent of whose members were AT&T employees. At the same time, a coalition of AT&T competitors stirred up its own pressure in favor of the break-up, mailing 70,000 envelopes bearing an imitation of the Bell System logo and this attention-grabbing warning: "Notice of Telephone Rate Increase Enclosed." The letter inside warned the reader that unless the recipient helped lobby in favor of the break-up, telephone rates would double.

Individual corporations also began using their employees and suppliers as lobbyists, a method previously used with great success by labor unions. The National Association of Home Builders—the 125,000-member trade association of the housing industry—developed one of the most comprehensive electoral strategies ever devised in the corporate world. Its 250-page manual, "Blueprint for Victory: Homebuilder's Political Offensive," outlined all aspects of what it called its G. I. (Get Involved) Program. The manual detailed telephone or house-to-house canvassing techniques, how to organize a "Victory Caravan" to transport campaign volunteers, and many other strategies previously reserved for political movements.

The Old and the New

In the postwar era, presidents continued to bash lobbyists. Harry Truman, whose presidency has been much discussed this campaign year, used these words: "There are a great many organizations with lots of money who maintain lobbyists in Washington. I'd say 15 million people in the United States are represented by lobbyists," he said. "The other 150 million have only one man who is elected at large to represent them—that is the president of the United States."

John F. Kennedy also attacked lobbyists, telling an audience at Ohio's Wittenberg College in 1960, "The consumer is the only man in our economy without a high-powered lobbyist in Washington. I intend to be that lobbyist." Yet throughout his presidency, he maintained a close friendship with one of Washington's prominent lawyer-lobbyists, Clark Clifford, remarking jovially at one point that Clifford was not like other consultants who wanted rewards for their assistance to him. "You don't hear Clark clamoring," Kennedy said. "All he asked in return was that we advertise his law firm on the back of the one-dollar bills." That lighthearted quip told much about the power of lobbyists and the personal relationships that nurture the business.

Lobbyists remain an integral part of the Washington establishment, but the scandals of the past continue to stigmatize their standing. One lobbyist captured the feeling: "My mother has never introduced me as 'my son, the lobbyist.' My son, the Washington representative, maybe, or the legislative consultant. But never as the lobbyist. I can't say I blame her." This explains a paradox of Washington life. While lobbyists are highly compensated and influential, they occupy a kind of underclass in the nation's capital. They are frequently left standing in hallways and reception areas for hours at a time. Theirs are the first

appointments canceled or postponed when legislators are pressed by other business calls. Their activity suffuses the culture of the city, but their status suffers
from a long history of lobbying scandals.

Summary Questions

1. How has Washington lobbying changed since the early days of the republic?
   What forces have brought about such changes? Is the negative image of
   lobbyists still warranted?
2. Why is it so difficult to regulate lobbying activity?

 9.4

The "Buying" of Public Policy

Frank J. Sorauf

The traditional American concern about the undue influence of interest groups is
nowhere better illustrated than in the furor over the impact of campaign contributions through political action committees. The huge rise in the number of
federally registered PACs from just over 600 in 1974 to nearly 4,200 in 1990 and
the tremendous increase in PAC contributions to candidates over the same period
have raised questions of "vote buying" by special interests. The national media
and a variety of reform groups regularly publish information correlating campaign
contributions by interest groups with legislative voting records on controversial
issues, implying a strong relationship between campaign giving and later congressional action.

According to Frank J. Sorauf, however, the causal link between receipt of a
campaign contribution and a representative's vote is quite difficult to demonstrate.
Most interest groups use other lobbying tactics as well, and it is hard to separate
the influence of campaign contributions from that of these efforts. Furthermore,
financial contributions are tangled with other factors that influence a legislator's

Frank J. Sorauf is a professor of political science at the University of Minnesota.

decision: ideological orientations, constituency interests, pressure from the party and legislative peers, and the like.

According to Sorauf, PAC contributions should be viewed as one tactic among many that interest groups use to influence legislators and only one factor among many that affect a representative's vote. PAC contributions may make a difference under certain circumstances, but the evidence simply does not support the "buying" of the Congress.

T he fear that contributors to campaigns, especially the contributors of large sums, will "purchase" leverage over public policy pervades Americans' views of their campaign finance. The issue centers very much on PAC contributions* and on recipients who are legislative candidates—hence the cliché about "the best Congress money can buy." There is, however, no logical reason to limit the issue that way. Contributors other than PACs, individuals especially, may want to affect specific public policies. . . . Nor are legislatures the only elected policy-makers; voters in the states select a wide range of executive, administrative, and judicial officials after campaigns of varying extensiveness. Yet whatever the scope of the issue, central to it is the link between campaign money and policy outcomes.

Common Cause and the mass media have popularized the issue in a predictable form: the case study of a link between PAC contributions and a congressional decision. Examples abound. Over the years the best publicized have involved the contributions of doctors, dairy farmers, realtors, used car dealers, bankers, and gun owners. For the limited space [here], the events surrounding the 1986 success of the National Rifle Association (NRA) in loosening the federal control of inter-state gun transactions will have to suffice.

In March and April of 1986, the House of Representatives voted to weaken the Gun Control Act of 1968 to permit interstate sales of rifles and shotguns and to ease the record-keeping in commercial gun transactions. (The Senate had earlier passed similar but not identical legislation.) It was a major legislative victory for the National Rifle Association, an association of about 3 million gun owners. In the defeated opposition were law enforcement officials and their much smaller and less well-funded organizations. The NRA, of course, was a major spender in

---

* A *political action committee (PAC)* is an organization that pools members' funds and contributions directly to the campaigns of those seeking public office. The Federal Election Campaign Act of 1971 and its amendments limit each multicandidate committee to contributions of no more than $5,000 per candidate. There is no limit, however, on the amount a PAC may contribute to a candidate's effort as long as its activities are not coordinated with those of the candidate or his or her campaign representatives. For example, unlimited amounts may be spent against a candidate, as long as the PAC's efforts are not coordinated with those of his or her opponent.

congressional campaigns in 1984 ($700,324 in contributions and $785,516 in independent expenditures).

NRA campaign spending did not go unnoticed in the press, and at the time of a crucial petition to force the bill out of committee, the *Washington Post* wrote that at least 129 of 156 (84 percent) of the signers of the discharge petition had received NRA money in 1984 or 1986. The next day a *Post* editorial proclaimed that the NRA "has done a bang-up job of buying support in Congress." But while some of the press assumed the PAC-policy connection, there were intimations in some of the nation's newspapers that the connection was not quite that simple. Sources of influence beyond the PAC and campaign finance seemed to be at work.

In various ways the nation's press provided a number of hints that the National Rifle Association's success in weakening the Gun Control Act of 1968 had roots in sources of influence other than money. From Minneapolis, New York, and Washington:

♦ The *Minneapolis Star-Tribune* quoted an anonymous Western Democrat as saying "It's the kind of an issue that could defeat me when nothing else could. In a typical year, this is an issue in a Rocky Mountain district that could move 4 to 5 percent of the people to vote the other way. . . ."

♦ The *New York Times*'s Linda Greenhouse attributed the outcome to "the power of the National Rifle Association, one of the best organized and most feared lobbies in Washington," noting in conclusion that the NRA had "dedicated $1.6 million of its $5 million annual legislative budget to the bill."

♦ Somewhat later the *Washington Post* printed a four-paragraph opinion piece by Rep. David S. Monson, a Republican from Utah, challenging its interpretation of the vote on the bill. Wrote Representative Monson: "As a recipient of NRA contributions, I can unequivocally assure voters that my votes would have been the same without one dime of support from the NRA. That is because my constituents and I believe that the current enforcement of gun control legislation is a disgrace."

Case studies such as this one raise all manner of questions. To begin, the direction of the cause is easily inferred, but less easily proven. Do the votes follow the money, or does the money follow the votes? While the votes in Congress may be influenced by the contributed money, it is more likely that the contributions result from the contributors' approval of the values and/or voting record of the candidate. PACs do give the greatest share of their money to incumbent candidates with well-established voting records; for candidates without a record of legislative voting, they usually try to discover basic values in interviews or questionnaires. PACs do not contribute at random; just as individual contributors do, they support candidates whose ideas and values they like. The key question—and a very difficult one it is—is not whether legislators vote in ways that please their contributors, but whether they would have done so in the absence of a contribution.

It is, moreover, very hard to separate the effects of lobbying and of constituency pressures from the effects of a campaign contribution. The NRA has three million loyal members who respond with considerable intensity to the alarms of the organization, either in grass-roots pressure or in voting. Its Capitol Hill lobbyists are experienced and well financed. To speak of the NRA is to speak simultaneously of a powerful lobby, an affluent PAC, and a potent grass-roots organization. It is also to speak of a group of voters with such intense feelings about gun control that they are the prototypical "single issue" voters—voters for whom a single issue overrides all others.*

Even if we can show that it was money that made the difference and that the votes did in fact follow the money, we have only explained a single case or instance. We have not even examined PAC activity on other sides of that issue. We have counted the winners, but not the losers. Nor do we know how typical our single case is of the whole business of a legislative session. To show the impact of campaign contributions on the legislative process, one would have to understand at least a good sample of roll calls and a map of PAC losses as well as victories. In recent years, indeed, it has been clear that some of the heaviest spenders in the PAC movement have been among the biggest losers in the Congress. One need only mention the American Medical Association's losses on Medicare cost containment and the National Realtors Association loss of real estate tax shelters in the income tax revision of 1985–86.†

Finally, most of the journalistic reports of PAC influence in legislatures suffer fatally from too simple a model of legislative decision-making. What of the role of constituency pressures; of legislative party; of the personal outlook and information of the legislator; of general public opinion; of the legislative peers and leaders; of groups and their lobbying; and, for at least some members, the programs and promptings of the president? One can hardly assume that the search for campaign contributions overrides all or even some of these imperatives. Any serious attempt to establish the independent effect of contributions must control for them, and many of the scholarly studies attempt to do so. Often, in fact, the argument shifts to the adequacy of the controls. Is a congressperson's previous record of liberal or conservative voting, for example, an adequate control for the aggregate effect of those external influences? That's a far tougher issue, of course, but at least all parties arguing it have rejected the simple correlation of PAC contributions and roll call votes.

---

* Single-issue voters would vote to support or not to support a candidate solely on the basis of the candidate's stand on one issue. The most publicized single issues of the past decade have probably been the Equal Rights Amendment (ERA) and those issues labeled pro-choice (permitting abortion) or pro-life (making abortion illegal).

† The National Realtors Association was not totally unsuccessful in the 1986 tax bill. Interest deductions from the mortgage payments for two residences were retained in the tax code, whereas consumer interest on other items, such as credit cards and car loans, is to be phased out as a deduction.

Scholars working on the problem have begun to approach it with strategies more complex and sophisticated than the usual journalistic treatment. In some instances they have expanded the relationship to more PACs and a broader set of roll call votes. In some, they have attempted to control for other factors such as party and constituency pressures. Yet others have extended the analysis over time, hoping to relate changes in contribution patterns with changes in votes. The results have been disappointingly mixed and ambiguous. Some studies find modest relationships and an independent effect of contributions, but others do not. . . .

From that diverse body of scholarship and its diverse conclusions, three conclusions seem warranted. First, and most important, there simply are no data in the systematic studies that would support the popular assertions about the "buying" of the Congress or about any other massive influence of money on the legislative process. Second, even taking the evidence selectively, there is at best a case for a modest influence of money, a degree of influence that puts it well behind the other major influences on congressional behavior. Third, in some of the studies with a time dimension, there is evidence that vote support for the PAC's legislative position leads to greater campaign contributions. They do not, however, answer the question whether the legislative votes changed in order to "earn" the reward of increased contributions.

Recent work has also begun to factor into the explanations the nature of PAC decision-making, the sources of PAC and group power, and the expectations of the contributors. They have, in other words, put the PACs into the equation! John Wright, for example, considers the way a group of large, often federated, PACs conduct their business:

> Because money must be raised at a local, grassroots level, local PAC officials, not Washington lobbyists, are primarily responsible for making allocation decisions. Consequently, congressmen who desire contributions must cultivate favorable relationships with local officials, and this arrangement tends to undercut the value of contributions as a bargaining tool for professional lobbyists.[1]

Janet Grenzke points to the effect of a different aspect of the PAC's basic organization and structure. Generally when one finds a positive causal relationship between contribution and pro-PAC change in a legislator's vote, she writes,

> the contribution is consistent with and may be considered a measure of the more important endorsement and campaign activities of the organization, which can influence member votes. Eliminating the contribution will not significantly change the organization's power because its power is based primarily on its ability to mobilize votes.[2]

In brief, PACs differ vastly in their organizations, goals, strategies, and decision-making; and those differences affect both their desire and their ability to use contributions to alter legislative votes.

When one considers PAC goals, one can of course take the PACs at their word; and the word has always been "access." Larry Sabato summarizes PAC expectations:

> While some legislators confess that PAC dollars affect their judgment of the issues before them, PAC officials are adamant that all they get for their investment is access to congressmen—a chance to "tell their story." Political analysts have long agreed that access is the principal goal of most interest groups, and lobbyists have always recognized that access is the key to influence. . . .
>
> A congressman's time is often as valuable as his vote because, as the Public Affairs Council's Richard Armstrong declares, "except maybe for some guy from Idaho . . . they haven't got time to see everybody. Some congressmen *say* they see everyone, but that's [expletive]."[3]

In the broader world of American politics, "access" has always been a slippery word, sometimes serving in fact as a code word for palpable, demonstrated influence. As the PACs use it, however, it most often has a literal meaning: a chance to persuade, an opportunity to make a case or argue a point. If that argument seems self-serving, it is honestly made in the great number of instances. More important, it squares with what systematic evidence we have about the money-vote relationship. It fits with the complex variety of PAC organizations and with the diversity of their goals, especially with their disposition to contribute to candidates for all kinds of reasons that have little or only something to do with specific policy goals. The more generalized goals of access simply fit the realities of PACs better than do assumptions of a more purposeful, impact-on-policy strategy.

To be stubbornly skeptical about it, however, we have no systematic evidence that contributions do in fact produce access. The testimony of journalists, members of Congress, and PAC leadership suggests that PACs do enjoy it. The harder question remains unanswered: would that access have been granted in the absence of the contribution? If one concedes the access, it is easy to spin out a broader hypothesis. What appears to be a limited independent influence of PAC contributions is achieved largely through the persuasion afforded or facilitated by access. Access thus converts to an edge in influencing the decisions of members of Congress. Moreover, persuasion is easier when other players in the legislative process are less exigent. Thus the influence of the contributors varies with the nature of the policy at stake; it is greater in the narrower, less salient issues that escape party, presidential, or popular attention.

Alternatively, one can recast the problem of money's influence on legislation in terms of pluralism—the struggle of competing interests and their PACs for access or influence in a diverse and many-sided legislative contest. It is a view of intricately divided and opposing influence, one in which countervailing interests check and offset each other. Such an argument about countervailing group power often stuns the ordinary citizen, for it leads to a conclusion that, all other things being equal, more PACs are "better" than fewer PACs. The view, moreover, is

Table 9.1

Dispersal of PAC Contributions to Major Party Candidates for the House of Representatives, 1982 and 1984

	1982	1984
Number of PACs contributing to average candidate	46	54
Number of PACs contributing to average incumbent	140	160
Average PAC contribution to average candidate	$816	$960
Average PAC contribution to average incumbent	$741	$890
Average total receipts from PACs (all candidates)	$37,904	$52,230
Average total receipts from PACs (incumbents)	$128,795	$142,352
Average PAC contribution as % of average candidate receipts	0.63%	0.76%
Average PAC contributions as % of average incumbent receipts	0.27%	0.28%

more than hypothetical; there are pieces of evidence that groups consciously attempt to offset the influence of their opponents. Certainly the success of conservative PACs in the late 1970s and early 1980s stimulated the formation of liberal PACs.* And one scholarly study has found evidence of corporate PACs making contributions to members of the House Education and Labor Committee about two months after labor PACs had done so. The resulting system of countervailing pressures thus liberates the legislator from the agonies of choice and gratitude. In the words of Rep. Barney Frank, a Democrat from Massachusetts, "Business PACs invest in incumbents. It's the banks against the thrifts, the insurance companies against the banks, the Wall Street investment banks against the money center commercial banks. There's money any way you vote."[4] The recipient may therefore be in a stronger bargaining position than the contributor.

The other side of the pluralist argument is that as PACs proliferate, the contribution of any one accounts for fewer and fewer of the receipts of the average candidate and, therefore, the political influence or leverage attached to it diminishes. The growing dispersal of PAC contributions and the diminishing dependence of a member of Congress on any one of them is apparent [see Table 9.1]. In fact, the dispersal is even greater than one might have expected because there are

---

* The *ideological PACs* are independent or nonconnected organizations, not merely the campaign arms of corporations or interest groups. In the late 1970s, for example, a small number of conservatives formed NCPAC, the National Conservative Political Action Committee. The organization spent huge sums of money against a number of liberal candidates in 1978, 1980, and 1982 and was credited by many observers with giving the Republicans control of the Senate in 1980.

two trends at work: the number of PACs is increasing *and* the "average" PAC is spreading its contributions to more candidates rather than sharply increasing the sums of money it gives to each. The bottom line, then, is that the share of the total receipts that the average PAC contribution represents is well under one percent; for incumbents it is less than a third of one percent. If money is leverage, the leverage is not very substantial.

To summarize once again, the evidence simply does not support the more extravagant claims about the "buying" of the Congress. Systematic studies indicate at most a modest influence for PAC contributors, a degree of influence usually far less important than the voting constituency, the party, or the values of the legislator. Moreover, several other studies suggest that the goals and capacities of most PACs are not congruent with assumptions that they set out to change congressional votes. In fact, both the extent of their influence and the nature of their operations fit much better their own stated goal of access. Finally, the development of PAC pluralism—both in the increase of countervailing PACs and in the wide dispersion of their contributions in small sums—also leads one to a more modest assessment of PAC influence. Such conclusions may serve few demonologies, but they are the only ones that serve the facts as we know them. . . .

Notes

1. John R. Wright, "PACs, Contributions, and Roll Calls: An Organizational Perspective," *American Political Science Review*, 79 (June 1985): 411.
2. Janet M. Grenzke, "Shopping in the Congressional Supermarket: The Currency is Complex," *American Journal of Political Science*, vol. 33, p. 12.
3. Larry J. Sabato, *PAC Power* (New York: Norton, 1984), 127.
4. Quoted in Robert Kuttner, "Ass Backward," *The New Republic*, April 22, 1985, p. 22.

Summary Questions

1. Why is it so difficult to demonstrate that PAC contributions have a major effect on public policy making?
2. Under what circumstances might PAC contributions be influential in determining how a legislator votes?
3. Can access to politicians be "bought"?

 Part III

INSTITUTIONS

 Chapter 10

CONGRESS

Of the three branches of government, the legislature is invariably the most open to scrutiny and influence. Members of Congress are directly accountable to their constituents. Even in our security-conscious age of metal detectors and concrete barriers, the U.S. Congress remains easily accessible to citizens who seek to influence their representatives and senators or merely to observe them in action. Just as the growth of government has affected the presidency and, to a lesser extent, the Supreme Court (see Chapters 11 and 13), Congress has changed greatly in the post-World War II era, especially since the mid-1960s.

Some of these changes are straightforward. For example, in 1947 members of Congress employed 2,030 staff aides in their personal offices. By 1991 the total had more than quintupled, to 11,572. Other developments have been more obscure, if no less important. The informal rules of legislative behavior have changed; today newcomers need not undergo a decade-long apprenticeship before wielding even a bit of power. Despite these and many other changes, however, contemporary legislators take on the same basic responsibilities as their predecessors: representing their constituents and making decisions about the major issues of the day.

Over the course of the American experience, Congress has received countless criticisms of its inefficiencies and its responsiveness to special interests. A bicameral (two-house) legislature is by nature difficult to control, even when a single political party holds majorities in both chambers. In addition, Congress often must face an executive branch whose interests run directly counter to its own. Differences in opinion between the two chambers or between Congress and the executive can and do produce deadlocks, such as the annual struggles over the budget.

Similarly, the representative nature of Congress makes it an appropriate target for interest groups. Legislators run expensive reelection campaigns. These require substantial contributions, which frequently come from the growing number of political action committees that represent a wide range of groups. The structure of Congress allows interest groups easy access to hundreds of subcommittees that deal with very specific issues ranging from oil exploration to air traffic control to military construction. The small membership and narrow focus of most House and Senate subcommittees provide attractive opportunities for a seemingly limitless number of lobbyists to influence public policies.

The readings in this section emphasize both continuity and change in congressional politics. They illustrate the rise of individualism on Capitol Hill. The days are gone when autocratic committee chairs could control the legislative agenda. To exercise real power as a committee chair in the House has ordinarily required at least twenty years' consecutive service on a given panel. This fact encouraged long careers and promoted the image of the Congress as a body of tottering graybeards who relied on seniority and the power of their committee positions, rather than the strength of their ideas or intellect, to dominate the process.

By the early 1970s, however, congressional structure and personnel had undergone a dramatic transformation, especially in the House. After the 1982 elections, more than two-thirds of the 535 members of Congress (100 senators, 435 representatives) had arrived on Capitol Hill since 1974. Accompanying this upheaval in personnel was a series of reforms that greatly dispersed power within the Congress. The changes of the 1969-1975 period profoundly affected the House of Representatives. Committee chairs lost much of their authority, and the big winners were the rank-and-file House members, especially the majority Democrats. These representatives demonstrated their new clout in 1975 by voting within the Democratic Caucus to oust three senior committee chairs.

Political scientist Kenneth Shepsle (10.3) assesses these changes by first sketching the "textbook Congress" of the 1950s and then noting the various ways in which it has diverged from the conventional wisdom of that era. In particular, the decline of committees has led to more variability and uncertainty in congressional politics. The seeming equilibrium of the 1950s Congress has given way to a less predictable, less coherent legislative process within a fragmented House of Representatives. Changing the way the House does business rests in large part on its replacement of veteran members with newcomers; although this turnover slowed substantially during the 1980s as incumbents dominated electoral politics, 110 new representatives entered the House in the wake of the 1992 elections. Bill Turque (10.2) examines the experiences of three first-term legislators who came to Capitol Hill with hopes of changing the direction of American politics. After a year of service, they were probably affected more by the House than vice versa. Even in a House that provides substantial resources to all its members, change comes neither quickly nor easily.

Formal changes in rules and procedures have affected the Senate less profoundly than they have the House, because the upper chamber has always relied on informal cooperation among its members. Nevertheless, some senators have become increasingly adept at tying the body into knots by relying on rules and traditions that evolved to protect minority rights. Senators such as Jesse Helms, Howard Metzenbaum, and Phil Gramm have acted to obstruct the regular flow of legislative business, acknowledging that in so doing they will win no popularity contests among their colleagues. Indeed, the obstructionism practiced by these and other senators has made leading the Senate a formidable—and perhaps impossible—task.

Historically, congressional politics has reflected continuing tensions between forces of centralization and decentralization. In the late 1970s, for example, decentralizing trends prevailed as subcommittees proliferated and individual legislators gained substantial personal resources, such as staff. Electoral competition for House seats has also declined, and most representatives are well insulated from any pressures that party leaders may seek to employ. Since the early 1980s, Speakers Tip O'Neill, Jim Wright, and Thomas Foley have instituted a strategy of "inclusive" leadership that has sought to give large numbers of the majority Democrats an increased stake in the process. But centralization is virtually impossible without strong party leadership, which seems outside the realm of realistic possibility. Certainly Senate Republican majority leaders Howard Baker and Robert Dole had little systematic success in rallying their troops in the 1981–1986 period. Democratic leader Robert Byrd did no better in 1987–1988, and in 1988 he chose not to seek reelection to this position. The retirement of Sen. George Mitchell (D-Maine), Byrd's successor, provides further evidence that the term "Senate leadership" may be a contradiction in terms. Further, divided government necessitates the resolution of many issues through negotiations between legislative leaders and the White House. Leaders not only must satisfy their legislative colleagues; they must also meet many of the president's demands.

After two centuries of development, Congress remains at the core of societal decision making. Its limitations are great, however, for almost all of its members are subject to reelection every two years and Congress is most effective when it enjoys strong executive direction. The closed congressional power system that existed in the early 1960s has given way to a much more open, democratic, decentralized system in the 1980s and 1990s. In neither era has Congress functioned as an efficient, completely representative body. In the first and last articles of this chapter, Nelson Polsby (10.1) and Catherine Rudder (10.4) argue against unwarranted attacks on the Congress, attacks mounted in the White House, within the press, and on Capitol Hill itself. As the most representative branch of government, the ability of the Congress to govern has been seriously questioned. It remains to be seen whether congressional leadership and presidential direction can produce coherent action and increased public support. Polsby and Rudder muster some optimism, but the task is formidable, to say the least.

10.1

Congress-bashing Through the Ages

Nelson W. Polsby

Congress has never been an especially popular institution—not in its early years, not in its partisan heyday circa 1900, and not in its contemporary manifestation. It may well be easier to joke about the legislature, or to "bash" it, than to seek an understanding of its quirks and complexities. In additon, a good deal of criticism comes from those who are unhappy—often profoundly so—with the policy decisions made on Capitol Hill. Congress's lack of popularity contrasts sharply with the good standing of individual legislators, who are usually reelected in overwhelming numbers.

In this article, political scientist Nelson Polsby takes on the Congress-bashers by arguing that the legislature gets more than its share of ill-informed criticism, often from those who have a particular policy ax to grind. He believes many of the "cures" for an unresponsive Congress, such as line item vetoes for the president or term limitations for legislators, are far worse than the "disease." Polsby sees the need for a vigorous, well-developed separation of powers in the United States so that varied interests can be effectively represented. A weakened Congress does not serve us well in an era of a strong, if not a completely dominant, president.

M y topic is Congress-bashing. You may find it hard to believe that there is much of anything to be said on this subject since Mark Twain around a century ago referred to Congress as America's only native criminal class. Twain's contemporary, the journalist Eugene Field, said "Some statesmen go to Congress and some to jail. It is the same thing, after all." "Reader," Twain said, "suppose you were an idiot. And suppose you were a Member of Congress. But I repeat myself."

As you can see, preparing for this essay hasn't been very difficult. Those quotations come out of standard reference works, and anybody who knows how to look under "C" can get a good start. What amazes me is how easy it is to

Nelson W. Polsby is professor of political science and director of the Institute for Governmental Studies at the University of California–Berkeley.

continue along in the same vein using more contemporary materials. During my lifetime, Congress-bashing has only been out of style very briefly: in the mid-'70s when Congressional resistance to the war in Vietnam provided a graphic illustration to liberals, used to putting Congress down, of the successful workings of a system of separation of powers; and during the impeachment drama itself, when the deliberations of the House Committee on the Judiciary were widely available to television viewers. Then, as everybody would see, Members of Congress were conducting public business in a non-idiotic, non-criminal way. Congress was rewarded with very high public opinion ratings. The Gallup Poll in 1974 found a plurality of 48 percent approving Congressional performance.

But this has not been the norm. Recently, public opinion has been more critical; a recent Harris Poll found approval rates falling to 15 percent. Moreover, a number of recent clippings in my file attest to the fact that Congress-bashing is back in style. Not that it has ever been far out of style. On a shelf not far from where I write sit half a dozen or so books disparaging Congress and complaining about the Congressional role in the constitutional separation of powers. These books have titles like *Congress: Corruption and Compromise; Congress: The Sapless Branch; House Out of Order; Congress Needs Help*, and so on. They date mostly from the late 1940s and the early 1960s, and typically their authors are liberal Democrats. In those years, Congress was unresponsive to liberal Democrats, and aggrieved members of that articulate tribe sought solutions in structural reform.

In fact, instead of reforms weakening Congress, what they—and we—got was a considerably strengthened presidency. This was mostly a product, and an after-effect, of World War II and not the result of liberal complaints. Before World War II, Congress balked at enacting most of the modest recommendations of the Brownlow Commission that included [giving] the president a handful of assistants with "a passion for anonymity," and it killed the National Resources Planning Board outright. After World War II, everything changed: Congress gave the president responsibility for smoothing the effect of the business cycle, created a defense department and two presidential agencies—the NSC [National Security Council] and the CIA [Central Intelligence Agency]—which enhanced the potential for presidential dominance of national security affairs, and laid the groundwork for the growth all over the government of an effective, appointed presidential branch, politically responsive to both Democratic and Republican presidents.

The growth of this presidential branch and its separation from the executive branch is the big news of the post-war era—indeed of the last half century in American government, though it took time for the presidential branch to grow into its post-war potential. It is customary today to acknowledge that Harry Truman's primary agenda, in the field of foreign affairs, was quite successfully enacted even though Congress was dominated by a conservative coalition [of Republicans and southern Democrats], and even though what Truman wanted in the way of peacetime international involvement was, for the US, quite unprecedented. Dwight Eisenhower's agenda was also largely international in its impact.

Looking back, it seems that almost all that Eisenhower really cared about was protecting the international position of the US from diminution by Republican isolationists. Everything else was expendable.

Congress responded sluggishly—and in its customary piecemeal fashion—to the swelling of the presidency. It was around John Kennedy's first year in office that liberals rediscovered that old roadblock in Congress, a deadlock of democracy, as one of them put it, that had thwarted the second New Deal, the packing of the Supreme Court, and Harry Truman's domestic program, and had sponsored the Bricker Amendment, stalled civil rights, and buried Medicare. Are memories so short that we do not recall those dear, departed days when Congress was the graveyard of the forward-looking proposals of a liberal president? Then, Congress was archaic, creaky 18th-century machinery unsuited to the modern age, and Congress-bashers were liberal Democrats. To be sure, Congress had a few defenders, mostly Republicans and Dixiecrats, who found in its musty cloakrooms and windy debates a citadel, as one of them said, of old-time legislative virtues, where the historic functions of oversight and scrutiny were performed, where the runaway proposals of the presidency could be subjected to the sober second thoughts of the people's own elected representatives, and so on.

Why rehash all this? In part, it is to try to make the perfectly obvious point that Congress-bashing then was what people did when they controlled the presidency but didn't control Congress. And that, in part, is what Congress-bashing is about now. Today, Republicans and conservatives are doing most of the complaining. It is worth a small bet that there are a fair number of editorial pages that used to think the separation of powers made a lot more sense in the Kennedy-Johnson years than it does today. On the other side, backers of FDR's scheme to pack the court have turned into vigorous defenders of the judicial status quo since Earl Warren's time. There is nothing wrong with letting the goring of oxen determine which side we take in a political argument. In a civilized country, however, it makes sense to keep political arguments civil, and not to let push come to shove too often.

There is something uncivil . . . about insisting upon constitutional reforms to cure political ailments. What liberal critics of Congress needed was not constitutional reform. What they needed was the 89th Congress [1965–1966], which enacted a great proportion of the agenda of the Democratic party as that agenda had built up over the previous two decades. History didn't stop with the rise of the presidential branch and the enactment of the second New Deal/New Frontier/Great Society. President Johnson overreached. He concealed from Congress the costs of the Vietnam War. He created a credibility gap. This, among other things, began to change Congress. The legislative branch no longer was comfortable relying on massaged numbers and other unreliable information coming from the presidential branch. During the 1970s, Members began to create a legislative bureaucracy to cope with this challenge. They beefed up the General Accounting Office and the Congressional Research Service. They created an Office of Technology Assessment and a Congressional Budget Office. They doubled and redoubled their personal staffs and committee staffs. Sentiments supporting this change began, oddly enough, in the mid-1960s, after a landslide election in which the Democratic party swept the presidency and both Houses of Congress. So, mistrust between the two branches in recent history has by no means entirely been a partisan matter.

Nevertheless, Richard Nixon's presidency, conducted entirely in unhappy harness with a Democratic Congress, did not improve relations between the two branches of Government. Johnson may have been deceitful, but Nixon, especially after his re-election in 1972, was positively confrontational. It was Nixon's policy to disregard comity between the branches. This, and not merely his offenses, fueled the impeachment effort in Congress. That effort was never wholly partisan. Republicans as well as Democrats voted articles of impeachment that included complaints specifically related to obstruction of the discharge of Congressional responsibilities. It is necessary to understand this recent history of the relations between Congress and the President in order to understand the provenance of the War Powers Act, the Boland Amendment [denying aid to Nicaraguan contras], and other instances of Congressional micromanagement; the unprecedented involvement of the National Security Council in the Iran-Contra affair; and similar manifestation of tension and mistrust between Congress and the president. . . .

This is about all of the historical context I want to give before turning to the three main issues that today are the chosen instruments of Congress-bashers. As is traditional in discussions of this kind, the people who favor these instruments are almost all people who are, at the moment, now powerful in Congress. So, mostly these are things Republicans want. My conscience is clear of partisan motivation, however. When Democrats did the Congress-bashing back in the late 1950s and early 1960s, I opposed them and defended Congress. Today, I am still against Congress-bashing, and therefore oppose the item veto and the limitation on terms of Members, both of which, by the way, would require constitutional amendments. I'm also in favor of paying Members proper salaries, as Congress-bashers are not.

The item veto says in effect that the President should be given the power to reach into bills passed by Congress and select those clauses and phrases and provisions he doesn't like and veto them, preserving those aspects of carefully crafted compromises and logrolls that he likes, and requiring those that he doesn't like to be passed by a two-thirds majority in each House of Congress. If such an arrangement were to come into existence, it is hard to see what incentives Members of Congress would have to undertake the arduous tasks of bargaining that legislation normally requires. What, indeed, in the give and take of bargaining would people on the president's side in Congress have to give, since the president could later, unilaterally, take back whatever hostages they gave? The item veto would effectively take Congressional politics out of the legislative process, and would weaken Congress. It would encourage Members of Congress, majority and minority alike, to be irresponsible and to stick the president with embarrassing public choices. It would reduce the incentives for Members to acquire knowledge about public policy or indeed to serve.

By allocating legislative responsibilities to Congress the Constitution, as originally and currently designed, forces Representatives of diverse interests to achieve cooperation. Because what Congress does as a collectivity matters, legislative work elicits the committed participation of Members. The item veto is, in short, a truly radical idea. It is also almost certainly unconstitutional. To espouse it requires a readiness to give up entirely on the separation of powers and on the constitutional design of the American government. There are plenty of people, some of them well-meaning, who are ready to do that. I am not, nor should people who locate themselves as conservatives or liberals or anywhere in the political mainstream. The separation of powers is actually a good idea. It gives a necessary weight to the great heterogeneity of our nation—by far the largest and most heterogeneous nation unequivocally to have succeeded at democratic self-government in world history. It would take a medium-sized book to make all the qualifications, and all the connections that would do justice to this argument. The conclusion is worth restating anyway: The item veto is a root-and-branch attack on the separation of powers and is a very radical and bad idea.

Less serious in its impact, but still destructive, is the proposal to limit the terms of Members of Congress. This proposal relies heavily for its appeal upon ignorance in the population at large about what it is that Members of Congress actually do. In order to take the limitation of service by Members seriously, one is required to believe that the job of Representative is relatively simple, and quickly and easily mastered. It is not. The job of a Member of Congress is varied and complex. It includes:

1. Managing a small group of offices that attempt on request to render assistance to distressed constituents, state and local governments, and enterprises in the home district which may have business with the federal government.
2. Serving on committees which oversee executive branch activity on a broad spectrum of subjects and which undertake to frame issues of national scope for legislative action. This entails the mastery of complicated subject matter, interacting with staff, expert outsiders, and colleagues.
3. Participating in legislative work more broadly. Members have to vote on everything, not merely on the work of their own committees.
4. Keeping track of their own political business. This means watching over (and occasionally participating in) the politics of their own states and localities, mending fences with interest groups, friends and neighbors, backers, political rivals, and allies.
5. Educating all the varied people with whom they come in contact about issues that are high on the agenda and about reasonable expectations of performance. This includes the performance of the government, Congress, and the Member.

Plenty of Members never try to master the job, or try and fail, and these Members would be expendable. Objection might still be raised that constituents, not a whole lot of constitutional limitations, ought to decide who represents whom in Congress. But that aside, what about the rather substantial minority of Members who learn the job, do their homework, strive to make an impact on public policy, and through long experience and application to work actually make a difference? Can we, should we dispense with them as well? Irving Kristol,* among others, thinks it may be worth it, since these Members are only a minority, and we would presumably be throwing out the majority who are not that good at the job.

This simply gives power to the people who do stay around: government bureaucrats, Congressional staff members, interest group lawyers, lobbyists, and so on, to whom the limitations wouldn't apply and who would have the advantage over all inexperienced Members—good and bad ones. And, of course, we could count on roughly the same proportion of bad Members as good Members being newly elected at each intake of Members. It is a delusion to think that good public servants are a dime a dozen in each Congressional district, and only the good ones would queue up to take their 12-year fling at Congressional office.

But suppose they did. In case they acquired expertise, what would they do next? Make money, I suppose. Just about the time their constituents and the American people at large could begin to expect a payoff because of the knowledge and experience these able Members had acquired at our expense, off they would go to some Washington law firm. And what about their usefulness in the meantime? Limited, I'm afraid, by the greater expertise, and better command of the territory by lobbyists, staff, downtown bureaucrats, career people one and all. So this is, once again, a proposal merely to weaken the fabric of Congress in the political system at large, and thereby to depress the effectiveness of the one set of actors most accessible to ordinary citizens. The standard objection to this statement is that Members aren't all that accessible. Well, neither is Ralph Nader, who has long overstayed the dozen years contemporary Congress-bashers wish to allocate to Members. Neither is the author of *Wall Street Journal* editorials in praise of limitations. And it must be said that a very large number of Members take their representational and ombudsman duties very seriously indeed. This includes holders of safe seats, some of whom fear primary election opposition, some of whom are simply conscientious. A great many of them do pay attention—close attention—to their constituents. That is one of the reasons—maybe the most important reason—so many of them are re-elected.

Much Congress-bashing these days actually complains about high re-election rates, as though a large population of ill-served constituents would be preferable. Actually, the number that you hear most often in connection with the proposal for term limitation is the famous 98 point something, the percentage of those

---

* Irving Kristol is a leading neoconservative.

seeking re-election who were actually re-elected in the last couple of Congressional elections [1986 and 1988]. This is a number that suggests that sitting Members are popular. They stand for election. Most of them have opponents in the general election and a fair number have opponents in the primary elections as well—and they get re-elected.

To some analysts, this number suggests that Congress is filled with tired blood, and there isn't enough turnover in the House of Representatives. I should say, by the way, that the percentage of incumbents seeking re-election in the Senate and who are re-elected has ranged in recent years from just over half in 1978 and 1980 to nine out of ten in 1982 and 1984. So, the argument about tired blood is presumably about the House. The point I would like to stress is this: The percentage of Members re-elected who are seeking re-election isn't the right number to measure turnover. There are 435 Members of the House. Thirty Members left in 1988, even though only seven were beaten in elections. Forty-six left in 1986. Forty-one in 1984. Seventy-nine in 1982. Seventy-one in 1980. These numbers exclude deaths, by the way. And they account for well over half the membership in the House (267 in fact) in a single decade. Mean terms of service in the House have hovered around five terms, or ten years of service, for at least 30 years. That's the right number—turnover—to consider if we wish to understand the real longevity of the House as a collectivity, and not that phony 98-point-something number that Common Cause and other self-righteous, but, I regret to say, intellectually careless Congress-bashers throw up at us.*

While we have intellectually careless Congress-bashers on our minds, it is certainly appropriate to pay our disrespects to Ralph Nader's off-the-wall effort, temporarily successful, at the head of a crazed phalanx of self-righteous disc jockeys and radio talk-show hosts, to deprive Members of salary increases. The issue of Congressional salaries is a straightforward one. Many Members, being well-to-do, don't need an increase. But some do. The expense of maintaining two places of residence—in Washington and at home—makes membership in Congress nearly unique and Members singularly burdened among Americans with upper-middle-class jobs. Here is the point once more: It is a job, requiring skill and dedication to be done properly. Moreover, membership in Congress brings responsibilities. National policy of the scope and scale now encompassed by acts of the federal government requires responsible, dedicated legislators. People with far less serious responsibilities in the private sector are paid considerably better than Members of Congress. Think, for example, how far down the organization chart at General Motors, CBS, or some other large corporation one would have to go before reaching executives making what Members of Congress do, and compare their responsibilities with those of Members. . . .

---

* Moreover, the 1992 elections brought 110 new members to the House, its largest "class" in more than 40 years. For details on their entry into congressional politics, see selection 10.2.

I don't begrudge the president of Reebok's salary of $14 million; or the Clorox president's total package of $1.4 million. And so forth. But let's get real. The responsibilities that these people have in the world don't begin to match the responsibilities that the 435 Members have. And it is clearly in our interest—not to pay Members like captains of industry (if that's what you call the presidents of Reebok and Clorox)—but decently as respectable upper-middle-class professionals, which is what they are. In short, there is a case for decent Congressional salaries to be made on at least two grounds: one is the rough-equity or opportunity-cost ground that we ought not to greatly penalize people financially who serve, and the second is the ground of need for those Members who have the expense of families, or college educations to think of and no extraordinary private means. . . .

The bottom salary for Major League baseball players is $100,000. Some law firms in New York start new graduates of good law schools at $90,000 or more. How can we argue that Members of Congress and others at the top of the federal government should not be paid at least a modest premium above beginner's wages? There is, evidently, no talking sense to the American people on this subject. I believe we can dismiss out of hand the charge that large numbers of Members individually, or Congress collectively, live in a world all of their own, divorced from the realities of everyday life.*

The sophomores who have written attacks of this sort in recent years in places like *The Atlantic, Newsweek,* and *Business Week* simply don't know what they are talking about. They abuse their access to large audiences by neglecting to explain the real conditions that govern the lives of Members, conditions that provide ample doses of everyday life. No doubt scandals involving various Members have in recent times made Congress as an institution vulnerable to criticism. But much of this criticism is irresponsible and irrelevant. Suppose we were to discover instances of cupidity, unusual sexual activity, and/or abuses of power among the rather sizable staff of an important daily newspaper like *The Wall Street Journal,* whose stock tip reporter was recently found to be selling stock tips? Or a symphony orchestra? Or, God forbid, a university?

I suppose that would impair our confidence in at least some of the collective output, but one would hope for relevant discriminations. The stock tips, perhaps, but not the Washington page. The ticket office, perhaps, but not the Mozart. The basketball program, perhaps, but not the Classics department. I do not think the existence of scandal excuses us from attempting to draw sensible conclusions about institutions and their performance. This sort of balanced and discriminating analysis isn't what proposals for item vetoes, limitations on terms of service,

---

* As of 1993–1994, U.S. House salaries stand at $133,600 and House members are prohibited from accepting honoraria.

or depressed rates of pay are all about. They are about the ancient but now slightly shopworn custom of Congress-bashing.

Summary Questions

1. Why is Congress so unpopular compared to, say, the president and the Supreme Court?
2. If Congress is so unpopular and so susceptible to "bashing," why do most incumbents win reelection? Do people evaluate the Congress as a whole and their own members of Congress differently? Explain.
3. What are the costs and benefits of term limitations for legislators? The president is limited to two terms. Is this a sound policy?

 10.2

Housebroken

Bill Turque

The U.S. Congress is simultaneously resistant to and capable of change. It is a 200-year-old institution that changes its membership every two years. During the 1980s, congressional turnover was modest, averaging only about 10 percent between 1984 and 1990. Then, in 1992, anti-incumbent sentiments as well as a well-publicized set of irregularities in the so-called House bank led to the election of 110 new members to the 435-member House of Representatives.

A year after their swearing in, reporter Bill Turque examined how three notable members of the "Class of 1992" had adjusted to life in the House. Whatever their initial expectations, each of these new members found it extremely difficult to move the House in new directions. In fact, after a year all three of these very different representatives had begun to act like the very Washington insiders they had campaigned to replace. Note that two of the profiles feature women; the Class of 1992 greatly increased female representation in the Congress. One question that you might ponder is whether the rising number of women on Capitol Hill will have much effect on the policies adopted by the Congress. Or, is the

Bill Turque is a reporter at *Newsweek*.

legislature so large and unwieldy that not even large-scale replacements will make much of a difference?

This time, Rep. Marjorie Margolies-Mezvinsky took no chances. The freshman Democrat from Pennsylvania was in no mood for eleventh-hour arm-twisting. The House clock had just started counting down the 15 minutes allotted for members to vote on NAFTA last Wednesday night. She slid her voting card into one of the chamber's electronic counters, punched "no" and bolted for the nearest door as if she were double-parked outside. She had already lived through one painful flip-flop. After a last-minute phone call from President Clinton on Aug. 5, she cast one of the two final votes that pushed his 1994 budget through the House. It didn't matter that NAFTA had been a done deal for hours. Margolies-Mezvinsky still observed a cardinal rule of survival for lawmakers who want to avoid trouble on tough issues: vote no and go. "The trick," says one senior House Democrat, "is to never let them find you."

It has been a punishing apprenticeship for the class of 1992. Voters elected 110 new members to the House last year, the largest group of freshmen in more than 40 years. Many of the newcomers ran as crusading outsiders vowing to reform an institution that seemed to capture under one roof everything that Americans hated about politics—partisan gridlock, pork-barrel spending, a commitment to careerism over principle and allegiance to moneyed special interests.

The freshmen have had their moments as agents of change. A bipartisan coalition of deficit-conscious first termers helped kill off a series of big spending programs this fall, including the Superconducting Super Collider and NASA's Advanced Solid Rocket Motor. They are a major force behind a new package of cuts—expected to come to the floor early next week—that would trim an additional $100 billion from the deficit over the next five years.

But more often, politics as usual prevailed over reform. Many of those who preached change ended up adopting the traditional hypocrisies of the House. Some have decried runaway spending while hustling for their own questionable projects close to home. Some have denounced Washington's money culture while raking in PAC contributions. These freshmen may have been outsiders to Washington, but they were not new to politics. Nearly half served in state legislatures before coming to Congress; more than 70 percent held some elective office before 1992. While some were genuine in their pursuit of reform, others cynically borrowed the rhetoric to win office.

After last fall's election, *Newsweek* selected three freshmen of the 103d Congress to follow through their first turbulent year in office. Margolies-Mezvinsky, a diminutive former television reporter, campaigned as a fiscally responsible "new" Democrat to win an upset victory in her suburban Philadelphia district. Republican Terry Everett, a millionaire newspaper publisher and real-estate developer from southeastern Alabama, garnered comparisons to Ross Perot for his conservative populism. Cynthia McKinney, a fiery liberal Democrat and the first African-American woman to represent Georgia in Congress, promised to bring government closer to the poor and disenfranchised in a newly created minority district. All three came to Washington talking about change. Before 1993 was over, Washington would change them instead.

Terry Everett

Pork, Peanuts and Promises Before 1992, Terry Everett was an unknown in Alabama Republican politics. But the bumper-sticker battle cry of his campaign, SEND A MESSAGE, NOT A POLITICIAN, captured the restive mood of Second Congressional District voters. What made Everett's anti-Washington populism especially unconventional was his refusal to accept PAC contributions. He was well positioned to turn his back on the cash. The son of a railroad section foreman, he'd made a fortune in newspapers and real estate. Everett spent more than $800,000 of his own money on the campaign, a sum that brought extraordinary exposure in a district where the most expensive media markets are Montgomery (population 190,500) and Dothan (54,500). He upset a widely favored Republican state legislator in the primary, and last November he narrowly beat Democratic state Treasurer George Wallace Jr., son of the former governor and presidential candidate.

Everett's up-by-the-bootstraps life story, unvarnished personal style and pledge to bring a businessman's approach to cutting the budget deficit spurred frequent comparisons to Ross Perot. As the 56-year-old Baptist Sunday-school teacher told a group of Alabama newspaper publishers in Washington last March, "I don't plan to be a willing convert to the way they do business in Washington."

One morning three months later, just after 8, Everett and his wife, Barbara, greeted each of their guests as they arrived at the Capitol Hill Club. They included representatives of General Dynamics, Hughes Aircraft, Lockheed, Florida Sugar, National Pork Producers and more than two dozen other PACs. The tribal rite of exchanging money for access is played out virtually every morning or evening in places like the club, a dining retreat for Republican lawmakers just across the street from Everett's office in the Cannon building. For their $500, PAC representatives got scrambled eggs, grits and a few minutes with a new member of the Armed Services and Agriculture committees, panels whose good will can mean millions in profits for defense contractors and agribusiness companies. For two hours of handshakes and small talk, the freshman Republican from Alabama netted nearly $30,000 for his 1994 re-election campaign.

Beneath Everett's reform fervor lurks the soul of a career politician. He insists he was clear during his campaign about the no PACs pledge—that it was a one-time offer, good only for 1992. But Everett's caveat was tantamount to the fine print on the side of a cereal box. It was nowhere to be found in his radio or television advertising—there was only a brief mention in the 15th paragraph of an August wire story that ran in some of the state's papers. "He left the impression he wasn't going to take any PAC money, period," says Bob Ingram, political columnist for The Montgomery Advertiser. "It looked like he was backpedaling on his promise. He was saying, 'PAC money was evil, it was sinful. You take it and you go to hell.' Suddenly, it's not so bad."

Everett says that as an unknown name in Alabama politics, he needed a dramatic gesture to attract attention. His idea was to give voters the chance to elect someone "who in their minds was not bought and paid for." But in 1994, he says, "they can make their own judgment from my voting record and the money I take from PACs." As proof of his independence, Everett pointed to his "no" vote on NAFTA despite $19,500 in donations from pro-NAFTA PACs (anti-NAFTA PACs kicked in $4,500). Until Congress passes new limits on PAC contributions—which he supports—Everett intends to play the game by the same rules as his opponents. He also wasn't keen on continuing to deplete his personal fortune (estimated at $8 million) to stay in office.

Everett did follow through on other parts of his reform message. He cosponsored measures calling for constitutional amendments that would limit terms, balance the budget and establish a presidential line-item veto. He was one of only 19 House members—nearly half of them freshmen—to sign Ralph Nader's "humility pledge" for term limits and reduced congressional pay. On his first day in office last January, he introduced a resolution barring Congress from voting itself salary increases if it passed a deficit budget the preceding year (it went nowhere). Everett also earmarked $40,000—his annual portion of the raise Congress voted itself in 1989—to establish a scholarship fund in his district.

But reform was on Everett's agenda only when it caused pain in someone else's district. Everett's predecessor, Bill Dickinson, was ranking Republican member of the House Armed Services Committee before his retirement last year and a zealous guardian of the district's military assets (Maxwell Air Force Base, its Gunter Annex and the army's Fort Rucker). Everett stepped effortlessly into his shoes. His fall newsletter to constituents is full of indignant references to wasteful government spending. In a column published by district newspapers, he railed against "outlandish special-interest projects." Yet this spring he worked hard to secure $14.4 million for a new "personnel-services facility" at Fort Rucker, the Second District's huge army base. He says the structure will replace pre-World War II-era buildings whose poor condition make them prohibitively expensive to maintain. "If it's cost-effective it's not pork," he insists. Says Auburn University political scientist Brad Moody, "He's so far successfully maneuvered to convince people he is against additional spending in general, but that he supports additional spending in the Second District. Not an atypical congressman."

Everett also positioned himself to safeguard one of Washington's most venerable pieces of pork: the peanut subsidy. Southeast Alabama's loose soil is ideal for goobers. In 1992 only two other congressional districts (both in Georgia) grew more of them than Everett's. The subsidy was a legacy of the New Deal, created to help farmers survive in the face of disastrously low Depression-era prices. But

---

Everett—October 6, 1993

7:00:   Meeting of GOP freshman class officers (Everett is secretary)

8:00:   Conservative Opportunity Society (group of GOP House members committed to pushing a conservative agenda)

9:00:   House Republican Conference meets to discuss crime bill and welfare reform

9:30:   Veterans' Affairs subcommittee on hospitals and health care

10:00:   NAFTA debate between political economist Pat Choate and GOP Rep. Duncan Hunter of California

10:00:   Joint press conference of Republican and Democratic freshmen to announce task force on implementing Vice President Al Gore's proposals on "Reinventing Government"

12:00:   Floor vote on NASA Advanced Solid Rocket Motor. (Everett votes to continue funding.)

12:30:   Floor votes

3:45:   Office meeting with National Propane Gas Association to discuss energy issues

5:30:   Fund-raiser for Rep. Dan Schaefer, Republican from Colorado

6:30:   Floor votes

7:30:   Office work

8:30:   Home

---

the price-support program, which bars nearly all foreign peanuts from the domestic market, has become a $34 million entitlement for a small group of U.S. growers. According to the General Accounting Office (GAO), the subsidized price of U.S. peanuts allows producers to make an average return of 51 percent after costs. As a result, American consumers are spending hundreds of millions of dollars a year more for peanuts—as much as an extra 40 cents on a $1.79 jar of peanut butter. (Growers say the GAO's figures are way off.) Everett himself even benefits—if modestly—from the price program. Tenants grow peanuts on part of his 400-acre farm near Enterprise, earning him about $8,000 a year.

Everett disputes the suggestion that there's a contradiction between his reform rhetoric and his fealty to the price supports. "The perception of pork is an individual one," he says. "What would you accomplish by cutting [the subsidy]? It doesn't cost that much money to start with, and it puts people to work. . . . What are we going to do? Put these people on welfare? You can't take a peanut farmer or laborer and teach them to run a computer. No disrespect. They're just not that inclined."

When Everett arrived in Washington, he immediately began searching for a strategic platform from which to safeguard the subsidy. His first idea was a peanut caucus, bringing together members from Alabama, Georgia, North Carolina and other growing states. But a better opportunity soon opened up—a vacancy on the House Agriculture Committee.

Everett was already stretched thin with two committee assignments (Armed Services and Veterans Affairs), which included seats on four subcommittees. He and other freshmen frequently complained about the bloated committee system. Plagued by redundant jurisdictions and pointless hearings, they said, it often diverted them from more substantive work. Everett once said he learned more from The Washington Post than from some of the classified Armed Services briefings he's received. "See how asinine this is?" he said one morning in May, leaving a VA Oversight and Investigations Subcommittee hearing to prepare for another meeting. "The combination of all this stuff makes it impossible to do a credible job on any one thing."

But even congressional freshmen understand that policymaking is only one function of the committee system—and often the least important. Committees are also about delivering largesse to the folks at home—and bulking up the official letterhead with as many credentials as possible. While Everett carped about the committee system, he lobbied strenuously for the Agriculture seat and won it.

The effort required him to overcome a natural reticence. Despite the comparisons to Perot, Everett's political act is low voltage. His knees shook when he delivered the speech announcing his congressional candidacy in the spring of 1992. His soft, listless voice and tongue-tied delivery often underwhelmed audiences. Where other lawmakers sweep into a crowded room and "work" it with backslaps and bonhomie, Everett's first impulse was to stand off to the side and watch. "He's very shy. People mistake it for humility," says an aide. He didn't especially enjoy the social rituals of Washington, and during his early weeks there, aides had to coax him into attending afterhours events. (At least once, he was glad he did. Last February he reluctantly attended a dinner at the German ambassador's residence and found himself seated at a table with Gen. Colin Powell, who was then chairman of the Joint Chiefs of Staff. Everett happily took the opportunity to lobby Powell on a new program for Fort Rucker.)

But the vanilla earnestness that fell flat in groups came across well in private with House colleagues. Everett persuaded members of the Agriculture panel and the House Republican Committee on Committees to waive rules barring members from sitting on more than one major committee. In a small plastic file box on his desk, he kept alphabetized index cards that tracked his contacts. Each card contained a small picture (he has trouble remembering the names and faces of his new colleagues), the member's phone extension, the date of their conversation and a notation: "Jennifer Dunn, 5/8, says she'll consider it." He also secured high-level help from Republican Whip Newt Gingrich, who often shared the same weekend flight to Atlanta's Hartsfield airport, where Everett caught a commuter plane to Alabama. "He's a natural networker," says Gingrich.

The Agriculture seat gave him a rare trifecta—three committees with powerful constituencies in his district. It also meant a total of 10 committee and subcommittee assignments, far above the average House workload that experts say is already swollen beyond reason. But Everett thought it was pretty good work, "especially for a freshman who was told he would spend his first term just trying to find his way around. I got news for you. This place ain't brain surgery. It's more endurance."

Everett believes he's done a good job this year, although he can't say the same for many of his fellow freshmen—especially the Democrats. In a series of interviews with local newspapers, he expressed disappointment with their lack of commitment to reform. "I don't see a lot of people living up to what they told the voters," he told the *Birmingham News*. Next year, when Second District voters ask him what he's done to promote change, Everett says he'll tell them that real reform won't be possible until more like-minded conservatives are elected to Congress. "I'd say, 'Send more people to Congress like Terry Everett.' "

Cynthia McKinney

The Learning Curve Cynthia McKinney got to the House floor early on the evening of Feb. 17. She wanted a seat on the aisle so she could shake hands—and be seen shaking hands—with Bill Clinton as he arrived to deliver his economic address to a joint session of Congress. The Georgia freshman passed some time chatting with an older member she didn't recognize. The Appropriations Committee was an anachronism, she said, with "staffers coming out of their ears." Listening to her critique was Appropriations chairman William Natcher, the 84-year-old Kentuckian who entered the House in 1953, nearly two years before McKinney was born. "I don't think he ever forgave me," she says.

McKinney had more than the usual freshman naiveté to overcome when she arrived in Washington. In a kingdom ruled by an aging white patriarchy of Brooks Brothers pinstripes, she stood in bold relief: a divorced, black, single mother with gold canvas tennis shoes, flowing, brightly patterned skirts and hair braided in elaborate cornrows. She felt more at home than she did during her four years in the Georgia Legislature—Congressional Black Caucus* mentors like Maxine Waters offered significant support. But the clubbiness of white, male Washington was omnipresent. There was always, as her chief of staff Andrea Young describes it, "the sense of disequilibrium when you walk into the steel-industry luncheon and there's nothing but middle-aged white men . . . in gray suits."

Months after most freshmen were recognizable figures on Capital Hill, McKinney still found herself treated like a wayward tourist. In February, a House elevator operator tried to order her off a members-only car. In April, a Capitol garage attendant confronted her and two staff members and asked edgily: "Who you

---

* The Congressional Black Caucus is one of dozens of groups organized by like-minded members to press for specific policies.

folks supposed to be with?" She had assumed that over time such institutional slights would cease. But in early August after a Capitol Hill police officer grabbed her by the arm at a metal detector that members are allowed to bypass, McKinney complained to House Sergeant-at-Arms Werner Brandt. "There's not that many people here who look like me," she told him.

It's not just the hallways that can be cold and inhospitable. In an institution run on windy rituals of deference and testimonial, the simplest kinds of recognition are sometimes elusive. A few minutes after she took a seat at her first meeting of a House Foreign Affairs subcommittee on Western Hemisphere affairs, she realized that no one on the panel was going to offer a welcome. "I was the only woman present, and the men were just having a backslapping good time. Never acknowledged that I walked in," said McKinney, a Ph.D. candidate at Tufts University's Fletcher School of Law and Diplomacy. "Then they got up and took a picture together. I finally figured maybe I was supposed to be in the picture. Then the chairman [Rep. Robert Torricelli of N.J.] gavels the meeting to order, goes through the agenda and gavels the meeting adjourned . . . I felt like Ralph Ellison's invisible man."

Her sense of alienation escalated into anger several weeks later. During a closed committee session, Torricelli delivered what McKinney described as an insulting lecture to exiled Haitian President Jean-Bertrand Aristide. "He wagged his finger in Aristide's face and said Americans were not going to send money down there," McKinney said, describing his demeanor as "pompous, arrogant and grandstanding."

Rep. Albert Wynn, a freshman Democrat from Maryland and the panel's other black member, recalls no rancor on Torricelli's part. Through a spokesman, Torricelli says only that the Haitian issue will be resolved through "a frank exchange of views, not an exchange of pleasantries." One subcommittee aide said that McKinney's spotty attendance (she missed nine of 14 open sessions between February and October) made it difficult to take her complaints seriously. "She would have more credibility if she were an active player," he said. (She says the committee sessions conflict with weekly Black Caucus luncheons.)

McKinney made her name in Georgia politics as a rhetorical bomb-thrower. Colleagues in the statehouse dubbed her "Hanoi Cynthia" after a 1991 speech denouncing the Persian Gulf War. At a hearing that same year on reapportionment, she frustrated a white legislator with persistent questions about how a particular plan would aid black representation. "I'm just a dumb ole country boy," said state Rep. Henry Reaves. "It shows," McKinney retorted. Her tenacious pursuit of a plan to create two new majority-black congressional districts paid off. Under pressure from the Justice Department, Georgia created two new "safe" black seats. She ran for Congress in the district she helped draw, winning and using her reapportionment victory to convey a message of black political and economic advancement.

Although healing is a consistent theme in her rhetoric, she hasn't hesitated to deal the race card. In her 1992 Democratic primary, she characterized two favored black opponents as tools of the party's white establishment. "She's a demagogue," says one of them, former state senator Gene Walker. When she learned this summer that a group of white constituents was considering a legal challenge to the 11th Congressional District's boundaries, she counted its opposition as a tactical asset. "This assures my reelection," she boasted while jogging one morning at Fort McNair in southwest Washington. "It shows that the redneck factor is alive and well."

But McKinney soon learned that scorched earth and victimization politics aren't enough on Capitol Hill. Some observers say she needs to exhibit the same relish for the complexities of legislating that she shows for incendiary quotes. "She needs to show that she can pull her share of the wagon," says one lobbyist who follows the Georgia delegation closely.

Last June's racially charged House debate over ending the ban on most federal funding for abortions for low-income women was a bitter lesson. She took on Rep. Henry Hyde, the amendment's sponsor, calling his measure "nothing but a discriminatory policy against poor women who happen to be disproportionately black." Hyde countered that abortion supporters were telling the poor, "We will give you a free abortion because there are too many of you people and we want to refine . . . the breed."

Hyde also won in part by employing an obscure parliamentary precedent that allowed him to outmaneuver the less experienced pro-choice women. "What we learned out of that is that we need to learn how to become legislators," she acknowledges.

McKinney faced a steep learning curve off the House floor as well. One major challenge was integrating single motherhood with the grinding congressional lifestyle—three days on the Hill and four working at home. Since a 1990 divorce McKinney has been raising a son, Coy, 9, by herself. Her workweeks usually begin before dawn on Tuesdays, when she leaves her suburban Atlanta home to fly to Washington. Until she returns late Thursday, child care falls primarily to her parents, Billy McKinney, a longtime state representative and civil-rights activist, and Leola McKinney, a retired nurse. Cynthia McKinney keeps Fridays clear to take Coy to Atlanta's Galloway School (her official schedule usually reads, "Reserved Coy Time"), but holdover House business can interfere. In his room one evening, she saw an entry in a journal he'd been keeping: "Mom is in D.C. again. Rats." "There's no way you can look at this and say, this is what it means to be a mom," she says.

Coy comes to Washington on vacations, where he follows her to the floor or roams the office, commandeering computer keyboards and leaving trails of baseball cards in his wake. When he's gone, so is most of McKinney's personal life. Her fiancé, Atlanta businessman Mohammad Jamal, visits when he can. But her few nonofficial hours are spent preparing her doctoral dissertation on former Soviet client states and reading briefing papers in a spartan southwest Washington condominium furnished with three Oriental rugs, two beds, a television and a chair, some of it donated by an aide.

McKinney—August 4, 1993

9:50:   Arrives Cannon House Office Building

10:00:   Finishes draft of speech she will deliver at noon rally for Clinton economic plan

10:50:   Slips out of an Agriculture subcommittee meeting for brief talk on NAFTA with UAW lobbyist

11:45:   Meeting at EPA with residents of an Augusta, Ga., neighborhood threatened by industrial pollution

12:55:   Addresses "Pass the Plan" rally sponsored by the DNC

1:45:   Shows up at Congressional Black Caucus weekly luncheon more than an hour late. Lunch is over.

2:40:   Joins members of the Black Caucus at a press conference asking the state of Texas for a stay of execution for Gary Graham

3:00:   Floor votes

4:15:   Meets with House sergeant at arms about Capitol Hill police who stop her at security checkpoints

6:00:   Reception for Democratic Sen. Barbara Boxer of California

7:10:   Staff meeting about Democratic Party-sponsored radio ads supporting Clinton budget to run in her district

8:00:   Home

McKinney spends weekends in Georgia on the road, trying to remain visible in a gerrymandered district devoid of any natural political identity. The 11th begins in the southern Atlanta suburbs, ribboning east across the impoverished rural counties of the old cotton belt to Augusta, then dips south along the South Carolina border into coastal Savannah. To keep in touch, McKinney puts herself back on a campaign footing. She rolled up 12,000 miles barnstorming in her aqua-green Mercury van during the first four months of 1993, maintaining a punishing schedule of town meetings, chamber of commerce luncheons, talk radio and community-center tours.

By mid-May, she was exhausted. Her voice was in shreds from overuse, her eyes bloodshot. Jamal would see the fatigue etched across her face as he picked her up at Hartsfield Airport on Thursday evenings. After an evening speech to the Optimists Club in Monticello, she threw up for 20 minutes. The next day Leola McKinney scheduled four appointments with medical specialists. The diagnosis was exhaustion. "Beach vacation," was the notation on one physician's prescription form.

When McKinney returned to Washington, aides tried to help, padding her daily schedule with more uncommitted time. Lunch, which had often been an orange-flavored diet powder, became a bona fide meal. But routine days ran deep into the evening, sometimes because of poor work by an inexperienced staff. Late one evening after a 12-hour day, McKinney was at her desk typing out a list of radio stations in her district. The Democratic National Committee wanted suggestions on where to air spots in support of Clinton's economic plan. "If all the radio stations aren't on the media list, then the media list doesn't do us much good, does it?" she scolded an aide over the phone. "We should never be in a position of having stuff offered to us and not being able to take advantage of it because we don't have our stuff together. Never, ever!"

Toward midsummer, McKinney seemed to turn a corner. She began to develop the kinds of personal connections that are at the heart of the legislative process. She lobbied—with some trepidation—Ways and Means chairman Dan Rostenkowski to make childless workers eligible for the earned-income tax credit. The beefy Chicago pol's lack of patience with freshmen was legendary. "I just got it all out, as quickly as I could . . . 'You know, Mr. Chairman, we've got to save childless workers,' " she recalls. "He winked at me, and he smiled. Then I knew I didn't have to be scared anymore."

McKinney's district agenda began to gain momentum as well. After months of prodding the Environmental Protection Agency, she was close to getting help for an Augusta neighborhood damaged by industrial pollution. As autumn began, she was pressing for a Justice Department investigation into charges that mining companies in central Georgia had defrauded landowners. And despite her problems with the pork-friendly Appropriations Committee, she quietly lobbied the panel to secure a $200,000 research grant for Savannah State College.

A White House in desperate search of congressional support on big votes also helped her learn to play the system. In August McKinney flatly told a United Auto Workers lobbyist that she opposed NAFTA. But in the weeks leading up to the vote, as the administration handed out incentives to soften up resistant members, her official position slid to "leaning no." She basked in VIP attention, including phone calls from Vice President Gore, former president Jimmy Carter, Vernon Jordan and Housing and Human Services Secretary Donna Shalala. Energy Secretary Hazel O'Leary even sent a single long-stemmed red rose and a card that read, "Thanks for listening."

Finally, last Tuesday, the day before the vote, McKinney met with Clinton in the Oval Office. In the end, she voted "no" on NAFTA. Was she holding out for a deal? She just smiled and said, "You never want to be so definitive that you can't take advantage of a changing situation."

Cynthia McKinney may find a home in the House after all.

Marjorie Margolies-Mezvinsky

The Maverick Game   The first few minutes after the vote on Aug. 5 were a blur. The hugs from fellow Democrats, the Republican men waving and chanting

"Goodbye, Marjorie" were all details she would reassemble later, like an investigator at a crash site.

Dazed and ashen, Rep. Marjorie Margolies-Mezvinsky retreated to the office of Vic Fazio, a senior Democrat from California, a mentor and a friend. At the moment, she needed both. After months of opposition to President Clinton's budget, she had become one of the two last-minute votes that pushed it over the top in the House, 218-216. The price for her conversion, which she'd named in a phone conversation with Clinton minutes earlier, seemed patently lopsided—the president's attendance at a one-day conference on entitlement spending to be held in her district. It had all the earmarks of a career killer.

Margolies-Mezvinsky's budget vote is the story of an ambitious newcomer who played and lost one of the oldest legislative games: trying to have it both ways on a tough issue. It also illustrates the perils of transforming bold campaign promises into reality. Like Clinton, she sold herself to voters in the Republican-dominated 13th Congressional District as a new kind of deficit-conscious Democrat—committed to reform without the expansive spending of welfare-state liberalism. "This is no time for politics as usual," she warned in campaign position papers. The tax increases and shallow deficit cuts of Clintonomics, she contended, were part of the party's past, not its future.

But in the end, the candidate who promised a new way of doing business operated with the same aggressive cynicism as the careerists she campaigned to replace. Despite her public opposition to Clintonomics, her private posture on the budget was far more elastic than most constituents ever realized. Ten weeks prior to her Aug. 5 switch, she assured the president of her support should he absolutely need it. She made the promise on May 27—two hours before the House voted on a measure called "reconciliation," which brings tax and appropriations bills into line with congressional spending guidelines.

It was an interim step in the budget process but a crucial test of the president's ability to govern. And the outcome was in doubt: conservative Democrats were in revolt against his proposed tax on the energy content of fuel. Republicans, smelling an opportunity to cripple a new Democratic president, were united in opposition. At 7:40 p.m. Clinton, hoarse from a day on the phone scrambling for votes, called to plead for Margolies-Mezvinsky's support. "We're so close, we're so close," he said, according to Margolies-Mezvinsky. A "yes" vote was extremely difficult, she explained.

But Margolies-Mezvinsky was also an innately cautious politician, with an almost compulsive desire to ingratiate. ("It's a hard habit to lose," she admits.) She found the prospect of voting "no" just as bleak: should reconciliation lose by a narrow margin, she and other fiscally conservative Democrats could be held responsible for sending Clinton into political free fall. Before the conversation was over, she'd left him a huge opening. "She told him that she would not be the one to sink his administration," said political adviser Ken Smukler. As it happened, her help wasn't necessary. The measure slipped through by six votes, with a much-relieved Margolies-Mezvinsky able to keep her opposition intact.

In the next morning's newspapers she retailed herself as the gritty fresh-man maverick who bucked the White House. "There was an overriding princi-ple which was more important than calls from the president and the vice president," she told the Philadelphia Daily News. "That was to keep my promise to the voters."

Everything about Margolies-Mezvinsky seemed calibrated for success in 1992. She was a celebrated working mother in the year of the woman; a first-time candidate in the year of the outsider, an indignant voice at a time when career politicians appeared especially arrogant and out of touch. She positioned herself on the issues with smart-bomb precision. For Republicans, there was her hard line on new middle-class taxes. Abortion rights and improved access to health care played well with women. Unions were drawn to her anti-NAFTA message.

Even in her early days on the Hill, Margolies-Mezvinsky moved with an insider's skill. She avoided a big role in the early reform initiatives pushed by Democratic freshmen—some of which irritated powerful senior members. To learn the three-card-monte pitfalls of House floor procedure, she sat for regular tutorials with a parliamentary expert. She also won a seat on the powerful Energy and Commerce Committee. Her gender and tenuous political situation at home helped. So did signals to chairman John Dingell of Michigan, zealous guardian of the automotive industry, that she would cooperate on votes he considered crucial. "There are two or three issues of importance to Dingell, all of which travel on four wheels," says one veteran Hill staffer.

The Energy and Commerce slot also helped her with another priority—money. Its broad jurisdiction (including health care, telecommunications and finance) makes it a magnet for PAC contributions. Several days each month, Margolies-Mezvinsky journeys to a small office in the Eastern Market section of Washington and settles into an unadorned "call room" set up by Tom Erickson, her fundraising consultant. (Federal law bars members from soliciting contributions in their offices.) There she works the phone to build a 1994 war chest that will re- quire anywhere from $500,000 to $1 million for re-election. Margolies-Mezvinsky, who supports legislation to limit the influence of PACs, collected $105,000 in special-interest money in the first six months of 1993, the second highest total among House freshmen, according to the public-advocacy group Common Cause.

Her background gave her a significant edge over other freshmen. Before running she'd spent 15 years as a reporter for WRC, Washington's NBC affili-ate. Her husband is attorney Ed Mezvinsky, a former Iowa congressman and ex-chairman of the Pennsylvania Democratic Party. An appealing personal story also made her stand out: she is the mother, stepmother or legal guardian to 11 children and the sponsor for several refugee families. Her sprawling English Sussex house in Narberth, Pa., from which she commutes to Washington two nights each week, has evolved into a sort of multicultural Brady Bunch commune. Her ability to juggle home and work is legendary among friends. "She craves sleeping late," says Bethesda, Md., attorney Nancy Chasen.

Margolies-Mezvinsky practices her politics with a disarming and occasionally earthy personal style that melds Hillary Rodham Clinton with Joan Rivers. Most freshmen fall back on forgettable stock answers to questions about their expectations for life in Congress. She uses her own distinctive metaphor. "A doctor asked his medical-school class, 'What organ grows to eight times its normal size when properly stimulated?' " she told a not-all-that-comfortable Lower Merion Civic Association one evening last April. After a female student flushed with embarrassment, Margolies-Mezvinsky said, another answered that it's the iris of the eye as it adjusts from light to dark. The doctor turned back to the woman. " 'I'd like to tell you three things. First of all, you have a dirty mind; second, you didn't do your homework, and third, you have to seriously realign your expectations.' "

As August approached, Margolies-Mezvinsky's greatest expectation was that she could avoid saying "yes" to the White House. On the afternoon of the final budget vote on Aug. 5, she huddled with her staff to draft a statement explaining her "no" vote. They agreed that Clinton's budget only chipped away at discretionary spending and timidly avoided the real source of the deficit—entitlements. They decided to call for a "summit" on entitlement spending. It was a safe nonstarter, carrying the veneer of reform without the dangerous details: No one would take it seriously. Or would they?

"You're saying nobody has courage here," Smukler said. "OK, where would you cut?"

"Well, first I'd resign," she joked.

"Attack entitlements and you won't need to," quipped one aide.

Several hours later the White House called to collect the chit Margolies-Mezvinsky put on the table in May. The administration was still six votes down, said Deputy Treasury Secretary Roger Altman. She could expect to hear from the president. "We didn't want to do it, but we had to," said a senior White House official. She now faced a crucial question: what did she ask of Clinton in exchange for her vote? No conventional piece of pork was rich enough to rationalize this kind of switch. It had to be something that seemed to transcend politics as usual.

Minutes before the vote, she spoke to Clinton in an anteroom just off the House floor. She told him that if she was needed, she had two conditions: one was an entitlement summit. the other was that she be the 218th vote—the White House's sole margin of victory. The more dramatic the flip-flop, she reasoned, the more political cover she would have.

It was never certain who was 218, and it hardly mattered. The story line was clear: valiant freshman saves Clinton. Shortly before 10:30 p.m. she was at the well of the House, encircled by House Speaker Tom Foley and other anxious senior members. At 5 feet 4, she seemed lost in an old-growth forest of pols. She made the leap with Pat Williams, a Montana Democrat, filling out green-colored cards to record "yes" after the official 15-minute voting period had expired. In Fazio's office a few minutes later a friend, Rep. Jim McDermott of Washington, cursed the cowardice of senior members from safer districts who took a walk on Clinton. He hugged Margolies-Mezvinsky and said, "You made your mark."

She didn't get to sleep until after 3 a.m. When the "Today" show called at 5:30, she knew she'd woken up to a nightmare. An aide in one of her district offices

---

Margolies-Mezvinsky—April 22, 1993

8:30:	Meeting with health insurers from her district
9:30:	Arrives Longworth House Office Building
10:00:	Attends Energy and Commerce subcommittee hearing on radioband space. Leaves early and gives written queries to staff to be inserted into the record.
10:45:	Cab to dedication of the U.S. Holocaust Memorial Museum
1:15:	Meets with Defense Secretary Les Aspin and members of Pennsylvania congressional delegation to discuss military-base closures
1:45:	Meets with vice president of a pharmaceutical company in her district to discuss investment tax credits
2:00:	Talks with two constituents representing a gay lobbying group
2:15:	Congressional Women's Caucus
4:15:	Photo shoot for *Jewish Times*, a Philadelphia newspaper
4:35:	Cab to Union Station
6:50:	Arrives Philadelphia. Drives to evening meeting.
7:30:	Speech to Lower Merion Civic Association
10:00:	Home

---

argued with a profane caller. "She's not a prostitute! She's not a whore!" For hours Margolies-Mezvinsky's Washington and district staffs were virtually cut off as calls kept every line lit. Liberal voices like the *Philadelphia Inquirer* praised her courage, but weeklies in the district lambasted the switch. "Just another run-of-the-mill, cheap, soiled, ward-heeling politician whose word was not worth a spit stain in the street," wrote the *Independent & Montgomery Transcript*.

She launched a frantic attempt to contain the damage. She justified her flip-flop as a historic opportunity for an honest national debate on spending. A poll of district voters suggested that she faced a hard sell. Asked whether they supported cuts in entitlements, 64 percent said yes. But questioned about specific decreases in programs like social security or Medicare, 71 percent said no. Nearly 9 in 10 voters believed the deficit could be cut by eliminating waste.

"It cannot be done!" she said at one of two scalding town meetings in her district on Aug. 28. Even if all discretionary money disappeared from the budget, she explained, a new deficit would begin accumulating by 2003 because of entitlements. But residents were in no mood for statesmanship. "Here comes the liar," said one woman as Margolies-Mezvinsky arrived at one of the sessions.

Her reversal arguably *was* the right thing, even the courageous thing. A budget defeat would have instigated the kind of legislative gridlock congressional candidates in 1992 swore to eliminate. But Margolies-Mezvinsky's path to the vote was also an exercise in calculated contempt for her constituents. "No" was "no" as long as it was meaningless. When the White House was unable to maintain a congressional coalition for its budget without her support, the strategy collapsed and forced her reversal. In many voters' eyes, it left her looking craven and manipulative. "I have to tell you, I don't know if you can be trusted," Joseph Simone, a district businessman, told her on Aug. 28, "I don't hear a set of basic beliefs on which you can base a program."

But Margolies-Mezvinsky's cynicism also reflected the voters' own confusion. Their anger over her switch was real enough. But they also sent mixed messages about what they truly wanted. Focus groups of district residents, convened by Margolies-Mezvinsky's polltakers vented their disgust ("They all thought she'd bought herself an ambassadorship," says media consultant Joe Trippi). Yet they were also sympathetic to her dilemma—fulfilling a critical campaign promise or saving a new president from a devastating defeat. As troubled as group participants were by the changes offered by Clintonomics, there was a larger fear: no change at all. "Every single one said they feared a failed presidency," Trippi said.

If there's any good political news for Margolies-Mezvinsky, it's that her 1994 re-election prospects are only marginally worse than they were before Aug. 5. Her narrow victory put her at the top of the GOP's national hit list long before the vote. "The option was a very difficult re-election, or a very, very difficult re-election," says Smukler. She hopes that the entitlement conference—set for Dec. 13 at Bryn Mawr—will boost her chances. To re-establish her deficit-cutting credentials, she is also cosponsoring a package of $100 billion in new reductions put together by Reps. Tim Penny and John Kasich.

Sitting in her office early one evening in late September, she insisted that she had been honest with voters despite the gulf between her public rhetoric and her private political strategy. "Absolutely," she said. But she also acknowledged that the vicious reaction to her switch had diminished her enthusiasm for the job somewhat. "Part of the beauty of being a freshman in Congress is that you don't know what you can't do," she said. "And it becomes more apparent with each day that there are lots of things that are very, very difficult to do."

Summary Questions

1. Was Rep. Margolies-Mezvinsky right to break her promise to her constituents to "save" the Clinton budget package? Should one always vote in line with one's constituents, who may be ill informed, even on well-publicized issues? Does the legislator have an obligation to educate her constituents? Can she always?

2. Representatives Everett and McKinney reflect two sides of the contemporary South: conservative Republicans and liberal Democrats from black-dominated districts. What implications does this have for decision making in

Congress, where compromise and conciliation have frequently been the order of the day?

 10.3

The Changing Textbook Congress

Kenneth A. Shepsle

Ordinarily, it takes a while for political scientists to agree that a certain article is a "classic" piece of work. With Kenneth Shepsle's "The Changing Textbook Congress," however, the recognition came quickly and virtually universally. A most imaginative and provocative theorist, Shepsle places congressional developments of the 1960s through the 1980s in a context of an institution that has changed profoundly since scholars painted their definitive portrait of the Congress of the 1940s and 1950s.

As a theorist, one of Shepsle's chief interests lies in determining how institutional equilibrium, or balance among forces, is established. Committees dominated the earlier era's equilibrium, but since the 1960s committees have come under pressure from individual members, with their considerable staff and technology resources, and from party leaders, who have gained substantial powers through a series of reform efforts. Moreover, most House members must represent increasingly large and diverse districts, which makes coalition building all the more difficult.

Shepsle does not identify a clear contemporary equilibrium within the Congress. With large numbers of power centers and stronger individual members, we may be entering an era marked more by uncertainty and fluidity than by a well-defined equilibrium.

When scholars talk about Congress to one another, their students, or the public, they often have a stylized version in mind, a textbook Congress characterized by a few main tendencies and described in broad terms. This is not to say that they are incapable of filling in fine-grained detail, making distinctions, or describing change. But at the core of their descrip-

---

Kenneth A. Shepsle is professor of government at Harvard University.

tions and distinctions are approximations, caricatures, and generalities. They are always incomplete and somewhat inaccurate, but still they consist of robust regularities. . . .

The textbook Congress I have in mind is the one that emerged from World War II and the Legislative Reorganization Act of 1946. Its main features persisted until the mid-1960s; its images remained in writings on Congress well into the 1970s. . . .

To illuminate the institutional dynamics of the past forty years, this chapter describes some early signs of change in the textbook Congress in the 1950s, suggests how events of the 1960s and 1970s disrupted the equilibrium, and looks at some of the emerging features of a new textbook Congress, though I am not convinced that a new equilibrium has yet been established. The story I develop here is not a historical tour d'horizon [overview]. Rather it addresses theoretical issues of institutional development involving the capacity of Congress and its members to represent their constituencies, to make national policy, and to balance the intrinsic tensions between these tasks. . . .

The Textbook Congress: The Late 1940s to the Mid-1960s

Any portrait of Congress after World War II must begin with the member and, in a popular phrase of the time, "his work as he sees it." Then, as now, legislators divided their time between Washington and home, the relative proportions slowly changing in favor of Washington during the 1950s. In Washington they divided their time between chamber, committee, and personal office; all three demands grew from the 1940s to the 1960s as chamber work load, committee activity, and constituency demands increased.

In 1947, just after passage of the Legislative Reorganization Act, the average House member had three staff assistants and the average senator six. Because even these modest averages would be the envy of a contemporary member of the British Parliament or of most state legislatures, they indicate that by midcentury the American national legislature was a highly professional place. Nevertheless, by the mid-1960s congressional staffs had swelled even further: a typical House member now had twelve assistants and a typical senator eighteen. Committee staffs, too, grew dramatically from an average of ten to nearly thirty in the House and from fifteen to more than thirty in the Senate. These numbers do not include the substantial staffs of the nearly 400 offices of institutional leaders, informal groups, and legislative support agencies.

Since most committee staffers during these twenty years were in fact under the control of committee chairmen, some of the more senior legislators came to head sizable organizations. Indeed, if most legislators in the Eightieth Congress (1947–8) could be said to have headed mom 'n pop businesses with a handful of clerks and assistants, by the mid-1960s they had come to oversee major modern enterprises with secretaries, receptionists, interns, and a variety of legislative, administrative, and political professionals (typically lawyers). A committee chair or ranking minority member, who might also head a couple of subcommittees or party committees, might have a staff exceeding one hundred.

This growth transformed legislative life and work. In the 1940s the House had its norms and the Senate its folkways, perhaps even an inner club.* Hard work, long apprenticeship, restrained participation of younger members, specialization (particularly in the House), courtesy, reciprocity, and institutional loyalty characterized daily life in each chamber. Even if these norms of behavior were only suggestions, frequent contact among colleagues made them a reality. Undoubtedly, members who were neighbors in the same office building, who shared a committee assignment, or who traveled back and forth to Washington from the same state or region came to know each other exceedingly well. But even more distant relationships were based on familiarity and frequent formal or informal meeting.

By the mid-1960s this had all changed. The rubbing of elbows was replaced by liaisons between legislative corporate enterprises, typically at the staff level. Surrounded or protected by a bevy of clerks and assistants, members met other members only occasionally and briefly on the chamber floor or in committee meetings. And many of the norms supporting work and specialization eroded.

With limited time and resources, legislators of the 1940s and 1950s concentrated on only a few activities. They simply did not have the staffs or money to be able to involve themselves in a wide range of policy issues, manage a network of ombudsman activities back home, raise campaign finances, or intercede broadly and frequently in the executive branch's administration of programs. Rather, they picked their spots selectively and depended on jurisdictional decentralization and reciprocity among committees to divide the legislative labor, on the legislative party for voting cues inside the chamber, and on local party organizations for campaign resources and electioneering.

During the 1960s, as congressional offices gained staff and funding, members began to take on many new activities. Larger staffs in district offices, trips home, and franking privileges enabled them to develop a personal presence before their constituencies. This permitted them to orchestrate electioneering, polling, voter mobilization, and campaign finance activities themselves. They grew less dependent on organizations outside their own enterprises—local parties, for example—which previously performed such functions. The geographic constituency had, of course, always been important, but it had often been mediated by party, both local and national. By the mid-1960s the members' relationships with their constituencies were growing increasingly unmediated (just as the relationships between members were growing increasingly mediated). They were constant presences in their districts, had begun to develop personal followings, and consequently achieved a certain independence from their parties (and hence some

---

* The consensus view of the Senate of this era emphasized its dominance by a core of generally senior senators, who came disproportionately, but not exclusively, from the South.

insulation from party fortunes). As members made more trips home and allocated more staff to district offices and more Washington staff to constituency service and constituency-oriented legislation, calculations of how they would present themselves to the folks back home and explain their Washington activities took on added importance. Constituents' needs (the geographic imperative) began to compete with party as a guide to behavior.

Personal and institutional arrangements in Washington also changed. In the 1950s members, especially in the House, limited themselves to work on a few issues, determined to a considerable extent by their places in the committee system. Most members were able to land assignments to committees that were directly relevant to their constituencies. Much of their time, energy, and limited staff resources were devoted to work inside these little legislatures. By partitioning policy into committee jurisdictions, and matching member interests with those jurisdictions, legislative arrangements permitted members to get the most out of their limited resources. Aside from those with institutional ambitions, who hoped one day to be appointed to the Appropriations, Rules, or Ways and Means committees (Appropriations, Finance, Foreign Relations, or Armed Services in the Senate), most members had only limited incentives to become actively involved in policy areas outside their own assignments and were content to serve on legislative committees that had jurisdiction over the issues of central importance to their constituents. Thus, with limited means and incentives, members sustained a system of deference and reciprocity as part of the 1950s equilibrium, especially in the House.

Because of the growth of resources within their own enterprises in the 1960s, members began to acquire enhanced in-house capabilities. Deference to expert committee judgments on policy outside the jurisdiction of committees on which a member served was no longer so necessary. Members could now afford to assign some of their staff to track developments in other policy areas. The charge to the staffer became "Find something of interest for the boss, something that will help the district." Members were also no longer so dependent on party signals; with greater resources they were better able to determine their interests. In short, greater resources led to vertical integration—the absorption into the member enterprise of activities formerly conducted outside it—and with that, to member independence. Consequently, the relationship in which jurisdiction constrained both interest and activism began to fray as the 1960s came to an end.

Incentives for members to break away from the institutional niches in which they found themselves also multiplied. In both the 1960s and the 1970s, reapportionments,* along with economic and demographic changes, produced congressional districts that were neither so purely rural nor so purely urban

---

* The Constitution mandates reapportionment of House seats among the states every 10 years. This became especially significant in the 1960s and 1970s as the Supreme Court interpreted the Constitution to mean that districts should be drawn as equally in population as possible.

as they had been. Increasingly, the districts were mixed, often including a major city and a number of towns, as well as perhaps some rural areas. Member
interests began to reflect this heterogeneity. Issues were also evolving in ways that
cut across existing interest-group configurations and committee jurisdictions.
Except in a few cases, one or two major committee jurisdictions could no longer
encompass the interests of a district. Members thus had to diversify their portfo-
lios of legislative activities. And this meant less specialization, less deference,
less reciprocity.

Thus the limited resources and truncated policy interests characteristic of
House members and to a lesser extent members of the Senate in the 1940s and
1950s began to give way in the 1960s and 1970s. Increased member resources and
more diverse constituencies provided both the means and the incentives for
members to break out of a now restrictive division and specialization of labor.
Geographic imperatives were beginning to supersede considerations of party and
seniority to become the principal basis on which members defined their responsibilities and work habits. Geography was also beginning to threaten jurisdiction
as the principal basis on which the House organized its business.

These changes were less dramatic in the Senate only because it had traditionally been a much less specialized institution. Resources were more plentiful and
constituencies more heterogeneous than in the House. And because the Senate
was smaller, members had to have more diverse activities and interests. Yet even
in the Senate the pressure toward less specialization was growing. Entire states
were becoming more heterogeneous as a result of the industrialization of the
South, the switch to a service economy in the North, and the nationalization of
financial matters (so that even South Dakota could become a center for credit
activities). And senators, like their House counterparts, were expanding their
enterprises. By the end of the period the Senate, though less dramatically than
the House, was also a less specialized place.

The argument I am making here is that geography, jurisdiction, and party hang
together in a sort of equilibrium. The 1940s and 1950s represented one such
equilibrium in which local parties helped the members get elected and legislative
parties loosely coordinated committee activity. But the division of labor and
committee dominance of jurisdiction were the central features of the textbook
Congress. Committees both accommodated member needs and controlled agendas and decisionmaking. This arrangement "advantaged senior members, committees, and the majority party, with the chairmen of the standing committees
sitting at the intersection of these groups." More heterogeneous constituencies
and increased member resources upset this textbook equilibrium. Members have
adapted by voting themselves even more resources and expanding their activities.
By the 1970s parties both inside and outside the legislature had become considerably more submissive holding companies for member enterprises than had
earlier been the case. Committees, too, had changed character. . . .

Beginning with the 1958 elections, however, and continuing throughout
the 1960s, a new breed of legislator was coming to Washington, one more

committed to legislative activism and policy entrepreneurship than in the past, one beginning to reflect demographic changes, and, most important, one that found ways to stay in office. By the early 1970s these legislators had accumulated considerable seniority. Thus the old equilibrium was disrupted and the stage set for institutional developments that would strike at the heart of the textbook Congress.

The Changing Textbook Congress: The 1970s and 1980s

An idiosyncratic historical factor had an important bearing on the institutional reforms of the 1970s that undermined the textbook Congress. For much of the twentieth century the Democratic party in Congress spoke with a heavy southern accent. In 1948, for example, more than 53 percent of the Democrats in the House and nearly 56 percent of those in the Senate came from the eleven Confederate states and five border states (Kentucky, Maryland, Missouri, Oklahoma, and West Virginia). These states accounted for only a third of all House and Senate seats. Beginning with the 1958 landslide, however, this distribution changed. In 1960 the same sixteen states accounted for just under 50 percent of Democratically held House seats and 43 percent of Democratically held Senate seats. By 1982 the numbers had fallen to 40 percent and 39 percent respectively, and have held at that level. . . . Increasingly, Democrats were winning and holding seats in the North and West and, to a somewhat lesser extent, Republicans were becoming competitive in the South.

The nationalization of the Democratic coalition in Congress, however, was reflected far more slowly at the top of the seniority ladder.* Although between 1955 and 1967 the proportion of southern Democrats (border states excluded) in the House had dropped from 43 percent to 35 percent (46 percent to 28 percent in the Senate), the proportion of House committee chairs held by southerners fell from 63 percent to 50 percent, and rose from 53 percent to 56 percent in the Senate. Southerners held two of the three exclusive committee chairs in the House and two of the four in the Senate in 1955; in 1967 they held all of them.

The tension between liberal rank-and-file legislators and conservative southern committee chairs was important in the 1960s but had few institutional repercussions. True, Judge Howard Smith (Democrat of Virginia), the tyrannical chairman of the House Rules Committee, lost in a classic power struggle with Speaker Rayburn in 1961. But the defeat should not be exaggerated. Committees and their chairs maintained both the power to propose legislation and the power to block it in their respective jurisdictions. In 1967 southern Democrats George

---

* *Seniority* means the number of consecutive terms a legislator has served on a committee. The most senior majority-party member would automatically become chair of the committee. This practice was modified, but not eliminated, in the 1970s.

H. Mahon of Texas, William M. Colmer of Mississippi, and Wilbur D. Mills of Arkansas chaired the Appropriations, Rules, and Ways and Means committees, respectively, in a manner not very different from that of the incumbents a decade earlier. Although the massive legislative productivity of the Eighty-ninth Congress (1965–66) did much to relieve this tension, it relieved it not so much by changing legislative institutions as by managing to mobilize very large liberal majorities. After the 1966 elections, and with the Vietnam War consuming more and more resources and attention, the Eighty-ninth Congress increasingly seemed like a brief interlude in the committee dominance that stretched back to World War II, if not earlier.

By the end of the 1960s a Democratic president had been chased from office, and the 1968 Democratic convention revealed the tensions created by the war in Vietnam and disagreements over a range of domestic issues. Despite a Democratic landslide in 1964, Republican gains for the decade amounted to thirty-eight seats in the House and eight in the Senate, further accentuating the liberal cast of the Democratic rank and file in Congress. As the 1970s opened, then, liberal Democratic majorities in each chamber confronted a conservative president [Richard Nixon], conservative Republican minorities in each chamber, and often conservative southern committee chairmen of their own party who together blocked many of their legislative initiatives. The liberals thus turned inward, using the Democratic Caucus to effect dramatic changes in institutional practices, especially in the House.

The Age of Reform   Despite the tensions it caused, the mature committee system had many advantages. The division of labor in the House not only allowed for decisions based on expertise, but perhaps more important, it sorted out and routinized congressional careers. Committees provided opportunities for political ambitions to be realized, and they did so in a manner that encouraged members to invest in committee careers. In an undifferentiated legislature, or in a committee-based legislature in which the durability of a committee career or the prospects for a committee leadership post depended on the wishes and whims of powerful party leaders (for example, the Speaker in the nineteenth century House), individual legislators have less incentive to invest effort in committee activities. Such investments are put at risk every time the political environment changes. Specialization and careerism are encouraged, however, when rewards depend primarily on individual effort (and luck), and not on the interventions and patronage of others. An important by-product is the encouragement given talented men and women to come to the legislature and to remain there. The slow predictability of career development under a seniority system may repel the impatient, but its inexorability places limits on risks by reducing a member's dependence on arbitrary power and unexpected events.

Even Voltaire's optimistic Dr. Pangloss, however, would recognize another side to this coin. When a committee system that links geography and jurisdiction through the assignment process is combined with an institutional bargain producing deference and reciprocity, it provides the foundation for the distributive politics of interest-group liberalism. But there are no guarantees of success. The legislative process is full of hurdles and veto groups, and occasionally they restrain legislative activism enough to stimulate a reaction. Thus in the 1950s, authorizing committees, frustrated by a stingy House Appropriations Committee, created entitlements as a means of circumventing the normal appropriations process. In the 1960s the Rules Committee became the major obstacle and it, too, was tamed. In the 1970s the Ways and Means Committee, which lacked an internal division of labor through subcommittees, bottled up many significant legislative proposals; it was dealt with by the Subcommittee Bill of Rights and the Committee Reform Amendments of 1974. The solution in the 1950s had no effect on legislative arrangements. The solution in the 1960s entailed modest structural reform that directly affected only one committee. In the 1970s, however, the committee system itself became the object of tinkering.

The decade of the 1970s was truly an age of legislative reform. In effect, it witnessed a representational revolt against a system that dramatically skewed rewards toward the old and senior who were often out of step with fellow partisans. It is a long story, admirably told in detail elsewhere. Here I shall focus on the way reforms enabled the rise of four power centers that competed, and continue to compete, with the standing committees for political influence.

First, full committees and their chairs steadily lost power to their subcommittees. At least since the Legislative Reorganization Act of 1946, subcommittees have been a significant structural element of the committee system in the House. However, until the 1970s they were principally a tool of senior committee members, especially committee chairmen, who typically determined subcommittee structure, named members, assigned bills, allocated staff resources, and orchestrated the timing and sequence in which the full committee would take up their proposals and forward them to the floor. Because the structures were determined idiosyncratically by individual chairmen, committees could be very different. Ways and Means had no subcommittees. Armed Services had numbered subcommittees with no fixed jurisdictions. Appropriations had rigidly arranged subcommittees. In almost all cases the chairman called the tune, despite an occasional committee revolt.

During the 1970s a series of reforms whittled away at the powers of the committee chairmen. In 1970 chairmen began to lose some control of their agendas. They could no longer refuse to call meetings; a committee majority could vote to meet anyway with the ranking majority member presiding. Once a rule had been granted for floor consideration of a bill, the chairman could not delay consideration for more than a week; after seven days, a committee majority could move floor consideration.

In 1973 the Democratic members of a House committee were designated as the committee caucus and empowered to choose subcommittee chairs and set subcommittee budgets. During the next two years, committees developed a procedure that allowed members, in order of committee seniority, to bid for subcommittee chairmanships. Also in 1973 the Democratic Caucus passed the Subcommittee Bill of Rights, which mandated that legislation be referred to subcommittees, that subcommittees have full control over their own agendas, and that they be provided with adequate staff and budget. In 1974 the Committee Reform Amendments required that full committees (Budget and Rules excepted) establish at least four subcommittees, an implicit strike against the undifferentiated structure of Ways and Means. In 1976 committee caucuses were given the authority to determine the number of subcommittees and their respective jurisdictions. Finally, in 1977 the selection procedure for committee chairs was changed, allowing the party caucus to elect them by secret ballot.

Full committees and their chairs thus had had their wings clipped. A chair was now beholden to the committee caucus, power had devolved upon subcommittees, and standing committees were rapidly becoming holding companies for their subunits.

Another center of power was created by the growth of member resources. Through House Resolution 5 and Senate Resolution 60, members were able to tap into committee and subcommittee budgets to hire staff to conduct their committee work. Additional resources were available for travel and office support. Budgets for congressional support agencies such as the General Accounting Office, the Congressional Research Service, and the Office of Technology Assessment, which individual members could employ for specific projects, also increased enormously. In short, member enterprises were becoming increasingly self-sufficient.

Committee power was also compromised by increased voting and amendment activity on the floor. The early 1970s marked the virtual end to anonymous floor votes. The secret ballot was never used in floor votes in the House, but voice votes, division votes, and unrecorded teller votes had allowed tallies to be detached from the identity of individual members. This changed as it became increasingly easy to demand a public roll call, a demand greatly facilitated by the advent of electronic voting in 1973. Roll call votes in turn stimulated amendment activity on the floor. In effect, full committees and their chairs, robbed of some of their control of agendas by subcommittees, were now robbed of more control by this change in floor procedure.

Floor activity was further stimulated by the declining frequency with which the Rules Committee was permitted to issue closed rules, which barred floor amendments to legislation. The specific occasion for this change was the debate on retaining the oil depletion allowance. Because this tax break was protected by the Ways and Means Committee, on which the oil-producing states were well represented, efforts to change the policy could only come about through floor amendments. But Ways and Means bills traditionally were protected by a closed rule. The Democratic Caucus devised a policy in which a caucus majority could instruct its members on the Rules Committee to vote specific amendments in order. Applying this strategy to the oil depletion allowance, the caucus in effect ended the tradition of closed-rule protection of committee bills. This encouraged floor amendments and at the same time reduced committee control over final legislation. It also encouraged committees to anticipate floor behavior more carefully when they marked up a bill.

Finally, committee dominance was challenged by the increased power of the Democratic Caucus and the Speaker. For all the delegation of committee operations to subcommittees and individual members, the changes in the congressional landscape were not all of one piece. In particular, before the 1970s the Democratic Caucus was a moribund organization primarily concerned with electing officers and attending to the final stages of committee assignments. After these activities were completed in the first few days of a new Congress, the caucus was rarely heard from. In the 1970s, however, as committees and chairmen were being undermined by subcommittees, there was a parallel movement to strengthen central party leadership and rank-and-file participation.

The first breach came in the seniority system. In 1971 the Democratic Caucus relieved its Committee on Committees—the Democratic members of the Ways and Means Committee—of having to rely on seniority in nominating committee chairs. This had the effect of putting sitting chairs on notice, although none was threatened ar the time. In 1974 it became possible for a small number of caucus members to force individual votes on nominees for chairs and later to vote by secret ballot. In 1975 the caucus took upon itself the right to vote on subcommittee chairs of the Appropriations Committee. In that same year three incumbent chairmen were denied reelection to their posts (a fourth, Wilbur Mills, resigned under pressure).

Next came the democratizing reforms. Members were limited in the number of committee and subcommittee berths they could occupy and the number they could chair. As the constraints became more binding, it was necessary to move further down the ladder of seniority to fill positions. Power thus became more broadly distributed.

But perhaps the most significant reforms were those that strengthened the Speaker and made the position accountable to the caucus. In 1973 House party leaders (Speaker, majority leader, and whip) were included on the Committee on Committees, giving them an increased say in committee assignments. The caucus also established the Steering and Policy Committee with the Speaker as chair. In 1974 Democratic committee assignments were taken away from the party's complement on Ways and Means and given to the new committee. In addition, the Speaker was given the power to appoint and remove a majority of the members of the committee and the Democratic members of the Rules Committee. In 1974 the Speaker also was empowered to refer bills simultaneously or sequentially to several committees, to create ad hoc committees, and, in 1977, to set time limits for their deliberations. Finally, in 1977 Speaker Thomas P. O'Neill started employing task forces to develop and manage particular policy issues. These task forces overlapped but were not coincident with the committees of jurisdiction and, most significant, they were appointed by the Speaker.

The caucus itself became more powerful. As mentioned, caucus majorities could instruct the Rules Committee and elect committee chairs and Appropriations subcommittee chairs. Caucus meetings could be called easily, requiring only a small number of signatories to a request, so that party matters could be thoroughly aired. In effect, the caucus became a substitute arena for both the floor and the committee rooms in which issues could be joined and majorities mobilized.

The revolt of the 1970s thus strengthened four power centers. It liberated members and subcommittees, restored to the Speakership an authority it had not known since the days of Joe Cannon,* and invigorated the party caucus. Some of the reforms had a decentralizing effect, some a recentralizing effect. Standing committees and their chairs were caught in the middle. Geography and party benefited; the division-of-labor jurisdictions were its victims. . . .

A New Textbook Congress?

The textbook Congress of the 1940s and 1950s reflected an equilibrium of sorts among institutional structure, partisan alignments, and electoral forces. There was a "conspiracy" between jurisdiction and geography. Congressional institutions were organized around policy jurisdictions, and geographic forces were accommodated through an assignment process that ensured representatives would land berths on committees important to their constituents. Reciprocity and deference sealed the bargain. Committees controlled policy formation in their respective jurisdictions. Floor activity was generally dominated by members from the committee of jurisdiction. Members' resources were sufficiently modest that they were devoted chiefly to committee-related activities. Constituencies were sufficiently homogeneous that this limitation did not, for most members, impose much hardship. Coordination was accomplished by senior committee members, each minding his own store. This system was supported by a structure that rewarded specialization, hard work, and waiting one's turn in the queue. Parties hovered in the background as the institutional means for organizing each chamber and electing leaders. Occasionally they would serve to mobilize majorities for partisan objectives, but these occasions were rare. The parties, especially the Democrats, were heterogeneous holding companies, incapable of cohering around specific policy directions except under unusual circumstances and therefore unwilling to empower their respective leaders or caucuses.

Something happened in the 1960s. The election of an executive and a congressional majority from the same party certainly was one important feature. Policy

---

* Rep. Joseph Cannon (R-Ill.) served as Speaker from 1903 to 1911. His power in this office was successfully challenged by a coalition of Democrats and dissident Republicans in 1910.

activism, restrained since the end of World War II, was encouraged. This exacerbated some divisions inside the Democratic coalition, leading to piecemeal institutional tinkering such as the expansion of the Rules Committee and the circumvention of the Appropriations Committee. At the same time the Voting Rights Act, occasioned by the temporarily oversized condition of the majority party in the Eighty-ninth Congress, set into motion political events that, together with demographic and economic trends, altered political alignments in the South. By the 1980s, Democrats from the North and the South were coming into greater agreement on matters of policy.

Thus the underlying conditions supporting the equilibrium among geographical, jurisdictional, and partisan imperatives were overwhelmed during the 1960s. The 1970s witnessed adjustments to these changed conditions that transformed the textbook Congress. Institutional reform was initiated by the Democratic Caucus. Demographic, generational, and political trends, frustrated by the inexorable workings of the seniority system, sought an alternative mode of expression. Majorities in the caucus remade the committee system. With this victimization came less emphasis on specialization, less deference toward committees as the floor became a genuine forum for policy formulation, and a general fraying of the division of labor.

One trend began with the Legislative Reorganization Act of 1946 itself. In the past forty years members have gradually acquired the resources to free themselves from other institutional players. The condition of the contemporary member of Congress has been described as "atomistic individualism" and the members themselves have been called "enterprises." The slow accretion of resources permitted members to respond to the changes in their home districts and encouraged them to cross the boundaries of specialization. These developments began to erode the reciprocity, deference, and division of labor that defined the textbook Congress.

The old equilibrium between geography and jurisdiction, with party hovering in the background, has changed. Geography (as represented by resource-rich member enterprises) has undermined the strictures of jurisdiction. But has the new order liberated party from its former holding-company status? In terms of political power the Democratic Caucus has reached new heights in the past decade. Party leaders have not had so many institutional tools and resources since the days of Boss Cannon. Committee leaders have never in the modern era been weaker or more beholden to party institutions. And, in terms of voting behavior, Democrats and Republicans have not exhibited as much internal cohesion in a good long while. Party, it would seem, is on the rise. But so, too, are the member enterprises.

What, then, has grown up in the vacuum created by the demise of the textbook Congress? I am not convinced that relationships have settled into a regular pattern in anything like the way they were institutionalized in the textbook Congress.

First, too many members of Congress remain too dissatisfied. The aggressive moves by Jim Wright* to redefine the Speaker's role are a partial response to this circumstance. Prospective changes in the Senate majority party leadership alignment in the 101st Congress convey a similar signal. The issue at stake is whether central party organs can credibly coordinate activities in Congress, thereby damping the centrifugal tendencies of resource-rich members, or whether leaders will remain, in one scholar's words, "janitors for an untidy chamber."

One possible equilibrium of a new textbook Congress, therefore, would have member enterprises balanced off against party leaders; committees and other manifestations of a specialized division of labor would be relegated to the background. Coordination, formerly achieved in a piecemeal, decentralized fashion by the committee system, would fall heavily on party leaders and their institutional allies, the Rules and Budget committees and the party caucuses. However, unless party leaders can construct a solution to the budgetary mess in Congress—a solution that will entail revising the budget process—the burden of coordination will be more than the leaders can bear. Government by continuing resolutions, reconciliation proposals, and other omnibus mechanisms forms an unstable fulcrum for institutional equilibrium.†

Second, any success from the continued strengthening of leadership resources and institutions is highly contingent on the support of the members. Strong leadership institutions have to be seen by the rank and file as solutions to institutional problems. This requires a consensus among majority party members both on the nature of the problems and the desirability of the solutions. A consensus of sorts has existed for several years: demographic and other trends have homogenized the priorities of Democrats; experience with the spate of reforms in the 1970s has convinced many that decentralized ways of doing things severely tax the capacity of Congress to act; and, since 1982, the Reagan presidency has provided a unifying target.

But what happens if the bases for consensus erode? A major issue—trade and currency problems, for instance, or war in Central America or the Middle East—could set region against region within the majority party and reverse the trend toward consensus. Alternatively, the election of a Democratic president could redefine the roles of legislative leaders, possibly pitting congressional and presidential factions against one another in a battle for partisan leadership.‡ The point here is that the equilibrium between strong leaders and strong members is vulnerable to perturbations in the circumstances supporting it.

---

* Jim Wright was Speaker from 1987 to 1989.

† *Reconciliation proposals* and *continuing resolutions* are budget-related bills that often combine many subjects in a catch-all (or omnibus) piece of legislation. Control by committees or other specialized groupings is rendered difficult by such practices.

‡ As of 1994, that has not happened much in the Clinton Administration, although House Democratic Whip Rep. David Bonior did lead the opposition to the Clinton-backed North American Free Trade Agreement in 1993.

. . . The member enterprises, however, will not go away. Members will never again be as specialized, as deferential, as willing "to go along to get along" as in the textbook Congress of the 1950s. For better or worse, we are stuck with full-service members of Congress. They are incredibly competent at representing the diverse interests that geographic representation has given them. But can they pass a bill or mobilize a coalition? Can they govern?

Summary Questions

1. How did the seniority system, which rewarded simple longevity rather than talent or political support, survive for so long? What are the advantages of promoting leaders based on seniority? The liabilities?
2. Reflect back on Reps. Everett, McKinney, and Margolies-Mezvinsky, from selection 10.2. In what ways are they part of the changing equilibrium of Congress? What role does the president play in this mix?

 10.4

Can Congress Govern?

Catherine E. Rudder

In this brief article, Catherine Rudder harks back to the themes of congressional unpopularity, membership turnover, the capacity to legislate, and the relations between the president and Congress that have been raised by the previous authors. She goes on to ask the central question: "Can Congress Govern?" Although she is scarcely the fount of optimism here, the ultimate message is clear: Congress should be able to govern, albeit cooperatively with the president. Congressional parties offer the possibility of providing coherent leadership without "muffling the voices of the rank and file."

Bringing us full circle from Polsby's discussion of "Congress-bashing," Rudder calls for greater public understanding of policy making, so that those we have elected may actually have the opportunity to govern, rather than simply occupy

Catherine E. Rudder is executive director of the American Political Science Association.

elective positions. It may well be the legislators themselves who will have to pull back from negative politicking and provide more insight into what the Congress can do in fashioning responsible, accountable policies. In the end, Rudder's prescriptions may be too much for an individualistic, partisan Congress to swallow. If that's the case, the branch of government closest to the people may cede its governing authority to the president, bureaucracy, the unelected judiciary, the clamoring interest groups, and the increasingly cynical media.

I t is ironic that Americans hold their national governing institutions, especially "the people's branch," in such low regard at a time when emerging democracies are striving to emulate those very institutions. U.S. citizens' contempt for Congress can be traced to four sources of varying degrees of seriousness and treatability. These include scandals in Congress, the poor performance of the economy, the policy performance of Congress and the president, and the public's lack of understanding of what Congress does.

The Public's Disenchantment with Congress

The most notable but least important source of contempt is scandal, a concept whose definition varies with time and place. In the contemporary Congress scandals range from poor ethical judgment of members to doubtful institutional practices. For example, in 1986 five senators allegedly gave preferential treatment to major campaign contributor and subsequent felon Charles H. Keating, Jr. One of the five, as chair of the Banking, Housing, and Urban Affairs Committee, was especially well situated to intimidate federal regulators overseeing Keating's activities. Another senator, Brock Adams, D-Wash., was accused of sexual improprieties and declined to run for reelection in 1992. Yet another David Durenberger, R-Minn., claimed questionable reimbursements and is reported to be under criminal investigation. The all-male Senate Judiciary Committee put on a salacious, unseemly spectacle in the 1991 Supreme Court confirmation hearings of Clarence Thomas and in the process gave the impression of institutional degradation.

Other recent scandals have included a poorly managed and perhaps pilfering House post office; a House restaurant that tolerated deadbeats; a House "bank" (more properly, a cooperative holding station for members' deposits) that allowed overdrafts without penalty; a congressional pay raise passed on the sly; exemptions for members from employment and workplace rules such as civil rights and safety laws; and a variety of longstanding perquisites for representatives and senators—such as free prescription medicine, cheap haircuts, and reserved parking spaces at Washington, D.C., airports—that were once generally accepted privileges of office.

These practices have come to be seen by the public as symptomatic of a Congress that has lost touch with those whom it represents. With reelection rates as high as 98 percent in the House, members have become, many have thought, removed from their electorates. Even if this analysis were correct, it does not get to the heart of the matter. (If anything, members of Congress are too responsive to their constituents' short-term, immediate interests—if not to their sensitivities—to legislate wisely, and those reelection rates support such a contention.)

Many of these problems, once they are defined as problems and exposed, are in effect self-correcting. The House bank has been closed. The House post office and other functions will be professionally run (and indictments have been handed down in the case of the post office). A record number of well-funded women ran competitive races for the Senate and House in 1992, with the result that 11 percent of the members of the House in the 103d Congress will be women—up from 7 percent (twenty-nine) in the 102d Congress—and that women's numbers in the Senate will rise from three to six.[1] The number of House incumbents defeated in primaries (nineteen) reached a post-World War II high in 1992, as did the number of voluntary retirements from the House. Almost one-quarter of the members of the 103d Congress will be new members. Perquisites are under review and are being curtailed. Term limits are not required to create turnover in Congress. A free, energetic press; competitive elections; and a mildly attentive public are.

A second reason for the public's disenchantment with Congress stems from the poor performance of the economy. Although in a technical sense the current recession has not been as severe as the one in 1982 (after which the United States experienced enormous economic prosperity), the recent downturn has been more protracted and has affected more white-collar workers. Moreover, the prosperity of the 1980s was not evenly shared: household incomes of the most wealthy one-fifth of the population soared, while those of the bottom one-fifth fell. Middle-class incomes—despite more workers per household—stayed about even.[2] If the economy were to improve, so would assessments of Congress.

A third reason stems from the policy performance of Congress and the president. Even when the government is divided by party, with a Republican in the White House and a Democratic majority in the House and Senate, the fortunes of the two branches are tied by whether they are producing public policy—although the public holds the president more accountable for program success than it does Congress.[3] From the congressional perspective, if the president does not set priorities and push for them effectively, and if he systematically vetoes legislation that Congress manages to conjure up on its own, he undermines Congress's reputation and its ability to govern.

Finally, even without scandals and with a booming economy and legislative accomplishment, Congress as an institution would probably be held in low esteem by the American public. Citizens, although they may like their own representative, do not appreciate what Congress does or understand the enormity of the tasks before it. This ignorance of both theory and process does not obviate the concern that the modern Congress may not be up to the task of governing; hence, the popularity of dubious constitutional amendments to tinker with the structure. This lack of public understanding may, however, reflect poorly on the civic education of Americans, the quality of congressional press coverage and attention to it, and the willingness of elected officials to perform their educative functions.

In sum, the cause of low public regard most amenable to treatment but least important to the ability of Congress to govern is scandal. It is, in fact, self-correcting under our system of government. Least controllable is the economy. In between are policy performance and public understanding. It is to these last two matters that this essay is addressed.

The Issues Confronting Congress

. . . [T]he most pressing issues that national lawmakers face are difficult domestic problems. These include the short-run and long-term need to strengthen the economy, to make an effective transition to a peacetime economy, and to reduce unemployment without triggering inflation or raising interest rates significantly. This difficult task is made more difficult by the quadrupling of the national debt since 1980, created by yearly deficits that absorb about 15 percent of annual federal spending. Thus the staggering size of the federal deficit not only constrains government's ability to use fiscal stimuli without causing other economic damage but it also uses up money that could be applied to employment and investment programs.

To the degree that yearly deficits (if not the overall, cumulated debt) are to be reduced, programs will have to be cut, not expanded, and taxes will have to be raised—a prescription opposite to what is needed if short-run economic problems are to be addressed. To the degree that a high-wage economy is to be created, spending for education, training, research, development, and infrastructure will have to be increased, not decreased as a deficit-reduction program would require. To the extent that the government is to have a role in resolving social problems such as crime, drugs, homelessness, deteriorating cities, and rising epidemics (including tuberculosis and AIDS), more, not less spending is needed.

These choices are not easy ones, nor is the proper course obvious. Furthermore, the nation has not reached a consensus as to which route to take. Similarly unpleasant trade-offs await the country in the areas of health care, energy consumption, and environmental protection. If not intractable, the problems confronting national lawmakers are daunting. Citizens have reason to believe that national governing institutions are not up to the task. This pessimism stems from a suspicion that modern problems are not amenable to democratic solutions, at least as American institutions have been designed and developed.

Paralyzing Forces　Under the American system of shared powers, creating and maintaining majorities has always been difficult. For a variety of reasons, the challenge seems to have grown in modern times.

Divided government. In the post-World War II period, divided government has become as much the norm as unified party control. The inherent conflict between institutions—between the executive branch and Congress and from 1981 to 1987 between the House and the Senate—is exacerbated by the overlapping cleavage of party. If Congress and the president have reasons to disagree, Democrats and Republicans certainly do. To sharpen party distinctions in the mind of the public and thus to try to create electoral advantage, parties have an incentive not to come to agreement on legislative matters unless there is some overriding reason for them to do so. According to this line of reasoning, governing is made that much more difficult by the increasingly common phenomenon of divided government.

This argument is vulnerable on two grounds, that of empirical evidence comparing policy performance under periods of divided and party government and that of research demonstrating the decline in importance of party in the electorate. In an already classic work, *Divided We Govern*, David R. Mayhew examines major legislation from 1946 through 1990 and finds that divided government makes little or no difference in the amount of important legislation enacted.[4]

Thus divided government does not necessarily produce more deadlock than unified government does. The Tax Reduction Act and the Omnibus Budget Reconciliation Act of 1981, the Social Security Amendments of 1983, the budget acts of 1982 and 1984, the Tax Reform Act of 1986, the Clean Air Act of 1990, and the Budget Enforcement Act of 1990 were all enacted under divided government.

Party division between institutions does, however, present a serious strategic choice, the outcome of which can lead to low legislative productivity. Party leaders can decide it is to their electoral advantage not to cooperate and to try to make the other party seem the villain. The president can decide not to present a realistic budget or not to set much of an agenda. He can decide not to compromise or not to bargain. He can veto major legislation. Like the Republican minority in Congress, the Democratic majority, for its part, must decide whether it is an opposition party or part of the governing coalition.[5]

Part of the complaint about divided government, however, is that it encourages dishonesty and destructive collusion, not just deadlock. To gain partisan advantage, the president may present a budget based on overoptimistic economic estimates in order to reduce the apparent need for painful tax increases or spending cuts. The more Congress is honest in its economic estimates, the more pain it will have to inflict on the American public. Not wanting to suffer the blame for tax increases or spending cuts that the president refuses to propose, Congress has an incentive to go along with the president's faulty estimates.[6]

A similar pattern can be seen in the proceedings leading to the Tax Reduction Act of 1981. These discussions degenerated into a bidding war and caused huge losses to the federal Treasury, much greater than President Reagan had originally proposed and greater than most disinterested observers felt could be justified—all to garner credit for being the most friendly to specific interests and to the

American taxpayer. Other examples of collusion include the savings and loan deregulation of 1982 (and the subsequent underwriting of that industry by the government) and the unwillingness or inability of the Republican president or the Democratic majority in Congress to curtail leveraged buyouts by altering tax incentives. Billions of federal dollars are being spent to guarantee the savings of Americans after the reckless behavior of savings and loan institutions, and tens of thousands of jobs are lost as companies are dismantled after buyouts. Yet neither party can be held responsible for either outcome. Because both parties are culpable, citizens have no party to vote for in protest of policies that many voters consider ill-conceived.[7]

This kind of party cooperation contributes to the low esteem in which Congress is held and to the anti-incumbency mood of the electorate. Thus Mayhew's analysis does not answer the less frequently articulated, but nevertheless serious, complaint about divided government—that it contributes to unaccountability and irresponsibility. His work does show that even when different parties control different branches of the government, important legislation can be enacted, not all of which, it should be added, is irresponsible.

Campaigns and elections. Evidence pointing to legislative performance under divided government is not the only reason to question the sufficiency of the deadlock thesis. To blame party conflict for the inability of Congress to act perhaps misses a major, but probably overstated, political development of our time—namely, the decline of party in the electorate and the emergence of the independent politician barely more than nominally connected to his or her party. This development complicates the task of governing and is contrary to the idea that the two parties are phalanxes locked in deadly combat.

The litany is familiar: Parties do not control who their nominees are; party organization at the local level has all but vanished; candidates create and maintain their own electoral organizations; many candidates shun their party label, raise their own money, get elected on their own, and owe little loyalty to their party. For their part, electorates are less strongly attached to parties than ever. They split their tickets and base their voting decisions more on candidates and candidate image than on party preference.[8] An attenuated connection to party means greater reliance on thirty-second advertisements and on episodic and noncontextual news reports.[9] The public becomes more volatile, less predictable, less reliable, and more susceptible to hit-and-run, negative attack campaign strategies.

If one were to extrapolate from these facts exclusively, the question whether Congress can govern must be answered in the negative. Members of such a Congress would not necessarily have anything in common and would have no apparent reason to work together. Members would act atomistically. There would be nothing to bring them together. The fortunes of Congress and the president, even if they were of the same party, would be disconnected.

Under such a system, it should be added, deadlock would be likely, absent other sources of coercion, but such inaction would be born of anarchy, not of divided party government. Furthermore, in such circumstances members not given to political suicide would have little inclination to cast public votes for painful policies that might be in the best long-run interests of the country.

Fortunately, the two parties bring about some cohesion. Difficult votes are cast. Still, candidate-centered campaigns and elections do weaken the ability of each party to create ongoing governing coalitions,[10] especially ones that can deal with problems involving unpleasant choices.

Congressional reforms.   The decentralizing effects of the congressional reforms of the 1970s, like the effects of the rise of the independent candidate, have perhaps been overstated, but they have in fact made governing more difficult. Ordinary members are more important than their counterparts were two decades ago. Committee chairs are less independent, they must pay more attention to the committee members of their party, and they must share their power with subcommittee chairs. This erosion of centralized power can, however, strengthen American democracy by giving voice to diverse constituencies and by reining in the exercise of arbitrary, dictatorial chairs. For Congress to govern, there must be a way of bringing these voices together rather than silencing them, as was the tendency before the reforms.

Thus, although creating majorities for legislation has never been easy, it is much more complicated now than previously. It is also worth noting that many of the elements that assisted action in the past are the same today. For Congress to retain its legitimacy, however, reforms were necessary, and, as will be apparent, several of the reforms provide Congress with the basis from which to govern accountably and responsibly.

Interest groups.   If divided government, independent politicians, and decentralizing congressional reforms are not sufficient impediments to policy performance by Congress, the sway that interest groups hold over Congress may be. Through their political action committees these organizations provide members with a large share of the campaign funds needed to wage expensive media campaigns. Such groups can often command voters' support, and they can threaten to generate election opposition. Because they control resources that members need, they gain access and members' attention.

Given the broad range and number of groups, one could reasonably argue that they represent the legitimate organization of interests in a free society. The problem such groups pose, however, is that many exist to protect the status quo—making such changes as health care reform or budget cuts very difficult propositions—and they are barriers to legislators' addressing virtually "constituentless" issues (such as deficit reduction, the poverty of 20 percent of the country's children, and other concerns representing "a diffuse, ill-organized interest") as opposed to "particularistic, well-organized, putatively very powerful interests."[11]

In short, the very issues facing Congress today, offering difficult choices and possibly painful results for some or all segments of the population, are those on which entrenched interest groups are most likely to obstruct action. Like the other barriers, however, this one is not impossible to scale, nor is it wholly negative.

How members spend their time. Not only has much of the American public given up on Congress, but so have many sitting members. A record number of representatives declined to run for reelection in 1992,* many expressing frustration with the system in which they found themselves. The complaints varied and were not new. Still, the inability of Congress to deliberate and legislate is a common concern. An important source of that inability is the amount of time members must spend, year-round, raising money for their next reelection campaign. The system of campaign finance distorts the legislative product here if nowhere else.

Countervailing Forces Although the constitutional structure makes enacting legislation difficult in any circumstances, modern developments—from the increasing frequency of divided government to the effects of some of the congressional reforms—heightens the challenge. The nature of the issues and the lack of consensus among the public, appropriately reflected in Congress, are complicating factors as well. Nevertheless, divided government does not necessarily lead to deadlock, nor is divided government always the case. Moreover, forces that paralyze action or lead to irresponsible collusion can be and sometimes are countervailed.

Presidential leadership. In study after study, legislative performance has been found to be dependent on the willingness of the president to set an agenda, to work for that agenda, to compromise, and to stay engaged in the process.[12] Congress must be willing to engage in negotiation as well.

It is true that a forceful congressional leader, such as former Speaker Jim Wright, D-Texas, can set out and effectively pursue his own agenda,[13] and Congress sometimes initiates action, as it did with the 1982 and 1984 budget acts. The president, however, can provide a sustained focus, can command the attention of the mass media, can reasonably claim to represent the nation, and can explain to the public the need for particular legislation in a way that Congress cannot.

Congressional parties and leaders. Far from describing the atomistic Congress of each member looking out for himself, David Rohde has documented the increasing degree to which roll call votes in the House, and to a lesser extent in the Senate, are divided along party lines.[14] Congressional reforms and changes in the party within the electorate account for this cohesion.

Specifically, although politicians may run candidate-centered campaigns they are still attached to a party. Thanks to the Voting Rights Act and the party realignment that has taken place in the South, Democrats are more similar in their constituencies and policy preferences than they were when southern Democrats were apt to vote with Republicans. By the 1980s the party caucuses had become more homogeneous. This wider difference between the congressional parties and greater similarity within them has resulted in "conditional party

---

* This pattern of substantial voluntary retirement continued in 1994, for both House and Senate.

government"—that is, a somewhat stable, continuous governing coalition.[15] The congressional parties can act as parties and by implication can be held account-able for what they do.

Congressional reforms have contributed to party coherence as well. It is true that the rank and file gained influence after changes in rules were instituted in the 1970s and that consequently party leaders must pay close attention to the needs and preferences of their members. The reforms, however, also strengthened the powers of leaders and the majority party. For example, the establishment of the Democratic Steering and Policy Committee—half elected and half controlled by the leadership—has the power to make Democratic committee assignments and to recommend actions concerning scheduling of legislation, legislative priorities, and party policy. Other reforms gave the Speaker the power to appoint the chair and Democratic members of the Rules Committee, with the concurrence of the caucus; to refer bills to multiple committees; and to set deadlines for committee action on legislation. An expansion of the whip system increased the likelihood that Democrats would vote together. The reforms strengthened not only the leadership but also the Democratic Caucus and caucuses within committees. As Rohde explains, the reforms help to "foster collective control."[16]

Speakers have varied in the extent to which they have used their powers to provide their congressional party with forceful leadership. Even Speaker Wright, who perhaps has most effectively exploited those powers to push a legislative agenda, saw his role as no more than "a hunting license to persuade."[17] The reforms require extensive consultation on the part of successful party leaders with their members. Leadership tools, however, must be used if they are to result in congressional policy performance. Taken together, the reforms provide Congress with a basis on which to govern—namely, through the majority party guided by forceful, consultative leadership.

Trumping interest groups. With the exercise of presidential leadership and the new coherence of the majority party in Congress, interest groups need not stymie the legislative process. On those occasions in which there is only a diffuse public interest on one side and well-defined interest groups lined up on the other, Martha Derthick and Paul Quirk and Randall Strahan have demonstrated that organized opposition can be overcome with the right combination of factors; among them are the development of consensus of elite opinion on an issue and the exercise of leadership by officials.[18] Alternatively, as Richard Cohen makes clear in his case study of the Clean Air Act, interest groups can be brought directly into the process and decent legislation can emerge.[19]

Public understanding. Despite the success of the Clean Air Act, the public was excluded from the process, though, ironically, its interests were represented. This neglect stemmed from the fact that many of the negotiations were held behind closed doors, that the press hardly covered the legislation as it was being devel-oped, and that members and the president did not bother to perform the educative function that is fundamental to informed consent.[20]

Many observers have noted that difficult compromises may be best hammered out in private, but before the bargains are made and once they are set, citizens must be engaged in knowing what the choices were and they must be told why a particular agreement was accepted. If the public is not brought in on the decisions and does not know when Congress and the president have effectively worked together, it should come as no surprise that citizens assess Congress and the president on what the media report: scandal, conflict, and stalemate.

When President Bush did not bother to explain to the public why he broke his pledge in 1990 not to raise taxes, he undermined his own political support and increased many voters' cynicism about the political system. A possibly admirable decision to compromise and develop a new budget enforcement mechanism was derided rather than appreciated. Further complicating the task of governing was the general unwillingness of the president and Congress to explicate the implications of issue choices and help the public to understand long-term, general interests. Although the pledge of "no new taxes" may have been effective campaign rhetoric, it made responsible governing considerably harder.

Conclusion

The issues facing the contemporary Congress are formidable and the task of legislating is made more difficult when the government is divided, politicians are independent of party and party leaders, voters are volatile in their loyalties, interest groups are powerful, and huge amounts of money are needed for reelection campaigns. Congress can govern, however, and most particularly it can govern when the president leads in a strategic and engaged manner. In fact, the stage is set for conditional party government, as Rohde calls it, by congressional reforms and by electoral forces that provide coherence without muffling the voices in the rank and file.

Reducing the power of Congress under the justification that the issues are too difficult and congressional conflict too rancorous for the legislative branch to govern sells democracy short. Such a justification is intellectually lazy and reduces the power of people to have a say in their government.

The low esteem in which Congress is held by the public and by some legislators speaks less to the question of whether Congress can govern than it does to the failure of Congress, the press, and educators to explain what Congress does, what citizens can expect and demand of it, and what voters can do to hold members accountable for their actions.

Notes

1. For a brief time three women served in the 102d Congress. Jocelyn Birch Burdick, D-N.D., was appointed to succeed her husband Quentin N. Burdick, who died Sept. 8, 1992.
2. Patricia Ruggles and Charles F. Stone, "Income Distribution Over the Business Cycle: Were the 1980s Different?" (Washington, D.C., Urban Institute, 1991, Research Paper).

3. Jon R. Bond and Richard Fleisher, *The President in the Legislative Arena* (Chicago: University of Chicago Press, 1990).
4. David R. Mayhew, *Divided We Govern: Party Control, Lawmaking, and Investigations, 1946–1990* (New Haven: Yale University Press, 1991).
5. Janet Hook, "Budget Ordeal Poses Question: Why Can't Congress Be Led?" *Congressional Quarterly Weekly Report*, Oct. 20, 1990, 3473.
6. Louis Fisher, "Elimination of Budget Resolutions" (Congressional Research Service, Washington, D.C., 1992, Mimeographed).
7. Donald L. Bartlett and James B. Steele, *America: What Went Wrong?* (Kansas City: Andrews and McMeel, 1992).
8. Martin P. Wattenberg, *The Decline of American Political Parties, 1952–1988* (Cambridge: Harvard University Press, 1990); and Wattenberg, *The Rise of Candidate-Centered Politics: Presidential Elections of the 1980s* (Cambridge: Harvard University Press, 1991).
9. Shanto Iyengar, *Is Anyone Responsible? How Television Frames Political Issues* (Chicago: University of Chicago Press, 1991).
10. Anthony King, "The American Polity in the Late 1970s: Building Coalitions in the Sand," in *The New American Political System*, ed. Anthony King (Washington, D.C.: American Enterprise Institute, 1978), 371–395.
11. Martha Derthick and Paul J. Quirk. *The Politics of Deregulation* (Washington, D.C.: Brookings Institution, 1985), 237.
12. Mark A. Peterson, *Legislating Together: The White House and Capitol Hill from Eisenhower to Reagan* (Cambridge: Harvard University Press, 1990); Bond and Fleisher, *President in the Legislative Arena;* David W. Rohde, *Parties and Leaders in the Postreform House* (Chicago: University of Chicago Press, 1991); Richard E. Cohen, *Washington at Work: Back Rooms and Clean Air* (New York: Macmillan, 1992).
13. Barbara Sinclair, "The Changing Role of Party and Party Leadership in the U.S. House" (Paper presented at the annual meeting of the American Political Science Association, Atlanta, September 1989); Rohde, *Parties and Leaders in the Postreform House*.
14. Rohde, *Parties and Leaders in the Postreform House*.
15. Ibid., 116.
16. Ibid., 28.
17. Hook, "Budget Ordeal Poses Question," 3472.
18. Derthick and Quirk, *Politics of Deregulation;* Randall Strahan, *New Ways and Means: Reform and Change in a Congressional Committee* (Chapel Hill: University of North Carolina Press, 1990).
19. Cohen, *Washington at Work: Back Rooms and Clean Air*.
20. Ibid.

Summary Questions

1. Even in an era of intense publicity and C-Span cable coverage of Congress, should we expect the public to understand the complexity of congressional policy making? Might well-structured congressional debates on broad issues, like health care or energy policy, add to citizen interest and understanding?

2. Rudder places much of her hopes for coherent legislating on "conditional party government." What does this mean? Does it require presidential leadership to work well? How has President Clinton done in providing legislative leadership to the Democratic Congress?

 Chapter 11

THE PRESIDENCY

On the surface, the public knows far more about the president than it does about any other political figure. What the president does—whether traveling to a summit or riding a horse—is news, virtually by definition. One major trend in American politics has been for presidents to become increasingly public figures, to the point where the public often holds unrealistically high expectations for their performance. Yet we usually know relatively little about how the president makes decisions and even less about how the institution of the presidency operates on a day-to-day basis.

A generation ago, Alexander Bickel called the Supreme Court "the least dangerous branch" because of its inability to implement decisions. Today, we might consider the presidency the most dangerous branch, because the possibility of exercising immense power, especially in military matters and foreign policy, resides there. From the Korean War to the Persian Gulf conflict, presidents have demonstrated their dominance. In domestic policy, on the other hand, the president is far more constrained by Congress and, occasionally, by the courts. This continuing difference between the domestic and foreign/military policy arenas has been aptly labeled the "two presidencies" phenomenon by political scientist Aaron Wildavsky.

Indeed, the power of the president has attracted the attention of presidential scholars. Without question the presidency has become much more powerful since Franklin Roosevelt recast its very nature in the 1930s. Even those presidents who have been most reluctant to increase the reach of the federal government, such as Dwight Eisenhower and Ronald Reagan, have sought to take advantage of the prerogatives of executive authority. At the same time, presidential power has waxed and waned in the modern era. In large part it is dependent on the president's relationship with the legislative branch and capacity to retain substantial support from the public.

The presidencies of Lyndon Johnson, Richard Nixon, Gerald Ford, and Jimmy Carter all demonstrated that Congress and the American people can impose major limitations on any president, even those, like Johnson and Nixon, who are eager to extend the limits of executive authority. Each of these presidencies was judged a failure, to a greater or lesser extent, by the public. These presidents were held accountable for actions and policies they could not completely control. As the presidency became more visible in the 1960s and 1970s, its occupants confronted an unwieldy Congress and an increasingly skeptical citizenry. Scholars, politicians, and journalists wondered whether the job had become impossible.

Then came the Reagan presidency (see 11.4). Its record will be the subject of debate for decades to come, but one thing is abundantly clear from the Reagan years: The presidency is not an unmanageable job. Reagan demonstrated that even without working congressional majorities in both houses, the president can act authoritatively and maintain relatively high popularity ratings well into a second term. George Bush, his successor, consistently received high popularity ratings, especially in the wake of Operation Desert Storm. Ultimately, however, he lost his base of electoral support.

If the role of the presidency in American politics has consistently grown, so has the potential impact of the president as an individual. It is often difficult to separate the individuals from their eras and political contexts. Some scholars have sought to eliminate this problem by examining the presidents' personalities and characters. Such approaches are often fascinating, if speculative, and they demonstrate how difficult it is to understand the intricate relationships among the president, the presidency, other political actors, and the public. For example, Reagan's ties to the American people often appeared to bypass the institutional presidency altogether, as he communicated directly on key issues. At the same time, Mayer and McManus note that Reagan's presidency was carefully orchestrated to maximize his command of the media. Thus, his links to the public were forged both by his own abilities and by his advisers' careful planning of what to present—and how. The influence of the president and that of the presidency are inevitably intertwined, especially in the modern era.

In the following selections, five scholars examine the modern presidency from both institutional and psychological perspectives. Richard E. Neustadt offers his now classic formulation of presidential influence: Presidents must protect their reputations and popularity as they seek to persuade legislators and even their own administrative appointees to support their policy initiatives. Political scientist Robert Dahl dissects the notion of the presidential mandate as an element in the "pseudodemocratization" of the American presidency. Indeed, Dahl sees the contemporary presidency as representing exactly what the framers sought to avoid: an executive who obtains office by pandering to an ill-informed and malleable public that is incapable of producing a meaningful mandate for action.

Finally, the journalistic profiles of Presidents Clinton and Reagan provide a fascinating juxtaposition of diametrically opposed executive styles. Maureen Dowd (11.3) describes the intense, "hands-on" style of Bill Clinton as he presses for health care reform with the knowledge of a think-tank policy wonk and the energetic verve of a Southern preacher. Conversely, Jane Mayer and Doyle

McManus offer a detailed picture of Ronald Reagan as literally acting his way through the presidency, relying on scripted actions and huge delegations of authority. For Reagan, the style worked well over the short term. He won a landslide reelection victory in 1984 and left office with his popularity intact, leaving his successor to confront the problems of a mounting debt that had fueled economic progress during the mid-1980s.

11.1

The Power to Persuade

Richard E. Neustadt

The American president generally is regarded as the most powerful elected official in the world. Some of this power derives from the presidential power of command. The president can order a wide range of policies to be carried out, especially when dealing with foreign affairs or defense issues. At the same time, any chief executive must confront the numerous obstacles to exercising presidential authority. Some of these are constitutional, such as the independent power bases of the Congress and the Supreme Court. Others are less formal but no less restrictive; for example, the bureaucracy often serves as a brake on presidential initiatives.

In this selection, political scientist Richard E. Neustadt fleshes out the nature of presidential power as the power to persuade—a classic formulation on which a generation of scholars has built. Not only are presidents obliged to persuade Congress of the virtues of their proposals; they must also persuade their own administrations, and often their top aides, that their proposals have merit, even after they have won legislative approval. (Although Neustadt added three chapters to his book *Presidential Power* in 1980, this excerpt appeared in the original edition, published in 1960, and replete with references to the Truman and Eisenhower administrations.)

T he limits on command suggest the structure of our government. The constitutional convention of 1787 is supposed to have created a government of "separated powers." It did nothing of the sort. Rather, it created a government of separated institutions *sharing* powers. "I am part of the legislative process," Eisenhower often said in 1959 as a reminder of his veto. Congress, the dispenser of authority and funds, is no less part of the administrative process. Federalism adds another set of separated institutions. The Bill of Rights add others. Many public purposes can only be achieved by voluntary acts of private institutions; the press, for one, in Douglass Cater's phrase, is a "fourth branch of

Richard E. Neustadt is a professor of government at Harvard University.

government." And with the coming of alliances abroad, the separate institutions of a London, or a Bonn, share in the making of American public policy.

What the Constitution separates our political parties do not combine. . . . The President and congressmen who bear one party's label are divided by dependence upon different sets of voters. The differences are sharpest at the stage of nomination. The White House has too small a share in nominating congressmen, and Congress has too little weight in nominating Presidents for party to erase their constitutional separation. Party links are stronger than is frequently supposed, but nominating processes assure the separation.

The separateness of institutions and the sharing of authority prescribe the terms on which a President persuades. When one man shares authority with another, but does not gain or lose his job upon the other's whim, his willingness to act upon the urging of the other turns on whether he conceives the action right for him.* The essence of a President's persuasive task is to convince such men that what the White House wants of them is what they ought to do for their sake and on their authority.

Persuasive power, thus defined, amounts to more than charm or reasoned argument. These have their uses for a President, but these are not the whole of his resources. . . . The status and authority inherent in his office reinforce his logic and his charm.

Status adds something to persuasiveness; authority adds still more. When Truman urged wage changes on his Secretary of Commerce while the latter was administering the steel mills, he and Secretary Sawyer were not just two men reasoning with one another.† Had they been so, Sawyer probably would never have agreed to act. Truman's status gave him special claims to Sawyer's loyalty, or at least attention. In [English political theorist] Walter Bagehot's charming phrase "no man can *argue* on his knees." Although there is no kneeling in this country, few men—and exceedingly few Cabinet officers—are immune to the impulse to say "yes" to the President of the United States. It grows harder to say "no" when they are seated in his oval office at the White House, or in his study on the second floor, where almost tangibly he partakes of the aura of his physical surroundings. . . .

A President's authority and status give him great advantages in dealing with the men he would persuade. Each "power" is a vantage point for him in the degree that other men have use for his authority. From the veto to appointments, from publicity to budgeting, and so down a long list, the White House now controls

---

* From the vantage point of the 1990s, Neustadt's language seems insensitive to gender. Remember, he wrote in 1960 when (1) there was little such sensitivity and (2) objectively, most top-level appointees were men.

† In 1952, President Truman seized control of the steel industry to prevent a strike during the Korean War. The Supreme Court ruled his action unconstitutional.

the most encompassing array of vantage points in the American political system. With hardly an exception, the men who share in governing this country are aware that at some time, in some degree, the doing of *their* jobs, the furthering of *their* ambitions, may depend upon the President of the United States. Their need for presidential action, or their fear of it, is bound to be recurrent if not actually continuous. Their need or fear is his advantage.

A President's advantages are greater than mere listing of his "powers" might suggest. The men with whom he deals must deal with him until the last day of his term. Because they have continuing relationships with him, his future, while it lasts, supports his present influence. Even though there is no need or fear of him today, what he could do tomorrow may supply today's advantage. Continuing relationships may convert any "power," any aspect of his status, into vantage points in almost any case. When he induces other men to do what he wants done, a President can trade on their dependence now *and* later.

The President's advantages are checked by the advantages of others. Continuing relationships will pull in both directions. These are relationships of mutual dependence. A President depends upon the men he would persuade; he has to reckon with his need or fear of them. They too will possess status, or authority, or both, else they would be of little use to him. Their vantage points confront his own; their power tempers his.

Persuasion is a two-way street. Sawyer, it will be recalled, did not respond at once to Truman's plan for wage increases at the steel mills. On the contrary, the Secretary hesitated and delayed and only acquiesced when he was satisfied that publicly he would not bear the onus of decision. Sawyer had some points of vantage all his own from which to resist presidential pressure. If he had to reckon with coercive implications in the President's "situations of strength," so had Truman to be mindful of the implications underlying Sawyer's place as a department head, as steel administrator, and as a Cabinet spokesman for business. Loyalty is reciprocal. Having taken on a dirty job in the steel crisis, Sawyer had strong claims to loyal support. Besides, he had authority to do some things that the White House could ill afford. . . . He might have resigned in a huff (the removal power also works two ways). Or, . . . he might have declined to sign necessary orders. Or, he might have let it be known publicly that he deplored what he was told to do and protested its doing. By following any of these courses Sawyer almost surely would have strengthened the position of [steel] management, weakened the position of the White House, and embittered the union. But the whole purpose of a wage increase was to enhance White House persuasiveness in urging settlement upon union and companies alike. Although Sawyer's status and authority did not give him the power to prevent an increase outright, they gave him capability to undermine its purpose. . . .

The power to persuade is the power to bargain. Status and authority yield bargaining advantages. But in a government of "separated institutions sharing powers," they yield them to all sides. With the array of vantage points at his disposal, a President may be far more persuasive than his logic or his charm could make him. But outcomes are not guaranteed by his advantages. There remain the counter pressures those whom he would influence can bring to bear on him from vantage points at their disposal. Command has limited utility; persuasion becomes give-and-take. It is well that the White House holds the vantage points it does. In such a business any President may need them all—and more.

I

This view of power as akin to bargaining is one we commonly accept in the sphere of congressional relations. Every textbook states and every legislative session demonstrates that . . . a President will often be unable to obtain congressional action on his terms or even to halt action he opposes. The reverse is equally accepted: Congress often is frustrated by the President. Their formal powers are so intertwined that neither will accomplish very much, for very long, without the acquiescence of the other. By the same token, though, what one demands the other can resist. The stage is set for that great game, much like collective bargaining, in which each seeks to profit from the other's needs and fears. It is a game played catch-as-catch-can, case by case. And everybody knows the game, observers and participants alike. . . .

In only one sphere is the concept [of power as give-and-take] unfamiliar: the sphere of executive relations. Perhaps because of civics textbooks and teaching in our schools, Americans instinctively resist the view that power in this sphere resembles power in all others. Even Washington reporters, White House aides, and congressmen are not immune to the illusion that administrative agencies comprise a single structure, "the" Executive Branch, where presidential word is law, or ought to be. Yet . . . when a President seeks something from executive officials his persuasiveness is subject to the same sorts of limitations as in the case of congressmen, or governors, or national committeemen, or private citizens, or foreign governments. There are no generic differences, no differences in kind and only sometimes in degree. The incidents preceding the dismissal of [Gen. Douglas] MacArthur* and the incidents surrounding seizure of the steel mills make it plain that here as elsewhere influence derives from bargaining advantages; power is a give-and-take.

Like our governmental structure as a whole, the executive establishment consists of separated institutions sharing powers. The President heads one of

---

* A strong-willed commander of U.N. and American forces in South Korea and a prospective Republican presidential nominee, Gen. MacArthur repeatedly challenged President Truman over Korean War strategies. Truman ultimately removed him from his command. This action reinforced the president's role as commander-in-chief, although MacArthur received much popular and legislative support upon his return to the United States.

these; Cabinet officers, agency administrators, and military commanders head others. Below the departmental level, virtually independent bureau chiefs head many more. Under mid-century conditions, Federal operations spill across dividing lines on organization charts; almost every policy entangles many agencies; almost every program calls for interagency collaboration. Everything somehow involves the President. But operating agencies owe their existence least of all to one another—and only in some part to him. Each has a separate statutory base; each has its statutes to administer; each deals with a different set of subcommittees at the Capitol. Each has its own peculiar set of clients, friends, and enemies outside the formal government. Each has a different set or specialized careerists inside its own bailiwick. Our Constitution gives the President the "take-care" clause and the appointive power. Our statutes give him central budgeting and a degree of personnel control. All agency administrators are responsible to him. But they *also* are responsible to Congress, to their clients, to their staffs, and to themselves. In short, they have five masters. Only after all of those do they owe any loyalty to each other.

"The members of the Cabinet," Charles G. Dawes used to remark, "are a President's natural enemies." Dawes had been Harding's Budget Director, Coolidge's Vice-President, and Hoover's Ambassador to London; he also had been General Pershing's chief assistant for supply in the First World War. The words are highly colored, but Dawes knew whereof he spoke. The men who have to serve so many masters cannot help but be somewhat the "enemy" of any one of them. By the same token, any master wanting service is in some degree the "enemy" of such a servant. A President is likely to want loyal support but not to relish trouble on his doorstep. Yet the more his Cabinet members cleave to him, the more they may need help from him in fending off the wrath of rival masters. Help, though, is synonymous with trouble. Many a Cabinet officer, with loyalty ill-rewarded by his lights and help withheld, has come to view the White House as innately hostile to department heads. Dawes's dictum can be turned around.

A senior presidential aide remarked to me in Eisenhower's time: "If some of these Cabinet members would just take time out to stop and ask themselves, 'What would I want if I were President?', they wouldn't give him all the trouble he's been having." But even if they asked themselves the question, such officials often could not act upon the answer. Their personal attachment to the President is all too often overwhelmed by duty to their other masters. . . .

Some aides will have more vantage points than a selective memory. Sherman Adams, for example, as the Assistant to the President under Eisenhower, scarcely deserved the appelation "White House aide" in the meaning of the term before his time or as applied to other members of the Eisenhower entourage. Although Adams was by no means "chief of staff" in any sense so sweeping—or so simple—as press commentaries often took for granted, he apparently became no more dependent on the President than Eisenhower on him. "I need him," said the President when Adams turned out to have been remarkably imprudent in the

Goldfine case, and delegated to him even the decision on his own departure.*
This instance is extreme, but the tendency it illustrates is common enough. Any
aide who demonstrates to others that he has the President's consistent confidence
and a consistent part in presidential business will acquire so much business on his
own account that he becomes in some sense independent of his chief. Nothing
in the Constitution keeps a well-placed aide from converting status into power
of his own, usable in some degree even against the President—an outcome not
unknown in Truman's regime or, by all accounts, in Eisenhower's.

The more an officeholder's status and his "powers" stem from sources independent of the President, the stronger will be his potential pressure *on* the
President. Department heads in general have more bargaining power than do
most members of the White House staff; but bureau chiefs may have still more,
and specialists at upper levels of established career services may have almost
unlimited reserves of the enormous power which consists of sitting still. As
Franklin Roosevelt once remarked:

> The Treasury is so large and far-flung and ingrained in its practices that I find it almost
> impossible to get the action and results I want—even with Henry [Morgenthau] there.
> But the Treasury is not to be compared with the State Department. You should go
> through the experience of trying to get any changes in the thinking, policy, and action
> of the career diplomats and then you'd know what a real problem was. But the Treasury
> and the State Department put together are nothing compared with the Na-a-vy. The
> admirals are really something to cope with—and I should know. To change anything in
> the Na-a-vy is like punching a feather bed. You punch it with your right and you punch
> it with your left until you are finally exhausted, and then you find the damn bed just as
> it was before you started punching.[1]

. . . Real power is reciprocal and varies markedly with organization, subject
matter, personality, and situation. The mere fact that persuasion is directed at
executive officials signifies no necessary easing of his way. Any new congressman of the Administration's party, especially if narrowly elected, may turn out
more amenable (though less useful) to the President than any seasoned bureau
chief "downtown." *The probabilities of power do not derive from the literary theory of
the Constitution.*

II

There is a widely held belief in the United States that were it not for folly or for
knavery, a reasonable President would need no power other than the logic of his

---

* Businessman Bernard Goldfine gave Sherman Adams, Eisenhower's top aide, the gift of a
vicuna coat. When it became public, Adams's acceptance of the gift caused substantial embarrassment to the president, and Adams subsequently resigned.

argument. No less a personage than Eisenhower has subscribed to that belief in many a campaign speech and press-conference remark. But faulty reasoning and bad intentions do not cause all quarrels with Presidents. The best of reasoning and of intent cannot compose them all. For in the first place, what the President wants will rarely seem a trifle to the men he wants it from. And in the second place, they will be bound to judge it by the standard of their own responsibilities, not his. However logical his argument according to his lights, their judgment may not bring them to his view. . . . An able Eisenhower aide with long congressional experience remarked to me in 1958: "The people on the Hill don't do what they might *like* to do, they do what they think they *have* to do in their own interest as *they* see it. . . ." This states the case precisely.

The essence of a President's persuasive task with congressmen and everybody else, is *to induce them to believe that what he wants of them is what their own appraisal of their own responsibilities requires them to do in their interest, not his*. Because men may differ in their views on public policy, because differences in outlook stem from differences in duty—duty to one's office, one's constituents, oneself—that task is bound to be more like collective bargaining than like a reasoned argument among philosopher kings. Overtly or implicitly, hard bargaining has characterized all illustrations offered up to now. This is the reason why: persuasion deals in the coin of self-interest with men who have some freedom to reject what they find counterfeit.

III

A President draws influence from bargaining advantages. But does he always need them? . . . Suppose most players of the governmental game see policy objectives much alike, then can he not rely on logic (or on charm) to get him what he wants? The answer is that even then most outcomes turn on bargaining. The reason for this answer is a simple one: most men who share in governing have interests of their own beyond the realm of policy *objectives*. The sponsorship of policy, the form it takes, the conduct of it, and the credit for it separate their interest from the President's, despite agreement on the end in view. In political government, the means can matter quite as much as ends; they often matter more. And there are always differences of interest in the means. . . .

Adequate or not, a President's own choices are the only means *in his own hands* of guarding his own prospects for effective influence. He can draw power from continuing relationships in the degree that he can capitalize upon the needs of others for the Presidency's status and authority. He helps himself to do so, though, by nothing save ability to recognize the preconditions and the chance advantages and to proceed accordingly in the course of the choice-making that comes his way. To ask how he can guard prospective influence is thus to raise a further question: what helps him guard his power stakes in his own acts of choice?

Notes

1. Quoted in Marriner S. Eccles, *Beckoning Frontiers* (New York: Knopf, 1951), 336.

Summary Questions

1. Why must presidents be able to "persuade" their own administrative appointees?
2. Can presidents *increase* their ability to persuade? How? By making good
   choices?

 11.2

Myth of the Presidential Mandate

Robert A. Dahl

The term *mandate* appears frequently in discussions of presidential elections.
Presidents claim mandates—often broadly defined—in the wake of their victories.
The people, they say, have spoken. After all, among elected officials only the
president has a national constituency. The problem comes in interpreting what
the people have to say. Many potential voters do not cast their ballots; in recent
presidential contests, these individuals constituted almost 50 percent of the potential electorate. Moreover, many reasons lie behind the millions of votes that
support a given candidate.

   Political scientist and democratic theorist Robert Dahl argues that it was not
until Woodrow Wilson's presidency that chief executives began to claim mandates for their policies and goals. Such claims have become commonplace, but
Dahl casts substantial doubt on their validity. Even with sophisticated sample
surveys, Dahl finds the complexities underlying mandates as exceedingly difficult to fathom. In addition, presidents frequently win by less than a majority of
the popular vote and often receive only a bit more than a quarter of the ballots
of all those eligible to vote. In sum, although presidents may be eager to claim

Robert A. Dahl is professor of political science emeritus at Yale University.

mandates for their actions, in most instances these claims will be self-serving rather than based on adequate criteria of clear relationships between the candidate and the electorate.

O n election night in 1980 the vice president elect enthusiastically informed the country that Ronald Reagan's triumph was

> . . . not simply a mandate for a change but a mandate for peace and freedom; a mandate for prosperity; a mandate for opportunity for all Americans regardless of race, sex, or creed; a mandate for leadership that is both strong and compassionate . . . a mandate to make government the servant of the people in the way our founding fathers intended; a mandate for hope; a mandate for hope for the fulfillment of the great dream that President-elect Reagan has worked for all his life.[1]

I suppose there are no limits to permissible exaggeration in the elation of victory, especially by a vice president elect. He may therefore be excused, I imagine, for failing to note, as did many others who made comments in a similar vein in the weeks and months that followed, that Reagan's lofty mandate was provided by 50.9 percent of the voters. A decade later it is much more evident, as it should have been then, that what was widely interpreted as Reagan's mandate, not only by supporters but by opponents, was more myth than reality.

In claiming that the outcome of the election provided a mandate to the president from the American people to bring about the policies, programs, emphases, and new directions uttered during the campaign by the winning candidate and his supporters, the vice president elect was like other commentators echoing a familiar theory.

Origin and Development

A history of the theory of the presidential mandate has not been written, and I have no intention of supplying one here. However, if anyone could be said to have created the myth of the presidential mandate, surely it would be Andrew Jackson. Although he never used the word mandate, so far as I know, he was the first American president to claim not only that the president is uniquely representative of all the people, but that his election confers on him a mandate from the people in support of his policy. Jackson's claim was a fateful step in the democratization of the constitutional system of the United States—or rather what I prefer to call the pseudodemocratization of the presidency.

As Leonard White observed, it was Jackson's "settled conviction" that "the President was an immediate and direct representative of the people."[2] Presumably as a result of his defeat in 1824 in both the electoral college and the House of Representatives, in his first presidential message to Congress, in order that "as few impediments as possible should exist to the free operation of the public will," he proposed that the Constitution be amended to provide for the direct election of the president.[3]

> "To the people," he said, "belongs the right of electing their Chief Magistrate: it was never designed that their choice should, in any case, be defeated, either by the intervention of electoral colleges or by . . . the House of Representatives."[4]

His great issue of policy was the Bank of the United States, which he unwaveringly believed was harmful to the general good. Acting on this conviction, in 1832 he vetoed the bill to renew the bank's charter. Like his predecessors, he justified the veto as a protection against unconstitutional legislation; but unlike his predecessors in their comparatively infrequent use of the veto he also justified it as a defense of his or his party's policies.

Following his veto of the bank's charter, the bank became the main issue in the presidential election of 1832. As a consequence, Jackson's reelection was widely regarded, even among his opponents (in private, at least), as amounting to "something like a popular ratification" of his policy.[5] When in order to speed the demise of the bank Jackson found it necessary to fire his treasury secretary, he justified his action on the ground, among others, that "The President is the direct representative of the American people, but the Secretaries are not."[6]

Innovative though it was, Jackson's theory of the presidential mandate was less robust than it was to become in the hands of his successors. In 1848 James Polk explicitly formulated the claim in a defense of his use of the veto on matters of policy, that as a representative of the people the president was, if not more representative than the Congress, at any rate equally so.

> "The people, by the constitution, have commanded the President, as much as they have commanded the legislative branch of the Government, to execute their will. . . . The President represents in the executive department the whole people of the United States, as each member of the legislative department represents portions of them. . . ." The President is responsible "not only to an enlightened public opinion, but to the people of the whole Union, who elected him, as the representatives in the legislative branches are responsible to the people of particular States or districts. . . ."[7]

Notice that in Jackson's and Polk's views, the president, both constitutionally and as representative of the people, is on a par with Congress. They did not claim that in either respect the president is superior to Congress. It was Woodrow Wilson who took the further step in the evolution of the theory by asserting that in representing the people the president is not merely equal to Congress but actually superior to it.

Earlier Views   Because the theory of the presidential mandate espoused by Jackson and Polk has become an integral part of our present-day conception of the presidency, it may be hard for us to grasp how sharply that notion veered off from the views of the earlier presidents.

As James Ceaser has shown, the Framers designed the presidential election process as a means of improving the chances of electing a *national* figure who would enjoy majority support. They hoped their contrivance would avoid not only the populistic competition among candidates dependent on "the popular arts," which they rightly believed would occur if the president were elected by the people, but also what they believed would necessarily be a factional choice if the president were chosen by the Congress, particularly by the House.[8]

In adopting the solution of an electoral college, however, the Framers seriously underestimated the extent to which the strong impulse toward democratization that was already clearly evident among Americans—particularly among their opponents, the anti-Federalists—would subvert and alter their carefully contrived constitutional structure. Since this is a theme I shall pick up later, I want now to mention only two such failures that bear closely on the theory of the presidential mandate. First, the Founders did not foresee the development of political parties nor comprehend how a two-party system might achieve their goal of insuring the election of a figure of national rather than merely local renown. Second, as Ceaser remarks, although the Founders recognized "the need for a popular judgment of the performance of an incumbent" and designed a method for selecting the president that would, as they thought, provide that opportunity, they "did not see elections as performing the role of instituting decisive changes in policy in response to popular demands."[9] In short, the theory of the presidential mandate not only cannot be found in the Framers' conception of the Constitution; almost certainly it violates that conception.

No president prior to Jackson challenged the view that Congress was the legitimate representative of the people. Even Thomas Jefferson, who adeptly employed the emerging role of party leader to gain congressional support for his policies and decisions,

> was more Whig than . . . the British Whigs themselves in subordinating [the executive power] to "the supreme legislative power." . . . The tone of his messages is uniformly deferential to Congress. His first one closes with these words: "Nothing shall be wanting on my part to inform, as far as in my power, the legislative judgment, nor to carry that judgment into faithful execution."[10]

James Madison, demonstrating that a great constitutional theorist and an adept leader in Congress could be decidedly less than a great president, deferred so greatly to Congress that in his communications to that body his extreme caution rendered him "almost unintelligible"[11]—a quality one would hardly expect from one who had been a master of lucid exposition at the Constitutional Convention. His successor, James Monroe, was so convinced that Congress should decide domestic issues without presidential influence that throughout the debates in Congress on "the greatest political issue of his day . . . the admission of Missouri and the status of slavery in Louisiana Territory," he remained utterly silent.[12]

Madison and Monroe serve not as examples of how presidents should behave but as evidence of how early presidents thought they should behave. Considering the constitutional views and the behavior of Jackson's predecessors, it is not hard to see why his opponents called themselves Whigs in order to emphasize his dereliction from the earlier and presumably constitutionally correct view of the presidency.

Woodrow Wilson   The long and almost unbroken succession of mediocrities who succeeded to the presidency between Polk and Wilson for the most part subscribed to the Whig view of the office and seem to have laid no claim to a popular mandate for their policies—when they had any. Even Abraham Lincoln, in justifying the unprecedented scope of presidential power he believed he needed in order to meet secession and civil war, rested his case on constitutional grounds, and not as a mandate from the people.[13] Indeed, since he distinctly failed to gain a majority of votes in the election of 1860, any claim to a popular mandate would have been dubious at best. Like Lincoln, Theodore Roosevelt also had a rather unrestricted view of presidential power; he expressed the view then emerging among Progressives that chief executives were also representatives of the people. Yet the stewardship he claimed for the presidency was ostensibly drawn—rather freely drawn, I must say—from the Constitution, not from the mystique of the mandate.[14]

Woodrow Wilson, more as political scientist than as president, brought the mandate theory to what now appears to be its canonical form. His formulation was influenced by his admiration for the British system of cabinet government. In 1879, while still a senior at Princeton, he published an essay recommending the adoption of cabinet government in the United States.[15] He provided little indication as to how this change was to be brought about, however, and soon abandoned the idea without yet having found an alternative solution.[16] Nevertheless, he continued to contrast the American system of congressional government, in which Congress was all-powerful but lacked executive leadership, with British cabinet government, in which parliament, though all powerful, was firmly led by the prime minister and his cabinet. Since Americans were not likely to adopt the British cabinet system, however, he began to consider the alternative of more powerful presidential leadership.[17] In his *Congressional Government*, published in 1885, he acknowledged that "the representatives of the people are the proper ultimate authority in all matters of government, and that administration is merely the clerical part of government."[18] Congress is "unquestionably, the predominant and controlling force, the center and source of all motive and of all regulative power." Yet a discussion of policy that goes beyond "special pleas for special privilege" is simply impossible in the House, "a disintegrate mass of jarring elements," while the Senate is no more than "a small, select, and leisurely House of Representatives."[19]

By 1908, when *Constitutional Government in the United States* was published, Wilson had arrived at strong presidential leadership as a feasible solution. He faulted the earlier presidents who had adopted the Whig theory of the Constitution.

> ... (T)he makers of the Constitution were not enacting Whig theory. ... The President is at liberty, both in law and conscience, to be as big a man as he can. His capacity will set the limit; and if Congress be overborne by him, it will be no fault of the makers of the Constitution, —it will be from no lack of constitutional powers on its part, but only because the President has the nation behind him, and Congress has not. He has no means of compelling Congress except through public opinion. ... (T)he early Whig theory of political dynamics ... is far from being a democratic theory. ... It is particularly intended to prevent the will of the people as a whole from having at any moment an unobstructed sweep and ascendancy.

And he contrasted the president with Congress in terms that would become commonplace among later generations of commentators, including political scientists:

> Members of the House and Senate are representatives of localities, are voted for only by sections of voters, or by local bodies of electors like the members of the state legislatures.[20] There is no national party choice except that of President. No one else represents the people as a whole, exercising a national choice. ... The nation as a whole has chosen him, and is conscious that it has no other political spokesman. His is the only national voice in affairs. ... He is the representative of no constituency, but of the whole people. When he speaks in his true character, he speaks for no special interest. ... (T)here is but one national voice in the country, and that is the voice of the President.[21]

Since Wilson, it has become commonplace for presidents and commentators alike to argue that by virtue of his election the president has received a mandate for his aims and policies from the people of the United States. The myth of the mandate is now a standard weapon in the arsenal of persuasive symbols all presidents exploit. For example, as the Watergate scandals emerged in mid-1973, Patrick Buchanan, then an aide in the Nixon White House, suggested that the president should accuse his accusers of "seeking to destroy the democratic mandate of 1972." Three weeks later in an address to the country Nixon said:

> Last November, the American people were given the clearest choice of this century. Your votes were a mandate, which I accepted, to complete the initiatives we began in my first term and to fulfill the promises I made for my second term.[22]

If the spurious nature of Nixon's claim now seems self-evident, the dubious grounds for virtually all such pretensions are perhaps less obvious.[23]

Critique of the Theory

What does a president's claim to a mandate amount to? The meaning of the term itself is not altogether clear.[24] Fortunately, however, in his excellent book *Interpreting Elections*, Stanley Kelley has "piece[d] together a coherent statement of the theory."

> Its first element is the belief that elections carry messages about problems, policies, and programs—messages plain to all and specific enough to be directive. . . . Second, the theory holds that certain of these messages must be treated as authoritative commands . . . either to the victorious candidate or to the candidate and his party. . . . To qualify as mandates, messages about policies and programs must reflect the *stable* views both of individual voters and of the electorate. . . . In the electorate as a whole, the numbers of those for or against a policy or program matter. To suggest that a mandate exists for a particular policy is to suggest that more than a bare majority of those voting are agreed upon it. The common view holds that landslide victories are more likely to involve mandates than are narrow ones. . . . The final element of the theory is a negative imperative: Governments should not undertake major innovations in policy or procedure, except in emergencies, unless the electorate has had an opportunity to consider them in an election and thus to express its views.[25]

To bring out the central problems more clearly, let me extract what might be called the primitive theory of the popular presidential mandate. According to this theory, a presidential election can accomplish four things. First, it confers constitutional and legal authority on the victor. Second, at the same time, it also conveys information. At a minimum it reveals the first preferences for president of a plurality of votes. Third, according to the primitive theory, the election, at least under the conditions Kelley describes, conveys further information: namely that a clear majority of voters prefer the winner because they prefer his policies and wish him to pursue his policies. Finally, because the president's policies reflect the wishes of a majority of voters, when conflicts over policy arise between president and Congress, the president's policies ought to prevail.

While we can readily accept the first two propositions, the third, which is pivotal to the theory, might be false. But if the third is false, then so is the fourth. So the question arises: Beyond revealing the first preferences of a plurality of voters, do presidential elections also reveal the additional information that a plurality (or a majority) of voters prefer the policies of the winner and wish the winner to pursue those policies?

In appraising the theory I want to distinguish between two different kinds of criticisms. First, some critics contend that even when the wishes of constituents can be known, they should not be regarded as in any way binding on a legislator. I have in mind, for example, Edmund Burke's famous argument that he would not sacrifice to public opinion his independent judgment of how well a policy would serve his constituents' interests, and the argument suggested by Hanna Pitkin that representatives bound by instructions would be prevented from entering into the compromises that legislation usually requires.[26]

Second, some critics, on the other hand, may hold that when the wishes of constituents on matters of policy can be clearly discerned, they ought to be given great and perhaps even decisive weight. But, these critics contend, constituents' wishes usually cannot be known, at least when the constituency is large and diverse, as in presidential elections. In expressing his doubts on the matter in 1913, A. Lawrence Lowell quoted Sir Henry Maine: "The devotee of democracy is much in the same position as the Greeks with their oracles. All agreed that the voice of an oracle was the voice of god, but everybody allowed that when he spoke he was not as intelligible as might be desired."[27]

It is exclusively the second kind of criticism that I want now to consider. Here again I am indebted to Stanley Kelley for his succinct summary of the main criticisms.

> Critics allege that 1) some particular claim of a mandate is unsupported by adequate evidence; 2) most claims of mandates are unsupported by adequate evidence; 3) most claims of mandates are politically self-serving; or 4) it is not possible in principle to make a valid claim of a mandate, since it is impossible to sort out voters' intentions.[28]

Kelley goes on to say that while the first three criticisms may well be valid, the fourth has been outdated by the sample survey,* which "has again given us the ability to discover the grounds of voters' choices." In effect, then, Kelley rejects the primitive theory and advances the possibility of a more sophisticated mandate theory according to which the information about policies is conveyed not by the election outcome but instead by opinion surveys. Thus the two functions are cleanly split: presidential elections are for electing a president, opinion surveys provide information about the opinions, attitudes, and judgments that account for the outcome.

However, I would propose a fifth proposition, which I believe is also implicit in Kelley's analysis:

> 5) While it may not be strictly impossible *in principle* to make a reasoned and well-grounded claim to a presidential mandate, to do so *in practice* requires a complex analysis that in the end may not yield much support for presidential claims.

But if we reject the primitive theory of the mandate and adopt the more sophisticated theory, then it follows that prior to the introduction of scientific sample surveys, no president could reasonably have defended his claim to a mandate. To put a precise date on the proposition, let me remind you that the first presidential election in which scientific surveys formed the basis of an extended and systematic analysis was 1940.[29]

I do not mean to say that no election before 1940 now permits us to draw the conclusion that a president's major policies were supported by a substantial majority of the electorate. But I do mean that for most presidential elections before 1940 a valid reconstruction of the policy views of the electorate is impossible or enormously difficult, even with the aid of aggregate data and other indirect indicators of voters' views. When we consider that presidents ordinarily asserted their claims soon after their elections, well before historians and social scientists could have sifted through reams of indirect evidence, then we must

---

* The sampling techniques allow a relatively small number of respondents (1,500 for a national sample) to accurately reflect the views of a much larger population (150 million adults).

conclude that before 1940 no contemporary claim to a presidential mandate could have been supported by the evidence available at the time.

While the absence of surveys undermines presidential claims to a mandate before 1940, the existence of surveys since then would not necessarily have supported such claims. Ignoring all other shortcomings of the early election studies, the analysis of the 1940 election I just mentioned was not published until 1948. While that interval between the election and the analysis may have set a record, the systematic analysis of survey evidence that is necessary (though perhaps not sufficient) to interpret what a presidential election means always comes well after presidents and commentators have already told the world, on wholly inadequate evidence, what the election means.[30] Perhaps the most famous voting study to date, *The American Voter,* which drew primarily on interviews conducted in 1952 and 1956, appeared in 1960.[31] The book by Stanley Kelley that I have drawn on so freely here, which interprets the elections of 1964, 1972, and 1980, appeared in 1983.

A backward glance quickly reveals how empty the claims to a presidential mandate have been in recent elections. Take 1960. If more than a bare majority is essential to a mandate, then surely Kennedy could have received no mandate, since he gained less than 50 percent of the total popular vote by the official count—just how much less by the unofficial count varies with the counter. Yet "on the day after election, and every day thereafter," Theodore Sorenson tells us, "he rejected the argument that the country had given him no mandate. Every election has a winner and a loser, he said in effect. There may be difficulties with the Congress, but a margin of only one vote would still be a mandate."[32]

By contrast, 1964 was a landslide election, as was 1972. From his analysis, however, Kelley concludes that "Johnson's and Nixon's specific claims of meaningful mandates do not stand up well when confronted by evidence." To be sure, in both elections some of the major policies of the winners were supported by large majorities among those to whom these issues were salient. Yet "none of these policies was cited by more than 21% of respondents as a reason to like Johnson, Nixon, or their parties."[33]

In 1968, Nixon gained office with only 43 percent of the popular vote. No mandate there. Likewise in 1976, Carter won with a bare 50.1 percent. Once again, no mandate there.

When Reagan won in 1980, thanks to the much higher quality of surveys undertaken by the media, a more sophisticated understanding of what that election meant no longer had to depend on the academic analyses that would only follow some years later. Nonetheless, many commentators, bemused as they so often are by the arithmetical peculiarities of the electoral college, immediately proclaimed both a landslide and a mandate for Reagan's policies. What they often failed to note was that Reagan gained just under 51 percent of the popular vote. Despite the claims of the vice president elect, surely we can find no mandate there. Our doubts are strengthened by the fact that in the elections to the House, Democratic candidates won just over 50 percent of the popular vote and a majority of seats. However, they lost control of the Senate. No Democratic mandate there, either.

These clear and immediate signs that the elections of 1980 failed to confer a mandate on the president or his Democratic opponents were, however, largely ignored. For it was so widely asserted as to be commonplace that Reagan's election reflected a profound shift of opinion away from New Deal programs and toward the new conservatism. However, from this analysis of the survey evidence, Kelley concludes that the commitment of voters to candidates was weak; a substantial proportion of Reagan voters were more interested in voting against Carter than for Reagan; and despite claims by journalists and others, the New Deal coalition did not really collapse. Nor was there any profound shift toward conservatism. "The evidence from press surveys . . . contradicts the claims that voters shifted toward conservatism and that this ideological shift elected Reagan." In any case, the relation between ideological location and policy preferences was "of a relatively modest magnitude."[34]

In winning by a landslide of popular votes in 1984, Reagan achieved one prerequisite to a mandate. Yet in that same election, Democratic candidates for the House won 52 percent of the popular votes. Two years earlier, they had won 55 percent of the votes. On the face of it, surely the 1984 elections gave no mandate to Reagan [for more on this, see 11.4].

Before the end of 1986, when the Democrats had once again won a majority of popular votes in elections to the House and had also regained a majority of seats in the Senate, it should have been clear and it should be even clearer now that the major social and economic policies for which Reagan and his supporters had claimed a mandate have persistently failed to gain majority support. Indeed, the major domestic policies and programs established during the thirty years preceding Reagan in the White House have not been overturned in the grand revolution of policy that his election was supposed to have ushered in. For eight years, what Reagan and his supporters claimed as a mandate to reverse those policies was regularly rejected by means of the only legitimate and constitutional processes we Americans have for determining what the policies of the United States government should be.

What are we to make of this long history of unsupported claims to a presidential mandate? The myth of the mandate would be less important if it were not one element in the larger process of the pseudodemocratization of the presidency—the creation of a type of chief executive that in my view should have no proper place in a democratic republic.

Yet even if we consider it in isolation from the larger development of the presidency, the myth is harmful to American political life. By portraying the president as the only representative of the whole people and Congress as merely representing narrow, special, and parochial interests, the myth of the mandate elevates the president to an exalted position in our constitutional system at the expense of Congress. The myth of the mandate fosters the belief that the particular interests of the diverse human beings who form the citizen body in a large, complex, and pluralistic country like ours constitute no legitimate element in the general good. The myth confers on the aims of the groups who benefit from presidential policies an aura of national interest and public good to which they are no more entitled than the groups whose interests are reflected in the policies that gain support by congressional majorities. Because the myth is almost always employed to support deceptive, misleading, and manipulative interpretations, it is harmful to the political understanding of citizens.

It is, I imagine, now too deeply rooted in American political life and too useful a part of the political arsenal of presidents to be abandoned. Perhaps the most we can hope for is that commentators on public affairs in the media and in academic pursuits will dismiss claims to a presidential mandate with the scorn they usually deserve.

But if a presidential election does not confer a mandate on the victor, what does a presidential election mean, if anything at all? While a presidential election does not confer a popular mandate on the president—nor, for that matter, on congressional majorities—it confers the legitimate authority, right, and opportunity on a president to try to gain the adoption by constitutional means of the policies the president supports. In the same way, elections to Congress confer on a member the authority, right, and opportunity to try to gain the adoption by constitutional means of the policies he or she supports. Each may reasonably contend that a particular policy is in the public good or public interest and, moreover, is supported by a majority of citizens.

I do not say that whatever policy is finally adopted following discussion, debate, and constitutional processes necessarily reflects what a majority of citizens would prefer, or what would be in their interests, or what would be in the public good in any other sense. What I do say is that no elected leader, including the president, is uniquely privileged to say what an election means—nor to claim that the election has conferred on the president a mandate to enact the particular policies the president supports. . . .

Notes

1. Stanley Kelley, Jr., *Interpreting Elections* (Princeton, N.J.: Princeton University Press, 1983), 217.
2. Leonard D. White, *The Jacksonians: A Study in Administrative History, 1829–1861* (New York: Free Press, 1954), 23.
3. Quoted in ibid., 23.
4. Cited in James W. Ceaser, *Presidential Selection: Theory and Development* (Princeton, N.J.: Princeton University Press, 1979), 160, fn. 58.
5. White, *Jacksonians*, 23.
6. Ibid., 23.
7. Ibid., 24.
8. Although Madison and Hamilton opposed the contingent solution of a House election in the event that no candidate received a majority of electoral votes, Gouverneur Morris and James Wilson accepted it as not too great a concession. Ceaser, *Presidential Selection*, 80–81.
9. Ibid., 84.

10. Edward S. Corwin, *The President: Offices and Powers, 1789–1948*, 3rd ed. (New York: New York University Press, 1948), 20.

11. Wilfred E. Binkley, *President and Congress* (New York: Alfred A. Knopf, 1947), 56.

12. Leonard D. White, *The Jeffersonians: A Study in Administrative History, 1801–1829* (New York: Free Press, 1951), 31.

13. Lincoln drew primarily on the war power, which he created by uniting the president's constitutional obligation "to take care that the laws be faithfully executed" with his power as commander-in-chief. He interpreted the war power as a veritable cornucopia of implicit constitutional authority for the extraordinary emergency measures he undertook during an extraordinary national crisis. (Corwin, *The President*, 277ff.)

14. "Every executive officer, in particular the President, Roosevelt maintained, 'was a steward of the people bound actively and affirmatively to do all he could for the people. . . .' He held therefore that, unless specifically forbidden by the Constitution or by law, the President had 'to do anything that the needs of the nation demanded. . . .' 'Under this interpretation of executive power,' he recalled, 'I did and caused to be done many things not previously done. . . . I did not usurp power, but I did greatly broaden the use of executive power.' " See John Morton Blum, *The Republican Roosevelt* (New York: Atheneum, 1954), 108.

15. Woodrow Wilson, *Cabinet Government in the United States* (Stamford, Conn.: Overbrook Press, 1947), orig. publication in *International Review*, 1879.

16. "He seems not to have paid much attention to the practical question of how so radical an alteration was to be brought about. As far as I know, Wilson's only published words on how to initiate the English system are in the article, *Committee or Cabinet Government*, which appeared in the *Overland Monthly* for January, 1884." His solution was to amend Section 6 of Article I of the Constitution to permit members of Congress to hold offices as members of the Cabinet, and to extend the terms of the president and representatives. See Walter Lippmann, *Introduction to Congressional Government* (New York: Meridian Books, 1956), 14–15.

17. Wilson's unfavorable comparative judgment is particularly clear in *Congressional Government: A Study in American Politics* (New York: Meridian Books, 1956; reprint of 1885 ed.), 181. Just as Jackson had proposed the direct election of the president, in his first annual message Wilson proposed that a system of direct national primaries be adopted. See Ceaser, *Presidential Selection*, 173.

18. Wilson, *Congressional Government*, 181.

19. Ibid., 31, 72–73, 145.

20. The Seventeenth Amendment requiring a direct election of senators was not adopted until 1913.

21. Woodrow Wilson, *Constitutional Government in the United States* (New York: Columbia University Press, 1908), 67–68, 70, 202–203.

22. Kelley, *Interpreting Elections*, 99.

23. For other examples of claims to a presidential mandate resulting from the election, see William Safire, *Safire's Political Dictionary* (New York: Random House, 1978), 398; and Kelley, *Interpreting Elections*, 72–74, 126–129, 168.

24. See "mandate" in *Oxford English Dictionary* (Oxford, England: Oxford University Press, 1971, compact edition); Safire, *Political Dictionary*, 398; Jack C. Plano and Milton Greenberg, *The American Political Dictionary* (New York: Holt, Rinehart and Winston, 1979), 130; Julius Gould and William L. Kolb, *A Dictionary of the Social Sciences* (New York: The Free Press, 1964), 404; Jay M. Shafritz, *The Dorsey Dictionary of American Government and Politics* (Chicago: The Dorsey Press, 1988), 340.

25. Kelley, *Interpreting Elections*, 126–128.

26. Cited in ibid., 133.

27. Cited in ibid., 134.

28. Ibid., 136.

29. Paul F. Lazarsfeld, Bernard Berelson, and Hazel Gaudet, *The People's Choice* (New York: Columbia University Press, 1948).

30. The early election studies are summarized in Bernard R. Berelson and Paul F. Lazarsfeld, *Voting* (Chicago: University of Chicago Press, 1954), 331ff.

31. Angus Campbell et al., *The American Voter* (New York: Wiley, 1960).
32. Quoted in Safire, *Political Dictionary*, 398.
33. Kelley, *Interpreting Elections*, 139–140.
34. Ibid., 170–172, 174–181, 185, 187.

Summary Questions

1. In what ways does the idea of a presidential mandate violate the assumptions of the Constitution's framers?
2. What is a mandate? Why is it so important, or at least useful, for a president to make such a claim in establishing a set of policy priorities?
3. Did Bill Clinton have a mandate after the 1992 election? Did he claim one?

 11.3

On Health, Clinton Finds Heaven Is in the Details

Maureen Dowd

This is a piece of daily journalism from *New York Times* reporter Maureen Dowd, who is noted for her lively prose and personality-oriented style. Written on deadline, this brief article depicts President Bill Clinton's combination of style and substance as he addresses the complexities of health care.

Clinton and his advisers chose a town meeting setting for his first televised appearance after his introduction of his health care plan in September, 1993. Comfortable with this format and at ease with health care details, Clinton put on a two and one-half hour performance that tested his host (ABC's Ted Koppel), his staff, the audience, and his voice. As Dowd reports, however, he kept his promise to answer questions as long as the audience posed them. Even after ABC ended its live broadcast, Clinton continued to respond, his voice growing hoarse, but his enthusiasm never waning. Dowd's brief portrait captures Clinton the policy wonk, never happier than when explaining how his plan will improve citizens' lives, on an individual-by-individual basis.

B efore ABC News's "town hall" on health care went on the air Thursday night, Ted Koppel came out to instruct the audience on the pace of live television.

The "Nightline" host told those in the crowd in the Tampa Bay Performing Arts Center to keep their questions for President Clinton "pithy and to the point."

Not one to mince words, even with a President, Mr. Koppel gave Mr. Clinton the same instructions, telling him to "zip" right along.

Mr. Clinton nodded sympathetically, as he is wont to do, and then unleashed two and a half hours worth of highly detailed "first, secondly" and "let me just add this" and "I want to make this very clear" and "Can I say one thing real quick?" and "I would like to amend that answer" answers about his health care plan.

Putting Me First

If health care is an issue that everyone in the country wants explained to them individually—What about *my* acupuncture bills? My aunt's lumbago? My massage therapy clients? My husband's favorite chiropractor? My protection against malpractice suits? My pharmacy's problems with drug manufacturers?—this is a President who is willing, nay, eager to do it.

"Bulimia?" he repeated after an elegant red-haired woman who had pushed up to the stage after the show. "That'll be covered."

The President had promised to stay as long as anyone had a question—a promise that alarmed his staff, who envisioned the policy equivalent of the dance marathon movie, "They Shoot Horses, Don't They?"

"Do you want a Xanax?" said Robert Boorstin, a White House health policy aide, jokingly offering a tablet of the anti-anxiety medication to a reporter who planned to stay up as long as the President.

Other Presidents would have retreated to a majestic distance after introducing the plan with a masterful speech to Congress: Float above the fray. Let the public absorb the general idea while the Administration experts fanned out to explain the tricky, politically thorny details. Preserve political capital.

Not this President. He did not wait a day, after his dignified, well-received speech on Wednesday night, to return to his cherished role as a chatty national talk show host. Although Ira Magaziner, the chief White House adviser on health care, was seated on the aisle of the fourth row so that he could field the questions that were too technical for Mr. Clinton, the President never called on him for help.

"It's the most personal, specific issue in the world," said Mandy Grunwald, a media adviser to the President who helped set up the show. "Why shouldn't he be the one to educate people and reassure them about their fears?"

And, in an insight into the gratification Mr. Clinton draws from this kind of format—the same enjoyment George Bush got from the freewheeling news

conferences that showed he was more a master of details than Ronald Reagan—
she added, "I don't know of any other President who could have answered those
questions about his own policy."

Mr. Clinton is supremely confident in this sort of setting, although Mr. Koppel
lost patience with the torrent of words at one point and complained that the
President was being glib to the point of obfuscation.

As the President was giving a long, equivocal, politically careful answer to a
woman who opposed the prospect of her health care payments going into a
common fund that could be used to pay for abortions, Mr. Koppel interjected,
saying, "Mr. President, this is a curious criticism to make, but sometimes I think
you're so specific in your answers or so detailed in your answers that it's a little
hard to know what the answer to the question was."

Mr. Clinton looked cross in reply, his mouth like the rim of a purse snapped
suddenly shut, just as he did at another moment when he was tossing around
remarks about things that would be covered in the year 1996 or 2000 and the
moderator drily noted: "There's a little thing called 're-election' that has to kick
in before you can be sure that you're going to be able to continue doing these
things into a second term."

As Mr. Koppel looked on bemusedly, the increasingly hoarse President continued to take questions from people in the front rows during commercial breaks,
even though his microphone was turned off—making him look, from the rear
of the hall, like a gesticulating figure on a television set when the mute button
is on.

At one point Mr. Koppel had to tap the President on the arm to get him to
watch a monitor showing pre-filmed clips of Tampa residents that would kick off
another live segment. The ebullient President did not mind; he watched a tape
of a Tampa woman insisting that middle-class people will get stuck, as usual,
financing the health care plan, and gave a big thumbs-up as if to reassure her
electronic image that it would not happen.

When Mr. Koppel interrupted a long story being told by a questioner with
AIDS, trying to speed up the man by saying "Do me a favor . . .", Mr. Clinton
jumped in breathlessly, like a high school contestant on "It's Academic."

"I know the question," the President proclaimed, proceeding to ask the question he felt the man was working up to, about Medicaid coverage of AIDS
patients, and then answer it at some length.

Long after Mr. Koppel, who had a bad cold and kept checking his watch, looked
like he was ready to be on his way, Mr. Clinton was still eagerly scanning the
crowd for questioners and jumping up from his black leather swivel chair to get a
little roving room while he talked.

He was deeply involved now in explaining things about comprehensive benefits, long-term care benefits and basic benefits, and about model forms for doctors,
variations on the model forms, and variations on the variations—all of this
intended to elucidate a plan that is supposed to simplify the process of getting
health care.

The President continued to take questions from people who crowded around the stage for another 20 minutes after ABC News finally pulled the plug on the show at 12:15 A.M. He ignored his advisers, David Gergen and Mandy Grunwald, and his personal aides, Andrew Friendly and Wendy Smith, who surrounded him like sheepdogs and, nipping, tugging and nudging, tried to herd him off the stage.

At one point, at 12:30 A.M., the usually smooth Mr. Gergen started to look a little desperate when the President stopped talking anorexia and got into an argument about the North American Free Trade Agreement.

"Prove it!" the President challenged a man who had yelled the Ross Perot argument at him that Nafta would cost American jobs. Then he began reeling off trade statistics and environmental data.

The President paid no attention to Mr. Koppel and Roone Arledge, the president of ABC News, who were waiting on stage to have their pictures taken with Mr. Clinton and to escort him to a private reception.

He Knew About Cobra

He paid no attention to the ABC technician who reached under his jacket and took off his microphone. He was busy with a question from a woman who had lost her job and was worried about transitional health insurance.

"That's the problem with Cobra," Mr. Clinton told the woman, easily using the acronym for the Consolidated Omnibus Budget Reconciliation Act of 1986, which concerns people who lose insurance coverage when they lose or leave their jobs.

Renata Major walked away impressed. "He knew what Cobra was right away," she said. "He told me I asked an excellent question."

Of course, with this President—who subscribes to that famous Dashiell Hammett line from "The Maltese Falcon" that "talking's something you can't do judiciously unless you keep in practice"—just about any question is an excellent question.

By 12:35 A.M., Mr. Gergen had coaxed Mr. Clinton over to the edge of the stage, close enough where they could actually pull him backstage without too much effort.

But the President was still looking longingly at the crowd, hoping to make a few more points, to win a few more converts. His hoarse voice could be heard fading in and out on dozens of different aspects of the plan:

"That's the problem with health centers in rural towns. . . . If you had a heart attack tonight? No. . . . Lifetime limits to the policy, the thing can turn out to be a real trap. . . . To my knowledge, the F.D.A. approved the drug. . . . The average person changes jobs seven or eight times in a lifetime. . . . We're in the process of redesigning the entire unemployment system, so there's a whole lot of these things that have to be readjusted because the nature of unemployment is different."

With one last tug from his advisers, the President was finally backstage. But it did not stop there. He went up to his health care advisers, Mr. Magaziner and Christine Heenan, wanting to go over various points he had made. "Now, was I right about this?" he asked them.

The President, who did not get back to his hotel until the wee hours, seemed happy with his all-talk special. "He was having fun," explained Ms. Grunwald.

Summary Questions

1. Is it a good idea for a president to understand his proposals in such intimate detail? Is it necessary?
2. How do Clinton's health care policy endeavors resemble a political campaign? To what extent is the public's backing crucial to Clinton's success on health care? Why?

 11.4

The No-Hands Presidency

Jane Mayer and Doyle McManus

If Bill Clinton (see 11.3) has proved to be the ultimate hands-on president in constructing and lobbying for such policies as health care reform, Ronald Reagan demonstrated how much a chief executive could delegate in performing the day-to-day responsibilities of the office. Especially after winning major tax reductions early in his term, Reagan's domestic policy was modest at best. Even with a landslide reelection victory in 1984, he took little advantage of his margin to push for major changes.

In this selection, Jane Mayer and Doyle McManus provide a host of details on Reagan's personal management style. Relying heavily on his staff, President Reagan delegated responsibilities to the point of detaching himself from much of the operations of government. While fully capable of focusing great attention on

Jane Mayer and Doyle McManus are Washington journalists.

a given issue, most frequently he maintained his distance from the hurly-burly of politics, even within the White House. Mayer and McManus describe a president who rarely initiated policies, as he left the substance of government to his aides. The contrast between Clinton and Reagan could hardly be more stark; even in an era of great demands on the presidency, the impact of individual style and personality remains great.

R eagan was unabashed about delegating many of the daily responsibilities of the presidency. When he cared deeply about an issue, he was outspoken and stubborn. His views were often strong, even radical. But his involvement in day-to-day governance—the actual running of the country—was slight. Since his days in Sacramento, he'd grown accustomed to letting others translate his goals into programs, much in the same way that he'd allowed others to run the 1984 campaign. Reagan portrayed this as a deliberate "management style," explaining to *Fortune* magazine (in an interview that pleased him more than most) that "I believe that you surround yourself with the best people you can find, delegate authority, and don't interfere."

Others in the office had delegated where possible, but Reagan's style of governing was unlike that of any other postwar president—each of whom had, in different ways, been strong chief executives who dominated not just the formation of policy but also its implementation. To a great extent, Reagan left the job of implementing his ideas to others—shunning personnel issues, rarely engaging in discussions about congressional strategy, and routinely following his subordinates' advice on media plans. Instead, he mastered the ceremonial and symbolic functions of the office so that he could act presidential even when he wasn't, in the traditional sense, functioning like one.

Reagan's day generally began between 7:00 and 8:00 A.M, when the White House operator would put through a wake-up call. By nine o'clock, after a light breakfast and a glimpse at the morning papers and television news shows, Reagan would ride the elevator downstairs from the second floor of the 132-room residence to the State Floor. There, a cadre of Secret Service agents would escort him out across the flagstone colonnade bordering the Rose Garden, past a well-disguised emergency box containing an extra pistol, and on through the armored door of the Oval Office. His chief of staff would greet him, and they would sit down for his first meeting of the day. If it was cold, the stewards would have a fire blazing; in the summertime, they would have already plumped the pillows on the wrought-iron chaises that graced the patio outside.

By the time he arrived in the Oval Office, Reagan had usually memorized most of the lines he would deliver in his public appearances that day. His nearly photographic recall—sharpened by his training as an actor—was as enormous asset. The night before, at seven, the staff would have sent an usher to the residence with a packet of the next day's instructions—whom he'd be meeting, for how long, and what he was expected to say. On carefully typed index cards, the staff composed most of his remarks, down to the greetings, and banter. They wrote out stage directions as well—where to turn and when. (One such cue card was accidently released publicly, directing Reagan to greet a member of his own cabinet and identifying him as the gentleman sitting under Coolidge's portrait.)

Reagan carried the cards with him when he came into the office in the morning, informing the staff of any changes he thought should be made. The cards were coded by size and filed by color: green for unclassified action, yellow for unclassified information, red for classified information, white for his statements. He had one size for his breast pocket, another, always folded in two, for his outside pocket. Longer remarks were typed in large print on what he called "half sheets." The president used these cards, not only for large meetings, but also for small gatherings of regulars, such as the congressional leaders, whom he usually saw weekly. Frequently he used cards to introduce members of his own cabinet, and, in one instance, he relied on them during a ceremony honoring James Brady, the press secretary wounded beside him in the 1981 assassination attempt. He also had "phone memos," which spelled out what his end of telephone conversations should be and left space for him to jot down what the interlocutor said, so that the staff could keep track. As he moved from one event to another, his staff first gave him a briefing on every move he would make. Over the years, many advisers tried to convince Reagan to dispense with his cue cards, but, conceded [Chief of Staff Donald] Regan, for the president "they were sort of like Linus's blue blanket."

By the standards of most other presidents, Reagan's office hours weren't long. After a 9:00 A.M. meeting with his chief of staff, Reagan attended a nine-thirty national security briefing with his national security adviser, the chief of staff, and frequently the vice president. After that the schedule varied, though usually the staff tried to give the president some private time late in the morning for reading; after lunch, some aides like David Stockman learned to avoid scheduling important business because the president was prone to nodding off. He was often finished for the day by four o'clock, and he usually took both Wednesday and Friday afternoons off. But he was organized and orderly in his habits. He spent about an hour almost every day lifting weights in the private gym—a habit developed under doctor's orders after the 1981 assassination attempt. Where other presidents grew gray in office, Reagan managed to put an inch and a half of muscle on his chest, and he loved to have visitors feel the tone of his biceps. Inside the Oval Office, though, Reagan was formal. He felt awed enough to say "I couldn't take my jacket off in this office," and aides said he never did. They also said he never left at the end of the day without first straightening his desk—a great slab of dark wood as imposing as its donor, Queen Victoria, who had it made for Rutherford B. Hayes from the timbers of the H.M.S. *Resolute*.

At the end of the day, Reagan usually returned upstairs with paperwork and spent the evening with his wife—both in their pajamas, eating supper from trays in his study, reading, studying the next day's lines, and watching television. Nancy Reagan said her husband generally fell asleep within minutes of going to bed, usually around 11:00 P.M. Just before he did, he would alert the thirty-six-person domestic staff, one of whom would then quietly turn off any remaining lights in the family quarters.

But Reagan was more complicated than liberal caricatures would suggest. He liked to joke about his image, using such lines as: "I hear hard work's never killed anyone, but I figure, why take a chance?" Yet those around him found to their surprise that he could be diligent—even compulsive—in performing the tasks they gave him. He was always immaculately dressed, and he was so punctual that he could time a statement or an appearance down to the second. His delivery and stage presence were honed by years of training. He would follow his daily schedule meticulously, drawing a line through each completed event with an arrow pointing to the next, exactly the way screen actors mark off completed scenes on a script. The president brought self-discipline and myriad skills to the White House; they simply were not the skills usually associated with the job.

Reagan's self-confidence was an important part of his appeal. In a complex world, he trusted his instincts, frequently to surprisingly successful effect. Although he occasionally worried about appearing ill informed in front of experts, he was generally relaxed about his ability to handle the job, perhaps because, as he once explained to [Michael] Deaver, he thoroughly believed that "God has a plan for me." The American public is especially intolerant of hesitation in its presidents, and Reagan simply wasn't agonized by self-doubt, as Carter had been. Nor was he needlessly concerned with controlling minor aspects of the office. Early on, Jimmy Carter's chief of staff Jack Watson had warned that by getting involved in too much, Carter was risking blame for too much. No one needed to give that lecture to Reagan. Both his strength and his weakness rested in an ability to leave the details to others.

White House communications director David Gergen had marveled at Reagan's similarity in this respect to Dwight Eisenhower, whom Reagan admired. But the Princeton historian Fred Greenstein, in his ground-breaking reassessment of the Eisenhower era, has termed Eisenhower's a "hidden-hand presidency" and has suggested that the former military commander ran his administration more forcefully than was immediately visible. By contrast, Reagan's rule bordered—far more than anyone wanted to admit—on a no-hands presidency.

A fundamental contradiction lay at the heart of the Reagan presidency: in public Reagan pursued the ideological agenda of an activist, but in the Oval Office he was just the opposite. As long as his record of achievements seemed strong, the way he ran the White House did not seem to matter to much of the press and the voting public. But many of those who worked on the inside—close enough to observe the inner workings of the presidency under these strange conditions—were privately astounded.

They found that Reagan was not just passive, he was sometimes entirely disengaged. He did not delegate in the usual sense; he did not actively manage his staff by assigning tasks and insisting on regular progress reports. Instead, he typically gave his subordinates little or no direction. Usually, he provided the broad rhetoric and left them to infer what he wanted. When it came to the fine points of governing, he allowed his staff to take the lead. "He made almost no demands and gave almost no instructions," conceded former advisor Martin Anderson. "Essentially, he just responded to whatever was brought before his attention." He seemed to have unquestioning trust in many of the small and large decisions others made for him—and when his staff could not reach a decision, he frequently made none either unless events forced him to do so. As Ed Rollins, who worked with Reagan for five years, concluded, "The job was whatever was on his desk."

Reagan's former campaign manager, John Sears, attributed this trait to Reagan's first career, as a movie actor in an age when the studios discouraged independent thinking. As such, Sears noted, Reagan had become professionally accustomed to learning his part and "following the prescribed rules—doing what they told you to do." If something went wrong on the set, Sears said, Reagan would most likely think, Hey, I'm just the star. I'm the performer. Others were supposed to worry about the rest of the show.

This complacency was evident in cabinet and staff meetings, where Reagan was a wonderful raconteur—frequently speaking as if he were still governor of California—as well as a good listener. But he rarely made substantive points. A staff member who had also served in the Ford White House said, "Ford led the discussion; Reagan followed it." When the public began to learn of Reagan's lack of involvement in meetings, aids explained it by saying the president wanted to hide his thought process in order to avoid leaks or that he was trying to spare the feelings of those with whom he disagreed. But, as Don Regan later admitted, Reagan "sent out no strong signals. It was a rare meeting in which he made a decision or issued an order."

If the president rarely played the leading role in meetings, his aides found he was even less likely to question the paperwork they sent him. Reagan obligingly read whatever he was given—all of it—at least in the early years. One aide early on was surprised to find that the president was staying up until the early hours of the morning trying to read all the materials his staff had sent him. "He reads indiscriminately," the aide marveled. "If you gave him eight hundred pages, he read every word. He used no judgment." Nancy Reagan finally stepped in and explained that her husband's workload needed to be reduced. Similarly, the staff had to monitor the amount of information they sent him to prepare for press conferences. As former communications director David Gergen recalled, "If you gave him too many pages, as good as his photographic memory is, he tries so hard to remember what he read that he sometimes gets mixed up." He was particularly susceptible to whatever arguments he had heard most recently. White House spokesman Larry Speakes used to joke that "the last thing you put in is the first thing that comes out."

Unlike other presidents, Reagan seldom requested information beyond the briefings and talking points his aides gave him. He enjoyed occasional luncheons with outside experts when they were brought in, but he rarely initiated invitations. He watched what Regan later called "a lot" of television and read a number of newspapers, although he claimed, possibly for effect, that he turned first to the comics. He was quite impressionable, particularly when it came to such arch-conservative publications as *Human Events*. After Reagan had seen it, Regan later said, "the goddamnedest things would come out of him—we had to watch what he read." He took great interest in the clippings and letters people sent him in the mail. One senior aide estimated that he opened more than half of his fifteen-minute national security briefings by reading selections from them.

Despite his position and power, Reagan often appeared to be living in contented isolation. Nancy Reagan was an inveterate telephone talker, and, in addition to acting as her husband's eyes and ears, she would occasionally put him on the line. But the president rarely initiated calls unless his staff asked him to. Nor did he keep in touch in other ways with those who were reputedly his oldest friends and advisers, on or off the White House staff. Holmes Tuttle, one of the few surviving members of Reagan's original California kitchen cabinet—the informal group of millionaires who financed his early campaigns—was usually advertised as one of the president's best friends. "We've had many years of togetherness," Tuttle affirmed. Yet when pressed he admitted, "No, he doesn't ask for advice. And as for picking up the phone and calling me, no." Similarly, Reagan's closest political friend in Washington, former Nevada senator Paul Laxalt, conceded that despite having known Reagan since 1964, "campaigning together, socializing together, camping together. . . . Do we talk about personal matters? Not at all."

Even on purely physical terms, Reagan's operating style was passive. Although he had 59 rooms in which to roam in the West Wing alone, he seldom ventured far beyond the Oval Office. In part, it was a necessary fact of life after the 1981 assassination attempt. Much as Eisenhower's schedule was restricted after his heart attack in 1955, the Secret Service became a protective wall around the president after the 1981 shooting, inevitably limiting his movement. He attended cabinet and congressional meetings, and delivered speeches in the rooms set aside for those activities, but one senior White House official doubted whether, beyond these ceremonial rooms, the press room, and the barber shop, he knew his way around the West Wing complex. He even seemed unsure about the location of most of his aides' offices, and he only visited his chief of staff, who worked a few yards down the hall, two or three times a year on special occasions, like birthdays.

Likewise, White House officials rarely wandered into the Oval Office except on official, prescribed business. In the second term only six officials—the chief of staff, the vice president, the national security adviser, the military aide, the White House doctor, and the president's personal aide—had walk-in privileges, meaning they could see the president without an appointment. And even those who could drop in seldom did so, in part because the president's workday wasn't all that long, and his time was filled by an unusually large number of ceremonial functions. A telling example of Reagan's isolation came out of the Iran-contra hearings, when the White House counsel's office tallied all the time the president had spent alone with his national security adviser, John Poindexter. The total—over eleven months and twenty-three days—came to eighty-one minutes.

The obvious danger was that Reagan could easily lose touch with political reality. It was always a peril of the office. As Woodrow Wilson noted, "Things get very lonely in Washington sometimes. The real voice of the great people of America sometimes sounds faint and distant in that strange city." But for Reagan, the hazard was exacerbated by his personality, which habitually screened out discord in order to paint the rosiest possible picture. One of his own children confided that "he makes things up and believes them." As a former senior White House official said, "He has this great ability to build these little worlds and then live in them."

In the first term, the single greatest safeguard against the president's losing touch was a staff structure as unusual as the president it served, an odd system that came to be known as the troika. It consisted of an uneasy triumvirate of top White House advisers—three extremely different men, with extremely different views and backgrounds—who policed not only each other but, in the process, the president too.

Chief of staff James A. Baker, a Princeton graduate, was the scion of one of Houston's most distinguished families, a former "Tory" Democrat who converted to the GOP in time to become undersecretary of commerce for Gerald Ford and campaign manager for George Bush in 1980. A dealmaker in pin stripes, he was as smooth as any political operator in Washington. Unlike Donald Regan, who would take his place,* he enjoyed the hurly-burly of politics—having made an unsuccessful run for attorney general of Texas in 1978—and counting a handful of congressmen and senators among his close friends. He never gained the trust of the president's more conservative backers for being too "pragmatic," but the alliances he forged so skillfully in Congress were the backbone of the first term's many legislative successes.

Deputy chief of staff Michael Deaver, the son of a gas station owner at the edge of the Mojave Desert, had come to know the Reagans through his administrative work for the Republican party in California. Uninterested in the substance of policy, he'd prove a master at the imperative of the eighties: producing the presidency for television. He had a sixth sense about how to play to Reagan's strengths and cover his weaknesses. And, more than any other White House hand, he understood how to deal personally with the president and his wife;

---

* During Reagan's first term, Baker was chief of staff and Regan was secretary of the treasury. They switched jobs in 1985. Baker was appointed secretary of state by George Bush in 1989.

legend had it that he'd once run through a glass door in his eagerness to retrieve a purse that Mrs. Reagan had left behind. Having spent all but four months of the previous nineteen years serving them, he was one of the few people who knew how to tell both of the Reagans when they were wrong and get away with it—a skill that would be lost to the White House with his departure.

Edwin Meese, the presidential counselor who would soon be attorney general, had attended Yale as an undergraduate and law school at the University of California at Berkeley; he went on to serve as deputy district attorney in California's Alameda County. Active in crushing the student demonstrations at Berkeley in the sixties, he had a fascination with law enforcement all his life. In Sacramento, he'd been Reagan's chief of staff, and in the White House he ran the Office of Policy Development. Though the office was ridiculed for its bureaucratic inefficiency and arch-conservative agenda, it nonetheless played an important role by translating Reagan's views into programs—a function largely abandoned with Meese's departure. If Baker was the political expert and Deaver the loyal retainer, Meese was the conservative conscience.

Many complained that the troika system was divisive and inefficient, since none of the three men could make a decision on his own. But in their jealousy, each helped ensure that before the president put his imprimatur on a decision, either there was a rare consensus or he heard all their views. The system was built on mutual distrust and, although no one said so, on the premise of an impressionable president vulnerable to whatever argument he heard last.

Each member of the troika thus spent much energy trying to neutralize the others. For instance, when in 1982 Meese got Reagan to back the Treasury and Justice departments' move to reestablish tax-exempt status for racially segregated schools, Deaver, recognizing the racist image it could give the administration, went into high gear. He successfully shepherded the few blacks serving in the White House into the Oval Office to change Reagan's mind.

At times the troika worked as a protective shield around the president, preventing interlopers from getting too close to him. Baker and Deaver, for instance, often became temporary allies in the fight against CIA director William J. Casey and other "hard-liners" on foreign affairs. After each of Casey's visits to the Oval Office, Deaver would saunter in casually and ask the president, "Did Bill have anything interesting to say?" Reagan would naturally tell his loyal retainer, and if the news was alarming, Deaver would notify Baker. Together they would then marshal some expert to make a counterargument—a congressman, family member, or longtime backer—to try to turn Reagan around. One issue given special surveillance was Casey's promotion of the secret war in Nicaragua, which Deaver believed "played to Reagan's dark side" in a dangerous way.

Baker had an equally great distrust of those serving as national security adviser—a post with a long history of back door communications aimed at getting the president's support. Baker attended the 9:30 A.M. national security meetings with the president and [Robert (Bud)] McFarlane. Even though Baker and McFarlane got along well, if the president nodded appreciatively during the briefing, as was his habit, Baker, according to a senior NSC aide, made a point of tracking McFarlane down later and saying, "If you think that was a go-ahead, think again."

Baker's deputy, Richard Darman, a skilled bureaucrat who had served in four federal agencies since 1971, set up what he proudly called "an authoritarian system" to monitor the NSC and others who sent paperwork to the president. The president's Out box became Darman's In box. If the president was out of the Oval Office and received, for instance, emergency correspondence elsewhere, Darman demanded that he get a facsimile immediately. If something was sent to the Executive Residence after hours, he insisted that the White House ushers deliver a copy to him by seven-thirty the next morning. The system was rigorous, but it wasn't foolproof.

One breakdown of the system resulted in the Strategic Defense Initiative. Two of the president's old political backers, Joseph Coors and Karl Bendetsen, managed to slip the nuclear scientist Edward Teller in to see Reagan without explaining to Baker and Deaver what the meeting was about. By the time Teller was done, the president had become a fervent convert to the untested and perhaps unfeasible notion that a shield could be built against nuclear weapons. It was a utopian concept that privately struck many of Reagan's arms control advisers as crazy; some privately rolled their eyes and called it "the dream." But once Teller had reached Reagan, the dream was policy.

When it worked, however, the troika forced Reagan to be exposed to diversity. Even if he raised no questions about an issue, his battling aides would. Moreover, they frequently forced him to play an active part in policy disputes. Ordinarily, a president would naturally serve this function, but as White House aide Johnathan Miller concluded, "Reagan is like a great race horse that performs well when you have a jockey that knows how to use a whip. If you don't use the whip, he'll just loaf." The troika wielded the crop that kept both the government and the president running.

Of course, Reagan wasn't completely pliant, as his first budget director, David Stockman, learned when he asked him to raise taxes. But those who knew him best, like John Sears, discovered that "you can't argue with him on the general, but on the precise you can see a tremendous amount of malleability." This characteristic inspired a maneuver that some staff members called "the Reagan argument." Its purpose was to persuade the president to change stubbornly held views by convincing him, in the face of contradictory evidence, that a switch in policy was only a change in tactics, not principles.

In order to make "Reagan arguments," former labor secretary William Brock recalled, senior advisers kept "Reagan files"—clips documenting his earlier stands, which could be marshaled to support whatever new position was being considered. Thus, levying $14 billion in new corporate taxes, which Reagan opposed on strong philosophical grounds, could be sold to him as "closing loopholes" in the Treasury's initial 1984 tax reform plan. Government surcharges on the price of gas could be sold, not as tax increases at all, but as "user fees" for highway use. The conservative social agenda—abortion, school prayer, and the other high-risk moral issues—was not being neglected, it was being postponed, so that his top priority, the economic program, would not be compromised.

By 1984, the more able advisers were masters of the technique. They liked to think they were saving Reagan from his own excesses—and frequently they were. But in the process, they ran the risk of manipulating the facts to fit their argument, politicizing intelligence, stretching rhetoric, and deluding a president not given to performing rigorous analysis of issues.

The troika also mastered techniques for managing the president in public. From Reagan's earliest days in politics, his advisers always feared the unpredictable results of his "going live." Although his aides never told him, they had engineered his most famous 1980 primary triumph—his insistence on opening a New Hampshire debate to all the candidates, not just front-runner George Bush—partly as a damage control maneuver. It was clear by the time of the debate that Reagan would win a narrow victory if nothing went wrong. But with Reagan, as his campaign aide James Lake explained seven years later, "if he went one-on-one against George Bush, there was a fifty-fifty chance he'd screw up." So they invited the other candidates, knowing that "if there were six guys, the risk would be spread out to one in six."

In the White House, Reagan's aides continued to limit his live exposure. They dispensed with an earlier idea of having him hold frequent "mini-press conferences," invented a rule trying to ban press questions at the daily "photo opportunities," and vetoed various proposed give-and-takes with youth groups because, as White House spokesman Larry Speakes explained, "he was too loose." Of course, spontaneous exchanges were sometimes unavoidable, but when the president's comments strayed too far afield, the White House press office sometimes managed to clean up his oral meanderings before a text was released for public consumption, thus altering the historical record along the way. In an Oval Office interview with the *Wall Street Journal,* in February 1985, for instance, Reagan mentioned that he had been talking "just this morning" about the biblical Armageddon. Some fundamentalists believe that it refers to an impending nuclear war, a provocative (and to some unnerving) notion for the president to entertain. "I don't know whether you know," he said with animation, "but a great many theologians over a number of years . . . have been struck with the fact that in recent years, as in no other time in history, have most of these prophecies been coming together." When the official transcript of the interview was released, the comments about Armageddon were gone. The White House later suggested that they had been "accidentally" omitted.

Similarly, his aides went to great lengths to conceal potentially embarrassing quirks. They were secretive about such matters as the president's and his daughter Maureen's apparently sincere belief that a ghost haunted the Lincoln Bedroom (Maureen claimed it had a "red aura"), the president's assertion that he had seen a flying saucer, and his acquiescence to Mrs. Reagan's reliance on astrology to determine his schedule.

Press access to the president was more tightly controlled than ever before; but complaints from journalists stirred little sympathy, perhaps because the problem was as old as the office. The question of how open the presidency should be to the public in this most democratic of governments was contentious right from the start. When George Washington announced that he would open his doors to the general public only twice a week, one senator fumed, "For him to be seen only in public on stated times, like an eastern Lama, would be . . . offensive." Despite such grousing, the presidency has grown progressively more closed to public inspection ever since. Herbert Hoover was the last president to set aside time once a week to receive any citizen who wanted to shake his hand. After that, the public had to rely on the press to serve as its eyes and ears—and there, too, access was progressively narrowed. Franklin Roosevelt used to give two press conferences a week, Eisenhower averaged more than two a month. Kennedy turned his frequent news conferences into witty jousting matches and took some members of the press into his closest confidence, getting protection in the bargain. But Reagan was the most remote. He didn't socialize with the working press, and he only gave five news conferences during all of 1984. Although a rotating pool of reporters traveled with him on *Air Force One* during the campaign, he never once came back to talk with them, though occasionally he waved from the Secret Service compartment. David Hoffman of the *Washington Post* used to joke that "covering Reagan means having to say you never saw him."

Yet the staff devoted huge amounts of energy to controlling and shaping the little the public did see of Reagan. This, too, was only new in the degree to which it took place. Many presidents before Reagan had harnessed public relations techniques to promote the office: Theodore Roosevelt may have created the modern "photo opportunity" by staging a press trip out West simply to dramatize his interest in conservation. The Nixon White House, more than any before it, perfected the art of controlling the press in the television age both by limiting access to the president and by planning no event without imagining the headline, photo, and story that would follow it. This system tried to ensure that every story was advantageous to the White House, no matter what the facts. This practice simply reached its apogee in Reagan's time, when in contrast to the Nixon era, the system served a consummate performer.

The result, as political essayist Leon Wieseltier described it, was that for the Reagan administration, "the truth was a problem to be solved." The solution was an art form known as "spin control," which referred to the "spin" the White House public relations experts put on news to make sure it bounced the desired way. Enterprising reporters tried to detect the spin and dig out the real story. Occasionally they were successful, but not without risking revenge. Press secretary Larry Speakes gave what he called "death sentences" to those reporters he deemed too critical or otherwise uncooperative. He would threaten to "put them out of business" by making sure their phone calls went unreturned and questions unanswered, putting them routinely at a competitive disadvantage. Speakes explained proudly, "The idea was to be subtle. They thought they were being screwed, but they were never quite sure." He froze out some reporters for years, but it is debatable how much they missed. Speakes later confessed to having fabricated several presidential quotes, even before his confession stirred a controversy, he admitted that he misled the public about how disengaged the president was. "As a rule," he said, "I did not think it was lying to suggest that the president might be aware of something when he wasn't."

These strategies shaped not only the written record but the photographic one as well. The official White House staff photographers shot an estimated eight to ten thousand pictures of Reagan every month, the best of which were released to the press. Mrs. Reagan usually determined which images the public saw, particularly when they included her. She personally went through the thousands of pictures, signing "O.K. per N.R." when they could be released and tearing off the corner of each of those she deemed unflattering.

Despite these many protective layers, someone close to the Oval Office would occasionally break ranks, providing a glimpse of a place that sounded quite strange. Terry Arthur, a staff photographer who spent countless hours quietly observing and documenting the president alone and with others, said he took the job partly "to find out who was running the show." After two solid years of traveling with the president, following him through meetings and on his weekend retreats, he concluded, "I never found out." Reagan, he said, "was like a Buddha. People would say, 'He wants this' or 'He wants that,' but you'd never really see him say so. He'd be shown the decisions others had made, and would say, 'Uh-huh.'"

Alexander Haig, Reagan's first secretary of state, was equally puzzled by the president's operating style. In his White House memoirs, he wrote, "To me, the White House was as mysterious as a ghost ship; you heard the creak of the rigging and the groan of the timbers, and sometimes even glimpsed the crew on deck. But which of the crew had the helm? . . . It was impossible to tell."

Summary Questions

1. The president must delegate much responsibility in conducting the affairs of state. Did Reagan delegate too much? In what ways?
2. Reagan's experience as an actor benefited him greatly as president. How much of any president's actions is essentially theater? Compare Reagan's performances with Clinton's televised town meeting on health care (11.3). Whose performance was more effective? Why?

 Chapter 12

BUREAUCRACY

The terms *bureaucracy* and *bureaucrat* evoke negative images for most Americans. To many, *bureaucracy* is a synonym for red tape, rigidity, insensitivity, and long waiting lines, and *bureaucrat* suggests a faceless government drone sitting at a desk, pushing papers, and stamping forms. In fact, a bureaucracy is any complex organization that operates on the basis of a hierarchical authority structure with job specialization. Corporations are bureaucracies, as are educational institutions. The dilemma is whether a bureaucracy complements democracy. On the one hand, it seems wise to have a government run by professionals whose jobs are not dependent on politics. But we seem to have created a class of government employees who are beyond the control of the voters.

In recent years, public officials and candidates for public office have nurtured the negative image of the public sector and those employed by it. Bureaucracy-bashing is good politics. Three recent presidents—Nixon, Carter, and Reagan—were first elected during campaigns that made opposition to the Washington bureaucracy a central theme. Every election year congressional candidates remind the public that the federal government has paid $91 for three-cent screws or $511 for a sixty-cent lightbulb. Contempt for the Washington bureaucracy may have reached a zenith during the Reagan presidency. Attorney General Edwin Meese once came to a cabinet meeting carrying a chubby, faceless, large-bottomed doll and announced that it was a bureaucrat doll—you place it on a stack of papers and it just sits there.

According to one student of American bureaucracy, Barry D. Karl, "the growth of the bureaucratic state may be the single most unintended consequence of the Constitution of 1787." The Constitution says little about the administration of government. It gives the president the appointment power and the obligation "to take care that the laws [are] faithfully executed," which suggests that the framers were well aware of the administrative needs of the new nation. But belief in limited government and fear of centralized power led them to envision a minimal role for the new federal government.

Thus, the administrative apparatus during the first few presidencies was very small. The State Department had only nine employees at its beginning, and the War Department had fewer than one hundred employees until 1801, at the start of the Jefferson presidency. Compared to Western European countries, the

United States bureaucracy experienced a rather late development, well after the growth of mass democracy under Andrew Jackson in the 1830s. By 1861, on the eve of the Civil War, roughly 80 percent of all federal personnel still worked for the Post Office Department.

The Civil War was one of the most significant events in the growth of American bureaucracy. Mobilization for the war effort led to the creation of many new agencies and the hiring of a large number of public employees. The growth of a national economy and rapid industrialization after the war also had a profound effect on the size and functions of the federal government, which began to pay attention to particular constituencies. "Clientele" agencies such as the Department of Agriculture (1889) and the Department of Commerce and Labor (1903) were created to service increasingly organized interests.

This period also marked the beginning of the development of a professional bureaucratic class. Before 1883, all federal workers were patronage employees, appointed by the president. When presidencies changed hands, many government employees were out of a job. The assassination of President James A. Garfield in 1881 by an unsuccessful patronage applicant provided the impetus for passage of the Pendleton Act (1882), which established the civil service system. Only about 10 percent of government employees were initially covered by the act, but today about 90 percent are; they receive their jobs on the basis of competitive merit, usually as the result of written examinations. Being fired for political reasons is illegal.

The New Deal and mobilization for World War II gave the federal bureaucracy the basic form with which we associate it today. As the federal government took on an expanded social and economic role, a myriad of new agencies were created. Today there are more than a hundred federal government agencies, and the government employs about 5 million people, 2.9 million of whom are civilians.

Despite the widely shared view that the federal bureaucracy has grown rapidly in recent decades, the number of federal employees has been relatively constant since 1945. Most of the growth in the public sector has been at the state and local levels. Nor do most federal bureaucrats work in or around the nation's capital. Only about 12 percent of federal employees work in Washington, and 300,000, or 10 percent, work in California. Federal government employment as a percentage of the total work force decreased over the past two decades. "Big government" is more dollars and rules than it is huge numbers of federal bureaucrats.

Whatever the size of the bureaucracy, its nature poses a dilemma. We need a bureaucratic organization and professional administrators so that government can carry out its basic functions without political interference. But the growth of a professional bureaucratic class has been considered at odds with American political values. Use of the term *civil servant* is an insistence that government employees serve the public, not their employer or themselves. Although Americans want state services, the fear of strong central government and administrative tyranny remains.

Because contemporary U.S. government involves so many activities, almost everyone can view some aspect of bureaucracy as illegitimate and threatening. Conservatives generally disapprove of government's redistribution of income and regulation of business, viewing it as intrusive and opposed to traditional free-market philosophy. Liberals are concerned about the bureaucracy's intelligence-gathering and domestic policing activities; the secrecy and potential violation of civil liberties raise concerns about "Big Brother" watching.

And the federal bureaucracy represents more than the passive administration of laws passed by the elected branches of government. Bureaucrats are given substantial authority: They issue rules, enforce compliance, allocate federal funds, and regulate economic activity. Because of their expertise, they often formulate policy, although the most successful bureaucratic policymakers work closely with Congress.

The American solution to the dilemma of bureaucracy and democracy is to keep the bureaucracy accountable through scrutiny by the other branches of government and by the nation's press. Congressional oversight of bureaucratic practices and spending, central direction in policy making by the president and his staff, and judicial review of administrative processes and rule making are all important restraints on bureaucratic discretion.

The articles selected for this chapter are intended to give the reader a sense of the impact of the bureaucracy on American politics, the controversial nature of its activities, and the difficulties facing those who wish to reform it. Charles Peters discusses some of the problems inherent in large organizations and how they can lead to flawed bureaucratic decisions. James Q. Wilson focuses upon the difficulties managers of public organizations confront because of their lack of control over agency revenues, productivity factors, and agency goals due to external political constraints. Finally, Jerry Hagstrom looks at one of the most controversial federal agencies, the U.S. Department of Agriculture, and describes recent efforts by the Clinton administration to reorganize the department and cut costs.

12.1

From Ouagadougou to Cape Canaveral: Why the Bad News Doesn't Travel Up

Charles Peters

On January 28, 1986, seven crew members of the space shuttle Challenger were killed in a midflight explosion. The tragedy was caused by the disintegration of a type of seal called an O-ring, which led to failure in the joint between segments of one of the eight solid booster rockets. It can be argued, however, that the fundamental reason for the shuttle disaster was a communication failure within the hierarchy of the National Aeronautics and Space Administration (NASA). Private engineers on the project were aware of a history of problems with the O-rings and had advised certain mid-level NASA officials not to launch under certain conditions. Had top-level officials known of the problems, the launch might not have taken place.

In this article, Charles Peters suggests that it is extremely difficult for top managers in a large organization to be aware of problems at various levels of a bureaucratic hierarchy. Officials at NASA were under tremendous political pressure to launch the shuttle, and so negative information was suppressed within the chain of command. Peters suggests that this problem is quite common and can be blamed for a number of the government's recent flawed decisions. The remedies, he suggests, are more direct government oversight and an active press.

Everyone is asking why the top NASA officials who decided to launch the fatal Challenger flight had not been told of the concerns of people down below, like Allan McDonald and the other worried engineers at Morton Thiokol.*

In the first issue of *The Washington Monthly*, Russell Baker and I wrote, "In any reasonably large government organization, there exists an elaborate system of information cutoffs, comparable to that by which city water systems shut off large

---

Charles Peters is editor in chief of *The Washington Monthly*.

* Morton Thiokol is the private engineering company that was in charge of the design and construction of the space shuttle booster rocket.

water-main breaks, closing down, first small feeder pipes, then larger and larger valves. The object is to prevent information, particularly of an unpleasant character, from rising to the top of the agency, where it may produce results unpleasant to the lower ranks.

"Thus, the executive at or near the top lives in constant danger of not knowing, until he reads it on Page One some morning, that his department is hip-deep in disaster."

This seemed to us to be a serious problem for government, not only because the people at the top didn't know but because the same system of cut-offs operated to keep Congress, the press, and the public in the dark. (Often it also would operate to keep in the dark people within the organization but outside the immediate chain of command—this happened with the astronauts, who were not told about the concern with the O-rings.)

I first became aware of this during the sixties, when I worked at the Peace Corps. Repeatedly I would find that a problem that was well-known by people at lower and middle levels of the organization, whose responsibility it was, would be unknown at the top of the chain of command or by anyone outside.

The most serious problems of the Peace Corps had their origins in Sargent Shriver's desire to get the organization moving.* He did not want it to become mired in feasibility studies, he wanted to get volunteers overseas and into action fast. To fulfill his wishes, corners were cut. Training was usually inadequate in language, culture, and technical skills. Volunteers were selected who were not suited to their assignments. For example, the country then known as Tanganyika asked for surveyors, and we sent them people whose only connection with surveying had been holding the rod and chain while the surveyor sighted through his gizmo. Worse, volunteers were sent to places where no job at all awaited them. These fictitious assignments were motivated sometimes by the host official's desire to please the brother-in-law of the president of the United States and sometimes by the official's ignorance of what was going on at the lower levels of his own bureaucracy.

But subordinates would not tell Shriver about the problems. There were two reasons for this. One was fear. They knew that he wanted action, not excuses, and they suspected that their careers would suffer if he heard too many of the latter. The other reason was that they felt it was their job to solve problems, not burden the boss with them. They and Shriver shared the view expressed by Deke Slayton, the former astronaut, when he was asked about the failure of middle-level managers to tell top NASA officials about the problems they were encountering. "You depend on managers to make a decision based on the information they have. If they had to transmit all the fine detail to the top people, it wouldn't get launched but once every ten years."

---

* Sargent Shriver, who was President Kennedy's brother-in-law, was the first director of the Peace Corps. The organization was set up to send American volunteers to help people in Third World countries. In 1972, Shriver was the Democratic vice-presidential candidate.

The point is not without merit. It is easy for large organizations to fall into "once every ten years" habits. Leaders who want to avoid that danger learn to set goals and communicate a sense of urgency about meeting them. But what many of them never learn is that once you set those goals you have to guard against the tendency of those down below to spare you not only "all the fine detail" but essential facts about significant problems.

For instance, when Jimmy Carter gave the Pentagon the goal of rescuing the Iranian hostages, he relied on the chain of command to tell him if there were any problems. So he did not find out until after the disaster at Desert One that the Delta Commandos thought the Marine pilots assigned to fly the helicopters were incompetent.*

In NASA's case chances have been taken with the shuttle from the beginning—the insulating thermal tiles had not gone through a reentry test before the first shuttle crew risked their lives to try them out—but in recent years the pressure to cut corners has increased markedly. Competition with the European Ariane rocket and the Reagan administration's desire to see agencies like NASA run as if they were private businesses have led to a speedup in the launch schedule, with a goal of 14 this year [1986] and 24 by 1988.

"The game NASA is playing is the maximum tonnage per year at the minimum costs possible," says Paul Cloutier, a professor of space physics. "Some high officials don't want to hear about problems," reports *Newsweek*, "especially if fixing them will cost money."

Under pressures like these, the NASA launch team watched Columbia, after seven delays, fall about a month behind schedule and then saw Challenger delayed, first by bad weather, then by damaged door handles, and then by bad weather again. Little wonder that [NASA's launch chief] Lawrence Mulloy, when he heard the warnings from the Thiokol engineers, burst out: "My God, Thiokol, when do you want me to launch? Next April?"

Mulloy may be one of the villains of this story, but it is important to realize that you need Lawrence Mulloys to get things done. It is also important to realize that, if you have a Lawrence Mulloy, you must protect yourself against what he might fail to do or what he might do wrong in his enthusiastic rush to get the job done.

And you can't just ask him if he has any doubts. If he's a gung-ho type, he's going to suppress the negatives. When Jimmy Carter asked General David Jones to check out the Iran rescue plan, Jones said to Colonel Beckwith: "Charlie, tell me what you really think about the mission. Be straight with me."

"Sir, we're going to do it!" Beckwith replied. "We want to do it, and we're ready."

---

* In the spring of 1980, President Carter made a decision to have a U.S. commando force attempt to rescue the American hostages held in Iran. A number of reasons have been suggested for the failure of the mission. The helicopters chosen for the mission evidently could not operate successfully in the sand and wind of the Iranian desert. One crashed on takeoff, killing a number of soldiers, and the mission was aborted.

John Kennedy received similar confident reports from the chain of command about the readiness of the CIA's Cuban Brigade to charge ashore at the Bay of Pigs and overthrow Fidel Castro. And Sargent Shriver had every reason to believe that the Peace Corps was getting off to a fabulous start, based on what his chain of command was telling him.

With Shriver, as with NASA's senior officials, the conviction that everything was A-OK was fortified by skillful public relations. Bill Moyers was only one of the geniuses involved in this side of the Peace Corps. At NASA, Julian Scheer began a tradition of inspired PR that endured until Challenger. These were men who could sell air conditioning in Murmansk. The trouble is they also sold their bosses the same air conditioning. Every organization has a tendency to believe its own PR—NASA's walls are lined with glamorizing posters and photographs of the shuttle and other space machines—and usually the top man is the most thoroughly seduced because, after all, it reflects the most glory on him.

Favorable publicity and how to get it is therefore the dominant subject of Washington staff meetings. The minutes of the Nuclear Regulatory Commission show that when the reactor was about to melt down at Three Mile Island, the commissioners were worried less about what to do to fix the reactor than they were about what they were going to say to the press.

One of the hottest rumors around Washington is that the White House had put pressure on NASA to launch so that the president could point with pride to the teacher in space during his State of the Union speech. The White House denies this story, and my sources tell me the denial is true. But NASA had—and this is fact, not rumor—put pressure on *itself* by asking the president to mention Christa McAuliffe. In a memorandum dated January 8, NASA proposed that the president say: "Tonight while I am speaking to you, a young elementary school teacher from Concord, New Hampshire, is taking us all on the ultimate field trip as she orbits the earth as the first citizen passenger on the space shuttle. Christa McAuliffe's journey is a prelude to the journeys of other Americans living and working together in a permanently manned space station in the mid-1990s. Mrs. McAuliffe's week in space is just one of the achievements in space we have planned for the coming year."

The flight was scheduled for January 23. It was postponed and postponed again. Now it was January 28, the morning of the day the speech was to be delivered, the last chance for the launch to take place in time to have it mentioned by the president. NASA officials must have feared they were about to lose a PR opportunity of stunning magnitude, an opportunity to impress not only the media and the public but the agency's two most important constituencies, the White House and the Congress. Wouldn't you feel pressure to get that launch off this morning so that the president could talk about it tonight?

NASA's sensitivity to the media in regard to the launch schedule was nothing short of unreal. Here is what Richard G. Smith, the director of the Kennedy Space Center, had to say about it after the disaster: "Every time there was a delay, the press would say, 'Look, there's another delay. . . . here's a bunch of idiots who can't even handle a launch schedule.' You think that doesn't have an impact? If you think it doesn't, you're stupid."

I do not recall seeing a single story like those Smith describes. Perhaps there were a few. The point, however, is to realize how large even a little bit of press criticism loomed in NASA's thinking.

Sargent Shriver liked good press as much as, if not more than, the next man. But he also had an instinct that the ultimate bad press would come if the world found out about your disaster before you had a chance to do something to prevent it. He and an assistant named William Haddad decided to make sure that Shriver got the bad news first. Who was going to find it out for them? Me.

It was July 1961. They decided to call me an evaluator and send me out to our domestic training programs and later overseas to find out what was really going on. My first stop was the University of California at Berkeley where our Ghana project was being trained. Fortunately, except for grossly inadequate language instruction, this program was excellent. But soon I began finding serious deficiencies in other training programs and in our projects abroad.

Shriver was not always delighted by these reports. Indeed, at one point I heard I was going to be fired. I liked my job, and I knew that the reports that I and the other evaluators who had joined me were writing were true. I didn't want to be fired. What could I do?

I knew he was planning to visit our projects in Africa. So I prepared a memorandum that contrasted what the chain of command was saying with what I and my associates were reporting. Shriver left for Africa. I heard nothing for several weeks. Then came a cable from Somalia: "Tell Peters his reports are right." I knew then that, however much Shriver wanted to hear the good news and get good publicity, he could take the bad news. The fact that he could take the bad news meant that the Peace Corps began to face its problems and do something about them before they became a scandal.

NASA did the opposite. A 1983 reorganization shifted the responsibility for monitoring flight safety from the chief engineer in Washington to the field. This may sound good. "We're not going to micromanage," said James M. Beggs, then the NASA administrator. But the catch is that if you decentralize, you must maintain the flow of information from the field to the top so that the organization's leader will know what those decentralized managers are doing. What NASA's reorganization did, according to safety engineers who talked to Mark Tapscott of the *Washington Times,* was to close off "an independent channel with authority to make things happen at the top."

I suspect what happened is that the top NASA administrators, who were pushing employees down below to dramatically increase the number of launches, either consciously or unconsciously did not want to be confronted with the dangers they were thereby risking.

This is what distinguishes the bad leaders from the good. The good leader, realizing that there is a natural human tendency to avoid bad news, traps himself into having to face it. He encourages whistleblowers instead of firing them. He visits the field himself and talks to the privates and lieutenants as well as the generals to find out the real problems. He can use others to do this for him, as Shriver used me. . . . But he must have some independent knowledge of what's going on down below in order to have a feel for whether the chain of command is giving him the straight dope.

What most often happens, of course, is that the boss, if he goes to the field at all, talks only to the colonels and generals. Sometimes he doesn't want to know what the privates know. He may be hoping that the lid can be kept on whatever problems are developing, at least until his watch is over, so that he won't be blamed when they finally surface. Or he may have a very good idea that bad things are being done and simply wants to retain "deniability," meaning that the deed cannot be traced to him. The story of Watergate is filled with "Don't tell me" and "I don't want to know."

When NASA's George Hardy told Thiokol engineers that he was appalled by their verbal recommendation that the launch be postponed and asked Thiokol to reconsider and make another recommendation, Thiokol, which Hardy well knew was worried about losing its shuttle contract, was in effect being told, "Don't tell me" or "Don't tell me officially so I won't have to pass bad news along and my bosses will have deniability."

In addition to the leader himself, others must be concerned with making him face the bad news. This includes subordinates. Their having the courage to speak out about what is wrong is crucial, and people like Bruce Cook of NASA and Allan McDonald of Thiokol deserve great credit for having done so. But it is a fact that none of the subordinates who knew the danger to the shuttle took the next step and resigned in protest so that the public could find out what was going on in time to prevent disaster. The almost universal tendency to place one's own career above one's moral responsibility to take a stand on matters like these has to be one of the most depressing facts about bureaucratic culture today.

Even when the issue was simply providing facts for an internal NASA investigation after the disaster, here is the state of mind Bruce Cook describes in a recent article in the Washington Post: "Another [NASA employee] told me to step away from his doorway while he searched for a document in his filing cabinet so that no one would see me in his office and suspect that he'd been the one I'd gotten it from."

It may be illuminating to note here that at the Peace Corps I found my most candid informants were the volunteers. They had no career stake in the organization—they were in for just two years—and thus had no reason to fear the results of their candor. Doesn't this suggest that we might be better off with more short-term employees in the government, people who are planning to leave anyway and thus have no hesitation to blow the whistle when necessary?

Certainly the process of getting bad news from the bottom to the top can be helped by institutionalizing it, as it was in the case of the Peace Corps Evaluation Division, and by hiring to perform it employees who have demonstrated courage and independence as well as the ability to elicit the truth and report it clearly.

Two other institutions that can help this process are the Congress and the White House. But the staff they have to perform this function is tiny. The White House depends on the OMB to tell it what the executive branch is doing. Before the Challenger exploded, the OMB had four examiners to cover science and space. The Senate subcommittee on Space, Science and Technology had a staff of three. Needless to say, they had not heard about the O-rings.

Another problem is lack of experience. Too few congressmen and too few of their staff have enough experience serving in the executive branch to have a sense of the right question to ask. OMB examiners usually come aboard straight from graduate school, totally innocent of practical experience in government.

The press shares this innocence. Only a handful of journalists have worked in the bureaucracy. Like the members of Congress, they treat policy formulation as the ultimate reality: Congress passed this bill today; the president signed that bill. That's what the TV reporters on the Capitol steps and the White House lawn tell us about. But suppose the legislation in question concerns coal mine safety. Nobody is going to know what it all adds up to until some members of Congress and some members of the press go down into the coal mine to find out if conditions actually are safer or if only more crazy regulations have been added.

Unfortunately, neither the congressmen nor the press display much enthusiasm for visits to the mines. Yet this is what I found to be the key to getting the real story about the Peace Corps. I had to go to Ouagadougou and talk to the volunteers at their sites before I could really know what the Peace Corps was doing and what its problems were. I wasn't going to find out by asking the public affairs office. . . .

Because the reporters don't know any better, they don't press the Congress to do any better. What journalists could do is make the public aware of how little attention Congress devotes to what is called "oversight," i.e., finding out what the programs it has authorized are actually doing. If the press would publicize the nonperformance of this function, it is at least possible that the public would begin to reward the congressmen who perform it consistently and punish those who ignore it by not reelecting them.

But the press will never do this until it gets itself out of Larry Speakes's office. Woodward and Bernstein didn't get the Watergate story by talking to Ron Ziegler,* or, for that matter, by using other reportorial techniques favored by the media elite, like questioning Richard Nixon at a press conference or interviewing other administration luminaries at fancy restaurants. They had to find lower-level sources like Hugh Sloan, just as the reporters who finally got the NASA story had to find the Richard Cooks and Allan McDonalds.

Eileen Shanahan, a former reporter for the *New York Times* and a former assistant secretary of HEW, recently wrote "of the many times I tried, during my

---

* Larry Speakes was Ronald Reagan's press secretary at the time this article was written. Ron Ziegler was President Nixon's press secretary. Bob Woodward and Carl Bernstein were the two *Washington Post* writers credited with unraveling the Watergate scandal.

tenure in the Department of Health, Education and Welfare, to interest distin-guished reporters from distinguished publications in the effort the department was making to find out whether its billion-dollar programs actually were reaching the intended beneficiaries and doing any good. Their eyes glazed over."

I have had a similar experience with reporters during my 25 years in Washing-ton. For most of that time they have seemed to think they knew everything about bureaucracy because they had read a Kafka novel and stood in line at the post office. In their ignorance, they adopted a kind of wise-guy, world-weary fatalism that said nothing could be done about bureaucratic problems. They had little or no sense about how to approach organizations with an anthropologist's feel for the interaction of attitudes, values, and institutional pressures.

There are a couple of reasons, however, to hope that the performance of the press will improve. The coverage of business news has become increasingly sophisticated about the way institutional pressures affect executive and corporate behavior, mainly because the comparison of our economy with Japan's made the importance of cultural factors so obvious. And on defense issues, visits to the field are increasingly common as reporters attempt to find out whether this or that weapon works.

But these are mere beachheads. They need to be radically expanded to include the coverage of all the institutions that affect our lives, especially government. This may seem unlikely, but if the press studies the Challenger case, I do not see how it can avoid perceiving the critical role bureaucratic pressure played in bringing about the disaster. What the press must then realize is that similar pressures vitally influence almost everything this government does, and that we will never understand why government fails until we understand those pressures and how human beings in public office react to them.*

Summary Questions

1. What factors operate within large organizations to prevent top leaders from learning about organizational difficulties? How might a leader of an organiza-tion overcome such factors?
2. According to the author, why don't congressional oversight and press scru-tiny of the bureaucracy uncover problems? How could such oversight be improved?

---

* In 1990, NASA experienced another public relations disaster when its $1.5 billion Hubble Space Telescope failed to focus clearly. NASA's investigating panel fixed the blame for the telescope flaw on the same management climate that led to the fatal explosion of the space shuttle *Challenger* in 1986. As in the shuttle case, the report indicated that engineers working on the telescope as far back as 1980 and 1981 were discouraged from bringing potential problems to the attention of their superiors.

12.2

Constraints on Public Managers

James Q. Wilson

Companies like AT&T or McDonald's rival in size and budget some of the largest government organizations and, on paper, are organized similarly, with a hierarchical authority structure and multiple layers of administration. They are bureaucracies in every sense of the term. Critics of government bureaucracy often point to the successes of such private sector organizations as efficient deliverers of services or products, in contrast to public bureaucracies that often are stereotyped as bound by rules or red tape and staffed by unmotivated and unresponsive workers. Every election sees candidates committed to reforming government bureaucracies, in an attempt to "run government more like a business."

Although government and private bureaucracies share many characteristics, they are different in fundamental ways, creating difficulties for those who aspire to make government agencies more like their private sector counterparts. In this selection, James Q. Wilson argues that all government agencies have certain characteristics that tend to make their management far more difficult than managing a business: "Government management tends to be driven by the *constraints* on the organization, not the *tasks* of the organization." Managerial control is particularly problematic because public managers have relative little control over revenues, factors of production, and agency goals, which are "all vested to an important degree in entities external to the organization—legislatures, courts, politicians, and interest groups." One result is that public managers become "averse to any action that risks violating a significant constraint," rigidly interpreting rules and avoiding innovation.

B y the time the office opens at 8:45 A.M, the line of people waiting to do business at the Registry of Motor Vehicles in Watertown, Massachusetts, often will be twenty-five deep. By midday, especially if it is near the end of the month, the line may extend clear around the building. Inside, motorists wait in slow-moving rows before poorly marked windows to get a driver's license or to register an automobile. When someone gets to the head of the line, he or she is

James Q. Wilson is professor of management and public policy at UCLA and past president of the American Political Science Association.

often told by the clerk that it is the wrong line: "Get an application over there and then come back," or "This is only for people getting a new license; if you want to replace one you lost, you have to go to the next window." The customers grumble impatiently. The clerks act harried and sometimes speak brusquely, even rudely. What seems to be a simple transaction may take 45 minutes or even longer. . . .

Not far away, people also wait in line at a McDonald's fast-food restaurant. There are several lines; each is short, each moves quickly. The menu is clearly displayed on attractive signs. The workers behind the counter are invariably polite. If someone's order cannot be filled immediately, he or she is asked to step aside for a moment while the food is prepared and then is brought back to the head of the line to receive the order. The atmosphere is friendly and good-natured. The room is immaculately clean.

Many people have noticed the difference between getting a driver's license and ordering a Big Mac. Most will explain it by saying that bureaucracies are different from businesses. "Bureaucracies" behave as they do because they are run by unqualified "bureaucrats" and are enmeshed in "rules" and "red tape."

But business firms are also bureaucracies, and McDonald's is a bureaucracy that regulates virtually every detail of its employees' behavior by a complex and all-encompassing set of rules. Its operations manual is six hundred pages long and weighs four pounds.[1] In it one learns that french fries are to be nine-thirty-seconds of an inch thick and that grill workers are to place hamburger patties on the grill from left to right, six to a row for six rows. They are then to flip the third row first, followed by the fourth, fifth, and sixth rows, and finally the first and second. The amount of sauce placed on each bun is precisely specified. Every window must be washed every day. Workers must get down on their hands and knees and pick up litter as soon as it appears. These and countless other rules designed to reduce the workers to interchangeable automata were inculcated in franchise managers at Hamburger University located in a $40 million facility. There are plenty of rules governing the Registry, but they are only a small fraction of the rules that govern every detail of every operation at McDonald's. Indeed, if the DMV manager tried to impose on his employees as demanding a set of rules as those that govern the McDonald's staff, they would probably rebel and he would lose his job.

It is just as hard to explain the differences between the two organizations by reference to the quality or compensation of their employees. The Registry workers are all adults, most with at least a high-school education; the McDonald's employees are mostly teenagers, many still in school. The Registry staff is well-paid compared to the McDonald's workers, most of whom receive only the minimum wage. . . .

Not only are the differences between the two organizations not to be explained by reference to "rules" or "red tape" or "incompetent workers," the differences call into question many of the most frequently mentioned complaints about how government agencies are supposed to behave. For example: "Government agencies are big spenders." The Watertown office of the Registry is in a modest building that can barely handle its clientele. The teletype machine used to check information submitted by people requesting a replacement license was antiquated and prone to errors. Three or four clerks often had to wait in line to use equipment described by the office manager as "personally signed by Thomas Edison." No computers or word processors were available to handle the preparation of licenses and registrations; any error made by a clerk while manually typing a form meant starting over again on another form.

Or: "Government agencies hire people regardless of whether they are really needed." Despite the fact that the citizens of Massachusetts probably have more contact with the Registry than with any other state agency, and despite the fact that these citizens complain more about Registry service than about that of any other bureau, the Watertown branch, like all Registry offices, was seriously understaffed. . . .

Or: "Government agencies are imperialistic, always grasping for new functions." But there is no record of the Registry doing much grasping, even though one could imagine a case being made that the state government could usefully create at Registry offices "one-stop" multi-service centers where people could not only get drivers' licenses but also pay taxes and parking fines, obtain information, and transact other official business. The Registry seemed content to provide one service.

In short, many of the popular stereotypes about government agencies and their members are either questionable or incomplete. To explain why government agencies behave as they do, it is not enough to know that they are "bureaucracies"—that is, it is not enough to know that they are big, or complex, or have rules. What is crucial is that they are *government* bureaucracies. . . . [N]ot all government bureaucracies behave the same way or suffer from the same problems. . . . But all government agencies have in common certain characteristics that tend to make their management far more difficult than managing a McDonald's. These common characteristics are the constraints of public agencies.

The key constraints are three in number. To a much greater extent than is true of private bureaucracies, government agencies (1) cannot lawfully retain and devote to the private benefit of their members the earnings of the organization, (2) cannot allocate the factors of production in accordance with the preferences of the organization's administrators, and (3) must serve goals not of the organization's own choosing. Control over revenues, productive factors, and agency goals is all vested to an important degree in entities external to the organization—legislatures, courts, politicians, and interest groups. Given this, agency managers must attend to the demands of these external entities. As a result, government management tends to be driven by the *constraints* on the organization, not the *tasks* of the organization. To say the same thing in other words, whereas business management focuses on the "bottom line" (that is, profits), government management focuses on the "top line" (that is, constraints). . . .

Revenues and Incentives

In the days leading up to September 30, the federal government is Cinderella, courted by legions of individuals and organizations eager to get grants and contracts from the unexpended funds still at the disposal of each agency. At midnight on September 30, the government's coach turns into a pumpkin. That is the moment—the end of the fiscal year—at which every agency, with a few exceptions, must return all unexpended funds to the Treasury Department. . . . Because of these fiscal rules agencies do not have a material incentive to econo-mize: Why scrimp and save if you cannot keep the results of your frugality?

. . . When a private firm has a good year, many of its officers and workers may receive bonuses. Even if no bonus is paid, these employees may buy stock in the firm so that they can profit from any growth in earnings (and, if they sell the stock in a timely manner, profit from a drop in earnings). Should a public bureaucrat be discovered trying to do what private bureaucrats routinely do, he or she would be charged with corruption.

We take it for granted that bureaucrats should not profit from their offices and nod approvingly when a bureaucrat who has so benefited is indicted and put on trial. But why should we take this view? Once a very different view prevailed. In the seventeenth century, a French colonel would buy his commission from the king, take the king's money to run his regiment, and pocket the profit. At one time a European tax collector was paid by keeping a percentage of the taxes he collected. In this country, some prisons were once managed by giving the warden a sum of money based on how many prisoners were under his control and letting him keep the difference between what he received and what it cost him to feed the prisoners. Such behavior today would be grounds for criminal prosecution. Why? What has changed?

Mostly we the citizenry have changed. We are creatures of the Enlightenment: We believe that the nation ought not to be the property of the sovereign; that laws are intended to rationalize society and (if possible) perfect mankind; and that public service ought to be neutral and disinterested. We worry that a prison warden paid in the old way would have a strong incentive to starve his prisoners in order to maximize his income; that a regiment supported by a greedy colonel would not be properly equipped; and that a tax collector paid on a commission basis would extort excessive taxes from us. These changes reflect our desire to eliminate moral hazards—namely, creating incentives for people to act wrongly. But why should this desire rule out more carefully designed compensation plans that would pay government managers for achieving officially approved goals and would allow efficient agencies to keep any unspent part of their budget for use next year?

Part of the answer is obvious. Often we do not know whether a manager or an agency has achieved the goals we want because either the goals are vague or inconsistent, or their attainment cannot be observed, or both. Bureau chiefs in the Department of State would have to go on welfare if their pay depended on their ability to demonstrate convincingly that they had attained their bureaus' objectives.

But many government agencies have reasonably clear goals toward which progress can be measured. The Social Security Administration, the Postal Service, and the General Services Administration all come to mind. Why not let earnings depend importantly on performance? Why not let agencies keep excess revenues?

I am not entirely certain why this does not happen. To some degree it is because of a widespread cultural norm that people should not profit from public service. . . .

But in part it is because we know that even government agencies with clear goals and readily observable behavior only can be evaluated by making political (and thus conflict-ridden) judgments. If the Welfare Department delivers every benefit check within 24 hours after the application is received, Senator Smith may be pleased but Senator Jones will be irritated because this speedy delivery almost surely would require that the standards of eligibility be relaxed so that many ineligible clients would get money. There is no objective standard by which the tradeoff between speed and accuracy in the Welfare Department can be evaluated. . . .

The closest we can come to supplying a nonpolitical, nonarbitrary evaluation of an organization's performance is by its ability to earn from customers revenues in excess of costs. This is how business firms, private colleges, and most hospitals are evaluated. But government agencies cannot be evaluated by this market test because they either supply a service for which there are no willing customers (for example, prisons or the IRS) or are monopoly suppliers of a valued service (for example, the welfare department and the Registry of Motor Vehicles). Neither an organization with unwilling customers nor one with the exclusive right to serve such customers as exist can be evaluated by knowing how many customers they attract. When there is no external, nonpolitical evaluation of agency performance, there is no way to allow the agency to retain earnings that is not subject to agency manipulation. . . .

Critics of government agencies like to describe them as "bloated bureaucracies," defenders of them as "starved for funds." The truth is more complicated. Legislators judge government *programs* differently from how they judge government *bureaus*. Programs, such as Social Security, have constituencies that benefit from them. Constituencies press legislators for increases in program expenditures. If the constituencies are found in many districts, the pressures are felt by many legislators. These pressures ordinarily are not countered by those from any organized group that wants the benefits cut. Bureaucrats may or may not be constituencies. If they are few in number or concentrated in one legislative district they may have little political leverage with which to demand an increase in numbers or benefits. For example, expenditures on Social Security have grown steadily since the program began in 1935, but the offices, pay rates, and perquisites of Social Security administrators have not grown correspondingly.

If the bureaucrats are numerous, well-organized, and found in many districts (for example, letter carriers in the old Post Office Department or sanitation workers in New York City) they may have enough leverage to insure that their benefits increase faster than their workload. But even numerous and organized bureaucrats labor under a strategic disadvantage arising from the fact that legislators find it easier to constrain bureaucratic inputs than bureaucratic outputs. The reasons are partly conceptual, partly political. Conceptually, an office building or pay schedule is a tangible input, easily understood by all; "good health" or a "decent retirement" or an "educated child" are matters of opinion. Politically, legislators face more or less steady pressures to keep tax rates down while allowing program benefits to grow. The conceptual ambiguities combine neatly with the political realities: The rational course of action for a legislator is to appeal to taxpayers by ostentatiously constraining the budget for buildings, pay raises, and managerial benefits while appealing to program beneficiaries by loudly calling for more money to be spent on health, retirement, or education. (Witness the difficulty schoolteachers have in obtaining pay increases without threatening a strike, even at a time when expenditures on education are growing.) As a result, there are many lavish programs in this country administered by modestly paid bureaucrats working on out-of-date equipment in cramped offices.*

The inability of public managers to capture surplus revenues for their own use alters the pattern of incentives at work in government agencies. Beyond a certain point additional effort does not produce additional earnings. (In this country, Congress from time to time has authorized higher salaries for senior bureaucrats but then put a cap on actual payments to them so that the pay increases were never received. This was done to insure that no bureaucrat would earn more than members of Congress at a time when those members were unwilling to accept the political costs of raising their own salaries. As a result, the pay differential between the top bureaucratic rank and those just below it nearly vanished.) If political constraints reduce the marginal effect of money incentives, then the relative importance of other, nonmonetary incentives will increase. . . .

That bureaucratic performance in most government agencies cannot be linked to monetary benefits is not the whole explanation for the difference between public and private management. There are many examples of private organizations whose members cannot appropriate money surpluses for their own benefit. Private schools ordinarily are run on a nonprofit basis. Neither the headmaster nor the teachers share in the profit of these schools; indeed, most such schools earn no profit at all and instead struggle to keep afloat by soliciting contributions from friends and alumni. Nevertheless, the evidence is quite clear that on the

---

* Elsewhere, government officials may enjoy generous salaries and lavish offices. Indeed, in some underdeveloped nations, travelers see all about them signs of public munificence and private squalor. The two may be connected.

average, private schools, both secular and denominational, do a better job than public ones in educating children.[2]

Acquiring and Using the Factors of Production

A business firm acquires capital by retaining earnings, borrowing money, or selling shares of ownership; a government agency (with some exceptions) acquires capital by persuading a legislature to appropriate it. A business firm hires, promotes, demotes, and fires personnel with considerable though not perfect freedom; a federal government agency is told by Congress how many persons it can hire and at what rate of pay, by the Office of Personnel Management (OPM) what rules it must follow in selecting and assigning personnel, by the Office of Management and Budget (OMB) how many persons of each rank it may employ, by the Merit Systems Protection Board (MSPB) what procedures it must follow in demoting or discharging personnel, and by the courts whether it has faithfully followed the rules of Congress, OPM, OMB, and MSPB. A business firm purchases goods and services by internally defined procedures (including those that allow it to buy from someone other than the lowest bidder if a more expensive vendor seems more reliable), or to skip the bidding procedure altogether in favor of direct negotiations; a government agency must purchase much of what it uses by formally advertising for bids, accepting the lowest, and keeping the vendor at arm's length. When a business firm develops a good working relationship with a contractor, it often uses that vendor repeatedly without looking for a new one; when a government agency has a satisfactory relationship with a contractor, ordinarily it cannot use the vendor again without putting a new project out for a fresh set of bids. When a business firm finds that certain offices or factories are no longer economical it will close or combine them; when a government agency wishes to shut down a local office or military base often it must get the permission of the legislature (even when formal permission is not necessary, informal consultation is). When a business firm draws up its annual budget each expenditure item can be reviewed as a discretionary amount (except for legally mandated payments of taxes to government and interest to banks and bondholders); when a government agency makes up its budget many of the detailed expenditure items are mandated by the legislature.

All these complexities of doing business in or with the government are well-known to citizens and firms. These complexities in hiring, purchasing, contracting, and budgeting often are said to be the result of the "bureaucracy's love of red tape." But few, if any, of the rules producing this complexity would have been generated by the bureaucracy if left to its own devices, and many are as cordially disliked by the bureaucrats as by their clients. These rules have been imposed on the agencies by external actors, chiefly the legislature. They are not bureaucratic rules but *political* ones. In principle the legislature could allow the Social Security Administration, the Defense Department, or the New York City public school system to follow the same rules as IBM, General Electric, or Harvard University. In practice they could not. The reason is politics, or more precisely, democratic politics.

The differences are made clear in Steven Kelman's comparison of how government agencies and private firms buy computers. The agency officials he interviewed were much less satisfied with the quality of the computers and support services they purchased than were their private counterparts. The reason is that private firms are free to do what every householder does in buying a dishwasher or an automobile—look at the past performance of the people with whom he or she previously has done business and buy a new product based on these judgments. Contrary to what many people suppose, most firms buying a computer do not write up detailed specifications and then ask for bids, giving the contract to the lowest bidder who meets the specifications. Instead, they hold conversations with a computer manufacturer with whom they, or other firms like them, have had experience. In these discussions they develop a sense of their needs and form a judgment as to the quality and reliability of the people with whom they may do business. When the purchase is finally made, only one firm may be asked to bid, and then on the basis of jointly developed (and sometimes rather general) guidelines.

No government purchasing agent can afford to do business this way. He or she would be accused (by unsuccessful bidders and their congressional allies) of collusion, favoritism, and sweetheart deals. Instead, agencies must either ask for sealed bids or for competitive written responses to detailed (*very* detailed) "requests for proposals" (RFPs). The agencies will not be allowed to take into account past performance or intangible managerial qualities. As a result, the agencies must deny themselves the use of the most important information someone can have—judgment shaped by personal knowledge and past experience. Thus, the government often buys the wrong computers from unreliable suppliers.[3]

Constraints at Work: The Case of the Postal Service

From the founding of the republic until 1971 the Post Office Department was a cabinet agency wholly subordinate to the president and Congress. As such it received its funds from annual appropriations, its personnel from presidential appointments and civil service examinations, and its physical plant from detailed political decisions about the appropriate location of post offices. Postal rates were set by Congress after hearings, dominated by organized interests that mail in bulk (for example, direct-mail advertisers and magazine publishers) and influenced by an awareness of the harmful political effects of raising the rates for first-class letters mailed by individual citizens (most of whom voted). Congress responded to these pressures by keeping rates low. . . . The wages of postal employees were set with an eye on the political power of the unions representing those employees:

Congress rarely forgot that there were hundreds of organized letter carriers in every congressional district.

In 1971, the Post Office Department was transformed into the United States Postal Service (USPS), a semiautonomous government corporation. The USPS is headed by an eleven-member board of governors, nine appointed by the president and confirmed by the Senate; these nine then appoint a postmaster general and a deputy postmaster general. It derives its revenues entirely from the prices it charges and the money it borrows rather than from congressional appropriations (though subsidies still were paid to the USPS during a transition period). The postal rates are set not by Congress but by the USPS itself, guided by a legislative standard. . . . The USPS has its own personnel system, separate from that of the rest of the federal government, and bargains directly with its own unions.

Having loosened some of the constraints upon it, the Postal Service was able to do things that in the past it could do only with great difficulty if at all. . . . When it was still a regular government department, a small local post office could only be closed after a bitter fight with the member of Congress from the affected district. As a result, few were closed. After the reorganization, the number closed increased: Between 1976 and 1979, the USPS closed about twenty-four a year; between 1983 and 1986, it closed over two hundred a year.[4] . . . When the old Post Office, in the interest of cutting costs, tried to end the custom of delivering mail to each recipient's front door and instead proposed to deliver mail (at least in new suburban communities) either to the curbside or to "cluster boxes,"* intense pressure on Congress forced the department to abandon the idea. By 1978 the USPS had acquired enough autonomy to implement the idea despite continued congressional grumblings.[5] Because the USPS can raise its own capital by issuing bonds it has been able to forge ahead with the automation of mail-sorting procedures. It now has hundreds of sophisticated optical scanners and bar-code readers that enable employees to sort mail much faster than before. By 1986 optical character readers were processing 90 million pieces of mail a day. Finally, despite political objections, the USPS was slowly expanding the use of the nine-digit zip code.

In short, acquiring greater autonomy increased the ability of the Postal Service to acquire, allocate, and control the factors of production. More broadly, the whole tone of postal management changed. It began to adopt corporate-style management practices, complete with elaborate "mission statements," glossy annual reports, a tightened organizational structure, and an effort to decentralize some decisions to local managers.

Though Congress loosened the reins, it did not take them off. On many key issues the phrase *quasi-autonomous* meant hardly autonomous at all. Congress at

---

* A cluster box is a metal structure containing twelve to one hundred mailboxes to which mail for a given neighborhood is delivered.

any time can amend the Postal Reorganization Act to limit the service's freedom of action; even the threat of such an amendment, made evident by committee hearings, often is enough to alter the service's programs. The nine-digit zip code was finally adopted but its implementation was delayed by Congress for over two years, thus impeding the efforts of the USPS to obtain voluntary compliance from the business community.

When the USPS, in a move designed to save over $400 million and thereby avoid a rate increase, announced in 1977 that it planned to eliminate Saturday mail deliveries, the service was able to produce public opinion data indicating that most people would prefer no Saturday delivery to higher postage rates. No matter. The House of Representatives by an overwhelming vote passed a resolution opposing the change, and the USPS backed down. It seems the employee unions feared that the elimination of Saturday deliveries would lead to laying off postal workers.[6]

Similarly, when the USPS in 1975–76 sought to close many rural post offices it had as an ally the General Accounting Office.* A GAO study suggested that twelve thousand such offices could be closed at a savings of $100 million per year without reducing service to any appreciable extent (many of the small offices served no more than a dozen families and were located within a few miles of other offices that could provide the same service more economically). The rural postmasters saw matters differently, and they found a sympathetic audience in Congress. Announcing that "the rural post office has always been a uniquely American institution" and that "service" is more important than "profit," senators and representatives joined in amending the Postal Reorganization Act to block such closings temporarily and inhibit them permanently.[7] As John Tierney notes, the year that the USPS timidly closed 72 of its 30,521 offices, the Great Atlantic and Pacific Tea Company closed 174 of its 1,634 stores, and "that was that.[8] . . ."

My argument is not that all the changes the USPS would like to make are desirable, or that every vestige of politics should be removed from its management. . . . Rather, it is that one cannot explain the behavior of government bureaucracies simply by reference to the fact that they are bureaucracies; the central fact is that they are *government* bureaucracies. Nor am I arguing that government (or more broadly, politics) is bad, only that it is inevitably (and to some extent desirably) sensitive to constituency demands. . . . For example, if Congress had been content to ask of the old Post Office Department that it deliver all first-class mail within three days at the lowest possible cost, it could have let the department arrange its delivery system, set its rates, locate its offices, and hire its personnel in whatever way it wished—provided that the mail got

---

* The General Accounting Office (GAO), a research agency of Congress, has the broad mission of overseeing and investigating how executive branch agencies spend appropriated funds. Its activities, often controversial, range from investigating cost overruns in the Department of Defense to assessing the adequacy of environmental regulations. GAO typically initiates its activities at the request of congressional committee leaders.

delivered within three days and at a price that did not lead mail users to abandon the Post Office in favor of a private delivery service. Managers then would be evaluated on the basis of how well they achieved these goals.

Of course, Congress had many goals, not just one: It wanted to please many different classes of mail users, satisfy constituency demands for having many small post offices rather than a few large ones, cope with union demands for wage increases, and respond to public criticism of mail service. Congress could not provide a consistent rank-ordering of these goals, which is to say that it could not decide on how much of one goal (e.g., keeping prices low) should be sacrificed to attain more of another goal (e.g., keeping rural post offices open). This inability to decide is not a reflection on the intelligence of Congress; rather, it is the inevitable consequence of Congress being a representative body whose individual members respond differently to different constituencies.

Neither Congress nor the postal authorities have ever supported an obvious method of allowing the customers to decide the matter for themselves—namely, by letting private firms compete with the Postal Service for the first-class mail business. For over a century the Post Office has had a legal monopoly on the regular delivery of first-class mail. It is a crime to establish any "private express for the conveyance of letters or packets . . . by regular trips or at stated periods over any post route."[9] This is justified by postal executives on the grounds that private competitors would skim away the most profitable business (for example, delivering business mail or utility bills in big cities), leaving the government with the most costly business (for example, delivering a Christmas card from Aunt Annie in Eudora, Kansas, to Uncle Matt in Wakefield, Massachusetts). In time the Post Office began to face competition anyway, from private parcel and express delivery services that did not deliver "by regular trips or at stated periods" (so as not to violate the private express statute) and from electronic mail and fund-transferring systems. But by then it had become USPS, giving it both greater latitude in and incentive for meeting that competition.

Faced with political superiors that find it conceptually easier and politically necessary to focus on inputs, agency managers also tend to focus on inputs. Nowhere is this more evident than in defense procurement programs. The Defense Department, through the Defense Logistics Agency (DLA), each year acquires food, fuel, clothing, and spare parts worth (in 1984) $15 billion, manages a supply system containing over two million items, and administers over $186 billion in government contracts.[10] Congress and the president repeatedly have made clear their desire that this system be run efficiently and make use of off-the-shelf, commercially available products (as opposed to more expensive, "made-to-order" items).[11] Periodically, however, the press reports scandals involving the purchase of $435 hammers and $700 toilet seats. Some of these stories are exaggerated,[12] but there is little doubt that waste and inefficiency occur. Congressional investigations are mounted and presidential commissions are appointed to find ways of solving these problems. Among the solutions offered are demands that tighter rules be imposed, more auditors be hired, and fuller reports be made.

Less dramatic but more common than the stories of scandals and overpriced hammers are the continuing demands of various constituencies for influence over the procurement process. Occasionally this takes the form of requests for special favors, such as preferentially awarding a contract to a politically favored firm. But just as important and more pervasive in their effects are the legal constraints placed on the procurement process to insure that contracts are awarded "fairly"— that is, in ways that allow equal access to the bidding process by all firms and special access by politically significant ones. For example, section 52 of the *Federal Acquisition Regulation* contains dozens of provisions governing the need to give special attention to suppliers that are small businesses (especially a "small disadvantaged business"), women-owned small businesses, handicapped workers, or disabled and Vietnam-era veterans, or are located in areas with a "labor surplus."*[13] Moreover, only materials produced in the United States can be acquired for public use unless, under the Buy American Act, the government certifies that the cost is "unreasonable" or finds that the supplies are not available in this country in sufficient quantity or adequate quality.[14]

The goal of "fairness" underlies almost every phase of the procurement process, not because the American government is committed heart and soul to fairness as an abstract social good but because if a procurement decision is questioned it is much easier to justify the decision if it can be shown that the decision was "fairly" made on the basis of "objective" criteria. Those criteria are spelled out in the *Federal Acquisition Regulation*, a complex document of over six thousand pages. The essential rules are that all potential suppliers must be offered an equal opportunity to bid on a contract; that the agency's procurement decision must be objectively justifiable on the basis of written specifications; that contracts awarded on the basis of sealed bids must go to the contractor offering the lowest price; and that unsuccessful bidders must be offered a chance to protest decisions with which they disagree.[15] . . .

To understand the bureaucratic significance of these rules, put yourself in the shoes of a Defense Logistics Agency manager. A decision you made is challenged because someone thinks that you gave a contract to an unqualified firm or purchased something of poor quality. What is your response—that in your judgment it was a good buy from a reliable firm? Such a remark is tantamount to inviting yourself to explain to a hostile congressional committee why you think your judgment is any good. A much safer response is "I followed the rules." . . .

---

* For example, the law requires that a "fair proportion of the total purchases and contracts" shall be "placed with small-business enterprises" and that "small business concerns owned and controlled by socially and economically disadvantaged individuals, shall have the maximum practicable opportunity to participate in the performance of contracts let by any Federal agency." [15 *U.S. Code* 637(d)(l)] In pursuance of this law, it is the government's policy "to place a fair proportion" of its acquisitions with small business concerns and small business disadvantaged concerns (*Federal Acquisition Regulation*, 19.201a). A "socially and economically disadvantaged individual" includes, but is not limited to, a black American, Hispanic American, Native American, Asian-Pacific American, or Asian-Indian American (Ibid., 52.219.2).

If despite all your devotion to the rules Congress uncovers an especially blatant case of paying too much for too little (for example, a $3,000 coffeepot), the prudent response is to suggest that what is needed are more rules, more auditors, and more tightly constrained procedures. The consequence of this may be to prevent the buying of any more $3,000 coffeepots, or it may be to increase the complexity of the procurement process so that fewer good firms will submit bids to supply coffeepots, or it may be to increase the cost of monitoring that process so that the money saved by buying cheaper pots is lost by hiring more pot inspectors. . . .

Public versus Private Management

The late Professor Wallace Sayre once said that public and private management is alike in all unimportant respects.[16] This view has been disputed vigorously by many people who are convinced that whatever problems beset government agencies also afflict private organizations. The clearest statement of that view can be found in John Kenneth Galbraith's *The New Industrial State*. Galbraith argues that large corporations, like public agencies, are dominated by "technostructures" that are governed by their own bureaucratic logic rather than by the dictates of the market. These corporations have insulated themselves from the market by their ability to control demand (through clever advertising) and set prices (by dominating an industry). The rewards to the technocrats who staff these firms are salaries, not profits, and the goals toward which these technocrats move are the assertion and maintenance of their own managerial autonomy. . . .

Professor Galbraith's book appeared at a time (1967) when American businesses were enjoying such unrivaled success that its beautifully crafted sentences seemed to capture some enduring truth. But the passage of time converted many of those eloquent phrases into hollow ones. Within ten years, it had become painfully obvious to General Motors that it could not, in Galbraith's words, "set prices for automobiles . . . secure in the knowledge that no individual buyer, by withdrawing its custom, can force a change."[17] Competition from Toyota, Nissan, and Honda had given the individual buyer great power; coupled with an economic slowdown, that competition led GM, like all auto manufacturers, to start offering cash rebates, cut-rate financing, and price reductions. And still the U.S. firms lost market share despite the "power" of their advertising and saw profits evaporate despite their "dominance" of the industry.

But Galbraith's analysis had more serious flaws than its inability to predict the future; it led many readers to draw the erroneous conclusion that "all bureaucracies are alike" because all bureaucracies employ salaried workers, are enmeshed in red tape, and strive to insure their own autonomy. The large corporation surely is more bureaucratic than the small entrepreneur, but in becoming bureaucratic it has not become a close relative of a government agency. What distinguishes public from private organizations is neither their size nor their desire to "plan" (that is, control) their environments but rather the rules under which they acquire and use capital and labor. General Motors acquires capital by selling shares, issuing bonds, or retaining earnings; the Department of Defense acquires it from an annual appropriation by Congress. GM opens and closes plants, subject to certain government regulations, at its own discretion; DOD opens and closes military bases under the watchful guidance of Congress. GM pays its managers with salaries it sets and bonuses tied to its earnings; DOD pays its managers with salaries set by Congress and bonuses (if any) that have no connection with organizational performance. The number of workers in GM is determined by its level of production; the number in DOD by legislation and civil-service rules.

What all this means can be seen by returning to the Registry of Motor Vehicles and McDonald's. Suppose you were just appointed head of the Watertown office of the Registry and you wanted to improve service there so that it more nearly approximated the service at McDonald's. Better service might well require spending more money (on clerks, equipment, and buildings). Why should your political superiors give you that money? It is a cost to them if it requires either higher taxes or taking funds from another agency; offsetting these real and immediate costs are dubious and postponed benefits. If lines become shorter and clients become happier, no legislator will benefit. There may be fewer complaints, but complaints are episodic and have little effect on the career of any given legislator. By contrast, shorter lines and faster service at McDonald's means more customers can be served per hour and thus more money can be earned per hour. A McDonald's manager can estimate the marginal product of the last dollar he or she spends on improving service; the Registry manager can generate no tangible return on any expenditure he or she makes and thus cannot easily justify the expenditure.

Improving service at the Registry may require replacing slow or surly workers with quick and pleasant ones. But you, the manager, can neither hire nor fire them at will. You look enviously at the McDonald's manager who regularly and with little notice replaces poor workers with better ones. Alternatively, you may wish to mount an extensive training program (perhaps creating a Registration University to match McDonald's Hamburger University) that would imbue a culture of service in your employees. But unless the Registry were so large an agency that the legislature would neither notice nor care about funds spent for this purpose—and it is not that large—you would have a tough time convincing anybody that this was not a wasteful expenditure on a frill project.

If somehow your efforts succeed in making Registry clients happier, you can take vicarious pleasure in it; in the unlikely event a client seeks you out to thank you for those efforts, you can bask in a moment's worth of glory. Your colleague at McDonald's who manages to make customers happier may also derive some vicarious satisfaction from the improvement but in addition he or she will earn more money owing to an increase in sales.

In time it will dawn on you that if you improve service too much, clients will start coming to the Watertown office instead of going to the Boston office. As a result, the lines you succeeded in shortening will become longer again. If you wish to keep complaints down, you will have to spend even more on the Watertown office. But if it was hard to persuade the legislature to do that in the past, it is impossible now. Why should the taxpayer be asked to spend more on Watertown when the Boston office, fully staffed (naturally, no one was laid off when the clients disappeared), has no lines at all? From the legislature's point of view the correct level of expenditure is not that which makes one office better than another but that which produces an equal amount of discontent in all offices.

Finally, you remember that your clients have no choice: The Registry offers a monopoly service. It and only it supplies drivers' licenses. In the long run all that matters is that there are not "too many" complaints to the legislature about service. Unlike McDonald's, the Registry need not fear that its clients will take their business to Burger King or to Wendy's. Perhaps you should just relax. . . .

Notes

1. John F. Love, *McDonald's: Behind the Arches* (New York: Bantam Books, 1986), 140ff.
2. James S. Coleman, Thomas Hoffer, and Sally Kilgore, *High School Achievement* (New York: Basic Books, 1982).
3. Steven Kelman, *Procurement and Public Management* [Lanham: American Enterprise Institute, 1990].
4. John T. Tierney, *The U.S. Postal Service* (Dover, Mass.: Auburn House, 1988), 101–2.
5. Tierney, *U.S. Postal Service*, 94–97.
6. John T. Tierney, *Postal Reorganization: Managing the Public's Business* (Boston: Auburn House, 1981), 67.
7. Ibid., 68–73.
8. Ibid., 72.
9. 18 *U.S. Code* 1696.
10. General Accounting Office, *Progress and Challenges at the Defense Logistics Agency.* GAO report NSIAD-86-64, Washington, D.C., 1986, p. 2.
11. Wendy T. Kirby, "Expanding the Use of Commercial Products and 'Commercial-Style' Acquisition Techniques in Defense Procurement: A Proposed Legal Framework." Appendix H in President's Blue Ribbon Commission on Defense Management (the "Packard Commission"), A *Quest for Excellence: Final Report*, June 1986.
12. I discuss these matters in chap. 17.
13. Kirby, "Expanding the Use," 106–7.
14. 41 *U.S. Code* 10(a).
15. Kirby, "Expanding the Use," 82–83, 91.
16. Quoted in Graham T. Allison, Jr., "Public and Private Management: Are They Fundamentally Alike in All Unimportant Respects?" in Frederick S. Lane, ed., *Current Issues in Public Administration*, 2d ed. (New York: St. Martin's Press, 1982), 13–33. The academic literature on public-private differences is summarized in Hal G. Rainey, Robert W. Backoff, and Charles H. Levine, "Comparing Public and Private Organizations," *Public Administration Review* 36 (1976): 233–44.
17. Galbraith, *New Industrial State*, 46.

Summary Questions

1. According to James Q. Wilson, in what ways is managing a private organization different from managing a public one?

2. Wilson suggests that "red tape" is more often the result of democratic politics than the preferences of bureaucrats. What does he mean by this? Would increasing citizen and group participation in politics lead to more or less bureaucratic rules and regulations?

 12.3

Down on the Farm

Jerry Hagstrom

The growth of the national bureaucracy over the past half century has been the inevitable consequence of the federal government's expanded role since the New Deal. Many federal agencies have become huge organizational entities, with large numbers of employees and ever-increasing budgets and expanding missions. A common criticism directed toward such bureaucracies, by conservatives and liberals alike, is that they have become bloated and inefficient, while at the same time, have continued to be impervious to change or reform.

Perhaps no government agency has been criticized more on such grounds than the U.S. Department of Agriculture (USDA). It has a budget of over $60 billion a year, employs roughly five percent of the federal civilian workforce in more than 14,000 offices, and administers a wide range of programs, from farm subsidies to management of the national forests to the food stamp and school lunch programs. Often its mission appears contradictory, as in efforts to promote the beef and pork of its producer clientele, while at the same time advocating that consumers eat a lean diet for nutrition and health reasons.

In this selection, Jerry Hagstrom looks at recent efforts to reform USDA. A number of proposals have been offered to reorganize and consolidate the department and its agencies, both by members of Congress and various presidential administrations. Currently, the department is the target of "reinventing government" efforts by the Clinton administration, led by Secretary of Agriculture Mike Espy. According to Hagstrom, reform efforts will "not come easily given the power of entrenched farm interests" who fear that "*reorganization* is a code word for downsizing," potentially diminishing services to the agriculture community.

<hr />

Jerry Hagstrom is a contributing editor at the *National Journal.*

I t seemed a simple request to Rep. Marcy Kaptur of Ohio. All she wanted was an organizational chart of the Agriculture Department, to help her understand various proposals for funding cuts or increases during this year's budget debate.

But in response, Kaptur's staff gave her a looseleaf notebook filled with page after page of diagrams of Agriculture's 42 agencies. Determined to get a picture of the whole department, Kaptur considered cutting and pasting the charts together—until staffers calculated that the assembled diagram would fill an entire wall.

Although she's both a Democrat and a member of the normally supportive Appropriations subcommittee on agriculture, there was a conservative cast to the conclusion Kaptur drew from the incident: that government had gotten "too big."

Kaptur is not alone in finding the Agriculture Department a prime example of bloat and inefficiency in government. Increasingly in recent years, this view has spread among budget analysts, congressional leaders, the press and even the farmers the department serves.

Now the Clinton Administration, pursuing its theme of "reinventing government," is planning to reorganize the department and cut costs. That the department is considered a prime candidate for "reinvention" was signaled when Vice President Gore made it the first stop on the tour he took last spring to spread the word about the Administration's National Performance Review. Secretary Mike Espy sounded the battle cry when he declared that he did not think "there is a department in this entire government in more dire need of being reinvented than USDA." On another occasion, Espy said he was committed to restructuring the department "from top to bottom." While devising his reorganization plan—due to be announced in early September along with results of the National Performance Review—Espy held back from filling high-level positions, including two assistant secretaryships and the leadership positions in several USDA agencies and state-level offices.

Espy's plan is expected to rationalize reporting relationships within the vast department, pulling together many farm-related agencies into three broad divisions reporting to three new high-level officials: one for farm services, one for international programs and one for rural development. The plan will entail reducing the number of agencies within USDA from 42 to 30, Espy said in an August speech.

Espy also has been under pressure to use the reorganization to strengthen food inspection and labeling, facilitate a tougher stand on environmental issues in rural America and cut fraud in food programs for poor people. It wasn't clear at press time whether the changes Espy is planning will do much to streamline the department's bureaucracy. President Clinton's fiscal 1994 budget proposed only a minor cut in the USDA workforce—to 110,800, from 112,100 in fiscal 1993. The budget projected a further cut, to 108,900 in fiscal 1995.

USDA old-timers say the plan draws upon a department "Streamlining Study" completed by USDA staff in October 1986 under the direction of John Block and

John Franke Jr., who were then, respectively, Secretary and assistant secretary for administration at Agriculture. That plan encountered strong resistance from leaders of USDA fiefdoms, notably including Forest Service chief Max Peterson. Mississippi Rep. Jamie Whitten, long known as the "permanent Secretary of Agriculture" on Capitol Hill, also was opposed. So the streamlining was stopped in its tracks.

Espy's reorganization plan may have a better chance than Block's, in part because his plan comes at the beginning of a new administration, when agency heads can be told to stay in line. And Whitten is gone—though obstacles remain on Capitol Hill. The number of farmers may have dwindled, but Members of Congress, including Republicans, from farm states may be counted upon to defend local USDA offices and programs.

A Proud History

President Lincoln established the Agriculture Department in 1862, but Franklin Roosevelt transformed it exactly 60 years ago. The New Deal agricultural programs, passed in 1933, were aimed at stabilizing farmers' incomes and assuring a regular and safe food supply. The department has given vast tracts of rural America access to basic infrastructure: roads, sewers, water systems, decent housing, telephones and electricity. Though many of these goals have long since been met, the department has continued to grow in size and complexity. Today, its 42 agencies employ about one out of every 20 full-time civilian employees in the executive branch, in more than 14,000 offices around the country. These employees oversee spending of some $62 billion a year.

The department's traditional mission has been to maintain or improve the standard of living of the nation's farmers. Federal farm programs ranging from grain subsidies to marketing orders that control the size of citrus crops still affect most of this country's 2.1 million farms. Most of the nation's food is grown by about 200,000 enterprises—prompting jokes that there is one Agriculture Department employee for every two "serious" farmers.

That picture is incomplete, however. Today the USDA staff works for a broad swath of American society. About 53 percent of its budget goes for food assistance programs, including the Food Stamp Program, whose beneficiaries number at least 28 million (10 percent of the U.S. population), the School Lunch program, which provides meals for 25 million children, and the Women, Infants and Children program, which provides money to 5.7 million people and which President Clinton is determined to expand. Also, the department's Forest Service manages 191 million acres—about 10 percent of the surface area of the lower 48 states—and employs 47,000 people, more than any other division of the department.

"A common misconception exists that USDA is mainly oriented toward farm production," Geoffrey Becker, an analyst with the Environment and Natural

Resources Policy Division of the Congressional Research Service, has written. "Based on where it spends most of its dollars, USDA might more appropriately be called the Department of Food and Nutrition. Based on employment, it might be called the Department of Forestry and Natural Resources."

Chorus of Criticism

The Agriculture Department has always had its critics among conservatives, who oppose its intervention in agricultural markets and its welfare programs. But in recent years, the outcry has broadened. A 1991 Pulitzer-prize-winning *Kansas City Star* series was the most colorful; it characterized the department as primarily responsive to commercial farmers and agribusiness interests. After an 18-month investigation published as a 24-page special edition, the *Star* editorialized that the Agriculture Department was "failing the grade. . . . It has gotten too big and appears to answer to no one. The government agency has in many ways failed in its missions to help to assure healthy food products for consumers, to conserve the environment and to boost the chances of survival for family farms."

A three-year General Accounting Office investigation, also published in 1991, found USDA's organizational structure "essentially unchanged since the 1930s" and "not responsive to new challenges facing the Department." Consolidating and integrating organizational functions, the report said, would allow USDA to provide the same services more efficiently to agribusiness customers and give it flexibility to meet its needs more efficiently. "In addition, organizational mechanisms are needed to coordinate and integrate USDA's diverse responsibilities in cross-cutting issues such as food safety, water quality and marketing," it continued. "Information, financial and human resources management systems need strategic planning to ensure that weaknesses are addressed in all agencies and that the systems operate as a unit."

The agriculture committees of both houses of Congress held hearings in 1992 to consider proposals to reorganize and consolidate the department and its agencies. USDA's most vocal critic was Sen. Richard Lugar, R-Ind., ranking minority member of the Senate Agriculture Committee. In February of last year, he unveiled a plan to cut the department down to a "leaner, healthier size," in part by closing 53 field offices in which office overhead costs exceeded the level of program benefits distributed to farmers. Senate Agriculture Committee chairman Patrick Leahy, D-Vt., also joined in the criticism.

In response to the pressure from Capitol Hill, then-Secretary of Agriculture Edward Madigan last year announced a plan to close or consolidate nearly 1,200 field offices of the Soil Conservation Service (SCS), the Farmers Home Administration (FmHA), the Agricultural Stabilization and Conservation Service (ASCS) and the Federal Crop Insurance Corp. (FCIC) into "farm service centers." "Savings from office consolidation would ultimately be in the range of

$400 million per year," Madigan said. That figure assumes a savings of $200,000 for each of 2,000 offices, leaving in place 12,300 offices.

The planned closures caused an uproar in rural towns around the country, and Madigan delayed issuing his orders until a few days before the Bush Administration left office. He also left behind a plan to replace the 14 subcabinet and other agency officials currently requiring Senate confirmation with just four new undersecretaries. Madigan also suggested reducing program operating agencies from 42 to 13.

Enter Espy

When Espy took office, he immediately put Madigan's plans for the field offices on hold and announced that his first priority would be streamlining the bureaucracy in Washington. The action won him immediate kudos on Capitol Hill and around the country.

Lugar's and Madigan's reform proposals, like those of most Republicans, contained an element of antagonism toward the department's activities. "Let farmers be farmers," Madigan would often say as he advocated reducing the department's bureaucracy.

While making the obligatory bow before the altar of cost savings, Espy says his greater goal is to make the department "farmer-friendly." That's in line with the Democrats' traditional faith in government—and is also a stand that could help shore up Espy's reputation among farm constituencies, which were caught off guard by appointment of a young (39), black Southerner to a post usually given to middle-aged white Midwesterners. Some farm groups feared that Espy's attention might be consumed by liberal groups shut out during the Republican years—notably those advocating more vigorous antipoverty efforts and food-safety programs. But Espy, who's well-known to Washington lobbyists as a willing recipient of campaign donations from agricultural political action committees, has toured the country to convince farmers that he will represent their interests.

In speeches to farm groups ranging from the corn growers to the rice millers to the National Farmers Union, Espy says, "I am from the South, but I am not of the South or for the South." People who think "cotton shirts grow on the racks at K-Mart and packets of rice somehow sprout from the bins at the A&P" are guilty of "urban narcissism," he adds. Urbanites, Espy continues, "always try to play this 2 percent game—that the farm population represents 2 percent of the American population and that each and every one of these farmers [is] like the Prince of Liechtenstein, so we need to cut and gut the farm programs. We need to remind them that agriculture is just like ripples in a pond. If you throw the rock in, the ripples will be seen everywhere."

When food poisoning broke out at Jack in the Box restaurants on the West Coast, Espy hired more meat inspectors and flew to Washington state to reassure consumers. But he also told producers that the Clinton Administration would not be too sympathetic to what it considers emotional consumerist and environ-mentalist appeals. "I remember the Alar-in-apples scare," he says in speeches. "So many from the western states remember that as well, when we had certain actresses and actors on television saying, 'Please don't eat those apples, those apples are tainted, those apples will kill you.' So much of that was just untrue. We had to admit error where error could be found, but also say, 'Listen, we in America have the safest food supply in the world.' "

Espy is also under pressure, however, to modernize the department. The Clinton Administration's transition team warned him that "the Carter Admini-stration began its tenure with a major reorganization of the department, which received much criticism, and which was reversed when the Administration left office in 1981." But it went on to say that the current pressures for reorganization were threefold:

- Farmers have to visit too many offices to receive services.
- Consumer advocates want food inspection and labeling responsibilities moved from the assistant secretary for marketing and inspection services to the as-sistant secretary for food and consumer services.
- USDA's traditionally weak management might be strengthened by taking functions currently located under the assistant secretary for administration and centralizing them under the deputy secretary.

The transition team recommended several "fundamental actions" to improve management, most having to do with improving financial management systems and administrative processes. The team recommended hiring a management expert to serve as assistant secretary of administration. Espy, however, chose Wardell Townsend Jr., his chief of staff in Congress, for the job, while putting deputy secretary Richard Rominger, a farmer from Delano, Calif., in charge of reorganization. Rominger, 65, is new to Washington, but he was director of the largest state agricultural department in the country, California's Food and Agri-culture Department, from 1977 to 1982. California farm leaders remember Rominger as their advocate and as the man who fought hard and successfully to get environmentalist Gov. Jerry Brown to eradicate the Mediterranean fruit fly.

Espy's few comments this past spring and summer about reinventing USDA suggested that he was interested in assigning new, high-level officials responsibil-ity for groups of agencies with allied functions.

USDA's top 25 officials held a two-day retreat in Annapolis, Md., in late June to discuss the reorganization. During a July interview, Rominger would not provide any details of the plan, beyond saying that staff cuts would come through attrition.

Espy has already announced that the department's public affairs offices will be reorganized. His press secretary, Steve Kinsella, gives an example of how one level of bureaucracy can be eliminated, thus cutting jobs and saving money: Press-release writers in each division of USDA will be taught to write in Associated

Press style. Then, they will no longer need to submit their work to a departmental press office, as they currently do so that editors there can rewrite it in news style.

The reinvention of USDA will combine such minor adjustments with a reshuffling of agency reporting relationships beneath a new superstructure of high-level officials.

But Espy is unlikely to deal quickly with what critics say are debilitating contradictions in the department's missions: promoting beef and pork, for example, while also inspecting them for safety, and at the same time telling the public to follow a lean diet. Consumer and environmental critics suggest that moving some of the department's regulatory functions to other agencies would both solve these conflict-of-interest issues and eliminate bureaucracy. But such proposals bring a firestorm of opposition from producers. In a congressional hearing earlier this year, Rep. Pat Roberts, R-Kan., asked whether reorganization might entail moving the Soil Conservation Service to the Environmental Protection Agency, the Food Safety Inspection Service to the Food and Drug Administration, the Foreign Agricultural Service to the Commerce Department and the Forest Service to the Interior Department.

Roberts urged his colleagues "to actively oppose these efforts, which would hamstring the department's role as production agriculture's spokesman."

It's more likely that Espy will try to increase inter-department coordination. He has begun meeting regularly with Babbitt, EPA administrator Carol Browner and Energy Secretary Hazel O'Leary. In July, Espy, Browner and FDA head David Kessler won praise when they issued a joint statement committing their agencies to overhauling the way the government regulates pesticides.

It is widely assumed that, once the Clinton Administration gets reorganization at headquarters in Washington under way, Espy will try to implement much of the Madigan plan for farm service centers—unless Democratic Members of Congress from rural areas complain too loudly that it may hurt their chances for reelection in 1994.

Rural Development

Reorganization also raises the question of how Espy will handle his own personal passion, rural development. At his confirmation hearing, Espy spoke eloquently about how, as a House member, he helped provide water service to a poor community in Mississippi where a little girl "had to go to a dirty creek just about every morning with a bucket into an insect-infected river, down a 12-foot incline, and draw it up, take it home and try to purify [it] through means of heat, just to brush teeth, just to go to school." Now that he is Secretary, Espy said in an interview, he would like "to fulfill the dream of the Roosevelt era—now that everyone has electricity, I'd like to make sure that everyone has water."

Espy's undersecretary for small community and rural development, Bob Nash, is the USDA official most likely to have President Clinton's ear; Nash was president of the Arkansas Development Finance Authority. But Espy's rural development priorities also face tests. Espy and Nash may have dealt personally with the need for water and sewer in the poor southern states, but rural residents outside the South seek more sophisticated development programs.

Bob Bergland, the former Minnesota congressman and Agriculture Secretary who is now executive vice president of the National Rural Electric Cooperative Association, wants Espy to establish a national commission to study rural development. A priority, according to Bergland, should be modernizing rural telecommunications systems so that rural areas can compete with cities and suburbs in the age of the electronic cottage. Earlier this year, Bergland tried to get the Rural Electrification Administration moved into the Rural Development Administration, which would in effect have meant that REA, which has a strong network of local institutions, would dominate RDA. The move has not gone anywhere so far.

The administration's commitment to rural economic development might also make it more difficult to close or consolidate field offices. Robert Christman, the outgoing state ASCS director in North Dakota, says that most of the complaints about the closings do not come from farmers, but from city officials in small towns, who say the offices increase traffic for other businesses. Rominger has said, however, that he doesn't consider the field offices a "substitute" for real economic development.

On the Hill

Any meaningful reorganization will require the assent of Congress, since much of the department's structure, and many of its ranking positions, are explicitly authorized by law. Change won't come easily, since many rural lawmakers fear that "reorganization" is a code word for downsizing.

Still, Espy may succeed where others have failed, in part because he is a Democrat dealing with Democrats in Congress. Espy was a protege of Agriculture Committee chairman Kika de la Garza, D-Texas, whose panel will have first crack at any "reinvention" legislation Espy wants. Farm-state lawmakers will demand hearings around the country before acting on such legislation, a House Agriculture Committee aide says.

Some Members have already introduced legislation to reorganize the department. Rep. Dan Glickman, D-Kan., has introduced a bill to put Agriculture's functions under six undersecretaries: for farm programs, rural development, international programs, consumer programs, natural resources and environment and research.

Over the years, congressional farm battles have become more complex. New Deal Democrats were the founders of the modern agricultural programs, while classic Republican conservatives always criticized farm support programs as disruptive of market forces and farm welfare programs as wasteful spending that added to tax burdens. But as the number of farmers has dwindled and the federal government has faced increasing budget pressures, agricultural politics have taken on a more regional cast. Republicans from farm states now often support farm programs, while urban Democrats see much farm spending as wasteful welfare for rich farmers.

In the 1992 presidential election, Clinton lost the Plains states as well as rural areas in many of the states that he carried overall. Although this would seem to strengthen reformers' hands, rural states have enormous power in the Senate. "Every Senator has farm constituents," notes a Senate Agriculture Committee aide. And while rural House districts have long voted Republican in the presidential race, many still send Democrats to Congress. The number of congressional districts with agriculture as a primary source of income has declined, but the number of districts with an audible farm presence may not have. In the redistricting after the 1990 census, for example, Ohio lost seats, and Kaptur's Toledo district was broadened to include more farmers. Many of the new districts in the South and the West contain farm territory.

Then there's the phenomenon of what a House Agriculture Committee aide calls "farm-state Republicans," who violate their party's general anti-government spending line when farm issues are up for vote.

Kansas Rep. Roberts, for example, has taken to debunking what he considers overblown critiques of USDA. He maintains that the department doesn't have 14,000 offices, but only 10,970; he argues that the 3,411 Cooperative Extension Service offices shouldn't be counted since they are under the jurisdiction of states and localities. Roberts labels as "unrealistic" suggestions that computers and faxes can substitute for local offices. "Virtually all of the county-level USDA offices currently have computers," he says, "and while the number of producers with computers has gone up considerably in the last 10 years, it does not begin to approach 15 percent—likewise for fax machines."

Roberts also disagrees with the assertion that Agriculture hasn't been reorganized in 50 years; over that period it has added many functions, he notes, from marketing and inspection to nutrition programs.

These additional responsibilities, added on year by year, "within a jumble of legislation," have created a department that lacks "a clear and current mission," write Neilson Conklin of Arizona State University and William Gahr of GAO in a recent issue of *Choices*, an American Agricultural Economics Association publication. So long as "fundamental questions about USDA's mission persist, reorganization will not solve the department's problems," they conclude. The two economists say that the department today should be focused less on helping producers than on four "opportunities and challenges [that] seem likely to sustain broad public interest and support: human health, the environment, renewable resources and regional development."

These proposals would indeed constitute a reinvention, and thus would not come easily given the power of entrenched farm interests. Espy's reorganization likely will require legislative action, but the kinds of sweeping change the two economists advocate couldn't be expected in that context. The first real chance would be during debate over reauthorization of expiring farm programs in 1995. Only then, in all likelihood, will it be possible to judge whether the Clinton Administration can live up to the sweeping change implied in Espy's reinvention rhetoric.

Summary Questions

1. What is the mission of the USDA and how has it changed since the New Deal?
2. Why is it so difficult to reform and "reinvent" a government agency like the USDA? What is the likelihood of the Clinton administration being successful in its reform efforts?

 Chapter 13

THE SUPREME COURT

Barely outlined in the Constitution, the Supreme Court and the American judiciary have been forced, almost from the beginning of the republic, to define their own roles within the political system. Historically, this has meant that the Court has engaged in a long-term balancing act, adhering to the rule of law while remaining conscious of the political environment of the times. At the heart of the American court system is a central irony—that we have relied on a profoundly undemocratic institution to safeguard our democratic state as well as to check the likely excesses of popular rule.

The Court's major tool in its work has been the power of judicial review; that is, the Court determines whether federal laws and regulations and state statutes are in accord with the Constitution and constitutional principles. Although the principle of judicial review was incorporated into American law with Chief Justice John Marshall's 1803 decision in *Marbury* v. *Madison* (reprinted in Selection 13.2), the Court has not, over the course of two centuries, invalidated many federal laws. Indeed, there was a fifty-four-year gap between *Marbury* and the next such ruling, the 1857 Dred Scott decision, which struck down the Missouri Compromise.

Since the New Deal, however, the Court has been somewhat more willing to overturn federal laws, especially when individual rights are at stake (see Chapter 3). State laws have received even more attention; almost a thousand such statutes have been declared unconstitutional. In a federal system, the power to strike down state legislation is essential, whereas the capacity to overrule national laws is less so. It is surely conceivable that Congress or the executive branch could interpret the Constitution as well as the Court. Still, the Supreme Court's role provides for a rough balance of power among the three branches. Lacking the authority to enforce its decisions, the Court can scarcely act in an arbitrary or capricious fashion. That does not mean, however, that it cannot have an impact, as indicated by its decisions on subjects such as school desegregation, the rights of the accused, access to executive branch material (the Nixon tapes case), and the separation of powers (the *Chada* case, which invalidated legislative veto sections of approximately two hundred laws).

In these and a host of other decisions, the Court clearly has acted in a policy-making role. Despite the continuing controversy over whether it should make policy or merely interpret the Constitution in light of the framers' intent, the fact remains that it has consistently rendered policy decisions from its earliest days. It can hardly work in any other way. For example, in *Boyle* v. *United Technologies* (1988), conservative justice Antonin Scalia, writing for a five-to-four majority, argued that members of the military service could not sue the manufacturers of possibly defective military equipment (such as a helicopter that crashed). Scalia reasoned that allowing suits would ultimately increase the cost of defense materiel to the federal government and the American taxpayer. But as dissenting justice William Brennan observed, "the Court lacks both authority and expertise to fashion [a rule that exempts military contractors from civil suits], whether to protect the Treasury of the United States or the coffers of industry. . . . I would leave that exercise of power to Congress, where our Constitution places it."

Justice Brennan, however, had previously written a broadly worded ruling that rendered the states almost superfluous in the face of federal power (*Garcia* v. *San Antonio Metropolitan Transit Authority*). In the end, both the conservative Scalia and the liberal Brennan have interpreted the Constitution broadly when it has suited their policy preferences. For further discussion of the question of intent and interpretation, see Leonard Levy's article (Selection 13.3) on the framers and the notion of original intent.

Mechanically, the Court sets its policy agenda by accepting a relatively small number of cases on which to rule. Although Congress and the president seem to have greater flexibility in setting their agendas, the Court can choose from among some 5,000 possible cases in selecting the 150 or so that it will hear in its annual October-through-June session. In fact, its docket often includes controversies from which Congress and the president traditionally have shied away. The most notable example is school desegregation, which the Court addressed in 1954, a full decade before Congress passed a major civil rights bill.

In this chapter, Alexander Hamilton's *The Federalist,* No. 78, and John Marshall's opinion in *Marbury* v. *Madison* provide the foundations for the Supreme Court's constitutional role. Hamilton articulates the classic formulation of the judiciary as "the least dangerous branch" because it "has no influence over either the sword [the executive] or the purse [the legislature]. . . . It may truly be said to have neither Force nor Will, but merely judgment; and must ultimately depend upon the aid of the executive arm even for the efficacy of its judgments." Marshall demonstrates the accuracy of Hamilton's observations in the *Marbury* decision, which involved a relatively trivial appointment but permitted Marshall to establish the principle of the judicial review of legislation.

The writings of Leonard Levy, Richard Posner, and Randall Kennedy contribute to our understanding of how the Supreme Court operates as a contemporary political institution. Historian Levy and federal appeals court judge Posner address the issue of constitutional interpretation; from differing perspectives both react to the assertion that the Court should be engaged principally in interpreting the so-called original intent of the framers. With typical assertiveness, Posner makes a strong case for substantial judicial leeway in constitutional interpretation. Indeed, he has often incorporated his own theories into both his judicial decisions and his numerous books. Writing on the appointment of Supreme Court justices, Kennedy argues that the president and the Senate should take "political vision" into account in the nominating and confirming processes. Much as Hamilton and Marshall understood the Court to be a political institution 200 years ago, so too do Levy, Posner, and Kennedy recognize its continuing nature as an inherently political body.

⊞ 13.1

The Federalist, No. 78

Alexander Hamilton

Of the three branches of government, the judiciary is the least fully outlined in the Constitution. To an extent this reflects the framers' greater concerns with the legislature and the executive, but it also indicates their perception that the judiciary simply did not pose the dangers the other branches did. For Alexander Hamilton, the key problem was to ensure that the judiciary remained independent of the legislature and the executive. One way to provide for this was to make court appointments lifetime positions, with removal impossible as long as the incumbents maintained "good behaviour"—a purposefully vague term.

Hamilton also laid out the case for judicial review of legislation. He observed that "no legislative act . . . contrary to the Constitution can be valid." And it is the Supreme Court that makes the final judgment on constitutionality. This seemingly great grant of authority is tempered, however, by the Court's inability to enforce its decisions without cooperation from the executive.

*T*o the People of the State of New York: We proceed now to an examination of the judiciary department of the proposed government.

In unfolding the defects of the existing confederation, the utility and necessity of a federal judicature have been clearly pointed out. It is the less necessary to recapitulate the considerations there urged; as the propriety of the institution in the abstract is not disputed: The only questions which have been raised being relative to the manner of constituting it, and to its extent. To these points therefore our observations shall be confined.

The manner of constituting it seems to embrace these several objects—1st. The mode of appointing the judges. 2d. The tenure by which they are to hold their places. 3d. The partition of the judiciary authority between different courts, and their relations to each other.

First. As to the mode of appointing the judges: This is the same with that of appointing the officers of the union in general, and has been so fully discussed in

---

Alexander Hamilton was the first secretary of the treasury and a consistent supporter of strong central government.

447

the two last numbers, that nothing can be said here which would not be useless repetition.

Second. As to the tenure by which the judges are to hold their places: This chiefly concerns their duration in office; the provisions for their support; and the precautions for their responsibility.

According to the plan of the convention, all the judges who may be appointed by the United States are to hold their offices *during good behaviour,* which is conformable to the most approved of the state constitutions; and among the rest, to that of this state. Its propriety having been drawn into question by the adversaries of that plan, is no light symptom of the rage for objection which disorders their imaginations and judgments. The standard of good behaviour for the continuance in office of the judicial magistracy is certainly one of the most valuable of the modern improvements in the practice of government. In a monarchy it is an excellent barrier to the despotism of the prince: In a republic it is a no less excellent barrier to the encroachments and oppressions of the representative body. And it is the best expedient which can be devised in any government, to secure a steady, upright and impartial administration of the laws.

Whoever attentively considers the different departments of power must perceive, that in a government in which they are separated from each other, the judiciary, from the nature of its functions, will always be the least dangerous to the political rights of the constitution; because it will be least in a capacity to annoy or injure them. The executive not only dispenses the honors, but holds the sword of the community. The legislature not only commands the purse, but prescribes the rules by which the duties and rights of every citizen are to be regulated. The judiciary on the contrary has no influence over either the sword or the purse, no direction either of the strength or of the wealth of the society, and can take no active resolution whatever. It may truly be said to have neither Force nor Will, but merely judgment; and must ultimately depend upon the aid of the executive arm even for the efficacy of its judgments.

This simple view of the matter suggests several important consequences. It proves incontestibly that the judiciary is beyond comparison the weakest of the three departments of power; that it can never attack with success either of the other two; and that all possible care is requisite to enable it to defend itself against their attacks. It equally proves, that though individual oppression may now and then proceed from the courts of justice, the general liberty of the people can never be endangered from that quarter: I mean, so long as the judiciary remains truly distinct from both the legislative and executive. For I agree that "there is no liberty, if the power of judging be not separated from the legislative and executive powers." And it proves, in the last place, that as liberty can have nothing to fear from the judiciary alone, but would have every thing to fear from its union with either of the other departments; that as all the effects of such an union must ensue from a dependence of the former on the latter, notwithstanding a nominal and apparent separation; that as from the natural feebleness of the judiciary, it is in continual jeopardy of being overpowered, awed or influenced by its coordinate branches; and that as nothing can contribute so much to its firmness and independence, as permanency in office, this quality may therefore be justly regarded as an indispensable ingredient in its constitution; and in a great measure as the citadel of the public justice and the public security.

The complete independence of the courts of justice is peculiarly essential in a limited constitution. By a limited constitution I understand one which contains certain specified exceptions to the legislative authority; such for instance as that it shall pass no bills of attainder, no *ex post facto* laws, and the like.* Limitations of this kind can be preserved in practice no other way than through the medium of the courts of justice; whose duty it must be to declare all acts contrary to the manifest tenor of the constitution void. Without this, all the reservations of particular rights or privileges would amount to nothing.

Some perplexity respecting the right of the courts to pronounce legislative acts void, because contrary to the constitution, has arisen from an imagination that the doctrine would imply a superiority of the judiciary to the legislative power. It is urged that the authority which can declare the acts of another void, must necessarily be superior to the one whose acts may be declared void. As this doctrine is of great importance in all the American constitutions, a brief discussion of the grounds on which it rests cannot be unacceptable.

There is no position which depends on clearer principles, than that every act of a delegated authority, contrary to the tenor of the commission under which it is exercised, is void. No legislative act therefore contrary to the constitution can be valid. To deny this would be to affirm that the deputy is greater than his principal; that the servant is above his master; that the representatives of the people are superior to the people themselves; that men acting by virtue of powers may do not only what their powers do not authorise, but what they forbid.

If it be said that the legislative body are themselves the constitutional judges of their own powers, and that the construction they put upon them is conclusive upon the other departments, it may be answered, that this cannot be the natural presumption, where it is not to be collected from any particular provisions in the constitution. It is not otherwise to be supposed that the constitution could intend to enable the representatives of the people to substitute their *will* to that of their constituents. It is far more rational to suppose that the courts were designed to be an intermediate body between the people and the legislature, in order, among other things, to keep the latter within the limits assigned to their authority. The interpretation of the laws is the proper and peculiar province of the courts. A

---

* A *bill of attainder* is a legislative act that inflicts punishment without a judicial trial. Crimes are thus defined by statutes that are general in nature, and the courts interpret those statutes. An *ex post facto* law either makes an act illegal after the fact or removes the legal protection from behavior after that behavior has been performed.

constitution is in fact, and must be, regarded by the judges as a fundamental law. It therefore belongs to them to ascertain its meaning as well as the meaning of any particular act proceeding from the legislative body. If there should happen to be an irreconcileable variance between the two, that which has the superior obligation and validity ought of course to be preferred; or in other words, the constitution ought to be preferred to the statute, the intention of the people to the intention of their agents.

Nor does this conclusion by any means suppose a superiority of the judicial to the legislative power. It only supposes that the power of the people is superior to both; and that where the will of the legislature declared in its statutes, stands in opposition to that of the people declared in the constitution, the judges ought to be governed by the latter, rather than the former. They ought to regulate their decisions by the fundamental laws, rather than by those which are not fundamental.

This exercise of judicial discretion in determining between two contradictory laws, is exemplified in a familiar instance. It not uncommonly happens, that there are two statutes existing at one time, clashing in whole or in part with each other, and neither of them containing any repealing clause or expression. In such a case, it is the province of the courts to liquidate and fix their meaning and operation: So far as they can by any fair construction be reconciled to each other; reason and law conspire to dictate that this should be done. Where this is impracticable, it becomes a matter of necessity to give effect to one, in exclusion of the other. The rule which has obtained in the courts for determining their relative validity is that the last in order of time shall be preferred to the first. But this is mere rule of construction, not derived from any positive law, but from the nature and reason of the thing. It is a rule not enjoined upon the courts by legislative provision, but adopted by themselves, as consonant to truth and propriety, for the direction of their conduct as interpreters of the law. They thought it reasonable, that between the interfering acts of an *equal* authority, that which was the last indication of its will, should have the preference.

But in regard to the interfering acts of a superior and subordinate authority, of an original and derivative power, the nature and reason of the thing indicate the converse of that rule as proper to be followed. They teach us that the prior act of a superior ought to be preferred to the subsequent act of an inferior and subordinate authority; and that, accordingly, whenever a particular statute contravenes the constitution, it will be the duty of the judicial tribunals to adhere to the latter, and disregard the former.

It can be of no weight to say, that the courts on the pretence of a repugnancy, may substitute their own pleasure to the constitutional intentions of the legislature. This might as well happen in the case of two contradictory statutes; or it might as well happen in every adjudication upon any single statute. The courts must declare the sense of the law; and if they should be disposed to exercise WILL instead of JUDGMENT, the consequence would equally be the substitution of their pleasure to that of the legislative body. The observation, if it proved any thing, would prove that there ought to be no judges distinct from that body.

If then the courts of justice are to be considered as the bulwarks of a limited constitution against legislative encroachments, this consideration will afford a strong argument for the permanent tenure of judicial offices, since nothing will contribute so much as this to that independent spirit in the judges, which must be essential to the faithful performance of so arduous a duty. . . .

That inflexible and uniform adherence to the rights of the constitution and of individuals, which we perceive to be indispensable in the courts of justice, can certainly not be expected from judges who hold their offices by a temporary commission. Periodical appointments, however regulated, or by whomsoever made, would in some way or other be fatal to their necessary independence. If the power of making them was committed either to the executive or legislature, there would be danger of an improper complaisance to the branch which possessed it; if to both, there would be an unwillingness to hazard the displeasure of either; if to the people, or to persons chosen by them for the special purpose, there would be too great a disposition to consult popularity, to justify a reliance that nothing would be consulted but the constitution and the laws.

There is yet a further and a weighty reason for the permanency of the judicial offices; which is deducible from the nature of the qualifications they require. It has been frequently remarked with great propriety, that a voluminous code of laws is one of the inconveniences necessarily connected with the advantages of a free government. To avoid an arbitrary discretion in the courts, it is indispensable that they should be bound down by strict rules and precedents, which serve to define and point out their duty in every particular case that comes before them; and it will readily be conceived from the variety of controversies which grow out of the folly and wickedness of mankind, that the records of those precedents must unavoidably swell to a very considerable bulk, and must demand long and laborious study to acquire a competent knowledge of them. Hence it is that there can be but few men in the society, who will have sufficient skill in the laws to qualify them for the stations of judges. And making the proper deductions for the ordinary depravity of human nature, the number must be still smaller of those who unite the requisite integrity with the requisite knowledge. These considerations apprise us, that the government can have no great option between fit characters; and that a temporary duration in office, which would naturally discourage such characters from quitting a lucrative line of practice to accept a seat on the bench, would have a tendency to throw the administration of justice into hands less able, and less well qualified to conduct it with utility and dignity. In the present circumstances of this country, and in those in which it is likely to be for a long time to come, the disadvantages on this score would be greater than they may at first sight appear; but it must be confessed that they are far inferior to those which present themselves under the other aspects of the subject.

Upon the whole there can be no room to doubt that the convention acted wisely in copying from the models of those constitutions which have established *good behaviour* as the tenure of their judicial offices in point of duration; and that so far from being blameable on this account, their plan would have been inexcuseably defective if it had wanted this important feature of good government. The experience of Great Britain affords an illustrious comment on the excellence of the institution.

Summary Questions

1. Why might a lifetime term for judges and justices be considered a good policy? Why did the framers make office holding contingent on continued "good behaviour" rather than on some more specific criterion?
2. Why did the framers consider the Supreme Court the weakest of the three branches? How can this be so if it has the final say over what the Constitution means?

 13.2

Marbury v. Madison (1803)

In March, 1801, during the waning hours of his administration, President John Adams appointed William Marbury to be a justice of the peace in Washington, D.C. James Madison, the secretary of state under incoming President Thomas Jefferson, refused to deliver the commission, following Jefferson's instructions. Marbury subsequently applied to the Supreme Court to obtain the position.

This minor controversy offered a great opportunity to John Marshall, whom Adams had appointed Chief Justice in the last months of his tenure. Marshall, no friend of Jefferson's, found in this case a way to establish the Court's power to declare a federal law unconstitutional. Although Hamilton argued strenuously in favor of the judicial review of legislation in *The Federalist,* No. 78 (Selection 13.1), the Constitution did not speak definitively on the topic. In this case Marshall ruled specifically that Marbury was entitled to his commission, but that the Court had no legitimate authority to order it done because the federal statute providing the

Court with the power to provide the appropriate remedy was unconstitutional. In short, this decision answered the open question posed by the Constitution: who has the authority to declare a statute unconstitutional? In *Marbury v. Madison,* Marshall won that power for the Supreme Court.

M r. Chief Justice Marshall delivered the opinion of the Court.
    At the last term on the affidavits then read and filed with the clerk, a
    rule was granted in this case, requiring the secretary of state to show cause why a *mandamus* should not issue, directing him to deliver to William Marbury his commission as a justice of the peace for the county of Washington, in the district of Columbia. . . .*

In the order in which the court has viewed this subject, the following questions have been considered and decided.

1st. Has the applicant a right to the commission he demands?

2dly. If he has a right, and that right has been violated, do the laws of his country afford him a remedy?

3dly. If they do afford him a remedy, is it a *mandamus* issuing from this court? . . .

This . . . is a plain case for a *mandamus*, either to deliver the commission, or a copy of it from the record; and it only remains to be inquired,

Whether it can issue from this court.

The act to establish the judicial courts of the United States authorizes the supreme court "to issue writs of *mandamus*, in cases warranted by the principles and usages of law, to any courts appointed, or persons holding office, under the authority of the United States."

The secretary of state, being a person holding an office under the authority of the United States, is precisely within the letter of the description; and if this court is not authorized to issue a writ of *mandamus* to such an officer, it must be because the law is unconstitutional, and therefore absolutely incapable of conferring the authority, and assigning the duties which its words purport to confer and assign.

The constitution vests the whole judicial power of the United States in one supreme court, and such inferior courts as congress shall, from time to time, ordain and establish. This power is expressly extended to all cases arising under the laws of the United States; and, consequently, in some form, may be exercised over the present case; because the right claimed is given by a law of the United States.

In the distribution of this power it is declared that "the supreme court shall have original jurisdiction in all cases affecting ambassadors, other public

---

* A *mandamus* is a binding directive, issued to individuals within the executive branch, that requires some action.

ministers and consuls, and those in which a state shall be a party. In all other cases, the supreme court shall have appellate jurisdiction."

It has been insisted, at the bar, that as the original grant of jurisdiction, to the supreme and inferior courts, is general, and the clause, assigning original jurisdiction to the supreme court, contains no negative or restrictive words, the power remains to the legislature, to assign original jurisdiction to that court in other cases than those specified in the article which has been recited; provided those cases belong to the judicial power of the United States.

If it had been intended to leave it in the discretion of the legislature to apportion the judicial power between the supreme and inferior courts according to the will of that body, it would certainly have been useless to have proceeded further than to have defined the judicial power, and the tribunals in which it should be vested. The subsequent part of the section is mere surplusage, is entirely without meaning, if such is to be the construction. If congress remains at liberty to give this court appellate jurisdiction, where the constitution has declared their jurisdiction shall be original; and original jurisdiction where the constitution has declared it shall be appellate; the distribution of jurisdiction, made in the constitution, is form without substance.

Affirmative words are often, in their operations, negative of other objects than those affirmed; and in this case, a negative or exclusive sense must be given to them, or they have no operation at all.

It cannot be presumed that any clause in the constitution is intended to be without effect; and, therefore, such a construction is inadmissible, unless the words require it.

If the solicitude of the convention, respecting our peace with foreign powers, induced a provision that the supreme court should take original jurisdiction in cases which might be supposed to affect them; yet the clause would have proceeded no further than to provide for such cases, if no further restriction on the powers of congress had been intended. That they should have appellate jurisdiction in all other cases, with such exceptions as congress might make, is no restriction; unless the words be deemed exclusive of original jurisdiction. . . .

To enable this Court, then, to issue a *mandamus*, it must be shown to be an exercise of appellate jurisdiction, or to be necessary to enable them to exercise appellate jurisdiction. . . .

It is the essential criterion of appellate jurisdiction, that it revises and corrects the proceedings in a cause already instituted, and does not create that cause. Although, therefore, a *mandamus* may be directed to courts, yet to issue such a writ to an officer for the delivery of a paper, is in effect the same as to sustain an original action for that paper, and, therefore, seems not to belong to appellate, but to original jurisdiction. Neither is it necessary in such a case as this, to enable the court to exercise its appellate jurisdiction.

The authority, therefore, given to the supreme court, by the act establishing the judicial courts of the United States, to issue writs of *mandamus* to public officers, appears not to be warranted by the constitution; and it becomes necessary to inquire whether a jurisdiction so conferred can be exercised.

The question, whether an act, repugnant to the constitution, can become the law of the land, is a question deeply interesting to the United States; but, happily, not of an intricacy proportioned to its interest. It seems only necessary to recognise certain principles, supposed to have been long and well established, to decide it.

That the people have an original right to establish, for their future government, such principles as, in their opinion, shall most conduce to their own happiness is the basis on which the whole American fabric has been erected. The exercise of this original right is a very great exertion; nor can it, nor ought it, to be frequently repeated. The principles, therefore, so established, are deemed fundamental. And as the authority from which they proceed is supreme, and can seldom act, they are designed to be permanent.

This original and supreme will organizes the government, and assigns to different departments their respective powers. It may either stop here, or establish certain limits not to be transcended by those departments.

The government of the United States is of the latter description. The powers of the legislature are defined and limited; and that those limits may not be mistaken, or forgotten, the constitution is written. To what purpose are powers limited, and to what purpose is that limitation committed to writing, if these limits may, at any time, be passed by those intended to be restrained? The distinction between a government with limited and unlimited powers is abolished, if those limits do not confine the persons on whom they are imposed, and if acts prohibited and acts allowed, are of equal obligation. It is a proposition too plain to be contested, that the constitution controls any legislative act repugnant to it; or, that the legislature may alter the constitution by an ordinary act.

Between these alternatives there is no middle ground. The constitution is either a superior paramount law, unchangeable by ordinary means, or it is on a level with ordinary legislative acts, and, like other acts, is alterable when the legislature shall please to alter it.

If the former part of the alternative be true, then a legislative act contrary to the constitution is not law: if the latter part be true, then written constitutions are absurd attempts, on the part of the people, to limit a power in its own nature illimitable.

Certainly all those who have framed written constitutions contemplate them as forming the fundamental and paramount law of the nation, and, consequently, the theory of every such government must be, that an act of the legislature, repugnant to the constitution, is void.

This theory is essentially attached to a written constitution, and, is consequently, to be considered, by this court, as one of the fundamental principles of our society. It is not therefore to be lost sight of in the further consideration of this subject.

If an act of the legislature, repugnant to the constitution, is void, does it, notwithstanding its invalidity, bind the courts, and oblige them to give it effect? Or, in other words, though it be not law, does it constitute a rule as operative as if it was a law? This would be to overthrow in fact what was established in theory; and would seem, at first view, an absurdity too gross to be insisted on. It shall, however, receive a more attentive consideration.

It is emphatically the province and duty of the judicial department to say what the law is. Those who apply the rule to particular cases, must of necessity expound and interpret that rule. If two laws conflict with each other, the courts must decide on the operation of each.

So if a law be in opposition to the constitution; if both the law and the constitution apply to a particular case, so that the court must either decide that case conformably to the law, disregarding the constitution; or conformably to the constitution, disregarding the law; the court must determine which of these conflicting rules governs the case. This is of the very essence of judicial duty.

If, then, the courts are to regard the constitution, and the constitution is superior to any ordinary act of the legislature, the constitution, and not such ordinary act, must govern the case to which they both apply.

Those, then, who controvert the principle that the constitution is to be considered, in court, as a paramount law, are reduced to the necessity of maintaining that courts must close their eyes on the constitution, and see only the law.

This doctrine would subvert the very foundation of all written constitutions. It would declare that an act which, according to the principles and theory of our government, is entirely void, is yet, in practice, completely obligatory. It would declare that if the legislature shall do what is expressly forbidden, such act, notwithstanding the express prohibition, is in reality effectual. It would be giving to the legislature a practical and real omnipotence, with the same breath which professes to restrict their powers within narrow limits. It is prescribing limits, and declaring that those limits may be passed at pleasure.

That it thus reduces to nothing what we have deemed the greatest improvement on political institutions, a written constitution, would of itself be sufficient, in America, where written constitutions have been viewed with so much reverence, for rejecting the construction. But the peculiar expressions of the constitution of the United States furnish additional arguments in favour of its rejection.

The judicial power of the United States is extended to all cases arising under the constitution.

Could it be the intention of those who gave this power, to say that in using it the constitution should not be looked into? That a case arising under the constitution should be decided without examining the instrument under which it arises?

This is too extravagant to be maintained.

In some cases, then, the constitution must be looked into by the judges. And if they can open it at all, what part of it are they forbidden to read or to obey?

There are many other parts of the constitution which serve to illustrate this subject.

It is declared that "no tax or duty shall be laid on articles exported from any state." Suppose a duty on the export of cotton, of tobacco, or of flour; and a suit instituted to recover it. Ought judgment to be rendered in such a case? ought the judges to close their eyes on the constitution, and only see the law?

The constitution declares "that no bill of attainder or *ex post facto* law shall be passed."

If, however, such a bill should be passed, and a person should be prosecuted under it; must the court condemn to death those victims whom the constitution endeavours to preserve?

"No person," says the constitution, "shall be convicted of treason unless on the testimony of two witnesses to the same overt act, or on confession in open court."

Here the language of the constitution is addressed especially to the courts. It prescribes, directly for them, a rule of evidence not to be departed from. If the legislature should change that rule, and declare *one* witness, or a confession *out* of court, sufficient for conviction, must the constitutional principle yield to the legislative act?

From these, and many other selections which might be made, it is apparent, that the framers of the constitution contemplated that instrument as a rule for the government of *courts*, as well as of the legislature. . . .

It is also not entirely unworthy of observation, that in declaring what shall be the *supreme* law of the land, the *constitution* itself is first mentioned; and not the laws of the United States generally, but those only which shall be made in *pursuance* of the constitution have that rank.

Thus, the particular phraseology of the constitution of the United States confirms and strengthens the principle, supposed to be essential to all written constitutions, that a law repugnant to the constitution is void; and that *courts*, as well as other departments, are bound by that instrument.

Summary Questions

1. What was the precise legal issue at the core of *Marbury v. Madison*? Why is this case so important to the ultimate workings of the separation of powers?
2. Is it absolutely imperative that the Constitution be interpreted as the supreme law of the land? Why shouldn't the legislature's interpretation of what is constitutional be weighed equally?

13.3

The Framers and Original Intent

Leonard W. Levy

The Constitution is essentially silent regarding how and by whom it should be interpreted. This is no mere academic matter; such review is central to any useful understanding of the Constitution. The framers did develop a means for amending the Constitution, but this was an exceptional event; only sixteen amendments have been accepted since the original Bill of Rights of 1790. The 1803 case of *Marbury* v. *Madison* (Selection 13.2) decided the issue of whether the Supreme Court could declare a law unconstitutional, but the question of what criteria are appropriate in interpreting the Constitution remains unanswered.

Various scholars and judges, mostly judicial conservatives, have argued that the Court should not go past the "original intent" of the framers in its interpretation. To do otherwise would be to place the Court in a political role that the framers sought to avoid. Leonard Levy argues to the contrary: that the framers did not agree on intent and did not want their discussions to be used in subsequent interpretations. In addition, emerging issues and new solutions would make reliance on intent a relatively useless basis for rendering judicial decisions for a government that was destined to be still going strong two centuries after its inception.

James Madison, Father of the Constitution and of the Bill of Rights, rejected the doctrine that the original intent of those who framed the Constitution should be accepted as an authoritative guide to its meaning. "As a guide in expounding and applying the provisions of the Constitution," he wrote in a well-considered and consistent judgment, "the debates and incidental decisions of the Convention can have no authoritative character." The fact that Madison, the quintessential Founder, discredited original intent is probably the main reason that he refused throughout his life to publish his "Notes of Debates in the Federal Convention," incomparably our foremost source for the secret discussions of that hot summer in Philadelphia in 1787.

We tend to forget the astounding fact that Madison's Notes were first published in 1840, fifty-three years after the Constitutional Convention had met. That

---

Leonard W. Levy is a professor of history at the Claremont Graduate School.

period included the beginnings of the Supreme Court plus five years beyond the entire tenure of John Marshall as Chief Justice. Thus, throughout the formative period of our national history, the High Court, presidents, and Congress construed the Constitution without benefit of a record of the Convention's deliberations. Indeed, even the skeletal Journal of the Convention was not published until 1819. Congress could have authorized its publication anytime after President George Washington, who had presided at the 1787 Convention, deposited it at the State Department in 1796. Although the Journal merely revealed motions and votes, it would have assisted public understanding of the secret proceedings of the Convention, no records of which existed, other than the few spotty and jaundiced accounts by Convention members who opposed ratification. The Convention had, after all, been an assembly in which "America," as George Mason of Virginia said, had "drawn forth her first characters," and even Patrick Henry conceded that the Convention consisted of "the greatest, the best, and most enlightened of our citizens." Thomas Jefferson, in Paris, referred to the "assembly of demigods." The failure of the Framers to have officially preserved and published their proceedings seems inexplicable, especially in a nation that promptly turned matters of state into questions of constitutional law; but then, the Framers seem to have thought that "the original understanding at Philadelphia," which Chief Justice William H. Rehnquist has alleged to be of prime importance, did not greatly matter. What mattered to them was the text of the Constitution, construed in light of conventional rules of interpretation, the ratification debates, and other contemporary expositions.

If the Framers, who met in executive sessions every day of their nearly four months of work, had wanted their country and posterity to construe the Constitution in the light of their deliberations, they would have had a stenographer present to keep an official record, and they would have published it. They would not have left the task of preserving their debates to the initiative of one of their members who retained control of his work and a proprietary interest in it. "Nearly a half century" after the convention, Madison wrote a preface to his Notes in which he explained why he had made the record. He had determined to preserve to the best of his ability "an exact account of what might pass in the Convention," because the record would be of value "for the History of a Constitution on which would be staked the happiness of a young people great even in its infancy, and possibly the cause of Liberty throughout the world." That seems to have been a compelling reason for publication as soon as possible, not posthumously—and Madison outlived all the members of the Convention. . . .

A constitutional jurisprudence* of original intent is insupportable for reasons other than the fact that the records of the framing and ratification of both the Constitution and the Bill of Rights are inadequate because they are incomplete and inaccurate. Original intent also fails as a concept that can decide real cases.

---

* *Jurisprudence* is a system or body of law.

Original intent is an unreliable concept because it assumes the existence of one intent on a particular issue such as the meaning of executive powers or of the necessary and proper clause, the scope of the commerce clause, or the definition of the obligation of contracts. The entity we call "the Framers" did not have a collective mind, think in one groove, or possess the same convictions.

In fact, they disagreed on many crucial matters, such as the question whether they meant Congress to have the power to charter a bank. In 1789 Hamilton and Washington thought Congress had that power, but Madison and Randolph believed that it did not. Although the Journal of the Convention, except as read by Hamilton, supports Madison's view, all senators who had been at the Convention upheld the power, and Madison later changed his mind about the constitutionality of a bank. Clearly the Convention's "intent" on this matter lacks clarity; revelation is hard to come by when the Framers squabbled about what they meant. They often did, as political controversies during the first score of years under the Constitution revealed.

Sometimes Framers who voted the same way held contradictory opinions on the meaning of a particular clause. Each believed that his understanding constituted the truth of the matter. James Wilson, for example, believed that the ex post facto clause extended to civil matters, while John Dickinson held the view that it applied only to criminal cases, and both voted for the clause. George Mason opposed the same clause because he wanted the states to be free to enact ex post facto laws in civil cases, and he believed that the clause was not clearly confined to criminal cases; but Elbridge Gerry, who wanted to impose on the states a prohibition against retroactive civil legislation, opposed the clause because he thought it seemed limited to criminal cases. William Paterson changed his mind about the scope of the ex post facto clause. Seeking original intent in the opinions of the Framers is seeking a unanimity that did not exist on complex and divisive issues contested by strong-minded men. Madison was right when he spoke of the difficulty of verifying the intention of the Convention.

A serious problem even exists as to the identity of the Framers and as to the question whether the opinions of all are of equal importance in the determination of original intent. Who, indeed, were the Framers? Were they the fifty-five who were delegates at Philadelphia or only the thirty-nine who signed? If fathoming original intent is the objective, should we not also be concerned about the opinions of those who ratified the Constitution, giving it legitimacy? About 1,600 men attended the various state ratifying conventions, for which the surviving records are so inadequate. No way exists to determine their intent as a guide for judicial decisions; we surely cannot fathom the intent of the members of eight states for which no state convention records exist. The deficiencies of the records of the other five permit few confident conclusions and no basis for believing that a group mind can be located. Understanding ratifier intent is impossible except on the broadest kind of question: Did the people of the states favor scrapping the Articles of Confederation and favor, instead, the stronger Union proposed by the Constitution? Even as to that question, the evidence, which does not exist for a majority of the states, is unsatisfactorily incomplete, and it allows only rough estimates of the answers to questions concerning popular understanding of the meaning of specific clauses of the Constitution. . . .

A Constitutional Jurisprudence of Original Intent?

A constitutional jurisprudence of original intent would be as viable and sound as Mr. Dooley's understanding of it. Mr. Dooley, Finley Peter Dunne's philosophical Irish bartender, believed that original intent was "what some dead Englishman thought Thomas Jefferson was goin' to mean whin he wrote th' Constitution." Acceptance of original intent as the foundation of constitutional interpretation is unrealistic beyond belief. It obligates us, even if we could grasp that intent, to interpret the Constitution in the way the Framers did in the context of conditions that existed in their time. Those conditions for the most part no longer exist and cannot be recalled with the historical arts and limited time available to the Supreme Court. Anyway, the Court resorts to history for a quick fix, a substantiation, a confirmation, an illustration, or a grace note; it does not really look for the historical conditions and meanings of a time long gone in order to determine the evidence that will persuade it to decide a case in one way rather than another. The Court, moreover, cannot engage in the sort of sustained historical analysis that takes professional historians some years to accomplish. In any case, for many reasons already described, concerning the inadequacies of the historical record and the fact that we cannot in most instances find a collective mind of the Framers, original intent analysis is not really possible, however desirable.

We must keep reminding ourselves that the most outspoken Framers disagreed with each other and did not necessarily reflect the opinions of the many who did not enter the debates. A point that Justice Rufus Peckham made for the Court in an 1897 case about legislative intent carries force with respect to the original intent of the Constitutional Convention. In reference to the difficulty of understanding an act by analyzing the speeches of the members of the body that passed it, Peckham remarked: "Those who did not speak may not have agreed with those who did; and those who spoke might differ from each other; the result being that the only proper way to construe a legislative act is from the language used in the act, and, upon occasion, by a resort to the history of the times when it was passed." We must keep reminding ourselves, too, that the country was deeply divided during the ratification controversy. And we must keep reminding ourselves that the Framers who remained active in national politics divided intensely on one constitutional issue after another—the removal power, the power to charter a corporation, the power to declare neutrality, the executive power, the power to enact excise and use taxes without apportioning them on population, the power of a treaty to obligate the House of Representatives, the power of judicial review, the power to deport aliens, the power to pass an act against seditious libel, the power of the federal courts to decide on federal common law grounds, the power to abolish judicial offices of life tenure, and the jurisdiction of the Supreme Court to decide suits against states without their consent or to issue writs of mandamus against executive officers. This list is not exhaustive; it is a point of departure. The Framers, who did not agree on their own constitutional issues, would not likely speak to us about ours with a single loud, clear voice. . . .

Conclusions

Fifty years ago, in his fine study of how the Supreme Court used original intent (not what the Framers and ratifiers believed), Jacobus tenBroek asserted, rightly, that "the intent theory," as he called it, "inverts the judicial process." It described decisions of the Court as having been reached as a result of a judicial search for Framers' intent, "whereas, in fact, the intent discovered by the Court is most likely to be determined by the conclusion that the Court wishes to reach." Original intent analysis involves what tenBroek called "fundamental misconceptions of the nature of the judicial process." It makes the judge "a mindless robot whose task is the utterly mechanical function" of using original intent as a measure of constitutionality. In the entire history of the Supreme Court, as tenBroek should have added, no Justice employing the intent theory has ever written a convincing and reliable study. Lawyers making a historical point will cite a Court opinion as proof, but no competent historian would do that. He knows that judges cannot do their own research or do the right kind of research and that they turn to history to prove some point they have in mind. To paraphrase tenBroek, Justices mistakenly use original intent theory to depict a nearly fixed Constitution, to give the misleading impression that they have decided an issue of constitutionality by finding original intent, and to make a constitutional issue merely a historical question. The entire theory, tenBroek asserted, "falsely describes what the Court actually does," and it "hypothesizes a mathematically exact technique of discovery and a practically inescapable conclusion." That all added up, said tenBroek, to "judicial hokum."

If we could ascertain original intent, one may add, cases would not arise concerning that intent. They arise because the intent is and likely will remain uncertain; they arise because the Framers either had no discernible intent to govern the issue or their intent cannot control it because the problem before the Court would have been so alien to the Framers that only the spirit of some principle implied by them can be of assistance. The Framers were certainly vaguer on powers than on structure and vaguer still on rights.

If, as Robert H. Bork* noticed, people rarely raise questions about original intent on issues involving powers or structure, the reason is likely that the

---

* Robert H. Bork was a U.S. Court of Appeals judge who was nominated by President Reagan for a Supreme Court appointment in 1987. After a bruising struggle, the Senate refused to confirm his nomination.

Constitution provides the answer, or it has been settled conclusively by the Court, making inquiry futile or unnecessary. For example, the question of constitutional powers to regulate the economy has overwhelmingly been put beyond question by the 1937 "constitutional revolution, limited," in Edward S. Corwin's phrase. Not even the most conservative Justices on today's Court question the constitutionality of government controls. Congress has the constitutional authority under Court decisions to initiate a socialist economy; political restraints, not constitutional ones, prevent that. There are no longer any serious limits on the commerce powers of Congress. The government can take apart the greatest corporations, like Ma Bell; if it does not proceed against them, the reason is to be found in national defense needs and in politics, not in the Constitution.

The states are supplicants before the United States government, beneficiaries of its largesse like so many welfare recipients, unable to control their own policies, serving instead as administrative agencies of federal policies. Those federal policies extend to realms not remotely within the federal power to govern under the Constitution, except for the fact that the spending power, so called, the power to spend for national defense and general welfare can be exercised through programs of grants-in-aid to states and to over 75,000 substate governmental entities; they take federal tax money and obediently enforce the conditions laid down by Congress and by federal agencies for control of the expenditures. Federalism as we knew it has been replaced by a new federalism that even conservative Republican administrations enforce. The government today makes the New Deal look like a backer of Adam Smith's legendary free enterprise and a respecter of John C. Calhoun's state sovereignty.

Even conservative Justices on the Supreme Court accept the new order of things. William H. Rehnquist spoke for the Court in *PruneYard*, Sandra Day O'Connor in *Hawaii Housing Authority*, and the Court was unanimous in both. In the first of these cases, decided in 1980, the Court held that a state does not violate the property rights of a shopping center owner by authorizing the solicitation of petitions in places of business open to the public. Rehnquist, finding a reasonable police power regulation of private property, asserted that the public right to regulate the use of property is as fundamental as the right to property itself. One might have thought that as a matter of constitutional theory and of original intent, the property right was fundamental and the regulatory power was an exception to it that had to be justified. Rehnquist did not explain why the regulation was justifiable or reasonable; under its rational basis test the Court has no obligation to explain anything. It need merely believe that the legislature had some rational basis for its regulation. . . .

The Constitution of the United States is our national covenant, and the Supreme Court is its special keeper. The Constitution's power of survival derives in part from the fact that it incorporates and symbolizes the political values of a free people. It creates a representative, responsible government empowered to serve the great objectives specified in the Preamble, while at the same time it keeps government bitted and bridled. Through the Bill of Rights and the great

Reconstruction amendments, the Constitution requires that the government respect the freedom of its citizens, whom it must treat fairly. Courts supervise the process, and the Supreme Court is the final tribunal. "The great ideals of liberty and equality," wrote Justice Benjamin N. Cardozo, "are preserved against the assaults of opportunism, the expediency of the passing hour, the scorn and derision of those who have no patience with general principles, by enshrining them in constitutions, and consecrating to the task of their protection a body of defenders." Similarly, Justice Hugo L. Black once wrote for the Court, "Under our constitutional system, courts stand against any winds that blow, as havens of refuge for those who might otherwise suffer because they are helpless, weak, outnumbered, or because they are nonconforming victims of prejudice and public excitement."

The Court should have no choice but to err on the side of the constitutional liberty and equality of the individual, whenever doubt exists as to which side requires endorsement. Ours is so secure a system, precisely because it is free and dedicated to principles of justice, that it can afford to prefer the individual over the state. To interpose original intent against an individual's claim defeats the purpose of having systematic and regularized restraints on power; limitations exist for the minority against the majority, as Madison said. Original intent analysis becomes a treacherous pursuit when it turns the Constitution and the Court away from assisting the development of a still freer and more just society.

The history of Magna Carta throws dazzling light on a jurisprudence of original intent. Magna Carta approaches its 800th anniversary. It was originally "reactionary as hell," to quote the chief justice of West Virginia. But the feudal barons who framed it could not control its evolution. It eventually came to signify many things that are not in it and were not intended. Magna Carta is not remotely important for what it intended but for what it has become. It stands now for government by contract of the people, for fundamental law, for the rule of law, for no taxation without representation, for due process of law, for habeas corpus, for equality before the law, for representative government, and for a cluster of the rights of the criminally accused. No one cares, or should, that the original document signifies none of this. The Constitution is comparably dynamic.

The Court has the responsibility of helping regenerate and fulfill the noblest aspirations for which this nation stands. It must keep constitutional law constantly rooted in the great ideals of the past yet in a state of evolution in order to realize them. Something should happen to a person who dons the black robe of a Justice of the Supreme Court of the United States. He or she comes under an obligation to strive for as much objectivity as is humanly attainable by putting aside personal opinions and preferences. Yet even the best and most impartial of Justices, those in whom the judicial temperament is most finely cultivated, cannot escape the influences that have tugged at them all their lives and inescapably color their judgment. Personality, the beliefs that make the person, has always made a difference in the Court's constitutional adjudication. There never has been a constitutional case before the Court in which there was no room for personal discretion to express itself.

We may not want judges who start with the answer rather than the problem, but so long as mere mortals sit on the Court and construe its majestic but murky words, we will not likely get any other kind. Not that the Justices knowingly or deliberately read their presuppositions into law. There probably has never been a member of the Court who consciously decided against the Constitution or was unable in his own mind to square his opinions with it. Most judges convince themselves that they respond to the words on parchment, illuminated, of course, by historical and social imperatives. The illusion may be good for their psyches or the public's need to know that the nine who sit on the nation's highest tribunal really become Olympians, untainted by considerations that move lesser beings into political office.

Even those Justices who start with the problem rather than the result cannot transcend themselves or transmogrify the obscure or inexact into impersonal truth. At bottom, constitutional law reflects great public policies enshrined in the form of supreme and fundamental commands. It is truer of constitutional law than of any other branch that "what the courts declare to have always been the law," as Holmes put it, "is in fact new. It is legislative in its grounds. The very considerations which judges most rarely mention, and always with an apology, are the secret root from which the law draws all the juices of life. I mean, of course, consideration of what is expedient for the community concerned." Result-oriented jurisprudence or, at the least, judicial activism is nearly inevitable— not praiseworthy, or desirable, but inescapable when the Constitution must be construed. Robert H. Bork correctly said that the best way to cope with the problem "is the selection of intellectually honest judges." One dimension of such honesty is capacity to recognize at the propitious moment a need for constitutional evolution, rather than keep the Constitution in a deepfreeze.

Summary Questions

1. Why did the framers not keep a more complete and definitive record of their proceedings of the 1787 Constitutional Convention?
2. Levy notes several different kinds of evidence that demonstrate the problems with ascertaining "original intent." Find as many of these as you can.
3. Levy concludes that constitutional interpretation is always a "legislative" activity. What does he mean by this?

13.4

What Am I? A Potted Plant?

Richard A. Posner

During the Reagan administration, there was a great deal of debate over the appropriate amount of discretion that appeals court judges and Supreme Court justices should exercise in interpreting the Constitution (see Levy, Selection 13.3). Liberals have generally argued for substantial leeway, noting that the framers could not have anticipated many key contemporary policy debates, such as those about abortion or the regulation of nuclear plants. By and large, conservatives have made a case for less discretion and a more literal interpretation of the Constitution. Nevertheless, some liberals, such as the late Supreme Court Justice Hugo Black, have adopted a literalist position, while some conservatives, such as Court of Appeals Judge Richard Posner, have taken a more discretionary approach.

In this article, Posner reacts to the strict constructionist or "legal formalist" view, labeling it virtually impossible to carry out. "Judges," he notes, "have been entrusted with making policy from the start." Posner endorses this notion in large part because of his tendency to approach legal reasoning from an economic perspective—one that has little, if any, grounding in the Constitution or the ideas of the framers. What is clear from his point of view is that all judges make policy and that both liberals and conservatives can benefit from expanded judicial discretion.

M any people, not all of conservative bent, believe that modern American courts are too aggressive, too "activist," too prone to substitute their own policy preferences for those of the elected branches of government. This may well be true. But some who complain of judicial activism espouse a view of law that is too narrow. And a good cause will not hallow a bad argument.

This point of view often is called "strict constructionism." A more precise term would be "legal formalism." A forceful polemic by Walter Berns in the June 1987 issue of *Commentary*—"Government by Lawyers and Judges"—summarizes the formalist view well. Issues of the "public good" can "be decided legitimately only

Richard A. Posner is a judge on the U.S. Court of Appeals for the Seventh Circuit and a senior lecturer at the University of Chicago Law School.

with the consent of the governed." Judges have no legitimate say about these issues. Their business is to address issues of private rights, that is, "to decide whether the right exists—in the Constitution or in a statute—and, if so, what it is; but at that point inquiry ceases." The judge may not use "discretion and the weighing of consequences" to arrive at his decisions and he may not create new rights. The Constitution is a source of rights, but only to the extent that it embodies "fundamental and clearly articulated principles of government." There must be no judicial creativity or "policy-making."

In short, there is a political sphere, where the people rule, and there is a domain of fixed rights, administered but not created or altered by judges. The first is the sphere of discretion, the second of application. Legislators make the law; judges find and apply it.

There has never been a time when the courts of the United States, state or federal, behaved consistently in accordance with this idea. Nor could they, for reasons rooted in the nature of law and legal institutions, in the limitations of human knowledge, and in the character of a political system.

"Questions about the public good" and "questions about private rights" are inseparable. The private right is conferred in order to promote the public good. So in deciding how broadly the right shall be interpreted, the court must consider the implications of its interpretation for the public good. For example, should an heir who murders his benefactor have a right to inherit from his victim? The answer depends, in part anyway, on the public good that results from discouraging murders. Almost the whole of so-called private law, such as property, contract, and tort law, is instrumental to the public end of obtaining the social advantages of free markets. Furthermore, most private law is common law—that is, law made by judges rather than by legislators or by constitution-framers. Judges have been entrusted with making policy from the start.

Often when deciding difficult questions of private rights courts have to weigh policy considerations. If a locomotive spews sparks that set a farmer's crops afire, has the railroad invaded the farmer's property right or does the railroad's ownership of its right of way implicitly include the right to emit sparks? If the railroad has such a right, shall it be conditioned on the railroad's taking reasonable precautions to minimize the danger of fire? If, instead, the farmer has the right, shall it be conditioned on his taking reasonable precautions? Such questions cannot be answered sensibly without considering the social consequences of alternative answers.

A second problem is that when a constitutional convention, a legislature, or a court promulgates a rule of law, it necessarily does so without full knowledge of the circumstances in which the rule might be invoked in the future. When the unforeseen circumstance arises—it might be the advent of the motor vehicle or of electronic surveillance, or a change in attitudes toward religion, race, and sexual propriety—a court asked to apply the rule must decide, in light of information not available to the promulgators of the rule, what the rule should mean in its new setting. That is a creative decision, involving discretion, the weighing of consequences, and, in short, a kind of legislative judgment—though, properly, one more confined than if the decision were being made by a real legislature. A court that decides, say, that copyright protection extends to the coloring of old black-and-white movies is making a creative decision, because the copyright laws do not mention colorization. It is not being lawless or usurpative merely because it is weighing consequences and exercising discretion.

Or if a court decides (as the Supreme Court has done in one of its less controversial modern rulings) that the Fourth Amendment's prohibition against unreasonable searches and seizures shall apply to wiretapping, even though no trespass is committed by wiretapping and hence no property right is invaded, the court is creating a new right and making policy. But in a situation not foreseen and expressly provided for by the Framers of the Constitution, a simple reading out of a policy judgment made by the Framers is impossible.

Even the most carefully drafted legislation has gaps. The Constitution, for example, does not say that the federal government has sovereign immunity —the right, traditionally enjoyed by all sovereign governments, not to be sued without its consent. Nevertheless the Supreme Court held that the federal government has sovereign immunity. Is this interpolation usurpative? The Federal Tort Claims Act, a law waiving sovereign immunity so citizens can sue the government, makes no exception for suits by members of the armed services who are injured through the negligence of their superiors. Nevertheless the Supreme Court has held that the act was not intended to provide soldiers with a remedy. The decision may be right or wrong, but it is not wrong just because it is creative. The 11th Amendment to the Constitution forbids a citizen of one state to sue "another" state in federal court without the consent of the defendant state. Does this mean that you can sue your own state in federal court without the state's consent? That's what the words seem to imply, but the Supreme Court has held that the 11th Amendment was intended to preserve the sovereign immunity of the states more broadly. The Court thought this was implied by the federalist system that the Constitution created. Again the Court may have been right or wrong, but it was not wrong just because it was creative.

Opposite the unrealistic picture of judges who apply law but never make it, Walter Berns hangs an unrealistic picture of a populist legislature that acts only "with the consent of the governed." Speaking for myself, I find that many of the political candidates whom I have voted for have failed to be elected and that those who have been elected have then proceeded to enact much legislation that did not have my consent. Given the effectiveness of interest groups in the political process, much of this legislation probably didn't have the consent of a majority of citizens. Politically, I feel more governed than self-governing. In considering whether to reduce constitutional safeguards to slight dimensions, we should be sure to have a realistic, not an idealized, picture of the legislative and executive branches of government, which would thereby be made more powerful than they are today.

To banish all discretion from the judicial process would indeed reduce the scope of constitutional rights. The framers of a constitution who want to make it a charter of liberties and not just a set of constitutive rules face a difficult choice. They can write specific provisions, and thereby doom their work to rapid obsolescence or irrelevance; or they can write general provisions, thereby delegating substantial discretion to the authoritative interpreters, who in our system are the judges. The U.S. Constitution is a mixture of specific and general provisions. Many of the specific provisions have stood the test of time amazingly well or have been amended without any great fuss. This is especially true of the rules establishing the structure and procedures of Congress. Most of the specific provisions creating rights, however, have fared poorly. Some have proved irksomely anachronistic—for example, the right to a jury trial in federal court in all cases at law if the stakes exceed $20. Others have become dangerously anachronistic, such as the right to bear arms. Some have even turned topsy-turvy, such as the provision for indictment by grand jury. The grand jury has become an instrument of prosecutorial investigation rather than a protection for the criminal suspect. If the Bill of Rights had consisted entirely of specific provisions, it would have aged very rapidly and would no longer be a significant constraint on the behavior of government officials.

Many provisions of the Constitution, however, are drafted in general terms. This creates flexibility in the face of unforeseen changes, but it also creates the possibility of multiple interpretations, and this possibility is an embarrassment for a theory of judicial legitimacy that denies that judges have any right to exercise discretion. A choice among semantically plausible interpretations of a text, in circumstances remote from those contemplated by its drafters, requires the exercise of discretion and the weighing of consequences. Reading is not a form of deduction; understanding requires a consideration of consequences. If I say, "I'll eat my hat," one reason that my listeners will "decode" this in non-literal fashion is that I couldn't eat a hat if I tried. The broader principle, which applies to the Constitution as much as to a spoken utterance, is that if one possible interpretation of an ambiguous statement would entail absurd or terrible results, that is a good reason to adopt an alternative interpretation.

Even the decision to read the Constitution narrowly, and thereby "restrain" judicial interpretation, is not a decision that can be read directly from the text. The Constitution does not say, "Read me broadly," or, "Read me narrowly." That decision must be made as a matter of political theory, and will depend on such things as one's view of the springs of judicial legitimacy and of the relative competence of courts and legislatures in dealing with particular types of issues.

Consider the provision in the Sixth Amendment that "in all criminal prosecutions, the accused shall enjoy the right . . . to have the Assistance of Counsel for his defense." Read narrowly, this just means that the defendant can't be forbidden to retain counsel; if he can't afford counsel, or competent counsel, he is out of luck. Read broadly, it guarantees even the indigent the effective assistance of counsel; it becomes not just a negative right to be allowed to hire a lawyer but a positive right to demand the help of the government in financing one's defense. Either reading is compatible with the semantics of the provision, but the first better captures the specific intent of the Framers. At the time the Sixth Amendment was written, English law forbade a criminal defendant to have the assistance of counsel unless abstruse questions of law arose in his case. The Framers wanted to do away with this prohibition. But, more broadly, they wanted to give criminal defendants protection against being railroaded. When they wrote, government could not afford, or at least did not think it could afford, to hire lawyers for indigent criminal defendants. Moreover, criminal trials were short and simple, so it was not ridiculous to expect a person to defend himself without a lawyer if he couldn't afford to hire one. Today the situation is different. Not only can the society easily afford to supply lawyers to poor people charged with crimes, but modern criminal law and procedure are so complicated that an unrepresented defendant will usually be at a great disadvantage.

I do not know whether Professor Berns thinks the Supreme Court was usurping legislative power when it held in the *Gideon* case that a poor person has a right to the assistance of counsel at the state's expense. But his article does make clear his view that the Supreme Court should not have invalidated racial segregation in public schools. Reading the words of the 14th Amendment in the narrowest possible manner in order to minimize judicial discretion, and noting the absence of evidence that the Framers wanted to eliminate segregation, Berns argues that "equal protection of the laws" just means non-discriminatory enforcement of whatever laws are enacted, even if the laws themselves are discriminatory. He calls the plausible empirical proposition that "separate educational facilities are inherently unequal" "a logical absurdity."

On Berns's reading, the promulgation of the equal protection clause was a trivial gesture at giving the recently freed slaves (and other blacks, whose status at the time was little better than that of serfs) political equality with whites, since the clause in his view forbids the denial of that equality only by executive officers. The state may not withdraw police protection from blacks (unless by legislation?) but it may forbid them to sit next to whites on buses. This is a possible reading of the 14th Amendment but not an inevitable one, unless judges must always interpret the Constitution as denying them the power to exercise judgment.

No one really believes this. Everyone professionally connected with law knows that, in Oliver Wendell Holmes's famous expression, judges legislate "interstitially," which is to say they make law, only more cautiously, more slowly, and in more principled, less partisan, fashion than legislators.* The attempt to deny this truism entangles "strict constructionists" in contradictions. Berns says both that judges can enforce only "clearly articulated principles" and that they may invali-

---

* Oliver Wendell Holmes (1841–1935) served first on the Massachusetts Supreme Court and then on the U.S. Supreme Court between 1882 and 1932. He was labeled "the Great Dissenter," and many of Holmes's minority opinions became the fodder for subsequent Court majority reasoning.

date unconstitutional laws. But the power to do this is not "articulated" in the Constitution; it is merely implicit in it. He believes that the courts have been wrong to interpret the First Amendment as protecting the publication of foul language in school newspapers, yet the words "freedom of speech, or of the press" do not appear to exclude foul language in school newspapers. Berns says he deduces his conclusion from the principle that expression, to be within the scope of the First Amendment, must be related to representative government. Where did he get that principle from? He didn't read it in the Constitution.

The First Amendment also forbids Congress to make laws "respecting an establishment of religion." Berns says this doesn't mean that Congress "must be neutral between religion and irreligion." But the words will bear that meaning, so how does he decide they should be given a different meaning? By appealing to Tocqueville's opinion of the importance of religion in a democratic society. In short, the correct basis for decision is the consequence of the decision for democracy. Yet consequences are not—in the strict constructionist view—a fit thing for courts to consider. Berns even expresses regret that the modern Supreme Court is oblivious to Tocqueville's opinion "of the importance of the woman . . . whose chastity as a young girl is protected not only by religion but by an education that limits her 'imagination.' " A court that took such opinions into account would be engaged in aggressively consequentialist thinking rather than in strict construction.

The liberal judicial activists may be imprudent and misguided in their efforts to enact the liberal political agenda into constitutional law, but it is no use pretending that what they are doing is not interpretation but "deconstruction," not law but politics, because it involves the exercise of discretion and a concern with consequences and because it reaches results not foreseen 200 years ago. It may be bad law because it lacks firm moorings in constitutional text, or structure, or history, or consensus, or other legitimate sources of constitutional law, or because it is reckless of consequences, or because it oversimplifies difficult moral and political questions. But it is not bad law, or no law, just because it violates the tenets of strict construction.

Summary Questions

1. Can the notion of "original intent" be defended as a serious legal doctrine according to Posner? Why not?
2. Do all judges make policy at least part of the time?
3. Posner has frequently been mentioned as a prospective Supreme Court nominee. Do you think the sentiments articulated in this article would make his nomination and confirmation more or less likely? Why?

13.5

The Political Court

Randall Kennedy

Of all the many appointive powers vested in the president, none is more important than that of selecting Supreme Court Justices, who often serve decades longer than those who appoint them. Chief Justice William Rehnquist, for example, was nominated by President Richard Nixon in 1971; he remains on the Court in the mid-1990s, more than two decades after Nixon left office. Some presidents have the good fortune to choose several justices, while others have less opportunity. Among past chief executives, Jimmy Carter was exceptionally unlucky, no vacancies having occurred during his four-year tenure, while Nixon appointed four justices in less than six years.

The contentious battle over several recent nominees, most notably Robert Bork in 1987 and Clarence Thomas in 1991, has rekindled the debate over the criteria for appointing and confirming high court justices. In this essay, written before President Bill Clinton appointed both Ruth Bader Ginsburg and Stephen G. Breyer to the Court, Harvard Law School Professor Randall Kennedy argues that the selection process is necessarily and properly political. Without pinning down a prospective justice on how he or she would rule on a specific case, the Senate, Kennedy asserts, should seek to understand a nominee's "political vision" before the candidate is confirmed for a lifetime appointment.

President Clinton will likely have the opportunity to fill several vacancies on the Supreme Court. How should he go about doing it? Although the president should look to a variety of considerations, by far the most important is a prospect's substantive political commitments. By substantive political commitments, I mean a prospect's stance towards the central, inescapable, politically significant controversies of our time. In the 1850s, a president should definitely have wanted to know where a prospect stood on the slavery question; in the 1930s, where a prospect stood on the New Deal; in the 1960s, where a prospect stood with respect to the civil rights revolution. Today President

Randall Kennedy is a professor at the Harvard Law School and editor of the journal *Reconstruction.* This article originally appeared in 1993.

Clinton should acquire knowledge that will let him know in detail and with confidence where a prospective nominee stands on all of the most vexing issues that trouble our society including reproductive freedom, race relations, freedom of expression, and the status of religion in a secular society. To acquire this information, the president (and the Senate) should directly ask prospects about their political beliefs. If a person declines to answer, the president should probably draw a negative inference, strike that prospect from the list of candidates, and move on to consider others who will allow the president access to his or her thinking.

One thing the president should not do is place a powerful branch of government in the hands of individuals whose political commitments are unknown to him. That would be folly. Yet, remarkably, that is what some observers urge.

Consider, for instance, the argument of Professor Stephen Carter of the Yale Law School. In an op-ed piece in the *New York Times*, Carter claims that the Reagan and Bush administrations "systematically eroded federal courts' independence" by applying "litmus tests to insure that those who became judges— particularly Supreme Court Justices—could be relied on to vote the way the conservatives preferred." He portrays "quizzing nominees about their views on controversial cases" as a politically depraved exercise of power heretofore practiced mainly by discredited politicos on the right.

According to Carter, "When William Brennan was badgered by Senator Joseph McCarthy about loyalty-security cases and Thurgood Marshall* was interrogated by several segregationist senators about civil rights and criminal procedure cases, liberals were properly outraged that a nominee would be asked, even indirectly, about his likely votes." Carter rails against searching for information that will allow the president to predict confidently how a nominee will vote as a justice. "Certainly it is true," he concedes, "that information is usually available from which it is possible to make educated guesses about how potential justices might vote. But to emphasize those predispositions as a prerequisite for appointment politicizes the Court." The president, Carter concludes, "should forgo litmus tests and turn to one of the many experienced federal or state appellate judges whose skills are respected across the political spectrum." Otherwise, Carter warns darkly, the cycle of judicial politicization will never end and "[t]here will be less and less reason to treat the 'opinions' of the courts as authoritative and no reason at all to grant the judges—and justices—life tenure."

Carter's argument reflects much of the confusion, mysticism, and sentimentality that commonly stymies realistic understandings of the judiciary. He objects that the course I advocate would "politicize" the Court. It would be helpful if he would point to a moment in our history in which the selection process was

---

* Brennan served on the Court between 1956 and 1993. Marshall, the former chief litigator for the National Association for the Advancement of Colored People (NAACP), served as Solicitor General of the U.S. before becoming a Supreme Court Justice in 1967.

*un*politicized—a point at which a president was blithely indifferent to the political associations and ideological predispositions of a prospective nominee and considered only "skill." He will be unable to make such a showing because, unsurprisingly, this moment has never existed. How could it? Members of the Supreme Court occupy seats with life tenure within a bureaucracy that wields considerable power. A president would be a fool or, worse, politically amoral to elevate to such an office anyone whose politics suggested a proclivity toward policies with which the president strongly disagreed.

Carter's references to the Reagan and Bush administrations' ideological screening of potential nominees and his allusions to the difficulties that William Brennan and Thurgood Marshall received as nominees at the hands of McCarthyists and segregationists should scare no one. There was, and is, nothing wrong with politicians of any ideological stripe demanding to know where prospective justices stand on political issues that are likely to be implicated in cases arising before the Court. What was wrong in the instances to which Carter alludes was not the questioning but an environment in which straightforward progressive responses to the inquiries posed a danger to candidates. Instead of seeking to insulate nominees from questions, liberals and the left should seek to persuade the public of the attractiveness of progressive answers.

Carter claims that insisting upon knowing the political predispositions of nominees—or, in his lingo, imposing a litmus test—erodes the independence of the judiciary. But how so? Judicial independence means placing individuals beyond the usual means of political discipline *after* that person has been elevated to judicial office. That insulation is attended to by constitutional provisions that explicitly mention two mechanisms that afford ample protection to the judiciary against interference from the other branches of government. One is life tenure: once appointed and confirmed, judges can be removed only pursuant to impeachment by the House of Representatives and conviction by the Senate—a costly, cumbersome process that has never been successfully invoked to oust a recalcitrant justice.

The second is income protection: the Constitution forbids Congress from decreasing the salaries paid to members of the federal judiciary. Neither Carter nor anyone else has set forth a convincing or even plausible explanation of why judicial independence—the autonomy of sitting justices—is eroded by subjecting a person to inquiries designed to inform a president of the political virtues of one candidate as opposed to another. After all, once a person is seated as a justice, the mechanisms protecting judicial independence ensure that person can change his or her mind without fear of losing office.

Moreover, contrary to what Carter suggests, it is precisely because justices are so fully insulated from the normal rigors of political discipline (that is, periodically standing for election) that it is especially important and appropriate for those responsible for elevating them to determine as fully as possible their political character. If the electorate makes a political mistake in selecting a president or a member of the House or Senate, the electorate must wait only two, four, or six years before rectifying that mistake. If the president makes a political mistake in the selection of a justice, only the indefinite and often painfully slow process of aging can remedy it.

Why is it important to know the political character of justices? Because their interpretation of statutes and determinations of the constitutionality of laws is inevitably influenced by that character. Expertise alone is an insufficient guide by which to determine who, from the point of view of a president, would best give meaning to the ambiguous, open-ended clauses that comprise the most important and controversial parts of our written constitution: due process, equal protection of the laws, freedom of speech. "Skill" of various sorts is important. A president should certainly insist on choosing someone who will be sufficiently adept, knowledgeable, and confident to persuade colleagues, isolate adversaries, and educate the public. But juristic skill is merely a tool; it does not guarantee that a justice will reach good results. For that to happen, expertise must be guided by a good political vision. It stands to reason that the president and the Senate should avail themselves of means by which to determine a prospect's political vision. Doing so shows no disrespect for the Court. Rather, it reflects a laudable determination to avoid putting the future of the federal judiciary into the hands of persons whose political commitments are unknown.

Carter and others claim that seeking to know in detail the political views of nominees or potential nominees is bad because it suggests a desire to select persons who are close-minded. "[A]ppointing justices who make up their minds before, not after, hearing arguments threatens judicial integrity," Carter writes, "and interferes with the Court's proper functioning. It was wrong for the Republicans to do it; it would be wrong if the Democrats do it." The specter Carter invokes is a straw man. Those with whom he argues do not advocate appointing justices who are closed to argument. Rather, they maintain that any person worthy of serious consideration has *already* considered arguments, that such a person has likely reached conclusions (that are possibly changeable in light of additional consideration), and that whatever conclusions he or she has reached should be accessible to a president. The idea that knowing a prospect's current views somehow taints the integrity of the selection process is hard to fathom, given that many of the best people any president is likely to consider for a justiceship are people with public careers whose stances on heated topics are already known.

Pleas to de-politicize the selection and confirmation process, to cherish unpredictability in the future course of nominees, to purposefully keep ourselves ignorant about the beliefs of people we empower represent a quasi-religious yearning to make the Court into a shrine above the messiness of politics. But what the process of selection and confirmation needs is *more* rather than less "politics"—more widely available knowledge about nominees, more debate, more participation by the governed, more presidential accountability for nominees, and more common sense. Neither the president nor the public should be asked to accept a pig in a poke. To know fully the political character of those he is considering selecting, the president must ask pointed questions—and demand clear answers.

Summary Questions

1. Should a prospective Supreme Court justice answer questions on his or her positions on controversial issues of the day, such as abortion?
2. Is it possible to "depoliticize" the selection process for justices? How would you seek to accomplish this?

 Part IV

Public Policy

Chapter 14

POLICYMAKING

The policymaking process brings together almost all of the elements in the structure of American politics. We can think of the Constitution as providing a framework within which policies are made—a framework that does not guarantee speedy action or governmental responsiveness to the wishes of the citizens. In addition, public opinion, as expressed through elections or interpreted in the media, is a basic element in policy formulation, yet it is often subject to change and adaptation. After all, presidents and legislators work diligently to generate public support for their own proposals.

The constitutional relationships outlined by the separation of powers and federalism impose serious limitations on policymakers. For example, education has traditionally been a state and local function in the United States; among national institutions, the Supreme Court, with its desegregation rulings, has affected local school districts more than the Congress or the president has.

Beyond these basic rules of the game, contemporary policymaking takes place within a context of a large and growing governmental establishment. Given an annual budget that approaches $1.5 trillion (an almost unimaginable sum), the permanent government of the federal bureaucracy is difficult for elected officials to control. In addition, the government extends its reach by providing guarantees in potentially risky undertakings (the banking industry, student loans, crop damage).

The growth of government has produced two other hallmarks of contemporary policymaking: (1) the extensive use of regulation, which has generated substantial debate, and (2) the influence of annual budgetary actions on almost all domestic policy decisions.

Traditionally, students of public policy have focused much of their attention on the legislature and its decisions. But as the reach of government has grown and problems such as environmental pollution have become increasingly complex, Congress has delegated more and more policymaking authority to the bureaucracy and to independent agencies such as the Food and Drug Administration. In terms of the gross number of policies, regulations far outstrip legislation. Both Congress and the president have sought to control this proliferation. Congress has enacted large numbers of legislative veto provisions, which gave it the opportunity to review various regulations, but in 1983 the Supreme Court declared these vetoes an unconstitutional violation of the executive's authority under the separation of powers. The president has had greater success in monitoring regulation. Through the Office of Management and Budget, the executive reviews regulations to determine their consistency with existing policies.

Still, since the late 1970s, movements toward less new regulation and substantial deregulation have gained ground. Although the Reagan administration generally reduced the number of new regulations, the first moves toward deregulation came in the Carter administration, when economist Alfred Kahn, then chairman of the Civil Aeronautics Board (CAB), began action to curtail regulations within the airline industry. In the end, Kahn succeeded in eliminating the CAB. Increased fare competition among airlines was one short-term result of deregulation, although in the 1990s airline consolidation and higher fares seem the order of the day.

If deregulation has generally been regarded as a success, the jury remains out on the budgetary reforms of the 1970s. The Congressional Budget and Impoundment Control Act of 1974 sought to establish a firm timetable for budget actions and to provide the legislature with tools to restrain the growing deficit. Neither of these goals has been met, and the 1980s witnessed almost yearly budget deadlocks in which massive packages (running as high as $600 billion) obtained grudging congressional approval. The normal legislative process, in which a single program or proposal is acted on, is often circumvented by these immense budget packages. The specialized congressional committees, such as Education and Labor, lose a good deal of control in this process, and almost no one knows exactly what the "omnibus" budget bills contain, because they are so long and complex. In 1994, a budget package placed strict caps on spending and almost completely tied the hands of the Congress, whose members could not increase spending in one area without reducing it in another.

No set of readings can adequately capture the diversity of domestic policymaking. In their articles, Christopher Georges (14.1) and Albert O. Hirschman (14.4) discuss the general problems of implementing policies and arguing for policy change, respectively. Georges argues that means for effective implementation need to be built into new initiatives, especially when local officials will ultimately be responsible for carrying out the legislative mandates. For his part, Hirschman analyzes three basic rhetorical patterns of opposition to policy change. The remaining articles examine two important contemporary policy arenas: crime and health care. Writing before the Clinton administration put forth its reform proposal, Joshua Wiener and Laurel Illston list six key questions that any health care reform plan will have to address. Finally, criminologist Jerome Skolnick takes lawmakers to task for their willingness to increase the likelihood and length of incarceration while doing little to enhance public safety. Taken together, these articles raise serious questions about the ability of the federal government to address, much less solve, the central issues of the day. In many ways, the government itself may be the problem. As Walt Kelly's cartoon character Pogo once put it, "We have met the enemy, and he is us."

14.1

Sign It, Then Mind It

Christopher Georges

The stepchild of American politics and American political science is policy implementation—what happens *after* Congress has acted and the president has signed the legislation. However noble, the intentions of policymakers often, perhaps inevitably, become twisted in the process of implementing laws. With a $1.5-trillion annual budget and literally thousands of separate governmental regulations, it is no wonder that policies regularly change as they are implemented.

In this article, Christopher Georges argues that policy engineers must give more thought to effective implementation as they are designing new legislation. Drawing upon past programs beset with implementation problems (1970s' crime legislation and 1988 welfare reform), Georges calls for careful construction and sensitive administration of policies put forward by the Clinton administration. Still, when reading this, we might wonder if implementation will ever be high on the list of those who write legislation. Can the government learn from its mistakes? It's a question worth pondering.

Ross Perot recently asked me for $15. Against my better judgment, I'm sending him a check. I did not vote for Perot. I hope he never becomes president. Even so, he earned my contribution based on a single remark midway through the second presidential debate. "Please understand," he said, "there are great plans lying all over Washington that nobody ever properly executes."

If the Clinton administration takes one lesson from Ross Perot, that should be it. It's no secret that the new president has more programs than Microsoft. Many are smart. Some are desperately needed. But most will surely follow the same failed path as the ones they are intended to replace—unless the Clinton administration pays heed to more than just turning good ideas into laws. Just as important is focusing equal attention on the nuts and bolts of how to *make the plans work* on the ground level.

Christopher Georges writes for *The Washington Monthly*.

Let's face it, policy implementation is boring. It's complex, and it makes terrible TV. But it's also the missing gene of American politics. Few people focus on it; even fewer care. But getting it right is especially relevant now as Washington gears up to push Clinton's brash new agenda. "All the pious announcements, all the laws that are passed will mean nothing," explains Richard Nathan, director of the Rockefeller Institute of Government at the State University of New York at Albany, "unless there is a commitment to carrying them out. Our failure to do this has been *the* endemic problem of American government."

And what exactly does that mean? It's no secret that countless plans, whether under Johnson or Reagan, in areas from crime to welfare, have failed to live up to their promise. Little matter that the best policy minds designed them, that ambitious new laws were passed, that billions were funneled to federal agencies and the states. Inevitably, it seems, our social ills have become worse. And when that happens, it's back to the drawing board to try a newer, better plan.

The assumption here is that the solutions—the laws themselves—are flawed. And in some cases that surely is part of the problem. But lawmakers and policy designers rarely stop to consider whether, for example, police officials charged with implementing the latest federal plan for community policing know how to train officers for the task, or whether welfare caseworkers actually sanction welfare recipients who fail to take job training classes, as the latest welfare law requires. In short, when the laws are written, is there enough thought given to how to implement the new policies?

In a word, no. Why not? Presidents and congressmen earn their stripes by passing legislation, not by making sure it works. To the constituents back home, a new law sends a signal that their man in Washington is on the ball, doing something—anything—to solve a problem. To the media, slavishly covering the signing of a new bill—as they did in broadcasting images of President Reagan's White House signing of the 1982 Garn-St. Germain Act, which helped cause the savings and loan disaster—is easy. Schlepping out to the hustings, on the other hand, to decipher the impact of the law on the banking industry, wasn't. About the only ones who seem to pay any attention at all to the implementation gap are professor-filled, blue-ribbon panels. (Foremost among them in recent years have been the 1990 Volcker Commission on Public Service,* the 1992 National Commission on State and Local Public Service, and a Brookings Institution team.) . . . Many have gone to great pains to illustrate that even the best laws will fail when implementation is ignored. Such warnings, however, seem to fall on deaf ears.

Of course, all politicians want their laws to succeed, but there is little incentive while designing new legislation to worry about the fine points of how it will be carried out. Unfortunately, it may take the failure of Clinton's vaunted agenda to prove the point. That's a particularly unsavory notion these days, as policy flops

---

* Headed by former Federal Reserve Board chairman Paul Volcker.

in the nineties will be more costly than those of the past. Considering the need to slash the deficit, we simply can no longer afford to play loosy-goosy with social programs; every penny spent must be producing tangible results. Just as important, further failures will push public confidence to the brink: How many times can Washington spend billions on reforms and then have nothing to show for them before taxpayers abandon faith in government solutions altogether?

There is, however, an easier way than waiting for the bright new agenda to become a wasted one: looking back to the causes of failed laws. Two areas, crime and welfare—where fully-debated, smartly-designed policy ideas in recent years failed—make the case.

Disorganized Crime

No issue was hotter in the 1968 election than crime. In the three years leading up to the election, the nation had been bled by riots in more than 100 cities. A 1968 Gallup poll revealed that most Americans believed lawlessness was America's number one domestic problem. After months of debate and with the input of special task forces comprised of the brightest stars in the field, Congress and the Johnson administration unveiled the 1968 Safe Streets Act. The cure to the crime problem would start with the creation of the Law Enforcement Assistance Administration (LEAA), through which $300 million in grants would be doled out to police departments across the nation. In order to win the grants, however, localities had to promise to use the money to fund crime prevention programs that the think-tank task forces had endorsed, namely plans like community-based policing, drug treatment on demand, hiring more police officers, and school-based drug education. Sound familiar? If you've followed Clinton's $3 billion crime program, it should. Of course, Clinton's plan is not identical (he's also pushing tougher ideas like boot camps for juvenile offenders), but the overlap is significant.

The bad news for Clinton is that the Safe Streets Act and the LEAA were dismal failures. (The LEAA, after a controversial, sorry existence, was abolished in 1982.) The good news, however, is that the failure had almost nothing to do with the quality of the policies proposed. In fact, libraries full of studies since 1982 have concluded that such reforms can, and have, worked—which helps explain why they're back on the agenda.

Instead, the failure was largely a product of how the act was carried out. Under Safe Streets, local police departments would submit funding proposals to "state planning boards," which would modify them as they saw fit and pass them along to the Washington-based LEAA for approval. If the plans contained the types of programs Congress and the administration had endorsed, the money would be released to the state boards, which would then dole it out to the local police units.

Of course, fighting crime, as the Safe Streets Act properly recognized, should intimately involve—and ultimately be controlled by—local governments, and not micromanaged from Washington. But Safe Streets' LEAA made a crucial blunder. It essentially threw the money at the states and the state planning boards. It cared only about who got what amount of money. When it came to considering whether the money was being used properly, and more importantly, what results the funding was producing, it was essentially hands off.

And how did that play out in towns and cities across America (where few Washington bureaucrats care to look)? For one, the state planning boards—made up for the most part of academics who were sold on the reforms—invariably locked horns with local police officials, blue-collar types who were often set in their ways. To the local officials, many of whom were quite comfortable running their local fiefdoms, the pointy-headed planners were perceived as a threat to their autonomy. Massachusetts's state planning board, made up mostly of liberal Harvard types, not surprisingly found itself slugging it out with the street-wise Boston police. "Morale here is zero," one Massachusetts state planner told the press in the early seventies. "We have no friends, no political base, no power." One southern state planner at the time said, "The police chiefs in this state come out of the Salem witch hunt. If a police chief doesn't want a training program, you can't do anything about it."

It wasn't long before the agenda began to unravel. While some local departments never applied for funds, others did and then used the money as they saw fit. In 1970, 37 percent of the LEAA funds had been used to pay for programs completely unrelated to crime. (The governor of Indiana, for example, dipped into the LEAA trough to buy himself an airplane.) And in 1971, it was later discovered that more than a dozen states had used LEAA funds for illegal purposes. "What had appeared to be a law officer's dream for badly needed help," stated a congressional report examining the LEAA in the mid-seventies, "was becoming merely a politician's dream for the biggest pork barrel of them all."

Even when the money did filter down to the local level, the new-fangled ideas were often resisted by local police officials wedded to their ways. Consider the Georgia sheriffs who, after a plan had been approved, refused to allow their local jails to be replaced by a multi-county prison slated as a model in providing the latest in rehabilitative programs. Why the stubbornness? To the sheriffs, local jails offered status, provided free labor when needed, and in many cases allowed them to put their wives on the county payrolls to cook meals for the inmates.

In the end, the local police simply beat the planners to a pulp. They were better organized and more politically connected. Linked by vocal, visible, and well-funded groups such as the International Association of Chiefs of Police and the American Correctional Association, they rolled over the friendless and politically unsophisticated planning agencies.

And what was Washington doing during the meltdown? "Their biggest concern was to get the money out in the field," explained one state planning official to the authors of *U.S. v. Crime in the Streets*, a late seventies study of the failure of the Safe Streets Act. "It's as if the people there held an a moral attitude about program standards—they just wanted to get the money out into the hands of the police." Federal myopia meant chaos ruled. Nevada's crime program, for example, failed to include an organized crime component. New York's had just one page detailing how it would deal with the state's drug problem (whereas Vermont's included 320 pages on the same problem). None of this seemed to matter to the LEAA, which approved the plans all the same.

Equally damaging was the fact that evaluation from the LEAA was virtually nonexistent. By the mid-seventies, the Office of Management and Budget (OMB), the General Accounting Office, and the White House had all concluded independently that the LEAA was in a fog. One 1976 OMB report criticized the LEAA for paying for millions of dollars worth of "interesting but unnecessary equipment." In fact, it wasn't until four years after the LEAA was created that Congress made the embarrassing discovery that the agency had not a single employee charged with collecting information on the success of programs.

Given the sloppy implementation of this act, it's little wonder that by the early eighties Washington was no longer enamored of the new crime-fighting ideas. But a decade later, we've come full circle. There is no question that localities must be tightly involved in implementing a federally initiated crime agenda, but unless the Clinton team is aware of why the grand ideas flopped the last time around, history is destined to repeat itself.

Class Act

Of course, the bungling of crime reform may well be the exception. Safe Streets' grand ideas, after all, were being *imposed* on local governments from faraway Washington—a situation sure to inspire distrust no matter how well the regulations were implemented. Perhaps the bulk of the blame in this case really lies with local governments, which were reluctant to accept the fashionable new programs in the first place.

The best way to test that objection is to examine a failed federal reform that was not handed down but was instead inspired by the states themselves—welfare reform.

Clinton's tough campaign rhetoric in this area, such as his promise to "scrap the current welfare system," played no small part in putting him in the White House. While he embraced the foundation of current federal law—forcing welfare recipients to enroll in job training programs—he went a step further, offering a plan that essentially would cancel benefits for those who fail to find a job after two years on assistance. That's no minor suggestion, and one that would require a reprogramming of Aid to Families with Dependent Children (AFDC).

Clinton's no-nonsense talk is justified. Public polls show that Americans are not happy with the welfare system, and plenty of policy experts agree. Nearly 5 million families receive AFDC benefits and the average aid recipient is on the rolls for more than six years. The most recent reform, the 1988 Family Support Act, sought to fix that. The sweeping measure, which came after nearly a decade of debate, turned the philosophy behind welfare inside out. Instead of simply providing recipients with money, the law demanded that those receiving aid must in return prepare themselves for a job through training courses, enrolling in college, or the like.

To make the new idea work, the 1988 law, in creating a program known as JOBS, turned much of the implementation responsibility over to the states. The federal government agreed to release more than $3.3 billion over five years in matching funds to state welfare agencies, which would be charged with creating specific programs to provide job counseling and training. The beauty of the 1988 act was that, unlike Safe Streets, many states, such as Arkansas and Massachusetts, had already experimented with so-called "welfare-to-work programs," giving Congress the confidence that it wouldn't be throwing money at a completely untested idea which the states didn't want.

The first round of evaluations of the act are just now filtering in, and while they don't point to a disaster on the scale of Safe Streets, about the brightest face that can be put on it is "mildly successful." In California, for example, welfare recipients who went through a job training program now earn an average of $1,900 a year. Those who did not, now earn an average of $1,600. Nationwide, the number of people on welfare in the past four years has gone sharply up—not down. "The hope that states would use JOBS to signal a change in the mission of the welfare system has not been realized," was the conclusion of the largest, and thus far only, in-depth study of the act, *Implementing JOBS*, a review of the welfare-to-work programs in 10 states by Jan Hagan and Irene Lurie of the Rockefeller Institute of Government in Albany, N.Y. The pace of progress has in part prompted Clinton and others to push the more radical reform agenda.

But before we leap into the next welfare overhaul, what exactly has gone wrong with the last one? While some critics of the act argue that the law itself is not tough enough (job training requirements, for example, can be fulfilled through taking self-esteem classes), the larger problem is that the act is "under-rated and under-implemented," explains Richard Nathan, author of a review of welfare implementation over the past three decades, *Turning Promise into Performance*. . . .

And what does that mean on the front lines? For one, there hasn't been enough money to make it work—partly because the federal government's $3 billion outlay isn't adequate, but also because the states simply have been slow to collect it. (Remember, the federal seed money is not a direct giveaway. In order for each state to receive its share, it must put up matching funds.) Of the $1 billion available to the states in 1991, only $600 million was actually claimed. Of the 10 states studied by Hagan and Lurie, only one, Oregon, even came close to pulling down all the funds to which it was entitled. And often the poorest states, which need the money the most, put up the least—and thus pull down the least. Mississippi, for example, drew less than 15 percent of the federal funds to which it was entitled.

In some cases, states facing serious fiscal problems simply haven't been able to make the investment. But in others, it's also a matter of leadership—or lack of it.

In fact, in none of the 10 states studied by Hagan and Lurie did welfare agencies make any "organizational changes" in the administration of their programs to incorporate the new federal mandates. Caseworkers, for example, were rarely trained for the dramatic shift from distributors of checks to counselors. Instead, in places like Tennessee, county welfare directors were taught how to market the JOBS program, but caseworkers were never trained for the tougher job of educating welfare recipients about where to get the actual job training and education.

In some cases, the failure of leadership is apparent not so much in what state officials do but in what they neglect. Some governors, such as Maryland's William Donald Schaefer and Massachusetts's Mike Dukakis in the eighties, sparked their welfare-to-work programs by holding press conferences to emphasize positive results, pushing for ad campaigns and the like. Others, such as Texas's Bill Clements in the late eighties, sat on their hands. While part of the resistance to push JOBS program in some states may have been due to a lack of funds, some of it was more intentional. "Don't underestimate the politics of it all," said one Texas welfare official, referring to the Clements administration. "They knew they could win political capital by keeping a safe distance from any program that smacked of welfare."

But as with Safe Streets, the implementation vacuum starts in Washington and filters down to the local level. National leadership has made little effort to inspire local welfare agencies to make the new plans work, allowing them to fall back on old ways. In Michigan, says Nathan, "Social workers simply did not believe in the idea of the program. That's what implementation is about, changing the mindset of the people, not just at the top but at the local level." Consider the attitude of welfare bureaucracy in New Jersey. Crucial to the success of the 1988 act, policy planners say, is sanctioning welfare recipients who refuse to take job training courses by withholding part of their welfare checks. But, explains Allan Zalkind, a top welfare administrator in Newark, which has one of the largest welfare populations in the nation, "We oppose the mandatory aspect of the act. We don't like to sanction anyone unless we feel it is absolutely necessary. Our job is not to hold the gun to someone's head."

One fallout from the lack of wallet and will has been that JOBS programs in most every state have been limited to helping only those who volunteer to get job training—in other words, those recipients who actively want to get off welfare. (In some states, like Minnesota, it is official policy to serve only those who voluntarily ask for job training.) That's fine for the volunteers, but it doesn't help much in ultimately lowering the number of people receiving benefits. Those who volunteer for assistance in finding a job are often the most ambitious who, with or without JOBS, would have left the dole after a relatively short period. It's the hard-core cases who are at the heart of America's welfare problem, and JOBS has offered little help in moving them off welfare. "Serving mostly volunteers means we are not reaching into the caseload," explains Judith Geuran, president of Manpower Development Research Corporation, a not-for-profit group that specializes in welfare reform. "The law has potential, but we are a long way from making it work."

The Promise Land

Making the Family Assistance Act or any law work should be just as high a priority as passing it—for Congress, the White House, and especially the federal agencies. Fortunately, there are road maps for this kind of success, especially on the state level. One is Massachusetts's Employment and Training welfare-to-work program. Here Chet Atkins, who headed the state's welfare agency in the eighties, not only played a hands-on role in creating the policy, but once it was designed, took his show out to the field, working with welfare workers across the state to ensure that the plan was accepted and understood. Atkins realized that before he could change the behavior of those receiving aid, he had to change the attitude of those handing it out.

Recognizing the significance of this missing link in American policy may well be the toughest step. Longtime friend of Bill and Hillary, Marion Wright Edelman, sure to be on the "A list" of White House guests, would do well on one of her visits to leave a copy of a speech she gave six years ago at the Kennedy School of Government's commencement ceremonies. There she spoke of the need for change—but not the kind of policy change most closely associated with Clinton's campaign. "Pay attention," she urged the new graduates, "to the nitty gritty steps of implementation. Passing a law or drafting a regulation is the easiest part of the change process. Making it work, informing the public . . . and getting and training sensitive and skilled personnel to administer it is just as crucial."

Summary Questions

1. Are the goals of legislators and bureaucrats different when it comes to implementing policies? How so, and with what implications?
2. Georges distinguishes between top-down policy making (Safe Streets) and bottom-up efforts (JOBS), yet both run into great difficulties. Can "top-down" legislation ever succeed? Why didn't the "bottom-up" policy produce better results?

14.2

Health Care Reform: Six Questions for President Clinton

Joshua M. Wiener and Laurel Hixon Illston

President Bill Clinton's ultimate place in history will largely be determined by his long-term success in addressing the various problems that fall under the umbrella of "health care reform." The stakes and complexity of health care policies are staggering, as witnessed by the extensive lobbying efforts of hundreds of interests. At the same time, many of the issues are basic, if not simple.

In this selection, two scholars at the Brookings Institution lay out six straightforward questions that any reform plan needs to address. Writing in 1993, before the Clintons unveiled their plan and before competing plans emerged, Joshua Wiener and Laurel Illston point out the difficulties in trying to accomplish various distinct goals, such as cutting costs and providing universal coverage, within a specific program. Still, large-scale change does not occur in a vacuum. All advocates of reform must deal with the basic issues raised by the authors.

Health care reform was high on Bill Clinton's agenda during the presidential campaign and is even higher now that he occupies the Oval Office, as evidenced by his quick appointment of a task force headed by Hillary Rodham Clinton, his most trusted adviser. The general direction of his plan "to control costs and cover everybody" is clear. He favors employer-mandated health insurance and cost containment based on managed competition and global budgets. But how will he flesh out the details of his plan? As he grapples with that problem, he must confront six questions.

How Minimum Is the Minimum Benefit Package?

Clinton's plan, like most proposals for health care reform, promises to provide all Americans with access to a "basic benefit package." But what is meant by "basic"?

Joshua M. Wiener and Laurel Hixon Illston are senior fellow and senior research analyst, respectively, in the Brookings Economic Studies program.

At one extreme is a bare bones package that will leave major health care needs uncovered and may impose large out-of-pocket costs on consumers. Since most people will want as comprehensive a set of benefits as possible, insurers will tend to compete by designing a benefit package that is attractive to the less-costly healthy population. At the other extreme is the package implied in Clinton's campaign blueprint, *Putting People First*: unlimited hospital care, preventive services, prescription drugs, and more than token amounts of mental health services. That package would be better than the one Medicare now provides to the elderly and better than at least 15 million Americans with insurance now have. It is not politically plausible to give younger people a better minimum benefit package than those over age 65. Upgrading the Medicare benefit package will probably cost between $15 billion and $20 billion. In addition, many companies will have to expand their health insurance coverage to include these services, raising their costs.

What Tax Breaks Should Go to Small Businesses?

Even though most small businesses already provide health insurance for their employees, most uninsured Americans work for small businesses that do not. Many work in low-wage or part-time jobs in businesses that cannot afford to pay $3,000 to $4,000 a year per employee in health insurance premiums. Clinton has endorsed tax breaks to ease that financial burden, but he has not specified what companies would be eligible, how big a tax benefit they would receive, or whether the tax breaks would be temporary or permanent.

The dilemma is that it is unfair to provide tax breaks only to small businesses that have not heretofore provided health insurance, but extremely expensive to provide them to all companies. Tying the tax breaks to lower-wage companies would create a perverse incentive for companies to hold down wages. For political if not economic reasons, large permanent tax credits are likely to be necessary to quell small businesses' opposition to being required to provide health insurance.

Can Managed Competition Control Costs?

Clinton has made clear that he plans to control costs through managed competition, not price controls. The aim of managed competition is to make employees and employers more cost conscious in their choice of insurance coverage. As a result, it is expected that employees will get their health services not from unfettered fee-for-service providers who have no incentive to control costs, but from health maintenance organizations and other forms of managed care—particularly those that do the best job of improving quality and cutting costs. Managed competition clearly fits Clinton's notion that the government should "steer, not row."

Advocates of managed competition believe that changing the tax treatment of health insurance is the key to cost containment. Employer contributions to the cost of health insurance are now an unlimited tax-deductible expense for employers. In addition, they are not counted as income (and are not taxed) for employees, who are thus encouraged to take their compensation in unduly generous health insurance. Most advocates of managed competition would limit this exclusion to the cost of an efficient health insurer providing the basic benefits. People who want to use a less efficient insurer or buy more comprehensive insurance benefits could do so, but they would have to pay income and payroll taxes on the incremental employer contribution toward the cost of the plan.

A tax cap has several policy virtues. It could raise a great deal of revenue, is reasonably progressive in its effects, and would provide more incentives for insurers to control costs. Still, it is unclear that by itself a tax cap could do much to reduce the rate of growth in health spending.

First, employers and employees are already painfully aware that spending is going up—for health care in general and health insurance in particular. According to a 1992 Gallup poll, 72 percent of Americans identify cost as the number one health care problem. Average out-of-pocket health care expenses rose from about $900 per family in 1980 to about $2,100 in 1990. Indeed, the soaring cost of insurance is directly responsible for the declining proportion of people covered by employer-sponsored insurance and for the widespread inability of sick and disabled people to buy insurance. Thus, a policy, that builds on making people pay more out-of-pocket for health insurance is politically risky, to say the least.

Second, the total federal revenue loss attributable to the tax treatment of employer-provided insurance was only about $65 billion in 1992. Even if losses can be cut by a third, it seems doubtful that $22 billion can have a dramatic cost containment effect when overall health care spending for the year was $838 billion. Furthermore, 45 percent of health expenditures are for government programs that would be exempt, for at least the foreseeable future, from this type of cost competition.

Even if this "excess" health insurance became taxable, it is unlikely that many people would move from a fee-for-service insurance plan to an HMO. Most people, after all, are in the 15 percent federal income tax bracket. For them, even a $1,000 increase in taxable income from choosing an "inefficient" insurer or a too-rich benefit package would increase taxes only about $150. (Social security and Medicare payroll taxes would also increase by about $75, but some of that would ultimately be returned to the employee in the form of higher retirement benefits.) The sickest 10 percent of the population who are responsible for 70 percent of health expenditures would be particularly unlikely to change insurance.

Although it has not gotten as much attention, a much stronger inducement would be to focus on the employer rather than employee side. If employers could deduct only the cost of efficient health insurance for the basic benefits, they would have a strong incentive not to contribute more than that amount. A worker who faced increased out-of-pocket costs of $1,000 (rather than $225 in increased taxes) for choosing an inefficient insurer would be much more likely to change to less costly insurance. But shifting compensation away from fringe benefits and back to income will take time, will conflict with existing collective bargaining agreements, and will not be popular with workers who prefer health benefits over cash even without the tax advantage.

If managed competition is to work, consumers must know which insurers are efficient and which are not. Insurers who provide coverage to older or sicker people will appear to be less efficient than those who enroll only healthy young people, but they must not be penalized for that fact. The key to measuring efficiency accurately is adjusting the employer contributions to account for differential health risk among employees. It is simple to adjust for age and sex, but these are extremely crude variables, and we are not yet able to make the necessary refinements on such a large scale.

How Do Global Budgets Fit In?

"Global budgets"—a new term of art meaning a fixed budget for health care— would force health care providers to live within a budget and end the cost shifting that has thwarted virtually all previous cost containment efforts in this country. For example, hospitals now evade tough Medicare reimbursement rates by charging higher rates to other third parties. Most other industrialized countries, including Canada, France, Germany, and the United Kingdom, control their health care spending through some form of fixed budget and rate setting. All provide near-universal access to basic health services and keep their health care costs, measured by spending per capita and as a percentage of gross domestic product, far below that of the United States.

Although the United States does not have much experience with global budgets, the state of Maryland's rate-setting system and an early 1980s Rochester, New York, demonstration successfully controlled hospital spending through variations on the global budget approach. And the new Medicare physician reimbursement system sets spending targets—an important component in establishing overall budget limits—that are enforced by the threat of future fee cuts. Clinton's call to integrate global budgets with managed competition is intellectually appealing, but it is not clear how it can be done. The role of rate setting in his plan is ambiguous: it exists as a "fallback," but not as a central part of his proposal.

Purists say that these regulatory strategies are antithetical to managed competition, the whole point of which is to rely on the market to deliver effective, efficient, affordable care. If prices are set by the government, plans will have far less incentive to compete on price. Managed competition advocates argue that regulatory strategies will end up protecting inefficient insurers and providers by setting rates high enough to sustain them at profitable levels. They also worry that global budgets and rate setting will drain political and intellectual energy from the difficult task of establishing market-based reform.

Finally, to the extent that the avowed goal of managed competition is to promote managed care and prepaid systems, a rate-setting approach may be counterproductive. Health maintenance organizations claim that they cannot convince people to join unless their premiums are at least 15 percent below those of the fee-for-service system. To do that, they say, they must negotiate price discounts from providers, which are likely to be less or nonexistent under an all-payer rate-setting system. But if the only value that managed care is supplying is provider discounts, why use managed care when the discounts can be obtained much more easily and universally by using the power of the government?

It is easy to see how global budgets work in government-run health programs like that of Canada or the United Kingdom, where the government is the sole payer. It is less obvious how they would be enforced in our private health insurance system with hundreds of insurers and thousands of providers. Every year the federal government announces annual health spending, but it is only an estimate and not a dollar-by-dollar accounting of expenditures.

Can national spending be capped and allocated, first among the states and then providers, without congressional logrolling and without institutionalizing existing inefficiencies and inequities? Clinton's solution is to take the task of setting and allocating the budget out of the hands of politicians and give it to a nonpolitical national health board. The problem is that although budget setting has a technical component, it is not primarily a technical problem. There is no one right or wrong level of health spending. If the health budget is to be societally determined, then it is a political decision in the highest and best sense of the word. It is a decision for which people should be accountable, which means that it must be agreed on by the president and Congress.

While tough rate setting and global budgets would fit with the common public perception that doctors and hospitals are gouging the system with high prices and waste, the political opposition among providers will be intense. Hospitals and physicians favor universal coverage, but oppose regulatory controls. The leader of at least one provider group has raised constitutional issues that could quite possibly delay the plan's implementation. President Carter, after all, made hospital rate containment one of his major legislative initiatives and lost.

Will the Savings Be Enough to Cover Everybody?

During the campaign, Clinton argued that health care for the uninsured should be financed through savings in the health care system and that new taxes would not be required. Over the long run, that may be possible, but it will not be easy. Most of the initial savings will accrue to the private sector rather than to government programs. Clinton may be able to argue that some of these savings should be channeled back into health care for the uninsured, but most people will call that a tax increase.

More narrowly, it may still be possible to fund health care for the uninsured through savings in Medicare and Medicaid. If the projected rate of increase in these two programs could be cut by 2 percentage points a year, then by 2000 there may be enough money to take care of the 36 million uninsured. Achieving these savings, though, will be hard because payment rates for both programs are already pretty tough, and upgrading Medicare to meet the minimum benefit package Clinton is likely to propose will take substantial additional funds. Integrating Medicaid into the private insurance system, a long-run goal of Clinton's, will cost at least another $20–30 billion for payment rate increases alone.

Aside from the ethical question of whether providing basic health care to the uninsured should be held hostage to achieving cost containment, three points argue against this strategy. First, the lesson of other countries is that the sure way to gain control over the health system as a whole is to assure health coverage for everyone. As long as a significant portion of the population has no coverage, cost shifting will allow providers to evade individual insurers' efforts at cost containment.

Second, savings of the size necessary are conceivable only because spending on Medicare and Medicaid—both entitlement programs with ever-expanding participation—is completely out of control and will be adding substantially to the federal budget deficit. If Clinton is to get control of the deficit, he will have to take at least some of these cost savings and apply them to deficit reduction.

Third, managed competition entails a long-run restructuring of the incentives of the health care system. It probably cannot save enough fast enough to provide meaningful coverage for the uninsured during Clinton's first term. Regulatory strategies have a better shot at producing near-term savings, but even that will be difficult.

Where Does Long-Term Care Fit on the Agenda?

Much to his credit, Clinton included long-term care in the list of necessary steps for national health reform. The current system of organizing and financing long-term care imposes catastrophic costs on nearly everyone who uses paid services. Only a trivial portion of total long-term health care bills is now covered by any form of insurance—public or private. In addition, the delivery system is heavily tilted toward nursing home rather than home care. Clinton wants to expand Medicare to cover more of the costs of long-term care, with a strong emphasis on home care services. But to do so will cost at least $40–50 billion in new spending, and even ardent supporters of long-term care reforms would agree that health care for the uninsured deserves higher priority. But if a full-fledged long-term care program is excluded from the initial health care reform proposal, how will it be addressed and when?

Two issues may cause Clinton to address long-term care sooner rather than later. First, as indicated earlier, the minimum benefit package for acute care is likely to be substantially more generous than existing Medicare benefits. The catch is that, with the exception of prescription drugs, most elderly already have this expanded coverage through their supplemental private insurance. For them, expanded acute care coverage will not be a new benefit. It might be better policy, and more politically popular, to put that extra $15–20 billion into significantly expanding long-term care services under Medicare and Medicaid.

The second issue is whether long-term care will be included in the global budget. Including it will risk institutionalizing the current inadequate system. Excluding it creates strong incentives either to substitute nursing home and home care for hospital services or, less benignly, to reclassify acute care services as long-term care. In either case, long-term care could become a huge escape hatch for the global budget.

No Perfect Answers

Americans universally believe that our health care system is fatally flawed and needs a radical overhaul. There is not, however, much consensus on what should be done [. . .]. His success or failure in pursuing health care reform will largely depend on how he answers these six questions. There are no perfect solutions, only difficult tradeoffs. Whatever answers Clinton develops, he will have to use every ounce of his leadership skills and political savvy to educate the American people on the decisions before us and to push his choices through Congress.

Summary Questions

1. How realistic is the notion of "managed competition"? Do we, as consumers of medical care, know enough to choose among complex plans and numerous providers?
2. Can American health care live within a budget while still allowing substantial choice, as well as universal coverage?
3. Wiener and Illston end the article by observing that "Americans universally believe that our health care system is fatally flawed and needs a radical overhaul." How important is such a belief to the success of health care reform?

14.3

Wild Pitch: "Three Strikes, You're Out" and Other Bad Calls on Crime

Jerome H. Skolnick

Nothing is quite so frustrating to policy makers as longstanding, seemingly intractable problems, especially when the public and the press are calling for rapid, effective actions. In the 1990s crime has become such an issue. Always difficult and expensive to address, by 1994 the crime issue rose to the top of pollsters' lists of the "most important single problem" facing Americans. Even though crime rates were relatively flat, the fear of crime had risen sharply. In response, legislators and other elected officials have proposed increasingly severe penalties for convicted felons. In particular, repeat offenders and those convicted of drug-related crimes have become the chief targets of policy makers.

In this piece, public policy scholar Jerome Skolnick argues that while extended prison sentences will not likely reduce rates of crime, they will take ever-larger chunks from state and federal budgets. Acknowledging that fear of crime can certainly be justified and that crime has increased greatly since the mid-1960s, Skolnick emphasizes the differences between satisfying an urge to exact retribution and implementing effective actions to prevent crime. His reasoning complements the argument put forth by Georges (14.1) that policy makers need to focus their attention on what works, rather than allowing emotions and intuition to produce simple, but ultimately unsatisfactory, answers to difficult questions.

A ccording to the pundits, the polls, and the politicians, violent crime is now America's number one problem. If the problem were properly defined and the lessons of past efforts were fully absorbed, this could be an opportunity to set national crime policy on a positive course. Instead, it is a dangerous moment. Intuition is driving the country toward desperate and ineffectual responses that will drive up prison costs, divert tax dollars from other vital purposes, and leave the public as insecure and dissatisfied as ever.

The pressures pushing federal and state politicians to vie for the distinction of being toughest on crime do not come only from apprehensive voters and the

---

Jerome Skolnick is professor of public policy at the University of California, Berkeley.

tabloid press. Some of the leading organs of elite opinion, notably the *Wall Street Journal*, have celebrated gut-level, impulsive reactions. In one *Journal* column ("Crime Solution: Lock 'em Up"), Ben J. Wattenberg writes that criminologists don't know what works. What works is what everyone intuitively knows: "A thug in prison cannot shoot your sister." In another *Journal* column ("The People Want Revenge"), the conservative intellectual Paul Johnson argues that government is failing ordinary people by ignoring their retributive wishes. Ordinary people, he writes, want neither to understand criminals nor to reform them. "They want them punished as severely and cheaply as possible."

Johnson is partly right and mostly wrong. Ordinary people want more than anything to walk the streets safely and to protect their families and their homes. Intuitively, like Wattenberg, many believe that more prisons and longer sentences offer safety along with punishment. But, especially in dealing with crime, intuition isn't always a sound basis for judgment.

The United States already has the highest rate of imprisonment of any major nation. The prisons have expanded enormously in recent years in part because of get-tough measures sending low-level drug offenders to jail. Intuitions were wrong: the available evidence does not suggest that imprisoning those offenders has made the public safer.

The current symbol of the intuitive lock-'em-up response is "three strikes and you're out"—life sentences for criminals convicted of three violent or serious felonies. The catchy slogan appears to have mesmerized politicians from one coast to the other and across party lines. Three-strikes fever began in the fall of 1993 in the wake of the intense media coverage of the abduction and murder of a 12-year-old California girl, Polly Klaas, who was the victim, according to police, of a criminal with a long and violent record. California's Republican Governor Pete Wilson took up the call for three strikes, and [in 1994] the California legislature overwhelmingly approved the proposal. Even New York Governor Mario Cuomo endorsed a three strikes measure. The [Congress] has passed a crime bill that adopts three strikes as well as a major expansion of the federal role in financing state prisons and stiffening state sentencing policy. . . .

But will three strikes work? Teenagers and young men in their twenties commit the vast majority of violent offenses. The National Youth Survey, conducted by Colorado criminologist Delbert S. Elliott, found that serious violent offenses (aggravated assault, rape, and robbery involving some injury or weapon) peak at age 17. The rate is half as much at age 24 and declines significantly as offenders mature into their thirties.

If we impose life sentences on serious violent offenders on their third conviction—after they have served two sentences—we will generally do so in the twilight of their criminal careers. Three-strikes laws will eventually fill our prisons with geriatric offenders, whose care will be increasingly expensive when their propensities to commit crime are at the lowest.

Take the case of "Albert," described in the *New York Times* not long ago by Mimi Silbert, president of the Delancey Street Foundation in San Francisco. At age 10, Albert was the youngest member of a barrio gang. By the time he was sent to San Quentin at the age of 19, he had committed 27 armed robberies and fathered two children. Now 36, he is a plumber and substitute teacher who has for years been crime-free, drug-free, and violence-free. According to Silbert, the Delancey Street program has turned around the lives of more than 10,000 Alberts in the past 23 years.

To imprison the Alberts of the world for life makes sense if the purpose is retribution. But if life imprisonment is supposed to increase public safety, we will be disappointed with the results. To achieve that purpose, we need to focus on preventing violent crimes committed by high-risk youths. That is where the real problem lies.

The best that can be said of some three-strikes proposals is that they would be drawn so narrowly that they would have little effect. The impact depends on which felonies count as strikes. Richard H. Girgenti, director of the New York State Division of Criminal Justice Services, says that the measure supported by Governor Cuomo would affect only 300 people a year and be coupled with the release of nonviolent prisoners. . . . Proposals like California's, however, will result in incarcerating thousands of convicts into middle and old age.

Regressing to the Mean

Before Governor Wilson signed the most draconian of the three-strikes bill[s] introduced in the legislature, district attorneys across the state assailed the measure, arguing that it would clog courts, cost too much money, and result in disproportionate sentences for nonviolent offenders. So potent is the political crime panic in California that the pleas of the prosecutors were rebuffed.

The prospect in California is ominous. Even without three-strikes legislation, California is already the nation's biggest jailer, with one out of eight American prisoners occupying its cells. During the past 16 years, its prison population has grown 600 percent, while violent crime in the state has increased 40 percent. As Franklin E. Zimring and Gordon Hawkins demonstrate in a recent issue of the *British Journal of Criminology*, correctional growth in California was "in a class by itself" during the 1980s. The three next largest state prison systems (New York, Texas, and Florida) experienced half the growth of California, and western European systems, about a quarter.

To pay for a five-fold increase in the corrections budget since 1980, Californians have had to sacrifice other services. Education especially has suffered. Ten years ago, California devoted 14 percent of its state budget to higher education and 4 percent to prisons. Today it devotes 9 percent to both.

The balance is now expected to shift sharply in favor of prisons. To pay for three strikes, California expects to spend $10.5 billion by the year 2001. The California Department of Corrections has estimated that three strikes will require the state to add 20 more prisons to the existing 28 and the 12 already on the drawing board.

By 2001, there will be 109,000 more prisoners behind bars serving life sentences. A total of 275,621 more people are expected to be imprisoned over the next 30 years—the equivalent of building an electric fence around the city of Anaheim. By the year 2027 the cost of housing extra inmates is projected to hit $5.7 billion a year.

But will California be better off in 2027—indeed, will it have less crime—if it has 20 more prisons for aging offenders instead of 20 more college campuses for the young?

Of course, Wilson and other politicians are worrying about the next elections, not the next century. By the time the twice-convicted get out of prison, commit a third major offense, and are convicted and sentenced to life terms, Wilson and the others supporting three strikes will be out—that is, out of office—leaving future generations a legacy of an ineffectual and costly crime policy. To avoid that result, political leaders need to stop trying to out-tough one another and start trying to out-reason each other.

The Limits of Intuition

H. L. A. Hart, the noted legal philosopher, once observed that the Enlightenment made the form and severity of punishment "a matter to be *thought* about, to be *reasoned* about, and *argued*, and not merely a matter to be left to feelings and sentiment." Those aspirations ought still to be our guide.

The current push to enact three strikes proposals is reminiscent of the movement in the 1970s to enact mandatory sentencing laws, another effort to get tough, reduce judicial discretion, and appease the public furies. But mandatory sentencing has not yielded any discernible reduction in crime. Indeed, the result has been mainly to shift discretionary decision-making upstream in the criminal justice system since the laws have continued to allow great latitude in bringing charges and plea bargaining.

Ironically, mandatory sentencing allowed the serial freedom of Richard Allen Davis, the accused murderer of Polly Klaas. Before 1977, California had a system of indeterminate prison sentencing for felony offenders. For such felonies as second-degree murder, robbery, rape, and kidnapping, a convict might receive a sentence of 1 to 25 years, or even one year to life. The objective was to tailor sentences to behavior, to confine the most dangerous convicts longer, and to provide incentives for self-improvement. However, in 1977, declaring that the goal of imprisonment was punishment rather than rehabilitation, the state adopted supposedly tougher mandatory sentences. Richard Allen Davis benefited from two mandated sentence reductions, despite the prescient pre-sentencing report of a county probation officer who warned of Davis's "accelerating potential for violence" after his second major conviction. Under indeterminate sentencing, someone with Davis's personality and criminal history would likely have been imprisoned far longer than the mandated six years for his first set of offenses. . . .

The Rise of Imprisonment

Two trends are responsible for the increase in imprisonment. First, the courts are imposing longer sentences for such nonviolent felonies as larceny, theft, and motor vehicle theft. In 1992 these accounted for 65.9 percent of crime in America, according to the Federal Bureau of Investigation's Uniform Crime Reports.

Second, drugs have become the driving force of crime. More than half of all violent offenders are under the influence of alcohol or drugs (most often alcohol) when they commit their crimes. The National Institute of Justice has shown that in 23 American cities, the percentage of arrested and booked males testing positive for any of ten illegal drugs ranged from a low of 48 percent in Omaha to 79 percent in Philadelphia. The median cities, Fort Lauderdale and Miami, checked out at 62 percent.

There has been an explosion of arrests and convictions and increasingly longer sentences for possessing and selling drugs. A Justice Department study, completed last summer but withheld from the public until February this year, found that of the 90,000 federal prison inmates, one-fifth are low-level drug offenders with no current or prior violence or previous prison time. They are jamming the prisons.

The federal prison population, through mandated and determinate sentences, has tripled in the past decade. Under current policy, it will rise by 50 percent by the century's turn, with drug offenders accounting for 60 percent of the additional prisoners. Three-strikes legislation will doubtless solidify our already singular position as the top jailer of the civilized world.

The Fear Factor

The lock-'em-up approach plays to people's fear of crime, which is rising, while actual crime rates are stabilizing or declining. This is by no means to argue that fear of crime is unjustified. Crime has risen enormously in the United States in the last quarter-century, but it is no more serious in 1994 than it was in 1991. The FBI's crime index declined 4 percent from 1991 to 1992.

In California, a legislative report released in January indicates that the overall crime rate per 100,000 people declined slightly from 1991 to 1992, dropping from 3,503.3 to 3,491.5. Violent crimes—homicide, forcible rape, robbery, and aggravated assault—rose slightly, from 1,079.8 to 1,103.9. Early figures for 1993 show a small decline.

On the other coast, New York City reported a slight decline in homicides, 1,960 in 1993, compared with 1,995 in 1992, and they are clustered in 12 of the city's 75 police districts, places like East New York and the South Bronx. "On the east side of Manhattan," writes Matthew Purdy in the *New York Times,* "in the neighborhood of United Nations diplomats and quiet streets of exclusive apartments, the gunfire might as well be in a distant city."

So why, when crime rates are flat, has crime become America's number one problem in the polls? Part of the answer is that fear of crime rises with publicity, especially on television. Polly Klaas's murder, the killing of tourists in Florida, the roadside murder of the father of former basketball star Michael Jordan, and the killing of commuters on a Long Island Railroad train sent a scary message to the majority of Americans who do not reside in the inner cities. The message seemed to be that random violence is everywhere and you are no longer safe—not in your suburban home, commuter train, or automobile—and the police and the courts cannot or will not protect you.

A recent and as yet unpublished study by Zimring and Hawkins argues that America's problem is not crime per se but random violence. They compare Los Angeles and Sydney, Australia. Both cities have a population of 3.6 million, and both are multicultural (although Sydney is less so). Crime in Sydney is a serious annoyance but not a major threat. . . .

Sydney's crime pattern explains the difference. Its burglary rate is actually 10 percent higher than L.A.'s, and its theft rate is 73 percent of L.A.'s. But its robbery and homicide rates are strikingly lower, with only 12.5 percent of L.A.'s robbery rate and only 7.3 percent of L.A.'s homicide rate.

Americans and Australians don't like any kind of crime, but most auto thefts and many burglaries are annoying rather than terrifying. It is random violent crime, like a shooting in a fast-food restaurant, that is driving fear.

Violent crime, as I suggested earlier, is chiefly the work of young men between the ages of 15 and 24. The magnitude of teenage male involvement in violent crime is frightening. "At the peak age (17)," Delbert Elliott writes, "36 percent of African-American (black) males and 25 percent of non-Hispanic (white) males report one or more serious violent offenses." Nor are young women free of violence. One in five African-American females and one in ten white females report having committed a serious violent offense.

Blacks are more likely than whites to continue their violence into their adult years. Elliott considers this finding to be an important insight into the high arrest and incarceration rates of young adult black males. As teenagers, black and white males are roughly comparable in their disposition to violence. "Yet," Elliott writes, "once involved in a lifestyle that includes serious forms of violence, theft, and substance use, persons from disadvantaged families and neighborhoods find it very difficult to escape. They have fewer opportunities for conventional adult roles, and they are more deeply embedded in and dependent upon the gangs and the illicit economy that flourish in their neighborhoods."

The key to reformation, Elliott argues, is the capacity to make the transition into conventional adult work and family roles. His data show that those who successfully make the change "give up their involvement in violence."

Confinement in what will surely be overcrowded prisons can scarcely facilitate that transition, while community-based programs like Delancey Street have proven successful.

Just as violent crime is concentrated among the young, so is drug use. Drug treatment must be a key feature of crime prevention both in prisons and outside. There is some good news here. In early 1994, President Clinton and a half-dozen cabinet members visited a Maryland prison that boasts a model drug-treatment program to announce a national drug strategy that sharply increases spending for drug treatment and rehabilitation. Although the major share of the anti-drug budget, 59 percent, is still allocated to law enforcement, the change is in the right direction. A number of jurisdictions across the country have developed promising court-ordered rehabilitation programs that seem to be succeeding in reducing both drug use and the criminality of drug-using offenders.

Drugs are one area where get-tough policies to disrupt supply have been a signal failure, both internationally and domestically. Interdiction and efforts to suppress drug agriculture and manufacture within such countries as Peru and Colombia have run up against what I have called "the Darwinian Trafficker Dilemma." Such efforts undercut the marginally efficient traffickers, while the fittest—the most efficient, the best organized, the most ruthless, the most corrupting of police and judges—survive. Cocaine prices, the best measure of success or failure, dropped precipitously in the late 1980s. They have recovered somewhat, but likely more from monopolistic pricing than government interference.

Domestically, get-tough intuitions have inspired us to threaten drug kingpins with long prison terms or death. Partly, we wish to punish and incapacitate them, but mostly we wish to deter others from following in their felonious paths. Unfortunately, such policies are undermined by the "Felix Mitchell Dilemma," which I named in honor of the West Coast's once notorious kingpin, who received a life sentence in the 1980s, albeit a short one since he was murdered in federal prison. Mitchell's sentence and early demise did not deter drug sellers in the Bay Area. On the contrary, drug sales continued and, with Mitchell's monopolistic pricing eliminated, competition reduced the price of crack. The main effect of Mitchell's imprisonment was to destabilize the market, lower drug prices, and increase violence as rival gang members challenged each other for market share. Drug-related drive-by shootings, street homicides, and felonious assaults increased.

Recently, two of Mitchell's successors, Timothy Bluitt and Marvin Johnson, were arrested and sent to prison. So will peace finally come to the streets? "When a guy like Bluitt goes down, someone takes his place and gets an even bigger slice of the pie," an anonymous federal agent told the *San Francisco Chronicle* this past January. "The whole process is about consolidating turf and power."

Youngsters who sell drugs in Oakland, Denver, Detroit, south central Los Angeles, Atlanta, and New York are part of generations who have learned to see crime as economic opportunity. This does not excuse their behavior, but it does intensify our need to break the cycle of poverty, abuse, and violence that dominates their lives. Prisons do not deter criminals partly because the Mitchells and Bluitts do not rationally calculate choices with the same points of reference that legislators employ. Drug dealers already face the death penalty on the streets.

History reminds us that gang violence is not novel, but it has not always been so lethal. The benchmark sociological study of the urban gang is Frederick Thrasher's research on 1,313 Chicago gangs published in 1927. The disorder and violence of these gangs appalled Thrasher, who observed that they were beyond the ordinary controls of police and other social agencies. He described gang youth, of which only 7.2 percent were "Negro," as "lawless, godless, wild." Why didn't more of them kill each other? They fought with fists and knives, not assault weapons.

Preventing Violent Crime

If violent crime prevention is our strategic aim, we need to test tactics. We need to go beyond the Brady Bill* and introduce a tight regulatory system on weapons and ammunition, and we need more research and analysis to figure out what control system would be most effective. Successful gun and ammunition control would do far more to stem the tide of life-threatening violence than expensive prisons with mandated sentences.

The Senate crime bill, however, promises to increase the nation's rate of imprisonment. Besides its three-strikes provisions, the legislation incorporates Senator Robert Byrd's $3 billion regional prison proposal. If enacted, states can apply to house their prisoners in 10 regional prisons, each with a capacity of 2,500 inmates.

To qualify, states must adopt "truth in sentencing" laws mandating that offenders convicted of violent crimes serve "at least 85 percent of the sentence ordered," the current average served by federal offenders. They also must approve pretrial detention laws similar to those in the federal system. And the states must ensure that four categories of crime—murder, firearms offenses resulting in death or serious bodily injury, sex offenses broadly defined, and child abuse—are punished as severely as they are under federal law. . . .

According to H. Scott Wallace of the National Legal Aid and Defender's Association, the mandate will add about 12,000 prisoners to the average state's correctional population but will offer only about 3 percent of the space needed to house them.

The most costly provision of the . . . crime bill—$9 billion worth—is its proposal for 100,000 more police, a measure endorsed by the administration. Its potential value in reducing crime is unclear. We need more research on constructive policing, including community policing, which can be either an effective

---

* Enacted in 1993, this law requires a five-day waiting period when purchasing hand guns, so that background checks can be conducted.

approach or merely a fashionable buzzword. We need to address the deficiencies of police culture revealed in the corruption uncovered by New York City's Mollen Commission and the excessive force revealed on the Rodney King beating videotape. More police may help in some places but not much in others. And they are very expensive.

A leading police researcher, David H. Bayley, has explained the ten-for-one rule of police visibility: ten cops must be hired to put one officer on the street. Only about two-thirds of police are uniformed patrol officers. They work three shifts, take vacation and sick leave, and require periodic retraining. Consequently, 100,000 new officers will mean only about 10,000 on the street for any one shift for the entire United States.

Even if we were to have more and better police, there is no guarantee they will deter crime. Criminologists have found no marginal effect on crime rates from putting more cops on the street. Indeed, Congress and the president need look no farther than down their own streets to discover that simply increasing police doesn't necessarily make the streets safe. Washington, D.C., boasts the highest police-per-resident ratio in the nation with one cop for every 150 civilians. It is also America's homicide capital.

We might get more bang for the patrolling buck by investing in para-police, or the police corps, or private police, rather than by paying for more fully sworn and expensive officers. Under the leadership of former Chief Raymond Davis, Santa Ana, California, had the most effective community-oriented policing department in the nation. Davis, who faced a weak police union, could innovate with community- and service-oriented civilians who wore blue uniforms but carried no guns—a new and cost-effective blue line.

The crime bill allocates approximately $3 billion for boot camps, another get-tough favorite. Criminologist Doris MacKenzie has found, contrary to intuition, no significant difference between camp graduates and former prison inmates in the rate at which they return to prison. Similarly, a General Accounting Office report concluded that there is no evidence that boot camps reduce recidivism.

If the public wants boot camps primarily for retribution, it doesn't matter whether they work. Under the Eighth Amendment's bar on cruel and unusual punishment, we're not permitted to impose corporal punishment with whips and clubs. In boot camps, however, we can require painful exercises and hard and demeaning labor to teach these miscreant youth a message of retribution. But if correctional boot camps are intended to resocialize youth and to prepare for them noncriminal civilian life, the camps are inadequate.

We need to experiment with boot camps plus—the "plus" including skills training, education, jobs, community reconstruction. Conservatives who stress moral revitalization and family values as an antidote to youth crime have the right idea. Yet they rarely, if ever, consider how important are the structural underpinnings—education, opportunity, employment, family functioning, community support—for developing such values.

Eventually, we are going to have to choose between our retributive urges and the possibilities of crime prevention. We cannot fool ourselves into thinking they are the same. The punishment meted out by criminal law is a blunt and largely ineffectual instrument of public protection. It deters some, it incapacitates others, and it does send a limited moral message. But if we want primarily to enhance public safety by preventing crime, we need to mistrust our intuitions and adopt strategies and tactics that have been researched, tested, and critically evaluated. In short, we need to embrace the values of the Enlightenment over those of the Dark Ages.

Summary Questions

1. Skolnick observes that Pete Wilson will have finished his stint as governor of California long before the geriatric prisoners who commit three felonies are released from incarceration. Do politicians often adopt policies that serve themselves, but place great burdens on their successors? Why is this so? Does it apply to other policy areas, such as the budget?
2. Even if crime rates are not increasing, should politicians take seriously a rising fear of crime? Short of simply pandering to, or even heightening, the public's worst fears, what can elected officials do to make coherent, effective policy on this most difficult issue?

 14.4

The Rhetoric of Reform

Albert O. Hirschman

Understanding policy change requires paying attention to how issues are framed. Is there a health care crisis or just a health care system in need of some modest adjustments? Looking at statistics may lead us to one conclusion; hearing a nightmare tale of an uninsured single mother might push us in another direction. A relative handful of social scientists, such as Murray Edelman, Deborah Stone,

Albert O. Hirschman is professor emeritus of social science at Princeton's Institute for Advanced Studies.

and Albert Hirschman, among others, have systematically emphasized how words structure our understanding and construction of societal problems and their possible solutions.

In this 1993 essay, Hirschman reflects on a recent (1991) book that examined the rhetoric of those who opposed reform proposals. He discovered patterns of opposition and, almost as an afterthought, noted that reformers themselves often used variants of these stock arguments. Hirschman here reemphasizes the power of rhetoric to shape policy debates and urges would-be reformers not to fall into language traps as they seek change.

T here are various reasons that an author may wish to return not to the "classic" that he wrote 30 years ago (this is a widely practiced form of narcissism) but to a book he has just recently published. The book I have in mind is my 1991 work, *The Rhetoric of Reaction*, in which I identified three staple claims of reactionary rhetoric which have recurred since the French Revolution. I labeled them *futility*—the claim that all attempts at social engineering are powerless to alter the natural order of things; *perversity*—the argument that interventions will actually backfire and have the opposite of their intended effect; and *jeopardy*—the idea that a new, possibly more radical reform will threaten older, hard won liberal reforms.

Largely drafted between 1985 and mid-1989, my book was no doubt written in part as a polemic against the then aggressive and seemingly triumphant neo-conservative* positions on social and economic policymaking. Since then, new opportunities have opened up for reformist policymaking, first in Eastern Europe with the collapse of Communism, then in the United States with the passing of the Reagan-Bush era. Under the circumstances, the question arises whether my book can lay claim to having acquired a new function.

Fortunately, I had inserted a chapter "From Reactionary to Progressive Rhetoric" for I had noted, in the course of writing, that some arguments typically used by "progressives" or reformers bear a distinct family likeness to my "reactionary" arguments. . . .

Actually, reformers should have first of all an interest in my historical survey of the futility, perversity, and jeopardy claims. That survey may help them anticipate, anatomize, and rebut the staple forms of reactionary rhetoric as they are used by conservatives and neo-conservatives. More subtly and perhaps more importantly, reformers are well advised not just to be prepared for conservative attacks against their proposals. They also should look out for the *real* dangers of these

---

* Often drawn from older, centrist elements of the Democratic Party, neo-conservatives reacted against what they considered the liberal excesses of the 1960s. Many, such as UN Ambassador Jeanne Kirkpatrick, strongly supported Ronald Reagan, while others, like pollster Ben Wattenberg, voiced their criticisms outside the party structure.

proposals, for which their adversaries will of course have a particularly sharp eye. For these reasons, reformers should know the principal reactionary arguments and take them seriously.

Begin with the perversity argument. Because some recent reforms have misfired (often because conservatives hobbled them with unattainable conditions), the watch for conceivable perverse outcomes is particularly intense. On occasion, it risks being overdone, even by advocates of reform.

For example, not long ago, various proposals for strengthening child support were made in the United States. In the case of single-parent children part of that increased support was proposed to be extracted from the absent or "non-custodial" parent (generally the father) by attaching his income through automatic withholding of wage payments. This way of improving the economic status of poor children had been pioneered in the state of Wisconsin and the proposal was to introduce it more widely, through federal legislation.

At that point, an interesting memorandum was circulated to the participants in the discussion. It attempted to list all the conceivable "unintended repercussions" that might flow from the proposed scheme. The list was surprisingly long and diverse. If future fathers who are unmarried face an assured long-term drain on their incomes, how might they react? They may insist on the woman they have impregnated having an abortion; or they may be attracted to "off-the-book" jobs whose wages could not be attached; or they might "disappear," move to another state, and assume a new identity and social security number; etc., etc. The strategies open to individuals intent on evading the proposed measure are obviously extremely varied. It is no doubt important to think in advance about such strategies and about the likelihood that they will be widely adopted, with the result that the proposed policy might be thwarted and that it might generate perverse results, such as a widespread increase in crime, abortions, etc.

The mere visualization of perverse reactions says, of course, very little about their likely incidence. Moreover, as I attempted to show in my chapter on the perversity thesis, many unintended consequences of public policies are not necessarily perverse, and even perverse effects are often such that "some positive margin survives [their] onslaught." In evaluating the prospective outcome of public policies, reformers should certainly be attentive to such possibilities as well as to the probable extent of truly perverse effects. Otherwise they would become affected by oversophisticated skittishness and, in general, be paralyzed by imaginary fears.

The point can be generalized: while the new fashion to look out in advance for dangers that may lurk in reform proposals is to be welcomed, reformers should be aware of the elementary economic principle that a search is not to be pushed beyond the point where the marginal cost of the search begins to exceed its marginal benefit.

Indeed, the relentless prospecting for perverse effects may itself have a perverse effect; it is apt to make the reformer insufficiently alert to emerging dangers. More important, reformers must realize that it is impossible to guard in advance against all possible risks and dangers. The most thorough prospecting will miss out on some negative effects that will appear only as events unfold. This inability to foresee future trouble will strike us as less disturbing once we realize that we are similarly unable to think in advance of the remedial measures that may become available or that we may devise once trouble occurs. . . .

Self-restraint in the Use of Progressive Rhetoric

. . . I implicitly counsel reformers to use self-restraint in using certain arguments on behalf of their programs and policies, no matter how effective and persuasive they may be or may seem to be. These arguments which I show to be progressive counterparts or equivalents of the reactionary perversity, futility, and jeopardy theses are essentially the following:

1. We should adopt a certain reform or policy because as things are we are caught, or will shortly land in, a desperate predicament that makes immediate action imperative regardless of the consequences—this argument attempts to deflect and neutralize the perversity thesis.

2. We should adopt a certain reform or policy because such is the law or tide of history—this argument is the counterpart of the futility thesis, according to which attempts at change will come to naught because of various "iron laws."

3. We should adopt a certain reform or policy because it will solidify earlier accomplishments—this is the progressive's retort to the jeopardy claim that the reform is bound to wreck some earlier progress.

How difficult would it be for reformers to give up these kinds of arguments? I have just listed them, I believe, in decreasing order of dispensability.

The most dispensable of the three arguments is, to my mind, the alarmist claim that disaster is upon us if we fail to take this or that progressive step. This way of arguing might be called "impending-disaster" or "impending-revolution" blackmail. It has been a common way for various Western progressives or reformers to present their programs, particularly since 1917 when the threat of social revolution appeared on the horizon of Western societies.* An important variant of this way of arguing became current after World War II in discussions on aid for the low-income countries of the Third World: here the joint disaster to be fought off—by extending generous financial aid—was revolution and the scary prospect of these countries being "lost" to the Soviet zone of influence.

For some time, these ways of arguing for national or international redistribution of income had gone stale from overuse. Since the events of 1989–91, they have become largely unusable as a result of the collapse of communism and the Soviet Union. As Gunnar Myrdal† argued long ago, progressives can and should make a

---

* With the Russian Revolution and the ascendancy of communism.

† A noted Swedish sociologist.

convincing case for the policies they advocate on the ground that they are *right* and *just*, rather than by alleging that they are needed to stave off some imaginary disaster.

What about the argument that a certain progressive policy should be adopted because such is the "tide" of history, the "wave of the future," which it is futile as well as knavish to oppose? This argument also should not be too difficult to discard, in part, I will admit, because, with the latest upheavals and *pace* Fukuyama,* the tide of history appears to run quite strongly against the tide-of-history view of things!

The argument that a certain policy should be adopted because it is in line with some inevitable drift of history so that any opposition to this drift will end up in history's dustbin is actually close to the view that disaster will inevitably strike unless we adopt a certain progressive program. While I was at pains to point out in my book the considerable differences between the perversity and the futility theses, the progressive counterparts to these two arguments turn out to have much in common. In both cases an appeal is made, not to human reason and judgment, but to anxiety and fear. And both views share the characteristic that, as a result of recent historical experience, they are highly discredited at the present time. Hence there is hardly any sacrifice involved in following my advice against using them.

Things are rather different in the case of yet another typical progressive argument which I implicitly ask my progressive friends to use sparingly. It is the argument that a proposed reform is not only compatible with previous progressive achievements, but will actually strengthen them and will be strengthened by them. Similarly, progressives will often argue that "all good things go together" or that there is no conceivable area of conflict between two desirable objectives (for example, "the choice between environmental protection and economic growth is a false one"). In itself, this is an attractive and seemingly innocuous way of arguing, and my advice to reformers cannot be never to use this argument. Given their considerable interest in arguing along mutual support rather than jeopardy lines, reformers may actually come upon, and will obviously then want to invoke, various obvious and non-obvious reasons why "synergy" between two reforms exists or can be expected to come into being.

My point is rather that reformers should not leave it to their opponents but should make an effort to explore the opposite possibility: that of some conflict or friction existing or arising between a proposed and a past reform or between two currently proposed programs. If reformers fail to look in this direction and, in

---

* Francis Fukuyama, a State Department official and scholar, argued that the demise of communism in Eastern Europe and the break-up of the Soviet Union effectively constitute an "end to history." That is, democracy and free markets have demonstrated their strength and virtue by surviving. Given the continuing tensions in much of the world and the fragmentation of the former Yugoslavia, Fukuyama's thesis has received little support in the 1990s.

general, are not prepared to entertain the notion that any reform is likely to have some costs, then they will be ill-equipped for useful discussions with their conservative opponents.

There is a worse scenario. The conviction, born from the mutual benefit thesis, that there is no conceivable cost to a given reform and that therefore nothing stands in its way can easily shade over into the feeling that nothing *should* stand in its way. In other words, those who have convinced themselves that there cannot possibly be any conflict between a reform they advocate and other worthwhile aspects of their society may resentfully turn against these very aspects if and when, against all expectations, they do turn out to be obstacles to "progress." The advocates of some reform will then be tempted to act in accordance with the maxim "the end justifies the means" and may well prove the jeopardy thesis right by their willingness to sacrifice positive accomplishments of their society for the sake of the specific forward step on which they have set their hearts.

An extreme version of this sort of dynamic is powerfully portrayed in Kleist's novella *Michael Kohlhaas*, where one man's boundless passion for justice makes him turn into a criminal. There is, of course, no logical necessity for progressives to go down this path or slippery slope, but the fact that they have been known to do so in the past is a strong argument for moderation and qualification of "mutual benefit," "synergy," or "false choice" claims in the future.

A Reformer's Primer

My "practical" advice for the reformer can be summed up in the following three points:

1. Reformers should be aware of the principal objections that are likely to be raised against their proposals and attempt to minimize the vulnerability of these proposals on perversity, futility, or jeopardy grounds. While doing so, reformers should not become unduly timorous; in particular, they need not endlessly search for all conceivable perverse effects.

2. Reformers should refrain from claiming that "history is on their side" or that, if a reform they advocate is not adopted, revolution or some other disaster is sure to follow. Since the Communist collapse, these types of arguments are no longer as appealing or persuasive as they once were; there is less need therefore to caution reformers against using or overusing them. Suddenly it has become far more expedient than heretofore to argue for reforms on purely moral grounds.

3. This does not mean, of course, that there are no longer any intransigent poses available to reformers. An example is the popular "synergy" thesis which holds that all reforms, past, present, and future, lend each other mutual support and that any conflict among them is inconceivable. Such an attitude disregards the complexity of the societies we live in and is injurious to democratic deliberations whose essence is tradeoff and compromise. Moreover, the amiable maxim

"all good things go together" can mask a reformer's readiness to push through one "good thing" at the cost, if need be, of the others.

Reformers would actually do well to canvass themselves what damage their proposals might inflict on other values and goals of their society. For example, it would be disingenuous to pretend that stimulating economic growth and correcting or attenuating inequalities that arise in the course of growth require exactly the same policies. The problem rather consists in finding an optimal combination of policies that does as little damage as possible to either objective. We are more likely to find something close to this optimum if we admit from the outset that we are in the presence of two objectives between which there exists normally a good deal of tension and conflict.

Virtue Rewarded?

As originally conceived, my book had a simple motive: I wanted to help stem the neo-conservative tide of the eighties. In this [article] I have shown how, in a changed political environment, the book may now have a very different use: to suggest a new style and rhetoric around progressive policymaking. Such versatility is unusual; it must be credited to my decision of following up some unintended thoughts that intruded in the course of writing. This decision thus carried a substantial and unexpected reward. The moral: even in intellectual pursuits, honesty can turn out to be the best policy.

Summary Questions

1. Why is the "perversity" argument so strong in a highly complex society such as that of the U.S. in the 1990s? How much should we worry about the unintended consequences of proposed policies?
2. Looking back at the other three articles in this section (Georges, Wiener and Illston, and Skolnick), to what extent can you see Hirschman's rhetorical patterns at work, either by reformers or opponents?

APPENDICES

The Declaration of Independence in Congress,
July 4, 1776

The Constitution of the United States of America

The Declaration of Independence in Congress   July 4, 1776

The unanimous declaration of the thirteen United States of America

When, in the course of human events, it becomes necessary for one people to dissolve the political bonds which have connected them with another, and to assume, among the powers of the earth, the separate and equal station to which the laws of nature and of nature's God entitle them, a decent respect to the opinions of mankind requires that they should declare the causes which impel them to the separation.

We hold these truths to be self-evident: That all men are created equal; that they are endowed by their Creator with certain unalienable rights; that among these are life, liberty, and the pursuit of happiness; that, to secure these rights, governments are instituted among men, deriving their just powers from the consent of the governed; that whenever any form of government becomes destructive of these ends, it is the right of the people to alter or to abolish it, and to institute new government, laying its foundation on such principles, and organizing its powers in such form, as to them shall seem most likely to effect their safety and happiness. Prudence, indeed, will dictate that governments long established should not be changed for light and transient causes; and accordingly all experience hath shown that mankind are more disposed to suffer, while evils are sufferable, than to right themselves by abolishing the forms to which they are accustomed. But when a long train of abuses and usurpations, pursuing invariably the same object, evinces a design to reduce them under absolute despotism, it is their right, it is their duty, to throw off such government, and to provide new guards for their future security. Such has been the patient sufferance of these colonies; and such is now the necessity which constrains them to alter their former systems of government. The history of the present King of Great Britain is a history of repeated injuries and usurpations, all having in direct object the establishment of an absolute tyranny over these states. To prove this, let facts be submitted to a candid world.

He has refused his assent to laws, the most wholesome and necessary for the public good.

He has forbidden his governors to pass laws of immediate and pressing importance, unless suspended in their operation till his assent should be obtained; and, when so suspended, he has utterly neglected to attend to them.

He has refused to pass other laws for the accommodation of large districts of people, unless those people would relinquish the right of representation in the legislature, a right inestimable to them, and formidable to tyrants only.

He has called together legislative bodies at places unusual, uncomfortable, and distant from the depository of their public records, for the sole purpose of fatiguing them into compliance with his measures.

He has dissolved representative houses repeatedly, for opposing, with manly firmness, his invasions on the rights of the people.

He has refused for a long time, after such dissolutions, to cause others to be elected; whereby the legislative powers, incapable of annihilation, have returned to the people at large for their exercise; the state remaining, in the mean time, exposed to all the dangers of invasions from without and convulsions within.

He has endeavored to prevent the population of these states; for that purpose obstructing the laws for naturalization of foreigners; refusing to pass others to encourage their migration hither, and raising the conditions of new appropriations of lands.

He has obstructed the administration of justice, by refusing his assent to laws for establishing judiciary powers.

He has made judges dependent on his will alone, for the tenure of their offices, and the amount and payment of their salaries.

He has erected a multitude of new offices, and sent hither swarms of officers to harass our people and eat out their substance.

He has kept among us, in times of peace, standing armies, without the consent of our legislatures.

He has affected to render the military independent of, and superior to, the civil power.

He has combined with others to subject us to a jurisdiction foreign to our constitution, and unacknowledged by our laws, giving his assent to their acts of pretended legislation:

For quartering large bodies of armed troops among us;

For protecting them, by a mock trial, from punishment for any murders which they should commit on the inhabitants of these states;

For cutting off our trade with all parts of the world;

For imposing taxes on us without our consent;

For depriving us, in many cases, of the benefits of trial by jury;

For transporting us beyond seas, to be tried for pretended offenses;

For abolishing the free system of English laws in a neighboring province, establishing therein an arbitrary government, and enlarging its boundaries, so as to render it at once an example and fit instrument for introducing the same absolute rule into these colonies;

For taking away our charters, abolishing our most valuable laws, and altering fundamentally the forms of our governments;

For suspending our own legislatures, and declaring themselves invested with power to legislate for us in all cases whatsoever.

He has abdicated government here, by declaring us out of his protection and waging war against us.

He has plundered our seas, ravaged our coasts, burned our towns, and destroyed the lives of our people.

He is at this time transporting large armies of foreign mercenaries to complete the works of death, desolation, and tyranny already begun with circumstances of cruelty and perfidy scarcely paralleled in the most barbarous ages, and totally unworthy the head of a civilized nation.

He has constrained our fellow-citizens, taken captive on the high seas, to bear arms against their country, to become the executioners of their friends and brethren, or to fall themselves by their hands.

He has excited domestic insurrection among us, and has endeavored to bring on the inhabitants of our frontiers the merciless Indian savages, whose known rule of warfare is an undistinguished destruction of all ages, sexes, and conditions.

In every stage of these oppressions we have petitioned for redress in the most humble terms; our repeated petitions have been answered only by repeated injury. A prince, whose character is thus marked by every act which may define a tyrant, is unfit to be the ruler of a free people.

Nor have we been wanting in our attentions to our British brethren. We have warned them, from time to time, of attempts by their legislature to extend an unwarrantable jurisdiction over us. We have reminded them of the circumstances of our emigration and settlement here. We have appealed to their native justice and magnanimity; and we have conjured them, by the ties of our common kindred, to disavow these usurpations, which would inevitably interrupt our connections and correspondence. They, too, have been deaf to the voice of justice and of consanguinity. We must, therefore, acquiesce in the necessity which denounces our separation, and hold them, as we hold the rest of mankind, enemies in war, in peace friends.

We, therefore, the representatives of the United States of America, in General Congress assembled, appealing to the Supreme Judge of the world for the rectitude of our intentions, do, in the name and by the authority of the good people of these colonies, solemnly publish and declare, that these United Colonies are, and of right ought to be, FREE AND INDEPENDENT STATES; that they are absolved from all allegiance to the British crown, and that all political connection between them and the state of Great Britain is, and ought to be, totally dissolved; and that, as free and independent states, they have full power to levy war, conclude peace, contract alliances, establish commerce, and do all other acts and things which independent states may of right do. And for the support of this declaration, with a firm reliance on the protection of Divine Providence, we mutually pledge to each other our lives, our fortunes, and our sacred honor.

JOHN HANCOCK
and fifty-five others

The Constitution of the United States of America*

Preamble

We the people of the United States, in order to form a more perfect union, establish justice, insure domestic tranquility, provide for the common defense, promote the general welfare, and secure the blessings of liberty to ourselves and our posterity, do ordain and establish this Constitution for the United States of America.

Article I

Section 1 All legislative powers herein granted shall be vested in a Congress of the United States, which shall consist of a Senate and a House of Representatives.

Section 2 The House of Representatives shall be composed of members chosen every second year by the people of the several States, and the electors in each State shall have the qualifications requisite for electors of the most numerous branch of the State Legislature.

No person shall be a Representative who shall not have attained to the age of twenty-five years, and been seven years a citizen of the United States, and who shall not, when elected, be an inhabitant of that State in which he shall be chosen.

Representatives and direct taxes shall be apportioned among the several States which may be included within this Union, according to their respective numbers, *which shall be determined by adding to the whole number of free persons, including those bound to service for a term of years and excluding Indians not taxed, three-fifths of all other persons.* The actual enumeration shall be made within three years after the first meeting of the Congress of the United States, and within every subsequent term of ten years, in such manner as they shall by law direct. The number of Representatives shall not exceed one for every thirty thousand, but each State shall have at least one Representative; *and until such enumeration shall be made, the State of New Hampshire shall be entitled to choose three, Massachusetts eight, Rhode Island and Providence Plantations one, Connecticut five, New York six, New Jersey four, Pennsylvania eight, Delaware one, Maryland six, Virginia ten, North Carolina five, South Carolina five, and Georgia three.*

When vacancies happen in the representation from any State, the Executive authority thereof shall issue writs of election to fill such vacancies.

The House of Representatives shall choose their Speaker and other officers; and shall have the sole power of impeachment.

Section 3 The Senate of the United States shall be composed of two Senators from each State, *chosen by the legislature thereof,* for six years; and each Senator shall have one vote.

---

* Passages no longer in effect are printed in italic type.

Immediately after they shall be assembled in consequence of the first election, they shall be divided as equally as may be into three classes. The seats of the Senators of the first class shall be vacated at the expiration of the second year, of the second class at the expiration of the fourth year, and of the third class at the expiration of the sixth year, so that one-third may be chosen every second year; *and if vacancies happen by resignation or otherwise, during the recess of the legislature of any State, the Executive thereof may make temporary appointments until the next meeting of the legislature, which shall then fill such vacancies.*

No person shall be a Senator who shall not have attained to the age of thirty years, and been nine years a citizen of the United States, and who shall not, when elected, be an inhabitant of that State for which he shall be chosen.

The Vice-President of the United States shall be President of the Senate, but shall have no vote, unless they be equally divided.

The Senate shall choose their other officers, and also a President *pro tempore,* in the absence of the Vice-President, or when he shall exercise the office of President of the United States.

The Senate shall have the sole power to try all impeachments. When sitting for that purpose, they shall be on oath or affirmation. When the President of the United States is tried, the Chief Justice shall preside: and no person shall be convicted without the concurrence of two-thirds of the members present.

Judgment in cases of impeachment shall not extend further than to removal from the office, and disqualification to hold and enjoy any office of honor, trust or profit under the United States: but the party convicted shall nevertheless be liable and subject to indictment, trial, judgment and punishment, according to law.

Section 4   The times, places and manner of holding elections for Senators and Representatives shall be prescribed in each State by the legislature thereof; but the Congress may at any time by law make or alter such regulations, except as to the places of choosing Senators.

The Congress shall assemble at least once in every year, and such meeting *shall be on the first Monday in December, unless they shall by law appoint a different day.*

Section 5   Each house shall be the judge of the elections, returns and qualifications of its own members, and a majority of each shall constitute a quorum to do business; but a smaller number may adjourn from day to day, and may be authorized to compel the attendance of absent members, in such manner, and under such penalties, as each house may provide.

Each house may determine the rules of its proceedings, punish its members for disorderly behavior, and with the concurrence of two-thirds, expel a member.

Each house shall keep a journal of its proceedings, and from time to time publish the same, excepting such parts as may in their judgment require secrecy; and the yeas and nays of the members of either house on any question shall, at the desire of one-fifth of those present, be entered on the journal.

Neither house, during the session of Congress, shall, without the consent of the other, adjourn for more than three days, nor to any other place than that in which the two houses shall be sitting.

Section 6   The Senators and Representatives shall receive a compensation for their services, to be ascertained by law and paid out of the treasury of the United States.

They shall in all cases except treason, felony and breach of the peace, be privileged from arrest during their attendance at the session of their respective houses, and in going to and returning from the same; and for any speech or debate in either house, they shall not be questioned in any other place.

No Senator or Representative shall, during the time for which he was elected, be appointed to any civil office under the authority of the United States, which shall have been created, or the emoluments whereof shall have been increased, during such time; and no person holding any office under the United States shall be a member of either house during his continuance in office.

Section 7 All bills for raising revenue shall originate in the House of Representatives; but the Senate may propose or concur with amendments as on other bills.

Every bill which shall have passed the House of Representatives and the Senate, shall, before it become a law, be presented to the President of the United States; if he approve he shall sign it, but if not he shall return it with objections to that house in which it originated, who shall enter the objections at large on their journal, and proceed to reconsider it. If after such reconsideration two-thirds of that house shall agree to pass the bill, it shall be sent, together with the objections, to the other house, by which it shall likewise be reconsidered, and, if approved by two-thirds of that house, it shall become a law. But in all such cases the votes of both houses shall be determined by yeas and nays, and the names of the persons voting for and against the bill shall be entered on the journal of each house respectively. If any bill shall not be returned by the President within ten days (Sundays excepted) after it shall have been presented to him, the same shall be a law, in like manner as if he had signed it, unless the Congress by their adjournment prevents its return, in which case it shall not be a law.

Every order, resolution, or vote to which the concurrence of the Senate and House of Representatives may be necessary (except on a question of adjournment) shall be presented to the President of the United States; and before the same shall take effect, shall be approved by him, or being disapproved by him, shall be repassed by two-thirds of the Senate and House of Representatives, according to the rules and limitations prescribed in the case of a bill.

Section 8 The Congress shall have power

To lay and collect taxes, duties, imposts, and excises, to pay the debts and provide for the common defense and general welfare of the United States; but all duties, imposts and excises shall be uniform throughout the United States;

To borrow money on the credit of the United States;

To regulate commerce with foreign nations, and among the several States, and with the Indian tribes;

To establish an uniform rule of naturalization, and uniform laws on the subject of bankruptcies throughout the United States;

To coin money, regulate the value thereof, and of foreign coin, and fix the standard of weights and measures;

To provide for the punishment of counterfeiting the securities and current coin of the United States;

To establish post offices and post roads;

To promote the progress of science and useful arts by securing for limited times to authors and inventors the exclusive right to their respective writings and discoveries;

To constitute tribunals inferior to the Supreme Court;

To define and punish piracies and felonies committed on the high seas and offenses against the law of nations;

To declare war, grant letters of marque and reprisal, and make rules concerning captures on land and water;

To raise and support armies, but no appropriation of money to that use shall be for a longer term than two years;

To provide and maintain a navy;

To make rules for the government and regulation of the land and naval forces;

To provide for calling forth the militia to execute the laws of the Union, suppress insurrections, and repel invasions;

To provide for organizing, arming, and disciplining the militia, and for governing such part of them as may be employed in the service of the United States, reserving to the States respectively the appointment of the officers, and the authority of training the militia according to the discipline prescribed by Congress;

To exercise exclusive legislation in all cases whatsoever, over such district (not exceeding ten miles square) as may, by cession of particular States, and the acceptance of Congress, become the seat of government of the United States, and to exercise like authority over all places purchased by the consent of the legislature of the State, in which the same shall be, for erection of forts, magazines, arsenals, dockyards, and other needful buildings;—and

To make all laws which shall be necessary and proper for carrying into execution the foregoing powers, and all other powers vested by this Constitution in the government of the United States, or in any department or officer thereof.

Section 9 *The migration or importation of such persons as any of the States now existing shall think proper to admit shall not be prohibited by the Congress prior to the year 1808; but a tax or duty may be imposed on such importation, not exceeding $10 for each person.*

The privilege of the writ of habeas corpus shall not be suspended, unless when in cases of rebellion or invasion the public safety may require it.

No bill of attainder or ex post facto law shall be passed.

No capitation, or other direct, tax shall be laid, unless in proportion to the census or enumeration herein before directed to be taken.

No tax or duty shall be laid on articles exported from any State.

No preference shall be given by any regulation of commerce or revenue to the ports of one State over those of another; nor shall vessels bound to, or from, one State, be obliged to enter, clear, or pay duties in another.

No money shall be drawn from the treasury, but in consequence of appropriations made by law; and a regular statement and account of the receipts and expenditures of all public money shall be published from time to time.

No title of nobility shall be granted by the United States: and no person holding any office of profit or trust under them, shall, without the consent of the Congress, accept of any present, emolument, office, or title, of any kind whatever, from any king, prince, or foreign state.

Section 10 No State shall enter into any treaty, alliance, or confederation; grant letters of marque and reprisal; coin money; emit bills of credit; make anything but gold and silver coin a tender in payment of debts; pass any bill of attainder, ex post facto law, or law impairing the obligation of contracts, or grant any title of nobility.

No State shall, without the consent of Congress, lay any imposts or duties on imports or exports, except what may be absolutely necessary for executing its inspection laws: and the net produce of all duties and imposts, laid by any State on imports or exports, shall be for the use of the treasury of the United States; and all such laws shall be subject to the revision and control of the Congress.

No State shall, without the consent of Congress, lay any duty of tonnage, keep troops or ships of war in time of peace, enter into any agreement or compact with another State, or with a foreign power, or engage in war, unless actually invaded, or in such imminent danger as will not admit of delay.

Article II

Section 1 The executive power shall be vested in a President of the United States of America. He shall hold his office during the term of four years, and, together with the Vice-President, chosen for the same term, be elected as follows:

Each State shall appoint, in such manner as the legislature thereof may direct, a number of electors, equal to the whole number of Senators and Representatives to which the State may be entitled in the Congress; but no Senator or Representative, or person holding an office of trust or profit under the United States, shall be appointed an elector.

The electors shall meet in their respective States, and vote by ballot for two persons, of whom one at least shall not be an inhabitant of the same State with themselves. And they shall make a list of all the persons voted for, and of the number of votes for each; which list they shall sign and certify, and transmit sealed to the seat of government of the United States, directed to the President of the Senate. The President of the Senate shall, in the presence of the Senate and House of Representatives, open all the certificates, and the votes shall then be counted. The person having the greatest number of votes shall be the President, if such number be a majority of the whole number of electors appointed; and if there be more than one who have such majority, and have an equal number of votes, then the House of Representatives shall immediately choose by ballot one of them for President; and if no person have a majority, then from the five highest on the list said house shall in like manner choose the President. But in choosing the President the votes shall be taken by States, the representation from each State having one vote; a quorum for this purpose shall consist of a member or members from two-thirds of the States, and a majority of all the States shall be necessary to a choice. In every case, after the choice of the President, the person having the greatest number of votes of the electors shall be the Vice-President. But if there should remain two or more who have equal votes, the Senate shall choose from them by ballot the Vice-President.

The Congress may determine the time of choosing the electors and the day on which they shall give their votes; which day shall be the same throughout the United States.

No person except a natural-born citizen, *or a citizen of the United States at the time of the adoption of this Constitution,* shall be eligible to the office of President; neither shall any person be eligible to that office who shall not have attained to the age of thirty-five years, and been fourteen years a resident within the United States.

In cases of the removal of the President from office or of his death, resignation, or inability to discharge the powers and duties of the said office, the same shall devolve on the Vice-President, and the Congress may by law provide for the case of removal, death, resignation, or inability, both of the President and Vice-President, declaring what officer shall then act as President, and such officer shall act accordingly, until the disability be removed, or a President shall be elected.

The President shall, at stated times, receive for his services a compensation, which shall neither be increased nor diminished during the period for which he shall have been elected, and he shall not receive within that period any other emolument from the United States, or any of them.

Before he enter on the execution of his office, he shall take the following oath or affirmation:—"I do solemnly swear (or affirm) that I will faithfully execute the office of the President of the United States, and will to the best of my ability preserve, protect and defend the Constitution of the United States."

Section 2   The President shall be commander in chief of the army and navy of the United States, and of the militia of the several States, when called into the actual service of the United States; he may require the opinion, in writing, of the principal officer in each of the executive departments, upon any subject relating to the duties of their respective offices, and he shall have power to grant reprieves and pardons for offenses against the United States, except in cases of impeachment.

He shall have power, by and with the advice and consent of the senate, to make treaties, provided two-thirds of the Senators present concur; and he shall nominate, and by and with the advice and consent of the Senate, shall appoint ambassadors, other public ministers and consuls, judges of the Supreme Court, and all other officers of the United States, whose appointments are not herein otherwise provided for, and which shall be established by law: but Congress may by law vest the appointment of such inferior officers, as they think proper, in the President alone, in the courts of law, or in the heads of departments.

The President shall have power to fill up all vacancies that may happen during the recess of the Senate, by granting commissions which shall expire at the end of their next session.

Section 3   He shall from time to time give to the Congress information of the state of the Union, and recommend to their consideration such measures as he shall judge necessary and expedient; he may, on extraordinary occasions, convene both houses, or either of them, and in case of disagreement between them, with respect to the time of adjournment, he may adjourn them to such time as he shall think proper; he shall receive ambassadors and other public ministers; he shall take care that the laws be faithfully executed, and shall commission all the officers of the United States.

Section 4   The President, Vice-President and all civil officers of the United States shall be removed from office on impeachment for, and on conviction of, treason, bribery, or other high crimes and misdemeanors.

Article III

Section 1   The judicial power of the United States shall be vested in one Supreme Court, and in such inferior courts as the Congress may from time to time ordain and establish. The judges, both of the Supreme and inferior courts, shall hold their offices during good behavior, and shall, at stated times, receive for their services a compensation which shall not be diminished during their continuance in office.

Section 2   The judicial power shall extend to all cases, in law and equity, arising under this Constitution, the laws of the United States, and treaties made, or which shall be made, under their authority;—to all cases affecting ambassadors, other public ministers and consuls;—to all cases of admiralty and maritime jurisdiction;—to controversies to which the United States shall be a party;—to controversies between two or more States;—*between a State and citizens of another State;*—between citizens of different States;—between citizens of the same State claiming lands under grants of different States, and between a State, or the citizens thereof, and foreign states, citizens or subjects.

In all cases affecting ambassadors, other public ministers and consuls, and those in which a State shall be party, the Supreme Court shall have original jurisdiction. In all the other cases before mentioned, the Supreme Court shall have appellate jurisdiction, both as to law and fact, with such exceptions, and under such regulations, as the Congress shall make.

The trial of all crimes, except in cases of impeachment, shall be by jury; and such trial shall be held in the state where said crimes shall have been committed; but when not committed within any State, the trial shall be at such place or places as the Congress may by law have directed.

Section 3   Treason against the United States shall consist only in levying war against them, or in adhering to their enemies, giving them aid and comfort. No person shall be convicted of treason unless on the testimony of two witnesses to the same overt act, or on confession in open court.

The Congress shall have power to declare the punishment of treason, but no attainder of treason shall work corruption of blood, or forfeiture except during the life of the person attained.

Article IV

Section 1   Full faith and credit shall be given in each State to the public acts, records, and judicial proceedings of every other State. And the Congress may by general laws prescribe the manner in which such acts, records, and proceedings shall be proved, and the effect thereof.

Section 2   The citizens of each State shall be entitled to all privileges and immunities of citizens in the several States.

A person charged in any State with treason, felony, or other crime, who shall flee from justice, and be found in another State, shall on demand of the executive authority of the State from which he fled, be delivered up, to be removed to the State having jurisdiction of the crime.

No person held to service or labor in one State, under the laws thereof, escaping into another, shall, in consequence of any law or regulation therein, be discharged from such service or labor, but shall be delivered up on claim of the party to whom such service or labor may be due.

Section 3 New States may be admitted by the Congress into this Union; but no new State shall be formed or erected within the jurisdiction of any other State; nor any State be formed by the junction of two or more States, or parts of States, without the consent of the legislatures of the States concerned as well as of the Congress.

The Congress shall have power to dispose of and make all needful rules and regulations respecting the territory or other property belonging to the United States; and nothing in this Constitution shall be so construed as to prejudice any claims of the United States, or of any particular State.

Section 4 The United States shall guarantee to every State in this Union a republican form of government, and shall protect each of them against invasion; and on application of the legislature, or of the executive (when the legislature cannot be convened), against domestic violence.

Article V

The Congress, whenever two-thirds of both houses shall deem it necessary, shall propose amendments to this Constitution, or, on the application of the legislatures of two-thirds of the several States, shall call a convention for proposing amendments, which, in either case, shall be valid to all intents and purposes, as part of this Constitution, when ratified by the legislatures of three-fourths of the several States, or by conventions in three-fourths thereof, as the one or the other mode of ratification may be proposed by the Congress; provided *that no amendments which may be made prior to the year one thousand eight hundred and eight shall in any manner affect the first and fourth clauses in the ninth section of the first article;* and that no State, without its consent, shall be deprived of its equal suffrage in the Senate.

Article VI

All debts contracted and engagements entered into, before the adoption of this Constitution, shall be as valid against the United States under this Constitution, as under the Confederation.

This Constitution, and the laws of the United States which shall be made in pursuance thereof; and all treaties made, or which shall be made, under the authority of the United States, shall be the supreme law of the land; and the judges in every State shall be bound thereby, anything in the Constitution or laws of any State to the contrary notwithstanding.

The Senators and Representatives before mentioned, and the members of the several State legislatures, and all executive and judicial officers, both of the United States and of the several States, shall be bound by oath or affirmation to support this Constitution; but no religious test shall ever be required as a qualification to any office or public trust under the United States.

Article VII

The ratification of the conventions of nine States shall be sufficient for the establishment of this Constitution between the States so ratifying the same.

Done in Convention by the unanimous consent of the States present, the seventeenth day of September in the year of our Lord one thousand seven hundred and eighty-seven and of the Independence of the United States of America the twelfth. In witness whereof we have hereunto subscribed our names.

GEORGE WASHINGTON
and thirty-seven others

Amendments to the Constitution*

Amendment I

Congress shall make no law respecting an establishment of religion, or prohibiting the free exercise thereof; or abridging the freedom of speech, or of the press; or the right of the people peaceably to assemble, and to petition the government for a redress of grievances.

Amendment II

A well-regulated militia being necessary to the security of a free State, the right of the people to keep and bear arms shall not be infringed.

Amendment III

No soldier shall, in time of peace, be quartered in any house without the consent of the owner, nor in time of war, but in a manner to be prescribed by law.

Amendment IV

The right of the people to be secure in their persons, houses, papers, and effects, against unreasonable searches and seizures, shall not be violated, and no warrants shall issue but upon probable cause, supported by oath or affirmation, and particularly describing the place to be searched, and the persons or things to be seized.

Amendment V

No person shall be held to answer for a capital, or otherwise infamous crime, unless on a presentment or indictment of a grand jury, except in cases arising in the land or naval forces, or in the militia, when in actual service in time of war or public danger;

---

* The first ten amendments (the Bill of Rights) were adopted in 1791.

nor shall any person be subject for the same offense to be twice put in jeopardy of life or limb; nor shall be compelled in any criminal case to be a witness against himself, nor be deprived of life, liberty, or property, without due process of law; nor shall private property be taken for public use without just compensation.

Amendment VI

In all criminal prosecutions, the accused shall enjoy the right to a speedy and public trial, by an impartial jury of the State and district wherein the crime shall have been committed, which district shall have been previously ascertained by law, and to be informed of the nature and cause of the accusation; to be confronted with the witnesses against him; to have compulsory process for obtaining witnesses in his favor, and to have the assistance of counsel for his defense.

Amendment VII

In suits at common law, where the value in controversy shall exceed twenty dollars, the right of trial by jury shall be preserved, and no fact tried by a jury shall be otherwise reexamined in any court of the United States, than according to the rules of the common law.

Amendment VIII

Excessive bail shall not be required, nor excessive fines imposed, nor cruel and unusual punishments inflicted.

Amendment IX

The enumeration in the Constitution, of certain rights, shall not be construed to deny or disparage others retained by the people.

Amendment X

The powers not delegated to the United States by the Constitution, nor prohibited by it to the States, are reserved to the States respectively, or to the people.

Amendment XI
[Adopted 1798]

The judicial power of the United States shall not be construed to extend to any suit in law or equity, commenced or prosecuted against one of the United States by citizens of another State, or by citizens or subjects of any foreign State.

Amendment XII
[Adopted 1804]

The electors shall meet in their respective States, and vote by ballot for President and Vice-President, one of whom, at least, shall not be an inhabitant of the same State with themselves; they shall name in their ballots the person voted for as President, and in distinct ballots the person voted for as Vice-President, and they shall make distinct lists of all persons voted for as President, and of all persons voted for as Vice-President, and of the number of votes for each, which lists they shall sign and certify, and transmit sealed to the seat of government of the United States, directed to the President of the Senate;—the President of the Senate shall, in the presence of the Senate and House of Representatives, open all the certificates and the votes shall then be counted;—the person having the greatest number of votes for President shall be the President, if such number be a majority of the whole number of electors appointed; and if no person have such majority, then from the persons having the highest numbers not exceeding three on the list of those voted for as President, the House of Representatives shall choose immediately, by ballot, the President. But in choosing the President, the votes shall be taken by States, the representation from each State having one vote; a quorum for this purpose shall consist of a member or members from two-thirds of the States, and a majority of all the states shall be necessary to a choice. And if the House of Representatives shall not choose a President whenever the right of choice shall devolve upon them, before the fourth day of March next following, then the Vice-President shall act as President, as in the case of the death or other constitutional disability of the President.

The person having the greatest number of votes as Vice-President shall be the Vice-President, if such number be a majority of the whole number of electors appointed; and if no person have a majority, then from the two highest numbers on the list the Senate shall choose the Vice-President; a quorum for the purpose shall consist of two-thirds of the whole number of Senators, and a majority of the whole number shall be necessary to a choice. But no person constitutionally ineligible to the office of President shall be eligible to that of Vice-President of the United States.

Amendment XIII
[Adopted 1865]

Section 1 Neither slavery nor involuntary servitude, except as a punishment for crime whereof the party shall have been duly convicted, shall exist within the United States, or any place subject to their jurisdiction.

Section 2 Congress shall have power to enforce this article by appropriate legislation.

Amendment XIV
[Adopted 1868]

Section 1 All persons born or naturalized in the United States, and subject to the jurisdiction thereof, are citizens of the United States and of the State wherein they reside. No State shall make or enforce any law which shall abridge the privileges or immunities of citizens of the United States; nor shall any State deprive any person of life, liberty, or property, without due process of law; nor deny to any person within its jurisdiction the equal protection of the laws.

Section 2 Representatives shall be apportioned among the several States according to their respective numbers, counting the whole number of persons in each State, excluding Indians not taxed. But when the right to vote at any election for the choice of electors for President and Vice-President of the United States, Representatives in Congress, the executive and judicial officers of a State, or the members of the legislature thereof, is denied to any of the male inhabitants of such State, being twenty-one years of age and citizens of the United States, or in any way abridged, except for participation in rebellion, or other crime, the basis of representation therein shall be reduced in the proportion which the number of such male citizens shall bear to the whole number of male citizens twenty-one years of age in such State.

Section 3 No person shall be a Senator or Representative in Congress, or elector of President and Vice-President, or hold any office, civil or military, under the United States, or under any State, who, having previously taken an oath, as a member of Congress, or as an officer of the United States, or as a member of any State legislature, or as an executive or judicial officer of any State, to support the Constitution of the United States, shall have engaged in insurrection or rebellion against the same, or given aid or comfort to the enemies thereof. Congress may, by a vote of two-thirds of each house, remove such disability.

Section 4 The validity of the public debt of the United States, authorized by law, including debts incurred for payment of pensions and bounties for services in suppressing insurrection or rebellion, shall not be questioned. But neither the United States nor any State shall assume or pay any debt or obligation incurred in aid of insurrection or rebellion against the United States, or any claim for the loss of emancipation of any slave; but all such debts, obligations, and claims shall be held illegal and void.

Section 5 The Congress shall have power to enforce, by appropriate legislation, the provisions of this article.

Amendment XV
[Adopted 1870]

Section 1 The right of citizens of the United States to vote shall not be denied or abridged by the United States or by any State on account of race, color, or previous condition of servitude.

Section 2 The Congress shall have power to enforce this article by appropriate legislation.

Amendment XVI
[Adopted 1913]

The Congress shall have power to lay and collect taxes on incomes, from whatever source derived, without apportionment among the several States, and without regard to any census or enumeration.

Amendment XVII
[Adopted 1913]

Section 1 The Senate of the United States shall be composed of two Senators from each State, elected by the people thereof, for six years; and each Senator shall have one vote. The electors in each State shall have the qualifications requisite for electors of [voters for] the most numerous branch of the State legislatures.

Section 2 When vacancies happen in the representation of any State in the Senate, the executive authority of such State shall issue writs of election to fill such vacancies: Provided, that the Legislature of any State may empower the executive thereof to make temporary appointments until the people fill the vacancies by election as the Legislature may direct.

Section 3 This amendment shall not be so construed as to affect the election or term of any Senator chosen before it becomes valid as part of the Constitution.

Amendment XVIII
[Adopted 1919, repealed 1933]

Section 1 After one year from the ratification of this article the manufacture, sale or transportation of intoxicating liquors within, the importation thereof into, or the exportation thereof from the United States and all territory subject to the jurisdiction thereof, for beverage purposes, is hereby prohibited.

Section 2 The Congress and the several States shall have concurrent power to enforce this article by appropriate legislation.

Section 3 This article shall be inoperative unless it shall have been ratified as an amendment to the Constitution by the legislatures of the several States, as provided by the Constitution, within seven years from the date of the submission thereof to the States by the Congress.

Amendment XIX
[Adopted 1920]

Section 1 The right of citizens of the United States to vote shall not be denied or abridged by the United States or by any State on account of sex.

Section 2 The Congress shall have power to enforce this article by appropriate legislation.

Amendment XX
[Adopted 1933]

Section 1 The terms of the President and Vice-President shall end at noon on the 20th day of January, and the terms of Senators and Representatives at noon on the 3d day of January, of the years in which such terms would have ended if this article had not been ratified; and the terms of their successors shall then begin.

Section 2 The Congress shall assemble at least once in every year, and such meetings shall begin at noon on the 3d day of January, unless they shall by law appoint a different day.

Section 3 If, at the time fixed for the beginning of the term of the President, the President-elect shall have died, the Vice-President-elect shall become President. If a President shall not have been chosen before the time fixed for the beginning of his term, or if the President-elect shall have failed to qualify, then the Vice-President-elect shall act as President until a President shall have qualified; and the Congress may by law provide for the case wherein neither a President-elect nor a Vice-President-elect shall have qualified, declaring who shall then act as President, or the manner in which one who is to act shall be selected, and such persons shall act accordingly until a President or Vice-President shall have qualified.

Section 4 The Congress may by law provide for the case of the death of any of the persons from whom the House of Representatives may choose a President whenever the right of choice shall have devolved upon them, and for the case of the death of any of the persons from whom the Senate may choose a Vice-President whenever the right of choice shall have devolved upon them.

Section 5 Sections 1 and 2 shall take effect on the 15th day of October following the ratification of this article.

Section 6 This article shall be inoperative unless it shall have been ratified as an amendment to the Constitution by the Legislatures of three-fourths of the several States within seven years from the date of its submission.

Amendment XXI
[Adopted 1933]

Section 1 The eighteenth article of amendment to the Constitution of the United States is hereby repealed.

Section 2 The transportation or importation into any State, Territory, or Possession of the United States for delivery or use therein of intoxicating liquors, in violation of the laws thereof, is hereby prohibited.

Section 3 This article shall be inoperative unless it shall have been ratified as an amendment to the Constitution by conventions in the several States, as provided in the Constitution, within seven years from the date of submission thereof to the States by the Congress.

Amendment XXII
[Adopted 1951]

Section 1 No person shall be elected to the office of President more than twice, and no person who has held the office of President, or acted as President, for more than two years of a term to which some other person was elected President shall be elected to the office of President more than once. But this article shall not apply to any person holding the office of President when this article was proposed by the Congress, and shall not prevent any person who may be holding the office of President, or acting as President, during the term within which this article becomes operative from holding the office of President or acting as President during the remainder of such term.

Section 2 This article shall be inoperative unless it shall have been ratified as an amendment to the Constitution by the legislatures of three-fourths of the several States within seven years from the date of its submission to the States by the Congress.

Amendment XXIII
[Adopted 1961]

Section 1 The District constituting the seat of Government of the United States shall appoint in such manner as the Congress may direct:

A number of electors of President and Vice-President equal to the whole number of Senators and Representatives in Congress to which the District would be entitled if it were a State, but in no event more than the least populous State; they shall be in addition to those appointed by the States, but they shall be considered for the purposes of the election of President and Vice-President, to be electors appointed by a State; and they shall meet in the District and perform such duties as provided by the twelfth article of amendment.

Section 2 The Congress shall have the power to enforce this article by appropriate legislation.

Amendment XXIV
[Adopted 1964]

Section 1 The right of citizens of the United States to vote in any primary or other election for President or Vice-President, for electors for President or Vice-President, or for Senator or Representative in Congress, shall not be denied or abridged by the United States or any State by reason of failure to pay any poll tax or other tax.

Section 2 The Congress shall have the power to enforce this article by appropriate legislation.

Amendment XXV
[Adopted 1967]

Section 1 In case of the removal of the President from office or of his death or resignation, the Vice-President shall become President.

Section 2 Whenever there is a vacancy in the office of the Vice-President, the President shall nominate a Vice-President who shall take office upon confirmation by a majority vote of both Houses of Congress.

Section 3 Whenever the President transmits to the President pro tempore of the Senate and the Speaker of the House of Representatives his written declaration that he is unable to discharge the powers and duties of his office, and until he transmits to them a written declaration to the contrary, such powers and duties shall be discharged by the Vice-President as Acting President.

Section 4 Whenever the Vice-President and a majority of either the principal officers of the executive departments or of such other body as Congress may by law provide, transmit to the President pro tempore of the Senate and the Speaker of the House of Representatives their written declaration that the President is unable to discharge the powers and duties of his office, the Vice-President shall immediately assume the powers and duties of the office as Acting President.

Thereafter, when the President transmits to the President pro tempore of the Senate and the Speaker of the House of Representatives his written declaration that no inability exists, he shall resume the powers and duties of his office unless the Vice-President and a majority of either the principal officers of the executive department(s) or of such other body as Congress may by law provide, transmit within four days to the President pro tempore of the Senate and the Speaker of the House of Representatives their written declaration that the President is unable to discharge the powers and duties of his office. Thereupon Congress shall decide the issue, assembling within forty-eight hours for that purpose if not in session. If the Congress, within twenty-one days after receipt of the latter written declaration, or, if Congress is not in session, within twenty-one days after Congress is required to assemble, determines by two-thirds vote of both Houses that the President is unable to discharge the powers and duties of his office, the Vice-President shall continue to discharge the same as Acting President; otherwise, the President shall resume the powers and duties of his office.

Amendment XXVI
[Adopted 1971]

Section 1 The right of citizens of the United States, who are eighteen years of age or older, to vote shall not be denied or abridged by the United States or by any State on account of age.

Section 2 The Congress shall have power to enforce this article by appropriate legislation.

Amendment XXVII
[Adopted 1992]

No law, varying the compensation for the services of the senators and representatives shall take effect, until an election of representatives shall have intervened.

CREDITS

Steele, Shelby. From "The Content of Our Character" by Shelby Steele. Copyright © 1990 by Shelby Steele. Reprinted by permission of St. Martin's Press, Inc., New York, NY.

Strossen, Nadine. Nadine Strossen, "The Constitutional Litmus Test," *American Prospect*, Summer 1993, #14, pp. 99–105. Reprinted by permission.

Teixeira, Ruy A. Reprinted by permission from "Voter Turnout in America: Ten Myths," by Ruy A. Teixeira, *The Brookings Review*, Fall 1992. Vol. 10, #2, pp. 28–31.

Theiler, Patricia. © 1990 *Common Cause Magazine*, 2030 M St., NW, Washington, DC 20036. Reprinted by permission.

Turque, Bill. From *Newsweek*, November 29, 1993, © 1993, Newsweek, Inc. All rights reserved. Reprinted by permission.

Wiener and Illston. From *The Brookings Review*, Spring 1993, pp. 22–25. Copyright © 1993. Used by permission.

Wilson, James Q. CHAPTER 7 (EDITED) from BUREAUCRACY: WHAT GOVERNMENT AGENCIES DO & WHY THEY DO IT by JAMES Q. WILSON. Copyright © 1989 by Basic Books, Inc. Reprinted by permission of Basic Books, a division of HarperCollins Publishers, Inc.

Wirth, Tim. Copyright © 1992 by The New York Times Company. Reprinted by permission.